INTRODUCTION TO PUBLIC RELATIONS

Second Edition

Sara Miller McCune founded SAGE Publishing in 1965 to support the dissemination of usable knowledge and educate a global community. SAGE publishes more than 1000 journals and over 800 new books each year, spanning a wide range of subject areas. Our growing selection of library products includes archives, data, case studies and video. SAGE remains majority owned by our founder and after her lifetime will become owned by a charitable trust that secures the company's continued independence.

Los Angeles | London | New Delhi | Singapore | Washington DC | Melbourne

INTRODUCTION TO PUBLIC RELATIONS

Strategic, Digital, and Socially Responsible Communication

Second Edition

Janis Teruggi Page

University of Illinois at Chicago

Lawrence J. Parnell

George Washington University

Los Angeles | London | New Delhi
Singapore | Washington DC | Melbourne

FOR INFORMATION:

SAGE Publications, Inc.
2455 Teller Road
Thousand Oaks, California 91320
Email: order@sagepub.com

SAGE Publications Ltd.
1 Oliver's Yard
55 City Road
London, EC1Y 1SP
United Kingdom

SAGE Publications India Pvt. Ltd.
B 1/I 1 Mohan Cooperative Industrial Area
Mathura Road, New Delhi 110 044
India

SAGE Publications Asia-Pacific Pte. Ltd.
18 Cross Street #10-10/11/12
China Square Central
Singapore 048423

Copyright © 2021 by SAGE Publications, Inc.

Printed in the United States of America

Library of Congress Cataloging-in-Publication Data

Names: Page, Janis Teruggi, author. | Parnell, Lawrence J., author.

Title: Introduction to public relations : strategies for digital and socially responsible communication / Janis Teruggi Page, University of Illinois at Chicago, Lawrence J. Parnell, George Washington University.

Description: Second edition. | Thousand Oaks, California : SAGE Publications, Inc., [2021] | Includes bibliographical references.

Identifiers: LCCN 2020017828 | ISBN 9781544392004 (paperback) | ISBN 9781544392011 (epub) | ISBN 9781544392028 (epub) | ISBN 9781544392035 (ebook)

Subjects: LCSH: Public relations.

Classification: LCC HM1221 .P34 2021 | DDC 659.2—dc23

LC record available at https://lccn.loc.gov/2020017828

Acquisitions Editor: Lily Norton
Editorial Assistant: Sarah Wilson
Content Development Editor: Jennifer Jovin-Bernstein
Production Editor: Andrew Olson
Copy Editor: Amy Hanquist Harris
Typesetter: Hurix Digital
Proofreader: Susan Schon
Indexer: Integra
Cover Designer: Scott Van Atta
Marketing Manager: Staci Wittek

This book is printed on acid-free paper.

20 21 22 23 24 10 9 8 7 6 5 4 3 2 1

BRIEF CONTENTS

DETAILED CONTENTS

iStock.com/PeopleImages

THE B○

CHAPTER 3: Ethics and Law in Public Relations 50

iStock 62926802

CHAPTER 4: Foundations of Public Relations: Research and Theory   74

CHAPTER 5: Strategic Communication Planning   100

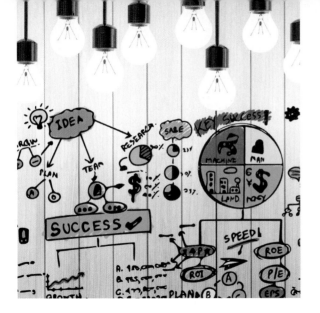

CHAPTER 6: Public Relations Writing: Persuasive and Audience Focused   122

iStock 504787947

CHAPTER 7: Media Relations in a Digital World 148

CHAPTER 8: Social Media and Emerging Technologies 172

Left: iStock 64967679
Right: iStock 540095978

CHAPTER 9: Corporate Social Responsibility and Community Relations — 198

iStock 69085708

CHAPTER 10: Employee Relations, Corporate Culture, and Social Responsibility　　224

CHAPTER 11: Corporate Communication and Reputation Management 246

CHAPTER 12: Issues Management and Crisis Communication 274

CHAPTER 13: Sports, Tourism, and Entertainment — 296

Getty 66350080¿

CHAPTER 14: Nonprofit, Health, Education, and Grassroots Organizations 320

CHAPTER 15: Public Affairs, Government Relations, and Political Communications 342

CHAPTER 16: Global Public Relations and Public Diplomacy · 362

PREFACE

What is it about the field of public relations (PR) that makes it so hard to define, detail, or document? How does the growing field of social responsibility (SR) intersect with PR in today's global and digital world?

This book answers these questions from a unique and contemporary perspective, explaining the process and purpose of PR by connecting it to business, social, and environmental trends and values. At the same time, this perspective is designed to augment—not replace—the traditional approach of an introductory text in PR and includes all the key elements of history, theory, skills, and strategy that you would expect.

The authors believe that SR is a global movement that businesspeople, public officials, and students at all levels understand, and as such, it will draw the reader into the text. Regardless of industry or position, most stakeholders appreciate the benefit of SR to companies, the public sector, and society. Corporations take a visible role in SR; thus, we use the terms "CSR" (corporate social responsibility) and "SR" interchangeably in this text.

For example, a corporation decreasing its carbon footprint, promoting more women into management, bringing fresh produce to urban food deserts, or improving water quality for distressed communities improves the quality of life for citizens and possibly benefits from business outcomes as well.

In its review of the trends and best practices of SR and PR, the connection of these key activities to the concept of organizational purpose will be explored as well.

Our goal in this text is to introduce PR as a *strategic* activity, put it into a business context using SR as a connecting point, and provide readers with the essential theoretical and practical foundations. Ultimately, we believe this approach will increase awareness of the vital role of PR in organizational success and launch the next generation of PR professionals toward effective and ethical leadership.

Organization of This Text

This book is specifically designed and structured in a user-friendly format for introductory public relations classes at both the undergraduate and graduate levels. It provides solid ground on which students can build their knowledge of the profession within a PR major or apply it to communications, business, law, or political science courses.

The book is organized into two progressive sections, separating the essentials from the specifics:

Understanding Public Relations (Chapters 1–5): The first five chapters of this text cover an introduction to the profession, its history, ethical and legal considerations, and the PR process: research, theory, strategy, programming, evaluation, and stewardship.

Practicing Strategic Public Relations in a Socially Responsible World (Chapters 6–16): The remaining chapters cover the major skills, functions, and practice areas in the field of PR.

New to the Second Edition

The second edition of *Introduction to Public Relations* includes refreshed content throughout the text along with new and updated features, including cases, chapter-opening scenarios, and profiles of both young and senior practitioners who provide tips and career guidance to students.

The new chapter-opening scenarios, a hallmark of the first edition, include cases on how Orlando tourism officials overcame the impact of the Pulse nightclub shooting and a review of the strategy and tactics deployed by the government of Puerto Rico to offset the devastating impacts of Hurricane Maria. Scenarios also feature the U.S. Custom and Border Protection (CBP) separation policy and its impact on nonprofits that shelter migrant children and the controversial tweet by the Houston Rockets GM that set off a global crisis between the NBA and China.

Chapter 2, which traces the history and development of public relations, now includes an expanded review of the role women and people of color played in the evolution of modern public relations. Many of these historical figures have been overlooked by PR textbooks, and we are pleased to share their stories to inspire the next generation of PR professionals.

The book's analyses of social media and the vital role of digital communications in strategic communications have been upgraded as well. Notably, the chapters on PR writing (6), media relations (7), social media and emerging technologies (8), corporate communications (11), and crisis and issues communication (12) have in-depth reviews of these game-changing factors.

This second edition provides new insights and updated information on government and political communications (15) in the Trump era and on global public relations (16). And it continues to highlight PR's role in socially responsible engagement and communications throughout, as well as adds new material in a dedicated chapter, "Corporate Social Responsibility and Community Relations" (9).

In the brief years since writing the first edition, there has been a rising tide of social responsibility and sustainability initiatives, CEO and investor social activism, employee preference for jobs with social purpose, and consumer demand for ethical brands. We have made an effort to address this sea change in our second edition.

Our goal throughout this new edition is to prepare students to move into public relations careers with confidence, ethics, and passion.

Features and Pedagogy

Each chapter of *Introduction to Public Relations* includes several learning tools to help students engage with the field of PR and connect the lessons in this book with present-day practice.

- **Learning Objectives** help prepare students to focus on concepts they will learn throughout the chapter.

- **Scenarios** are how we start each chapter, highlighting a contemporary issue that ties directly to the concepts discussed in the chapter. The opening scenario presents a problem—students are provided with an overview of the situation and some guiding questions they can use to reflect on these issues as they progress through their reading. We revisit the scenario at the end of each chapter, where we outline the solution and provide students with some major takeaways.

- **Insights** are special-topic boxes that add depth or expose practices that make PR such a fascinating field.

- **PR Profiles** feature current practitioners or subject matter experts describing challenges they have faced in their own careers. These veterans and rising stars share their combined experience and backgrounds to help the next generation of leaders of the PR profession. These profiles will inform, entertain, and educate readers and students using this text.

- **Social Responsibility in Action** boxes feature short, specific cases that highlight best practices and effective tactics, showing the link between sound public relations strategy and meaningful social responsibility programs.

- **Social Responsibility** callouts use symbols to identify where focused social responsibility examples appear throughout each chapter.

- **Wrap Up** sections provide the reader with a chapter summary to reinforce students' understanding of the content.

- **Key Terms** in each chapter are listed, with definitions in a glossary at the end of the book.

- **Think About It** exercises encourage students to apply what they have learned through focused individual and group discussion prompts.

- **Write Like a Pro** exercises provide students with a specific writing assignment to practice in the context of PR.

- **Case Studies** present current practices involving well-known companies, agencies, and organizations, such as AT&T, Unilever, Samsung, Mastercard, Gerber, Edelman, and WorldPride. These chapter case studies illustrate the key responsibilities of a modern PR professional: media relations, crisis communications, employee communications, applied communications research, and corporate- and government-specific communications. The cases encourage student discussion through ***Engage*** and ***Discuss*** prompts and problem-solving questions.

We hope you find this text an insightful and valuable introduction to the field of PR through the unique lens of SR and how they can blend together to provide strategic communications leadership for an organization. Our intent is to build students' knowledge and confidence in pursuing successful careers in this dynamic and exciting profession.

ACKNOWLEDGMENTS

We would like to thank our students and alumni for inspiring and challenging us to create this book and extend our practical, applied approach to PR education to the broader market. We also want to acknowledge our colleagues and administrators at The George Washington University and the University of Illinois at Chicago for their support during the research and writing of this book.

As we completed this second edition, our country and the world faced a global health crisis. During this challenging time, the importance of credible and consistent communication from every sector—including the government, nonprofit, and corporate communities—was reinforced on a daily basis. In our view, the crisis emphasized the critical role of strategic communications and the need to prepare today's students to meet other critical challenges in the future.

For their assistance in developing this second edition, the authors deeply appreciate the contributions from the professionals and academics who shared cases, insights, and profiles in our chapters. We would also like to extend thanks to the reviewers for their expertise and their insightful suggestions throughout the development of this book.

Charles F. Byers, Santa Clara University

Tori Martin Cliff, The University of Memphis

Kay Colley, Texas Wesleyan University

Colleen Fitzpatrick, Saint Mary's College

S. Catherine Foster, Canisius College

Maxine Gesualdi, West Chester University of Pennsylvania

Kirk Hazlett, Curry College

Carolyn J. Higgins, Purdue University Northwest

John Kerezy, Cuyahoga Community College

Lucyann S. Kerry, Middlesex University Dubai

Kate S. Kurtin, California State University, Los Angeles

Anne Marie Males, Humber College

Christopher J. McCollough, Columbus State University

Scott Morton, Catawba College

Dana Alexander Nolfe, Bryant University

Peggy O'Keefe, New York University

Megan K. O'Rourke, University of Montana

Maxey Parrish, Baylor University

Pam Parry, Eastern Kentucky University

Claire M. Regan, Wagner College

Arien Rozelle, St. John Fisher College

Amy Sauertieg, Penn State Harrisburg

Shirley Ann Serini, Valdosta State University

Xu Song, Stockton University

Ann Strahle, University of Illinois

We are especially grateful for the clear guidance from the editors at SAGE, particularly Jennifer Jovin-Bernstein, who continuously provided essential critique, advice, and assurance throughout the long process of this project.

Janis is grateful to her past colleagues, employers, and clients who inspired her with worthy projects and challenges that increased her knowledge and professionalism. She is especially grateful to her husband, William S. Page, for his assistance in researching and editing stages of this project. And she thanks her children—Johanna, Ben, Nick, and Marguerite—who offered support and encouragement throughout the process. Janis dedicates this book to her older brother Frank Teruggi Jr., whose life of pursuing social justice drives her commitment to build a better world through socially responsible advocacy and communication.

Larry would like to dedicate this book to his parents, Pat and Bill Parnell, lifelong educators who taught him at an early age that teachers don't just teach—they care. Over the years, he has had mentors, colleagues, and friends in both business and academia too numerous to mention here. Collectively, they have contributed to his professional growth and development, and he is indebted to them for their advice and continuing friendship. Larry is also dedicating this book to his four children—Sara, Matthew, Erin, and Jessica—and four grandchildren—Maya, Isaac, Kyla, and Lucy.

Finally, we would like to thank our spouses, William Page and Janice Parnell, for their constant encouragement and patience as we updated this second edition. We know that it took away from family time, and we hope you are as proud of it as we are.

Janis Teruggi Page, PhD

Lawrence J. Parnell, MBA

ABOUT THE AUTHORS

Our combined professional backgrounds—representing deep experience as PR practitioners, academic researchers, and classroom instructors at leading universities—inform the text and underscore the conclusions and recommendations within.

Janis Teruggi Page draws from 20 years of executive experience managing strategic communications for regional and national media companies. She managed corporate, consumer, and media relations, creating programming partnerships with major TV networks, directing PR for national industry trade show events, and supervising new product launches. She is a member of PRSA and continues to serve clients through her consultancy, MediawerksPR.

An award-winning educator, Janis is a faculty member of the Department of Communication, University of Illinois at Chicago and a Fulbright Distinguished Chair scholar. She has developed and taught both undergraduate- and graduate-level PR courses that instruct principles, writing, cases, campaigns, corporate advocacy, issues management, sustainability, and visual communication.

Janis has produced more than 50 conference papers, book chapters, and refereed articles. Her work appears in the *Journal of Public Interest Communication,* the *Journal of Public Relations Education,* the *Journal of Political Management*, and the *Handbook of Strategic Communication*, among others. Janis is also coauthor of the 2021 textbook *Visual Communication Insights and Strategies*. She earned a PhD from Missouri School of Journalism in 2005.

Lawrence J. Parnell is an award-winning practitioner and educator. In 2003, he was selected the PR Professional of the Year by *PRWeek*; in 2009, he was named to the PR News Hall of Fame; and in 2015, The George Washington University Master's in Strategic Public Relations program, which he leads, was named Best PR Education Program by *PRWeek*. He is an active member of PRSA and the Page Society.

He offers the practical experience of more than 30 years of communications work in government, corporate, and agency settings and 12 years in academia as an associate professor of strategic public relations and program director at The George Washington University (GW). As well, he has served as an adjunct professor at the GW School of Business and teaches strategic communications to MBA candidates.

During his career, he has advised elected officials, government leaders, and corporate executives at the national and global levels on major business and communications issues. He continues to provide high-level communications consulting and training to corporations, nonprofits, and government organizations through his firm Parnell Communications.

His research on CSR, PR, and public diplomacy has been presented at national and global industry and academic conferences and published in *Shaping International Public Opinion: A Model for Nation Branding and Public Diplomacy*.

1

Strategic Public Relations

A Constantly Evolving Discipline

Learning Objectives

1.1   Define and understand the perception of PR

1.2   Define corporate social responsibility

1.3   Explore the growth of the PR industry in the United States and globally

1.4   Review roles, functions, and career options

1.5   Review career options in the field of PR

Scenario

Orlando's Big Thank You: An Integrated Communications Campaign to Revive Tourism

Visit Orlando, the travel and tourism association serving the hospitality industry in Greater Orlando, faced two critical external events that could have seriously impacted the number of visitors in 2017 to the area's restaurants, resorts, theme parks, and hotels.

First, in June of 2016, the Pulse nightclub in Orlando was the site of a mass shooting, an act of domestic terrorism that shocked the city and the country. A report by Maxim Group (PRSA, 2018), "Evaluating the Impact of a Potential Florida Tourism Slowdown From the Orlando Terror Attack," stated, "We believe this weekend's tragic terror-related shooting in Orlando has the potential to reduce tourism-related spending . . . for at least the next couple of quarters."

Second, in early 2017, the Trump administration issued an executive order restricting immigration. This helped create the global perception that the United States was not welcoming to foreign visitors. Following the executive order, the Global Business Travel Association estimated "a loss of over $1.3 billion in overall travel-related expenditures in the US in 2017 . . . that inbound travelers would have spent."

Orlando is the most visited tourist destination in the United States, and the hospitality industry generates more than $66 billion in economic impact per year, accounting for one out of every three jobs in Orlando. According to *Visit Orlando,* the area is home to more than 450 resorts, hotels, and inns and attracted over 68 million visitors in 2016.

A decline in the reputation of the area as a safe and welcoming destination represented a serious economic challenge that demanded immediate attention.

Faced with this potential crisis, *Visit Orlando* needed a communications campaign to reassure potential visitors that Orlando was still a welcoming, safe, and worthwhile place to visit. To assist them with meeting the challenge, the company retained the services of Edelman, a leading global PR firm, and the resulting program they developed and executed won a Silver Anvil, the top award from the Public Relations Society of America (PRSA), in 2018.

As you read through this chapter, consider what public relations (PR) strategies and tactics you would recommend to offset the potential damage to Orlando's global reputation created by these two unrelated events. What would you recommend that Orlando tourism officials say as they prepare to announce their annual numbers? Consider the following questions:

1. What kind of research would you recommend?
2. Who would be your target audiences?
3. What special event(s) or media relations strategy would you propose?
4. What role should social media play in your response plan?

At the end of this chapter (as with all the chapters in this text), you will see how the organization responded and the outcome(s) the public relations program produced. Pay special attention to demonstrating return on investment (ROI) for the resources allocated to meet the challenge, reduce the impact of the crisis or issue, and enhance **corporate reputation**.

The authors hope you will find this approach interesting and challenging and that it will help you connect the key takeaways of each chapter to real-life examples of strategic public relations. ●

Source: PRSA, 2018.

The goals of this introductory chapter are to provide a foundation and understanding of the field of PR (public relations) and its development into a strategic management function, as well as outline how you might pursue a career in this dynamic industry.

The chapter will also connect PR to the growing field of corporate social responsibility (CSR)—also referred to as sustainability or corporate philanthropy—and illustrate how one discipline informs and enriches the other. Later in the chapter, you will read the first of a series of "Profiles in PR." In this section, you will be introduced to a successful PR professional who will share her or his experience and advice for building a career in PR and/or social responsibility (SR).

In subsequent chapters, the profiles will feature professionals and experts who share their experiences and advice on the topics covered in each chapter, such as media relations, crisis management, or research.

The Image of Public Relations in Popular Culture

>> LO 1.1   Define and understand the perception of PR

In this chapter, you will read about the public perception—accurate and not-so-accurate—of PR and how it contributes to an organization or cause. This issue has been discussed and debated since the early days of the profession. Historically, PR professionals focused primarily on generating publicity, versus today when the goal has shifted to impacting public opinion, influencing behavior, and driving business results (see Chapter 2). The historical image among nonpractitioners of the **publicist**, or "flack," has been driven, in part, by how the profession has been depicted in movies, the media, and on television.

According to Joe Saltzman (2011), director of The Image of the Journalist in Popular Culture project at The Norman Lear Center at the University of Southern California (USC), "Many public relations practitioners believe that the image of the publicist and the public relations professional (in the media) is one of the most negative in history" (para. 5). In Saltzman's research, he studied more than 300 films and TV programs from 1901 to 2011. The negative images of PR range from devious press agents who will do anything—including lie, cheat, steal, and even commit crimes—to save their reputations and protect clients. For example, the character Don Draper (played by Jon Hamm) is portrayed as a powerful and unethical communications executive on the A&E Network show *Mad Men*.

Olivia Pope (played by Kerry Washington), on her hit ABC show *Scandal*, is involved in high-stakes crisis and political communications work each week. The hit show, still running in syndication, is based on the life and career of Judy Smith, a Washington, DC-based crisis manager. Notably, Smith served as a consultant to the show, providing her input on how PR and crisis management in Washington, DC, works. However, she insists her work, while demanding, is nowhere near as dramatic as the life and

When two recent crises threatened Orlando's global reign as a top vacation destination, the PR firm Edelman created a reputation recovery campaign to welcome back tourists.
iStock.com/SeanPavonePhoto

career of Olivia Pope. "Moving dead bodies from crime scenes—that doesn't happen in my office in Washington, DC," explained Judy Smith (Burton, 2014).

In her pioneering study, *Public Relations in Film and Fiction, 1930 to 1995*, Karen Miller wrote that today's "fictitious characters . . . display very little understanding of PR or what practitioners do" (1999, p. 24). Miller explained, "Sometimes (in the movies) PR is magic," and other times, "it is almost embarrassingly easy."

Nowhere in these shows or movies do you see PR people working on a serious issue, such as protecting Orlando's critical tourism industry, as outlined in the chapter-opening scenario. Perhaps that is because while the work benefits the employees of thousands of large and small businesses in Orlando, it is not as entertaining as watching the high-stakes, dramatic storylines of PR professionals common in films and on television.

These stereotypes should not be taken lightly and must be countered with facts, as with any profession. The best way to do that is by engaging professionally with people and clients and showing the value PR brings to the management table and global marketplace.

Defining Public Relations: What's in a Name?

Moving beyond the *perception* of public relations, let's examine the various definitions of PR to see if there is a consensus. Defining PR has been a goal for much of the profession's history. Often, practitioners have relied on saying what PR was not—for example, *advertising*, which traditionally relies on paid media "ads," or *sales*, which is an in-person transactional exercise. At its best, PR involves an information exchange between people or "publics" with the goal of sharing information and influencing the behavior of the recipient.

Other key elements of PR that distinguish it from advertising include the need for specialized skills, such as issues and crisis management, internal communications, and providing strategic communications advice. These and other related elements are unique to PR and are not found in advertising, sales, or other marketing activity.

While the strategies, tactics, and vehicles differ over time, PR professionals are constantly engaged in delivering messages and influencing behavior or public opinion. Whether it is buying a certain brand or product, voting for a candidate, donating to a cause or charity, or investing in a **public company**, in PR your role is to build reputation and create trust. This must be done in an ethical and transparent manner in order to serve your client or company's interests as well as your own career.

A Crowd-Sourced Definition From the Public Relations Society of America

In response to the need for an agreed-upon definition, the Public Relations Society of America (PRSA), the leading professional organization for public relations professionals, launched an effort to develop a more "current and accurate definition of public relations."

Judy Smith, a Washington, DC–based crisis manager (*right*), was the inspiration for the character Olivia Pope, played by Kerry Washington (*left*), on the television show *Scandal*.
Frederick M. Brown / Stringer / Getty Images

The project took the form of a "crowd-sourced" effort involving PRSA members, academics, and industry leaders to solicit input for an "official" definition of PR to be used going forward. That months-long process produced the following definition, which was first published in 2012: *Public relations is a strategic communication process that builds mutually beneficial relationships between organizations and their publics.*

Chartered in 1947, the PRSA is the world's largest and foremost organization of PR professionals with more than 22,000 members. In addition, it has a sister organization, the Public Relations Student Society of America (PRSSA), which consists of over 370 chapters and more than 9,700 undergraduate members, students majoring in or considering a career in public relations. PRSA provides professional development, sets standards of excellence, and upholds principles of ethics for its members. It also advocates for greater understanding and adoption of public relations services and acts as one of the industry's leading voices on pivotal business and professional issues (see www.prsa.org).

Public Relations Scholars Weigh In

Over the years, academics and authors have developed their own definitions that share many of the same elements. Scott Cutlip, Allen Center, and Glen Broom, in the seminal text *Effective Public Relations* (first published in 2000), defined PR as the "management function that identifies, establishes and maintains mutually beneficial relationships between an organization and the various publics on whom its success or failure depends" (Cutlip et al., 2000).

This definition has echoes both in the PRSA version as well as the one put forth by leading PR scholars James E. Grunig and Todd Hunt (1984), who suggested that "public relations is the management of communication between an organization and its publics."

What Is "Public Relations"?

If you Google "public relations," you see it is defined by the Oxford English Dictionary as "the professional maintenance of a favorable public image by a company or other organization or a famous person" and "the state of the relationship between the public and a company or other organization or a famous person" (Lexico Oxford Dictionary, n.d.).

Despite the varied definitions for the profession, Paul Holmes, founder and chair of The Holmes Group, notes that he likes the term "public relations" (2017a). Holmes has been writing about public relations for more than 25 years, and he suggests reducing the term to its component parts. The words "public" and "relations" are in common usage and appear to be well understood: "public" (of or concerning the people as a whole; done, perceived, or existing in open view; or ordinary people in general; the community) and "relations" (the way in which two or more people or things are connected or the way in which two or more people or groups regard and behave toward each other).

Holmes offers his own definition, rooted in the meaning of the two words: "Public relations is the discipline of managing the relationship between an organization and the people upon whom it depends for success and with whom it interacts, and ensuring that those relationships facilitate the organization's strategic objectives" (Holmes, 2017a, para. 10).

There are significant reasons why he likes this definition, he notes.

First, it makes it clear that the end product of public relations—and therefore the main focus of every campaign—is a relationship: hopefully, a stronger, more rewarding relationship with employees, consumers, shareholders, regulators, or the communities in which organizations operate.

Second, if you think about how relationships are formed, one thing should be clear: Communication is important, but it is far from the most important factor. Ad agencies, digital firms, and even management consultancies can all claim to be in the communications business. PR is unique in looking beyond the transactional and focusing on the long-term, mutually beneficial value of relationships. To remove that key element would be to surrender the critical differentiator between

what PR pros bring to the table and what others offer.

Holmes dismisses the current angst around the term "public relations," suggesting it's the result of a particular moment in time, of changes in the relationship between marketing and corporate communications, and of increased competition among advertising agencies, digital firms, management consultancies, and others.

At a time when public relations people are anxious to define themselves more broadly than ever before, when senior in-house people are needed at the policy-making table more urgently than ever before, and when public relations firms have embraced integrated campaigns that use paid, shared, and owned channels, Holmes suggests that PR professionals need to double down on the term "public relations." By jettisoning the term "public relations," practitioners might be turning their backs on the one thing that differentiates PR from all of those other related disciplines: the focus on relationships. ●

Source: Holmes, 2017a.

Regardless of which definition you find most relevant, each has elements and concepts in common. Note the use of the terms "mutually beneficial," "management function," "strategic," and "publics." At its heart, PR is, in fact, a communications process that keeps the interests of all parties—pro and con—in mind. It is strategic, not tactical. It is a relationship, not a one-way street where policies or positions are taken onboard verbatim by your audience. It is an interactive process that occurs over time, not a transaction or isolated event or activity.

These distinctions convey a give-and-take relationship in which the interests of all parties can be addressed and communications goals more likely achieved—all within the context of that "relationship."

Public Relations Versus Advertising: Understanding the Difference

While the lines between PR and advertising/marketing are increasingly blurred, there are distinct differences, even though both work through the public media to convey a message. To begin with, as noted earlier, PR involves persuasion, not purchasing. The result the PR pro is seeking (obtaining news coverage, influencing public opinion, enhancing a reputation or rebuilding one, etc.) comes through interaction between the PR professional and a gatekeeper (e.g., a journalist, blogger, or influencer). This process of outreach and persuasion of a reporter to write or film a story is referred to as "earned" media and is central to the practice of media relations.

On the contrary, advertising is a transaction, thus the term "paid" media. A company that wants public attention for a product or a cause pays for the print ad space, broadcast airtime, or paid social media posts, and it is usually run as is with no interpretation. This distinction—between earned and paid media—has been captured in a short but accurate quote: "PR is what you *pray* for. Advertising is what you *pay* for" (Wynne, 2014).

Defining Corporate Social Responsibility and Sustainability Communications: Doing Well by Doing Good, or Is It More Complex?

>> LO 1.2   **Define corporate social responsibility**

Many PR campaigns incorporate corporate social responsibility (CSR) engagement, defined as the "economic, legal, ethical, and *discretionary* expectations that society has of organizations" (Carroll & Buchholtz, 2014, p. 36) to give back or contribute to society. In 2007, a peer-reviewed study of the top 50 global business schools defined CSR as "the sum of the *voluntary* actions taken by a company to address the economic, social and environmental impacts of its business operations and the concerns of its principal stakeholders" (Christensen et al., 2007, pp. 347–368). The use of the word "voluntary" is key here—no one is making these companies do this activity.

Ideally, CSR should function as a built-in, self-regulating mechanism whereby a business monitors and ensures its support of the law, ethical standards, and international norms. Consequently, businesses would embrace responsibility for the impact of its activities on the environment, consumers, employees, communities, stakeholders, and all other members of the public sphere.

Evolution of Corporate Philanthropy Into Corporate Social Responsibility

Carol Cone, generally regarded as the pioneer of CSR as a business and communications strategy, described the evolution of CSR in a seminal 2010 study published by Edelman (2010):

Nearly two-thirds of consumers feel that it is not adequate for corporations to simply give money away to charity or good causes, they need to integrate them into their day-to-day business. . . . It is no longer enough to slap a "green" ribbon on a product and call it CSR. Americans seek deeper involvement in social issues and expect brands and companies to provide various means of engagement . . . we call this the rise of the "citizen consumer."

In 2004, CVS pharmacies across the United States stopped selling cigarettes after the company decided that doing so was incompatible with its goal of promoting health.
Andrew Burton / Staff / Getty Images

Essentially, CSR is the deliberate inclusion of public interest into corporate decision-making, and it honors a triple bottom line: people, planet, and profit.

Examples of the close relationship between PR and CSR are found throughout this book, and Chapter 9 offers an in-depth exploration of the practice.

Growth of Public Relations Into a Global Industry

>> **LO 1.3** **Explore the growth of the PR industry in the United States and globally**

Looking ahead to Chapter 2, you will learn how the PR industry has roots throughout U.S. history, business, and politics. In addition to its long heritage in the United States, PR has become a global business; several countries in Europe—such as Great Britain—have long traditions of PR as well. Within the United States, PR remains an attractive career choice with steady growth in employment opportunities and salaries driven by increasing spending by clients and companies on PR-related activity.

The U.S. Department of Labor's Bureau of Labor Statistics (BLS) estimates job growth in the PR field at 6% per year from 2018 to 2028, with a median income of $60,000 per year (BLS, 2020b).

The BLS's most recent report indicates that as of the end of 2018, there were 240,700 people nationwide employed in the PR industry as public relations specialists. The BLS projected about 14,000 new jobs in PR will be added each year until 2024 (BLS, 2020b).

Social Media and Digital Communications Key to Growth

A lot of this steady growth is attributable to the demand for skilled communicators who can leverage social media for their employers or clients. For those of you with these skills, the career upside is almost unlimited. For the rest of you, this is an area of opportunity once you have these skills mastered.

The BLS noted in its most recent report that the growth of the PR industry "will be driven by the need for organizations to maintain their public image, especially with the growth of social media" (BLS, 2020b).

While much of the increase in PR spending in the United States is attributable to an improving economy, its growing recognition as an effective platform for supporting business and corporate social responsibility activity is a major factor as well.

There is no doubt that social media has accelerated this trend, moving rapidly from a few major platforms for leisure time use to dozens of powerful marketing and communications platforms for organizations all over the globe.

Global Public Relations Spending Trends

Industry data shows that between 2012 and 2018, global investments in marketing services were experiencing continuous growth, with the latest figures expected to surpass $450 billion. Marketing services encompass areas such as public relations, data investment management, sponsorship, health care, and direct marketing (Duffin, 2019).

Global spending on PR itself is hard to track as there are different terms or activities included in the category (e.g., advertising, marketing, special events) in different countries, and the documentation is not as reliable as it is in the United States. Two leading PR industry publications, *PRWeek* and *The Holmes Report*, reported continued global growth in 2018.

PRWeek's April 2019 Agency Business Report shows that overall global agency revenue for the larger, established firms rose 5% in 2018, to $11.9 billion, up 1% on prior year growth. The 2018 U.S. number increased slightly less than the rise reported for 2017, but it was still up 4% to $5.64 billion (Barrett, 2020).

The Holmes Report's (now part of PRovoke) April 2019 estimate, which includes smaller and newer firms outside of the top 250, along with the vast number of firms that do not provide revenue figures, puts the size of the global PR agency industry at $15.5 billion, up from $15 billion in 2018 (PRovoke, 2019b).

Both publications noted particularly strong markets worldwide (besides the United States), including the world's second-largest China, Europe, India, and the Middle East.

Emerging and Developing Nations

In developing countries where traditional media is limited or a free, independent press is not a given, PR's growth is being driven by social media platforms that are easily accessible and largely uncensored. In these economies, private citizens and advocacy groups use social media to spread their message(s), build followers, and conduct business without ever dealing with a newspaper or broadcast media outlet.

Pew Research reported in its 2016 online media report (Poushter, 2016) that the majority of adult Internet users in developing nations surveyed say that they use social networking sites, such as Facebook and Twitter, for news and information, as well as to keep in touch. The report adds that adults in emerging and developing nations are more likely to use these two forms of social media compared to citizens in more developed countries (Poushter, 2016).

Smartphones in developing nations, such as India, Mexico, and Vietnam (*left to right*), can be essential tools for the spread of information, given the lack of traditional press.
iStock.com/boggy22; Jeff Greenberg / Contributor / Getty Images; HOANG DINH / Staff / Getty Images

Roles and Functions for Public Relations Pros

>> LO 1.4 **Review roles, functions, and career options**

As noted earlier, some organizations rely on PR professionals solely to "play defense," which means essentially to offset bad news or manage a crisis or major issue facing the organization. However, enlightened organizations see the benefit of using the PR staff to "play offense" as well and enhance the reputation of the company, cause, or candidate.

What are the key roles PR professionals play in an organization? What are the key strategies and tactics they use? How do you get started and build a career in PR? Let's examine these questions now and set the stage for a more in-depth discussion of strategies and tactics in subsequent chapters.

Roles

Writer

First and foremost, to be effective as a PR professional, you *must* be an accomplished writer, and you must continue working to maintain the quality of your work as well. To succeed, you will need to be able to take complex or controversial subject matter and prepare press releases, statements, opinion pieces, and, occasionally, speeches and white papers for your clients or senior management team. In addition, your writing must not only be succinct and complete, but it must be persuasive. After all, your goal is to influence the audience and stimulate behavior (e.g., making a purchase, supporting a cause or candidate, or raising funds for a charity), so being persuasive, accurate, and honest is key.

Strategic Advisor

Good PR professionals are a strategic resource to their company or client. They keep them abreast of current issues, trends in public opinion, and on marketplace developments. No communications plan occurs in a vacuum. Knowing what competitors are doing, how the public is feeling, and what government officials might do or say that impacts your organization is critical to developing strategic plans and selecting tactics. To do this well, you will need to stay current on your company and industry and on overall business trends. You will also need to be comfortable with PR strategies and tactics to advise your company on the best path to follow given the situation.

Marketing Communications Expert

Occasionally, the role of PR is to support product introductions or ongoing sales and marketing programs. While this is most often the case with consumer product companies—sometimes referred to as **business-to-consumer (B-to-C) communications**—increasingly PR is being leveraged to boost sales and launch new products across many types of industries, including **business-to-business (B-to-B)** and **business-to-government (B-to-G)** situations.

This can take the form of news conferences or events to introduce new products, testimonials, and case studies and posting content on social media platforms (e.g., Facebook, Instagram, Twitter, and Snapchat) to create interest and conversation about the product or service. This has evolved to a practice referred to as **integrated marketing communications (IMC)**.

While many have forgotten the details of what happened on the Deepwater Horizon rig, they probably recall that BP was responsible.
iStock.com/landbysea

Crisis Manager

This is one of the most well-known and often glamorized roles for PR (e.g., *Scandal*), and most PR pros see it as the ultimate test of their abilities. In a crisis, something *big* has gone wrong: A disaster has occurred; negligence or discrimination within an organization has been discovered; a product is being recalled; or financial wrongdoing by management is uncovered. Your company is in the spotlight. The so-called court of public opinion is in session, and its judgments can be harsh and swift—especially in a 24/7 digital media world. Working under these circumstances is challenging and exciting, so be aware that this work is very stressful and the stakes are high. It is not for the inexperienced, unprepared, or timid.

Also, keep in mind that what people remember the most about a crisis is not the details but how well the company (and the PR team) handled the situation and responded to the issues. One need only look at the Deepwater Horizon explosion and oil spill in April 2010 to see what happens when a crisis is poorly managed. More people recall the dramatic underwater footage of oil pouring into the Gulf of Mexico, the damaged coastline, and stricken wildlife than remember what happened to cause the damage. But they have not forgotten the name of company responsible: BP. The same is true for airline accidents (e.g., Boeing Max crashes); banking industry scandals (Wells Fargo), or cell phones that spontaneously combust (Samsung Galaxy).

The Public Relations Tool Kit

As a PR professional, you will learn to deploy tools and tactics to accomplish your communications goals. While there are many skills you will use in your career, there are basic ones you must master to be successful. Later in this text, in the chapters on key practice areas, there will be a more in-depth discussion of each of these. For now, we will summarize them as follows: media relations, employee communications, research and strategic planning, and social media (see Figure 1.1).

Let's examine each one separately.

Media Relations

Media relations and PR are often used interchangeably, especially by nonpractitioners. However, while they are related, they are not the same thing. Generally, media relations strategies are designed to accomplish one specific goal—for example, to create or manage publicity.

Images like this one, of a pelican slicked with oil after the Deepwater Horizon disaster, stick with people, as does the company responsible—in this case, BP.
MCT / Contributor / Getty Images

FIGURE 1.1

The Public Relations Tool Kit

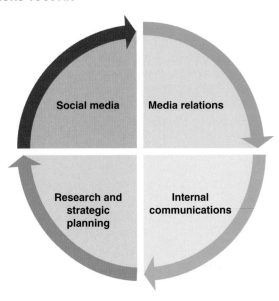

Media relations can be described as a company's interactions (directly or through intermediaries) with editors, reporters, and journalists from national, local, specialty, and trade publications or online and broadcast outlets. The goal is to communicate a message, story, or information by convincing the journalist(s) it is newsworthy and deserves mention or focus in their publication or broadcast outlet.

On occasion, media relations can mean working with the media to avoid a "bad" story or "balance" one to minimize the damage. For example, a reporter may approach you with a story idea or tip that you know is based on a rumor or misleading information. Your role is to provide sufficient data and details to convince them that the story idea is flawed or incomplete and provide the information needed to support that conclusion. Sometimes, this means they will abandon the story; at other times, they will just include your company's point of view more prominently and thereby minimize the "blame game."

Another component of media relations critical to your success is to be an effective liaison between the company and the media. Dana Perino, who served as White House Press Secretary to President George W. Bush (September 2007–January 2009) and is now a commentator on Fox News, explains it this way: "Your job (*in the White House*) is to represent the President to the media, as most people expect, but it is also to represent the media to the President—both roles are crucial to your success in the job" (D. Perino, personal communication, 2017). This has clear relevance to the role you will play between your client or company and the media.

Employee Communications

Those of you whose career path leads you to work for a company or inside a large organization may find yourselves asked to manage the communications to your fellow employees. This can concern routine matters such as employee benefits and updates to company policy or involve more complex matters like communicating before, during, and after a merger or similar major corporate event. Generally, employee communications can involve creating newsletters, websites, videos, intranets, or frequently asked questions (FAQs) and preparing remarks for senior management to convey their vision for the company to employees.

However, communications can be a crucial factor in whether the benefits of a major organizational change (e.g., a merger) are achieved or not, research shows. Depending on which research source you use, it is estimated that anywhere between 50% and 85% of mergers fail to deliver on the promises made the day the deal was announced. Often, one of the reasons cited for the failure is poor communication to the employees impacted by the transaction and lack of clarity on the vision and goals going forward.

More recently, activism among employees and encouraging their employer to take public stands on controversial issues (e.g., immigration, gender equality, discrimination) is on the rise. The firm Weber Shandwick, a popular thought leader on the topic of CEO activism, (see "CEO Activism in 2017: High Noon in the C-Suite," Weber Shandwick, 2017) recently produced a new report ("Employee Activism in the Age of Purpose: Employees (Up)Rising") that documents this trend: "Nearly four in 10 employees (38%) report that they have spoken up to support or criticize their employers' actions over a controversial issue that affects society" (Weber Shandwick, 2019, para. 2).

Research and Strategic Planning

In a time when documenting your results matters more and more, PR professionals need to develop their strategic planning and research capabilities. As such, a full chapter will be spent reviewing this topic in detail later in the book (see Chapter 4). Whether you conduct the research yourself or delegate it to a colleague or an outside firm, your plans will be much more likely to succeed if they are based on solid research. This can take the form of **secondary research** (reviewing already available materials) or **primary research** (e.g., conducting new surveys and/or focus groups).

In an ideal situation, your communications plan will benefit from both of these forms of research. Ironically, secondary research often precedes primary research in that the material/data to review already exists (secondary) and does not need to be designed, fielded, and the results evaluated (primary) before any insights are available.

Your research plan should include testing your message(s), identifying your target audience, and measuring progress toward the goals you have set. The up-front investment of time and resources on research will provide a strong foundation and greatly enhance the outcome of your plan (Stacks & Michaelson, 2010). The importance of the research and planning element was outlined well in the case presented at the beginning of the chapter. The research efforts undertaken by *Visit Orlando* and Edelman included both secondary and primary research on tourist and visitor attitudes about Orlando following the two tragic events. Both were key to developing their recommendations to respond.

As noted, there will be a more in-depth discussion of research and strategic planning in Chapter 4.

Social Media

The explosive growth in digital or social media as an alternative media and information source—particularly in the developing world—has dramatically increased the need for social media skills as a prerequisite for a career in public relations (Elliott, 2011; Perrin, 2015). Deirdre Breakenridge, a noted author and social media expert, suggests that "people in the PR industry need to become hybrid professionals" (Cision, 2012), combining traditional PR and cutting-edge social media skills.

Breakenridge recommends the following goals for young PR pros:

The explosive growth in social media has required companies to combine traditional PR and cutting-edge social media skills. PR crises can quickly go viral online, as United learned after several incidents in which passengers were mistreated and, in one instance, injured by their employees.
iStock.com/Laser1987

- Integrate traditional PR practices with digital and social communications while moving the best of both practices forward.

- Work outside of the PR "silo" and cross-functionally with marketing, including learning and applying marketing tactics.

- Collaborate with other departments, such as web/IT, sales, customer service, human resources, and so on.

- Be flexible and adaptable in an ever-changing global communications environment (Cision, 2012).

Given this trend, employers will be looking for professionals who are comfortable in this space and competent in leveraging this resource to accomplish business and communications goals. It is no longer sufficient to know how to use Facebook, Instagram, Twitter, or Snapchat for personal outreach. Employers are looking for staff that know how to work with social media to reach new customers, engage with them, drive sales and marketing programs, or impact public opinion.

In the corporate arena, this can include managing the social media profile, monitoring online conversations, and developing and posting content on company-owned sites to enhance reputation and support business objectives.

In the nonprofit arena, social media is a very cost-efficient way to build followers and raise money for operations and charitable activities, as well as activate and engage people to support a cause or issue.

Finally, in government and in politics, social media represents a direct communications channel to reach citizens and voters to inform and educate them about government services, policy, candidates, and—in the case of elections—serve as a get-out-the-vote weapon.

Career Paths for Public Relations Professionals: Which Way Is Right for You?

>> LO 1.5   Review career options in the field of PR

While there are many variables and options, there are generally four paths your PR career might take: agency (such as a PR or consulting firm); corporate, in a communications staff role; government (e.g., local, state, or federal), or working for a nonprofit organization (like World Wildlife Fund) or an association (such as the National Restaurant Association; see Figure 1.2).

Let's review each one individually and put them into perspective.

FIGURE 1.2

PR Career Paths

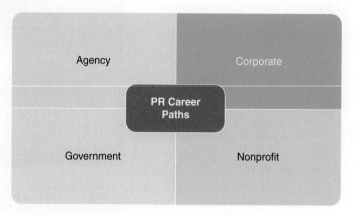

Agency

The path of working in an agency setting is one many PR professionals take, especially early in their careers when they are first learning their craft. As a young PR professional, joining an agency has many advantages. First and foremost is that the focus of the business is on public relations—that is what they do for clients every day. As such, you are in an environment where nearly everyone you work with is a PR professional. The opportunity to learn new tactics and strategies, benefit from a colleague's previous work, or bounce an idea off someone with more experience is actively encouraged. Some people make an entire career of working for an agency, rising to become practice leaders, office managing partners, or even part of the senior management of a firm.

PR PROFILE

How I Started and Built My Career

Erin Munley DeWaters

Photo courtesy of Erin Munley DeWaters

Research shows millennials change jobs four times before the age of 32—I beat that average.

By the age of 32, I had held six jobs with titles ranging from "assistant" to "strategist" to "vice president." I've done many types of communications—from digital to crisis—and helped launch an award-winning CSR program. I have had an interesting, challenging, and rewarding career so far. I joke that I must have good career karma, but I also know my success has been achieved by leveraging two things: education and opportunities.

Careers start with decisions about education. When you select a college, you start to create your network. Professors, counselors, and peers will be avenues to career opportunities. People you know from childhood, like friends of your parents, are also your initial network. That's how my career started.

My mom had a friend whose daughter worked on Capitol Hill. Through that connection, I got an internship in a congressional office. When I graduated from the University of North Carolina at Chapel Hill, I wanted to go back to DC, so I scoured the job boards online and applied to entry-level roles. I was open to *all* opportunities, and I encourage you to be, too.

My first job was in a nonprofit membership organization. It wasn't a PR agency or well-known company, yet today, I do PR for a company that is part of a global retail group. So when you're evaluating roles, please know there is no "typical" career path.

Another major step in my career was graduate school. Two years after college, I got my master's in PR at The George Washington University. I learned a ton, broadened my network, and built confidence. Based on that confidence, I've raised my hand many times to take on new professional responsibilities so I could learn and gain experience.

Raising my hand helped me get the chance to launch a new CSR program for Food Lion, the southeastern U.S. regional grocery chain. There was a vacant position, and I stepped into a lead role on the project. Food Lion was looking to integrate PR and CSR, and that's exactly what we did through "Food Lion Feeds." It was the most rewarding experience of my career.

After that, I joined MetLife, where I managed PR for two of its U.S. divisions. MetLife's reputation as a good corporate citizen is one of the things that drew me to the company.

Today, I'm the director of communications for the services company of Ahold Delhaize USA, the largest grocery retail group on the East Coast. Ahold Delhaize is the parent company to Food Lion and other top grocery chains across the United States. In this role, I've had the opportunity to help the newly formed subsidiary company establish its community engagement program.

In my experience, I have learned that CSR isn't a nice-to-do; it's a must-do, and smart companies get that. An integrated PR/CSR strategy creates opportunities to tell stories, reach consumers, and build corporate reputation. If you're entering PR today, you'll be at a significant advantage by understanding the intersection.

As you think about the road ahead, lean into your education and value the relationships it helps you create. Be open to opportunities. Raise your hand and learn. You'll build competency and credibility, and they will be the foundation for your career path—wherever it takes you. ●

Erin DeWaters is a self-described "older millennial" and a working wife, mom, and graduate of the University of North Carolina at Chapel Hill and The George Washington University. She serves as director of communications for Retail Business Services, the services company of leading grocery retail group, Ahold Delhaize USA.

Barri Rafferty, worldwide president of Ketchum Public Relations, got her start in the industry working at Cone Communications while in graduate school in Boston. She then moved to New York and experimented with a big agency (Burson-Marsteller), the corporate side (SlimFast), and at a small beauty boutique PR agency (Lippe Taylor). Rafferty decided that a big agency would provide her with a supportive environment as she started her family, so she joined Ketchum as a vice president and account supervisor in New York.

Working her way up to her present position of president and CEO of Ketchum, Rafferty has held several key roles, including group manager for the New York brand practice, associate director of the New York office, and director of the global brand marketing practice. She previously relocated to Atlanta to be director of that office and later became director of the Ketchum's South region. She came back to New York to serve as its office director. In 2012, Rafferty became CEO of North America, and in 2016, she was named worldwide president. Since her appointment

Barri Rafferty was the first woman to lead a global PR firm.
Photo courtesy of Barri Rafferty

in 2017 as the first woman to lead a global firm, several other major firms have followed suit and named female leaders.

After working in an agency for a few years, you might decide to move to an internal (or client-side) position in a government, corporate, or nonprofit setting. Others decide to start their own firms or set up shop as independent counselors to leverage the skills and contacts gained while working for a larger firm. Still others move into the academic arena to share their knowledge and experience with the next generation.

Corporate

For those PR professionals who pursue a career in a corporate setting, there are challenges and opportunities to develop skills not found in other work settings. As a corporate PR professional, you would generally work in the communications department, although it may have many different names depending on the nomenclature and culture of the company. Some companies refer to the department as public relations; others will use variations of corporate communications, external affairs, corporate affairs, public affairs, and/or just communications or marketing.

The name of the department is often dependent on the reporting relationship of the function. According to a recent study by USC Annenberg Center (Holmes, 2017b), in most companies, PR reports to marketing or the CEO, but in a few cases, it reports to others, including legal or human resources (HR). Reporting to the CEO is viewed as desirable because it positions the function as a key corporate department with direct access and interaction with top management (see Figure 1.3).

These individuals often have responsibility for writing the company's annual report to stockholders, news releases on quarterly financial results, announcement on mergers and acquisitions, and senior management changes. These are known as **material events**, and publicly traded companies are required to report them to the public in a timely manner.

A career in corporate PR can be challenging and rewarding, and the compensation and benefits are often quite good. As well, corporate PR positions can be more stable and less susceptible to client budget shifts or staffing changes that often impact agency work.

Recent research suggests that succeeding in a corporate role requires communications executives "to be knowledgeable about the business—from strategy to operations—so they are able to provide strategic input on issues that span business functions" (Arthur W. Page Society, 2017). The Page report quotes one anonymous CEO as suggesting, "I don't think a healthy organization can do much without (communications) being involved in every part of the strategy and every part of the operation" (p. 2).

A cautionary note about this path: Unlike the agency world, PR teams are relatively small in most companies, and most likely, you will be one of only a few people who work on PR for your company. This can limit your internal network and

FIGURE 1.3

In-House Reporting Lines

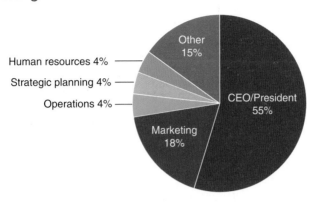

Regardless of the reporting relationship, staff members in a corporate communications department are usually responsible for media relations, executive, internal (sometimes shared with HRO, and financial communications if the company has public shareholders and is listed on a stock exchange (e.g., the New York Stock Exchange or NASDAQ).

Source: "2017 Global Communications Report Predicts Convergence of Marketing And PR," Paul Holmes, March 30, 2017. Reprinted with permission.

be challenging because your fellow employees may not understand what you do and how it adds value to the company's business objectives. As a result, many PR pros wait to pursue corporate opportunities until later in their careers when they have more general PR experience. As such, building and maintaining a good personal network of mentors and colleagues outside of your current employer is strongly recommended.

Government

Many professionals have long careers in a government communication role, working at the federal or state level. In the federal government, the function is more commonly referred to as **public affairs**. Most every cabinet department—from the U.S. Department of Agriculture (USDA) to Health and Human Services (HHS) and the Department of Homeland Security (DHS)—has a public affairs office. In larger departments with a national or international focus (like the U.S. State Department), there are often regional offices outside the United States where communications professionals interact with the global and local media and serve constituents (e.g., U.S. citizens and companies) locally.

Similarly, at the state, county, or city level, public information and public service are the driving forces and primary focus. Most cities' locally elected officials (e.g., governor, county commissioner, or mayor) have a dedicated press secretary, who serves at the pleasure of the elected official. In each major city or state department, there is usually also a public information office, focused on responding to the media and the public, providing information about essential services and responding in crisis or disaster situations. As with some of the other career paths noted here, the government PR professional (or public affairs officer) is usually part of a small group of dedicated professionals. As such, there are few others in the office who understand your role and can offer suggestions or advice, making your external network all the more important. Here again, having an outside network of colleagues—or participating in organizations such as the National Association of Government Communicators (NAGC)—is strongly advised.

Nonprofit and/or Association Public Relations

Nonprofit and association work is an increasingly popular path for young PR professionals, especially in the Washington, DC, area and in New York City, where many of these national and global organizations are headquartered. However, success in this setting is measured in awareness, membership growth, and fundraising success, as well as by traditional PR activities. Nonprofits such as the United Way, the Red Cross, and the World Wildlife Federation are focused on a key cause or issue, such as community service, disaster relief, or protecting endangered species. The PR professionals in this environment handle media relations and provide executive counsel as well as support ongoing fundraising efforts and membership communications and development.

Nonprofit company members frequently look to their association to monitor events and activity of the local, state, and federal government as well as advance the profession through research, training, and overall visibility. Often, these organizations take on the additional role of managing industrywide issues and crises on behalf of their members or assist member companies as they work their way through the situation.

Jeff Joseph was formerly senior vice president of communications and strategic relationships at the Consumer Technology Association (CTA), based in northern Virginia. According to the CTA website, the group "advocates for the entrepreneurs, technologists and innovators who mold the future of the consumer technology industry" (J. Joseph, personal communication, 2017). The CTA (formerly the CEA—the Consumer Electronics Association) is best known as the host of the huge Consumer Electronics Show (CES) each year in Las Vegas, which draws thousands of tech suppliers and customers to see what's new and cool in high technology and popular entertainment from the biggest names in technology. "Association PR allows you to engage in a variety of PR disciplines. One moment you're focused on public affairs. The next, media relations, or crisis communications. All while supporting our singular mission—to help grow the industry," Joseph said. Currently, he serves as president of the Software & Information Industry Association (SIIA).

Scenario Outcome

In this chapter, you were introduced to media relations, research, crisis management, and other foundations of strategic public relations. Now, it is time to apply that knowledge to a "real-world" business challenge.

The Red Cross PR team is actively involved in community outreach and fundraising support along with community and media relations activity when the organization responds to disaster situations across the United States and around the world.
Orlando Sentinel / Contributor / Getty Images

At the start of the chapter when the *Visit Orlando* case was outlined, you were asked to think about how the organization should respond to two external events—the Pulse nightclub shooting and President Trump's executive order on immigration—as it prepared to release its annual visitation reports for 2017.

The following questions were suggested to guide your thinking:

1. What kind of research would you recommend?
2. Who would be your target audiences for the announcement of the annual results?
3. What special events or media relations strategy would be most effective?
4. What role should social media play?

To begin with, the communications team (*Visit Orlando* and Edelman) gathered key stakeholders to brainstorm new approaches. The team set the overarching objectives of reinforcing Orlando's brand identity as a top vacation and meetings destination and creating a personal and emotional connection between Orlando and its core audiences, which included consumers, media (travel and national outlets), travel professionals, meeting planners, convention attendees, and families.

The brainstorm resulted in an idea to create a major, one-of-a-kind event: sending thank-you cards to *all* the tourists who visited Orlando in 2017. To capture the creative spirit of Orlando, the team decided to seek a Guinness world record for "the most hand-written thank you cards collected within a 24-hour period."

The effort succeeded, as more than 19 million consumers were reached with "thank-you" messages in one day, through tactics such as thank-you cards, postcards, advertising, client events, newsletters, and more. There was significant media coverage in target publications and a high volume of social media posts and traffic created by this event as well. The "Big Thank You" event was timed to coincide with the release of the annual visitation numbers to add color and excitement to the news conference.

The project's goal was to engage Orlando's tourism community (owners and employees) to maximize the impact of the positive news on the annual visitation numbers for 2017, which increased compared to the prior year. The Guinness stunt, combined with the positive news on visitation numbers, shone an international spotlight on the area's desirability as a resort destination and reinforced the key message that all are welcome in Orlando.

Here is a summary of how the event was covered (PRSA, 2018):

- Overall coverage garnered globally reached the target media in the United States, Canada, United Kingdom, Brazil, Mexico, and China.

- More than 65 broadcast stories ran in markets across the United States. More than 30 local media attended the launch event. The Associated Press article featured quotes from *Visit Orlando* president and CEO (George Ague) and was syndicated in 130 news outlets around the country.

- Social media impressions reached 6.9 million, with over 4,000 engagements and more than 17,000 views on the Facebook Live of the announcement.

- More than 19 million consumers were reached with "thank-you" messages through combined tactics such as thank-you cards, postcards, advertising, client events, newsletters, and more.

(Adapted from 2018, Public Relations Society of America, Inc., Silver Anvil Winners)

WRAP UP

This initial chapter discussed the definitions of PR throughout history and the "official" one by the PRSA, first developed in 2012. The chapter also examined the differences between PR and advertising, noting the credibility gap between what people read and see on the news versus paid advertisements. The impact of social media was addressed, with a focus on "sponsored" and "owned" content used to bridge the gap between "paid" and "earned" media.

In addition, the skills that PR professionals use in their work—including media relations, employee communications, research, and strategic planning—were reviewed. Finally, the chapter looked at the career paths a PR professional might follow.

As you move through the remainder of the text, there will be detailed chapters on these concepts as well as the areas of specialization for a career in this dynamic and exciting industry.

KEY TERMS

Blogger 8
Business-to-Business (B-to-B) 11
Business-to-Consumer (B-to-C) 11
Business-to-Government (B-to-G) 11
Corporate Reputation 3
Influencer 8
Integrated Marketing Communications (IMC) 11
Material Events 18

Primary Research 14
Public Affairs 19
Public Company (Publicly Traded Company) 5
Publicist 4
Secondary Research 14
Stakeholders 8
Sustainability Communications 9

THINK ABOUT IT

Early in the chapter, you read about the perception of PR and PR people based on the research from USC and others on how popular culture (movies, television, etc.) have portrayed PR over the years. As part of that research, they produced a YouTube video with a compilation of scenes from movies and television over the past 50-plus years. For this activity, it is suggested that you form small work groups. You can find this video at https://www.youtube.com/watch? v=hqGCgg68Wt4.

Here is your task:

1. View the YouTube video from USC.
2. Discuss your thoughts and reactions to how it portrays PR.
3. Capture your notes from the discussion and share them with the class.
4. Brainstorm ideas to change the perception (if necessary).
5. Determine if you can (or feel you need to) improve the public's understanding of PR.

WRITE LIKE A PRO

Assume you are on the PR team for a regional bank nearing its 150th anniversary. The bank serves both its economically challenged headquarters city and an affluent state in the northeastern United States. As such, the bank's customers have a variety of challenges, including home affordability, paying for college and health care, and caring for family members, such as senior citizens. Remember, as a bank your company's expertise in financial services lends itself more to some challenges than others. How do you decide which ones to take on and which to leave for others? How do you leverage and engage your employees and customers?

1. Develop an outline of a plan (250 words) to celebrate the bank's anniversary, based on these suggestions.
2. Make sure to include tactics from PR (media relations and community events) and social responsibility initiatives (employee volunteers, contributions, or fundraising) into one comprehensive outline.

Allstate Foundation Purple Purse: Raising Awareness and Funds for Victims

The issue of domestic violence has become a national phenomenon in recent years. Research indicates that one in four women will be a victim of domestic violence in her lifetime and that financial abuse occurs in 98% of those cases. Financial abuse (withholding funds, destroying credit, jeopardizing jobs) provides abusers with another way to control and punish their victims.

The Allstate Foundation created the Purple Purse in 2010 to ignite a national conversation about domestic violence and financial abuse. The Allstate Foundation committed to an expanded Purple Purse program in 2014, including a fashion statement around the Purple Purse imagery, a social statement on a serious issue, and better financial support for the local organizations that victims depend on to rebuild their lives. The actress Kerry Washington has served as the national spokesperson for the campaign since its inception.

According to the program's website, www.purplepurse.com, through year-end of 2018 the program had invested $66 million dollars in programming for domestic abuse survivors and helped over 1.7 million victims (Allstate Foundation Purple Purse, n.d.).

Research and Strategy

The Allstate Foundation commissioned a 2014 national survey (*Silent Weapon: Domestic Violence and Financial Abuse*), which showed that two thirds of Americans believe domestic violence is a serious problem, while revealing that just over one in three has ever talked about it. Further, nearly eight in 10 said they were not familiar with financial abuse and considered it the least likely form of abuse to be recognized by others. In fact, 65% believed their own family or friends would not know if they were in a financially abusive relationship, and 70% said family or friends would not know how to help them. Strategies included media relations, social media, celebrity involvement, and fundraising challenges (Allstate Foundation Purple Purse, 2014).

Execution

The centerpiece of the program was a launch event held in New York City, timed to coincide with Fashion Week and featuring a purple purse designed by Kerry Washington. An Associated Press exclusive interview with her was placed to break the story the morning of the announcement of the event, creating a cascade of media coverage. Washington also appeared in a public service announcement (PSA) about the Purple Purse program, conducted interviews with national media, engaged fans through her social media feeds, and introduced new audiences to the cause by showcasing her personally designed purple purse at numerous high-profile events during Fashion Week.

At the local level, the Allstate Foundation issued the Purple Purse Challenge to 140 nonprofits across the country. The goal was to raise money for domestic-violence survivors and the organizations that serve them. The challenge was launched through www.purplepurse.com, with $650,000 in incentives from the Allstate Foundation. Each program partner company received a package of purple purses, purple purse charms, and other collateral to generate awareness and promote fundraising.

The Allstate Foundation delivered program kits internally to help company employees and allied Allstate agents involve their local communities in the campaign, thereby expanding the program's impact.

To engage the Hispanic audience fully, the Allstate Foundation placed an exclusive on the Hispanic survey statistics with the international news agency Agencia EFE. A Spanish-language satellite media tour, audio news release, and a new Spanish-language site—www .espanol.purplepurse.com—completed this outreach initiative and provided key information to an essential program audience.

Evaluation

In only one month in its first year, the Purple Purse Challenge raised nearly $2.5 million to benefit financial empowerment services for survivors, a 614% increase from the revenues raised in 2013. More than half of all donations were at $25 and under, demonstrating that this was truly a successful grassroots fundraising campaign. The progress in fundraising and assisting victims has steadily increased since then. The program resulted in more than 23,000 media placements through earned media and social platforms as well as through paid amplification, a 447% increase in program media results from 2013.

Earned broadcast placements included ABC's *Good Morning America*, MSNBC's *Morning Joe*, CNN, and E! *Extra* and *Access Hollywood*. Top print and online placements included stories in the Associated Press, WSJ.com, Huffington Post, CBSNews.com, Yahoo! Celebrity, TIME.com, and many more. Other print placements appeared in *People, Living, Ebony, ESPN The Magazine, Money, Martha Stewart Living, TIME*, and *Working Mother*.

Online, the Allstate Foundation Purple Purse became a continuing topic of conversation, with more than 13,500 #PurplePurse social posts across Twitter, Facebook, and Instagram. On September 17, 2014, a few days after the Purple Purse Challenge program launch, Kerry Washington was trending on Facebook due to her involvement in the Purple Purse campaign.

Source: Adapted from PRSA Silver Anvil Case Study. PRSA, 2015.

Engage

1. Explore the National Network to End Domestic Violence (www.thehotline.org) and Purple Purse (www.purplepurse.com) websites to see how they communicate with their various stakeholders.
2. Do a Google search for "controversial celebrity endorsements" and learn what can go wrong and what can be done.

Discuss

1. The Purple Purse campaign deals with a very sensitive and controversial topic. Do you think it is wise for the Allstate company to connect itself so visibly? What are the downsides of this approach for customers, employees, and the public?
2. How do the issues of domestic violence and financial abuse connect or relate to the business of the Allstate insurance company?
3. Is there a risk of tying your CSR campaign to a celebrity so closely? What if he or she gets into difficulty or has his or her own crisis? How does Allstate protect itself from any backlash?
4. The case mentions special outreach to the Hispanic community. Why do you think this is a key part of the program?

THE BOSTON TEA

2

The History of Modern Public Relations

From Barnum to Lee, Bernays to Page, and Introducing Other Pioneers

Learning Objectives

2.1   Identify key developments in the modern history of PR

2.2   Explain the growth of the PR agency business model

2.3   Summarize the challenges PR will face in the years to come

Belle Moskowitz: Pioneer and Innovator in Advocacy and Issues Management

Anyone who has ever visited New York City—or viewed its skyline—recognizes the Empire State Building in Midtown Manhattan.

The 102-story art-deco style building features the world-famous Observatory, which has been featured in movies (e.g., *Sleepless in Seattle*, *Annie Hall*, and *King Kong*) and on television since it opened April 11, 1931, 12 days ahead of schedule. In November 2019, the Observatory was reopened after a major renovation with great fanfare, including an on-location broadcast of the network program *CBS This Morning*.

Without question, it is an iconic building with a rich history and serves as a lasting symbol of one of the world's great cities.

However, few people know the story of the landmark building's construction during the Great Depression (1929–1939) or the many challenges that creating "the world's tallest building" posed for city leaders and the project's developers. During the construction phase, when several other tall buildings were also going up in New York, residents were reportedly concerned about construction accidents, worker safety, and the long-term impact on the city's quality of life.

Constructed during the Great Depression, the Empire State Building was the first client of PR pioneer Belle Moskowitz.
Science & Society Picture Library / Contributor / Getty Images

Fewer still know the critical role played by Belle Moskowitz—an innovative public relations and advocacy professional—who advised the developer and helped to reassure the public. Her work helped pave the way for creation of an international landmark and popular tourist attraction that attracts 4 million visitors a year.

According to research by the Museum of Public Relations (2018), Moskowitz was a communications practitioner during the Progressive Era (1890–1920). She began her career in the early 20th century as a social worker, focusing her efforts on social and education reforms for young women.

Belle Moskowitz became the first woman to serve as a political consultant and the first woman to open a PR firm, Publicity Associates in 1928. Moskowitz was highly visible in New York, working as campaign manager for Al Smith, a successful gubernatorial candidate who served four terms beginning in 1918.

One of her first clients was the developer's company behind the Empire State Building. She helped manage communications during the planning and construction of the landmark up to and including the grand opening on May 1, 1931 (Perry, 2009).

Her challenge was to manage public perceptions during the Great Depression, which was a time of great stress and tension in the United States. Specifically, some citizens of New York saw the new building as a symbol of hope and evidence of America's construction and engineering prowess. Others were concerned about the risks to workers and citizens associated with the massive project.

(Continued)

(Continued)

Student Challenge

Put yourself in Belle Moskowitz's shoes. Think about what you would have recommended to offset public concern and simultaneously celebrate the hope this project embodied for New York and the United States at a critical time in our history.

Answer the following questions—and remember the time period of this Scenario is the early 20th century, so adjust your answers to the technology and media available at the time:

1. What tactics would you use to manage the issues and prevent a crisis?
2. How could the company be more open and responsive?
3. How would you minimize public concerns about safety and disruption?
4. How would this case be different today versus in the 1930s? ●

This chapter will take the reader through a brief history of the public relations (PR) industry—with an emphasis on the "modern era" since it is most relevant to the PR business today. In the pages that follow, you will learn about some well-known industry pioneers like Ivy Lee, Edward Bernays, and Arthur W. Page and some of the colorful figures in history—such as P. T. Barnum—who practiced early forms of PR and advertising to generate awareness for their businesses.

You will also read about some other industry pioneers—notably women and minorities—whose contributions are not as well-known, but no less significant. Their contributions to PR history have been largely overlooked, but they are essential to provide you with a complete picture of the development of the profession. They may also provide you, as a PR student, with role models you can relate to as you build your own career.

Later in the chapter, you will also learn about the PR agency business and how it has become a force in the industry and a rewarding career path for many practitioners. Many of the innovations and creative strategies commonly deployed by PR professionals (e.g., media tours, thought leadership, competitive intelligence) originated in agencies. Further, as we will outline later, the agency business is an excellent training ground for young professionals regardless of their ultimate career path in PR.

Finally, to help you prepare and respond, this chapter looks at some key trends—digital, global, and social responsibility (SR)—that will impact the future of the PR industry.

A History of Public Relations in the Modern Era

>> LO 2.1   Identify key developments in the modern history of PR

The biggest challenge in writing a history of PR is this: Where do we start?

Do we begin with Plato and the ancient Greeks? Or examine the communication tactics used by the Catholic Church in the 1500s to spread Christianity? Or the efforts of leaders in the Middle Ages and Renaissance to expand their empires, build followers, and stabilize their leadership position using communications tactics?

After all, when viewed through the lens of influencing public opinion or driving change, we can see public relations elements at work in the Norman Conquest, the

Crusades, and both the French and American Revolutions (Bates, 2006). When America was a British colony in the late 1700s, PR tactics like the Boston Tea Party led by Sam Adams built support for the American Revolution by encouraging dissent and disagreement with British rules and regulations. Thomas Paine's *Common Sense*, an influential pamphlet on American independence, may have been the first political communications campaign and was an early example of PR designed to support activism. The *Federalist Papers*, authored by Alexander Hamilton, John Jay, and James Madison, were written to support ratification of the U.S. Constitution, and are very similar to the opinion pieces (op-eds) written and published today to influence public opinion.

Public Relations and Press Agentry: The Era of the 1800s

As America expanded in the 18th century, PR moved from building support for American independence to a more commercially focused enterprise. Driven by the dramatic expansion of newspapers and entrepreneurs launching new businesses and/or promoting authors and celebrities, PR moved into what is referred to as the "Golden Age of Press Agentry."

The period saw the rise of the press agent, whose job it was to "hype" companies, products, entertainment, and "celebrities"—by almost any means necessary. The tactics were often short on ethics and focused solely on achieving publicity. Exaggeration, lies, and outright fabrication became common practice among many of these "publicists," along with free tickets, gifts, or other compensation to get reporters to write about their clients. Characters such as Davy Crockett, Daniel Boone, Annie Oakley, or Buffalo Bill were created, or their exploits exaggerated, to sell tickets, win votes, or get news coverage. Unfortunately, this approach to PR remains a common perception of the profession even today.

One of the best-known figures of these freewheeling times was P. T. Barnum—considered the Great American Showman—whose namesake circus and museum continued to operate long after his death. Many believe Barnum, who was reportedly the second millionaire in the United States, was the originator of the *publicity stunt*, which is a *press event* or activity created solely to get news coverage. Former Librarian of Congress Daniel Boorstin described these as "pseudo-events" (1992, p. 9) and suggested Barnum was the acknowledged master of his time at this tactic. "Whatever your occupation, whatever your purpose, if you need the support of the public then take the steps necessary to let them know about it," P. T. Barnum said (Quoteswise, n.d.).

Examples of Barnum's creativity and style include Joyce Heth, whom he promoted as the 161-year-old former nursemaid to George Washington, and the Feejee Mermaid, a stuffed half-monkey/half-fish creature. Both of these were exhibited at his American Museum in New York and drew big crowds. Barnum knew that both controversy and curiosity sell, and he used that knowledge to draw people in to see if the hype was accurate. Once they paid for admission and were in the door, other exhibits and shows were there to entertain and educate.

P. T. Barnum is credited by some as the originator of the "press event" or "publicity stunt."

Hulton Archive / Stringer / Getty Images

SOCIAL RESPONSIBILITY AND BARNUM

Kathleen Maher, curator of the Barnum Museum in Bridgeport, Connecticut (Barnum's adopted hometown where he served as mayor in 1875), has studied his legacy and suggests that Barnum's contributions go beyond eccentric exhibits and bombast. His worldwide tours for General Tom Thumb, a midget who could sing, dance, and act, and his promotion of Jenny Lind, the "Swedish Nightingale," may be considered precursors to today's reality television and musical contest shows. As well, Barnum would often donate a portion of the proceeds of his shows to local charities to generate positive publicity—an early example of SR, also called strategic philanthropy. Maher writes,

Whether fact or fiction, the conclusion was less relevant than the experience or opportunity. Barnum was ingenious in presenting speculation within a world of curiosity. He offered a chance to explore the irrational, examine imaginative possibilities, and derive new opinions and truths. His pioneering spirit of promotion and his acumen for business transformed popular conceptions of the era, in turn defining many ideals of today. (K. Maher, personal communication, 2017)

A colorful character to be sure, Barnum deserves further study—and perhaps some reevaluation—for his contributions to the growth and development of promotional PR and strategic philanthropy.

Railroads Drive Public Relations' Development

We know from U.S. history that the railroad industry was a major factor in the growth and development in the country. In the latter stages of the 19th century, the railroad industry initiated and used many PR tactics now seen as commonplace. These include distribution of pamphlets and materials promoting migration to the western United States; creating publicity and information offices in new market areas; and staging promotional "road shows" that traveled the country on railroad cars (naturally) and featured murals, artwork, and artifacts promoting the quality of life in the western United States.

By all accounts, these tactics worked, and westward migration swelled—with 5 million people resettling in the Midwest and more than 2 million farms being established. Commenting on this achievement, Andy Piasecki (2000), a lecturer at Queen Margaret College in Edinburgh, Scotland, and a PR historian, suggests that "none of this could have been achieved without complex communications strategies closely linked to business objectives." Clearly, as the 1800s wound down, PR had begun yet another transformation, moving away from publicity for its own sake to communications strategies designed to achieve specific business objectives.

Building on the work of late 19th century anti-segregation activists like Ida Wells and John Muir, PR professionals began to take on more substantive social issues as the 20th century approached. These two activists, and others like them, made significant contributions that paved the way for the *modern era of PR*.

Ida Wells was born a slave and rose to adulthood to fight discrimination as a speaker, editor, and founder of an antisegregation newspaper in Memphis. She was also a cofounder and early leader of the National Association for the Advancement of Colored People (NAACP). Lesser known is that in 1884, at the age of 22, Wells refused to move to the "colored section" when ordered to do so by a railroad conductor, many years before Rosa Parks became famous for a similar act on a bus in Alabama in 1955 (Hannah-Jones, 2017).

The movement of public relations into social issues in the 20th century built upon the work of 19th-century activists like Ida B. Wells (*left*) and John Muir (*right*).
Chicago History Museum / Contributor / Getty Images; Bettmann / Contributor / Getty Images

---

SOCIAL RESPONSIBILITY AND ADVOCACY

Like Wells, John Muir was also an activist, although his focus was on preserving and protecting nature. John Muir was most active in the 1860s. He wrote books and magazine articles, gave speeches to engage U.S. citizens on conservation efforts, and led the creation of national parks across the country (National Park Service, n.d.). Muir founded the Sierra Club, and his environmental activism helped preserve the Yosemite Valley, Sequoia National Park, and other wilderness areas for future generations. He was an early proponent of sustainability, and because of his efforts, the government and the business community came to exercise restraint in dealing with America's natural resources.

Pioneers of Modern Public Relations

Most scholars agree that the pioneers of the modern style of PR were Ivy Lee, regarded as the originator of the *public relations counsel* concept; Edward Bernays, often referred to as the *father of modern public relations;* and Arthur Page, revered for his groundbreaking work as the *first corporate PR officer* at AT&T. These leaders took PR into the corporate boardroom, politics, and government. Through the work of these and other trailblazers, PR professionals began to take on major social issues and critical business challenges, moving beyond the bombast of P. T. Barnum and the late 19th-century publicists.

Ivy Lee

With the opening of one of the first firms in 1904 in New York, Ivy Lee and his partner George Parker raised the bar for the PR industry, declaring themselves as "public relations counselors." The firm was called Parker & Lee, and its major clients

Ivy Lee, alongside his partner George Parker, opened one of the first PR firms in New York in 1904. His successful campaign in support of a rate hike for the Pennsylvania Railroad is considered a landmark in the history of PR.

ullstein bild Dtl. / Contributor / Getty Images

were the Pennsylvania Railroad, the Rockefeller family, and the American Tobacco Company, as well as some Hollywood studios and the New York subway system.

One of the firm's first clients, the Pennsylvania Railroad Company, hired them to build support for a 5% rate hike. Ivy Lee developed a comprehensive PR campaign, reaching out to the company's key stakeholders—the media, railroad employees, passengers, customers, and state and federal elected officials—as well as to college presidents, religious leaders, and other opinion leaders to help make the company's case and convince the government regulators to approve the increase (St. John, 2006). These efforts paid off. Public opposition declined, multiple outside groups supported the rate hike, and the federal government ultimately approved the 5% rate hike. This campaign is heralded as "a landmark in the history of advocacy public relations" (St. John, 2006, p. 225).

However, Ivy Lee was not without his detractors. While he is generally lauded for his pioneering role as a PR counsel, he was also accused of not being transparent regarding some controversial clients. He was criticized for working for the American Russian Chamber of Commerce during the Stalin era and for promoting the German Dye Organization, later discovered to be an organization owned by the Nazi party. Notwithstanding these issues, Ivy Lee made major contributions to the practice of modern PR. Commenting on Lee's contributions, Fraser P. Seitel (2013) concluded that Lee, more than any other, brought the practice of PR into the 21st century.

Edward L. Bernays

Following in the tradition of Lee, Edward L. Bernays was another pivotal figure in the development of modern PR. He believed PR was most effective when social science and behavioral psychology were leveraged in PR campaigns to change behavior or shape public opinion (Bernays, 2015). Reflecting his family heritage as the nephew of Sigmund Freud, his PR model was based on using scientific persuasion techniques to advocate for a position or product. He was one of the first to emphasize identifying your target audience, conducting research to understand their views, and tailoring your message accordingly.

He detailed this view in his seminal book *Crystallizing Public Opinion* (2015), first published in 1923 and still read today by students and scholars of the discipline. Later in his career, Bernays was invited to join the faculty of New York University (NYU) and teach one of the first courses on PR in the United States. He wrote,

> The public relations counsel is the pleader to the public of a point of view. He acts in this capacity as a consultant both in interpreting the public to his client and in helping to interpret his client to the public. He helps to mold the action of his client as well as to mold public opinion. (Bernays, 2015, p. 57)

As his many innovative campaigns demonstrate, Bernays was an innovator and a creative genius. Whether it was his work for the Ivory soap brand, when he created a children's soap carving contest that sold millions of bars of soap; the famous "Torches of Freedom" campaign for American Tobacco in 1929, in which he hired fashion models to smoke in public (then considered taboo for women) during New York's Easter parade; or his campaign for a "Hearty American Breakfast," which included eggs and bacon (Hormel was his client), he was all about the "big idea" (The Museum of Public Relations, n.d.).

According to Larry Tye (2002), the author of *Father of Spin: Edward L. Bernays and the Birth of Public Relations*, Bernays was "the first to demonstrate for future generations of PR people how powerful their profession could be in shaping America's economic, political and cultural life."

Lesser known, but well appreciated within the PR industry, was the role Bernays's wife— Doris E. Fleischman, a writer, feminist, and former editor of the *New York Tribune*—played

Edward Bernays was one of the first PR professionals to use social science and behavioral psychology in developing his techniques.
Bettmann / Contributor / Getty Images

in his work. She was his partner in life and in business and took on many of the responsibilities behind the scenes for their clients, as well as writing and editing books and articles on her own (Tye, 2002).

Among her other duties, Fleischman wrote the firm's newsletter for clients called *Contact*. This publication explained the value of public relations and was vital to the firm's growth and success. Bernays described his wife as his most valuable asset and their relationship as a "twenty-four-hour-a-day-partnership" (Schroeder, 2015).

Bernays and Fleischman were also active in promoting causes and charities, pioneering the concept of *pro bono work* in PR, a still common form of social responsibility (SR).

Arthur W. Page

The philosophy and approach of Arthur W. Page, a pioneer in the world of corporate PR and career executive at AT&T, is summed up in this statement:

> All business in a democratic country begins with public permission and exists by public approval. If that is true, it follows that business should be cheerfully willing to tell the public what its policies are, what it is doing, and what it hopes to do. This seems practically a duty. (Arthur W. Page Center, 1932)

AT&T had a long history of pioneering the use of publicity to build its business, and Page was a pivotal figure in that effort (Block, n.d.).

As far back as the early 1900s, AT&T hired the Publicity Bureau of Boston, one of the first PR agencies in the United States, to promote its products and services. One of the staff members on their account was James Ellsworth, whom the company later enticed to join them and create their first PR department at AT&T.

One day early in his career at the publishing company owned by his family, Page received a telephone call from Walter Gifford, the chief executive of AT&T. When the two met a few days later, Gifford asked Page if he would write a book about AT&T. Page declined, explaining that while it might be a nice ego boost for management, it wouldn't do the company any good. This advice reflected Page's belief that reputation was earned by actions, not just through publicity. As their conversation drew to a close, Gifford asked Page if he would like to put his ideas about communication and reputation into practice at AT&T. Page agreed, but only if it would be in a policy-making position (Block, n.d.).

Arthur Page was hired in 1927 and served as the company's first vice president of PR and was appointed as a corporate officer. He remained with the company until his retirement in 1948. During his career, he was elected to the AT&T Board of Directors and later served on other corporate boards and was an advisor to several presidents of the United States. Years later, communications leaders from major companies and top PR firms would form the Arthur W. Page Society (now called simply "Page") to further the study and practice of public relations as a management function.

PR PROFILE

Ofield Dukes

The Washington Post / Contributor / Getty Images

There were many firsts in the life of Ofield Dukes.

Dukes was described by Robert Johnson, founder of Black Entertainment Television (BET) and publisher of *Ebony* and *Jet* magazines, as a "brilliant PR strategist." A former journalist, his milestone accomplishments include the following:

- His first job in Washington, DC, was at the U.S. Department of Labor, serving as the Deputy Director of Public Affairs of the President's Committee on Equal Employment Opportunity (appointed by President Kennedy in 1961).

- He was the first African American PR professional to open an office at the National Press Building, two blocks from the White House in April of 1969. His early clients included Motown Records, Lever Brothers (now Unilever), and Anheuser-Busch.

- In 1971, he helped establish the first Congressional Black Caucus, which is a leading voice on Capitol Hill for civil rights and equality.

- He was one of the first PR professionals to teach a course at Howard University's

School of Communications on Public Relations (1971).

- In July of 2001, he was the first person of color to win the coveted Gold Anvil Award from the Public Relations Society of America (PRSA) for his lifetime of achievement.

Yet for someone who advised presidents that included both Lyndon Johnson and Bill Clinton and civil rights leaders such as Dr. Martin Luther King, John Lewis, and A. Phillip Randolph, Dukes was by all accounts a modest and sincere practitioner for whom "public relations was his passion and truth his guiding force," suggests his daughter, Roxi Trapp-Dukes Victorian in his autobiography (Smith & Anderson, 2018).

Born in August 1932 in Rutledge, Alabama, a small community between Mobile and Montgomery, Dukes's parents were sharecroppers, picking cotton on land owned by whites. In 1940 when he was 6, his family joined the migration of southern Blacks to the big cities of the North. His father had found work at a Ford Motor Company factory, and he and his mother and sisters moved to Detroit to be with him soon after.

After serving in the Army in Korea, he returned home to Michigan and entered Wayne State University to study journalism, graduating in 1958. As a freelance journalist and later editor at the *Michigan Chronicle*, a Black weekly newspaper, and in between as news director at WCHB, a Black-owned radio station, Dukes had a front-row seat for many of the major news stories of the day.

During his time as a reporter, he won several awards from the National Newspapers Publishers Association for his writing and caught the eye of senior advisors to President Lyndon B. Johnson. Soon after, he was invited to come to Washington to work in the Johnson–Humphrey administration. Dukes describes this experience in his autobiography, *Ofield: The Autobiography of Public Relations Man Ofield Dukes*, as a "significant change in my life and my professional identity" (Smith & Anderson, 2018). "Washington, DC, is the public relations capital of the world. Nothing happens in the city without a mixture of public relations and politics," he wrote.

Summing up his remarkable career, Ofield Dukes wrote this in the opening chapter of his autobiography:

During my 32 years in public relations, I had struggled, worked extra hard, with a passion to be excellent and the best I could be. I wanted to prove that a Colored man, a Negro, a Black, an African-American professional could successfully operate in the mainstream of the public relations industry. (2018)

By all accounts, Dukes proved he could "operate" with the best of them in Washington, DC, and nationally. He was a pioneer among 20th-century PR practitioners and a mentor and role model to countless young African American scholars and PR professionals. ●

Source: Adapted from *Ofield: The Autobiography of Public Relations Man Ofield Dukes*, Rochelle L. Ford, PhD, and Rev. Unnia L. Pettus, PhD, PRMuseum Press, 2017.

Other Innovators of Modern Public Relations

While Ivy Lee, Edward Bernays, and Arthur Page were towering figures in the development of modern PR practice, others made significant contributions to the profession but are not as widely known or celebrated. For example, innovators in the political and governmental communications arena include George Creel, Amos Kendall, Leonne Baxter, and Elmer Davis (see Table 2.1).

George Creel's work on behalf of the war effort (World War I) under President Woodrow Wilson was groundbreaking for several reasons. Among Creel's many accomplishments was the creation of the "Four Minute Men" group, who traveled the country speaking to the public about World War I and supporting the president's positions and views (Creel, 1920). They worked under the supervision of the U.S. Committee on Public Information, which Creel led.

In those early days, the local movie theater was a primary gathering spot for communities across the country—especially on the weekends. However, the projectors in these older theaters were manually operated, and the film canisters usually had to be changed midmovie. During this downtime—usually about 4 minutes—speakers from the Committee would update moviegoers on current events and the progress of the war, thus the name "Four Minute Men." This effort is regarded as one of the first instances of a *speaking tour* to support a communications objective (Creel, 1920).

Other notable PR pioneers in other sectors of the industry include Warren Cowan, whose firm Rogers and Cowan remains one of the leaders in *entertainment PR* today with a stable of global celebrities as clients, and Eleanor Lambert, a major figure in *fashion PR* who first introduced designers like Bill Blass and Calvin Klein and created the "Best Dressed List."

TABLE 2.1

Notable Early Political Communicators

NAME	PROFESSION	CONTRIBUTION
George Creel	Headed U.S. Committee on Public Information during WWI	Use PR to sell liberty bonds and build the Red Cross
Amos Kendall	First White House press secretary	Worked for President Andrew Jackson in the 1830s
Leone Baxter	Founded the first political consulting firm in the United States	Founded his firm in 1933 with partner Clem Whitaker and developed strategies still used today
Elmer Davis	Conceived and promoted WWII victory gardens	Worked for President Franklin D. Roosevelt to encourage citizens to grow their own vegetables to help the war effort

Other pioneers, like Chester Burger, made major contributions in the planning and implementation of *corporate PR*. Burger pioneered the use of television news by PR professionals and advised major companies (e.g., AT&T) on how to package news stories for the new medium when it debuted in the 1950s (Gregory & Kirschenbaum, 2012).

Growth of the Public Relations Agency Sector

>> **LO 2.2**   **Explain the growth of the PR agency business model**

No review of the evolution of modern PR would be complete without a discussion on the PR agency business and the contributions of its early pioneers, including Harold Burson, Daniel J. Edelman, and John W. Hill. While there are many outstanding businesspeople who founded, or now head up, small and large PR firms or agencies, there is almost universal agreement that Burson, Edelman, and Hill are three of the pioneers and builders of the PR agency business.

Harold Burson

Regarded by his peers, clients, and current and former employees as a legend in the agency business, Harold Burson began his career in the 1940s as a journalist working for the Armed Forces Radio Network. In this capacity, he was assigned to cover the post–World War II International War Crimes Trial in Nuremberg, Germany, of Nazi officers and sympathizers.

He founded his firm in 1953 with Bill Marsteller when they began working on the Rockwell Manufacturing account. In the early 1960s, the partners saw the potential of PR as a worldwide business and opened Burson-Marsteller's (B-M) first overseas office in Geneva, Switzerland.

PRWeek, citing a recent survey of industry leaders, described Harold Burson as one of "the 21st century's most influential PR figures" (*PRWeek*, 2016). Throughout its history, B-M has been viewed as a great place to work and as a leader in crisis communications and reputation management. Most famous among its work in this arena was the Johnson & Johnson Tylenol poisoning case in 1982 (see the Case Study at the end of this chapter).

As with many major figures in the industry, B-M and Harold Burson are not without their critics. In the case of B-M, this was due to some controversial clients and assignments over the years. These include controversial government leaders in Nigeria, Argentina, and Indonesia; corporate clients facing crises like the Three Mile Island nuclear plant, Union Carbide, and the big tobacco companies; and certain companies seeking to discredit a competitor through negative media coverage, such as B-M client Facebook allegedly did with Google in 2011 (Benady, 2014).

Burson's thoughts on professional ethics and the firm's work for controversial clients were noted in a story about his death in *The Washington Post*:

> We are in the business of changing and molding attitudes, and we aren't successful unless we move the needle, get people to do something. But we are also a client's conscience, and we have to do what is in the public interest. (Smith, 2020, para. 3)

His easygoing manner, years of experience, and extensive global contacts made Burson a beloved figure in the industry, and as such, his views on client service, staffing, and agency management were closely followed. Burson passed away in early 2020 at the age of 98. He was still going in to work a few days a week right up until the end of his life. Befitting his status and universal respect, his memorial service in New York drew a veritable who's who of the global PR industry.

Daniel J. Edelman

Dan Edelman founded his PR firm, Daniel J. Edelman, Inc., in 1952 and led its growth to become the world's largest independent PR firm as ranked by fee income (*PRWeek*, 2018). He began his career as a sports reporter in Poughkeepsie, New York, after World War II and became a news writer for CBS. Later, he served as PR director for the Toni Company (hair and beauty products) before founding his own firm in Chicago.

His initial focus was on marketing communications or PR to support sales and new production introductions. "He is credited by many as the father of marketing PR; he understood the potential of earned media to enhance the marketing message," his son, Richard Edelman, noted in a memorial speech to the Arthur Page Society in 2014.

Dan Edelman is credited with creating the idea of a *media tour*, during which company spokespeople travel to meet with local media and promote a product or service through events, interviews, and public appearances. One of the earliest versions of this tactic was for his client Toni, where Edelman had worked before starting the firm. The veteran publicist sent six pairs of identical twins—one with a Toni home permanent and one with a salon permanent—on a tour of 72 cities to publicize the "Which Twin Has the Toni?" ad campaign (Wisner, 2012). The concept was very successful, earning extensive media coverage for the client, and media tours soon became commonplace across the PR industry. It is now a staple tactic used by PR pros to promote products and services as well as companies and issues.

As the firm grew, Edelman expanded into all forms and disciplines of PR—corporate, public affairs, sustainability, employee communications, financial communications, social media, and, of course, marketing communications. As have the other global firms, Edelman has encountered criticism for some of its client work as it has grown. For example, in 2015 the firm faced controversy over advocating for climate change at the same time it represented several so-called "climate change deniers," such as the American Petroleum Institute (API). Soon after, the firm resigned from its work for the API, which was a multimillion-dollar account (Edelman, 2015; Goldenberg, 2015).

Although Dan Edelman is gone now, his son Richard, who is CEO of the firm, and staffers worldwide believe that the spirit and philosophy of their founder is evident in their work with clients every day.

John W. Hill

John Hill, who established Hill & Knowlton (H&K) in 1933, began his career as a newspaper reporter, editor, and financial columnist. He established his first firm in 1927 in Cleveland, Ohio, and developed a clientele of banks, steel companies, and industrial companies operating in the midwestern United States. The firm became known as Hill & Knowlton in 1933, when Donald Knowlton, a former client, joined the firm as a partner. One year later, the partnership moved to New York to serve a major new client (the American Iron and Steel Institute [AISI]), and the beginnings of a major global firm were in place.

H&K was the first American PR firm to establish an office in Europe and, at its high point, was said to have "hung out its shingle" in hundreds of countries around the world. In building his firm with Knowlton, Hill was known for a simple business philosophy guided by "the essential requirements for PR: integrity and truth; soundness of policies, decisions and acts, viewed in the light of the public interest and use of facts that are understandable, believable and presented to the public with imagination" (PRSA New York, 2016). As with other major firms, there have been controversial clients (e.g., Church of Scientology, the government of Kuwait, the tobacco industry). However, the firm has also been recognized for its outstanding work for clients, promoting diversity, and being a good place to work by leading industry publications such as *PRWeek*.

INSIGHTS

African American and Women Pioneers in the Agency Field

MOSS HYLES KENDRIX
Educational Supervisor, N. Y. A.

Moss Kendrix
Moss H. Kendrix, November 1940 via Wikimedia Commons

Although not as widely known as Burson, Edelman, or Hill, other key figures in the PR agency field are also recognized as pioneers. These include Joseph V. Baker, Moss Kendrix, Barbara Hunter, Muriel Fox, Inez Kaiser, and Donald Padilla.

Joseph V. Baker

After working for the *Philadelphia Inquirer* as the first African American journalist (and also its city editor), in 1934 Baker opened the first Black-owned PR firm in the United States. He went on to acquire significant accounts from large corporations and became the first Black president of the Philadelphia PRSA chapter.

Moss Kendrix

An African American, Kendrix founded his own PR firm in Washington, DC, in 1944 to advise Coca-Cola and other major brands. He was instrumental in advising several large consumer product companies to stop using stereotypical images like Aunt Jemima and Uncle Ben in their advertising and promotions.

Barbara Hunter

Hunter purchased the PR firm Dudley-Anderson-Yutzy (known as DAY) in the early 1960s along with her sister Jeanne Schoonover, becoming the first female owners/proprietors of a major PR firm. Over the years, the sisters made DAY into a force in consumer PR and marketing communications. Hunter founded a new firm, Hunter PR, when she was 65 years old. It's still in operation today.

Muriel Fox

Fox was the first female PR executive at Carl Byoir & Associates. In 1966, she cofounded with Betty Friedan the National Organization for Women (NOW). Fox also served for many years as NOW's communications director, responsible for both media and government relations. In 1974, she founded NOW's Legal Defense and Education Fund.

Inez Kaiser

In 1957, Kaiser opened a public relations firm in Kansas City, the first African American woman in the United States to do so. Her firm, whose clients included 7 Up, Lever Brothers, and Sears Roebuck, was also the first African American–owned business in Kansas City, Missouri. In the 1970s, Kaiser counseled the Nixon and Ford administrations on issues related to minority-owned businesses.

Don Padilla

Don Padilla was a journalist prior to creating his own PR firm in Minneapolis, Minnesota. In 1961, he joined forces with David Speer to form what was to become one of the largest PR firms in the Midwest, Padilla and Speer (today known as Padilla). As a leader in the Latino community, Padilla was active throughout his life in supporting civic, education, and arts organizations in his Minneapolis hometown. In 1996 following his death, the PRSA Minneapolis chapter created the Padilla Community Excellence Award in his honor. ●

Source: Compiled with the assistance of Museum of PR, personal communications, 2019.

Public Relations Comes of Age

Following the path set by these and other leaders, PR came of age in the 1960s and moved into an era of growth—both in the United States and around the world. Many experts attribute this to the booming economy in the post–World War II era, rapid advances in technology, and growth of the media—particularly television—as well as more active and more politically aware citizens.

Another key factor was the recognition by leaders in business, government, and nonprofit communities of the potential that PR offered to help their businesses or organizations prosper. They had witnessed firsthand the positive impact PR had in building support for the war effort and how Bernays, Lee, Page, and other leaders had helped businesses build awareness and market share.

The 1960s was also a period of social unrest and change, including the civil rights, anti-Vietnam War, and women's liberation movements—all of which featured high-profile activists, adept in working with the media and shaping public opinion.

PR News Award for Best Corporate Social Responsibility Annual Report—Viacom

Each year, *PR News*, one of the leading publications covering the PR industry and the sponsor of numerous workshops and recognition events, sponsors the CSR Awards competition. The awards, which culminate in a major event at the National Press Club in Washington, DC, have more than 20 categories into which companies and agencies submit their CSR work for review by a panel of distinguished judges.

Best Annual Report on CSR Activity

One of the key categories, and an area where PR professionals are often called in to assist, is the annual corporate report on sustainability, or CSR. In some cases, this can be part of the corporate annual report (a yearly document required of publicly traded companies), or it can be a separate document. In any case, it is a key document in which organizations and companies report on their CSR activities to the community and employees.

Raising Voices: Viacom Wins Award

At the 2016 awards ceremony, the winner in this category was Viacom. A major global entertainment company, Viacom's media networks include Nickelodeon, Comedy Central, MTV, VH1, Spike, BET, CMT, TV Land, Nick at Nite, Nick Jr., Channel 5 (UK), Logo, Nicktoons, TeenNick, and Paramount Channel, and together they reach a cumulative 3.4 billion television subscribers worldwide.

Viewers, Employees, and Management Involved

In selecting it as the winner, the judges noted Viacom's "deep commitment to telling viewers' stories, amplifying their voices to educate and empower people to make a difference."

"Viacommunity" Celebrated

Viacom's CSR efforts are detailed in a 100-page report that covers its "Viacommunity" initiatives and achievements for the year ending December 31, 2014. President and CEO Philippe Dauman explained that similar to its global business, Viacom's social initiatives are constantly accelerating. "To ensure our efforts are at their strongest and push further forward, we have laid out a series of social responsibility goals for the company," he said.

Opportunities for Women, Young People, and Minorities

A few of the company's noteworthy results include partnering with community organizations to increase opportunities for women, young people, and underrepresented minorities in tech; expanding employee volunteerism and supporting social change in underserved communities across Viacom's business network ●

Source: Seymour, 2016.

Public Relations' Focus Differs by Organization

For the business community, media relations research, planning, and implementation are crucial in understanding public opinion and identifying market opportunities. As the media has grown and shifted, the need for media relations specialists to accomplish corporate goals has also grown. Whether it is the mainstream business media (e.g., *The New York Times*, *The Wall Street Journal*, or *Fortune* magazine), the television networks that grew to include cable news (e.g., CNN, MSNBC, etc.), or the many publications covering every major trade from accounting to zoology, getting a firm's story told and defending its reputation are paramount.

For government agencies and elected officials, PR strategies and tactics are now critical tools in delivering information and government services to people more effectively. For elected officials, mounting election or reelection campaigns requires effective media and community outreach, deep research to understand public opinion, and efficient message delivery to reach voters.

Nonprofit organizations have benefited as well from strategic PR. Fundraising is more successful, and campaigns have more impact. Working with the public and generating awareness via media coverage have become fundamental to a positive outcome. Digital media and social media have "democratized" the process of reaching the public, reduced costs, and increased efficiency. As a result, most nonprofit organizations have an active social media presence and understand it must be constantly updated.

Issue-based activist organizations like Greenpeace or Occupy Wall Street and political causes like Rock the Vote or the Conservative Political Action Conference (CPAC) also have made effective use of PR strategies to advance their agendas. These groups have leveraged social media to develop coalitions, attract donations, and put pressure on government leaders.

Social media drove the Women's March on Washington, DC, first held on January 21, 2017, the day after President Trump's inauguration. The event drew close to a million protesters to the nation's capital and to cities and towns on all seven continents. The protest movement began with a Facebook post by a concerned woman in Hawaii and grew through "shares" and "likes" by others who felt similarly about the results of the 2016 election. After the event, all four of the women who led the effort were selected by *Time* magazine as among the 100 most influential people of 2016.

In addition to social media, activist groups have made effective use of traditional PR tactics that include media relations, thought leadership, staged events, and original research to promote their causes and create awareness and conversation. These will be explored in greater detail in subsequent chapters.

The Future of Public Relations

>> **LO 2.3** **Summarize the challenges PR will face in the years to come**

Looking ahead, what are the key trends to watch and understand to become valued as a strategic advisor to your clients, companies, and candidates? For the PR industry specifically, there are a few key issues worth examining: the growth of digital media, an increased emphasis on measurement and return on investment (ROI), integration of PR and marketing, the integration of PR and CSR and the need to improve diversity and inclusion, and to embrace globalization.

A native of Colombia, Maria Cardona leads the multicultural and public affairs practices for the Dewey Square Group based in Washington, DC.

Alexander Tamargo / Contributor / Getty Images

Growth and Impact of Digital Media

Without question, digital media is changing the way traditional PR is performed and, in the process, raising the expectations of management and clients for results. Recent research indicates that this is not an easy challenge. More people are online more often and consuming news and information, and fewer are getting their news from the traditional newspapers and cable and broadcast news stations. This will require a whole new set of skills for tomorrow's PR professionals.

According to the Pew Research Center Social Media Usage 2018 study (Smith & Anderson, 2018), nearly three quarters of American adults (73%) use social networking sites (e.g., Facebook, YouTube, Twitter, LinkedIn), up from 7% when it began systematically tracking social media in 2005. This is more than a tenfold increase in usage in the past 10 years (Perrin, 2015). Key statistics from Pew's research on media and news consumption show the following: A majority of U.S. adults (62%) get their news on social media, and 43% do so often (Smith & Anderson, 2018), compared to 49% of U.S. adults in 2012 who reported seeing news on social media (Gottfried & Shearer, 2016).

Increased Emphasis on Measurement and Return on Investment (ROI)

With the advent of social media and more sophisticated measurement techniques now available, detailed measurement of PR campaigns has become more commonplace. For years, the PR industry relied on unscientific and barely defensible measurement tools such as advertising value equivalency (AVE; e.g., what purchasing the airtime or ad space in the publication would cost) and/or tracking media impressions (calculations based on the circulation or viewership ratings of a media outlet). Management and clients have become sophisticated and are demanding measurement of specific outcomes (vs. outputs) and evidence of ROI for company resources allocated to PR activity.

Forrest Anderson, a leading PR research expert and founding member of the Institute for PR's Measurement Commission, explained, "The single most important thing people need to remember when measuring the impact of a communications program is their definition of impact, which should come from the initial, measurable objectives of the program" (2014, para. 1).

However, as Jo Ann Sweeney noted, "Often, clients want to dive in and measure before we are all clear what we are measuring and why" (Anderson, 2014, para. 2). Anderson agreed, saying, "I believe this is why many PR efforts fail—they don't have objectives to guide the strategies and tactics" (2014, para. 3).

In Chapter 4, this topic will be reviewed and discussed in greater detail.

Integration of Public Relations and Marketing

One of the more significant trends in recent years is the integration of marketing and product-related publicity into a field called integrated marketing communications (IMC). In this concept, PR, advertising, product development, and research professionals all work together to identify a need for a product, assess competitive activity or presence, identify and understand the target audience, and reach out to them via traditional and social media platforms.

The concept of integrated marketing communications, as described by Phillip Kotler, a noted professor and author of several foundational books on marketing, involves coordinating the promotional elements to deliver a "clear, consistent, and compelling message about the organization and its products" (Kotler & Gertner, 2002). It calls for more than just developing a product, pricing it, and making it available to customers, he notes, "Companies must also communicate with current and prospective customers, and what they communicate should not be left to chance. All their communications efforts must be blended into a consistent and coordinated communications program" (Kotler & Gertner, 2002).

Intersection of Public Relations and Corporate Social Responsibility

While the practice of CSR has come a long way since its inception in the 1970s, some companies are just now beginning to capitalize on the bottom-line benefits and reputation enhancement potential that strategic CSR can produce. John Browne (former CEO of BP) and Robin Nutall (Partner, McKinsey) suggest that companies may be failing to deliver on their CSR efforts due to poorly "integrated external engagement" (Browne & Nuttall, 2013).

"In practice, most companies have relied on three tools for external engagement: a full-time CSR team in the head office, some high-profile (but relatively cheap) initiatives, and a glossy annual review of progress," write Browne and Nuttall (2013). In their view, more effort and resources are merited, given the positive returns of strategic CSR.

This is an area for focus and emphasis in the coming years. Many (if not all) company or client stakeholders are expecting leadership in CSR activities and initiatives as they seek to identify the winners and losers in this critical corporate activity. The expectations have grown along with the CSR field, and the role of the PR profession going forward in this will be paramount. See Chapter 9 for a more in-depth discussion of this emerging field of communications activity.

Improve Diversity and Inclusion

In a multicultural society, PR professionals need to understand and reflect the diverse racial, religious, and sexual orientation differences in the workplace and in their strategies and tactics. For employers, the industry is well past the point where there is an excuse for a lack of diversity. Whereas in the past the contributions of female and minority professionals might have been overlooked, today's companies and PR firms are actively seeking diversity in their employee base to more accurately reflect the marketplace they are trying to serve. While that is a positive step, clearly more work needs to be done.

According to the Bureau of Labor Statistics (2020a), the demographics of advertising, marketing, and PR jobs in the United States indicate that 9.9% are held by African Americans/Blacks and 13.6% by Hispanics/Latinos. This compares to the demographics of the U.S. population that indicate it is 14% Black and 17% Hispanic for the same period (U.S. Census, 2011).

The diversity hires in the United Kingdom (England, Scotland, Wales, and Northern Ireland) are equally low. According to a 2012 report by the U.K. Office of National Statistics, 14% of the British population have minority or ethnic backgrounds, but only 9% of U.K. PR practitioners identify themselves as being from these groups, according to research from the Public Relations Consultants Association (Stimson, 2013).

Many industry groups—including PRSA, the International Association of Business Communicators (IABC), the Page Society, and the PR Council—recognize that to be successful the industry must have employees who reflect all of society.

Clearly, to be effective at delivering messages, motivating behavior, and influencing public opinion, PR professionals (and companies) need to be representative of the audiences they are trying to reach. Simply translating copy or messages into different languages or using different models or celebrities to endorse products is not sufficient. More work needs to be done in this important area.

Globalization

Given the rate of change globally and the ever-present nature of social media, the world is now a very small, interconnected place. Events—good or bad—in one part of the world become known, discussed, and debated around the globe in a matter of minutes. Each day brings another example of this new reality. There are no unique, "local" markets anymore, and PR professionals must be aware and capable of managing this reality. Cision, a media monitoring service and source of industry thought leadership, said in a recent post, "PR is facing challenges. But they're NOT insurmountable," and suggests that glocalization—thinking globally and acting locally—is the new normal (Mireles, 2014).

Stakeholders all over the world, and especially in key markets, expect a meaningful relationship with companies with whom they do business or who operate in their country. The media and public in these areas expect a culturally aware attitude and a level of transparency and accountability from corporations that was not the case a few years ago. The penalty for not meeting these requirements can be harsh—both in terms of sales and profits as well as reputation, government support, or market acceptance. Strategic CSR, as we will learn later, is a key tool to meet this new global reality.

Scenario Outcome

At the beginning of this chapter, you were presented with a scenario and a challenge. Put yourself in the place of Belle Moskowitz and make recommendations to the developer of the Empire State Building and the City of New York to manage public concerns about a massive construction project in Midtown Manhattan.

Specifically, you were asked to think of how to (a) reassure the public and demonstrate that the project was moving ahead smoothly and safely and (b) alleviate public fears about accidents or disruption of city life.

Several questions were suggested to guide your thinking as you read through the chapter:

1. What tactics would you use to manage the issues and prevent a crisis?

2. How could the company be more open and responsive?

3. How would you minimize public concerns about safety and disruption?

4. How would this case be different today versus in the 1930s?

As you discuss these questions with your classmates, consider how Moskowitz responded. What did she recommend?

In a breakthrough strategy for the time, she convinced company management to be open to the media and the public throughout the construction phase of the project.

Specifically, she recommended the company provide frequent, scheduled access of the news media—news photographers in particular—to the construction site so they could take photographs to show the steady progress and highlight the skilled tradesmen doing the complex and challenging work.

One iconic photo from the time featured a group of construction workers casually seated on a steel beam high above the city, taking a lunch break. This photo has been published and featured in the media, on souvenirs, posters, and any number of promotional items since it was first published.

This groundbreaking tactic of providing access and transparency reassured the public that the workers were capable and safe, showed the citizens the project was progressing nicely, and helped build excitement (rather than concern) about the project. Reportedly, the positive publicity and goodwill this strategy created lasted right up until the grand opening.

By being open and transparent, Moskowitz provided an early example of strategic issues management and how it can minimize—or even prevent—a crisis. We will delve deeper into this key topic in Chapter 12. For now, it is important to recognize the strategic thinking displayed by an early PR pioneer to facilitate the construction and development of an international landmark.

WRAP UP

This chapter covered a lot of topics, introduced some key figures, and summarized many years of history. You learned how communications has been a part of civilization as long as there have been different groups of people—rulers and subjects, activists and citizens, politicians and voters, and businesses and customers—trying to understand and influence each other.

You read short profiles of some of the well-known leaders of the modern era of PR, including Bernays, Lee, and Page, and you discovered other PR professionals—minorities and women in particular—who made major contributions. You then took an in-depth look at the PR agency business and its pioneers as well as learned about lesser known, but equally important, women and African Americans who have made significant contributions to its growth.

The chapter closed with a look at the issues impacting PR in the next 5 to 10 years and the social issues that will challenge PR professionals throughout the rest of the 21st century.

KEY TERMS

Media Tour 37
Modern Era of PR 30

Press Event/Publicity Stunt 29
Pro Bono Work 33

THINK ABOUT IT

The issue of diversity and inclusion continues to be a challenge for the PR profession. Since the early 1900s, minorities and women have been underrepresented or underappreciated for their contributions. The problem is evident by the disconnect between the demographics of the U.S. population and the employment trends in the PR industry.

As a reminder, in the section of this chapter outlining key challenges for the future of the PR profession, you read the following statistic: *According to the Bureau of Labor Statistics (2020a), the demographics of advertising, marketing, and PR jobs in the United States indicate that 9.9% are held by African Americans/Blacks and 13.6% by Hispanics/ Latinos. This compares to a population in the United States that is 14% Black and 17% Hispanic.*

Your challenge is to break into groups, discuss this issue, and develop proposals on how the PR industry can improve its diversity and inclusion performance. This might take the form of CSR initiatives between companies catering to minority customers or women and/or affiliations with nonprofits such as the United Negro College Fund, La Raza, or the National Organization for Women.

Prepare a short memo listing your ideas and an outline of a plan of action to discuss in class to address this challenge.

WRITE LIKE A PRO

In this chapter, you read a lot about the history of PR, notably the modern era and some industry leaders whose contributions helped create the PR practices of today.

You were also introduced to The Museum of Public Relations, an organization in New York City that highlights the leaders of the early days of PR. The Museum of PR has an amazing collection of artifacts exhibited there from PR professionals—many of them people of color or women. It can be accessed online (www.prmuseum.org) and is a must visit for PR students, scholars, and practitioners when you are in New York.

Visit the site and prepare a short "backgrounder" that summarizes the work of a featured pioneer that appeals to you. The document should be suitable in style and format to one that could be submitted to a reporter seeking coverage or a potential donor to encourage their interest in the museum and its mission.

Note: A backgrounder is a short overview that provides information to encourage the reader to learn more about a given topic. In this case, you could describe the purpose and history of the Museum, as well as your chosen personality in detail, and then summarize the information and materials available there to learn more. You should start by visiting the museum's website at www.prmuseum.org.

CASE STUDY

Johnson & Johnson's Tylenol Crisis

As noted earlier in this chapter, Burson-Marsteller (BM) advised Johnson & Johnson during the now-famous Tylenol crisis—a case regarded as one of the classic historical examples of managing a crisis properly.

In the fall of 1982, random packages of Tylenol Extra-Strength already on store shelves were opened and had cyanide-laced capsules placed in them by an unidentified individual or individuals. The perpetrator(s) then resealed the containers and put them back on the shelves of several pharmacies and food stores in the Chicago area, where they were sold.

Seven people died after ingesting the poison capsules they thought were Tylenol. Johnson & Johnson, parent company of McNeil Consumer Products Company, which makes Tylenol, suddenly, and with no warning, had to explain to the world why its trusted product was killing people (Ten Berge, 1990).

Research and Strategy

Robert Andrews, assistant director for PR at Johnson & Johnson at the time, recalls how the company reacted in the first days of the crisis:

> We got a call from a Chicago news reporter. He told us that the medical examiner there had just given a press conference—people were dying from poisoned Tylenol. He wanted our comment. As it was the first knowledge we had here in this department, we told him we knew nothing about it. In that first call we learned more from the reporter than he did from us. (Ten Berge, 1990)

Johnson & Johnson Chair James Burke reacted to the media coverage by forming a seven-member strategy team, and he engaged their PR agency, Burson-Marsteller. The strategy guidance to the agency from Burke was, first, "How do we protect the people?" and, second, "How do we save this product?"

Execution

Johnson & Johnson, acting on the advice of its agency and internal team, moved ahead by stopping the production and advertising of Tylenol and withdrawing all Tylenol capsules from the store shelves in Chicago and the surrounding area. After finding two more contaminated bottles elsewhere, Johnson & Johnson ordered a national withdrawal of every capsule (Cutlip et al., 1994).

By withdrawing all Tylenol, even though there was little chance of discovering more cyanide-laced tablets, Johnson & Johnson showed that they were not willing to risk the public's safety, even if it cost the company millions of dollars. The result was the public viewing Tylenol as the unfortunate victim of a malicious crime (Cutlip et al., 1994).

Subsequently, Johnson & Johnson announced the creation of new triple-safety-seal packaging with a press conference at the manufacturer's headquarters. Tylenol became the first product in the industry to use the new tamper-resistant packaging just 6 months after the crisis occurred (Ten Berge, 1990).

Evaluation

Throughout the crisis, more than 100,000 separate news stories ran in U.S. newspapers, and there were hundreds of hours of national and local television coverage. A postcrisis study by Johnson & Johnson said that more than 90% of the American population had heard of the Chicago deaths due to cyanide-laced Tylenol within the first week of the crisis. Two news clipping services found more than 125,000 news clippings on the Tylenol story. One of the services reported that this story had been given the widest U.S. news coverage to date since the assassination of President John F. Kennedy (Kaplan, 2005).

Scholars and PR practitioners have come to recognize Johnson & Johnson's handling of the Tylenol crisis as the top example for success when confronted with a threat to an organization's existence. Ten Berge (1990) lauds the case in the following manner:

> The Tylenol crisis is without a doubt the most exemplary case ever known in the history of crisis communications. Any business executive, who has ever stumbled into a public relations ambush, ought to appreciate the way Johnson & Johnson responded to the Tylenol poisonings. They have effectively demonstrated how major business has to handle a disaster. (p. 19)

Engage

- Explore Johnson & Johnson's CSR website at www.jnj.com/caring/citizenship-sustainability to see how it communicates what it's achieved.

- Drawing from its website, put together a list of the internal and external stakeholders touched by its current CSR activity. How are employees involved?

Discuss

- In the Tylenol poisoning case, there is no discussion of how the news and the company's response were communicated to Johnson & Johnson's employees. While this no doubt happened then, how would you recommend a company faced with a similar crisis now manage its internal messaging?

- Should the company have considered reworking the packaging and handling of all its over-the-counter medications? Or was this just a random incident?

- If you worked for a competitor of Johnson & Johnson, how might you have recommended your company respond? What, if anything, should your company have done to make sure it was not the next victim of this criminal behavior?

Source: Crisis Communications Strategies, n.d.

3

Ethics and Law in Public Relations

Learning Objectives

3.1   Identify ethical issues in PR and explain the three moral guidelines

3.2   Survey professional codes of ethics and describe the responsibilities of the individual practitioner

3.3   Understand key legal issues confronting PR practitioners and identify the links among social responsibility, ethics, and law

Good Works Upended by U.S. Border Policy

Heartland Alliance opened its doors in 1888 in Chicago, pioneered in part by Jane Addams, founder of Chicago's famed Hull House. In the beginning, Heartland's mission was focused on bringing "health care, housing and support" to those facing homelessness. Over the years, it offered those services to immigrant families separated at Ellis Island, to those affected by the Great Depression, and to returning veterans of both World Wars. Later in the 20th century, its outreach included providing health care and services during the height of the HIV/AIDS crisis. In 2020, the nonprofit worked throughout the midwestern United States and 20 other countries and served more than 500,000 people.

Central American asylum seekers wait as U.S. Border Patrol agents take them into custody on June 12, 2019, near McAllen, Texas.

John Moore / Staff / Getty Images

Caring for Migrant Children

Since 1996, Heartland's affiliate, Heartland Human Care Services (HHCS), has operated shelters to care for migrant children who arrive at the U.S. border unaccompanied. According to its website, these children "are vulnerable to trafficking and other abuses" (Heartland Alliance, n.d., para. 2). They arrive "alone, scared and often traumatized from their journey fleeing a dangerous situation. Heartland Human Care Services provides a compassionate, peaceful, and healing setting until they can be united with family or sponsor in the U.S." (para 3). However, in order to qualify as an organization able to receive and care for the unaccompanied children, Heartland was required to execute a contractual agreement with the U.S. Department of Human Services that included, among other things, strict compliance with the government's policies on immigration.

The Controversy

In June 2018, Heartland became caught up in the controversy surrounding the Trump administration's policy that separated children from their parents at the border when it received 73 children who had been separated under this new directive.

As the controversy unfolded and journalists traveled to the detention centers along the southern border to investigate and report on the living conditions in the government-run facilities, horrifying images of children lying on cement floors in chain link cages began to flood the news cycle. Unfortunately, those same images often ran concurrently with news reports that some of the minors were being transported to and housed at the Heartland-run shelters in the Chicagoland area. And while Heartland's shelters offered comfortable and ample bedroom and living spaces for the children in their care, along with access to health care, in-house daily education, multilingual teachers, therapeutic clinicians, and daily outdoor activities and field trips, none of these differences were displayed or even mentioned in the news coverage.

Suddenly, one of its core missions—one it had performed for over 20 years without controversy—was being depicted in a negative light, and the organization was being excoriated as being complicit in the separation of families. Protests began outside its locations in Chicago, with activists calling the facilities "detention centers" and demanding the release of the border children who had been placed with Heartland.

(Continued)

(Continued)

The Threats

In short order, stories appeared in the press: one claiming a 5-year-old child had been drugged by staff members; another saying a 10-year-old boy had broken his arm playing soccer, but had been treated by Heartland staff, not a doctor. Several lawsuits were filed, challenging the government's separation policy and demanding that the children be reunited with their families. As the temporary custodian of the minors residing in their shelters, Heartland inevitably found itself swept into these suits, a codefendant alongside the government, despite openly decrying the government's immigration position. As the number of lawsuits and amount of media coverage increased, so did public outcry for local officials to get involved, eventually leading to a powerful Chicago alderman who threatened to place harsh restrictions on Heartland's ability to provide any services.

How Should Heartland Respond?

Imagine you are Heartland's director of communications. Consider how you'd deal with the following:

- Internal stakeholders (employees) and external stakeholders (volunteers, donors, political allies) are anxious for Heartland to express a position adverse to the government's change in policy. How do you cope with the demand from these stakeholders while remaining in compliance with Heartland's contractual obligations?

- Heartland's reputation has, rightly or wrongly, been damaged. What are some of the tactics you'll use to repair the damage?

To find guidance in handling sensitive issues like this, you'll need to engage in the discussion of ethics, ethical issues, and ethical decision-making that takes place in this chapter. ●

In this chapter, you will learn how ethical concerns and legal issues impact the practice of public relations (PR). As a practitioner, you'll be confronted with many decisions based not only on rules and expectations but also on the possible outcomes affecting various publics and the resulting degrees of harm versus good. Knowing in advance what might be the negative results of a decision will help guide your actions.

This chapter first reviews the main ethical philosophies relevant to PR and also takes a magnifying glass to the professional codes of ethics. The codes are the standards by which you'll practice and that provide you with guideposts to help with decisions. Case studies help illustrate how companies are striving to operate ethically and what PR's role is in assisting with that effort. You'll also learn how ethical lapses lead to reputation loss and how PR and CSR (corporate social responsibility) help recovery. The chapter also guides you on how to make important ethical decisions when serving your organization or client.

You'll become familiar with the most common legal concerns that should flash warning signals to any PR practitioner: the First Amendment, defamation, disclosure, privacy, and copyright. The takeaway lesson is to vigilantly respect legal parameters when serving your organization.

Ethics in Public Relations

>> LO 3.1   Identify ethical issues in PR and explain the three moral guidelines

Ethics is the study of what is morally right and wrong, what's fair and unfair, and how we should make decisions. PR practitioners have power in both management and communication decisions to shape society—providing information, forming attitudes, and encouraging behaviors. With power comes the obligation to their organization, to their stakeholders, and to themselves—as well as to the public in general—to perform ethically.

PR practitioners hold a unique internal and external perspective—knowing and understanding the organization itself as well as the multiple publics it impacts. This broad understanding is developed through constantly nurtured relationships and open, effective communication. They are the strategic link between the organization and key stakeholders, with two broad areas of critical responsibility:

- An obligation to function ethically
- An opportunity to serve as ethics counsel to the organization

Actress Kim Cattrall played Samantha Jones, the owner of a PR firm, on the television show *Sex and the City*, which first aired in 1998 and is still in syndication. She was seen as a poster child for the industry, stereotyping the PR professional as self-centered, frivolous, and focused on celebrity management and the planning of star-studded events and glamorous parties.
Getty Images / Staff / Getty Images

Public Relations Mix-Ups and Ethical Deficits

The profession can be misunderstood as simply a one-way message-pushing service that promotes only the good sides of a product, service, or entity. You've likely heard the phrase "PR spin" to describe persuasive communication or "spin doctor" in reference to a persuasive communicator. This language suggests PR practitioners intend to make ideas, products, events, politicians, and so on seem better than they really are. This misconception of PR as a practice of manipulation can be attributed to the profession's early history; its portrayal in film, television, and news reporting; and also some well-publicized cases of unethical clients and ethically questionable services provided by some PR firms.

For example, the year after the federal government's multibillion-dollar bailout of multinational insurer AIG in 2008, MSNBC's Rachel Maddow reported some of the money was used to hire PR firm Burson-Marsteller (B-M) to "shine up" AIG's image.

Harold Burson, considered one of the founders of the PR industry (as you read in Chapter 2), launched B-M in 1953. It then developed an expertise in the field of reputation and crisis management.

In 1982, B-M was credited with creating the template for effective and appropriate crisis management by guiding Johnson & Johnson's response to the Tylenol deaths. As you read in the case study "Johnson & Johnson's Tylenol Poisoning Crisis" in Chapter 2, seven people in metropolitan Chicago died from ingesting capsules laced with cyanide due to criminal tampering. B-M advised the company to remove all products from the market, stop advertising, and keep communication open and available.

Today, B-M is one of the top-10 global public relations and communications firms.

But on her 2009 MSNBC news broadcast, Maddow described B-M in the following way:

- "Who is Burson-Marsteller? Well, let me put it this way. When Blackwater killed those 17 Iraqi civilians in Baghdad, they called Burson-Marsteller. When there was a nuclear meltdown at Three Mile Island, Bobcock and Wilcox, who built that plant, called Burson-Marsteller."

- "The Bhopal chemical disaster that killed thousands of people in India; Union Carbide called Burson-Marsteller. Romanian dictator, Nicolae Ceausescu—Burson-Marsteller. The government of Saudi Arabia, three days after 9/11—Burson-Marsteller. The military junta that overthrew the government of Argentina in 1976, the generals dialed Burson-Marsteller."

- "The government of Indonesia, accused of genocide in East Timor—Burson-Marsteller. The government of Nigeria accused of genocide in Biafra—Burson-Marsteller. Philip Morris—Burson-Marsteller. Silicone breast implants—Burson-Marsteller. The government of Colombia, trying to make all those dead union organizers not get in the way of a new trade deal—they called Burson-Marsteller."

- "Do you remember Aqua Dots, little toy beads coated with some thing that turned into the date-rape drug, when . . . all those kids ended up in comas? Yes, even the date-rape drug Aqua Dots people called Burson-Marsteller." (MSNBC, 2009, paras. 137–140)

Maddow concluded, "When evil needs public relations, evil has Burson-Marsteller on speed dial" (MSNBC, 2009, para. 141).

In response, B-M's CEO Mark Penn addressed his employees (Gordon, 2009) in an internal memo, clarifying the work for AIG "has nothing to do with 'burnishing their image' but is all about helping this company handle the massive volume of media, government and employee interest in their situation" (para. 6). What about the other controversial clients? Penn wrote, "Our work for Aqua Dot was to help remove a dangerous product off the shelves as quickly as possible" (para. 7). Alluding to the Maddow segment, Penn clarified,

> Just like lawyers and management consultants, PR firms are often called in to help when companies face difficult problems. Our role is crucial to companies operating in open and transparent business and media environments . . . we always counsel our clients to be open and honest. (Gordon, 2009, para. 8)

In a later interview (Benady, 2014), Harold Burson admitted some mistakes, such as following State Department advice to help the Argentine junta (which eventually murdered and disappeared more than 30,000 citizens). He explained other client controversies as mischaracterized: working for Romania before the leader Ceausescu became a tyrant and representing Nigeria as a legitimate country engaged in a civil war (he alleged the Biafrans themselves misused PR by propagating myths).

Public relations professionals continue to handle tough issues facing corporations, and this chapter provides guidelines in best practices.

Contemporary Public Relations Serves the Public Good

Since its beginning fewer than 100 years ago, the PR profession in the United States has experienced negative misperceptions of its responsibilities and practices and also suffered some notorious cases of unethical PR. Yet discovery of the truth and open, honest communication are its primary concerns—leading to the dominant practice of issues management. For the benefit of all, PR professionals work to discover and address potential issues, such as customer dissatisfaction with a service, *before* they become a problem or even a crisis. Skills involve asking, listening, and empathizing to function as the ethical conscience in the organization—and then evaluating and recommending to resolve issues, often resulting in customer retention, positive social sharing, and possible economies in legal, lobbying, media relations costs.

What Ethical Guidelines Should Be Used in Public Relations?

Most PR practitioners have done little formal study of ethical philosophies; rather, they tend to rely on situational ethics. PR ethics scholar Shannon Bowen finds limited usefulness with this route: "It sees no universal or generally applicable moral norms but looks at each situation independently" (2013, p. 306). There are three major types of normative ethics that guide moral actions: teleological, deontological, and virtue ethics. Bowen suggests the first two, the teleology theory of utilitarianism (or consequentialist theory) and the deontological theory of absolutism (or nonconsequentialist theory) are the most appropriate ethical guides for PR (see Table 3.1).

How to Apply Utilitarianism

1. Do not be guided by established rules or duties.
2. Predict the possible consequences of decisions and weigh the good and bad of each potential outcome (see Figure 3.1).

TABLE 3.1

Normative Ethics

CATEGORY	NAME	DESCRIPTION	CRITICISM
Teleological (values)	Utilitarianism	Emphasizes consequences of actions—the greatest good for the greatest number of people	Is it possible for someone to accurately predict outcomes?
Deontological (rules)	Absolutism	Emphasizes duties or rules—what's morally right applies to everyone	Should we act as if our own ethical choices are universal law?
Virtue (character)	Agent-Based	Emphasizes individual moral character—guided by one's virtue and practical wisdom	Different people may have quite different concepts of what constitutes virtue.

FIGURE 3.1

Utilitarianism Challenge

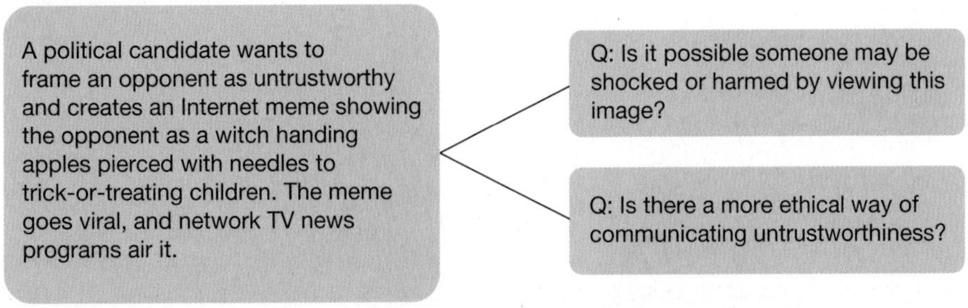

A political candidate wants to frame an opponent as untrustworthy and creates an Internet meme showing the opponent as a witch handing apples pierced with needles to trick-or-treating children. The meme goes viral, and network TV news programs air it.

Q: Is it possible someone may be shocked or harmed by viewing this image?

Q: Is there a more ethical way of communicating untrustworthiness?

3. Draw a conclusion: The ethical choice will be the decision or outcome that has the *most* positive consequences and *least* negative consequences.

4. Another way to view this is to choose to produce the greatest good for the greatest number of people.

How to Apply Absolutism

1. Do not use possible outcomes as a decision-making guide.

2. Rather, determine what is morally right, applying equally to all people (see Figure 3.2).

3. Follow moral principles objectively: The ethical choice is doing what's morally right for everyone.

How to Apply Virtue Ethics

1. Do not weigh the consequences to project best outcomes.

2. Do not be guided by rules or proscribed duties.

3. Individual moral character guides motivation for a decision.

4. Decisions are guided by courage, honesty, benevolence, compassion, justice, and temperance (see Figure 3.3).

FIGURE 3.2

Absolutism Challenge

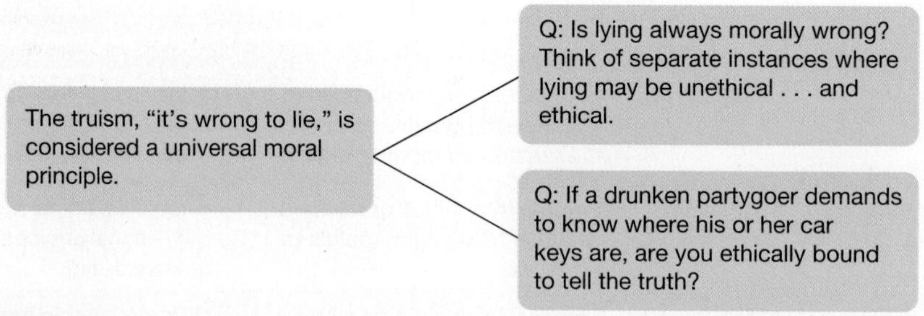

The truism, "it's wrong to lie," is considered a universal moral principle.

Q: Is lying always morally wrong? Think of separate instances where lying may be unethical . . . and ethical.

Q: If a drunken partygoer demands to know where his or her car keys are, are you ethically bound to tell the truth?

FIGURE 3.3

Virtue Ethics Challenge

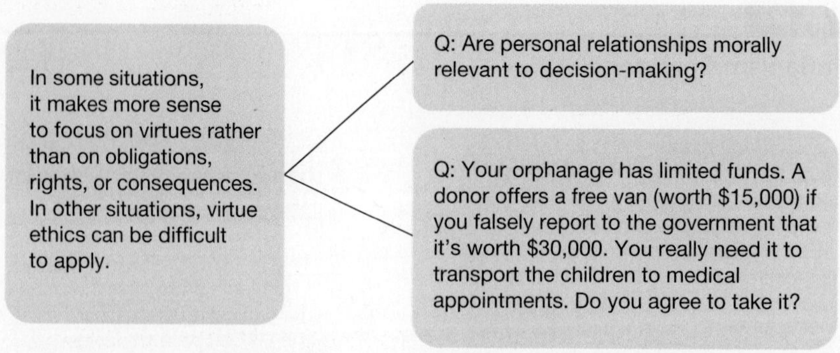

In some situations, it makes more sense to focus on virtues rather than on obligations, rights, or consequences. In other situations, virtue ethics can be difficult to apply.

Q: Are personal relationships morally relevant to decision-making?

Q: Your orphanage has limited funds. A donor offers a free van (worth $15,000) if you falsely report to the government that it's worth $30,000. You really need it to transport the children to medical appointments. Do you agree to take it?

A Personal Framework for Ethical Reasoning in Public Relations

To bridge all three approaches to ethical reasoning—utilitarianism, absolutism, and virtue ethics—Martin and Wright (2015) propose a personal framework for ethical reasoning in public relations. It has four parts:

1. Define the issue.
   A. Describe the issue in one or two sentences; then, list the facts in order of relevance. Include any external pressures you feel: political, economic, interpersonal, or social.

2. Identify stakeholders.
   A. List all people who might be affected and all people to whom you owe a duty. Suggest their current state of mind and heart.

3. Define and evaluate options.
   A. Consider all three ethical approaches, listing best and worst cases for each.
   B. For each of the approaches listed, identify pros and cons (benefits and costs) for each of the stakeholder groups, including the client. Take into account the following:
      i. *Harms/Cares.* How would they benefit? Would anyone be harmed? What costs may have to be paid?
      ii. *Duties.* What are your duties? Do they respect the integrity and freedom of those affected? Are you free of vested interest or ulterior motives? Would you expect others to follow this as a rule?
      iii. *Rights.* What are stakeholders' rights? Might any invalidate any of your options? Does your relationship with stakeholders carry any explicit or implicit rights?

4. Make and justify a decision.
   A. Now choose your course of action, selecting the option that allows you to fulfill your most important duties, in keeping with your own values, and that has best consequences for the affected people. If the choice is among harmful actions, choose the least harmful. Then, justify your decision based on ethical reasoning—as if you were addressing the person least likely to agree.

Can Public Relations Ethics Be Applied to Social Movement Organizations?

Published ethical guidelines for PR focus on corporate, nonprofit, government, or otherwise mainstream organizations. Yet social movement organizations (SMOs) often have the unique challenge of using persuasive communication campaigns to redefine accepted social practices into social problems. They may use forceful appeals to gain attention or even purposely cause contention (Freeman, 2009). However, SMOs must communicate about problems perceived as severe and unresolved by authorities, creating a sense of urgency that motivates social intervention. SMOs must walk a line between extremes; if they are too moderate, they risk being assimilated and "blunted" (Gitlin, 2003, p. 290), yet if they are too critical, they risk being marginalized and trivialized.

Visual Spectacles or Strategic Actions?

SMOs have gained leverage through disruptive actions deliberately staged for the media. Greenpeace flotillas, the AIDS Coalition to Unleash Power (Act Up) die-ins, and the unruliest aspects of the antiglobalization body World Trade Organization (WTO)—such as sit-ins and street theater—are examples of successful visual communication that was newsworthy. More playfully, protestors have used carnivalesque street performances to highlight contradictions and the absurdity of social, environmental, or economic issues.

(Continued)

(Continued)

Ethical Questions of the Social Movement Organization

Freeman (2009, pp. 287–288) suggests asking the following about the organization:

- "To what extent it is marginalized (both in terms of lack of power and resources and in terms of posing a challenge to hegemony (those in power)."

- "To what extent its goals are socially responsible and in the public interest (such as promoting truth, justice, and minimization of harm)."

- "To what extent its primary moral claimants (potentially victimized parties) are experiencing harm or disadvantage (this could include the cause's urgency and severity)."

- "To what extent it is targeting its message at parties directly responsible for causing the problem or who have more control in solving it."

Ethical Questions of Its Communication Means and Messages

- Freeman (2009, pp. 287–288) suggests asking the following about its communications: "To what extent its goals are confrontational and critical of hegemony and social norms."

- "To what extent it uses persuasion (asymmetry) versus dialogue (symmetry)."

- To what extent it will cause audience members to experience dissonance or emotional discomfort."

The more an SMO matches the organizational factors, the more ethically justified it is employing the communication means and messages. ●

Source: Freeman, 2009.

Stay Informed, Be Vigilant, Develop Professional and Personal Ethics

≫ LO 3.2   Survey professional codes of ethics and describe the responsibilities of the individual practitioner

PR practitioners must actively observe, evaluate, and often respond to the many issues that organizations face—frequently unexpected or at first appearing harmless. Social media posts, comment threads, meme generators, and YouTube videos can amplify criticisms or concerns about an organization's behavior. To guide ethical choices and behaviors in any situation, PR practitioners should follow the ethical code her or his employer has adopted, as well as be guided by professional and personal ethics (see Table 3.2).

Professional Ethics

PRSA (n.d.c) offers a Member Code of Ethics, which serves as a model for all U.S. organizations and professionals that practice PR. The code is structured into two broad sections: guiding professional values and ethical conduct provisions. The Professional Values Statement sets the industry standard for the professional practice of PR. These core values include the following (paras. 7–12):

- *Advocacy*—We serve the public interest by acting as responsible advocates for those we represent. We provide a voice in the marketplace of ideas, facts, and viewpoints to aid informed public debate.

TABLE 3.2	
Helpful Third-Party Sources of Communication Ethics Codes	
INTERNATIONAL, NATIONAL, AND REGIONAL PROFESSIONAL PUBLIC RELATIONS ASSOCIATIONS	
Global Alliance for Public Relations and Communication Management (GA)	Code of Ethics http://www.globalalliancepr.org/code-of-ethics
International Association of Business Communicators (IABC)	Code of Ethics https://www.iabc.com/about-us/purpose/code-of-ethics/
International Public Relations Association (IPRA)	Code of Conduct https://www.ipra.org/member-services/code-of-conduct/
Arthur W. Page Society	Page Principles http://www.awpagesociety.com/site/the-page-principles
Canadian Public Relations Society (CPRS)	Code of Professional Standards https://www.cprs.ca/About/Code-of-Professional-Standards
UK's Chartered Institute of Public Relations (CIPR)	Code of Conduct and ethics resources: https://www.cipr.co.uk/ethics
Public Relations Society of America (PRSA)	Member Code of Ethics https://www.prsa.org/ethics/code-of-ethics

- *Honesty*—We adhere to the highest standards of accuracy and truth in advancing the interests of those we represent and in communicating with the public.

- *Expertise*—We acquire and responsibly use specialized knowledge and experience. We advance the profession through continued professional development, research, and education. We build mutual understanding, credibility, and relationships among a wide array of institutions and audiences.

- *Independence*—We provide objective counsel to those we represent. We are accountable for our actions.

- *Loyalty*—We are faithful to those we represent while honoring our obligation to serve the public interest.

- *Fairness*—We deal fairly with clients, employers, competitors, peers, vendors, the media, and the general public. We respect all opinions and support the right of free expression.

The Code Provisions of Conduct (PRSA, n.d.b, paras. 13–18) provides detailed recommendations in the following categories, briefly explained here:

- *Free Flow of Information*—Protecting and advancing the free flow of accurate and truthful information, [which is] essential to serving the public interest and contributing to informed decision-making in a democratic society

- *Competition*—Promoting healthy and fair competition among professionals [to] preserve an ethical climate while fostering a robust business environment

- *Disclosure of Information*—Fosters informed decision-making in a democratic society
- *Safeguarding Confidences*—Client trust requires appropriate protection of confidential and private information
- *Conflicts of Interest*—Avoiding real, potential, or perceived conflicts of interest builds the trust of clients, employers, and publics
- *Enhancing the Profession*—Public relations professional work constantly to strengthen the public's trust in the profession

Personal Ethics

Derina Holtzhausen, professor and past editor of the *International Journal of Strategic Communication*, argues that professional and corporate codes interfere with individual ethical decision-making, making ethical decisions a group responsibility that people "hide behind" (2015, p. 771). This is not an isolated criticism: Other critics (Curtin & Boynton, 2000) reason that most professional codes of practice, while good guidelines, are "vague, unenforceable, or applied inconsistently" (p. 411) and as such cannot account for the variety of views in a globalized society.

A **moral impulse** should guide individual PR practitioners, steering them to consider perspectives of multiple stakeholders. While admittedly often tempered by binding laws, contracts, financial expediency, or strategic intent, the practitioner has to accept responsibility in ethical decision-making. This ideal application of virtue ethics—one that's individually guided by moral responsibility and selflessness—then yields subsequent actions, words, and images that are manifestations of the ethical choice.

Social Responsibility Ethics

There is a common direction between both schools of business and communication to encourage students to become leaders that transform not just organizations but the societies that house them. Corporate ethics codes are also drivers of PR ethics. Economic events in the early 21st century, including the 2007–2008 financial crisis and increased globalization, have greatly influenced business behaviors and decision-making, as have activist movements powered by social media. Along with this shift to social responsibility (SR), notable firms are evaluating the companies' codes and compliance and publishing rankings of the world's most reputable or ethical companies. Among them are Ethisphere, GMI Ratings, and the Reputation Institute.

Images spread fast with tech-savvy Gen Xers and millennials, so PR visual messaging must be based on ethical decision-making. Some practitioners might consider it unethical to use this image to raise awareness and donations for disadvantaged children.

iStock.com/olesiabilkei

Visual Communication Ethics

Visual ethics involves "how images and imaging affect the ways we think, feel, behave, and create, use and interpret meaning, for good or for bad," writes visual scholar Julianne Newton in her chapter "Visual Ethics Theory" in the *Handbook of Visual Communication* (2005, p. 433). She understands visual ethics as an ecological system of process and meaning—how visuals are made and received—and calls them the soul of communication.

Concern for the ethical use of visuals in PR is critical, as we continuously adapt to evolving communication technologies and our publics quickly adopt and embrace them. Today, visual media is the dominant mode for creating, sharing, and consuming information through many social media platforms. Brands are quick to interact with consumers in these spaces, yet for a PR practitioner, there is both power and responsibility in designing or using visual messages for organizational communication.

Does Public Relations Mean Deception?

Shannon A. Bowen, Arthur W. Page Society

Photo courtesy of Shannon A. Bowen

Studies often report that public relations professionals routinely rely on deception. One study reported that 65% of public relations professionals report telling a lie "occasionally" to keep their jobs (Ragan Communications, 2008). Likewise, a *PRWeek* study indicated that 25% of PR pros said they lied on the job (Kuczynski, 2000).

In the 2015 BledCom International Public Relations Research Symposium, a researcher reported that of over 20 interviewees, 17 acknowledged regularly lying to the media; of those, 16 said they would lie again. One of the CCOs in the study explained, "Sure, I lie, we are professional manipulators. That is what we do." And another: "I am the one really pulling the strings." Is it any wonder that the public relations profession often has a persistent reputation as untrustworthy?

Relationships with journalists suffer, the credibility of PR suffers, and communicators have to work daily to conquer these negative impressions. Perhaps worst of all, lies erode trust of the stakeholders and publics we seek to serve, as well as the managements we counsel.

The annual Edelman Trust Barometer (2019) finds that the government and the media are widely distrusted. For business, 76% of participants say that their CEOs should lead change rather than wait for government to impose it. They are most trusting of "my employer" but demand ethical behavior. Findings on the actions that erode perceived ethics include failure to show responsibility during a crisis, using unethical business practices, failing to keep information secure, providing substandard working conditions, or misrepresenting the organization. PR is involved in most or all of these practices, so we are part of the trust problem—but we can also help solve it through fostering ethical behavior. Our responsibility to stakeholders and publics necessitates honesty and ethical reflection in the organization's actions, as well as how they are communicated.

We need honesty to foster a reputation that can help organizations grow, achieve their goals, and meet the needs of stakeholders and publics. Telling the occasional "white lie," either out of pressure, fear, or obligation, does not serve our management or clients well, undermines the credibility of the profession, and may harm our own career interests.

A better model for the PR professional is to be a counselor and advocate of honesty—sometimes even when that honesty is damaging to the organization. Refusing to engage in dishonesty, manipulation, or even white lies helps one to become a counselor to management, helping

(Continued)

(Continued)

participate in determining the correct course of action for an organization.

When issues or crises emerge, PR practitioners will be called upon to provide counsel in how to handle these uncomfortable situations. My 2009 and 2016 studies showed that this opportunity opens a chance for the organization to respond with ethical behavior, thereby enhancing relationships. Maintaining honesty at all times is the best policy, but having a model, approach, or guideline to really examine the ethics of a situation thoroughly is the best practice.

Consider the Ethical Implications

Considering the ethics of your decision, in addition to using honest communication, helps advance not only the responsibility of the organization but also the value of the PR counsel within it. Issues of ethics are even more crucial when PR is defined as building relationships with publics and stakeholders that are based on credible and accurate communication. Good ethics is good business for everyone involved. My research (2009) found that public relations acts as the ethical counsel in many organizations and must be prepared to do so with analytical rigor. Guidelines for analysis of ethical problems are as follows:

- *Be rational.* Gather data from multiple sides and points of view and analyze it logically. Be as objective as possible and determine which arguments have the most merit.

- *Be consistent.* Follow the vision, mission, values, and ethics statement of your organization. What do your publics and stakeholders expect you to reliably deliver? How can you do that?

- *Be principled.* Strive to maintain the principles that can be valued across situations and even cultures. Defeat deception and manipulation with honesty and candor. What decision maintains equity, liberty, responsibility, honesty, and so on?

- *Respect other views.* Listen to the perspectives of those on the other side of an issue. When it makes sense, incorporate some of their values into your decision-making. Even those who disagree with your decision can likely understand it when they feel heard and it maintains a common value or principle.

- *Do the right thing.* Even when things go awry, a good intention can help get matters back on the right footing. Advise your team and your management on what you should be doing, not just what you could be doing. Ethics always prioritizes should over could. Act with good intention in all decisions.

Shannon A. Bowen, PhD, University of South Carolina, is a member of the Arthur W. Page Society and a board member and part of the board of directors of the International Public Relations Research Conference.

Source: S. Bowen, personal communication, 2020.

Suggested Reading: Bowen, S. A. (2005). A practical model for ethical decision making in issues management and public relations. *Journal of Public Relations Research, 17*(3), 191–216.

Note: BledCom research is discussed in more depth in my *PRWeek* columns that can be found at http://www.prweek.com/article/1359922/we-professional-manipulators-pr-pros-lying-ourselves and in a large archive at https://www.sc.edu/study/colleges_schools/cic/journalism_and_mass_communications/news/professional_manipulators.php#.Xern-G5FxPY

Ms. Bowen's Sources:

Bowen, S. A. (2009). What communication professionals tell us regarding dominant coalition access and gaining membership. *Journal of Applied Communication Research, 37*(4), 427–452.

Bowen, S. A., Hung-Baesecke, C. J., & Chen, Y. R. (2016). Ethics as a pre-cursor to organization-public relationships: Building trust before and during the OPR model. *Cogent Social Sciences, 29*(1). http://dx.doi.org/10.1080/23311886.2016.1141467

Edelman. (2014). Edelman trust barometer. https://www.edelman.com/sites/g/files/aatuss191/files/2019-02/2019_Edelman_Trust_Barometer_Global_Report.pdf

Kuczynski, A. (2000, May 8). In public relations, 25% admit lying. *The New York Times*, sec. C, p. 20, col. 5.

Ragan Communications. (2008, January/February). Polls indicate public relations pros must lie to remain employed. *Journal of Employee Communication Management*, p. 8. http://www.lexisnexis.com.pallas2.tcl.sc.edu/hottopics/lnacademic/? verb=sr&csi=314324retrieved8/24/16viaLEXIS-NEXIS ●

The PRSA ethics code doesn't specifically address visual communication, but if pictorial imagery is employed, ethical issues may be raised—especially if they mislead or wrongfully influence viewers negatively. As we now have the vast capacity to create, manipulate, and quickly transmit visual messages, we must be aware of the potential for ethical issues. A familiar issue is with imagery used by nonprofits to raise awareness and donations for disadvantaged children. Sometimes called "poverty porn," the images can be viewed as unethical.

How Does Law Affect Public Relations?

>> LO 3.3 Understand key legal issues confronting PR practitioners and identify the links among social responsibility, ethics, and law.

Morality and ethics are often confused with a question of legality: Something thought of as unethical may not be illegal, and something considered unethical or immoral may be completely legal. This section deals with PR decision-making based on considerations of *legality*, as public communication in the United States is conditioned by legal rights and legal restrictions. Issues of **free speech, defamation**, **disclosure, privacy**, and **copyright** in the ever-expanding boundaries of the Internet all concern the PR practitioner. We also cover the field of litigation PR.

Free Speech

The U.S. Constitution's First Amendment reads in part, "Congress shall make no law . . . abridging the freedom of speech, or of the press." However, there are exclusions, for example, due to national security needs, obscenity laws, and prohibited language that incites hatred or violence. Freedom of speech also permits gathering of information, protected by the federal Freedom of Information Act (FOIA, n.d.), a law granting citizens the right to get information from the federal government. Thanks to FOIA, each state has "sunshine" laws, under various names, granting public access to state records (Ballotpedia, n.d.).

SOCIAL RESPONSIBILITY

Socially responsible business practices include respecting human rights and fair labor practices. The UN (United Nations, n.d.) Global Compact is the world's largest corporate sustainability initiative, asking companies to follow and advance its universal principles concerning human rights, labor, the environment, and anticorruption. All members must submit an annual "communication on progress," reporting on their progress in meeting the principles. Although not all comply, this reporting is a voluntary effort to provide open access of information to interested publics.

Turning from external to internal communication, the U.S. National Labor Relations Board (NLRB) has policies that prohibit restrictions on employee speech. As much of this dialogue flows through social media, often it's the PR practitioner who sets policy and monitors activity. There are many issues to be aware of; for example, a social media policy must be written carefully to avoid restricting public criticism—it's OK to complain, but the policy must protect the company's business interests. And while companies invest time and expense in establishing their names and logos—which are protected under copyright laws against any use for profit—the NLRB allows employees to freely use them to communicate workplace grievances (Myers, 2013).

Defamation

Defamation is the act of making a statement that can be proven to be false with the intention of causing harm to another's reputation or livelihood. It has two categories: libel is a written or published defamatory statement, while spoken defamation is considered slander (NOLO, n.d.a).

Technology invites the PR professional to explore many ways to engage with key publics. Likewise, customers, employees, investors, and sometimes adversaries may use digital platforms to express dissatisfaction or objections with your organization. The easy access to a public court of opinion can be influential and potentially damaging if the content is defamatory.

The Communications Decency Act of 1996 has significant jurisdiction on Internet and online speech. It protects "interactive" websites and Web hosts from being held liable for content provided by its third-party users. In other words, the harmed party can take action only against the actual author of defamatory content, not the websites (Facebook, Twitter, etc.) themselves. Online defamation, or "cyberlibel," can appear on blogs, in forums, on websites, and within social networking platforms. For example, Reddit, the online news aggregator that brands itself as a source for what's new and popular on the Web, rarely removes defamatory content, even though it tends to go viral (Gibson, 2014).

INSIGHTS

The Ethical Implications of *Citizens United v. Federal Election Commission*

Attorney David J. Dale, a former PR practitioner, offers this scenario on the legal and ethical issues raised by the Citizens United ruling. Dale is a partner with Staub Anderson in Chicago, Illinois.

You are the PR manager for ABC, Inc., a midsized for-profit corporation with a strong regional presence that employs around 5,000 workers. It's an election year, and your boss, the founder and current president of the company, is solidly behind the Republican candidate for president. You've heard that he's been considering using his business's goodwill and resources to help get the word out in support of his candidate. Thus, it comes as no surprise when he emails you to schedule a one-on-one meeting to discuss some of his latest ideas, and ahead of the meeting, he asks you to consider the following questions:

- Can ABC, Inc., use its social media presence to spread the word about the candidate's political platform and even openly endorse this candidate?

- Can ABC, Inc., offer incentives to its customers in return for promises of support and perhaps even donations to the candidate's campaign?

- Can ABC, Inc., use its own workforce to get out and support the candidate by attending rallies, canvasing communities, and even soliciting donations?

- More importantly, does ABC, Inc., have to reimburse its workers for their time?

- What if an employee refuses to take part?

Only 5 years ago, your answer would have been markedly different than it is today, thanks to a single Supreme Court decision, most commonly known and referred to as *Citizens United*.

Citizens United v. FEC, 130 S. Ct. 876 (2010), involved a nonprofit, tax-exempt corporation (Citizens United) and its attempts to publicly advertise and promote its documentary film titled *Hillary the*

Movie, an unabashed appeal to voters not to vote for Hillary Clinton for president. Under existing federal laws, specifically the Federal Election Campaign Act of 1971 (FECA), corporations (both for- and nonprofit) were barred from making "a contribution or expenditure in connection with any election to any political office."[1] The statute was purposefully written to define "contribution" in the broadest sense, restricting not only monetary contributions but "anything of value," which included funding communications, compensating employees for time contributed to campaign activities, and even uncompensating time if the employees were directed to participate by management.[2] In addition to restricting corporations from using their employees to outwardly support political campaigns, businesses were also restricted from engaging in election-related communications with its employees.[3]

Thus, in a pre-*Citizens United* landscape, and based on the then-existing restrictions, you might have advised your boss to err on the side of caution and steer clear of any ideas or initiatives that purported to use ABC, Inc.'s, resources or its employees to support a specific candidate. However, in its landmark *Citizens United* decision, the ban on independent political expenditures was struck down by the Supreme Court, which held the First Amendment prohibited restrictions on corporations' use of its own money to fund communications advocating for specific candidates or political parties.

As a result, corporations (both for- and nonprofits) now have the authority to "use [their] own resources, including paid work-hour time of its employees, for independent expenditures" in support of a chosen political candidate or party.[4] And while companies are still prohibited from making direct contributions to candidate campaigns or firing an employee for voluntary participation in political efforts, they are no longer prohibited from firing an employee for declining to participate in employer-mandated political activity. In the wake of this decision, company executives now openly urge employees to support specific candidates, solicit donations directly from their workforce, invite political candidates to speak at company meetings, and even disseminate political advertisements via employees' payroll checks. While most companies readily acknowledge the difficulty of forcing its employees to participate in political endeavors in practice, the fact remains that under *Citizens United*, there is no federal restriction prohibiting it.

Having reviewed the state of the corporate/political world post–*Citizens United*, and considering both the ethical and practical ramifications of his proposed plans, you tell your boss that the question is not "Can we do it?" but "Should we do it?" You explain that while your company may be legally permitted to issue communications on behalf of a specific candidate and even direct its employees to participate in campaign-related events, you remind your boss that doing so may alienate not only your customers but also your workers. And given the repeated criticisms of the *Citizen United* decision and calls for its repeal, any perceived gain from forcing ABC, Inc., and its workers to campaign for a candidate may be quickly lost in the long run. ●

---

[1] 2 U.S.C. §441b(a).

[2] 2 U.S.C. § 441b(b)(2); see also 11 C.F.R. § 100.54 (2014); FEC MUR 5664, General Counsel's Report #2, supra note 14, at 5.

[3] 11 C.F.R. § 114.2(b)(2)(ii). While employers were permitted to discuss basic policy issues and pending litigation, they were not permitted to advocate for specific candidates or political parties.

[4] FEC MUR 6344, First General Counsel's Report at 7.

Because of the often anonymous and pseudonymous nature of Internet posts, the best strategy for a PR practitioner is watchfulness and quick response, as well as maintaining a strong Web presence.

Disclosure

"Bloggers who make endorsements must disclose the material connections they share with the seller of the product/service," stated the Federal Trade Commission (FTC) when it amended its guidelines regarding endorsements and testimonials (FTC, 2009). Even the mere sharing of a link on social media to show

songofstyle
Paid partnership with …   Follow

songofstyle Today was amazing. Thank you @volvocarusa for letting me drive the #volvoxc90. I really don't want to give it back.

Load more comments

kikinassaustin 🖤🖤🖤🖤🖤
soo7755 Nice photo! 🌷😍
millerrodrigues1 Linda Foto!
inlust_forlife You got this💜
sophoebelous Love this!!!
malikamancia So cute🌸
theanitte 🖤🖤🖤
meriliis_krais Wow🖤 😊
nesmahoumami Wow! This Photo is amazing!
gigiscupoftea Oh I love Jacarandas 🖤

44,777 likes
JUNE 28

Log in to like or comment.   …

Instagram now requires that users mark posts for which they have been paid. Here, Aimee Song's post has a banner noting that it is a paid partnership with Volvo.
Instagram/@songofstyle

you're a fan of a particular business or product requires disclosure *if* you're being rewarded by that entity for your action. This legality supports the PRSA's established advocacy of full disclosure of information.

While bloggers seek access to goods to review, they prefer to retain editorial control over the review process (Lahav & Zimand-Sheiner, 2016; Walden et al., 2014). Thus, it's important for PR professionals who help to place products with bloggers to confirm the issue of transparency with them. Consumers are increasingly turning to blogs for product information, and when PR practitioners encourage trustworthy and open communication with their publics, it has the potential to positively impact attitudes about the product company and translate into bottom-line outcomes.

Celebrities or experts have a responsibility to disclose their relationships with companies when they give endorsements outside the context of traditional advertising, such as in talk show appearances or on social media (FTC, 2009). This applies to their promotional statements on their blogs or websites as well. When in doubt, send questions to endorsements@ftc.gov.

SOCIAL RESPONSIBILITY IN ACTION

Nike and Sweatshop Labor

After a lawsuit accused Nike of lying about conditions in its factories, the company vowed to improve conditions and root out child labor.
Peter Charlesworth / Contributor / Getty Images

The Suit

Nike was sued for lying about sweatshop labor in 1998 by San Francisco resident Marc Kasky under California's unfair business practices law, which prohibits false claims and advertising. The suit centered on the company's news releases and other public statements regarding accusations its athletic shoes were manufactured in Asian sweatshops. The lawsuit charged Nike had lied about its reliance on sweatshop labor.

Nike's Defense

Although Nike claimed its comments were protected free speech—aspects of public debate and not commercial speech—opponents counterargued that the First Amendment doesn't extend to making false statements designed to make products more acceptable to consumers.

Enter the California Supreme Court

The court ruled 4-to-3 against Nike, stating that "when a business enterprise makes factual representations about its own products or its own operations, it must speak truthfully" (Savage, 2002). The company then took its case to the U.S. Supreme Court. Subsequently, the high court decided against ruling on it, leaving the earlier ruling to stand.

The Settlement: Nike Embraced CSR

Kasky agreed to drop the suit because Nike had improved workplace conditions and had accepted outside scrutiny. Nike CEO Phil Knight vowed to root out child labor to overcome the issue: "The Nike product has become synonymous with slave wages, forced overtime and arbitrary abuse" (Banjo, 2014, para. 24). Nike's payment of $1.5 million to settle the charges went to the Fair Labor Association for factory monitoring in developing countries worldwide. The association's executive director, Auret Van Heerden, celebrated Nike's agreement that "even though it doesn't own the factories, it will be responsible for conditions in any supplier plant" (Girion, 2003).

Nike's Social Responsibility Wins and Losses

In 2005, not long after the lawsuit was resolved, Nike became the first corporation in its industry to publish a complete list of its contract factories, along with its first CSR report (Newell, 2015). By 2006, Nike ranked in the top 10 for its social responsibility reporting, according to the SustainAbility Global Reporters Program ranking (Nike, 2006). In 2015, Triplepundit.com published "How Nike Embraced CSR and Went From Villain to Hero," documenting the company's CSR leadership (Newell, 2015). In 2018, the Reputation Institute ranked Nike second in the U.S. top 100 companies with the best reputations (Reputation Institute, 2018b).

However, Nike took a big loss in reputation in 2019 as the public quickly judged it amidst product weaknesses, controversial CSR, scandals, and lawsuits. George-Parkin (2019) summarized Nike's blunders in *Footwear News*; for example, when college basketball star Zion Williamson's foot tore through his Nike sneaker in the middle of a nationally televised game, leaving him with a knee injury, Twitter erupted. Nike's stock dropped more than 1%. Subsequently, its reputation took a hit, descending from #2 to #60 in the U.S. RepTrak 100. Contributing to the drop was *The New York Times* exposé on its "boys' club" culture and widespread sexual harassment, its controversial campaign with former NFL quarterback, Colin Kaepernick who protested police brutality by kneeling during the national anthem), and ongoing lawsuits regarding a hostile work environment and leadership's failure to investigate.

Despite these troubles, Nike maintains a healthy commitment to CSR, particularly in its manufacturing responsibility. Visit www.purpose.nike.com to explore how Nike communicates its CSR engagement. ●

Copyright and Fair Use

Social media affords PR practitioners vast potential to engage stakeholders, yet it also presents legal challenges when it comes to copyright law. "A copyright provides legal protection for any creative work that is published, broadcast, or presented or displayed publicly, including video, audio, or written work on the Web" (Conway, 2012, para. 5). However, the Internet legal site www.Nolo.com states that in some situations, under the **fair use** rule, you "may make limited use of the original author's work without asking permission" (NOLO, n.d.b, para. 4).

What determines fair use can be complex, but factors include the purpose of its use, nature of copyrighted work itself, amount of use, and effect of use on the work itself. Former Cision CEO Dawn Conway (2012) advises the PR professional on what *not* to do:

- Don't copy a whole article and distribute it via email or elsewhere on a public network.
- Don't distribute reprints of an article without written permission from the copyright holder. This might entail a fee.
- Quoting short excerpts from copyrighted material needs source identification, and extensive quoting needs permission.
- On your blog or website, you may illustrate your own points or thoughts with an excerpt from another source, but you must identify it and link to it.

Further advice from Cision cautions that negotiating copyright is complex and offers some tips (Feldman, 2015):

- *Attribution.* Citing sources is the golden rule of copyright compliance.
- *Education.* Don't violate another person's copyright due to lack of knowledge. Feldman recommends creating an internal copyright wiki that houses up-to-date information and resources.
- *Monitor.* Keep track of your own content with alerts and social listening software to learn where and how your content is being used.

The PR Council also offers copyright guidance at www.prcouncil.net/resources.

Privacy

The right of privacy protects citizens from harm caused by the public dissemination of truthful but private information about them (Heath, 2001). Invasion of privacy is divided into four legal actions: **intrusion**, disclosure, **false light**, and **appropriation**. Most states include a fifth **right of publicity**, meaning a citizen may control the commercial use of his or her identity. See Table 3.3 for a more detailed look into a citizen's right to privacy.

TABLE 3.3

Privacy Legal Actions

Intrusion	It's important for a PR professional to secure permission from a private or secluded individual to protect against intrusion—the intentional disturbance, physically or otherwise, upon the solitude or seclusion of another that causes offense, mental anguish, or suffering (praccreditation.org, n.d.).
Disclosure	It's equally important to know, regarding disclosure, that photos taken publicly and facts already publicly known (either released by the person or on public record) are not seen as private information, and publishing them is not an invasion of privacy (Heath, 2001).
False Light	False light requires that the information be either untrue or suggestive of false impressions and be widely publicized.
Appropriation	Appropriation involves using some aspect of a person's identity that causes mental or physical distress.
Right of Publicity	Heath (2001) advises that the right of publicity belongs to those whose celebrity gives their names, images, or identities financial value.

Working for the Law: Litigation Public Relations

A media strategy is particularly important during high-profile litigation. When PR firms represent law firms as clients, under U.S. law they are granted legal protection to confidential information—an extension of attorney–client privilege to nonlawyers—although this is a complex issue that may be contested.

For firms practicing PR litigation and claiming attorney–client privilege, Cayce (2015) recommends it is important to be hired by the client's lawyers, not by the client; that PR is involved with actual litigation strategy or preparation; and that PR is involved with the immediate effects of litigation and not the aftermath—these are easier to prove for in-house PR counsel than for outside consultants.

Using PR methods without a professional to support litigation strategy can be controversial. In a civil lawsuit against professional basketball player Kobe Bryant for sexual assault, the judge said his lawyers engaged in "public relations litigation" by using pleadings to attract media attention. Rather, a better approach would have been for a PR professional to have responsibly used court documents to communicate with the public (Terilli et al., 2007).

Scenario Outcome

At the beginning of this chapter, you read about Heartland's reputation crisis that began in June 2018, regarding refugee children separated from their parents at the U.S. border. You were asked to consider how the organization should respond.

In fact, the summer of 2018 left an indelible mark on Heartland. The organization faced harsh criticism and was forced to release several statements, refuting the allegations leveled by the press and lawsuits and reassuring stakeholders, political allies, and the general public that it was committed to its core mission and values. Regarding the abuse allegations, Heartland couldn't issue a response because the investigation was confidential, and issuing any statement to the press might be viewed as divulging confidential information or interfering with an ongoing investigation. Consider the following evidence of Heartland's communication efforts:

- On June 21, 2018, the *Chicago Tribune* quoted the organization: "Heartland has nothing to do with the decision to separate kids from their parents at the border, but we have everything to do with keeping children safe while they are in our care." The Heartland statement continued, "Children and families who arrive at our borders are seeking safety. They are fleeing violence and unrest in their home countries. Heartland Alliance stands with them. And we ask you to stand with us" (Briscoe, 2018a, para. 14).

- The next day, Heartland president Evelyn Diaz welcomed U.S. Senator Dick Durbin for a visit to one of Heartland's nine shelters accommodating some of the separated children. As reported again in the *Chicago Tribune*, upon seeing toddlers and infants, Durbin described it as "a kindergarten or day care situation" (Briscoe, 2018b, para. 5).

- The following month, ProPublica reported, "Heartland has tried to distance itself from administration policies . . . (publishing) a fact sheet about its shelters showing photos of tidy bedrooms as well as children sitting in class and outside playing volleyball" (Sanchez et al., 2018).

Ultimately, the decision was made to shutter several facilities and move employees into the remaining Chicago shelters in order to, according to Heartland's executive director, "streamline our efforts and maximize our efficiency in providing care" (Sanchez et al., 2019, para. 16).

In the summer of 2019—a full year after the initial crisis—due to new media reports of appalling conditions for children held at Border Patrol detention centers, Diaz issued a statement on Heartland's website titled "Where We Stand on Immigration." She distanced Heartland from the border conditions, emphasizing, "Let me be clear—there is no comparison" (Diaz, 2019, para. 2). The statement linked to a "Facts About Our Shelters" page with photos of cheerful bedrooms, classrooms, and playgrounds.

WRAP UP

In this chapter, you learned ethical guidelines, drawing from both professional codes of ethics and a personal framework for ethical decision-making in PR. You considered examples of ethical challenges facing corporations and how they were addressed. You learned how some decisions created bigger issues for a corporation while others correctly addressed a problem. The key legal issues facing PR practitioners were introduced, with examples of the issues and how they continue to add complexities to the practice. You also studied the ethics and legal considerations of social responsibility and practiced making ethical and legal decisions in the role of a PR professional.

KEY TERMS

Absolutism 55
Appropriation 68
Consequentialist Theory 55
Copyright 63
Defamation 63
Deontological Ethics 55
Disclosure 63
Fair Use 67
False Light 68
Free Speech 63
Intrusion 68

Libel 64
Moral Impulse 60
Nonconsequentialist Theory 55
Normative Ethics 55
Privacy 63
Right of Publicity 68
Slander 64
Teleological Ethics 55
Utilitarianism 55
Virtue Ethics 55

THINK ABOUT IT

Some business practices that are considered normal in many parts of the world are frowned upon here and are even illegal by U.S. standards. Assume you work for a U.S.-based company, So-Chai, which owns tea leaf plantations in the West African country of Burkina Faso. You travel there twice a year to manage PR for its sustainability programs—supporting relationships with in-country managers, supply chain partners, and government officials. You've developed positive relationships and established that both the company and its leadership are honest and trustworthy. On a recent trip, several newly appointed government officials asked for "gifts" and money to give the necessary approvals for So-Chai. What do you do? (*Hint*: First, investigate the Foreign Corrupt Practices Act at www.justice.gov; then, consider cultural norms for Burkina Faso found at www.geert-hofstede.com/Burkina_Faso.html.)

You're the PR manager for Swift Airlines. During a recent heat wave, one of its planes was stranded on the runway for 4 hours due to a baggage handlers' strike. More than 175 passengers and crew were kept on board with limited food and beverages and backed-up toilets. Many tweeted about the situation, and their photos went viral, prompting the media (and late-night comics) to cover the incident. Draft an email to be sent to all Swift Airlines employees under the CEO's name. Acknowledge the situation, reveal the airline's position, and emphasize its concern for both the passengers and employees. Choose an ethical perspective or a professional code to guide your response (and identify it as a note at the bottom of your draft). Separately, draft a cover memo to the CEO explaining your rationale for the content of the email.

SOCIAL RESPONSIBILITY CASE STUDY

Social Media Highlights Dove's Crisis of Sincerity

Situation

Dove's parent company, Unilever, is a recognized leader in social responsibility, especially under the guidance of Paul Polman as CEO for 9 years until 2018. Dove has led its award-winning Campaign for Real Beauty, championing inclusivity and female empowerment in the personal care industry, since 2004. However, in October 2017, Dove released a 3-second body wash video GIF ad to Facebook, featuring a dark-skinned woman pulling off her brown shirt to transition to a white woman in a cream shirt. The visual echoed racist hygiene ads dating back to the late 19th century in which white bodies were clean and Black bodies were dirty.

Research and Strategy

Back in 2000, to make its brand more relevant to women, Dove commissioned a Harvard University and London School of Economics survey, "The Real Truth About Beauty," to discover how ideal portrayals of feminine beauty that's neither attainable nor authentic impacted women's happiness. The findings? Only 2% of participants saw themselves as beautiful. This study grounded Dove's outreach in 2004 to connect with women on a deeper emotional level by portraying beauty in a more egalitarian way. Beyond advertising, the resulting Campaign for Real Beauty included women's forums, artistic exhibitions, publications, and performances, as well as a self-esteem education project for youth. The campaign contributed to a rise in sales of Dove products from around $2.5 billion in 2004 to $4 billion by its 10-year anniversary (Neff, 2014).

Execution

In its 2017 iteration of the campaign, Dove made the unfortunate choice to create and place the "transformation" ad on Facebook. On the day the ad posted to Dove's U.S. Facebook page, a follower, Naomi Blake, commented that Dove should consider the perspectives of people of color. After getting a generic response from Dove extolling its product benefits and its commitment to diversity in beauty, Blake shared screengrabs of the ad, along with her conversation with Dove, on her Facebook account—

AFP Contributor / Contributor / Getty Images

which went viral across Facebook and Twitter. The next day, #BoycottDove emerged on Twitter. Many pointed to the realities of subtle racism, a daily reality for many people of color. Data analysis found that online attitudes toward Dove in the wake of the ad were primarily critical, with 45% of posts conveying negative sentiment and more than 40% mentioning Dove along with a variant of the word "racist."

Evaluation

Within an hour after #BoycottDove appeared, Dove responded by pulling the ad and tweeting a partial apology: "An image we recently posted on Facebook missed the mark in representing women of color thoughtfully. We deeply regret the offense it caused" (Zed & Dasher, 2019, p. 11). Over the next couple of days, *The Independent UK* criticized the apology in an op-ed, *The New York Times* covered the issue, Dove elaborated on its apology on its U.S. Facebook page, and Lola Ogunyemi, the Nigerian model featured in the ad, defended it in *The Guardian*, stating her experience was positive while acknowledging the public's new lack of trust in Dove. Ad Age called the campaign one of the biggest campaign fails of 2017.

Engage

- Despite its 2017 fail, the Dove Campaign for Real Beauty won *PR Week's* "Best Campaign of the Past 20 Years" award in 2019. Edelman PR received the award jointly as its agency of record. Search to discover the breadth of Dove's 15-year-long campaign for Real Beauty, noting both its positive and negative reception throughout its history.

Discuss

- With social media, everyone's a critic, and it is unrealistic for companies to be concerned with every online detractor. How do organizations discern what they should take seriously and when to respond?

- Given the growing importance of corporate activism and heightened sociopolitical tensions in the United States and worldwide, how did a brand like Dove "miss the mark" so drastically?

- Is it possible for multinational corporations like Dove–Unilever to pursue corporate activism and social responsibility and have such efforts perceived by the public as genuine?

Source: Zed and Dasher, 2019.

4

Foundations of Public Relations

Research and Theory

Learning Objectives

4.1 Understand the importance of research in the PR planning process

4.2 Identify the common methods used in PR to plan a research strategy

4.3 Recognize the role theory plays in PR

Farm Town Strong: Overcoming the Rural Opioid Epidemic

The United States is in an opioid overdose epidemic, and rural areas have been hit much harder than the rest of the country. The nation's two largest general farm organizations—the American Farm Bureau Federation (AFBF) and National Farmers Union (NFU)—joined forces in 2018 to find out why and how to address this public health crisis.

Opioids include those prescribed and also heroin and fentanyl. Existing research from the U.S. Centers for Disease Control and Prevention (CDC) reported opioids killed more than 42,000 people in 2016—a number higher than in any year on record, and more than had died from gun-related violence or motor vehicle accidents.

Rural America has been hit hard by the opioid epidemic, requiring a strategic communications campaign to provide solution-based information and resources.
iStock.com/Dmytro Diedov

The situation is grave in rural America. According to a CDC press release in late 2017, rural drug overdose death rates are higher than in urban areas. Despite under-reporting of illicit drug use in rural areas, its effects appear to be greater.

To help the AFBF and NFU address this crisis, as their newly hired PR consultant you must consider the following:

1. What questions would you need to answer through conducting primary research?
2. What specific primary research methods would you use?
3. What publics would be involved?
4. How would you carry out this research?

To begin to answer this challenge and make meaningful recommendations to your client, you'll need to get a foundational understanding of how to begin the PR process. ●

In this chapter, you will be introduced to the first step of the PR (public relations) process—research—which is foundational in PR for solving any problem or addressing any situation. Asking and answering key questions are critical: What is the situation? What is the organization's goal? Who is the target audience? How can they be reached? What is the essential message?

After you're armed with good and vital information, you'll then need to use it strategically—and that's another focus of this chapter: how to draw on communication theory to guide your strategy. A primer on communication theory explains its role in predicting and analyzing outcomes of PR efforts. You'll understand *why* the media have the power to influence public opinion, *how* to best approach certain people you absolutely need to reach, and *when* to advise your client to say, "I'm sorry."

Of course, the PR challenge of solving a client's problem with a PR campaign involves more than research and guiding theory. It requires that you use theory to determine a communication strategy (objectives), what you'll specifically do (tactics), how you'll know if they're working (evaluation), and how to maintain the good relationships gained (**stewardship**). But those steps are for the next chapter; now, let's start at the beginning.

How to Begin

>> **LO 4.1**   **Understand the importance of research in the PR planning process**

Having vital information is essential to making life's big decisions. How did you decide which college to attend? What laptop to buy next? What guides your path to good health and fitness? Which car, or which job, do you *really* want? You may first be thinking of **word-of-mouth (WOM)** advice and recommendations from close friends and family members. But you're also likely to be considering the numbers: how popular *is* that new laptop, what are its ratings, and how much does it cost? If possible, you'll want to get a closer look at these critical choices . . . visit the college campus, interview a current employee, test drive some cars. The more you look, it's likely the more questions you'll have. Eventually, the *big* questions will be asked and answered to your satisfaction, and you'll be confident about making a decision.

This is research, and you've been doing some form of it all your life. So as we turn to the important first step in the practice of PR—research—you can understand it's a vital key to knowledge that leads to smart decisions. Nearly all PR practitioners and educators agree that PR should begin with research, leading to a clearer understanding of a situation and how to address it with a PR plan. Successful PR entails careful research that not only guides initial activities but also evaluates programs when they are ongoing as well as once they are completed. With good research, PR practitioners can plan strategically and produce effective tactics and various components that will ultimately lead to the achievement of end goals. In Chapter 5, you will learn about the evaluation stage of the PR process: using research to measure the results of a campaign. The focus of this research discussion is how to begin.

Researching products and services online, particularly reading reviews written by past customers, has become an essential part of the decision-making process for many Americans.
iStock.com/ilkercelik

Research: First Step in the Public Relations Process

There are various acronyms for the PR planning process that are all essentially in agreement, including the following: RACE (research, action, communication, evaluation), RPAE (research, planning, action/communication, and evaluation), ROPES (research, objectives, programming, evaluation, and stewardship), and RPIE (research, planning, implementation, and evaluation). Chapter 5 will go into depth on the entire planning process, but as you see, all models begin with *R* for research because it plays a critical foundational role. Consider the important tool of social media where timing is critical. Research from Kissmetric tells us that the best time to post on Twitter is on weekdays at 5 p.m., and the best time to post on Facebook is Thursdays and Fridays from 1 p.m. to 3 p.m.

(Fontein, 2016). PR practitioners use both secondary and primary research to guide planning decisions. Secondary research is gathering essential information that already exists—the research findings of others (e.g., published reports), whereas primary research is gathering essential information through research that you conduct—or contract out for (e.g., surveys). You will need to research your client organization, its business environment, the PR problem or opportunity, and the affected public.

Organizational Background

If you are handling internal PR for your own organization, likely you already have good knowledge of its business, the publics it serves, its competition, and the current state of your industry—perhaps both nationally and locally. What shapes the environment in which it does business? Research the competition, the organization's share of the market, and its position in the market. In a client situation, you'll need to have an adequate understanding of the organization and all the factors that affect it. It's important to consider the implications of this information and how it might apply to the planning of a PR campaign.

Communications Analysis

Communications analysis involves the collection and evaluation of relevant external public messaging about the organization (including from mainstream and specialized sources and social media content), as well as that produced by the organization itself (internal messaging, such as press releases, newsletters, websites, etc.). Externally, what are the organization's image and reputation? Internally, what PR initiatives have been engaged in recently? What communication channels have been and are currently being used? Look at what is being said *about* the organization both externally and internally. Once answered, you must consider how this information might impact your PR plan.

Issue Analysis

Consider the organization's history to help you understand its current situation. Also evaluate the organization's relationship with its publics and communities and how it may be unique in any way. Be sure to identify the *key* opportunity or challenge that faces the organization. Ancillary issues are important to note. With all this knowledge, you should now be able to concisely state the central issue the PR campaign will address, determine the goal for the client, and PR's role in achieving it. It's important now to also anticipate problems that may be encountered. A complete issue analysis should reveal some pathways for your PR campaign.

Target Publics and Public Opinion

Issues usually affect more than one public, but a single public may be evident as a primary focus for a PR campaign. Consider both internal (e.g., employees) and external (e.g., customers) publics, identify and describe the primary public, and then those publics of secondary and tertiary importance. These are the targets your PR campaign should consider when planning. Know what their relationships are with the organization and what their knowledge, attitudes, and behaviors are concerning the organization and/or the issue at hand. Publics can be classified into three types: latent (they do not recognize the problem or opportunity); aware

Learning as much as you can about your client's organization, history, and past PR efforts is essential to planning your campaign.
iStock.com/ferrantraite

(they develop from **latent publics** after they recognize the problem or opportunity); and **active publics** (they develop from **aware publics** after they begin to *do something* about the problem or opportunity; Dozier & Grunig, 1992, p. 400). A careful evaluation of the target publics will help you strategically develop your plan.

SWOT Analysis

Once you have made a good effort to complete the aforementioned secondary research steps, organizing your findings into a SWOT analysis helps you determine some strategic pathways for your plan. A SWOT analysis is a planning technique to help you identify strengths, weakness, opportunities, and threats related to project planning. It guides you to look internally at the organization for its strengths and weaknesses, as well as externally for opportunities and threats. The website Business News Daily advises, "Use your SWOT analysis to discover recommendations and strategies, with a focus on leveraging strengths and opportunities to overcome weaknesses and threats" (Schooley, 2019, para. 4).

Primary Research Methods

>> LO 4.2   Identify the common methods used in PR to plan a research strategy

Once you've thoroughly conducted secondary research, you have a clearer understanding of what you still *need to know*. Depending on the need, decide which types of primary research to conduct and specifically with whom and for what purposes. Formulate research questions for each method. PR challenges very often require multiple research methods, and there are important considerations when choosing which ones to use and in what order (see Table 4.1).

TABLE 4.1

Common Public Relations Research Methods

TYPE	METHODS
Quantitative	Survey
	Content analysis
	Digital analytics
Qualitative	Focus group
	Depth interview
	Participant observation

Research Ethics Do's and Don'ts

A practical list of do's and don'ts when conducting professional research is found in the PR Measurement Standards on the Institute for Public Relations (IPR) website (Institute for Public Relations, n.d.). This summary reveals the importance of correct research procedures and behaviors.

Before doing research, *do* the following:

- Accurately and honestly communicate to your colleagues and clients the precise way you plan to report the results.
- Establish a baseline for measurement, and track results against the baseline.

When reporting research results, *don't* do the following:

- Use terminology loosely; for example, don't use "ROI" (return on investment) unless it involves financial investment and return.
- Measure something against an "industry standard" unless, indeed, it is that—and not just a collective opinion.
- Claim that PR results, such as media hits or impressions (numerical evidence), suggest changes in attitudes or behaviors.
- Compare PR value to advertising value—the fields have distinctly different characteristics.

Another good source for best practices in research methods and findings is found in *A Practitioner's Guide to Public Relations Research, Measurement and Evaluation* (Michaelson & Wright, n.d.):

Research methods should have the following characteristics:

- Clear and specific research objectives

- Well-defined and well-selected sample of respondents
- Well-designed research instruments that are appropriate, unbiased, and accurate
- Rigorous execution to generate reliable results
- Detailed supporting documentation with full transparency

Findings should accomplish the following:

- Demonstrate effectiveness of the PR campaign
- Link outputs (what you did) to outcomes (what resulted)
- Aid in development of better communications programs
- Include data to demonstrate impact on business
- Apply to a broad range of business activities—for example, marketing, product development, and corporate reputation

In an academic setting, any research involving people as subjects must first be approved by the university's institutional review board (IRB). Check with your institution's IRB (or ask your instructor) to see if a classroom research project must undergo IRB evaluation and approval. The reason for this procedure is to ensure your subjects will be treated ethically: with decency and dignity; without coercion; with full awareness of what will be asked of them; with full knowledge of the purpose for the research; with knowledge of who is conducting the research and who, whether a person or organization, is sponsoring it; and who will have access to the results (Smith, 2013). ●

Quantitative Methods

Quantitative methods observe effects, test relationships, and generate numerical data that is considered objective. Results can be obtained through computerized statistical analysis and can be projected to a larger population than just those studied.

Surveys are a key form of primary research in planning a PR campaign.
iStock.com/kasayizgi

Survey

Surveys are one of the most common methods used in PR research for various reasons: their capacity to reach a large sample of a desired group of people, their low cost, their wide geographic distribution, the analytical data they generate, and the ease of execution via software solutions on the Internet or via mobile apps or email. Phone or in-person surveys allow for immediate results. In all surveys, you can ask both closed questions (multiple choice, yes or no, and true or false) and open-ended questions that allow for individual statements. The facility of survey data to make correlations can help better define publics. For example, questions about attitudes or behaviors can be measured against questions about demographics or social or economic characteristics, providing a clearer understanding of active and passive publics. The anonymity and structure of surveys help encourage participation. The disadvantages of the survey method are that the people who choose to respond only represent a sample of your public, and you will omit hard-to-reach respondents. Likewise, responses may not be entirely truthful, and the survey itself may be flawed if not properly designed and worded.

INSIGHTS

Survey Reveals Expectations of CSR Communication

Two researchers (Kim & Ferguson, 2014) sought to discover what and how to communicate for effective corporate social responsibility (CSR) communication. To find the answers, they asked a representative sample of American consumers what they expect from companies' CSR communications.

The Survey. First, they based their survey questionnaire on several previous CSR communication studies, collecting a total of 46 items to measure. These items included information sharing, personal relevance, third-party endorsement, message tone, consistency and frequency, and transparency. They also measured consumers' preference for 22 CSR communication media channels and nine communication sources. Finally, they included 10 demographic questions.

The Sample. The sample of publics was chosen from a list of consumer panels managed by Researchnow. This U.S. marketing research firm specializes in consumer surveys. After emailing invitations, their data collection was completed in 10 days, totaling 663 responses, approximately half female and half male.

The Findings. Kim and Ferguson reported that "publics wanted to know 'who is benefiting' from the companies' CSR the most, followed by information about specific social causes that a company supports . . . specific commitments . . . a company's CSR goal . . . and previous CSR achievements or results of the company" (p. 7). The researchers emphasized the most important finding: "publics wanted to know information about CSR beneficiaries significantly more than any of the other information" (p. 7).

Regarding CSR communications, Kim and Ferguson found, in order of priority, "(1) people who benefit from the company's CSR initiative . . . (2) non-profit organizations, (3) the company itself, (4) participants of the CSR initiative, (5) activist groups . . . , (6) the company's employees, (7) the company's CEO, and (8) the company's public relations spokesperson" (p. 9).

The Practical Implications. For effective CSR communication, messages should avoid a promotional tone, offer facts in a transparent way (including both positives and negatives), share third-party endorsements, and focus on the CSR beneficiaries with specific examples on how lives/society benefited. To read the authors' full implications and recommendations, access the open-source publications at https://prjournal.instituteforpr.org/wp-content/uploads/2014KIMFERGUSON.pdf. ●

Content Analysis

Content analysis is a method of examining and categorizing existing communication and involves a structured coding system. It can be helpful for communication audits to get a good idea of *what's* being said and *how*—perhaps to compare across media, or over time, or to contrast against an opponent's messaging. It has the benefit of being relatively low cost, but one must be very careful to design the coding system to note all essential information and how it should be counted. It also *does not* consider characteristics of storytelling, metaphoric constructions, and other forms of rhetoric—which a qualitative rhetorical analysis would do.

Digital Analytics

Digital analytics tools allow you to collect, organize, and analyze online data—for example, from websites and social media platforms about customer and user conversations, activities, trends, and patterns. This allows you to get insights fast and accurately from multiple sources. As with other measurement and analytical methods, you may not be responsible for this process, but you should be aware of its value and application in listening to publics, guiding decision-making, and informing content changes.

Qualitative Methods

Qualitative methods are useful to explore attitudes, perceptions, values, and opinions. They are useful to confirm or refute your hunches and overall can help guide direction. Your research questions typically ask, "How do participants feel about X, and why," "How do participants interpret X," or very simply, "What is going on here?" Some reasons PR professionals use qualitative methods are to build understanding of an issue by getting some preliminary information, to gather immediate information needed to address a pressing issue, and to inform the development of further research tools. Qualitative research is descriptive and interpretive, and results cannot be generalized to a larger group.

Focus groups allow you to conduct essentially multiple depth interviews simultaneously.
Ammentorp Photography / Alamy Stock Photo

Depth Interview

A **depth interview** is a probing, one-on-one conversation that helps answer questions that ask how and why. It's also appropriate for engaging response on sensitive topics or with anyone who may have difficulty completing a questionnaire. A researcher typically uses a semistructured list of questions and can adapt questioning to follow important threads in content that may be revealed. Thus, the intimacy helps establish comfort and trust, and one can get a lot of detail and discover unexpected information. There are some disadvantages to be aware of: availability of time is a factor, as you will have *a lot* of material to transcribe and interpret, and there is no preliminary guarantee that your interviewee will be as cooperative as you wish.

PR PROFILE

Ask, Answer, Recommend: Using Research to Understand Business Goals and Develop Innovative Public Relations Strategies

Forrest Anderson, Forrest W. Anderson Consulting

Photo courtesy of Forrest Anderson

My career has been built on these two simple premises:

1. Asking and answering the right questions

2. Making the leap from information to recommendations

I began my communications career as a technical writer at a research institute and moved into their PR department. While the salary was low, the institute reimbursed education, so I got my MBA in marketing and management policy from The Kellogg School of Management at Northwestern University.

My studies taught me to develop strategies for organizations by understanding their business goals, strengths, weaknesses, stakeholder wants and needs, and trends and issues in the business environment. When I joined a major PR agency, I was assigned to write strategies for the PR programs we proposed to prospective clients because my MBA enabled me to link communications strategies to prospective business goals.

But I encountered a problem. The agency had very little information to guide the strategy. It did, however, have a research department, which I soon joined. In my research role, I would gather information about potential clients, their target audiences, and their business environments—everything necessary to build communications strategies that would support meeting goals, such as increasing sales or reducing employee turnover.

Then, another problem arose. Many of the client contact staff were unable to translate this information into logical communications recommendations. So I advised them to tell the client this:

> Based on this information, the communications program to help you achieve your business goals needs to do the following:
>
> **Target this audience** (clearly defined and drawn from demographic and psychographic research) . . .
>
> **With this message** (developed and tested through secondary research, qualitative and quantitative primary research, and assessment of external trends and issues) . . .
>
> **Via these media** (identified through researching the targets' media choices for similar information).

There also is growing evidence from ongoing research that communications practitioners, who use research to understand stakeholder wants and needs and their organization's business environment and who share this information internally, have an extraordinary influence within their organizations. And this includes influence on the C-suite.

A Favorite Project

At one agency, I worked with a major bank that had grown after acquisition and wanted to position itself as very customer oriented. Their own customer research and new employee research indicated the bank was *not* customer oriented. For example, a customer in one state could not cash a check at the bank's kiosk in another state. The issue was technology. While this is hard to imagine now, not too long ago many technology platforms did not talk to each other.

We recommended against the customer-oriented positioning because it wasn't true. Moreover, customers and employees would not have believed it. Instead, we suggested the bank explain how it was working *to become* more customer oriented. To reach this goal, we observed, they needed to fix their technology issues.

This is an example of communications professionals recognizing a business problem that couldn't be solved by communications, advising management of the issues needing attention, and recommending an alternative path. ●

Before starting his own research firm, Forrest W. Anderson Consulting, Anderson led research at Golin, Applied Communications, and Text 100.

Source: F. Anderson, personal communication, 2019.

Focus Group

Focus group research is a very common method for PR as well as advertising. It is relatively inexpensive and allows for recruiting and assembling participants rather quickly, yielding immediate findings. It is essentially a collective depth interview ideally conducted with between six and 12 participants. Thus, it allows for the flexibility of follow-up questions, and the group situation stimulates discussion. It's typically video recorded for later analysis of both spoken and visual expressions. However, there are some disadvantages. Depending on circumstances, it may be hard to get a group of suitable participants all together at the same time in the same place. It's also unpredictable: Some participants may be inhibited by public speaking or being recorded. And the moderator's skill is crucial in establishing rapport, posing questions, probing for insight, and managing any participants who might tend to control the conversation. As with any qualitative methods, results cannot be generalized to a larger population.

Participant Observation

Participant observation involves the researcher participating in an activity to observe and better understand those involved in that activity and their perspectives.

For example, if a client needs an internal communication plan, observing office dynamics in the workplace could lead to conclusions your client may be unaware of. Or if your client has physical venues for events or products, engaging in the attendee experience may give you a clearer understanding of what the publics encounter and how they behave. A researcher should be aware of several considerations:

- Maintain objectivity; don't "go native."
- Be unobtrusive; don't change group dynamics.
- It can be difficult to record observations.
- It's easy to confuse recollections with interpretations.

The Big Ideas Behind Public Relations Strategies

>> LO 4.3   Recognize the role theory plays in PR

How do the findings from *formative* research, undertaken to help understand and solve a problem, translate into a PR campaign? By guiding your strategy and tactics. Research clarifies what your campaign needs to achieve and how to get there. It allows you to confidently confirm the end goal you first identified—or were assigned—and also helps reveal any modifications needed in that goal. Research also helps guide your strategy to achieve that goal through specific objectives. Theory enters the space between research and strategy.

The How and Why of Theory

Research guides your PR strategy, but theory helps explain how and why things should work the way you intend them to. There are three types of theory (see Figure 4.1). Typically, one of the first ways we try to understand a problem is to draw from anecdotal information—our past experiences, stories we've heard, and situations we've observed. That's called **commonsense theory,** and it's a good start but only as a warm-up.

Certain job-related generalizations are called **working theory**—agreed-upon ways of doing things, such as shooting a film with specific camera shots to evoke specific emotions. In higher education, where we are preparing for leadership

FIGURE 4.1

Three Types of Theory

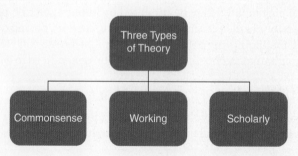

positions in the communication field, we need to think in a more structured way by drawing on **scholarly theory**.

Systematic research to understand human behavior and events has provided more thorough and accurate explanations behind why things did—or didn't—work. These scholarly explanations are what we call "capital T" theories. For example, the widely tested theory of agenda setting might support an aggressive media campaign to help launch a new business. Why agenda setting? Because different levels of the theory explain that the news media set the agenda with the public on both *what* to think about and *how* to think about it.

Thus, it's important to develop some perspective, based on theory, on how PR can address and solve a problem or turn an opportunity into a success. There are many different scholarly theories on why things work the way they do, drawn from the study of communication but also from psychology, sociology, cultural studies, and even art history (such as telling us why certain symbols can evoke cultural meanings).

Theory goes beyond description to prediction. When studying the PR approach to a past situation, theory is explanatory: Why *did* something succeed or fail? When preparing a PR recommendation, theory is visionary, telling us what *should* guide our strategies to succeed. Theories provide an understanding of the relationships between actions and events. As a PR practitioner, you'll need to explain why and how your plans will work. Knowing and being able to explain the science behind your proposals bolsters both your confidence and credibility.

Applying Theory in Public Relations

There are many theories relevant to the practice of PR. Ten are listed and described in Table 4.2 to provide a baseline in your understanding of how theory connects to practice. These selected theories of media and mass communication, persuasion, and management include examples to illustrate how theory can be both predictive and explanatory—examples from the classroom and the world beyond.

TABLE 4.2

Ten Theories for Public Relations

Media and Mass Communication Models	Agenda setting/framing Two-step flow Spiral of silence Diffusion of innovations Uses and gratifications

Persuasion Models	Elaboration likelihood model (ELM)
	Cialdini's principles of influence
	Reciprocation
	Commitment and consistency
	
	   • Social proof
	
	   • Liking
	
	   • Authority
	
	   • Scarcity
	
	Inoculation theory

Management Models	Excellence theory Image restoration theory

Media and Mass Communication

These theories concern the sender, the message, and the audience via various forms, including traditional television, radio, newspapers, and more recently, film, music, and all the new communication technologies. We'll briefly introduce five theories here: agenda setting (including framing), two-step flow, spiral of silence, diffusion of innovations, and uses and gratifications. Once we look at examples, you should recognize them in your own media experiences.

Agenda-Setting Theory

Agenda-setting theory, developed by McCombs and Shaw (1972), states that the media have a large influence on audiences by choosing which stories to make prominent, thus influencing what publics should think about (known as first-level agenda setting). The media also uses selective attributes to shape the stories, influencing publics in how to think about them (known as second-level agenda setting). Thus, the theory says the media determine for the public what's important and why. Consider, however, are the news media always influencers of public opinion? Actually, alternative media, advertising, film, entertainment TV, and music may have a greater effect than news. But no matter the conduit, when the content is no longer user created, there is always a gatekeeper author that controls the story that sets the agenda for your audience.

- *A Student's Example:* In a campaign plan for the U.S. Secret Service, students applied agenda-setting theory to their strategy to change the tone of media coverage by driving specific messages that media relay to the public.

- *Agenda Setting in Action:* Puerto Rico has experienced an economic crisis since 2014, resulting in the migration of qualified talent (a "brain drain"). Researchers found that existing political and economic factors primarily influenced the brain drain. However, media emphasis on social factors (the promise of better education, better health services, and better public services) set an agenda that encouraged higher valuing of these social factors and thus increased interest in migration (Flecha et al., 2017). Thus, as a PR practitioner, funneling select information to traditional media, or placing it in social media, can help to set an agenda favorable to your messaging goals.

Framing Theory

Framing theory is a concept first put forth by Erving Goffman and is similar to second-level agenda setting. It suggests the way we present something to our audience (called "the frame") influences how they think about that information. You may be familiar with the word mastery of Frank Luntz, the Republican strategist who skillfully renamed "global warming" as the much more benign "climate change." And in the attack mode, why was his phrase "death taxes" more effective than "estate taxes" in persuading Americans and eventually Congress to reduce estate taxes? Framing is the careful choice of words, imagery, sound, motion, or any rhetorical device to influence a certain meaning. And that makes it also a persuasion theory as well.

- *A Student's Example:* A campaign plan for Sprint applied framing theory to support a strategy of portraying the offer of their competitor, Verizon, not as a "deal" but really as "quite an expense" for consumers and businesses.

- *Framing in Action:* (*Note*: This example illustrates both framing and two-step flow theory.) Direct-to-consumer advertising (DTCA) of prescription drugs is allowed in the United States and only a few other countries. In most countries, it is banned, and the pharmaceutical industry relies primarily on PR to publicize its products. An analysis of press releases used by pharma companies in Israel, where DTCA is banned, found their content predominantly used third-party influencers such as leading experts and physicians to frame the message as credible and the drugs as heroes. Conversely, the messages also villainized the diseases and used negative framing of patients as "ticking time bombs" (Shir-Raz & Avraham, 2017, p. 387).

SOCIAL RESPONSIBILITY IN ACTION

"Color, Way of Love" Beautifies, Repairs, and Improves Schools Across China

The exterior walls of Chinese school buildings like this one were transformed with large, colorful murals. To view them, do an image search for "Nippon Color of Love Murals."
Xinhua News Agency / Contributor / Getty Images

Launched in 2009, "Color, Way of Love" is a CSR program of Japanese paint company Nippon Paint. It beautifies and repairs campuses for schoolchildren in poor, remote areas of China. A number of the students are "left-behind children" whose parents have gone to bigger cities to find work. By 2017, the program was active in more than 100 cities and towns across China, benefiting nearly 300 schools. Each year, the project adds something new for the media to cover.

Nippon Paint painted 12 schools and 10 urban wall paintings in 2018. Since its beginnings, the project has painted nearly 100 wall paintings. Nippon works with global artists and muralists to create the wall paintings, drawing on talent from France, Argentina, Germany, Italy, Brazil, Russia, Colombia, Poland, and the United States. And the company provides more than visual enhancements; its principle purpose is to create equal opportunities for children to be educated in art, inspiring artists of the future. receive art education and inspire future artists. Its success has allowed Nippon to replicate the project in countries throughout the Asia Pacific region.

Award-Winning Media Event. The company put "Color, Way of Love" at the heart of its effort in 2018 to communicate its core values and CSR vision. It held a media event at a kindergarten, allowing reporters to interview artists, learn about their projects, and express their inner child through a variety of activities. The event was also a showcase for "Dream Making," highlighting the visually impressive wall painting. The event generated 180 media reports in print, new media, network and video sites, earning Nippon's project the 2019 "Media Relations Campaign of the Year" prize from *PR Daily*. Additionally, media featured exclusive interviews with 11 participating artists, explaining the stories behind their work. ●

Source: PR Daily, n.d.

Two-Step Flow

Two-step flow theory was conceived by Paul Lazarsfeld and Elihu Katz. It says the media can also influence key spokespeople, experts, and leaders—early adopters of new ideas—who then influence certain groups of publics. These opinion leaders receive mass media messages and then pass on the content filtered through their own interpretations. Individuals with this "personal influence" can significantly aid in getting people to change their attitudes and behaviors. The concept of **upward flow theory** reverses direction—for example, employees advising management on existing or potential issues; a grassroots movement organized to sway political leaders; and generally, any opinion study with the goal of discovering public interests and concerns.

- ***A Student's Example:*** A class team applied two-step flow to a campaign plan to "recover, reclaim, sustain" a failing college by influencing community opinion leaders to then influence other publics about positive steps taken by the college.

- ***Two-Step Flow in Action:*** A study on the flow of information in Twitter-based discussion groups found opinion leaders emerged during the information flow. While not creators of the content, these opinion leaders had an influential function. This finding is important as it suggests that, beyond the purposeful incorporation of opinion leaders in a PR plan, leaders may emerge independently and with opinions not necessarily aligned with the plan's goals.

Spiral of Silence

Ideas and opinions expressed in mass media can discourage expressions by people who hold dissenting opinions due to their sensitivity of feeling isolated or rejected. Elisabeth Noelle-Neumann's **spiral of silence theory** helps explain the power of public opinion, especially regarding topics that have moral arguments. PR professionals wanting to encourage expression from those in the "minority" should publicize some minority opinion to draw out the silent voices; also, surveys and questionnaires should carry carefully worded questions to encourage response on controversial topics.

- ***A Student's Example:*** A campaign plan to build awareness of child abuse in the southwestern United States held intimate focus groups with similar participants to encourage open discussion on a topic that's culturally sensitive.

- ***Spiral of Silence in Action:*** A major public health goal is reducing the rate of college binge drinking. Favored by young adults, Facebook and other social media platforms could potentially magnify the reach of health campaign messages. What predicts the likelihood to share health-related messages on social media? Researchers (Luo et al., 2019) found that people were more willing to share when they had an anti- rather than a pro-binge drinking opinion, when the messages included "how-to" information, and when people were asked to share via private messaging rather than via public status updates. Here, spiral of silence theory explains the reticence in expressing opinions publicly on sensitive topics. Acknowledging the effect of the spiral of silence helps PR practitioners to predict which types of publics would be more or less likely to express their opinion and, knowing so, to find ways to encourage those less likely.

Diffusion of Innovations

Diffusion of innovations theory draws from the fields of both marketing and psychology, stating that a new idea or a product must pass through a sequential process with a public to ultimately be adopted. Everett Rogers's theory has a six-step process: awareness—knowledge—evaluation—trial—adoption—reinforcement. Research shows that a public's response to a certain persuasive appeal that calls for behavior change depends on where it lies in the diffusion process. Note the steps that must be accomplished before you reach "trial." Also consider how other theories may fit in; for example, early adopters can wield personal influence to spread awareness.

- *A Student's Example:* General Motors introduced its breakthrough Chevy Volt in 2008, but the company didn't adequately explain the concept of a plug-in hybrid to people. Early adopters understood, but the general public didn't. Students tackled this problem, recommending a campaign plan for rebranding the Chevy Volt. The plan was guided by principles of diffusion of innovations because a reorientation process was needed to build understanding and acceptance for an electric vehicle with new technology components.

- *Diffusion in Action:* Between 2010 and 2018, the use of social media by police departments increased substantially. Researchers (Hu et al., 2018) applied diffusion of innovations theory to understand police departments' adoption and implementation of new technologies. As of 2018, about 94% of U.S. police departments had adopted Facebook. Hu et al. studied 14 of the most popular police Facebook pages (ones with the most "likes") and analyzed posts during a 1-year period. The study found five major themes and 24 noteworthy subthemes. Clustering them, the researchers identified four principal types of social images of police on Facebook. These included crime fighter, traditional cop, public relations facilitator, and mixer (a balance of the three previous types). Because of the departments' long history on Facebook, their high post rate, and their use of a designated poster, they were likely in the routinization phase of the implementation process.

Uses and Gratifications Theory

Uses and gratifications theory was developed by Elihu Katz and says that users of media take an active role by choosing and using certain media. They're goal oriented. A person selects a source that best meets that individual's needs. Uses and gratifications theory holds the assumption that the user has alternative choices to satisfy a need. When it was first developed, the theory defined four types of need by users of mass media:

- *Diversion:* Media fills the need to escape from everyday life, to relax.
- *Personal relationships:* We use media to fulfill needs for companionship and to form relationships with others (e.g., interest groups).
- *Personal identity:* We tend to use media to find out about ourselves; people profiled may reflect our desires, needs, fantasies, or secrets.
- *Surveillance:* We use media to find out what is going on around us.

For a strategic campaign planner, the application is clear: Determine the needs of your target public, and then address them using appropriate media channels and tactics. With the predominance of digital technologies, modern applications of uses and gratifications can be adapted to study the use of mobile phones, the Internet, social media, instant messaging, online gaming, and more.

- *A Student's Example:* A campaign plan recognized that millennials shared music preferences in social media platforms to both express identity and support relationships, so YouTube and Facebook were chosen as channels to communicate the client's message.

- *Uses and Gratifications in Action:* Hashtags are prolific on social media; however, we don't yet fully understand what motivates and predicts their use. Using uses and gratifications (U&G), researchers (Erz et al., 2018) identified two categories of users on Instagram—potential influencers and followers—and found six motives of hashtag use: self-presentation, chronicling, inventiveness, information seeking, venting, and etiquette. These motivations influenced the frequency of clicking and adding hashtags, as well as the number of hashtags used in a post. Potential influencers were heavy users of hashtags, primarily driven by motives of self-presentation and status seeking. Thus, those who manage social media managers wanting to increase users' hashtagging of a brand must consider the different motives, provide visually appealing content, and create hashtags that are meaningful and add value to users' presentations of self in their posts.

Persuasion

Persuasion is considered human communication designed to influence others by changing their beliefs, values, attitudes, or behaviors. Three persuasion theories relevant to the PR process are elaboration likelihood model (ELM), Cialdini's influence principles, and inoculation theory.

Elaboration Likelihood Model

Elaboration likelihood model (ELM) is a major persuasion theory developed by Richard Petty and John Cacippio. It states that persuasive messages are received by people through two different routes: either the central route or the peripheral route.

- Via the central route, one's mental processing is based on thought, analysis, and reflection. Active thinking internalizes the message, and attitudes formed are more persistent and resistant to change. Some publics *are* central processors by nature, so when addressing them, it's extremely important that your argument has cognitive strength.

- Via the peripheral route, one's processing is based on mental shortcuts with little effort, thus attitudes formed are more short-lived. With the crescendo of chatter in our world, most messages are processed this way. Although the listener may immediately change an attitude, it's not long-lasting.

As PR strategists, because we know the central route to mental processing is more likely to stick and affect attitude and behavior change, we need to know how to motivate the central route! Here's how:

- Increase motivation to engage: Explain why your message is relevant and how it affects the receiver personally.

- Increase ability to engage: Adapt to the receiver's level of understanding and experience. Eliminate distractions. Make it accessible.

As a result of this, receivers will actively think about your message and are more likely to change attitude.

SOCIAL RESPONSIBILITY

- **A Student's Example:** A campaign plan for Military OneSource used ELM to guide its detailed and compelling strategies and tactics, with the goal of changing attitudes on posttraumatic stress disorder (PTSD) in service members and their families.

- **ELM in Action:** Water is vital in our lives; however, water that's safe to drink is a limited resource. Public awareness campaigns, including public service announcements (PSAs), are crucial to fighting the global water crisis. Researchers (Krajewski et al., 2019) examined environmental communication efforts on YouTube, specifically the content of global water crisis PSAs. The elaboration likelihood model helped them evaluate the potential effectiveness of the PSAs. They found that central route processing cues are more prevalent than peripheral route cues. This holds practical implications for organizational messaging: For topics like water security that have great personal relevance to people, viewers are likely more highly motivated to engage with the statistics and clearly articulated arguments of a cognitive message strategy.

FIGURE 4.2

Influence Principles

Principles of Influence

Social psychologist Robert Cialdini identified six different cues (see Figure 4.2) that trigger peripheral route processing (as explained with ELM, peripheral routes are mental shortcuts). Here are **Cialdini's influence principles**:

- *Reciprocation:* This refers to the drive to respond to another's positive action with your own positive action. It also can be used persuasively and is a principle behind negotiating with concessions.

- *Consistency and commitment:* These are the desire to be (and to appear to be) *in agreement, in harmony, and compatible* with who we think we are or what we have already done. Once we make a choice or take a stand, we experience intrapersonal and interpersonal pressures to behave consistently with that stand (our commitment). A strategist seeking influence might consider the power of the highly valued consistency principle.

- *Social proof:* This is Cialdini's term for behavior influenced by the fact that "everyone's doing it." Cialdini explains, "We view a behavior as correct in a given situation to the degree that we see others performing it," (2001, p. 100). It can be a very powerful weapon of influence.

- *Liking:* Cialdini's studies showed that people tend to say yes to those they like. There are multiple components of liking: repeated contact, similarity, flattery, and physical attractiveness.

- *Authority:* Most cultures have a sense of duty to it. Our obedience to authority often takes place with little deliberation and makes so much "sense" to us that we comply when it does not make sense. It's automatic. This principle can explain the persuasive power of visual "trappings" of authority (clothing, status symbols, titles, etc.).

- *Scarcity:* This accounts for people's behavior when confronted with limited numbers, time, opportunities, and loss in general. We want something more when there's less of it. And we are more motivated by the prospect of losing something than we are by the prospect of gaining something of equal value. In fact, known as psychological reactance, we react against any interference by wanting and trying to possess the item more than we did before.

- **A Student's Example:** A campaign plan to help the National Football League (NFL) manage its crisis with chronic traumatic encephalopathy (CTE) applied all of Cialdini's influence principles in its messaging strategy.

- **Authority in Action:** Phishing is the fraudulent email attempt to obtain online financial and personal information. Phishing email subject lines can appear authentic, carrying persuasive power in only a few words. Researchers (Ferreira & Teles, 2019) analyzed a random sample, finding that Cialdini's influence principles of "authority" and "reciprocity" were used most prominently. The use of "you" and "your" were more evident in "authority" characterizations, while the use of "we, us, our" more often appeared in the "reciprocity" category. As PR practitioners are tasked with protecting organization-public relationships, being aware of phishing and antiphishing strategies is an important responsibility.

Inoculation Theory

Here's a theory that we call a "weapon" of influence, as it was developed and tested in competitive situations. Inoculation theory by William J. McGuire, a social psychologist, states that inoculation builds resistance to persuasive messages. Based on the metaphor of a medical inoculation or vaccination, the theory says that if you give your audience a small dose of your opponent's argument and then you immediately provide a counterargument, it triggers a process of counterarguing by the audience members themselves—on their own, within their own minds— which eventually makes them resistant to later, stronger persuasive messages from your opponent. For example, often used in litigation and political campaigns, the inoculation strategy might begin: "My opponent (or defense counsel) will tell you..."

- *A Student's Example:* A campaign plan for a political candidate proposed a series of videos telling her story and touching on negative aspects of her opponent's story, which were then refuted.

- *Inoculation in Action:* Corporate advertising usually is seen as promotional, but during a corporate crisis, it can have an inoculation effect. Ads that run before a crisis occurs can increase audience resistance toward later negative news about the organization and weaken any resistance by the audience toward future corporate ads. Researchers (Ho et al., 2017) also suggest a halo effect (the carry-over of favorable impressions) contributes to the positive reception of organization news. For PR professionals, ongoing positive communication programs are a safety net against negative fallout when troubling issues affect an organization.

U.S. police departments favor Facebook for community engagement.
Associated Press

Management Models

Management theories consider input from and relationships with various stakeholders in an organization. Next, we describe excellence theory, which supports PRSA's principle of mutuality, and Benoit's image restoration theory, which guides response to, and evaluation of, issues that negatively impact reputation.

Excellence Theory

Excellence theory is a major PR theory of mutuality developed by James Grunig (1992; 2013) and others. An organization's good relationships with its stakeholders (publics) helps it develop and attain the goals of both the organization and its publics. The theory can also guide organizations to reduce costs of negative publicity and to increase revenue by providing needed products and services. To maximize PR value, a campaign must first identify important publics and then cultivate long-term relationships through two-way symmetrical communications. This means the organization and its publics both talk and listen to each other with mutual respect and willingness to adapt. Organizations that embrace this theory put PR professionals in a critical management function.

- *A Student's Example:* In this campaign plan, the Port of Houston Authority confronted alleged misconduct, negative media attention, and a state investigation. The students chose excellence theory to guide public-organization relationships through social media.

- *Excellence in Action:* Today, local governments are using social media for two-way communication with their citizens to build and maintain good relationships. Those in charge of community relations see it as an important tool to encourage citizens to be more active in social and political issues. Guided by excellence theory, a study (Galvez-Rodriguez et al., 2018) examined the Twitter and Facebook profiles of local governments, finding low involvement by citizens. To increase citizen engagement, the researchers recommend that communication managers should be trained and empowered to discover citizen interests, allowing them to provide content suitable for attracting citizens' online involvement.

Image Restoration Theory

Image restoration theory, developed by William Benoit, helps evaluate—or recommend—a response to a harmful situation. Depending on situational contexts, it suggests five strategies: denial, evading responsibility, reducing offensiveness, corrective action, and mortification. Many case studies have applied Benoit's theory to analyze damaging situations involving celebrities, politicians, and corporations.

- *A Student's Example:* A case study applied image restoration theory to evaluate how Carnival Cruise Line rebuilt its image and reputation.
- *Image Restoration in Action:* In 2008, four leading Chinese milk companies were involved with the largest food safety crisis in China that caused sickness and death in infants. Examining the crisis recovery stage, researchers (Zeng et al., 2018) found that three of the companies survived the crisis, attributing their survival to the image restoration strategy of reducing offensiveness during the postcrisis stage. Specifically, they used the component of bolstering, which means to mitigate negative effects by strengthening a positive impression with publics based on a company's previous good acts or good reputation.

Note: Em Griffin's A First Look at Theory helped inform some of these descriptions (Griffin, 2017).

Scenario Outcome

At the beginning of this chapter, you read about the opioid overdose epidemic in rural areas of the United States and the commitment of America's two largest general farm organizations to address it. Putting yourself in the role of their newly hired PR consultant, we ask how you would plan and conduct the necessary primary research as foundation for a campaign. Here is what actually happened.

Primary Research

To understand the impact of the opioid epidemic in farm country, AFBF and NFU commissioned a Morning Consult research poll of 2,201 rural adults in October 2017. The results showed the following:

- 74% of farmers and farm workers had been directly impacted by opioid abuse, and 77% said it would be easy to access opioids illegally.
- Rural adults were largely unaware that rural communities are impacted the most, and 57% said opioid abuse is more a problem in urban communities.
- 61% said there is stigma associated with opioid abuse, and 68% said increasing public education about resources and reducing that stigma would be effective means for solving the opioid crisis.

Many target audiences were identified, including farmers and farm families, rural adults, agricultural youth organizations, USDA Rural Development, and the media.

Planning

The findings from primary research helped to identify three goals: raise awareness about the opioid epidemic, address stigma, and provide information and resources to farmers and farm families. To meet these goals, the campaign intended to meet the following objectives:

1. Generate media coverage in at least 200 news stories about rural opioid addiction.
2. Engage audiences to use a campaign hashtag an average of 100 times per month.
3. Focus rural audiences on resources, with at least 5,000 views of a website offering information about opioid addiction, prevention, and treatment.

A campaign theme, "Farm Town Strong," resulted from message testing during the research stage. A key strategy was to demonstrate the urgency of addressing the crisis. The messaging strategy framed the story about addiction as an epidemic that must be addressed rather than to be ashamed of—a message research had shown would resonate in rural America. Given the longstanding respect and trust for USDA among rural audiences, the campaign worked closely with USDA Rural Development, jointly shaping strategy and participating in opioid stakeholder meetings and advisory groups.

"Farm Town Strong: Overcoming the Rural Opioid Epidemic" received a 2019 PRSA Silver Anvil Award of Excellence.

WRAP UP

In this chapter, you were introduced to the first step in the PR planning process—research—and gained a specific understanding of necessity and value. You also explored the common research methods in PR, both quantitative and qualitative: content analysis, survey, data analytics, focus group, depth interview, and participant observation. And you explored the relationship between theory and PR strategy, seeing how mass communication, persuasion, and management theories help guide strategic planning. Beyond guidance, you discovered theory is also useful to diagnose what *might* have been done to achieve a better outcome and to explain why something did work well or missed the mark.

KEY TERMS

Active Publics 78
Agenda-Setting Theory 86
Aware Publics 78
Benoit's Image Restoration Theory 93
Cialdini's Influence Principles 91
Commonsense Theory 84
Content Analysis 81
Depth Interview 82
Diffusion of Innovations Theory 89
Digital Analytics 81
Elaboration Likelihood Model (ELM) 90
Excellence Theory 93
Focus Group 83
Framing Theory 86

Inoculation Theory 92
Latent Publics 78
Participant Observation 83
Qualitative Methods 81
Quantitative Methods 79
Scholarly Theory 85
Spiral of Silence Theory 88
Stewardship 76
Survey 80
Two-Step Flow Theory 87
Upward Flow Theory 88
Uses and Gratifications Theory 89
Word-of-Mouth (WOM) 76
Working Theory 84

THINK ABOUT IT

Simulate a focus group in class. First, use your university or college to identify an issue that the administration should monitor. It may be the level of satisfaction of commuter students, safety on campus, or the experience of international students—issues like this. Ideally, choose an issue that impacts students in your class. Then, choose a moderator (it's OK if several students moderate together) and develop a script with questions to ask focus group members. About eight students should be the focus group participants. Remaining students will serve as the "client" (members of the administration) who will quietly observe the focus group, noting facial expressions, body language, and making general observations. After the focus group is conducted, critique and debrief with each student, sharing how they experienced the process.

WRITE LIKE A PRO

As a newly hired PR assistant at the West Coast agency, JDG-PR, you are expected to be an expert in social media. One of your first assignments is to support the social media team for their client, Tee-Shirt Winery. The client's nearest competitor is Barefoot Wines, and their wines are quite comparable in price point and quality. Tee-Shirt's brand positioning is fun, quirky, carefree, and organic. Your assignment is to conceive of a Snapchat video that tells part of the brand's story and then prepare a storyboard for it. The goal of the video is to send fans to the client's YouTube channel. Cialdini's influence principles are good sources to guide your narrative strategy as they explain how influence transfers in momentary experiences. (Identify how Cialdini's principles guided you at the end of your submission).

SOCIAL RESPONSIBILITY CASE STUDY

Tylenol Gives Caregivers a Helping Hand

Situation

Not all pain relievers are created equal. Johnson & Johnson's Tylenol (acetaminophen) is often recommended for patients with serious health conditions. This differentiator and its emotional component motivated J&J to appeal to a specific audience making health decisions for the people they love—caregivers. Every year, nearly 44 million Americans take care of love ones. Past research has shown the following:

- Two thirds of the U.S. population expect to be caregivers in the future.
- Approximately 90% of care for a sick or disabled relative is given by one individual for over 4 years.
- Unpaid caregiving amounts to approximately $375 billion every year.

Research and Strategy

J&J recognized the often-unexpected responsibility of caregiving, while taxing, can also bring loved ones closer together. To learn how Tylenol could make a difference with a CSR initiative, J&J conducted quantitative and qualitative research:

- Issued a consumer survey
- Interviewed current and former caregivers and care receivers
- Created an advisory board of caregiving experts

Findings revealed that while caregiving is hard, there are benefits: 97% reported a positive impact on their lives, and 86% found caregiving one of the most rewarding things they've ever done. However, often no one is really "there" for them: 64% said they lack support from others, and 93% would like some help, either with moral support, running errands, giving them a day off, household chores, or transportation for doctor's visits.

These insights revealed a unique opportunity: Tylenol could celebrate caregivers by providing tangible resources to make their daily tasks easier. The #HowWeCare campaign was born with the goal of elevating care for caregivers while elevating awareness, preference, and engagement with the brand. Partners included Handy (a platform connecting people with household service professionals) and the ride-hailing company Uber. J&J developed Tylenol-branded care cards that offered 3 hours of home cleaning (via Handy) and a safe ride to a doctor's appointment (via Uber). By visiting the tylenol.com/howwecare site, people could purchase a card and send it to a specific caregiver via email. To give an authentic, notable, and gently humorous voice to the campaign, Tylenol partnered with the "clean comic" Jim Gaffigan—a caregiver for his wife who'd been diagnosed with a brain tumor.

Execution

#HowWeCare launched in the summer of 2018 and was amplified through strategic communications:

Video storytelling featured the stories of three families whose lives were suddenly turned upside-down, but through loving care, they experienced emotional rewards and gratification. Along with a fourth video of Jim and Jeannie Gaffigan, all were placed on WebMD, YouTube, and the Tylenol/HowWeCare website.

- Earned media included interviews with Jim and Jeannie in New York and LA, which sent people to the website and encouraged care card purchases.
- Influencer ambassador partnerships included 605 micro- and macro-influencers who drove traffic to the #HowWeCare videos and website and also cocreated content.
- Social sharing of all partners' social channels increased reach and awareness.
- An online strategy included #HowWeCare display ads, CRM email, and targeted banners to those who engaged, reinforcing why the brand may be the right pain reliever for care recipients.

Evaluation

Messages of support and thanks for #HowWeCare poured in from caregivers, and measurement methods revealed it exceeded its objectives. The campaign increased brand affinity: Those who saw the videos at least twice were 88% more likely to search for Tylenol compared to the average Google user. It increased brand awareness, generating more than 934 million total impressions across earned, influencer, and paid media, driven by 15 national interviews in top outlets such as *Today,* AP, *Parents, Hollywood Reporter, People,* Sirius radio, *Access Hollywood Live, Health,* BuzzFeed, *USA Today,* and more. Key messages were delivered in 93% of interviews. And it increased consumer action: Social engagement reached one of the brand's all-time highs when roughly 20,000 people mentioned the campaign across platforms, and 93% of posts were positive/neutral. Plus, the videos received 300,000-plus views.

Engage

- Go to www.tylenol.com/howwecare and explore its resources. Then, check to see how the campaign is using social channels.

Discussion

- From your research, would you conclude this CSR campaign is one that still thrives, or was it just a 1-year effort? As the #HowWeCare case study acknowledged, the pain reliever category is crowded. What would you recommend for new CSR campaign for Tylenol to help differentiate itself from the competition?

Note: This case was winner of a 2019 PRSA Silver Anvil Award of Excellence, © 2019, Public Relations Society of America, Inc.

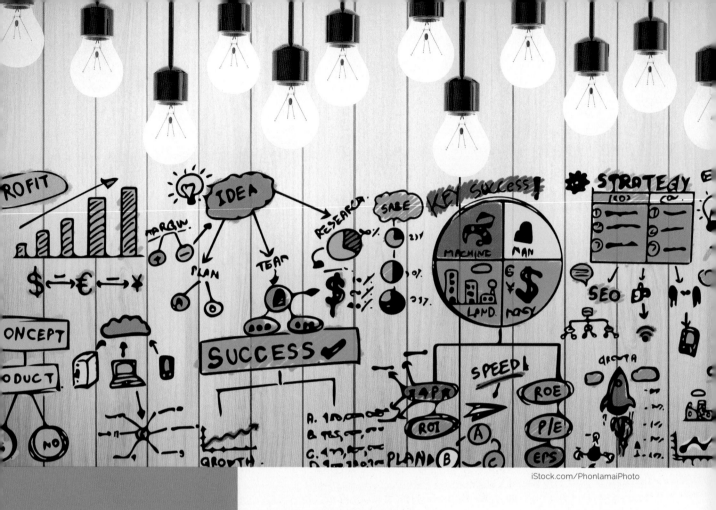

iStock.com/PhonlamaiPhoto

5 Strategic Communication Planning

Learning Objectives

5.1	Understand the models for and structure of strategic communications plans
5.2	Learn how to formulate communications objectives
5.3	Illustrate how to prepare strategic PR programs to meet business objectives
5.4	Explain the roles of evaluation, ongoing research, and measurement

Creating Awareness of Skin Cancer Among African Americans

Sixty-five percent of African Americans say they have never used sunscreen (Skin Cancer Foundation, 2016). The American Association of Dermatologists (AAD) reports that darker skinned people are equally susceptible as Caucasians to many forms of skin cancer, particularly melanoma, which is one of the deadliest forms. Bob Marley, the pioneering reggae musician and Jamaican cultural icon, died from a form of melanoma in 1981 (Skin Cancer Foundation, n.d.).

Despite the risk of skin cancer, most African Americans do not use sunscreen.
iStock.com/XiXinXing

The AAD and SkinCancer.org have worked together and supported Skin Cancer Awareness Month each May for several years. The program has achieved good visibility and awareness in the spring and summer time frame.

Focus on behavior change. Moving forward, the AAD wanted to develop and launch a new program focused on the African American community, encouraging the daily use of sunscreen and regular visits to the dermatologist. The overall goals included stimulating an increase in dermatological office visits and the sale and use of sunscreen by African Americans. AAD was interested in working on a combined PR/CSR (public relations/corporate social responsibility) program with a major partner on this project. It also believed this was an excellent vehicle for the right company to engage in corporate philanthropy and/or a cause-related marketing campaign.

Campaign challenge. Your agency has been retained by the AAD to develop and implement a plan to raise awareness about skin cancer prevention and detection as a daily, year-round activity. AAD has corporate partners that market over-the-counter (e.g., conventional sunscreens) and prescription-strength products to prevent and treat severe sun damage to the skin. The association was confident that with the right concept and plan it could get additional corporate sponsors to sign on and support the efforts with product, promotion, and publicity to build awareness and achieve key objectives.

As you read through this chapter, consider the following:

1. How would you get started in developing a plan?
2. What type(s) of research would you undertake?
3. What specific objectives would you propose?
4. What tactic(s) would you propose?
5. How will you measure progress or success?
6. What budget considerations are there to consider?
7. Does your plan reflect best practices in PR and CSR communications? ●

In this chapter, we review several models for the strategic communications planning process, including ROPES (research, objectives, programming, evaluation, stewardship; see Figure 5.1), RPIE (research, planning, implementation, evaluation; see Figure 5.2), and others. In the prior chapter, we reviewed the role of research in developing a strategic communications plan. We also identified the major communications theories that form the foundation for PR planning.

In this chapter, you will review the process of completing your plan, implementing it, and measuring progress toward achieving the desired objectives. This is critical to understand because strategic planning is central to both strategic public relations (SPR) and social responsibility (SR) initiatives.

As you go through this chapter, you will learn the building blocks of strategic planning and the importance of measurement and evaluation before, during, and after the planning stage. Clients or senior managers you encounter during your career will want to be assured that resources put into communication programs produce plans with a clear return on investment (ROI). This will require a dedication to strategic planning and an understanding of how to build a communication plan that delivers meaningful results.

Foundations of Strategic Planning in Strategic Public Relations

>> LO 5.1   Understand the models for and structure of strategic communications plans

The communication planning process is, by definition, fluid and dynamic, but there is a recommended structure and process. Following the steps and maintaining the planning discipline as you move through the process will be key to accomplishing your goals. Dozier and Broom (1995, p. 23) describe this process, noting, "Strategic planning is deciding where you want to be in the future (the goal) and how to get there [the strategy]. It sets the organization's direction proactively—avoiding 'drift' and routine repetition of activities." Each of the components of a PR plan is critical. Each section has its own purpose and challenges if the plan is to have the desired outcome.

Situation Analysis

The situation analysis (developed through research, as covered in Chapter 4), or summary, is one of the most important parts of the plan, which is why it is the first step. It is designed to set the stage and define the problem or opportunity. A well-written, succinct summary is key to achieving consensus among your management team or from a client. It allows you to explain why the plan is needed and how it reflects the situation facing the company. If properly drafted, it also demonstrates to management or a client that you understand the company and the factors—positive or negative—that are impacting it currently. Finally, it sets up the communication plan that follows and introduces the solution (e.g., the *objectives*) you are proposing.

Example

An employee-driven project by Food Lion serves as a good example of how important the situation analysis is in planning. Food Lion is a regional supermarket chain based in North Carolina that operates over 1,000 stores in the mid-Atlantic and southeastern United States. It is owned by Ahold Delahaize, a Dutch holding

FIGURE 5.1

ROPES Process

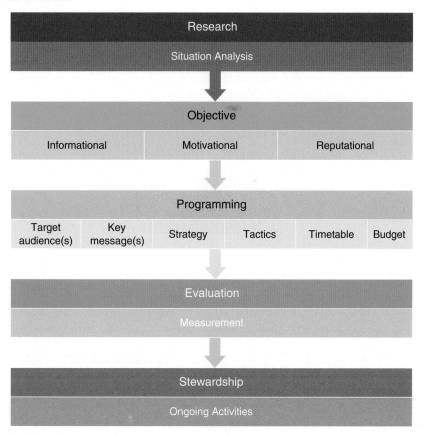

company that operates grocery and retail stores across Europe and the United States. Based on consumer and employee research, Food Lion set as its key objective to realign its charitable programs into **strategic philanthropy** and more closely align it to the company's core grocery business.

The situation analysis, prepared by the Food Lion communications team, included a summary of its internal and external research, an assessment of customer and employee awareness of the company's current SR efforts, and a recommended way forward. This helped set up the new strategic plan that led management to approve the recommended initiatives.

The launch of the "Food Lion Feeds" program was extremely successful by all accounts. It garnered considerable positive press, increased community goodwill, built employee pride, and produced a clear understanding among key stakeholders of the company's sustainability programs. The program also won several awards in the communications and SR arenas. A strong, clear situation analysis was key to convincing management to approve the project and for Food Lion to successfully reposition its charitable activity.

In any situation, there will be those who advocate for business as usual and keeping the status quo. However, the Food Lion Feeds program was based on solid research, was consistent with the company's core business, and was creative in its tactics and execution. This combination allowed the PR/SR team to overcome internal resistance to change and succeed.

FIGURE 5.2

RPIE Model

RPIE

As noted earlier, there are several other models for the planning process in public relations. These include RACE (research, action, communication, evaluation), RPAE (research, planning, action/communication, evaluation), and RPIE, among others.

RPIE is recognized by the Public Relations Society of America (PRSA) as the preferred planning model (PRSA, n.d.d). RPIE stands for research, planning, implementation, and evaluation (see Figure 5.2). Given its prominence and its importance to students and professionals interested in pursuing APR accreditation from the PRSA, a more robust discussion of this model in particular is in order.

RPIE, like other PR planning acronyms, emphasizes a staged approach to public relations, based on research and evaluation. This reflects the fact that the days of moving straight to PR tactics (e.g., implementation) without preliminary research or follow-up evaluation are long gone. Senior executives and clients want to know the reasons for each tactic and expect specific evidence of results consistent with their business or organizational objectives afterward. Neither of these is possible without meaningful up-front research as well as careful after-action evaluation of PR activity.

For example, suggesting a media relations effort without testing the messages, picking the audience, choosing the right media, or assessing the impact of the coverage would be pointless. It would be like beginning a journey without a GPS to guide you and provide alternatives should roadblocks occur or the destination change. Ronald Smith, in his 2013 book *Strategic Planning for Public Relations*, suggests, "Careful planning leads to programs that are proactive and preventive rather than to activities that are reactive and remedial" (p. 14).

Though RPIE does not explicitly include the concept of stewardship (as in the *S* in the ROPES model), scholars and practitioners agree that it is implied since the process is designed to be continuous. Specifically, the *evaluation* step should lead you back to do follow-up *research*, updated *planning*, and additional *implementation* in order to ensure the progress made, and relationships built, are lasting.

Perhaps the best way to illustrate this is with a PR campaign. In the following example, see how each component—research, planning, implementation, and evaluation—plays a critical role.

EcoPlanet Bamboo (EPB) is a U.S.-owned bamboo plantation and processing company practicing what it calls "conscious capitalism" in Nicaragua, the poorest country in Central America. According to the social responsibility media platform Triple Pundit (Peyok, 2019), EPB transforms degraded land to cultivate bamboo, is developing ways to use bamboo pulp to make tissue products, and plans to form the pulp into disposable containers, replacing plastics and Styrofoam. Its overall goal is to generate value for specific stakeholders, including current and prospective employees and the local community.

EPB's growth did not come without some challenges. In its early years, one key challenge was educating employees in the ethical mission of the company and making them proud to work there in order to encourage retention and recruitment. Guided by the RPIE model, to meet this challenge as EPB's PR consultant you might have done the following.

Research

Secondary. Review existing available research on cultural characteristics in Nicaragua, the Nicaraguan worker, demographic information from EcoPlanet's human resources team, and any prior communication with/from employees. These resources will help you draw conclusions to guide your plan development.

Some key findings include the following:

1. Employees have a strong personal appreciation of the company, as it provides a fair wage and supplements their health and nutritional needs.

2. Many company employees are poorly educated or illiterate.

Primary. Initiate face-to-face gatherings (focus groups) with the employees and listen to their concerns, points of view, and expectations to learn how they experience EcoPlanet Bamboo as employees and how that experience can be improved.

Planning

Goals. Increase employee commitment to the company and its sustainability and human rights philosophy.

- *Objectives*
  - Build awareness of company mission.
  - Generate understanding and respect for company operations.
  - Motivate employee retention and community recruitment.
- *Strategies*
  - Bring the corporate mission to life on a daily basis.
  - Reward workers for performing in support of the mission.
  - Include families and community members.
- *Tactics*
  - Rewrite company mission statement to communicate with key publics.
  - Celebrate workers' contributions through internal and external publicity.
  - Hold regular public events to explain the company's mission, praise workers, and include community members and leaders in major events.

Implementation

- Design and produce a visual mission statement in the form of a bilingual comic book and signage (necessary due to low literacy rate and limited comprehension of English among employees).
- Create videos to communicate "good works" achieved by employees.
- Produce and distribute an internal bilingual newsletter.
- Launch a microsite focused on employee and community members.
- Hold picnics, cultural events, a health care fair, and community meetings for workers, families, and community members/leaders.

Evaluation

Use research tools and techniques such as the following to measure impact:

- Distribution and reception of comic book and signage
- Airing and reception of videos
- Employees' awareness and attitudes
- Event attendance and participants' awareness and attitudes
- Levels of employee retention
- Hiring results from community recruitment efforts

In this example, we can see how decisions made at each step of the process shape a successful campaign. The company's ability to meet its challenges was rewarded in 2014 when it was recognized by the U.S. State Department as a recipient of the department's Award for Corporate Excellence (ACE). These awards recognize global achievements in supporting sustainable development and respecting labor and human rights by U.S. businesses (U.S. State Department, 2014).

In your career, it will be very important to choose and follow a strategic planning model that works for you. RPIE, ROPES, RPAE, or RACE are just handy tools designed to help plan and demonstrate the value of the PR programs you undertake. This is the most important takeaway from any discussion of PR planning models and acronyms. They help make sure your PR activities are research based, well planned, effectively implemented, and evaluated on a continuous basis.

By following one of these models, your strategic PR plans will be consistent with organizational strategy, focused on the target audience, and will maximize the positive outcomes for your client or company.

Objectives

>> LO 5.2 Learn how to formulate communications objectives

In developing your strategic objectives, two or three are recommended, according to most practitioners. A smaller number provides focus and discipline to the planning process and avoids overwhelming the plan and PR staff with too many objectives. Further, to be useful your objectives need to be specific, measurable, and tied to the corporate strategy and mission. Dozier (1985, p. 21) explained this critical connection in an article in *Public Relations Review*: "The prudent and strategic selection of a few specific public relations goals and objectives linked to organizational survival and growth serves to justify the public relations program as a viable management activity." Dozier's key point is that objectives are vital to creating an effective plan. Management buy-in and support for the plan or activity often hinges on the quality of the objectives. While your management team may not be PR experts, they know their business, and by connecting your plan to the overall corporate strategy, you create a basis for a mutual understanding. As you draft your objectives, keep this vital connection in mind.

Consider also the overall goals and time frame—for example, short term or long term—and factor that into your plan. These items will impact your approach to developing objectives, which are the building blocks to meet your goal. In practice, strategic objectives can be *informational, motivational,* or *reputational* (see Table 5.1), depending on the audience and purpose of the plan you are developing (Regester & Larkin, 2008).

Informational Objectives

Informational objectives are focused on creating awareness of a product, company, or issue by sharing information and attributes. It is worth noting that these can be harder to measure because awareness and perceptions are more difficult to quantify. A recent example of a campaign with informational objectives is one implemented by Johnson & Johnson, one of the world's leading health care companies and its former agency Cone Communications (see the PR Profile box in this chapter, page 109). The company wanted to address the lack of awareness among health care providers of the benefit of adopting sustainability initiatives in the workplace.

Example

According to the company's research, the health care industry generates more than 5.9 million tons of waste each year, contributes 8% of U.S. greenhouse gas emissions, and spends almost $8 billion on energy alone. Yet audience surveys showed there was little to no awareness of these statistics within the industry, and thus participation in Johnson & Johnson-sponsored sustainability initiatives had been inconsistent (Sutter, 2012).

In response, the company launched the "Metrics That Matter, Messages That Motivate: Making the Right Case for Sustainability in Healthcare" campaign to address this issue. The short-term plan designed for Johnson & Johnson had two clear informational objectives:

TABLE 5.1

The Three Types of Strategic Objectives

TYPE OF OBJECTIVE	FOCUS
Informational objectives	Creating awareness by sharing information and attributes
Motivational objectives	Changing the attitude and influencing the behavior of your target audience
Reputational objectives	Rebuilding or enhancing trust and confidence around a corporate event or crisis

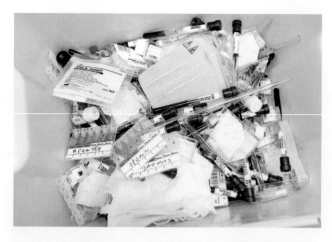

Johnson & Johnson's "Metrics That Matter, Messages That Motivate: Making the Right Case for Sustainability in Healthcare" campaign successfully raised awareness of the environmental impact of the health care industry.
BSIP / Contributor / Getty Images

1. Engage and educate health care professionals about sustainability best practices.

2. Increase dialogue and media coverage on the intersection of sustainability and health care.

The overall goal was to develop an awareness program that would "equip healthcare professionals with insights on how to advance the organizational (Johnson & Johnson) commitment to and investment in sustainability" (Cone Communications, 2014). The plan was successful by all accounts. In other cases—where it is necessary to change behavior or offset misperceptions—a different set of objectives is required, as we'll discuss in the next section.

Motivational Objectives

Motivational objectives are designed to educate and inform your target audience so that the desired behavior or activity is more prevalent. By definition, motivational objectives are more complex because they are designed to share information, change attitudes, and influence behavior. Ironically, these objectives can be easier to measure than informational ones. This is because you are trying to drive a specific change in attitude and behavior. With the proper tools, you can measure that progress among your target audiences easier than you can gauge awareness created by a media-focused, informational campaign (Stacks, 2010).

Example

A good example of a long-term plan with motivational objectives was the one created for the American Academy of Pediatric Dentistry (AAPD) by its agency (Weber Shandwick) in 2015 (AAPD, 2014). The principal concern for the organization was that the role of the pediatric dentist was not well understood among the target public—parents with young children.

Working with their agency, the group created "The Monster-Free Mouths Movement" to respond to this concern with a goal of raising awareness about children's oral health and accomplishing two motivational objectives:

1. Establish pediatric dentists and the AAPD as trusted sources and champions for children's oral health.

2. Encourage parents to take their young children to pediatric dentists for preventative oral health care.

The objectives in this plan were specific and measurable. For example, the AAPD tracked the increase in first visits by children to member dentists, monitored inquiries and visits to its dedicated campaign website, and logged requests for campaign materials by member dentists. Media coverage in target publications and on social media were monitored and measured as well. In addition, the objectives were tied directly to the goals of the organization (AAPD), whose purpose includes building awareness of pediatric dentistry and the need for early oral health care for children. Finally, the objectives were geared toward changing behavior—in this case, among parents with young children.

Reputational Objectives

Reputational objectives are objectives and plans that are tied to a major corporate event or crisis. The timing can be either short or long term, and they are designed to change perceptions and rebuild or enhance trust and confidence (Stacks, 2010).

The reputation of Princess Cruises, another Carnival line, took a major hit when two of its ships—the *Diamond Princess* and *Grand Princess*—were quarantined at sea for weeks due to an outbreak of COVID-19 as the coronavirus pandemic escalated in early 2020.
MediaNews Group/East Bay Times via Getty Images / Contributor / Getty Images

Example

A program developed by Carnival Corporation to respond to a series of events that shook the company and the entire cruise line industry is a clear example of a reputational objective. As you may recall, the company and its reputation suffered, beginning in 2012 with the sinking of the *Costa Concordia* ship (a Carnival brand) off the coast of Italy. Then, in 2013 a Carnival cruise had multiple passengers get sick, and the ship's services and facilities were overwhelmed. These two incidents received worldwide publicity—most of it negative—that damaged the company's reputation and put its brand at severe risk.

How Public Relations Planning Drives Social Change

Aaron Pickering, Vice President, Cone Communications

Photo courtesy of Aaron Pickering

I work in PR and social responsibility because I believe it is one of the best drivers of political, environmental, and social change. As director of brand strategy at FIRST Robotics—an $80 million nonprofit organization with a presence in over 100 countries—I develop and execute partnerships with Fortune 500 brands to advance STEM (science, technology, engineering, math) learning to help young people prepare for the future. Given that approximately 65% of students entering school today will work in jobs that don't currently exist (McKinsey Global Institute, 2017), many global brands see value in supporting workforce development and increasing STEM learning.

Because of all these factors, I believe it is an exciting time to work at the intersection of PR, SR,

(Continued)

(Continued)

and business because the case for sustainability has never been as compelling:

- In 2020, a third of all retail sales are expected to come from millennials—and 87% of them prefer to purchase products with a social or environmental benefit.

- Most people prefer to work for socially responsible companies, and recent research shows that 62% of millennials are willing to take a pay cut to do so (Cone Communications, 2015).

As PR professionals, we can support this by calling the public's attention to social issues and engaging business leaders and other key stakeholders in the process of addressing them.

Previously, I was senior vice president at Cone Communications, a Porter Novelli company. In this role, I developed PR strategies to enhance the reputation of brands that respect people and the planet and provide reliable, quality products to the marketplace.

I began my career as a defense contract analyst in Washington, DC, while pursuing a graduate degree in strategic public relations. After graduating, I pivoted to the nonprofit sector to apply my skills to the causes and issues I care about. In my work, I learned that PR and SR could be the "secret sauce" to driving social change. I also recognized that large corporations had the most resources to support these efforts and had a stake in the outcome.

In 2012, I began managing communications for the Fair Labor Association—the multistakeholder initiative formed by former President Clinton to improve working conditions globally. I handled PR for the organization throughout our investigation of Apple's largest supplier, Foxconn in China, and I saw firsthand how CR and PR could impact an industry. Following our investigation, other suppliers and major brands in tech and other industries began to address labor challenges in their own supply chains.

While the current political landscape may be highly polarized, the issues facing all of us remain clear. Strategic planning will continue to be critical for developing PR and CSR initiatives to address pressing social issues. I look forward to continuing to contribute to this important work and hope many of you will join us. ●

Sources: Cone Communications, 2015; McKinsey Global Institute, 2017; A. Pickering, personal communication, 2019.

A major brand renovation and corporate image repair were clearly required. The company developed and launched a reputation-based, long-term communications plan built around the core objective of increasing "collaboration, cooperation, and communication"—or the "three Cs," as they became known inside the company.

By the end of the program, the company's brand and corporate image had improved dramatically; media coverage became more balanced, some positive news articles also appeared, and passenger bookings began to rebound (Marzilli, 2014). This plan succeeded due to its specific, measurable reputational objectives, which included the following:

1. Mitigating negative news with good news about the company and its new CEO

2. A company-wide focus on improving the passenger experience

These objectives were designed to reposition the company's cruise lines as "safe, well-run operations" and restore consumer confidence in the brand. The company's sustained outreach and focus on the plan and its objectives produced the desired improvements, its reputation was rebuilt, and its bottom-line results at the time improved as well.

Unfortunately, high-profile crisis situations—such as the novel coronavirus/COVID-19 pandemic that began in late 2019—continue to impact the entire cruise line industry, making reputation management a critical skill for PR practitioners in this business.

Programming

>> LO 5.3   Illustrate how to prepare strategic PR programs to meet business objectives

The programming stage involves the execution of the campaign plan. It encompasses defining a target audience, determining strategy, choosing key messages, and implementing tactics (activities).

Target Audience

One of the fundamental rules of PR is this: Know your audience. This is especially true in strategic planning and program implementation. In most cases, you will have a definite target group you are trying to reach with a specific message and a limited time to accomplish that objective. Budgets are a factor because resources are not unlimited. Researching and identifying your target audience is a critical step in developing a viable communications plan that focuses your resources on the right audience. Target audience segments, if they are not already known, can be identified through market research—secondary or primary—as outlined in Chapter 4.

For example, in the Monster-Free Mouths Movement program, the AAPD knew it wanted to reach three specific groups: parents of young children, child care workers, and members of the AAPD itself. The AAPD plan's primary audience was parents of young children, and the plan was designed with them front and center. However, the children themselves were identified as a secondary audience, and cartoon characters and kid-friendly materials were created to make the dental visit fun.

Strategic communications plans can have more than one audience, and your objectives, program, tactics, and evaluation need to take this into consideration and be tailored accordingly. In this case, creating awareness about the need for oral health care for young children was a great start. However, providing the AAPD member dentists with collateral material to make that first visit enjoyable for kids was equally important to delivering on the overall objective.

Strategy

When you get to this part of the plan, you have already established the situation, identified your objectives, and segmented your target audience. This is where you develop the approach that will produce the results identified in the objectives section of the plan.

Your strategy should be a clear statement of how you will achieve the objectives and what will guide your tactics (the specific activities you will undertake to meet the objectives). At some point in your career, management may come to you with a tactic in mind that was used previously—

Identifying your target audience is an essential step in planning a successful campaign.
iStock.com/Rawpixel

for example, hiring a celebrity spokesperson, launching a competition, or holding an event or press conference—and suggest that tactic again, before you have done your research or planning. You need to resist the urge to do this, noting that the tactic, and others, will be fully considered when you get to that stage of your plan.

You will not succeed by jumping ahead to tactics without doing the foundational work: defining the situation or opportunity, settling on your objective(s), identifying the audience you are trying to reach, and preparing the message(s) you are trying to convey. Plus, you will be the one held accountable because you are supposed to be the expert, not the executive who suggested the tactic. In this instance, your best option is to step back, acknowledge the request, and get all the planning steps done as quickly as possible. After the process is completed, you can identify which tactic or tactics will have the best chance of accomplishing your goals and let all the principals know what you are planning and why.

Key Messages

Simply put, a **key message** is what you want your target audience to understand and accept after the program has been implemented. This is not an easy process and should be done thoughtfully. The messages must be clear, have interest or relevance to the recipient, and include a call to action to drive the change or the impact you are seeking.

Example

An example of a key message from the Johnson & Johnson medical waste case was *Johnson & Johnson is the leader in sustainability in the health care industry.* The message was based on research conducted on health care professionals in Europe, South America, and the United States. The results showed there was a gap between health care facilities' desire to participate in sustainability initiatives to manage waste and the awareness of how to get started. This central message positions the company to help in both cases.

INSIGHTS

Social Responsibility Planning: A Competitive Advantage?

Corporate social responsibility can create new revenue streams and give companies a competitive advantage with customers.
Getty Images

CSR is getting a lot of attention today and is a major focus of this text.

In her book *Just Good Business*, UC Berkeley business professor Kellie McElhaney (2008, p. 16) cites an IBM Institute for Business Value study that reports 68% of business leaders see CSR as a means to create new revenue for their companies, and a little more than half (54%) believe that CSR activities they undertake have given them an advantage in the marketplace.

McElhaney suggests the process of developing a CSR plan should include five key steps:

1. **Develop a vision.** Conduct internal research about your industry, company strategy, and management's definition of success. Armed with this information, you can prepare a summary statement of the company's "purpose" and consider CSR options and activities against this vision.

2. **Connect CSR outreach and events to your vision, purpose, and strategy.** Using the vision/purpose statement, carefully review potential social responsibility programs and choose only those that are consistent with your vision/goals. As well, you should seek opportunities to promote your business, products, and services by choosing programs than connect with your business and strategy.

3. **Ongoing monitoring and evaluation are critical.** After you launch your CSR initiative, maintain the effort and don't allow the momentum to disappear. Too many companies launch a new initiative with great fanfare and then let it drift or decline. This undermines your credibility, creates expectations, and may do more damage than not having launched in the first place.

4. **Engage customers and the public in your activity.** Look for CSR activities that connect with your customers' needs and personal goals. The public will be more engaged and participation will increase if they can relate and believe in the program. There is plenty of research documenting that customers want to buy products and support corporations they feel are doing good things in the world.

5. **Well-managed CSR supports recruitment and retention.** Similar to its positive impact on customer relationships, CSR has been shown to enhance the perception of a company as a great place to work. Employees want and expect to work for a company that shares their values and for CEOs they feel care about what they care about. Properly done, your CSR activity can attract employees who will engage in and support your CSR activities. Harnessing this powerful connection and communicating internally to build employee engagement will pay off in more productive employees as well as attract top talent to your company versus your competitors. ●

Source: Economy, 2017.

Tactics

SOCIAL RESPONSIBILITY

Tactics are the part of the plan where the "rubber meets the road," so to speak. Tactics always follow strategy; they are the how, not the what, of the plan. These are the specific activities you recommend be implemented to convey the message(s) to the target audience. Depending on the objectives, this could entail placing stories in target media, staging an event or activity to convey the messages, conducting outreach online or directly to the public, or any number of other ideas in the PR toolbox that fit the needs of the plan.

There are good examples of tactics in these cases as well. For example, in the Johnson & Johnson case, to accomplish its objective of "engaging and educating health care professionals about sustainability best practices," the company used the primary tactic of a major industry conference on that specific topic. Its second objective, "increase dialogue and media coverage," was accomplished through a targeted media relations program focused on key health care and sustainability publications and influential social media platforms.

Timetable and Budget

As with any strategic plan, the timetable for the program is a critical element. It provides all parties with a sense of the timing of key elements and when results can be expected in the marketplace.

The timetable allows the company or client to coordinate new product offerings, website updates and enhancements, and employee briefings to coincide with the program rollout and to get maximum benefit. It is also useful as a budget management tool, as it indicates when certain expenditures are likely to occur and when resources, such as additional staff, volunteers, experts, or spokespeople, will need to be mobilized or ready. Finally, it is a tracking mechanism to monitor the plan's rollout and allows you to know if things are on schedule and progressing as expected.

Similarly, the program's budget is a resource-focused document—it provides a plan for expenditures related to the plan. It also helps create a discipline on how resources are used, as there is a finite budget set aside for the plan, and it is up to the program manager(s) to use these resources carefully and in accordance with the plan. Finally, a clearly defined budget will allow you to calculate return on investment (ROI) because the expenditures for each step can be more easily identified and compared.

Evaluation, Research, and Measurement

>> LO 5.4   **Explain the roles of evaluation, ongoing research, and measurement**

Winston Churchill once said, "However beautiful the strategy, you should occasionally look at the results." As the quote suggests, strategic planners should always build measurement and evaluation steps into their plans to improve overall results.

Evaluation

Every plan should have a built-in **evaluation phase** at the end of the program's implementation. Here is where the specific, measurable objectives you built into the plan are critical. If the objectives are properly crafted and reflect the company's business strategy, the PR professional can more easily demonstrate progress against those objectives. This can be very helpful in seeking budget and resources to continue the plan (if needed) or supporting budget requests for plans in the future. A track record of delivering on objectives and meeting overall program goals can be very helpful in getting management or client support for the next one you develop.

The cases examined in this chapter contain several examples of measurement inclusion in program planning and implementation. In the Food Lion case, the company did extensive, up-front, primary, and secondary research on internal and external awareness of its sustainability initiatives. This data served as a benchmark to measure awareness among its key publics after the campaign was completed.

Ongoing Research

The strategic planning process begins and ends with research. To develop your plan, you must make sure it is based on current and accurate information about the company, industry, market, and key audiences. The research in the preliminary phase can draw insights from available materials—secondary research—or can be based on new, specific data—for example, primary research. In most cases, secondary research is the basis for developing PR plans because it is already available and less expensive and time-consuming to produce.

Moving From Charity to Strategic Philanthropy—SAP Leads the Way

Companies worldwide are implementing corporate philanthropy programs. Some encourage or match employee donations. Levi's participated in back-to-school programs, donating school supplies and their employees' time.
Tim Mosenfelder / Stringer / Getty Images

Is philanthropy good for business? Many leading global companies, like SAP, believe so. These organizations are implementing strategic programs to donate money or provide in-kind goods and services to causes that fit their overall strategy and meet a need in their local or global market. This is a concept known as **corporate philanthropy**.

Business and Social Benefit

SAP, a leading international IT and management consulting company, recently ramped up donations of its technologies and management consulting talent to organizations across the world. At first glance, this might seem to be just a charitable donation, but there is more to distributing software and expertise than just supporting a worthy cause. Consider that for many global companies, developing markets offer a growth market. So the donation of equipment and management talent there is both strategic and philanthropic. The key is to make a sustained and transparent effort in these emerging markets to support access to technology and economic growth. Over time, this will benefit both the company and the country.

Increasing Employee Engagement

Research shows that employees—both current and potential—want more from their employer than a paycheck and benefits. They want to work for a company they believe has a clear social purpose that is consistent with their own views and beliefs. Programs like SAP's provide a foundation for employee engagement and position it as an employer of choice in a crowded and competitive market for talent.

Developing Talent for the Future

For SAP, this is more than about engaging employees at its headquarters or in its regional offices. It is about establishing programs for social good and developing talent to sustain the company's future.

Boosting Economic Opportunity

According to Kaye (2011), "With its mantra of providing software products that 'make the world better' the company [SAP] is on a mission to foster a supportive business climate and create opportunity." For many communities across the globe, SAP and other firms create economic opportunities in developing markets where unemployment is a daily challenge. Through software donations and sharing management expertise with local nonprofits and community organizations, SAP's efforts will contribute to a healthy population, an improving climate for business, and a more educated, employable workforce.

It's Just Good Business

The logic of this strategic philanthropy is clear: SAP needs both highly skilled employees and successful customers. The local entrepreneurs they support will develop businesses that can benefit from the company's products and its people, and the communities they help build together will help SAP maintain and grow its business worldwide. ●

Source: Kaye, 2011.

Research also comes into play during the implementation of the plan—to measure your progress and course adjust if needed—and at the end when you are looking to determine the impact of your efforts. Ideally, your plan will benefit from all three of these types of research—preplanning, interim, and postimplementation. Each of the examples used in the chapter demonstrates the value of up-front and ongoing research to develop and fine-tune a program to maximize your results. These concepts are explored in more detail in Chapter 4.

Stewardship to Maintain Momentum

SOCIAL RESPONSIBILITY

The final letter in the ROPES model (see page 103) stands for stewardship. In other models, like RPIE, this step is implied, as noted. Depending on the context, stewardship can be an important consideration; some say it's essential. Once a campaign has successfully engaged your key publics, stewardship helps ensure a healthy, ongoing relationship and sustains the momentum achieved. Dr. Kathleen Kelly of the University of Florida conceived of this concept based on her research in fundraising. She identified stewardship's four dimensions or elements (see Figure 5.3): reciprocity, responsibility, reporting, and relationship nurturing. She proposes,

> Without stewardship, the practice of PR and SR is incomplete. PR practitioners must ensure that expressions of appreciation are provided, recognition activities are planned, responsibility is monitored, a system of reporting is in place, and strategies for relationship nurturing are carried out. (Kelly, 2001, pp. 279–289)

FIGURE 5.3

The Four Dimensions of Stewardship

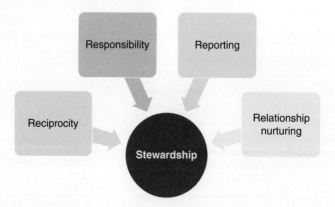

Scenario Outcome

At the beginning of this chapter, you were given a challenge: Develop a plan for a combined PR/CSR program with a partner company for the American Association of Dermatologists (AAD). Based on the content in this chapter, you can follow the strategic process to develop a plan:

Research is your foundation. First, you will want to review the medical research the AAD has on hand to get background information. You should also examine industry marketing data to see if there is a pattern to African Americans purchasing and using sunscreen products. Armed with this secondary research, you might choose to recommend some primary research—for example, focus groups, email surveys, or one-on-one interviews or mall intercepts, where research staff interview people while they are shopping, to quantify your initial findings.

Objectives are critical. You will need to set specific, measurable objectives to help increase sunscreen use and office visits to the dermatologist. The objectives can stress visits to a campaign website by the target audience or requests for information kits and samples by member doctors. They can also be focused on articles for target media and/or new postings on social media sites (e.g., Twitter, Instagram, Facebook, etc.).

Program development follows. First. craft campaign messages that convey key data about skin cancer to the members of the target audience. These should connect to the next programming step, tactics. To address the CSR angle or opportunity, you could work with the AAD to identify current partners or new companies to approach about a cause-related marketing program to increase sales and/or use of sunscreen. Think of companies that target the skin care or African American markets. To increase awareness, conduct a media outreach program that targets general interest magazines, major newspapers, and local television as well as African American-focused media. To drive office visits, the program could include a coupon for an initial appointment with an AAD-member dermatologist. The AAD and its partner might also engage a spokesperson with a strong following in the target audience—for example, a sports, entertainment, or public figure—to launch a media tour or a series of community appearances.

Evaluation measures your progress. The remaining pieces of the plan, notably measurement and evaluation, should follow. For example, performance against the CSR goals and objectives can be measured in terms of visits to the dermatologist or community-based screenings and traffic on campaign websites for campaign information and materials.

Stewardship keeps good relationships strong. The goal is to produce results that show progress toward the goals of the program and a return on the investment made by the AAD and its corporate partner(s). The relationships created with key publics need to be maintained through ongoing communications and outreach to keep all parties informed and engaged.

WRAP UP

Strategic planning and successful PR programs are inextricably linked. Planning is the difference between the practitioner who executes tactics and the strategic advisor who designs, develops, and implements strategic communications plans to achieve business objectives. One will likely be viewed as a technician, the other as a strategist.

Which would you rather be?

In this chapter, we reviewed the steps after research in the strategic planning process. We also considered the elements of a strategic plan—situation analysis, objectives, target audience(s), key message(s), strategy, tactics, measurement and evaluation, timetable, and budget—and introduced the idea of stewardship to maintain the relationships the plan helped build.

The strategic planning process need not be time-consuming and can flow smoothly and quickly, especially in crisis situations. By practicing this discipline routinely in your daily work, you will be able to do so again, even under the most difficult of circumstances.

KEY TERMS

Corporate Philanthropy 115
Evaluation Phase 114
Informational Objectives 107
Key Message 112

Motivational Objectives 108
Reputational Objectives 109
Strategic Philanthropy 103

THINK ABOUT IT

In this chapter, you read about several organizations and how they developed communications plans for a market opportunity or to manage an issue they faced. Pick one that is of interest to you and your fellow students.

Assume you all work for a PR firm that has been engaged to continue or sustain (e.g., stewardship) the progress it made with the initial program. What strategy or tactics would you suggest the organization or company implement now, and how would you measure your results to determine if you were on target?

WRITE LIKE A PRO

Identify a company or organization in the news in your area or nationally. Taking into consideration the RPIE approach to communications planning, develop an outline of a plan for the company or organization to manage the newsworthy issue or crisis or take advantage of the opportunity the situation presents.

Consider if this situation is an industry problem—for example, the impact of consuming sugary drinks or soda on the health of young people—or a company-specific problem—for example, a food handling or sourcing problem that creates health concerns for customers.

If it is both a company and an industry concern, what role might a trade group or association play in addressing the problem? For example, would you recommend working with government officials in Washington, DC? If it is solely a company concern, what role might employee relations or CSR initiatives play?

Outline your response to the situation, noting each of the planning steps.

CASE STUDY

The African American Community Steps Up to Save Lives

It has been reported that African Americans are the least likely demographic group to find matching marrow donors. For many African Americans, this disparity can be the difference between life and death. "Be the Match," a nonprofit that operates a national registry of volunteer marrow donors, worked with its PR firm (PadillaCRT) to create awareness during National Marrow Donor Month, which occurs in July.

Research and Strategy

Research shows donors between the ages of 18 and 44 are preferred by transplant doctors more than 90% of the time and provide the greatest chance for transplant success due to their relative health. However, the same research indicates a lower number of volunteers for transplants among African Americans. This subgroup—African Americans between the ages of 18 and 44—became the target audience for the program.

The team confirmed that sharing personal stories of patients and donors would drive the most media interest and target audience engagement. African American marrow donors and patients were identified and interviewed to find personal stories that would inspire others to participate.

Prior media coverage was analyzed by the agency to determine the best method and opportunities for media outreach. Ten key markets were identified, including New York, Los Angeles, San Francisco, Philadelphia, Baltimore, Chicago, Miami, Dallas, Houston, and Minneapolis.

An aggressive media outreach campaign was planned, targeting African American media outlets, including print, broadcast, and online media in the target markets.

The campaign's objectives were these:

- Increase the number of African Americans joining the bone marrow registry by 20%.
- Achieve significant media coverage from African American-focused media as well as national and local media print and broadcast media outlets.
- Place news stories in target media outlets to create awareness and stimulate inquiries about the foundation.
- Drive traffic to the organization's dedicated website, www.BTMItsOnYou.org.

Execution

The team created and launched "It's on You," a monthlong awareness campaign and call to action to the African American community to step up and help save lives. They found ways to share stories about the relationships between donors and patients: Blog posts emphasized the need for more diverse donors and dispelled the myths of donation. Compelling human-interest story angles beyond the basic awareness-month messages were supplied to media outlets. Interviews, live shots, and additional media requests were coordinated.

The campaign delivered the key message that more African American registry members are needed now, and it only takes a few minutes to join the "Be the Match" registry. An invitation to visit www.BTMItsOnYou.org and a call to take some action were included in all communications. Local media outreach guidelines were created, along with media lists, media materials, and a list of local African American-focused events to assist staff with media outreach in the 10 target markets.

Evaluation

The first objective was to increase African American donorship by 20% during the month of July. In fact, nearly 250 African Americans joined the registry online—26% more than average.

Second was to achieve coverage from African American-focused media outlets. The campaign gained extensive coverage through stories incorporating the key messages from those outlets: 100% of news segments included target messages, and 94% mentioned the BTMItsOnYou.org or BeTheMatchBlog.org links.

Third was to land at least three or four national media stories in African American–focused media outlets to drive awareness beyond local market efforts. In reality, nine national media stories were secured, including ones in *Essence Magazine, Today's Black Woman, Juicy Magazine*, American Urban Radio Networks (AURN), Journey to Wellness, Arise.tv, *Real Health, The Tom Joyner Morning Show*, and BlackAmericaWeb.com.

The final objective was to create more activity on the campaign landing page. The campaign resulted in over 41,000 unique visitors to the site over the period of June 26 to July 31.

Engage

- While this was only a monthlong event, the problem it was designed to address is national and growing. Visit Be the Match (www.BTMItsOnYou.org) to get an overview of the issue and the scope of the challenge the group is facing.

Discuss

- What ideas do you have to help increase the number of donor volunteers?
- Is there a company or fraternal organization that might be a good partner organization?
- Is there an employee volunteer or fundraising opportunity for a company with a market focus on African Americans or other ethnic groups with a need for more matching donors?
- How about a celebrity or athlete—with a connection to the issue—as a spokesperson?

6

Public Relations Writing

Persuasive and Audience Focused

Learning Objectives

6.1	Understand the style and structure of PR writing and foundational models of communication
6.2	Identify the characteristics of compelling, persuasive, newsworthy, and targeted messaging
6.3	Develop proficiencies in effective writing for essential PR tactics

What Do Taylor Swift, Ben Harper, and Beatie Wolfe Have in Common?

To put it another way, what special connection do pop rock, folk rock, and bluegrass share? The answer is the rich acoustic tones of a Taylor guitar.

Guitar hero. Cofounded by Bob Taylor in 1974 and based in El Cajon, California, the guitar maker is a global leader in the manufacture of premium acoustic and electric guitars, with a prestigious international reputation and a loyal following in the music industry. Its quality guitars rely on quality materials, and that includes the wood in their fingerboards—the rare high-density black ebony. The best musicians and guitar makers demand it. In fact, beyond manufacturing, Taylor is also a major supplier of black ebony to the industry.

Taylor Guitars, a maker of high-quality instruments, is known for strict attention to ethical sourcing of sustainable materials.
Guitarist Magazine / Contributor / Getty Images

As a fundamental part of its corporate ethos, Taylor Guitars is devoted to best practices throughout its building process, starting with sound forest management, ethical sourcing of tonewoods, and rigorous attention to environmental sustainability. Their green practices extend to the final steps in the process, with repurposing of wood scrap and sawdust and the use of recyclable packing materials.

The West African country of Cameroon has one of the world's last ebony rain forests. However, ebony's journey from a tree in the rain forests of Africa to an instrument in an artist's hands is long, complicated, and fraught with environmental concerns, social issues, and strict regulations.

Over the years, a combination of market demands, poor economic conditions in Cameroon, and lack of sufficient forest management has caused stress on the supply of ebony. Such factors have led to problems for suppliers, low worker wages, and an environment of irresponsible procurement. In 2011, Taylor Guitars stepped in to secure its supply of ethically sourced ebony by purchasing Crelicam, the largest ebony mill in Cameroon.

Situation. Once Taylor Guitars learned more about the social and environmental issues impacting the Cameroonian ebony trade, it commenced to make improvements. It did this by "enhancing local incomes by hiring local workers; training workers to use state-of-the art equipment; and encouraging Cameroonian legal and policy reforms to improve transparency and traceability of logging permits and respect for the rights and needs of other forest users" (Taylor Guitars, n.d. para. 9).

Bob Taylor also made a shocking discovery: 90% of the harvested ebony was left lying to decay on the forest floor simply because it was not pure black but variegated in color. Bob then made a decision to change the industry standard by using all of the harvested variegated ebony for guitar fretboards—and to save the rain forest at the same time.

After reading this chapter, you should be able to answer the following questions:

1. How can Bob Taylor convince the musicians and manufacturers who are diehard fans of black ebony to change their perception of what defined ebony—to abandon their views and accept what was considered "inferior" as the new standard?

(Continued)

(Continued)

2. To achieve the above, the public's knowledge, attitudes, and behaviors need to change. As the PR manager for Taylor Guitars, what PR tactics would you recommend? ●

Source: This scenario is drawn from Page and Page, 2018.

In this chapter, you'll first get a basic understanding of various communication models that help explain the communication process—a process you will often lead as a PR (public relations) writer. Effective communication doesn't just happen; it's the result of careful adherence to established guidelines. Instructions and examples are included to help you understand how to produce the most common writing tactics in contemporary PR for both external and internal publics. Different writing styles are used when addressing the general public, which may be unfamiliar with industry jargon, versus those used within the company workforce.

Essential for future PR professionals, emphasis is given to the critical need to improve and maintain quality writing skills. Nothing hurts communication more than poorly written copy; grammatical errors and unnecessary typos will get your release, pitch, or op-ed tossed into a real or virtual trash can. To support this goal, you'll find detailed examples of the written tactics most frequently required in internships, introductory, and midlevel positions.

Although some may seem dated, such as a standard press release designed for a print outlet, the structures are not. An effective communicator is a good writer who knows the proper formats. (*Note:* Social media and new technologies are covered in a separate chapter.)

For a Public Relations Career, You Had Better Become a Good Writer

>> LO 6.1 Understand the style and structure of PR writing and foundational models of communication

Good PR writing starts with research and an understanding of how the process of communication works. Your research should make you a near expert about your topic, your reader, and your PR goal (Inform? Entertain? Influence attitudes? Encourage behavior?). You will know enough about your reader that your words will be interesting, useful, helpful, and so on. Even if you know a lot about your topic at the start, you still should find out what's new. With our 24/7 information cycle, some strategic searches will ensure you've found credible and insightful news and not just hobbyists' blogs.

Understanding your reader allows you to write concisely and effectively. Who are you writing to and for what purpose? What do they know already, and what do they need to know? What are your goals?

In most writing for PR, providing the "5Ws and H"—who, what, when, where, why, and how—up front gives readers enough critical information and encourages them to read on. The facts, themes, words you use, and knowledge of your reader will help increase interest and engagement. We talked about framing in Chapter 4—that is, how journalists and PR writers selectively use content that tells a story in a certain way to appeal to readers and clearly make intentional points.

Understanding Communication

In 1948, political scientist Harold Lasswell wrote, "A convenient way to describe an act of communication is to answer the following questions: 'Who? Says what? In which channel? To whom? With what effect?'" (McQuail & Windahl, 1993, p. 13), thereby establishing an early model of communication. However, notice there is no consideration of interrupted speech, flawed channels, inattentive listening, or varying reactions.

The following year, Shannon and Weaver offered a more exacting communication model that included the concept of **noise** (McQuail & Windahl, 1993, p. 17), meaning unplanned factors that affect the communication process, including whether the listener is distracted due to illness, worries, or preoccupations or whether physical noise in the environment sidetracks the listener or nullifies a message. The prospect of a message being interrupted or filtered through internal or external noise is of great concern to PR practitioners, which explains the multipronged tactical approach—the PR campaign that repeats and reinforces messaging—as a standard PR practice. As well, PR recognizes and values two-way symmetrical communication; thus, the need for *feedback* is crucial. This concept was first developed by Norbert Wiener (1988), a leading scholar of **cybernetics**, a theory of message transmission. Feedback responds to the PR practitioners' need to talk *with* publics, not *at* them.

Schramm's Model of Mass Communication

Wilbur Schramm then developed a classic model of mass communication (McQuail & Windahl, 1993, p. 19) in 1954 (see Figure 6.1). Schramm's model looks complicated, but it's really very linear. Consider the following example:

1. "Message **encoded** by the transmitter" is the starting point in Schramm's model—I type an email message about coffee beans, selecting words and content (encoding) drawn from my knowledge (transmitter's field of experience).

FIGURE 6.1

Schramm's Model of Mass Communication—1954

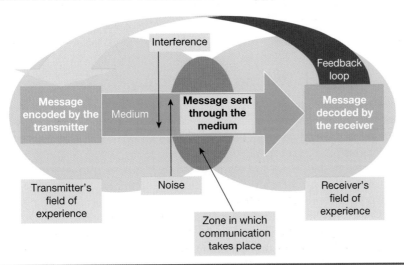

Source: http://sk.sagepub.com/books/key-concepts-in-marketing/n46.xml
Wilbur Schramm then developed a classic model of mass communication (McQuail and Windahl, 1993, p. 19); in 1954 (Figure 6.1).

2. It travels via the Internet (medium) but ends up in a spam folder (interference).

3. When the intended recipient locates it, she's annoyed and exhausted, as it's midnight (noise) and she's still in her office communicating online via her computer (zone).

4. She's familiar with coffee beans, as Starbucks is a regular stop (receiver's field of experience), and she understands my message is about some exotic new sources (message decoded by receiver).

5. Yet she's fatigued and not fully processing some information (noise). She shoots back an email (feedback loop) telling me she's not ready to purchase any yet but needs more time to investigate the offer.

Public Relations Writing Strategy and Style

>> LO 6.2   Identify the characteristics of compelling, persuasive, newsworthy, and targeted messaging

Beginning with an understanding of how the communication process works, PR writers must then proceed strategically. Whatever the tactic, if it requires the written word, you should always ask and answer these basic questions before beginning:

1. Why are you writing?

2. Who are the target readers—and what is most relevant to them?

3. What is the PR's desired objective? What do I want to happen?

4. What is the organization's need and key message?

5. What communication channel will be used?

6. When is the deadline?

7. What are the legal aspects, and who needs to approve it?

The answers to the seven basic questions will help you reach your reader, focus on the core message, and write more easily and quickly, increasing the likelihood of it being approved and released.

Always Approach Writing Strategically

Your strategy can differ, depending on the context, but it generally gives you a framework or path to achieve a goal. You must begin at the end: Know what you want to achieve. What is the big idea or takeaway? This knowledge allows you to proceed with a conscious plan to get there.

The answer to the "How do I want to end up?" question may also guide your writing to support your client's brand positioning—a marketing term that typically guides corporate communication. Being strategic about your writing gives you a course of action to confidently follow. Your writing may seek to inform, impress, influence, and/or persuade. These objectives support various goals—for example, publicizing, building relationships, reinforcing a brand, resolving crises, generating votes, attracting investors, and so on. However, always remember to ask yourself the question, "Have I addressed the readers' interests or only mine?"

Recipe for Success

For most purposes, following Chip and Dan Heath's SUCCESs principles will sharpen your writing and increase its effectiveness. In their book *Made to Stick: Why Some Ideas Die and Others Survive* (Heath & Heath, 2007), they introduce the acronym SUCCESs, which stands for simple, unexpected, concrete, credible, emotional, and storytelling (see Table 6.1). While the authors left the last *S* unattributed, we see it standing for strategic.

TABLE 6.1

SUCCESs Principles

SIMPLE	UNEXPECTED	CONCRETE	CREDIBLE	EMOTIONAL	STORYTELLING
Simplicity asks writers to identify the essential core of their ideas; exclude the nonessentials to get to the heart. Don't just make it short; make it simple yet meaningful.	The unexpectedness principle asks the writer to engage people's curiosity by opening gaps in their knowledge and then filling them.	Concreteness requires that ideas be clearly understood through the use of selective wording that evokes mental images—do not be ambiguous.	Credibility in writing helps make people believe our ideas; achieve credibility through knowing your readers' interests and needs and speaking to them.	Emotions expressed in writing help people care about our ideas; look for the right emotions to harness.	Storytelling, one philosopher wrote, characterizes all human communication. It's how we judge what's believable and what's not—and what motivates us to accept an idea because it resonates with stories we've heard and know to be true.

INSIGHTS

AP Style "Cheat Sheet"

Months/Dates

RULE OF THUMB	EXAMPLE
For dates and years, use figures. Do not use *st*, *nd*, *rd*, or *th* with dates, and use Arabic figures.	March 14 Jan. 2, 2002
Spell out the month unless it is used with a date.	In the month of December
When used with a date, abbreviate only the following months: *Jan., Feb., Aug., Sept., Oct., Nov.,* and *Dec.*	Sept. 13 May 6
If you refer to an event that occurred the day prior to when the article will appear, do not use the word *yesterday*. Instead, use the day of the week.	On Thursday, the Eagles scored two touchdowns.
If an event occurs more than 7 days before or after the current date, use the month and a figure.	On June 7
Capitalize days of the week, but do not abbreviate.	Monday Tuesday

(Continued)

(Continued)

Numerals/Money

RULE OF THUMB	EXAMPLE
Never begin a sentence with a figure, except for sentences that begin with a year.	One hundred students attended. 1999 was the last year of a tumultuous century.
Use Roman numerals to describe wars and to show sequences for people.	World War I King Henry VIII
For ordinal numbers, spell out *first* through *ninth* and use figures for *10th* and above when describing order in time or location.	Third base 10th time she tried
For cardinal numbers, spell out numbers below 10 and use figures for numbers 10 and above.	The teacher had two teaching assistants and 50 students.
When referring to money, use numerals.	$75.50 $500,000
For cents or amounts of $1 million or more, spell the words *cents, million, billion, trillion,* etc.	8 cents $5 million

Punctuation/Abbreviations/Quotes

RULE OF THUMB	EXAMPLE
Use a single space after a period.	She ran home. He ate lunch.
Commas and periods go within quotation marks.	"I'm sorry to be late," he said. She said, "I'm hungry."
Do not use commas before a conjunction in a simple series.	The rainbow was blue, purple, red, yellow and green.
Some widely known abbreviations are required in certain situations (consult the *AP Stylebook* for exceptions).	Gov. Dr.
Use quotation marks around the titles of books, songs, television shows, computer games, poems, lectures, speeches and works of art.	The parent read the book, "The Little Fur Family." They sang "This Old Man."
Do not use quotations or italics for the names of magazine and newspapers.	The New York Times Sports Illustrated

Source: Purdue Online Writing Lab. (2020). *Associated Press style.* https://owl.purdue.edu/owl/subject_specific_writing/journalism_and_journalistic_writing/ap_style.html

The Curse of Knowledge

According to Steven Pinker, a linguist at Harvard University, the "curse of knowledge" is a major writing pitfall (Sleek, 2015). It's a cognitive bias that many adults must fight to overcome. "We assume others understand the words we use, share the same skills we possess, and know the obscure facts that we perceive as common knowledge," Pinker explains. "I think the curse of knowledge is the chief contributor to opaque writing" (para. 5):

> It simply doesn't occur to the writer that readers haven't learned their jargon, don't seem to know the intermediate steps that seem to them to be too obvious to mention, and can't visualize a scene currently in the writer's mind's eye. And so the writer doesn't bother to explain the jargon, or spell out the logic, or supply the concrete details—even when writing for professional peers. (Sleeker, 2015, para. 6)

To escape this curse, Pinker suggests trying to empathize with your reader, show early drafts to a reader, and use a simple yet visually descriptive and conversational style of writing.

Beyond Strategy: Form

Good PR writing is concerned with style, grammar, and punctuation. The range of writing styles for PR is wide—using AP style (touched upon in the Insights box) for news releases, persuasive strategies for pitch letters and PSAs (public service announcements), conversational narratives for blogging, informative approaches for newsletters, analytical writing for white papers and reports, and so on. Examples in this chapter reflect some of these styles.

If you need to refresh your knowledge of correct grammar and/or punctuation, ask your instructor to direct you to resources provided by your college or university. There are also good online resources, including at the Purdue Online Writing lab (OWL) at www.owl.purdue.edu.

Generating Content: Public Relations Writing Essentials

>> **LO 6.3** Develop proficiencies in effective writing for essential PR tactics

The focus of PR writing will range widely due to the varying communication needs of a corporation, nonprofit organization, or government agency.

- Corporations usually focus on customers or consumers, financial relations, internal relations, and social responsibility (SR) or sustainability communications.

- Not-for-profit organizations typically concentrate on issue advocacy, membership development, service promotion, and fundraising support.

- Government agencies stress public information and public awareness.

At times, all these entities may have specific needs—for example, in issue or crisis management, reputation enhancement or repair, general relationship

PR writers are often tasked with creating video scripts, along with brochures, presentations, website content, and more.
iStock.com/sturti

building, media relations, and/or lobbying. The writing tactics that address these situations and goals are multiple, but the most common forms when dealing with the media are news releases, pitch letters, fact sheets, and alerts.

PR writers will often also create newsletters, brochures, or presentations and serve many online needs, including content for blogging, websites, wikis, and social media platforms. As with today's journalists, the PR writer also now has moved into writing for video, podcasts, websites, social media platforms, and more. Advanced forms of PR writing include op-eds, speeches, feature articles, briefing reports, white papers, and annual reports. These generally require more background research and careful thinking before they're written. Usually, they also require more persuasive or more polished writing, owing to their varied purposes and specific audiences.

When you consider these many communications and their importance to the credibility of an organization or individual, it should be clear why they should be written not only strategically but to respect legal, societal, and professional norms. Seeing how important content is, it is also clear why PR writers should become experts in their subject areas and support their views with fact, not fiction or exaggeration.

That First Job

A "first job" in PR for the intern or newly graduated student typically requires a lot of writing and technical skills—for example, drafting various media releases, contributing blog entries, providing website content, and even updating Wikipedia pages. The writing styles differ, depending on the tactic. Writing in AP style is required for any news item sent to newspapers, whether print or online, because that is their established writing style. Experience shows that releases that are not in AP style do not get serious consideration. When it's your job to write about your organization or client and see it through to media placement, following the "rules" of writing is essential.

Even if you start out on the local level, you should be ready to step into the shoes of the seasoned journalist because times have changed in the news business. Newsrooms were once staffed with dozens of reporters, each with a different specialty or "beat." If you handled PR for a school district, you'd send news about a new superintendent to the education reporter, alert the sports reporter about athletic awards, and announce the drama club's spring musical to the entertainment editor.

Unfortunately, at too many newspapers, those beats and the reporters who covered them are long gone. However, the newsworthy stories still need to be shared with the public. Thus, your news release must be complete, accurate, and correctly formatted from the beginning, as there is a possibility it may be run as you wrote it—with little or no changes by the editors.

SOCIAL RESPONSIBILITY IN ACTION

Nespresso in South Sudan

Nespresso has worked with South Sudanese coffee farmers to improve their welfare and revive the coffee industry harmed in the country's civil war.
Reza / Contributor / Getty Images

Nespresso works with coffee farmers in war-torn South Sudan to improve their welfare and revive the industry that was nearly decimated prior to 2011 during a period of war leading up to the country's independence from Sudan. South Sudan's eastern border is one of the very few places where the coffee bean grows in the wild. The plant has a deep connection to this area's history, but the conflict and violence saw production brought to a virtual halt. However, despite all obstacles, with the determination of some courageous South Sudanese farmers, coffee is making a comeback.

Partnering With an NGO

Nespresso's work in South Sudan is part of its "The Positive Cup" strategy. Improving farmer welfare and driving sustainability is the goal—for both coffee sourcing and consumption. Nespresso began working to revive coffee production in South Sudan with the help of the nonprofit organization

TechnoServe, which helped build partnerships with local farmers. The nonprofit provided tools, technical assistance, and training to farmers, all to enable them to grow a crop suitable for export. At first, around 300 farmers were part of the coffee cooperatives; that number grew to 730 before development was halted in 2016 due to armed conflict in the country. At that time, 1,270 households had experienced at least one of the training sessions, providing them with vital agricultural skills and knowledge.

Communicating Through Celebrity

Nespresso brand ambassador George Clooney has made many trips to South Sudan in support of efforts to end the country's conflict. Coffee is critical for the country's future, and his involvement has helped spread the story of Nespresso's efforts. Clooney's attention-getting ads for Nespresso have featured a road trip through Hollywood history, dropping him into *Easy Rider, Psycho, The Muppet Movie,* and a *Game of Thrones*-like fantasy. Nespresso communicates its efforts to reduce poverty of smallholder coffee farmers on its website and in its annual CSR report featuring a case study (use the search terms "Nespresso South Sudan case study").

Communicating Across the Battleground

With the resurgence of conflict in 2016 that inhibited TechnoServe's work on the ground, it began supporting the farmers through a weekly radio broadcast that offered seasonal advice and follow-up training to the farmers—many who had fled to safer locations. The program is produced from neighboring Uganda and is broadcast in three different languages on Spirit FM, a popular radio station in South Sudan. With an improving security situation in 2019, TechnoServe hoped to resume on-farm training in 2020 (Sainz, 2019). ●

The News Release

Traditionally, one of the most important tools used in PR is this tactic requiring precise writing: the news release. It is used to secure attention and coverage with multiple media outlets—radio, television, newspapers, magazines, and appropriate Internet sites and social media platforms. The news release has been the gold standard vehicle, recognized and respected, to get essential news and information to members of the media. No matter who or what your organization or client is—a corporation, nonprofit, celebrity, politician, government agency, university, and so on—the news release is a common mode of communicating to the media. According to the media database company Cision (2017), its 2017 State of the Media Report confirms that journalists rank news releases as one of their most valuable resources.

A valuable news release will have newsworthy content. You must determine what is of interest to the viewers, readers, or listeners of a news outlet. Gatekeepers at the news outlets are looking for news and information that fits their specific scope of interest (entertainment, sports, lifestyle, features, business, politics, etc.). Thus, you must be careful to deliver your specific news to the right media source or news worker. It should be targeted and relevant to their audience. Don't hope for it to be passed along to the right person; with pared-down staffs and tight deadlines, it's unlikely your news will be handed off. So do your research. Watch, read, and listen to the sources you think are right for your client. This is generally the case with mainstream media. Typically, trade and specialized business media are more accommodating about moving news to the right department.

Inverted Pyramid

When writing a news release, follow the **inverted pyramid** formula (see Figure 6.2), designed for ease of use by the media outlet, leading off with the most important information and continuing in diminishing levels of importance. This format helps news professionals decide if the news is relevant to their audience and gives them a clear structure for editing. The content flow is nearly identical to how a journalist would write a news story but with a significant difference: your choice of what's most important reflects your organizational goals.

For example, when announcing a change in company leadership, your lead paragraph might reference a major honor or accomplishment of the incoming CEO to frame the organizational shift as positive and noteworthy. A journalist might have the same facts yet place them later in a story. Your role as a PR writer is to respect the inverted pyramid structure that privileges the five Ws and H, but to also prioritize the information important to the organization.

FIGURE 6.2

The Inverted Pyramid

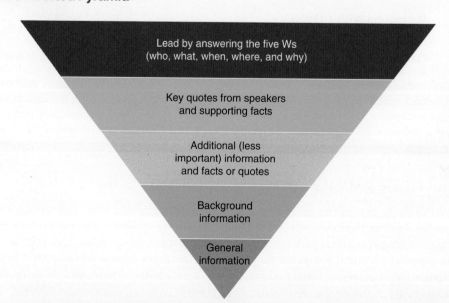

The Format, Step by Step

The main mode of distribution for a news release is via email, which dictates its structure. The email's subject line should carry the release's headline—in about 20 words or fewer. Note the wording in the subject line is critical to having it opened and read. In the body of the email (not in an attachment), the release content begins with the name of the organization (or logo), followed by the date of distribution. The third line carries the headline in boldface (and often a subhead).

The body of the release then begins. Its first paragraph (called the lead) begins with the city from which the news originates and continues with just one or two sentences on the most important elements of your "news." A second paragraph, also short, provides the *next*-most important elements. Often, the third paragraph is a quote from the CEO or a person significant to the news—and it should be highlighted by indenting or boxing. The rest of the release concisely provides all the necessary facts that help explain your earlier information or provide necessary background information. End with a brief, summary paragraph on the organization (called the boilerplate).

It's Digital! And That's Good

Since it's digital, within the release be sure to include *relevant* URL links with further information. The release ends with the PR person's full contact information so a news writer can easily identify how to get any questions answered.

Look at actual, current news releases on the websites of PR Newswire, Business Wire, and CSRwire. These releases are written by in-house or agency PR practitioners, but keep in mind they're all not necessarily good releases. However, all of them are written for the online environment, single-spaced, with the news portion ideally about 250 words long. Due to cyberspace considerations—including the spread of viruses, increase in spam, restrictive bandwidth, computer screen constraints, and so on—news releases now are delivered to the media in the body of an email (not in an attachment) or are previewed with a 100- to 200-word summary in an email with a hyperlink to the organization's online newsroom or to another server, where the full text can be read. Figure 6.3 shows an example news release from Yum! Brand's online newsroom.

Multimedia News Releases

The multimedia news release is delivered digitally and not only offers a written component but has embedded live URL links to relevant material, including social media sites, downloadable JPEGs of posters and logos, and in many cases, accompanying visual elements such as links to photos, videos, and PSAs.

Princess Cruises produced a multimedia news release to announce the christening of its new ship, *Sky Princess*, with a moving tribute to pioneering women of the U.S. space program. The release carries not only a traditionally written news release with embedded hyperlinks but separately offers images for downloading and a link to more still photos, video A-roll (footage that tells the story through an interview or news segment), and B-roll (supplemental footage to visually support A-roll). View it by using the search terms "Princess Cruises Sky Princess dedication PR Newswire." Browse more multimedia news releases by searching for "PR Newswire multimedia news release."

Writing for Social Media

Before engaging in social media, public relations practitioners must understand the contexts of the conversation and the nature of the platforms. They must also get a good sense of the community by observing who's participating in the dialogue and

FIGURE 6.3

Sample News Release

sodexo
QUALITY OF LIFE SERVICES

U.S. Department of Labor Presents Sodexo With Platinum HIRE Vets Medallion

GAITHERSBURG, Md., Nov. 26 /CSRwire/ - Sodexo, a leading food services and facilities management company, announced today that its United States Marine Corps (USMC) East Coast operations earned a Platinum Award through the HIRE Vets Medallion Award Program. This is the only federal-level veterans' employment award that recognizes a company or organization's commitment to veteran hiring, retention, and professional development. This is also a very prestigious award with the U.S. Department of Labor and firmly establishes Sodexo as a preferred employer for our veterans.

The Honoring Investments in Recruiting and Employing American Military Veterans Act of 2017 (HIRE Vets Act) required the Secretary of Labor to establish a program recognizing employer efforts to recruit, employ, and retain veterans. Employer-applicants meeting established criteria receive a HIRE Vets Medallion Award.

"As the largest federal government foodservice provider and a company that serves members from all military branches on a daily basis, Sodexo keenly understands the incredible value veterans bring to the workforce," said Kim Mullahey, Vice President, Human Resources, Sodexo Government, North America. "Not only are we proud of our work hiring veterans, we created programs and initiatives designed specifically to attract veterans to our company and retain them once on board. The HIRE Vets Medallion Award validates those efforts."

Sodexo and all other 2019 award winners were formally recognized at a ceremony on Wednesday, November 6 in Washington, D.C. Sodexo representatives accepted a framed medallion certificate, which was signed by United States Secretary of Labor, Eugene Scalia. Lori Ready-DiGiovanni, PHR, from Sodexo's East Coast USMC Operations represented Sodexo at the awards ceremony.

With more than 40 years of experience working with municipal, state, federal and military clients, Sodexo's Government segment and its nearly 3,000 employees improve the Quality of Life for the people it serves at 150 military and U.S. Federal Government locations in 26 states. Headquartered in the Washington, D.C., metropolitan area, Sodexo provides a variety of integrated food and facilities management solutions and is the nation's largest federal foodservice contractor – serving 45.6 million meals annually with a focus on wellness and nutrition.

CONTACT
Madison Brennan
+1 (301) 987-4636
Madison.Brennan@sodexo.com
Sodexo

Source: Press release issued by Yum! Brands, Inc., over Business Wire, September 7, 2016.

what is being said. You'll read more about writing for social media in Chapter 8, Social Media and Emerging Bloggers Technologies. Here are some of the writing opportunities and challenges these tools offer.

- **Blogging.** Blogs arrived before any other social media writing platform. Today, you'll find many blogs authored by organizations and individuals. As a public relations tool, blogs often offer an author's more personal point-of-view, helping to build authenticity and cultivate relationships with readers. A good blog post can have some length, connect to social channels, welcome reader comments (a policy is essential), and be tracked with analytics.

- **Microblogging.** A microblog carries shorter and more frequent posts. While you may not think of strategic social media posting on Twitter, Instagram, or Snapchat this way, essentially a well-maintained social media account allows you to "microblog." Many PR practitioners use this method to disseminate news to audiences other than just journalists: bloggers, publishers, and the public at large.

- **Search engine optimization (SEO).** You want to be found via searches, so understanding SEO and the various ways to get results (keywords, headlines, page title, meta tags, and links) figures in critically. Most importantly, keep up with the constant updates and changes that search engines release.

Fact Sheet

Often, a fact sheet is a companion release to the traditional news release, carrying only the five Ws and H in an outline format, with bold heads and short explanatory paragraphs. It may be bulleted, organized by dates, or structured in some other obviously relevant way. It allows the news worker to quickly see the entire scope of the "news" and provides a clear reference tool for specific information. As with the news release, it should end with a summary paragraph on the organization (called the "boilerplate"). It may or may not be labeled "Fact Sheet" at the top and provides a headline and dateline, similar to the news release (see Figure 6.4).

Backgrounder

A common component in a media kit is the **backgrounder**. It offers the news worker the "story behind the story." How did this issue arise? Why did this event become so notable? Where did the company come from? It offers some history, illustrations, or vignettes that a journalist might use to appeal to reader interests but also summarizes the current situation. The backgrounder allows a news worker to develop a deeper story beyond the facts in the news release. A "reference" piece must be fact-checked and the content approved by the client before use.

The One-on-One Pitch

The written pitch is a short letter, typically emailed to specific people you've identified as gatekeepers at their media outlets. Unlike the news release, it is not a mass distributed one-size-fits-all letter but is personalized to each specific media outlet and contact person. Its goal is to put a spotlight on a news item or a story angle that is distinctive and of interest to the gatekeeper's readers or audience—and to hopefully begin a one-on-one, back-and-forth process that results in coverage. Consider it an exchange relationship: You have some important news, or an attractive news "opportunity," of high interest to a community targeted by your chosen media. Often, the pitch parcels out the news with tidbits versus giving it all away in the first contact. If you get a response indicating interest, provide more details and work to secure the placement.

Depending on the news, you may be offering one media outlet an exclusive, or at least a "first" opportunity in their media category. Again, depending on the news,

FIGURE 6.4

Sample Fact Sheet

A Celebration of the Arts in Downtown Lapeer, Michigan

Art on Nepessing Street 2018

WHAT	A celebration of the arts in historic Downtown Lapeer including an exhibit of high quality original artwork. Pieces are donated by artists, displayed in downtown Lapeer businesses, and then become part of a silent auction during the street festival. There are two ways to participate:

1. Get a free vendor booth when you donate a piece of original artwork for the silent auction – your donated piece will be exhibited in a local business and automatically be entered into our Best of Show competition for a grand prize of $1,500
    OR
2. Pay for a vendor booth and join us for just the street festival. This event will also include an art walk, pub crawl, food vendors, and three days of entertainment. Proceeds benefit the Center for the Arts of Greater Lapeer and the Lapeer Main Street DDA.

WHEN
Art Walk Exhibition from **May 8th – May 30th**
Art Walk Pub Crawl: **Friday May 18th from 6 – 10 pm**
Street Festival: **June 1st – 4 pm to 10 pm**
                 June 2nd – 10 am to 6 pm
                 June 3rd – 10 am to 4 pm

WHERE
Exhibition throughout downtown Lapeer culminating with a three-day Art Festival on Nepessing St.

WHO
The Center for the Arts of Greater Lapeer, Inc. which is made up of Gallery 194 and the PIX Theatre
Lapeer Main Street DDA
Local and National Artists
Downtown businesses exhibiting art during the art walk
YOU when you come out to enjoy the festival and see the artwork!

PUBLICITY
This event is widely covered by newspapers and electronic media. Print materials: ads, press releases, posters, flyers, signs. Postings, including artists' names, bios, and images of representative artwork.

Contact:
Artist Contact:
Katie Beth Chrismer/Gallery 194
194 West Nepessing St. Downtown Lapeer, Michigan 48446
Email: info@gallery194.com   phone: (810)667-1495

Business Contact:
James Alt – DDA Executive Director
Email: james@lapeerdda.com   phone: 810-728-6598

CENTER FOR THE *Arts* OF GREATER LAPEER   *Lapeer* DOWNTOWN

Source: Art on Nepessing St.

you may choose one or more newspapers, a TV news or radio program with a large or devoted audience, perhaps a specialized magazine with a targeted audience, or even just local media outlets. All likely have online components, but pitching influential bloggers should also be considered.

The written pitch must quickly communicate its value and substance to the recipient. This is not the place for tentative phrases or polite "How are yous?" However, because this is a personal letter, use a professional yet friendly tone.

Transmitted in the body of an email, the best pitches have a succinct yet alluring subject line—use your creativity. Once opened, the email begins with a personal salutation and immediately describes the newsworthy item and suggests why she or he should cover it. Knowing your chosen media well is critical here as your goal is for the recipient to react with: "That's a perfect fit for us!"

If you are pitching an event to a TV news editor, be sure to use descriptive language to help the reader visualize the camera shots. If you're pitching a guest for a soft news program, bring the guest to life with suggestions of what he or she would show, do, say, and so on. Or your objective may be to secure an in-depth story, so you would provide enough significant and compelling facts to secure interest to know more. Make it as long as only one screen length, and do include relevant URL links. Always close your pitch with your direct contact information and a promise to follow up within a day or two—then do it.

News Features and Op-Eds

News features and op-eds are similar in that they both require a more sophisticated style of writing and far more ambitious content than news releases and pitch letters. News features are relatively timeless "soft news" that tell a good story as opposed to the time-limited "hard news" of news releases. They can be published immediately, but they can also be published weeks, even months, later. They may be one page or several pages in length, but they typically provide a behind-the-scenes perspective on the topics addressed. They're also creatively composed—for example, an insider's how-to for gardening in the city or a profile of a person who does magic tricks at your restaurant chain. They "go beyond the facts." Look for material within your organization for feature treatment. This could be an executive's experience in a hands-on CSR initiative or your company's creative solution for day care alternatives.

Op-eds, alternatively, are opinion pieces that usually concern current issues. They're more analytical and focused than a feature, providing insight rather than information. The best op-eds usually provide a provocative and insightful perspective on topics of great interest to the public.

In writing both features and op-eds, the PR writer controls the content; however, the writing has to be of journalistic quality. Thus, you would research carefully, write clearly, and structure tightly. The idea is to mimic the media's approach because your aim is to have the media use what you've written because it conforms to accepted journalistic standards. If you meet these standards, your piece will probably run pretty much as you wrote it or with modest editing.

A PR professional must be prepared to speak on TV, at news conferences, and at media presentations of new products.
iStock.com/wdstock

Features

Feature writing begins with generating ideas for stories. This requires a creative and inquisitive mind. An employer expects a PR writer to be an expert in releases and pitches, but the one who generates ideas for stories to be published or covered is a step above the rest and more likely to become a valued and respected member of the management team. These ideas should contribute, first and foremost, to the success of your client or employer. The best ones connect in some way to current events or trends and tie in your company or client. For example, a health-branded nutrition product ties in with the arrival of summer or Heart Awareness month.

Once a topic is approved by your supervisor or client, and once you've researched the topic sufficiently, good storytelling skills are required. It may be light or serious, but it should have the essential elements of narrative: characters, setting, and plot. It requires descriptive writing and often even dialogue. You should strive for engaging and entertaining language with substantive quotes and also provide photos or illustrations. Good endings to features usually deliver some surprise—an aha detail or resolution that satisfies the reader. A PR feature is typically 1,000 to 2,000 words in length and, if accepted, often uses the author's (or client's) byline.

Well-written news features are welcome by the media for several reasons, but the most important is that they need help getting content. No medium today has enough money and/or staff to write about everything interesting or important that goes on in their community or state or region. Outside contributions enhance the media's ability to write about and publish news and information that is beneficial to their readers.

Often, the media prefers topics that have a how-to or service angle—that is, features that help improve their readers' lives. You likely can't go wrong if you write about improving physical, emotional, psychological, economic, educational, and social well-being. For examples of good features, browse some of the major lifestyle or special-interest magazines online, such as *Vanity Fair* or *Men's Health*. While longer than a PR feature, you'll see some top-quality writing by experienced authors.

You may be wondering where you should send your feature, and there are many options: newspapers, both local and national, and particularly the lifestyle, arts, and business sections; general magazines or ones with local, regional, and national lifestyle titles; specialty and trade magazines, where their special-interest editorial targets a more devoted reader interested in golf, cars, fitness, travel, or specialty business topics; and in-house and internal publications—many large corporations publish magazines where your content might be appropriate.

Op-Eds

The term "op-ed" originated in 1970, when *The New York Times* published the first op-ed page. The name referred to the page's placement opposite the editorial page. Today, the term is also thought of as "opinion editorial."

The op-ed is typically submitted to a newspaper by a reader or an outside expert with a view on a timely and relevant topic. The writing may be informational, persuasive, critical, and even satiric. As a PR writer, you would research and write an op-ed to be submitted under the name of your client or CEO—or you would edit and finalize one already drafted. Your topic must be relevant to the news outlet's readers and must be well argued, defended, or articulated.

As well, an op-ed must be carefully proofed and edited before submission; it is then reviewed and, if chosen for publication, carefully edited again. Op-eds are longer than news releases—*The Washington Post* caps them at 800 words; however, other newspapers may draw the limit at 500. They are exclusively offered to one media outlet and not sent to other outlets or posted online.

Placing an op-ed in a prestigious newspaper can lend credibility to your organization, its author, and the issue. For a strategically written and placed op-ed, read Mark Zuckerberg's op-ed in *The New York Times* from October 2019 (https://www.nytimes.com/2019/10/25/opinion/sunday/mark-zuckerberg-facebook-news.html). He argued that Facebook can help the news business and announced the launch of Facebook News, dedicated solely to high-quality news, with tools to help publishers increase their subscribers.

PR professionals may be closely involved in the crafting of op-eds, either by determining the information to be conveyed, editing the piece, or writing it on behalf of a client.
Joseph Clemson / Alamy Stock Photo

Media Kit

Due to the unfortunate decrease in the size of news organizations' staffs, journalists are left to multitask for both online and print editions. However, a positive outcome is the need for more content supplied by PR practitioners. It is, in fact, easier today than in the past to place a story *if* it is well written and appropriate to the specific outlet. This new dynamic also gives the media kit (also called press kit) more importance now in providing all the elements needed for the journalist to work with. What should go into a media kit? In many cases, the following are included:

1. A hard news release giving the latest information about your client and the product, event, announcement, or campaign

2. A soft feature release with the same focus

3. A fact sheet with key bullet point details to accompany the press release (usually the five Ws and H, a quote, and selective ancillary information)

4. A background article about your client organization and background details about the product, event, or campaign itself

5. A bio sheet with biographical material about a key leader or leaders of the organization

6. A photo opportunity sheet, offering specific occasions for still photos and video shoots, to help the media better illustrate their stories or segments

7. Photographic images/digital artwork, if available and appropriate, of your "newsworthy" item

A physical media kit, with the multiple components placed in a pocketed folder, should be produced for distribution at a press conference. However, most journalists prefer a digital media kit, which should be stored and accessible in your website's online newsroom.

Speechwriting

Writing speeches is a challenging art form—crafting words and selecting visuals to inform, entertain, influence, or inspire. As with all PR writing, it begins with knowing the speech's purpose and audience.

I Love What Public Relations Is All About

Don Bates, Management Consultant and PR Writing Instructor

Photo courtesy of Don Bates

I began my career at Northeastern University in Boston. As a sophomore, I got an after-class gig in the public information office. I wrote "hometown" news releases. These announce the names of students who make the dean's list, receive scholarships, win awards, get elected to student organizations, and otherwise distinguish themselves on campus. Letting their hometown media know about their achievements is a great way to say, "Job well done." It's also a great way to make the students and their families feel proud, to attract local college-bound high schoolers, and to enhance the university's reputation.

I didn't know how to write releases, but my freshman journalism professor told me to try because I had "a knack for words." What he didn't tell me is how difficult it can be to turn that knack into workable copy. In any event, I learned because I had a mentoring boss who gave me wings and student-writer friends who taught me to edit like Ernest Hemingway. Later, I got a co-op job as a *Quincy Patriot Ledger* reporter. There, I got my first daily newspaper byline. I began to study and practice writing like my pants were on fire. I still feel the heat.

After graduation, I moved to New York City and got my first job in PR, a profession about which I knew zip. A headhunter said it paid twice what journalism paid. I was married. Money was important. I jumped at the chance. I'm thrilled I did. I love what PR is all about, warts and all. And I love the role writing plays in its delivery.

Methodically, I evolved from wordsmith to what I call "wordworker"—someone who intentionally crafts language to make favorable things happen to those for whom he or she is employed. I went from FYI (for your information) to FYA (for your action) writing. One of my writing rules is everything written for PR purposes must include a concrete call for action. If it's not obvious, make it so. Create something recipients can buy, write for, or take part in. Don't waste people's time with information-only documents. PR is doing, not diddling.

Writing isn't the only skill one needs in PR, but it's one of the essentials because just about everything practitioners do requires something written: plan, program, publication, speech, video and, sooner than we think, virtual reality and human-like robot scripts. It's also the tool we use to think through and solve employer or client problems with commonsense logic built around strategic messages that persuade audiences to purchase, invest, volunteer, donate, organize, vote, create, or otherwise engage the world.

More to the point, I like the influence, however modest, I have as a PR writer, even though I and all PR professionals handle many other responsibilities and challenges in a given week. I like the feeling I get when what I write leads to something tangible, meaningful, and helpful for others. I think everyone else in PR feels the same.

Don Bates, New York University PR and business writing instructor, is a PR management consultant for corporate communication executives and PR agencies interested in growing their businesses or merging with another agency. He is author of "The PR Writer's Code of Conduct: The Time Has Come" in O'Dwyer's, *a PR magazine.* ●

Sources:

Bates, D. (2019). Personal communication.
Bates, D. (2019, July 2). PR writer's code of conduct, the time has come. *O'Dwyer's: The inside news of PR and marketing communications.* https://www.odwyerpr.com/story/public/12742/2019-07-02/pr-writers-code-conduct-time-has-come.html

Let's assume you are drafting a speech for the company president to give to employees. This fact makes your audience research easier but can also present challenges in writing, depending on the purpose (is the company downsizing, merging, relocating, shifting strategic direction, etc.).

Most speeches follow the same formatting guidelines: double- or triple-spaced using large typeface with **serifs** (short lines attached to ends of letter strokes) for ease of reading, indented paragraphs, numbered loose pages, and annotated in the margins (in the text) or with cues for the speaker (such as "pause for emphasis").

Regarding the structure of the speech, the old golden rule of speechwriting applies: First, tell your audience what you're going to tell them; next, tell them; and last, tell them what you've told them. The language of a speech is unlike other PR writing; it can be elegant, poetic, emotional or persuasive, rational, and plain-spoken. It often incorporates story elements, visual imagery, and a sense of **immediacy**. The purpose and topic of the speech will guide what language is appropriate. A reasonable time length for a speech is 20 minutes or less; anything longer and there's serious risk of losing, if not annoying, the audience. For speech ideas, visit www.ispeeches.com.

Writing for Organizational Media and Digital Environments

More readers and viewers are getting their news online and via social media. This diverse and fluid field of media consumption represents challenges, opportunities, and dangers for the PR profession. Writers must shift from a more traditional style, structuring content to the social and digital environment.

These environments provide opportunities to deliver content directly to specific publics—employees, clients, special interest bloggers, and so on—without concern for geographical boundaries or the need to place a news item with traditional media for it to be disseminated. However, there are drawbacks; most critically, the standards required in the traditional press release can loosen without a gatekeeper to check facts and format. What goes out on the Web and on social media may not have the rigor, clarity, and veracity of carefully vetted information. Yet, with the evolution of digital and social media, the PR writer benefits from access to forms of distribution that allow for reaching more people, more frequently, and at less cost. It's essential that professional standards are maintained in this cornucopia of media to ensure your organization is well represented: clear, accurate, and concise writing that communicates credibility. Anyone who follows the news can recall more than one incident when an ill-conceived Tweet or Facebook post has damaged the reputation of the writer and reflected badly on his or her organization.

One of the reasons the PR profession is growing is that while newspapers have suffered from loss of readers and advertising revenue due to free online content, PR's utility has expanded with the ability to directly reach specific publics expeditiously and at less cost. You'll explore writing for social media, digital environments, and emerging technologies in Chapter 8.

Innovative Storytelling in CSR Reports

It's a PR writer's job to help produce an annual sustainability or SR report for companies who choose to issue one. Such reporting is of great interest to investors of publicly held companies as well as to the media, consumers in general, and partners

iStock.com/cnythzl

in a company's supply chain. These reports can be dense, but there are creative ways to go beyond a traditionally written report. Interactive graphics, data visualizations, and short videos and documentaries offer an appealing way to present topics.

Digital innovations in CSR reporting include those of Virgin Media, one of the first businesses to stop producing hard-copy versions of its CSR reports in 2010. It now invites people to join a conversation through interactive scrolling PDFs, GIFs, and a 360° sustainability video. It also engages employees on its goals with a quiz to help them find out what role they can play in helping the company meet its goals (Buchanan, 2018).

A study of 200 CSR videos created and published between 2000 and 2015 found critical insights on how they communicate competence and concern (Bortree, 2016). Competence is communicated through quality products that meet society's needs and concern through socially and environmentally responsible behaviors.

The study found that competence is communicated in CSR videos most often through the presence of numbers and statistics, and concern is communicated most often in the videos through the presence of an employee or employees. Videos that focused on social responsibility addressed "community" more often than did the environmental videos. Take a look at some recent videos by searching in YouTube for "CSR reports," adding the current year.

Scenario Outcome

At the beginning of this chapter, we provided a real-life scenario of Taylor Guitars' need to communicate an industry-changing decision with its various stakeholders. To review, due to the diminishing supply of black ebony wood in the world's rain forests, Bob Taylor made a decision to cease using only black ebony in premium acoustic guitars. As a supplier of guitars to celebrity musicians and guitar retailers, and as a supplier of black ebony to other guitar manufacturers, Taylor was faced with the major challenge of convincing everyone that ebony with variegated color is just as "good" as black ebony and to accept it in place of the rare black ebony. As the PR manager for Taylor Guitars, we asked you how you would advise him to achieve this goal—what messaging strategies would be most effective?

To shift the mindset, Taylor Guitars used the industry stature and influence of its CEO to launch a concerted PR campaign aimed at multiple publics. Bob Taylor began a series of presentations and meetings with other guitar makers who were end users of Crelicam ebony. To these manufacturers, he explained the ebony trade in Cameroon and the threat to the future of the wood. He then set out the new direction the company was taking to provide ethical, legally sourced, and sustainable ebony. He explained Crelicam's intent to use variegated wood, and he shared what he had learned from his cutters. Almost all the manufacturers Taylor spoke with agreed to use the variegated wood. This acceptance of the different coloration by virtually the entire industry spurred a PR effort to encourage consumer acceptance, too.

Taylor Guitars's PR campaign was spearheaded by a company-produced 13-minute online video, featuring Bob Taylor: *The Truth of the Forest: The State of Ebony in the World*. Watch it on YouTube and note how the spoken words reflect the components of a well-written speech. In the video, Taylor relates the story of the acquisition of Crelicam, explains the threat to the world's supply of ebony, and informs guitar buyers of the inclusion of variegated ebony in new products from Taylor Guitars. Using a guitar with a fretboard made of variegated ebony as an example, Taylor makes the case for the change as being environmentally and ethically sound without compromising the guitar's tone or quality.

The PR efforts also included a series of articles on the subject. The acquisition of Crelicam, the obstacles that Taylor faced, the ethical and social issues, and the case for using variegated ebony were featured in Taylor Guitars' magazine for owners, *Wood&Steel*. In addition, the PR campaign resulted in featured media coverage on the firm's sustainability efforts in Cameroon, which appeared in lifestyle and industry magazines, websites, and major metro U.S. newspapers.

The unique feature of this PR thrust was that it had a very specific audience to address with a very specific message. The real targets of all the efforts were the guitar-buying public and guitar manufacturers and distributors. Bob Taylor's personal presentations, the online video, and the in-depth articles all reached these publics with a consistent message that changed the perception of what is and what is not acceptable ebony. It is an evolving initiative. Visit www.taylorguitars.com/ebonyproject to learn about the company's latest efforts on ebony sourcing in Cameroon and how they're communicated. One offshoot is using scrap ebony for household products: In 2018, Taylor quietly launched a premium line of socially responsible ebony kitchenware, named Stella Falone for two women working at the Crelicam mill. It can be explored at www.stellafalone.com.

WRAP UP

In this chapter, you honed your PR skills by analyzing how a company should communicate to multiple stakeholders about a significant change in its product. You solved this problem for Taylor Guitars through a journey that began with a look at the communication process.

As PR is a profession guided by strategy, you learned that when writing, too, you must ask and answer essential questions. Both the quality and structure of PR writing are keys to engaging your reader; while diverse tactics require differing structures, they always must be exceptionally well written. With this chapter, you now have a good understanding of the widely used writing tactics in PR, and you've been challenged to read, review, and practice them.

KEY TERMS

Backgrounder 135
Boilerplate 133
Channel 125
Cybernetics 125
Encoded 125
Immediacy 141

Inverted Pyramid 132
Lead 133
Noise 125
Op-Eds 137
Serifs 141

THINK ABOUT IT

Brainstorm how you would pitch a client's new product to a news writer or media outlet.

Your client manufactures PeakStrength products aimed at the active athlete and is rolling out a new product, Barknola, an organic energy bar for dogs. Research shows that athletes in the more challenging sports tend to have canine companions who accompany them into remote areas. Feeding these dogs is a problem because it requires "packing in" pouches of food, resulting in extra weight and less backpack storage space for the athlete's own needs. A single Barknola bar is the size of a normal granola bar and provides the average dog with all the nutrition needed for 8 hours. In product pretrials, cases of Barknola have been donated to dog owners at climbing competitions and bike races, 12 police departments with K-9 units, and a Wounded Warriors program that provides companion dogs to veterans suffering from PTSD. Determine a news angle or opportunity and then choose a specific (and real) person at a media outlet to email your pitch to. Most critical is what the wording in your subject line will be.

WRITE LIKE A PRO

As the PR director for Taylor Guitars, you are in charge of producing its first sustainability report video.

Considering what you now know about both Taylor Guitars' environmental and social engagement, draft a storyboard for a 60- to 90-second video. Use PowerPoint to create 9 to 12 slides that suggest the visual sequencing and the verbal narrative. Also propose one interview in your video.

Defend your proposed video in a memo to Bob Taylor:

- Specify the target audience(s).
- Identify some of the SUCCESs principles used: simple, unexpected, concrete, credible, emotional, and/or storytelling (covered earlier in this chapter).
- Explain your interview choice.

SOCIAL RESPONSIBILITY CASE STUDY

Whirlpool: Clean Clothes for School From Care Counts™

Situation

Whirlpool is the world's leading home appliance company. For more than 20 years, it has also been one of Habitat for Humanity's largest corporate partners. It donates a refrigerator and range to every home the charity builds in North America.

In 2015, a simple request from an elementary school principal in Fairfield, California, provided a new giving opportunity. The request? Donate a washer and dryer to the school. Why? Because when students didn't have clean clothes, they stopped coming to school. They chose to stay home to avoid bullying and mockery.

Research and Strategy

A Whirlpool survey conducted together with its PR firm, Ketchum, learned that one fifth of American students have problems accessing clean clothes. In response, Care Counts by Whirlpool was born. According to Whirlpool, it worked with "school teachers, administrators, and Dr. Richard Rende, PhD, internationally recognized developmental psychologist and researcher" (Whirlpool Corporation, 2016, para. 9) to design this pilot laundry program, exploring the relationship between accessible clean clothes and the rates of attendance.

The program asked each school to identify the students who needed clean clothes and then to anonymously track how often they used the laundry service, their attendance, and their grades over the course of the school year. Other behavioral changes were also observed. Their primary teachers completed a survey asking qualitative questions exploring their thoughts on how access to clean clothes improved a student's ability to participate in class, enjoy school, and other aspects of the school experience.

Execution

In the 2015–2016 school year, the first program placed washers and dryers in 17 schools in St. Louis, Missouri, and Fairfield, California. Program leaders used tools to track data, allowing students to manage their own schedules for doing laundry. That year, 2,000 loads of clothes were cleaned. After looking at the data comparing student attendance and washed loads, more than 90% of tracked students had better attendance, increasing their days in school by 6.1 days over the previous year. The most at-risk students benefited even more, averaging nearly two more weeks in school than the prior year.

"When we learned that a child's education could be at risk because they do not have access to clean clothes, we were determined to help," said Chelsey Lindstrom, brand manager. "It's incredible to see how the simple act of laundry can have such a profound impact on students' lives, and we are excited to bring this resource to even more schools across the country" (Whirlpool Corporation, 2016, para. 5).

Evaluation

In the pilot program, students enjoyed improvements beyond just attendance rates. Whirlpool reported that teachers surveyed saw the results listed in Table 6.2 (2016, para. 4).

TABLE 6.2

Pilot Program Results

- 95% of participants showed increased motivation in class.
- 95% of participants were more likely to participate in extracurricular activities.
- 95% of participants interacted with peers and enjoyed school more.
- 89% of participants got good grades.

"Every single day of school matters. When students miss school, they are missing an opportunity to learn," said Martha Lacy, principal, David Weir K–8 Academy. "Absenteeism strongly impacts a student's academic performance. In fact, students with excessive absence rates are more likely to fall behind, graduate late and even drop out" (Whirlpool Corporation, 2016, para. 3).

Due to its first year of success, the Care Counts program continued providing students access to clean clothes by adding more school districts. A documentary-style video, media materials, microsite, school officials, and brand spokespeople all told the story of the program. That first year earned more than 600 stories in outlets including *ABC World News Tonight*, Today.com, *Business Insider*, *U.S. News & World Report*, and NPR.

Update

By its fifth year (2019), Care Counts was supporting needy 38,000 students in 18 cities and 82 schools throughout the United States (Whirlpool Corporation, 2019). The program also experienced notable increases in attendance by elementary and middle school students at risk for chronic and problematic levels of absenteeism. In the 2018–2019 school year, high-risk elementary school students who participated in the program attended 11 more days per year, and more than two thirds increased their grades. To increase the number of students it serves, Care Counts began inviting qualified schools to apply for a washer and dryer. The program has an ambitious communications effort, as you'll discover in the following Engage section.

Engage

- Whirlpool issued a press release timed for Attendance Awareness Month. Find it at https://www.multivu.com/players/English/8589951-whirlpool-care-counts-school-laundry-program/. Watch the short videos, then scroll down to "Connect With Whirlpool" and open the "Fact Sheet" link.

- Explore the program's main site at www.whirlpool.com/care-counts.

Discuss

- Whirlpool's Care Counts program appears to have a great impact on the students who benefit from having access to clean clothes. Did you know this issue existed? If so, do you think there's enough attention brought to the subject? What tactics would you employ to spread the word about Care Counts?

- Whirlpool partners with Teach for America to help bring the Care Counts program to other areas of the country. Suggest corporate or product manufacturers they might consider as other partners and explain why.

7

Media Relations in a Digital World

Learning Objectives

7.1   Understand the current state of the news media

7.2   Explore communications theory and its application to media relations

7.3   Measure the impact of news coverage toward achieving business goals

7.4   Identify global trends and practices in media relations

Scenario
Building Awareness for Aflac's CSR and Philanthropy

Despite its well-deserved profile as one of *Fortune's* Best Places to Work and Most Admired Companies (2017), Aflac's research reflected that their long-standing CSR and philanthropy efforts were not well known or appreciated by its stakeholders. Aflac is a Fortune 500 company, providing supplemental insurance protection to more than 50 million people in Japan and the United States.

360b / Alamy Stock Photo

This perception gap was concerning for the communications team and senior management since Aflac had raised over $120 million for childhood cancer treatment and been recognized by *Ethisphere* magazine's list of the Most Ethical Companies for 11 straight years.

Based on their research on the reputation gap, the team set about to develop a communications initiative for 2018 with the following objectives:

- Raise awareness of Aflac's philanthropy and commitment to ethical leadership.
- Elevate national discussion about funding for childhood cancer research and support.
- Increase Aflac's reputation rankings—as measured by the Reputation Institute.
- Increase the visibility of Aflac's executives as thought leaders on CSR.

The communications team decided to launch a new CSR project to offer emotional support to children diagnosed with cancer, stimulate fundraising for cancer research, and enhance Aflac's corporate reputation.

To start, the team reviewed award-winning CSR Annual reports to identify best practices and provide direction for revising their own report. The research revealed four categories that were most relevant to their key stakeholders, including consumers, investors, and employees. The four "pillars" identified were ethics, workplace, philanthropy, and environmental sustainability. These would become the outline for the new CSR campaign and report.

As you read through this chapter focused on media relations, consider the challenge and opportunity before the Aflac corporate communications team. Your company has a well-defined program for sustainability and philanthropy, yet it is not evident to the marketplace or your key stakeholders. Management has to be questioning the time, effort, and resources committed to these activities and seeking answers.

How would you respond? Here are some questions to consider and discuss as you develop your response:

How would you respond to this challenge?

What are the key elements of your awareness program?

What role should media relations play in raising awareness of your CSR and philanthropy?

How would you measure and report the results to management and other stakeholders?

(Continued)

(Continued)

This real-life scenario is one that many communications professionals face. How do you get credit for the good works of your company or client to make sure this translates into a more complete corporate reputation?

At the end of the chapter, you will learn how the company responded and the outstanding results they achieved. ●

For most non-PR practitioners, *media relations* and *PR* are viewed as synonymous. This has been the case since the early days of the profession, when PR pros were often referred to as "publicity agents" or "flacks." As discussed in Chapter 2, these publicists worked mostly on behalf of major companies and politicians and later on for celebrities. But there is a difference between generating publicity and engaging in more strategic public relations (SPR) activities. In 1942, Baus described publicity as "the dissemination of information for a motive." But he also noted that "all publicity is public relations, but not all public relations is publicity."

This chapter will lay the foundation to prepare you to generate meaningful publicity as part of a PR (public relations) or SR (social responsibility) campaign. It begins with an overview of the current state of the news media, specifically the economic and demographic trends impacting both journalists and news organizations.

Then, the basics of media relations will be reviewed, along with the communications theories that inform it. Finally, we will look at how media relations practices differ around the world and explore how U.S.-based PR professionals should interact with the global media to accomplish their global communications goals.

The State of the News Media Today

>> LO 7.1   Understand the current state of the news media

One of the first, and most basic, rules of PR is to *know your audience*. This entails reviewing research data, talking with the target audience to learn what motivates them, and determining the key messages you want to communicate. The practice of modern media relations is no different. To work effectively with reporters, bloggers, or other influential people (i.e., influencers), you need to understand the state of the news media now and the trends that are impacting the industry for the future.

The rationale is simple. As Lori Beecher, executive vice president and director of media and content strategy for Ketchum, explained:

> The ability to be successful in your media relations efforts is directly proportionate to an understanding of the reporters, editors, and producers and the industry in which they work. You will be much more successful if your outreach efforts are consistent with their needs and reflect the realities of today's news media. (L. Beecher, personal communication, 2016)

Research on the Media

There is no question that the media industry—which includes newspapers, magazines, television, and radio as well as the online media—is vastly different from the media industry just a generation ago (Barthel, 2019).

In most of the major U.S. metropolitan areas today, there are fewer daily papers, more cable television, and three or fewer television network affiliates, along with a variety of radio formats, including talk, all news, music, sports, and entertainment. In addition, there are new entrants. These range from online news outlets, podcasts, broadcasts on demand, and news aggregator sites that collect stories and videos and deliver them directly to your Facebook or Twitter page based on your preferences and search history.

To get a sense of how much things have changed and what is ahead for the U.S. media, let's review some recent research from the Pew Research Center (Smith & Anderson, 2018). However, do not assume that these changes in the news media mean that the practice of media relations is less important. The targets may have increased or shifted, but news coverage and media visibility—in all its forms—is what management and clients still want and expect from PR pros. In fact, a recent study of the PR profession estimates that approximately 80% of PR practitioners practice media relations, in one form or another, during their typical workweek (Darnowski et al., 2013, cited in Supa, 2014).

In its annual *State of the News Media Report* for 2018, Pew (Barthel, 2019) paints a challenging picture for the media industry in the United States and globally. For example, Pew reports that the newspaper sector "had perhaps its worst year since the 2008 recession." Some key indicators support this conclusion (Barthel, 2019):

- Average weekday circulation (print and digital combined) fell 8% in 2018, reflecting a steady decline since 2010. This is now at its lowest level since 1940, when the data began to be collected.

  ○ Cable news viewership: It increased 8%, due in part to the ongoing political drama in Washington, DC.

  ○ Network TV viewership: The morning news show audience declined by 4%, and the evening news ratings were flat with the prior year.

  ○ Local TV news viewership: It declined in both segments—morning by 10% and evening by 14%.

- Total advertising revenue (for publicly traded media companies) declined 8%.

- Readership of daily newspapers is on the decline overall (digital and print) as more and more people get their news delivered online or from other sources.

- Network TV grew ad revenues 6% for evening programming and 14% for the morning shows.

- Cable television increased ad and subscriber revenue by 10%.

- Local TV (network affiliates and independents) showed increases in advertising revenue as well—particularly in areas where political advertising is prevalent, reflecting the 2018 midterm elections.

However, there are troubling trends for the television industry as well due to decline in viewing trends and so-called "cord cutting." Cord cutting is a phenomenon in which people discontinue (or "cut") their cable subscriptions and rely on Internet-based providers or "streamers" (e.g., Hulu, Netflix, Amazon, etc.) for their entertainment and news content. This trend, by most accounts, is expected to accelerate as costs of basic cable increase and patterns of viewing change. *Variety* magazine reported that in 2018, 32.8 million U.S. adults (compared to 24.9 million in 2017) have "cut the cord" (Spangler, 2018).

Among minority and special interest publications, the situation is in flux as well. Pew reports that Hispanic weekly papers saw some circulation growth in 2018, but the major Hispanic dailies (such as *La Opinión*) posted declines in subscriptions and advertising, and the largest Hispanic-focused television networks (e.g., Univision and Telemundo) had mixed results. Univision's average news audience declined (12% in the evening, 14% for late night, and 11% for the morning news time slots). Telemundo, however, bucked this trend somewhat in 2018, posting increases of 7% in the evening and holding its audience numbers steady for late-night news programming.

The African American newspapers that publish audited circulation figures (there are 12) had mixed results in 2018, according to Pew. Three papers remained flat, two posted increases in circulation, and seven suffered a decline in circulation. As we learned in the profile of Ofield Dukes in Chapter 2, many of today's African American journalists got their start in the Black media, so this trend is concerning for the future. Diversity and inclusion in hiring and promotion by the mainstream media will be critical to creating a representative media industry in the future.

The rise of the digital news outlets—so-called "digital native" sites—has leveled off since the last report from Pew in 2016. These sites have changed the reading and viewing habits of Americans—especially millennials (defined as those currently between the ages of 18 and 34 at the time of the research). The Pew data indicates an increase in the total audience and in the time spent on these sites—often at the expense of time on the sites of traditional media organizations or reading the actual, physical publications.

Pew reports that 27% of those under 30 years old are more likely to name social media as a main source of news than a traditional outlet. And, Pew adds, this is increasingly common among *all* adults in the United States, noting that 67% of all U.S. adults now get their news on social media sites (Smith & Anderson, 2018).

To be clear though, most of these sites do not generate their own news stories. So working with reporters to obtain coverage in target publications is still critical since the impact and reach of the article is extended by these services when they rerun the article.

Another key consideration for media relations professionals is the trend in U.S. population demographics that is shifting toward millennials (the generation born between 1980 and 1990) and away from the baby boomer generation (born between 1946 and 1964, after World War II). This is significant because this latter group has driven the media's business model and strategy for the past 20 to 30 years.

With this industry data and demographic trends as a backdrop, let's examine the implications for the practice of media relations and suggest how PR professionals can and should respond.

Current Practice of Media Relations

Dustin Supa (2014) of Boston University suggests that media relations continue to be an integral part of PR and SR. He offers a definition of media relations that speaks to both its "tactical" and "strategic" importance: "Media relations is the systematic, planned, purposeful and mutually beneficial relationship between a public relations practitioner and a mass media journalist" (p. 4).

In the current environment, Supa suggests, most PR practitioners would agree that "media relations is an integral part of the strategic plan for any public relations campaign" (Supa & Koch, 2009, cited in Supa, 2014, p. 4). Supa suggests five guiding principles to understand media relations:

1. "Media relations should be viewed as a strategic function" of PR, not just tactical.

2. "Every organization has different media relations goals"; some want or need coverage, some don't, and some only want it in specific publications versus the national media.

3. "In media relations, the relationship is key"—for example, you need to understand the needs and expectations of both parties (reporters and PR professionals).

4. Media relations is "not a means to an end"—journalists are a stakeholder group, not a vehicle to reach stakeholders.

5. The "tools used in media relations do not define media relations"—media relations are defined by the use of the tools to achieve goals, not the tools themselves.

Generating media coverage is what management expects PR people to do and what PR people spend a great deal of their professional lives doing. Yet it is important to note that as a PR professional you have the responsibility to seek fair and balanced news coverage. The reporters and producers have a responsibility as well—to provide reliable information that informs, entertains, or improves the lives of their audience in a meaningful fashion. No one wins in the long run if a news story is fabricated, incomplete, misleading, or "fake."

The issue of **fake news** became a major talking point during the 2016 U.S. presidential elections, surfaced again in national elections across Europe in the spring of 2017, and remains an issue still today. Paul Chadwick (2017), writing in a May 2017 column in the *Guardian* newspaper (U.S. edition), suggests that "fake news is not new," (para. 7), but it is a more serious threat now than ever before to journalism and thus to the practice of media relations. He suggests this definition of fake news: "Fake news means fiction deliberately fabricated and presented as nonfiction with the intent to mislead recipients into treating fiction as fact or into doubting verifiable fact" (para. 15). PR professionals must reject fake news and expose it when it occurs if the profession is to be regarded as trustworthy and ethical. For more discussion on ethics and PR, see Chapter 3.

To examine how the process of media relations works, the next section of this chapter focuses on the role of the PR professional and how to get the job done without misleading the public, journalists, or the media. It all comes back to understanding your target audience, learning what motivates them, and being ethical in all your dealings with the news media.

Monitor the Media for Best Results

As a PR professional, you have many roles to play in contributing to a successful media relations effort. To begin with, you must be a constant observer of the news media—who is

The issue of fake news became a major one during the 2016 U.S. presidential campaign and is still prevalent in the 2020 campaign, as evidenced by 143,000,000 results in an online search of "fake news in 2020 campaign."
Joris Van Ostaeyen / Alamy Stock Photo

covering what topics, and what types of stories are of interest to which publications? You also need to know the answers to these questions: How is the media covering your industry, competitors, and company or client? Which reporters are interested in topics that connect with the story you want them to tell?

Once you have determined the answers to these and other preliminary questions, you can begin to develop your approach, or **pitch**, as it is referred to in the PR industry. The pitch, to be effective, should include a short summary of the story, a connection or relevance to the publication and its readers, and be accurate, intriguing, and complete.

Given the demands on the media today, you must summarize the story idea succinctly because they will not read a long, drawn-out note. Think "elevator pitch" (e.g., short and to the point), and keep it simple and straightforward so they can tell right away if it is of interest. If they want to know more, give them the tools to do that—for example, links to studies, new research, or access to experts. If they don't, accept that outcome and move on.

PR people and the media share a "tenuous working relationship at best" and a "distrustful, non-communicative relationship at worst" (Supa, 2014). This potential disconnect is at the center of strategic media relations: Two parties with different goals and agendas must find common ground where a fair, accurate, and balanced news story can result.

Paul Farhi, longtime media reporter for *The Washington Post*, suggests that PR professionals can be "helpful" to a reporter (and help themselves in the process) by identifying stories of interest and suggesting them to the right reporter, with some caveats.

> PR people can be vital to reporters . . . *if* they can supply timely and accurate information, *if* they are responsive to inquiries on deadline, *if* they are knowledgeable and trustworthy, and *if* they can be a conduit for reporters to the newsmaker. (P. Farhi, personal communication, 2017)

A key element in a successful media pitch is to determine the right reporter to approach. This requires that you do the research to find reporters interested in the topic and leave others out of the pitch altogether. Pitching multiple reporters when only a handful will be interested is counterproductive and annoying to the reporter or producer. This analysis is best accomplished by using a commercial database—such as Meltwater, Cision, or BurrellesLuce—to search the topic, media, and geographic area you are interested in. Some services can also scan social media platforms, locate conversations about your client/company or competition, and assess them in terms of the tone and frequency.

Begin by doing your research, then develop a tightly focused and current media list, and finally craft a simple but persuasive pitch to get targeted reporters interested. It helps if you have worked with them or interacted before you make the "pitch" so you are not a total stranger seeking news coverage. This familiarization process can entail sending them new research, providing names of experts for background information, or commenting constructively on stories they have written—whether they involve your company/client or not. Remember, it is called "media relations" for a reason. It is a *relationship*, and both parties have needs and expectations to be fulfilled.

Hyundai Motors Introduces Drivers to the Future

Hyundai's launch of the Tucson Fuel Cell, the first mass-produced fuel cell car, was preceded by a yearlong media campaign to prepare the marketplace for the vehicle's arrival.
Ethan Miller / Staff / Getty Images

Hyundai Motor Company was ready to bring its new Tucson fuel cell vehicle to market. This was to be the first mass-produced fuel cell vehicle that consumers could purchase and drive right away. Working with their agency (Ketchum), Hyundai launched a yearlong media relations-based campaign to educate both the industry and consumers on the benefits of fuel cells and introduce drivers to a different take on the future of the automobile.

Launching the First Fuel Cell Car

In supporting the launch of the Tucson fuel cell vehicle, the first of its kind, the agency recognized that changing the minds of a highly skeptical industry and consumer base would not be easy. The task was made more difficult by the opposition to fuel cell-powered vehicles from automotive industry leaders like Elon Musk (Tesla) and Bob Lutz (GM).

Focus on Building Consumer Awareness, Then Demand

The company mounted a yearlong campaign that relied on media relations and events/activities

focused on customers, not industry leaders. Through creating a groundswell of publicity and reaching the public directly, the communications team was able to help achieve its goals and help make sure that the entire allotment of these vehicles was leased or sold *before* they reached the dealer.

Preparation Is Key

This case demonstrates that when seeking to publicize an event, product, person, or activity, you need to put yourself in the reporters' and public's shoes. Your questions should include these:

- Is the news I want to share important to the readers, viewers, or listeners of the media outlet?

- Is my news current and actual news? Are there elements or details to the story that bring new insights or benefits to the readers or viewers?

- Is the reporter or producer I am contacting interested in the topic? Is he or she covering the industry and knowledgeable about it?

- Is my information accurate, timely, and truthful?

Set for Success

With these questions answered, you are prepared to pursue a story opportunity. You should also be familiar with the various reporters' points of view and be prepared that they may seek comments and experts to balance the story. In this case, the agency and client had done the work, knew who covered automotive news, and had a sense of what competitors might say when contacted. As a result, the launch goals were met, and the coverage was balanced, not critical. ●

Source: Hyundai Motor America with Ketchum, 2015.

Media Relations—It's All About Building Relationships

Michelle Leff Mermelstein, APR, Wireless Device Public Relations—Sprint

Photo courtesy of Michelle Leff Mermelstein

Initially, I was laser-focused on a career as a journalist. I was fortunate enough to have an inspiring teacher in high school who helped me develop a love of writing and covering the news of the day.

After studying journalism and political science in college, I landed a job as an associate editor for a magazine covering insurance, finance, and tax law. I often had to reach out to financial services companies to get a comment on legislation that impacted their industry. Some of the media relations professionals I reached out to were incredibly helpful and buttoned-up. As a reward for getting me the information or executive quote I needed to complete my story, I would go back to them again and again. But the PR people who weren't particularly helpful, or only focused on what they needed from me, didn't get a lot of coverage in the magazine. It was simple—the relationship needed to work for both of us.

It wasn't long before I "switched sides of the desk." As a new PR professional, I remembered the talented PR pros who helped me get my story done when I was a journalist and, in turn, got featured in my coverage.

Good media relations is not complicated—it is all about walking a careful line between serving the media and your employer or client. The best campaigns begin with the premise that the news media and PR staff work on parallel tracks and come together when it is mutually beneficial. PR practitioners should strive to be a resource to the media—this is true with traditional, broadcast, and online reporters.

In my experience, there are three things that define the best media relations practitioners:

1. They are strong writers and don't view writing as a chore. They can translate a complicated issue into concise messages so reporters can make it relevant to their readers.

2. They are smart and know their subject matter as well—or better—than their management or spokespeople. One of the greatest compliments I have ever received was when a senior executive told me I knew the product we were launching better than he did. Also, I have never had a reporter give me grief if I tell them I need to get more details before I respond to a question.

3. They respect all reporters and treat them as peers. *The Wall Street Journal* has an audience that can be just as important as a tech blog or a fashion magazine.

I am extremely grateful to have a career focused on media relations. I see media relations as a puzzle: With each project, my challenge is to put the right pieces together so that they resonate with the reporter and position my company in the best light. This specialty of public relations is right for you if you are passionate about being a storyteller. You will be amazed at how rewarding it can be to build positive, professional relationships with the media. You may even create some lifelong friendships along the way. ●

Source: M. Leff Mermelstein, personal communication, 2019.

Media Relations in Political Communications

The practice of media relations in the political arena has many similarities to so-called "traditional media relations" for a company or nonprofit. In short, the tactics may be similar, but the goals are different. In a political environment, your goal is to generate support, raise money, and ultimately, secure votes for your candidate or cause. In a business situation, you are more likely promoting a new product or service or seeking recognition of your company's charitable and sustainability efforts.

Traditionally, most candidates for elected office seek coverage in the mainstream and social media and then "echo" it in handouts, Facebook posts, or other materials. Others will generate their own content—position papers, statements, photo opportunities, and so on—and post them on the campaign site, supplementing or even bypassing the traditional media.

There can be no doubt that social media—in all of its forms—will continue to be a major factor in national and local elections (including the 2020 presidential campaigns). Candidates appreciate and understand the direct access that social media provides to voters, and we will have to be on our guard against abuse of this vehicle as we consider whom to vote for and support. A more detailed discussion of political communications appears in Chapter 15.

Media Relations in Crisis Situations

No discussion of the topic of media relations would be complete without a mention of the critical role the function can play in a crisis. While there is a full discussion of crisis and issues management in Chapter 12, it is worth a brief note here. Most PR professionals agree that how well you manage media relations in a crisis is usually a major factor in the duration of the event and the damage done. Sometimes, the impact of the media coverage on a company's reputation can be as bad as the crisis itself, especially if it is not well handled.

By definition, a crisis—whether it is a natural disaster, a product recall, questionable behavior by management, or any other situation that impacts the company—is a major news story and will generate a lot of inquiries and coverage, but not all accurate or flattering.

Crisis expert and author James Lukaszewski suggests, "Crisis situations are sloppy, random affairs that slowly reveal the

While the goals of public relations in the political arena may be different from the corporate world, the tactics are similar.
Bloomberg / Contributor / Getty Images
Bloomberg / Contributor / Getty Images

PR professionals must be prepared to respond in a crisis, such as the revelation that Volkswagen had programmed their diesel cars to cheat on emissions tests, which prompted congressional hearings.
Bloomberg / Contributor / Getty Images

extent of the damage and the actual response requirements." He adds, "Those who actually have survived a crisis understand that they tend to happen explosively, but resolving them happens incrementally" (J. Lukaszewski, personal communication, 2017).

In other words, crises are dynamic and changeable, and the media is both an audience/stakeholder and a vehicle to address the public. And, fair or not, the rules and expectations are different for the company involved than everybody else, he suggests. Any crisis, or natural disaster, will generate media inquiries and coverage, as noted by Lukaszewski. How well they are handled, and the tone of the response, is a critical consideration in managing and surviving the situation with your personal and corporate reputation intact. Lukaszewski adds, "In crisis, breaking news is too often 'broken news.'"

According to Tim Coombs, PhD, author and professor, who researches and writes extensively about crisis management, the PR team plays an important role in this process.

> Public relations can play a critical role in preparing spokespersons for handling questions from the news media. The media relations element of public relations is a highly valued skill in crisis management. The public relations personnel provide training and support because in most cases they are not the spokesperson during the crisis. (Coombs, 2014a)

Bloggers

There are a variety of media outlets—national, local, trade, and online—a PR practitioner should consider to accomplish media relations goals. Historically, media relations efforts have been directed primarily at the major business and local papers and broadcast outlets that reach the majority of your target audience. This is logical, but remember that everyone—including your competitors—is also seeking coverage from the same reporters and outlets. In addition, you cannot overlook the digital media—for example, bloggers, influencers, and online media—as they can extend your story and reach more of your target audience.

Sony Electronics' imaging division, which includes Sony's top-of-the-line Alpha cameras and other optical products like the lenses used in Apple's latest iPhones, has found including bloggers and influencers in its product launches very effective. According to Matt Parnell, director of marketing at Sony Electronics,

> As the media landscape continues to change, we have to be flexible in our media outreach efforts to accomplish our goals. We've made it a priority to include the top bloggers and major influencers at our launch events, right alongside the traditional trade and mainstream media. The results have been better than we could have ever imagined. They bring a level of excitement that simply wouldn't exist at a typical product or campaign launch event, and the resulting media coverage and social buzz reflects that. (personal communication, 2019)

Trade and Professional Media

Another area of the media often overlooked in media relations is the trade or professional media. Coverage in a key trade publication, which is read by industry members and/or enthusiasts, can be very beneficial to generating interest in your product or service.

SOCIAL RESPONSIBILITY

Coverage in key trade publications is vital when you are promoting CSR initiatives—since these publications cover innovation in their industries in more depth than traditional national or local media due to a more general focus.

An example might be an industrial manufacturing company that has improved its water management process and, in the process, saved money and made better use of a key natural resource. This story may not be interesting to a reporter at a daily paper, but it would be to one who covers that industry in depth and whose readers are interested in this issue. Professional journals and trade papers cover new products and industry trends and developments for more than the traditional media, and they are read closely by industry leaders and insiders.

Equally important, articles in trade journals often spark interest among journalists who cover the industry for the **mainstream media**. Also keep in mind that when the mainstream media organizations are looking to hire a new reporter to cover an industry, they often look to the leading trade and technology industry publications for their candidates. Thus, one of the advantages in working with trade reporters is that they may someday work at mainstream media outlets. In the meantime, coverage in a leading trade journal can be very useful in reaching your short-term communications goals—both generally, among investors, and in CSR-related activity.

Communications Theory and Media Relations

>> LO 7.2   Explore communications theory and its application to media relations

The study of communications theories that support the practice of media relations is a developing area, but most scholars agree that a few traditional theories have application (Supa, 2014). These include *gatekeeping, agenda setting*, and *framing* (Entman, 1993).

Gatekeeping

Kurt Lewin coined the term **gatekeeper** in 1947 (Davie, n.d.), describing a process in which a person of authority decides what information should move forward to a group or individual and what information should not. Soon afterward, David Manning White (1950) related it to journalism in the first study of its kind, "The 'Gate Keeper': A Case Study in the Selection of News." In a media setting, the editor or producer plays this vital role. They decide which news items will be published, broadcast, or posted on social media and what will not. For PR professionals seeking news coverage or visibility, it is important to identify the gatekeepers and appeal to them specifically and convincingly to get a positive response.

Agenda Setting

Maxwell McCombs and Donald Shaw were among the first communication scholars to argue that public opinion is shaped, in part, by media coverage. Their seminal study, "The Agenda-Setting Function of Mass Media" (McCombs & Shaw, 1972), established agenda-setting theory. It states the news media have an agenda; they tell audiences what news to consider important. Further studies revealed that the media also influence people's perceptions—*how* to think about the news.

FIGURE 7.1

Communications Theory and Media Relations

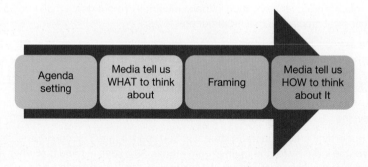

Framing

Robert Entman (1993) reinforced the media's *shaping* of news by explaining it as "framing" that affects how people think about it. He extended Erving Goffman's (1974) scholarship on how people make sense of the world based on frameworks that help them to interpret data. Thus, the *way* the story is told by the media (without any altering of actual facts)—the "frame" surrounding an issue—may influence readers' or viewers' perceptions.

Ron Smith, a professor and author who writes on PR theory and strategic planning, suggests,

> Much can be said about the role of the media in influencing the way people perceive public relations messages. . . . [S]ometimes the media influence is intentional, sometimes apparently accidental. Regardless of the motivation, media influence is inevitable. Public relations practitioners [who are] aware of the media's role can consider [the best] ways to deal with it. (Smith, 2011, para. 1)

The news media tells us what to think *about* (agenda setting) by choosing how and if to report a story. In the process, they influence the public (readers, listeners, and/or viewers) to understand or evaluate the issue or situation (framing; see Figure 7.1).

A more detailed discussion of these and other key communications theories is provided in Chapter 4. These theories inform the interaction between the journalist and the PR practitioner and the process of placing a story in target media. The good news is that if you are successful with your pitch and the reporter produces a story that meets his or her needs and yours, the benefits are significant.

Richard Branson (2013)—a global entrepreneur, multibillionaire, influencer, and opinion leader—summarized it as follows: "Publicity is absolutely critical. . . . You have to get your brand out and about, particularly if you're a consumer-oriented brand. A good PR story is infinitely more effective than an ad."

Measuring News Coverage

>> LO 7.3   Measure the impact of news coverage toward achieving business goals

There is growing widespread industry agreement that the focus of measuring the impact of media relations and PR in general should be on outcomes—for example, business created or opinions changed—and not on outputs—for example, the total number of articles generated or a dollar figure estimating the benefit of news coverage.

Advertising Value Equivalence

A reporter from *The Wall Street Journal*, Carl Bialik (2011), looked into the ways that PR people assess the impact of media coverage after some PR "experts" were quoted as estimating that a photo of former President Obama drinking a Guinness (while on a trip to Ireland) had "$32 million in publicity value."

While the company that manufactures Guinness, Diageo, was likely pleased to see this great photo published globally and "go viral" on social media, they declined to comment on the estimated PR value of the photo for the story. Most likely because the dollar figure—which they did not issue—was not substantiated nor could anyone prepare a verifiable estimate on the value of the news coverage. Actually, when the "PR expert" who gave the "$32 million in PR value" quote was pressed by the reporter to provide supportive details, he replied that it was an "estimate" and not an actual, documentable number (Bialik, 2011).

You have no doubt heard and seen examples like this where someone will say "that's a million dollars in free publicity," but you know this is not an actual hard number or fact. This practice reflects an older standard of PR measurement known as **advertising value equivalency (AVE)**, which seeks to estimate the relative value of a news story generated by PR by comparing it with a paid advertisement.

Over the years, many publicists have tried to translate news coverage into dollar figures, and some have used a simplistic approach. For example, a newspaper article was said to be "worth" as much the cost of a newspaper ad of the same size. In broadcast news, 30 seconds of news coverage is given a valuation comparable to a 30-second advertisement on the same station. Some PR specialists, reasoning that news coverage is more credible than paid advertising, maintained that a multiple of "value" should be applied—sometimes two or three times more—of an equivalent ad. However, there is no scientific documentation for either approach, and this approach has fallen out of popular use as a result.

David Rockland (2010), former global director of research and measurement for Ketchum, says the main problem with "publicity and advertising equivalency" calculations is that they assume all news stories are equally effective and are seen and read. Yet, he notes, the coverage might make only a glancing mention of your company/product or even be negative, while other coverage might focus entirely on the client. Surely, these cannot be seen as equivalent, but in this simplistic approach they are, he maintains.

To bring more order and clarity to measuring the impact of media relations and PR in general, the industry has been actively debating the issue. In 2010, after a landmark conference in Barcelona, Spain, the PR industry publicly stated that AVE is not a valid measure of PR (Michaelson & Stacks, 2011). The Barcelona Principles established in 2010 took a

Photographs of President Barack Obama drinking Guinness beer while in Ireland went viral, providing the brand with valuable exposure. The exact value of that exposure, however, is difficult to calculate.

BRENDAN SMIALOWSKI / Staff / Getty Images

FIGURE 7.2

Barcelona Principles

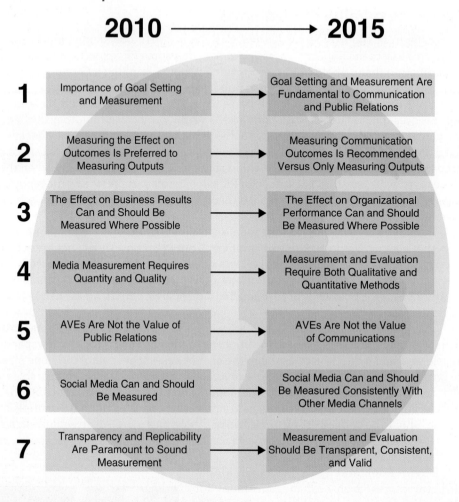

Source: Reprinted with permission from the Institute for Public Relations.

more scientific approach to measuring the impact and value of PR and were updated in 2015 (see Figure 7.2).

Impressions—Better, but Not Good Enough

Another common means of assessing the impact or value of media relations is a metric referred to as **impressions**, which is supposed to indicate the impact of a story or product mention in the media. Under this approach, the value of the coverage is calculated using the number of readers or viewers who *might* have read the story or seen the broadcast. This is usually done using audited subscription numbers of the publication or viewership of a given broadcast media outlet. For example, if a story ran in *The New York Times* on a weekday morning, the number of impressions cited under this approach would be based on the number of subscribers to the daily issue—or 590,000 (Ember, 2016).

Similarly, if a news segment is broadcast on local TV in New York during the 6 p.m. local newscast, the number of impressions might be estimated at hundreds of thousands, using network affiliate WNBC Channel 4 as an example. If the segment made the network news, the number would be 8.6 million, based on the reported viewership of the network newscast NBC's *Nightly News* (Katz, 2016).

While this approach may be a clear improvement over AVE in that it is based on audited subscription and viewership numbers, there are flaws to this approach as well. For example, no one would suggest that all 590,000 readers of *The New York Times* read the story on the given day it ran. As well, no one can guarantee that all the viewers of WNBC in New York or the 8.6 million viewers who watch NBC's *Nightly News* nationally saw the piece and/or remember it.

Guidelines for Measuring Media Coverage Impact

"Impressions are definitely not what they seem," Tim Marklein (2016), a well-regarded PR research expert and CEO of Big Valley Marketing, suggested in a recent post on the Institute for Public Relations (IPR) website:

> At first, impressions were used as a foundational unit of measure for publishers and advertisers, who built an entire economy negotiating to buy impressions by the thousands. They then evolved into a lingua franca of marketing measurement, providing a comparable way to evaluate reach (impressions) and efficiency across marketing vehicles and media outlets. They were then adapted to digital and social channels, as "visits" and "unique visitors" are used alongside impressions to compare reach among old and new media. (Marklein, 2016, para. 2)

"The reality is that impressions . . . only count how many people *potentially* had the opportunity to see your ad, story and/or content," Marklein (2016, para. 6) explains. Impressions "are typically calculated based on a publication's reach [circulation] or a site's traffic, but unless you own the site [and monitor it constantly], you don't know how many people *actually* saw the individual piece of content" (para. 6).

One of the reasons that AVE and impressions—and other simplistic methods—are used by some practitioners is that no verifiable alternative has emerged for putting a financial value on the worth and impact of PR outputs. While the effort to quantify these measurements continues, there are some more reliable ways to estimate the impact of media coverage that can help quantify the results. The most common one involves assessing the tone and the degree of visibility of key messages in the news coverage that results from PR outreach.

Positive, Negative, and Neutral Analysis and Key Message Visibility

Once a collection of news stories has been generated, it can be collected and analyzed. Once these are in hand, you can conduct a basic analysis to get a sense of the tone of the articles and whether the key messages are coming through to the reader or viewer. This analysis can be very helpful in demonstrating the value of PR efforts, determining if the assessments are fair and objective. Clients and management can understand and trust these more than other measures because they are observable and do not depend on a false formula like AVE or impressions that estimate the potential audience.

The approach to measuring the tone of news coverage is to read the entire article or view or listen to the broadcast and make an independent assessment of the tone of the article. The most common process is to use a scale of "positive, negative, or neutral" and assess the article and its impact accordingly.

Let's return to the example earlier in the chapter, where you are serving as the PR director of a regional bank and you have developed a target media list to place a story about your company's CSR activity. Once your news release has been distributed and covered by some of the key media, you can conduct this analysis.

Measuring impact can be made easier by purchasing reports from an online monitoring service that provide an analysis of the target media you reached and providing an assessment on the tone of the stories that appeared. If the tone of the article is primarily supportive, it can be said to be *positive*. If it has some good and some bad but is accurate and balanced, it can be categorized as *neutral*. And, of course, if it is highly critical or supports a different product or point of view, it would be scored as *negative*.

Message Testing

Another useful tool is to review the coverage and examine it to see if the message(s) you wanted to convey are present. The process involves assessing if the messages are *highly visible*, *mentioned briefly*, or *not mentioned* at all in the story. While this method is more subjective, it is useful to provide a sense of whether your messages are getting through to your target audiences. This method allows you to "score" the story from a point of view of message visibility and impact and adjust or enhance the message if necessary.

Global Media Relations Trends and Tactics

>> **LO 7.4** **Identify global trends and practices in media relations**

The challenge of global media relations is an undertaking that most PR professionals will face at some point in their careers. In today's rapidly changing, globally connected world, the field is a challenging one. Making sense of emerging markets, keeping tactics local, finding the influencers, and determining how to be flexible and adapt to widely differing cultures and changing conditions are problems that PR scholars have researched.

INSIGHTS

Effective Global Public Relations Requires Specific Knowledge and Strategy

In her book *Pitch, Tweet, or Engage on the Street: How to Practice Global Public Relations*, Kara Alaimo (2016a) suggests that global PR practitioners adapt their strategies and approaches to reflect the customs and culture of each country.

"I conducted interviews with 74 global public relations practitioners from 31 countries. I asked them how they advise global organizations to adapt their strategies for particular cultures and what factors they need to take into account when implementing global public relations strategies in

their countries," she noted in a post on the Institute for Public Relations site (Alaimo, 2016b, para. 2).

First, Alaimo notes (2016b), expectations of global companies or organizations differ dramatically throughout the world. In some parts of the world, the local government and citizens may expect companies to provide services outside of that company's area of expertise. For example, she mentions infrastructure projects (roads and schools) and "high expectations for corporate social responsibility" by local citizens of companies operating in their country. Often, the local or national government is not viewed as capable of mounting major improvement projects; as such, they look to companies operating—or seeking to operate—in their country to pay for these projects. These companies are asked to build roads, housing, schools, and medical facilities to obtain permits for development projects or market entry. These projects are beneficial to the country while the project is underway, and when the company leaves, the improved infrastructure is left behind.

The second category relates specifically to media relations by large U.S. companies. The standard practice in the United States is for companies to seek news coverage of their CSR activity and then repurpose it on the company's social media platforms (Yu, Asur, & Huberman, 2011, cited in Alaimo, 2016b).

However, the interviews of experts in the study suggest that in many countries people do not respect the media because it is government controlled and censored. Instead, she found, the citizens often rely on influencers or opinion leaders for insights and information. These individuals have a reputation for sharing independent and accurate information on social media. As such, her research concludes, global PR practitioners with CSR projects to promote in these countries might be better off targeting these people instead of the state-controlled media (Alaimo, 2016b). ●

Sources:

Alaimo, K. (2016a). *Pitch, tweet, or engage on the street: How to practice global public relations and strategic communication.* Routledge.

Alaimo, K. (2016b). *Updating the generic/specific theory of international public relations: More factors to consider when practicing in new markets.* Institute for Public Relations. http://www.instituteforpr.org/updating-genericspecific-theory-international-public-relations-factors-consider-practicing-new-markets/.

Yu, L., Asur, S., & Huberman, B. A. (2011). What trends in Chinese social media. *arXiv.* https://arxiv.org/pdf/1107.3522.pdf

Excellence Theory and Global Applications

One of the most well-known theories of international PR, put forth by Verčič, Grunig, and Grunig (1996) and Grunig, Grunig, and Verčič (1998), is based on the excellence theory. The scholars determined that the core principles of PR are the same worldwide, but specific applications differ in different settings.

Excellence theory considers PR as strategic—not tactical—and part of senior management's role, and it advocates a two-way symmetrical model of communication (see Chapter 4 for a more detailed discussion of this important theory).

However, specific variables apply, depending on the country context. Professionals should keep in mind five different dimensions when practicing international PR and media relations.

The five dimensions for global PR and media relations include (1) the political and economic system, (2) culture(s), (3) levels of activism, (4) level of economic development, and (5) the media system in a given country. Based on her research, Alaimo (2016b) suggested two additional dimensions: social expectations and local influencers.

Ethical Standards in Global Media Relations

Another key challenge in global media relations is the ethical challenge of paying for news coverage. It is not at all uncommon for the media in a developing country to expect payment in the form of advertisements—or cash payments to their reporters—to get editorial coverage. In addition, in some markets it is common for journalists to expect to be paid "expenses" to attend a press event and then write a story or broadcast a news segment afterward. In some cases, PR practitioners even get to review the copy before it is published.

"Pay for play" is an issue researched by Katerina Tsetsura (2011), PhD, of the University of Oklahoma, who conducted interviews with both global PR practitioners and locally based journalists. In both groups, the notion of paying for coverage was viewed as a "problem" and "inappropriate"—with 84% of the respondents indicating that the practice is *not* acceptable in their view. This does not mean that it doesn't happen—some respondents noted that such arrangements happen at higher levels of the media outlet or broadcast company—for example, editors and publishers and company management—but both the journalists and practitioners interviewed said they are not party to it.

"I think it can be a fuzzy line. It's hard to know if they do or they don't unless senior management is working with the magazine or newspaper leadership separately to advertise," commented one global PR professional who participated in the study (Tsetsura, 2011).

A journalist who also participated in the study added,

> In my experience, such things are seldom if ever direct. The publisher and senior editors will of course be acquainted with some of the ad sales folks, who will of course have opinions about whatever industry is being covered and about how major advertisers feel about the work (e.g., coverage) the publication is doing. I've never received specific guidance on such things, but one always knew who the big players were. (Tsetsura, 2011, p. 172)

This is a rare practice in the United States, especially where there is a clear separation between the editorial and advertising side of most publications and networks. The relatively new phenomenon of working with social media influencers is testing these boundaries since many of them receive travel or advertising support from companies whose events or products they support. More and more, these influencers are opting to note in their post that they are sometimes compensated by the subjects of their posts.

However, for companies that operate on a global scale, especially if they have plants or marketing/sales offices in other countries, this might be expected. While there are clear PR industry guidelines on ethics, it comes down to each company making a policy decision and enforcing it across all geographies.

Scenario Outcome

At the beginning of this chapter, you read about the challenges facing the Aflac communications team. Despite a strong track record in philanthropy and CSR, research had shown that this was not carrying through to the brand or reputation of the company.

Their challenge was to develop a new initiative consistent with their brand and make sure it connected to their corporate strategy and met a defined need in the marketplace. What follows is a summary of the campaign's execution and results.

Do you see any of your ideas and suggestions represented?

Execution

As noted in the chapter-opening scenario, Aflac began by conducting new research—both primary and secondary—to identify best practices and an opportunity to promote their CSR activity to stakeholders.

This research showed that the main attributes of a successful CSR program were ethics, workplace, philanthropy, and environmental sustainability.

Aflac focused on these attributes when compiling its CSR annual report for 2017 (published in 2018). As well, they included them in a new initiative designed to bring attention to its philanthropic efforts to combat childhood cancer.

The communications team, along with their outside agencies (Fleishman Hillard with KWI and MMC) developed and launched a new program featuring My Special Aflac Duck™, a plush robotic duck (consistent with their well-established branding). The program included distribution and hospital visits nationally to offer emotional support and goodwill to children (and their families) recently diagnosed with cancer.

My Special Aflac Duck™ made its debut at the 2018 Consumer Electronics Show (CES) in Las Vegas in early 2017. CES is one of the biggest and most well-covered trade shows of all. The show was chosen due to the innovative technology used to make the plush toy and the opportunity it provided to showcase senior management and address the issue of sustainability and social responsibility.

The communications team, and its outside advisors, leveraged the momentum created by the CES launch and the media coverage it created nationally, locally, and in key trade media. Awareness of the need to address childhood cancer increased as well, which helped kick-start national fundraising efforts.

Beyond these events and the initial coverage obtained, another key goal was to position Aflac's senior management and CSR spokespeople as thought leaders on the CSR and corporate philanthropy. After the CES kickoff, company executives participated in leading forums throughout the year on treatment and prevention and in discussions/conferences on helping families cope with childhood cancer.

The team's expectation was that through this awareness and fundraising program, the marketplace and Aflac's key stakeholders would be more aware of the company's track record and expertise. The long-term goal was for Aflac's corporate reputation to "catch up" with the reality of the company's long-term commitment to CSR and philanthropy.

Results

CES Show—Launch

- Media outreach at the CES show in Las Vegas resulted in eight major interviews with target national media. These, along with a satellite media tour done from CES, created over 800 stories during and after the show.
- The My Special Aflac Duck™ plush toy won three awards at the CES show: Innovation, Best Robotics, and Best of CES.
- Follow-up research by the Reputation Institute (2018b) showed a significant increase in the company's overall reputation score, moving it beyond an "average" to a "strong" rating in all the key categories.
- Fundraising benefited as well, and Aflac met its goal of $1.5 million for the year.

Executive Visibility—CSR-Related

- Aflac executives were interviewed about the company's CSR and philanthropic activity by national media, including *USA Today, Associated Press, Forbes, Yahoo!,* and *The Huffington Post,* as well as the key PR trades, *PRWeek and PR News.*
- Awareness for pediatric cancer was raised through speeches, panels, and op-eds featuring the Aflac executives, according to independent research.

- Campaigns on LinkedIn for key Aflac executives produced significant increases in followers, comments, posts, and likes and generated online contributions as well.

- The Aflac corporate Facebook page experienced a major increase in traffic in the months and year following the launch. Analytics show a 12% increase in page likes, a 260% increase in average monthly engagement, a 134% increase in average monthly reach, and a 168% increase in average monthly impressions for 2017.

Source: Granger, 2018.

WRAP UP

In this chapter, the groundwork was set to help you develop or enhance your strategic media relations skills. As noted, while there are many aspects of PR that you will be asked to execute during your careers, media relations will nearly always be one of them. This chapter included data from the Pew Research Center on the current media environment and looked at the different types of media you might include in your outreach plans. This discussion introduced the concepts of *paid* (advertising) and *earned* (PR/media relations) as well as company/client-*sponsored* and -*owned* media. Measuring the impact of media relations results was covered as well—noting what works and what does not—and examples were provided to illustrate the difference. The current state of global media relations as well as media relations in politics and crisis communications were introduced.

KEY TERMS

Advertising Value Equivalency (AVE) 161
Demographics 152
Fake News 153
Gatekeeper 159

Impressions 162
Mainstream (Traditional) Media 159
Pitch 154
Spokesperson 158

THINK ABOUT IT

Working with your instructor, form into small groups and choose a current news story, preferably with a CSR or philanthropy focus. Review the story for details and then develop an outline for a media relations strategy to respond on behalf of the company or organization involved. (*Note:* CSRwire.com is a great source for recent news releases and studies on CSR.)

Your outline should include an overview of the situation and a summary of the tone and focus of the news coverage to date (using the positive, negative, or neutral scale).

Develop one objective for your media relations plan, one key message you want to convey, and one tactic to create media coverage. Finally, you should include one example of research you would use to measure the impact of your media relations activity. This can include news clips (their tone and message prominence), coverage in target media, increased visits to a dedicated website, or donations or sign-ups by volunteers, for example.

This exercise is designed to help you look at a situation and develop a framework for a strategy and an approach to responding. Once the framework is in place, you can fill it in with objectives, messages, target audiences, and goals.

WRITE LIKE A PRO

Assume you work for an agency that has been retained to advise a regional grocery chain on increasing visibility of its CSR activity. Your task is to prepare a media pitch for a new CSR initiative for your company—a food drive to generate donations to a local food bank that is struggling. You also want to include expanded CSR plans of the company.

Your firm has prepared a target media list—including the local papers, television and radio stations, and influential bloggers who cover CSR topics in your area. You also have a good list of influential people in the local nonprofit community who are supportive of the company's decision to expand its local sustainability activity. Remember what you read in this chapter about the need to localize the story and provide a visual element for best results.

Send the pitch to your instructor—remember the premium is on short, succinct requests and targeted story suggestions.

SOCIAL RESPONSIBILITY CASE STUDY

Deepwater Wind: Launching America's First Offshore Wind Farm

American dependence on fossil fuels and our knowledge of the harmful effects of its emissions have created a need to explore and employ alternate energy sources. Solar and wind power are two of the most common "clean" energy producers in use, but these generators are located on land, creating aesthetic and environmental concerns.

The summer of 2016 would see that change when Deepwater Wind, America's first offshore wind farm—located 3 miles off the coast of Block Island, Rhode Island—would finally power up and usher in a new era for renewable energy in the United States.

Research and Strategy

"Communicating clearly and effectively about a new technology—in this case, offshore wind energy—can be a challenge," said Jon Duffy, president of Duffy & Shanley (D&S), the wind farm's local PR firm. "We've worked hard to build our own understanding of offshore wind and become trusted resources for news media explaining this new technology to their audiences. Our role was as much about educating the news media as it was publicizing our client's project," he explained (Carufel, 2017, para. 5).

Getting national news coverage was a top priority of the campaign. The PR team wanted to portray the new wind turbines off the coast of Block Island as "symbols of American innovation" and Deepwater Wind as a leader of a new American industry (para. 2).

In preparing to launch the facility, the PR team developed close media relationships with top national and international energy and environmental journalists. They knew that to tell the story of the Block Island Wind Farm's completion, they needed to "demystify" a project that people believed might never actually be completed.

Execution

To bring media close to the action, D&S chartered a Block Island-based fishing boat for eight tours over the course of 2 weeks. They also used visual storytelling—web and social media videos, photography, aerial and time-lapse footage—to make this pioneering project real for all the project stakeholders and the public. The visuals became an important tool to help media outlets that couldn't travel to Block Island.

One of the firm's most important media targets was *The New York Times*, and the D&S team provided guided access of the farm to the newspaper's environmental reporter and photographer and set up a 2-hour interview with Deepwater Wind's CEO. As a result, the *Times* ran a cover story (with several photos) in its "Science" section and featured it prominently on its online site. That coverage led to a *Times* editorial that pushed for growth of the offshore wind industry in the United States, featuring Deepwater Wind as leading that charge. In another extremely valuable promotion, then-President Obama shared the *Times* story in a tweet that was "liked" more than 7,000 times and retweeted nearly 3,000 times.

Evaluation

In just a 4-month period, PR efforts for the Deepwater Wind campaign led to over 350 print, online, and broadcast stories in some of the country's most influential media, including *The Wall Street Journal*, Associated Press, Reuters, *Bloomberg BusinessWeek*, *USA Today*, *The Washington Post*, *CBS Evening News*, *NBC Nightly News*, CNBC, MSNBC, *PBS News Hour*, NPR, Yahoo!, Mashable, and more.

D&S's work for Deepwater Wind helped position the company as a leading offshore wind developer. The campaign also won the Bulldog Reporter Award for Media Relations in 2017—the only major PR award competition whose entries are judged by working journalists.

As evidence that the Block Island Wind Farm had set America's offshore wind industry in motion, just a month after it began operations, Deepwater Wind secured contract approval for its larger South Fork Wind Farm off Long Island, New York, and the company began design for additional projects in Massachusetts, Rhode Island, and Maryland.

Engage

- Visit the Deepwater Wind website (www.dwwind.com) to learn about this technology and its expected benefits.

- Review other sites and research to assess if this approach and technology are viewed as effective. What, if any, criticisms are there that need to be addressed?

- Read *The New York Times* article (https://nyti.ms/2jGVAzz) and visit the D&S site (www.duffyshanley.com) to learn more about the company, technology, and the firm advising support for both.

Discuss

- How did D&S make the story compelling enough to merit media coverage? Note recent research on reluctance of the media to cover CSR initiatives.

- How might Deepwater Wind use social media more to extend their impact and results?

- What best practices or new ideas should D&S (and Deepwater Wind) consider for future wind farms approved or planned elsewhere in New England and the United States?

- With a new administration in place in Washington, DC, what ideas or options should the company consider to build on its momentum from this event?

Source: Carufel, 2017.

8

Social Media and Emerging Technologies

Learning Objectives

8.1   Describe social media's historical context and its contemporary place in society

8.2   Understand the purpose and use of various social media tools in the field of PR

8.3   Evaluate PR best practices in social media and digital communications

8.4   Identify how to measure social media effectiveness, and craft a strategy for staying abreast of trends

Scenario
Owning a VW Is Like Being in Love

Or so proclaimed *Popular Mechanics* magazine in 1956, marking the beginning of a decades-long love affair between Volkswagen (VW) and American car buyers and reviewers.

The ad agency DDB's iconic "Think Small" campaign, which ran from 1959 to the early 1970s, turned the VW Beetle's drawbacks—small size, air-cooled engine, rear-wheel drive—into virtues (Garfield, 1999).

Sales of the model exploded in the 1960s, fueled by the innovative ad campaign and the "Bug's" status as something of an antiestablishment vehicle. This was the era of finned, chromed, and high-horsepower automobiles rolling out of Detroit, and the Beetle was the perfect counter to those behemoths.

The VW van: an alternative to station wagons. Embraced by many young people in the 1960s, the vans were painted and modified to create what became known as a "hippie van."

The Volkswagen Beetle gained popularity in the 1950s and eventually became one of the most influential cars of the century.
Evan Kirby on Unsplash

- In 1999, the VW Beetle was named one of the most influential cars of the 20th century (Cobb, 1999). By 2014, VW was one of the biggest car makers in the world, with factories in 31 countries (Bowler, 2015). In 2015, the Golf MK7 won the *Motor Trend* Car of the Year award (Jurnecka, 2015).

That same year, a monumental scandal broke. On September 18, 2015, the U.S. Environmental Protections Agency (EPA) publicly filed a notice of violation of the Clean Air Act to the Volkswagen Group. It accused VW of designing "defeat device" software and installing it in 500,000 diesel vehicles to intentionally trick regulators and deceive the EPA's emissions tests.

- VW had admitted this deception to the EPA 15 days earlier but hadn't publicly disclosed it. This now publicized situation was critically damaging to the VW brand. Four days after the news broke, VW admitted its emissions fraud was much larger, involving up to 11 million vehicles. The CEO announced his resignation the next day. A headline in a German newspaper announced, "'Made in Germany' in the Gutter" (Leveille, 2015).

Organizations use social media as an effective way to communicate quickly during a crisis. Consumers also access social media sites (e.g., Twitter) during crises to seek and share information, often offering their opinions.

- During a 10-day period shortly after the news broke, a researcher examined conversation on Twitter about VW's emission crisis (Whytas, 2016). More than 40,000 English-language tweets were examined that contained at least one of these hashtags: #VW, #VWGate, #DieselGate, #VWscandal, or #Volkswagenscandal. Three main concerns were voiced: loss of trust in VW, sales staffs worried about their livelihoods, and alarm at the implications to health with so many VWs on the road with higher emissions.

As you read this chapter, consider the following:

1. How should VW PR have handled this crisis via social media? What repercussions might arise if not handled properly?

(Continued)

(Continued)

    2. If you were VW's PR counsel, what publics would be critical to communicate with, through which social channels, and with what messaging?

To answer these questions, you can begin to outline your recommendations as you engage with the lessons in this chapter. At the end, you will find how VW responded—and continues to respond. ●

This chapter explores the dynamic world of social media and emerging technologies and their impact on the PR profession. First, it considers the antecedents of social media and how it evolved through innovation after innovation, each expanding the ability of people and organizations to communicate with each other in real time. Peeling back the labels and personalities of social media platforms, the chapter explains how social networking theory, first developed in the mid-20th century, helps us understand the usefulness of social media and why it has spread so fast.

Then, the chapter illustrates how organizations effectively use social media tools to reach their communication goals, which include establishing credibility and building relationships. To illustrate, you'll find specific explanations and case examples of major digital platforms used in PR—Facebook, Instagram, Twitter, LinkedIn, YouTube, TikTok, second screens, podcasts, apps, augmented reality, and microsites.

Cases and tips from PR executives also teach how digital communications strategies interrelate with more traditional communications methods and how to effectively use both. As Linda Descano of Havas PR reveals, "The best communications campaigns today take a merged media approach, threading stories across paid, earned, and owned media channels, and through online social activations, offline marketing experiences, and PR stunts" (L. Descano, personal communication, 2020).

Social Media

>> LO 8.1 Describe social media's historical context and its contemporary place in society

Social media has undoubtedly transformed how PR is practiced. Social media allows PR practitioners to speak directly with target audiences without interference or alteration by a media gatekeeper as in traditional media relations. It's 24/7. It's a world of voices, words, and images converging without restriction. It's ever changing. It demands engagement, dialogue, content, and constant watchfulness.

Historical Context

In PR, one major goal of social media is to encourage visitor interaction—to like, comment, share, pin, vote, buy, and travel to the client's various other social media sites or to its main website.

We can trace the idea of social media back to the groundbreaking invention of the telegraph that allowed long-distance transmission of messages in real time. It laid the foundation for a revolution in communications that now has our world spinning with innovations (see Figure 8.1). Assuredly, as you read this now, some

FIGURE 8.1

Antecedents and Timeline of Social Media

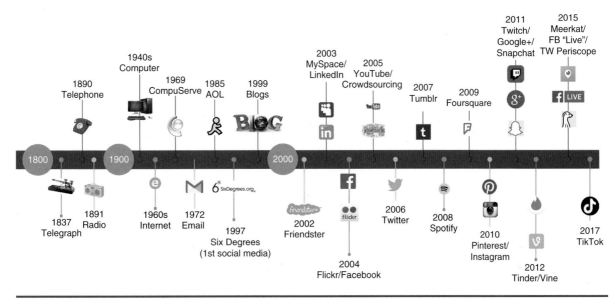

Source: Miriam Johnson; Center for the Study of Women in Society.

platforms have disappeared as more innovations have arrived. Let us consider the contemporary state of social media within American society—what many have dubbed "the revolution in communication."

Social and Emerging Media Use

Various sources rank and publish social media site data with some variation. One of the most reputable is the Pew Research Center. According to Pew, as of 2019, 81% of Americans said they go online on a daily basis, and nearly 50% of young adults (18–29) go online "almost constantly" (Perrin & Kumar, 2019). The GlobalWebIndex Gen Z Audience Report 2019 found the Internet habits of Gen Z (defined by the study as those born 1998–2013) differ from the rest. They devote 3 hours each day exclusively on social media, and they don't see it as a place for communicating or staying up to date, but rather for using apps such as YouTube and Instagram as an entertainment source and a time-filler (Global WebIndex, 2019).

According to the Pew study (Perrin & Kumar, 2019), nearly three quarters of American adults were using YouTube, 69% using Facebook, and 37% using Instagram (Perrin & Anderson, 2019; see Figure 8.2). A Nielsen study (2019) revealed that Black American adults were the heaviest users of Instagram—using it 20% more than does the total U.S. population. Regarding age demographics, the Pew study found Facebook relatively common across age groups: 68% of those aged 50 to 64 and nearly half of those 65 and older said they used the site. Other platforms exhibited substantial age differences, especially Instagram and Snapchat, which were used by 67% and 62% of 18-to 29-year-olds, respectively. And women were nearly 3 times as likely as men to use Pinterest (Perrin & Kumar, 2019). All of these statistics should be watched and respected when it comes to planning social media communication strategies.

FIGURE 8.2

Social Network Dominance, 2019

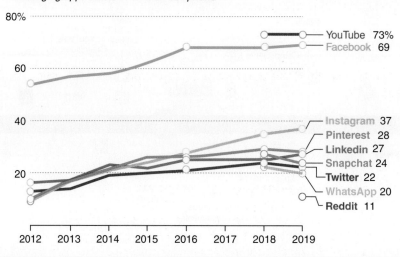

Percentage of U.S. adults who say they ever use the following online platforms or messaging apps online or on their cell phone

Note: Pre-2018 telephone poll data is not available for YouTube, Snapchat, and WhatsApp. Comparable trend data is not available for Reddit.

Source: "Facebook, YouTube continue to be the most widely used online platforms among U.S. adults." Pew Research Center, Washington, DC (April 9, 2019) https://www.pewresearch.org/ft_19-04-02_socialmediaplatforms_feature/

FIGURE 8.3

Unique Monthly U.S. Visitors, January 2020

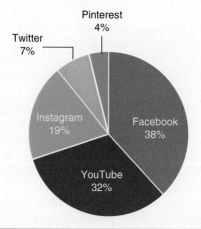

Source: Data from eBizMBA.

The Pew data is based on users' own reports of their habits. When we consider the data on site visitors, we see an alignment—users report strong preferences for Facebook and YouTube, and this is confirmed by monitoring the number of site visitors (see Figure 8.3). According to the social media monitor eBiz/MBA (2020), which measures both popularity and influence, in January 2020 Facebook led in both influence and unique monthly visitors—over 2.2 billion. The next-most influential site, YouTube, had 1.8 billion. Third in influence, Instagram's users totaled 1.1 billion. Next came Twitter at 375 million users, and then Pinterest with 250 million.

How can the explosion of social media be explained? One way to understand its role in our lives is explained by social network theory (SNT), which we'll learn more about in the next section.

The Value and Strategies of Social Media

>> LO 8.2 Understand the purpose and use of various social media tools in the field of PR

Social Network Theory

Social media opens up a world of networking and relationship-building for PR practitioners. The concepts behind social media can be found in **social network theory (SNT)**, a model researched by sociologists and organizational behavior scholars beginning in the 1950s (Granovetter, 1973).

The theory examines the web of interrelationships among people and organizations. Its concepts of network *size and quality, social distance, network diffusion,* and *complexity* all help explain the usefulness of social media platforms. *Business Communication Quarterly* explains how SNT connects to familiar social media platforms (Sacks & Graves, 2012):

- While Facebook only arrived in 2004, it illustrates the SNT concepts of *size* and *quality*: Within organizational PR, often larger networks are attractive

Within the wide world of social media networking, PR professionals zero in on the specific platforms used by a client's publics.

Photo by Luc Legay on flickr

but require time and energy to maintain high-quality ties and nurture meaningful relationships. Network quality isn't necessarily dependent on size.

- LinkedIn demonstrates the principle of *social distance*, which states that people are more inclined to do favors for those with whom they have close connections. Even second-order and third-order connections have more power than nonrelationships. You can see why PR is in the business of building and nurturing relationships.

- Twitter's speed and ease mirror the principles of *network diffusion* (how quickly a positive or negative message spreads) and *complexity* (the simpler the message, the faster and wider it spreads).

Understanding that the dynamics of social media have deep roots in tested theory reinforces the need to be strategic about using the various platforms.

PR Embraces Digital and Social Media

With people's social media activity strong and growing both in the United States and worldwide, the PR practice has embraced it—as it's radically changed the way we consume information. While traditional media outlets and press releases have a purpose for specific kinds of news, "brand journalism" on social media connects publics with engaging digital storytelling in social feeds, blogs, podcasts, and other outlets. Content is king in storytelling. Strategically, the PR practitioner needs to analyze target publics and their social media use to identify platforms that work best for a particular client's needs. In an expansive survey of global PR professionals (*The Global State of PR* report), three quarters reported their top offerings were in social media management and content marketing, with influencer marketing following as a close third (Talkwalker, 2020).

Social media tactics should focus on conversations. However, the tactics aren't always guided by strategic planning—although they should be, according to new research (Plowman & Wilson, 2018). Drawing from in-depth interviews and a national survey of PR practitioners, the study also revealed that respondents saw a disconnect between research and strategic planning: Formative research was not always used to develop social media strategy. The researchers conclude,

> If organizations are merely using social media research to evaluate objectives or track engagement, their strategy runs the risk of (1) being asymmetrical, focused on advocating for the organization instead of seeking to build mutually beneficial relationships with publics that result in long-term benefits, and (2) being misaligned with the realities of their operating environment. (Plowman & Wilson, 2018, p. 141)

This reinforces the RPIE (research, planning, implementation, evaluation) process as a pathway for all PR programs, including social media.

Driver of Public Relations Growth

Looking to the future, both agency and client-side PR practitioners globally predict considerable change in the PR industry over the next 5 years (USC Annenberg, 2019), and a sizable 83% of the practitioners identify technological innovations

FIGURE 8.4a

Percentage of PR Practitioners in 2019 Expecting Social Media Purpose to Be More Important by 2024

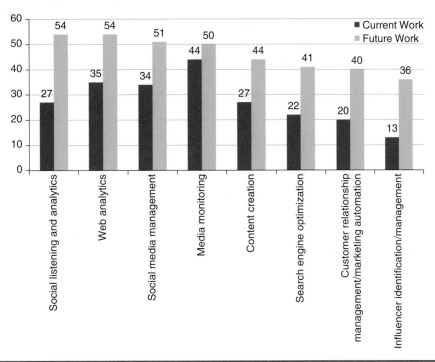

Source: Based on USC Annenberg Center for Public Relations. (2019). Global Communications Report, PR:Tech, the future of technology in communication.

as a significant driver of this change. "Shared media" (social media and online influencers) will be the most valuable communication strategy—good news for students who are digital natives well prepared to deal with social media. Social media tools should see the biggest jump in importance within the next 5 years (see Figure 8.4a). And as paid, earned, shared, and owned channels are colliding, in the future it's likely many consumers won't be able to differentiate between information written by a reporter, sponsored by a brand, or promoted by an influencer. Engaging influencers in PR campaigns is a dominant strategy for more than two thirds of practitioners—another key finding of *The Global State of PR* report (Talkwalker, 2020).

Visual images are engaging storytellers and will only grow in importance and use in the coming years, especially on YouTube and Instagram. This is unfortunately, but realistically, based on our decreasing attention spans. Professional communicators need to increase their visual literacy to use images ethically and strategically. According to visual communication scholar Paul Martin Lester, "The most powerful, meaningful, and culturally important messages are those that combine words and pictures equally and respectfully" (2014, p. xi). This is especially important with artificial intelligence (AI), as its use (prominently supported by Google) will also expand (see Figure 8.4b).

FIGURE 8.4b

Percentage of PR Practitioners in 2019 Expecting Social Media Platforms to Be More Important by 2024

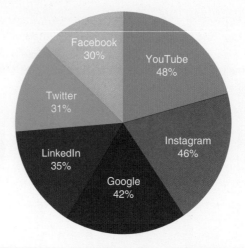

Source: Based on USC Annenberg Center for Public Relations. (2019). Global Communications Report, PR:Tech, the future of technology in communication.

Media Relations

With the crescendo of social media use and the shrinking traditional media landscape, it's no surprise that Cision's *State of the Media* report (2019) found journalists overwhelmed, overworked, and challenged by new complexities in social media. However, journalists do rely on social media to stay connected with sources, and they find images and infographics to be most useful. Essentially, PR outreach to media needs to be more relevant and targeted to stand out in the crowded social field and our fragmented, ever-shifting media environment.

The ability via social media to communicate directly and interactively should not overshadow the other ways in which digital communication has affected PR. In particular, it has made media relations a 24-hour-a-day job, with reporters expecting websites to have up-to-the-second information available without them having to go through a PR staffer. As a result, Internet content must be carefully screened and diligently organized so that journalists' investigative efforts will bear fruit. Both academic research and professional surveys suggest that while social media has increased the ability to connect with publics, its 24-hour nature has increased both workload and job-related stress (Argenti, 2016).

Social Influencers

While reaching media gatekeepers—usually journalists—has always been a traditional media relations goal in PR, companies have routinely used celebrity affiliations to boost brand image and credibility, like Nike's with Tiger Woods. Now, influencers, those online experts with a ubiquitous presence who've cultivated a recognized and respected personal brand, are the social media ambassadors . . . and gatekeepers. They offer a level of credibility and trust in supporting your client's PR objective and can be highly effective in getting publics talking about your brand.

As noted earlier, influencer marketing is a top offering of many PR firms, and these relationships evolve with new social media platforms, features, and metrics. The most common ways PR pros work with influencers for brand collaborations is via discounts, competitions, and giveaways—less frequently, through attending events. Certainly, the influencer's audience must be right for the brand and the campaign, and the relationship must be managed well. There are potential risks of a brand affiliating itself with influencers, such as when they fail to stay aligned with your content strategy or if they experience a scandal. When done successfully, PR firms often use engagement rates and potential reach to prove the ROI (return on investment) of influencer collaborations (Talkwalker, 2020).

Crisis Situations and Risk Management

The use of social media in a crisis is essential. A future chapter (Chapter 12) covers crisis management in depth, so we'll just briefly mention it here. In a crisis, companies know that Twitter is the major link to the media and their customers. It reveals how information about the crisis is spreading and reflects what's across social media. Public comments may favor outrage and punishment over understanding, and this conversation cannot be downplayed or disregarded. Social conversations must be vigilantly monitored and addressed expeditiously, guided by transparency and sincerity. Corporations should encourage nonprofit partners and supportive influencers to collaborate on issues and initiatives important to them. Intel advises employees engaged in corporate social media to be, among other things, honest yet respectful of Intel's privacy, confidentiality, and legal guidelines (Inside Social Media, 2009).

PR professionals must also be prepared to deal with the dark side of social media, negative **memes**, and cyberattacks. Unfortunately, it is far easier now for bad actors to communicate. Your organization or issue may be targeted with fake news to influence beliefs that support a deliberate agenda. A widely discussed example is the Russian propaganda that infiltrated the 2016 U.S. presidential election. In 2019, a site named NPC News published a story reporting that Rep. Alexandria Ocasio-Cortez (D-NY) opposes daylight savings time because it speeds up climate change. Although it was fact-checked as false, the story had 21,000 Facebook engagements (Brandwatch, 2019).

Viral outrage can spark around misrepresented issues; it can incense and engage publics sometimes entirely removed from your brand use or experience. For example, when United Airlines prohibited two teenage girls from boarding a flight for wearing leggings, social channels erupted in sharp criticism despite United's explanation that the girls, flying on employee passes, were subject to the airline's dress code. United did it right: It responded directly, communicated with its own publics, and provided the facts.

Hootsuite, the social media management platform, warns of these common social media security risks (Newberry, 2018):

1. Reserve your brand's handle on all social media channels so when you're ready to use one, your presence will be consistent across networks.

2. Don't neglect social accounts. Idle, unmonitored accounts can be targeted by hackers posting deceptive or false messages under your name.

3. Be cautious of human error, such as clicking on the wrong link or downloading the wrong file.

4. Beware the third-party apps that integrate with social networks and their vulnerabilities for hackers to gain access. For example, hackers accessed *Forbes'* and Amnesty International's Twitter accounts through a flaw in the Twitter Counter app associated with Twitter analysis.

How should businesses and public relations professionals handle potential social media threats?

1. Create a social media policy that includes guidelines on messaging, confidentiality and personal use rules, expectations for updating, how to identify problems, and how to respond when concerns arise.

2. Provide training on social media security best practices.

3. Limit social media access, especially the ability to post and knowledge of passwords.

4. Set up a system of approvals, especially to avoid content that offends and reflects negatively on the organization. Put someone in charge.

5. Monitor accounts and engage in social listening. Follow up on anything unexpected.

INSIGHTS

Vaccines: Social Media and Misinformation

Dr. Jeanine Guidry, Assistant Professor, Robertson School for Media and Culture, Virginia Commonwealth University

Vaccines are among the world's greatest public health triumphs. They have greatly contributed to the reduction in morbidity and mortality of many infectious diseases—smallpox, polio, and measles, just to name a few. In fact, in the year 2000 measles was declared virtually eliminated in the United States. However, since then several outbreaks of the disease have appeared, apparently linked to skepticism about vaccine safety.

Much of the current antivaccine sentiment appears to start with a now-discredited British ex-physician, Andrew Wakefield, who published a paper in *The Lancet* in 1998, asserting that there was a link between the measles, mumps, and rubella vaccine on the one hand, and autism on the other. The problem? The study was found to be what the *British Medical Journal* termed an "elaborate fraud," and *The Lancet* retracted the article. Wakefield was stripped of his medical degree in 2010, but he continues his antivaccine activities. In the meantime, at least a dozen major studies, some covering as many as 100,000 children, have shown no link between vaccines and autism.

Much of the current spread of vaccine misinformation has been taking place on social

media platforms, and studies have shown that people relying on social media for vaccine information are more likely to be misinformed about the issue compared to those relying on traditional media. An example is social media platform Pinterest, most frequently known for its posts about recipes, decorating inspiration, and craft tutorials. When researchers started studying Pinterest and vaccine communications in 2015, they found that about 75% of all vaccine-related pins were questioning vaccine safety.

In the past few years, social media platforms have started to address the presence of misinformation on their platforms. Pinterest started in early 2019 by restricting access to vaccine-related videos and followed this up in August of 2019 with an announcement that vaccine-related searches now will be shown results from reliable public health organizations such as the World Health Organization (WHO) and the Centers for Disease Control and Prevention (CDC). Facebook implemented similar practices for its platform, as well as reduced the ranking of pages and grounds that spread misinformation about vaccines in search results and its newsfeed. In addition, the company stopped recommending content that included vaccine misinformation on sister-platform Instagram.

Finally, cognitive psychology tells us that it is easier for people to accept a specific piece of information than to evaluate whether it is true or not. In addition, misinformation is often described as "sticky"—meaning it tends to be resistant to correction. However, correction can have a positive effect, particularly when originating with a reputable organization—something particularly relevant for public relations professionals working for public health-related entities.

In addition, one of the most powerful dynamics in social media use is that it makes individual users into both content creators and content publishers, which can work for reliable *and* unreliable information. As public relations professionals, our challenge is to increasingly use it for reliable information. ●

Using Social Media to Build Credibility

Publics have high expectations for how organizations interact with them, typically expecting communication that is authentic, honest, candid, and two-way. We can sum up these expectations in one word: credibility. Research on social media concludes credibility is an umbrella term that encompasses the dimensions of *personal interaction, expertise, welcoming language,* and *trustworthiness* (Kim & Brown, 2015).

- *Personal interaction* is the single most significant aspect of credibility. Organizations should interact and relate in a personal way with their publics. This humanizing communication shows a level of transparency and altruism.

- *Expertise*—long before social media—was identified as a foundational aspect of credibility, and it remains key to the social media space. Both content and appearance—well developed and visually attractive—help communicate expertise.

- *Welcoming language* (also called "invitational rhetoric") is language that invites others' perspectives and does not try to control or censor conversations. It recognizes the mutuality concept of relationship building and emphasizes the value of listening.

- *Trustworthiness*, as with expertise, has long been identified in media studies as essential to credibility. With social media, it can be considered the sum of the preceding factors: Well-performed personal interactions, well-formed expressions of expertise, and consistent use of welcoming language all contribute to building trust between a public and an organization. Trust is foundational to long-term relationships.

Corporate Social Responsibility

A robust communication strategy is needed for any CSR engagement, and that means social media plays a key role. As seen in examples of award-winning social media campaigns, the authenticity of social media is an important part of their success. Business professor Paul Argenti (2016) notes that transparency and authenticity are particularly important for businesses trying to explain their understanding of and their efforts in sustainability and social responsibility (SR). Boston College's Center for Corporate Citizenship conducts research on social media's facility to amplify CSR communication. One strategy it suggests is encouraging employees to engage in the corporate social media content to put a human face to the company.

Social media allows these businesses to connect with target publics in meaningful ways. Examine the following examples:

- In 2005, Canadian Tire launched Jumpstart, a national charity that benefits kids who face financial and accessibility barriers to sports and recreation. To expand awareness and increase donations, the firm used social media to launch its "Toasters" campaign. For $25, Canadians could buy . . . yes, toasters! Three versions would either burn the image of hockey legend Wayne Gretsky or images of two other hockey stars onto the toast. While the goal was to raise $250,000 over the lifespan of the campaign, the toasters sold out in 24 hours (Ragan's PR Daily, 2018b).

- PepsiCo was one of the first CSR-focused companies to use **crowdsourcing** to build an online CSR campaign, the Pepsi Refresh Project. Its social media campaign was such a success that 1 month after its January launch, it opted out of traditional advertising in the Super Bowl after a 23-year commitment (Argenti, 2016).

PR PROFILE

Why a Communications Campaign Is Only as Good as Its Social Media Strategy

Linda Descano, Executive Vice President, Red Havas PR North America

Photo courtesy of Linda Descano

I can't think of a bigger game changer for communications than technology. It's empowered consumers to set the terms for the way brands communicate with them. And as people have increasingly gone to different places to find news and information (places that can often be held in the palm of the hand), traditional media has become only a part of the recipe for engagement.

The best communications campaigns today take a merged media approach, threading stories across paid, earned, and owned media channels and through online social activations, offline marketing experiences, and PR stunts. Social media is key to establish brand voices, fuel larger stories, elevate individuals into industry thought leaders, and extend the reach of events beyond their attendees.

The biggest opportunity that the social space holds for brands is that it allows them to engage in conversation with their audience and listen to what they have to say. As opposed to the more traditional monologue style of communication, now brands get to enjoy a real-time dialogue with their customers and followers. Although pay-to-play social media is a powerful way to get a message in front of an audience (e.g., buying ads or promoting posts), the real payoff is in getting an audience to interact organically with your content and especially to share it across their own social networks—basically to cultivate individuals as brand ambassadors. The trick is to craft a message in a way that draws people in and moves them to care and to share what you have to say.

Another reason to make social media part of every PR plan is that our raucous multichannel news cycle demands a constant supply of sensational news that it will either find or create. An old-fashioned communication strategy could be compromised by anybody anywhere who has a connection. Although the social space is a place where any cranky comment can grow legs, it's also the only place where messaging and audience targeting can be adjusted in real time to capitalize on fast-moving media opportunities and to head off negative events.

Whatever you do, don't forget the most important part: Output is not the same as outcome, so measure what you do. Start every social media campaign with an understanding of what **ROI** (return on investment) means for a client and its business efforts. (For some clients, the primary objective of social media is to generate engagement in the form of social shares, while others may want to drive newsletter sign-ups, downloads of an app, sales, or traffic to a destination page.) By extension, determine whether ROI means the total number of social conversations about the company or year-over-year growth in the number of advocates (people sharing its content).

And today, there is more data to parse than ever. Once you've established clear metrics, track those metrics using social analytics platforms. Historical performance is one necessary benchmark for tracking performance and optimizing ongoing efforts. Another way of gauging effectiveness: Look holistically at the total reach and engagement through a campaign, and track what percentage is earned versus paid and owned.

As the very definitions of who is making the news and how it's being made are shifting beneath us, social media may just be the best way to get a client's messages into the news. Once you figure out how to blow up the Internet, you've figured out the hard part—at least for now. ●

Before joining Red Havas, Linda Descano, CFA®, served as managing director and global head of content marketing and social media for Citi.

Source: L. Descano, personal communication, 2020.

A Showcase of Digital and Social Media PR Practices

>> LO 8.3 **Evaluate PR best practices in social media and digital communications**

Top PR agencies, brands, and nonprofits are using multiple social media platforms and digital communications creatively and successfully. The following examples offer instruction and inspiration, but remember—it's an evolving social media world out there, so be sure to refer to industry blogs and websites to keep current.

Industry News Sources

- Edelman, a leading global PR firm, shares digital news at www.edelmandigital.com/insights.
- Ragan's PR Daily is a hub for the PR industry with a dedicated social media page: www.prdaily.com/SocialMedia/SocialMedia.aspx.
- Meltwater, the media monitoring company, offers news on social media at www.meltwater.com/blog.
- Social Media Examiner is a widely respected social media marketing blog: www.socialmediaexaminer.com.

Facebook

As the social media leader, Facebook offers great opportunities for PR. However, in 2018 Mark Zuckerberg announced algorithm changes that prioritized community-centric content. Many companies feared the changes would drive down their visibility, leading to decreased engagement with brand posts. However, Airbnb managed to keep Facebook working for it with some successful strategies (Barnhart, 2018).

To fill its Facebook feed, Airbnb relies heavily on user-generated content from satisfied customers. The images of exotic locations posted by users help to attract and engage followers. Luckily, Facebook's algorithm favors visual content over links, so Airbnb's strategy works with it. Airbnb also goes back and forth with customers, emphasizing customer care and exploring their thoughts and ideas; thus, posts gain more engagement as a result.

With internal publics, Facebook offers the breadth to tell an evolving story when an organization is going through change. While technology company NCR was building a new and expansive global headquarters in Atlanta, it also increased its digital visibility with Facebook. It used the platform to engage with employees in the area, alerting them to major changes, providing updates, and building enthusiasm. Employees discovered a "Silicon Valley of the East" with glamorous lifestyle and culture enhancements like a fitness center and inviting outdoor green spaces—all in an upscale Atlanta neighborhood. For its creative use of Facebook, NCR's effort was named best PR campaign in *PR News*'s social media awards.

Instagram

The ubiquitous GIF, popular culture, and university milestones gave life to an Instagram campaign by Northern Arizona University (NAU; Ragan's PR Daily, 2019c). Because GIFs are now available in Instagram Stories, the university developed unique NAU GIFs. Through them, the university tells the story of its "Louie the Lumberjack" mascot, inviting students to tell their personal stories.

First, the NAU GIF stickers featured a "Back to NAU" theme with connections to popular culture references. For example, the Louie mascot was refashioned to look like Super Mario punching boxes to unpack his belongings. Another pack of GIFs featured "Game Day-Ready" themes. And others encouraged prospective students to announce their decision to attend NAU with the addition of the hashtag #NAUSaidYes.

When NAU won first place in the "Instagram Stories" category of PR Daily's 2019 Digital Marketing & Social Media Awards (Ragan's PR Daily, 2019c), they had been viewed 92.4 million times.

How Can a Small Brand Use Social Media to Grow?

Just a few years ago, Shannon Peppeard, an entrepreneur with a growing interior design business in a distant Chicago suburb, never had to seek out clients. With a combination of luck and good fortune, her small business was thriving on referrals alone.

"To me, marketing and advertising were not needed. But then I attended a designer conference called Bold Summit in Chicago, and it completely changed my outlook on social media. Before this conference, I wasn't using social media at all. I went into the conference not really knowing what it was all about and still thinking I didn't need it for my business. Boy, was I wrong" (S. Peppeard, personal communication, 2020)!

Peppeard learned about the value of social media to brand yourself and attract the clients she wanted—and weed out the others. After the conference, she hired a web designer to create a professional website. In that process, she changed her business name and rebranded. What resulted was a beautiful, elevated, and branded website and Instagram account.

"It was a game changer for my work to finally be 'out there.' Now, not only was I documenting my work in pictures on Facebook, Instagram, and the website, but I was also invited into a community of other interior designers I had no idea were there. Social media allowed me to engage my peers and people in my industry. It opened up so many doors with industry contacts and high-end clients."

Peppeard's Instagram account that had earlier been started with five followers grew to over 12,000 in 2 years. She learned that the right content attracted the right followers. Soon, she found that social media was a full-time job, so she sought PR experts to help her business grow.

On the strength of her dynamic Instagram account, professional website, and her blog PepTalk, Peppeard was nominated within her industry as "Influencer of the Year 2020"—a prestigious honor placing her in the company of fellow nominees that include renowned designers, bloggers, and social media gurus.

Twitter

With the immediacy of a tweet, Twitter has transformed citizen engagement in politics, popular culture, product experience, customer service, news consumption, issue advocacy, and more—as well as influenced the communication practices of organizations, media professionals, personalities, politicians, and most definitely the field of PR. Many brands use Twitter to thrust their campaigns into the realm of popular culture because Twitter users can influence movements within cultures and inject creativity into new and surprising places (Trinder, 2020).

Adidas and UNHCR are among brands and organizations that found creative ways to use Twitter successfully. For nighttime runners, Adidas used Twitter to launch the #nitejogger trainers—shoes that light up in the dark. It unveiled the world's first "invisible emoji" that users can see in the Twitter timeline only when they switch to the app's dark mode. During the campaign, the brand significantly increased its share of conversations.

The United Nations High Commissioner for Refugees (UNHCR) teamed up with the fashion-tech start-up Kniterate and Twitter to build awareness about the plight of refugees in winter, an especially difficult time for millions of people displaced from their homes. Beside an urgent call for donations, the 5-month long #Knitforrefugees campaign collected usernames of participating Twitter accounts that were then physically knitted *live* onto scarves by an automated knitting machine. In the United Kingdom, the UNHCR global goodwill ambassador and author Neil Gaiman urged his followers to tweet their thoughts about "warmth and winter," which inspired a short story that was knitted onto a shawl and released as a thread on Twitter (Trinder, 2020).

Adidas introduced running shoes that lit up in the dark on Twitter, unveiling the world's first "invisible emoji" that lit up when the app was in dark mode.
vgajic / Getty Images

TikTok

Not all brands will have a compatible fit with the TikTok social video app, but if they're serving (or looking to serve) a younger demographic and can embrace a casual and comedic tone, it's where the party is. Favored by Gen Z, TikTok offers brands a way to reach a new public in a very personal way. And many users respond to the app's hashtag challenges. For example, Chipotle part-nered with influencers on a TikTok challenge to celebrate #NationalGuacDay. It offered free guacamole on digital orders and asked customers to use TikTok to share a video of an avocado-themed dance (performed to "The Guacamole Song")—hashtagging it #GuacDance. It earned 250,000 submissions and 430 million views in the first 6 days. As a result, avocado use at Chipotle jumped 68% for National Avocado Day (Morris, 2019).

Professional sports communications have also leaned into TikTok. To celebrate its 100th season, the NFL arranged a 2-year partnership with TikTok (as did the NBA and Wimbledon) to create weekly content. Its goal: to connect with younger viewers and create future fans through engaging them with game highlights, sideline moments, and hashtag challenges (Morris, 2019).

Apps

A dating app for cows? This clever campaign was named winner of the 2019 "Most Effective Use of Social Media" PR Award given by The Drum, Europe's largest media and marketing website. U.K.-based Hectare Agritech (HA) had several goals for its PR agency, Octopus Group: raise the profile of SellMyLivestock, its online trading platform; build awareness of the possibilities for online livestock trading in general; and determine if there was demand for its services in new, international markets (The Drum, 2019).

The solution: HA created and launched a Tinder-inspired app called Tudder. It let farmers match up potential "partners" for their cattle by swiping right on cattle they like. HA promoted the app with a Valentine's Day-focused media campaign, securing coverage by both national and international mainstream media. Significant trade titles in agriculture and farming also reported on the app. Tudder led users to SellMyLivestock, where they could browse more pictures and data about the animals before making a buying decision. The results? HA reported a surge in both traffic and new subscribers to the platform, and the far-reaching media coverage of Tudder drew business inquiries from farmers in new regions, including the United States and Australia (The Drum, 2019).

A Tinder-inspired app called Tudder lets farmers match up potential "partners" for their cattle by swiping right on cattle they like.
MATTHEW STOCK/REUTERS/Newscom

LinkedIn

The business networking site LinkedIn offers myriad ways for an organization to use it stra-tegically as an extension of its professional brand. A company page should carry impres-sive images and content, some ideally written by employees—humanizing it *and* establish-ing it as a thought leader. It is definitely more time-consuming to set up than are some other social media tools, but here's an example of one company using LinkedIn for PR value.

#RepresentLove

Tinder petitioned the Unicode Consortium to permit users to create multiracial couples.
NurPhoto / Contributor / Getty Images

Emojis!

The 2,500-plus emojis in our texting and typing world let us show emotions, clarify our thoughts, and in general illustrate our communication. Another function of emojis is to express our identities, including race and sexual orientation. However, emojis didn't always allow us to do that. The dating app Tinder, which had introduced nonbinary gender identities into its app, decided to do more.

Tinder is available in 190 countries and offered in more than 40 languages. Concurrent with the rise of online dating was an increase in interracial marriages. Tinder recognized this as an opportunity to differentiate itself among competitors and decided to use emojis as both a means to shape its brand and create a more inclusive space.

#RepresentLove resulted as a means of celebrating interracial love.

Research Drives Action

A survey developed and conducted on Tinder's behalf, the "Global Tinder Survey on Interracial

Relationships," showed nearly 60% have been in a romantic relationship with a person of a different race. It was time to rally for these singles and their ability to express themselves using emojis—the universal language of the digital age. Tinder petitioned the Unicode Consortium to permit users to create multiracial couples, allowing representation for the nearly 75% of Tinder users who have dated a person of a different race.

Planning

To build global public backing for Tinder's petition and #RepresentLove initiative, Tinder employed these strategies:

- To emphasize Tinder's commitment to fostering diversity and inclusion, it positioned the emoji launch as proof of this pledge, accomplished through earned and owned communications channels.

- To create a broader narrative about users' openness to interracial relationships, Tinder developed factual and emotional content to inspire sharing by its users.

Strategies Come to Life

These strategies succeeded in generating earned media storytelling, global survey data, and an inspirational video. To magnify the attention, a digital influencer program enlisted celebrities to share their own interracial couple emojis. As a result, in 2019 Unicode updated its bank of emoji symbols to allow users to select the race and gender of both people when choosing an emoji that features a couple. ●

Source: PRSA, 2019c.

In an effort to take advantage of popular concern around email security issues, the Zix Corporation's PR firm, The Hoffman Agency, took a four-pronged approach with its LinkedIn page (see Table 8.1). Zix's followers grew from 600 to 2,400, nearly two thirds of them senior executives, managers, and directors, and LinkedIn began driving more than 85% of the company's social traffic.

TABLE 8.1

LinkedIn Transformation

ISSUE	APPROACH
1. Executive profiles	Updated to be: • More compelling • More discoverable through key words like "email encryption" and "BYOD"
2. Presentation	Polished to: • Humanize • Use a storytelling approach
3. Content	Posts emulated most popular content on the Web: • Customer spotlight features • Thought leadership on industry news • Highlights of consumer surveys • Best-practice Q&As
4. Action strategies	Executive participation: • Used for promotion • Drove engagement

YouTube and Second Screens

Pampers was the ultimate Super Bowl underdog in 2019 with no TV airtime purchase. However, with about three quarters of fans on social media during the game and more looking to ads for entertainment, Pampers' strategy was to own the second screen—where conversations about the game and ads take place. To kick off its new campaign "Love the Change," Pampers released a new video remix of John Legend's popular hit "Stinky Booty Duty," starring Legend and his young family, along with Adam Levine and his infant daughter.

The video's big idea was to challenge traditional parenting roles by celebrating dads and the unique bond they share with their babies. Working with MSL, Publicis Groupe's PR network, the campaign strategy was designed to earn attention from millennial parents by tying the video's release and promotion to the multiscreen reality of how consumers engage during live events (The International Business Awards, 2019).

This is how it played out: A social media teaser campaign began the day before the game, leading to organic pickup. On game day, celebrities Legend and his wife, model Chrissy Teigen, and Levine shared the video on their

Pampers stole the 2019 Super Bowl ad show with a social media video strategy starring John Legend.

Phillip Faraone / Stringer / Getty Images

social channels. Hundreds of influencers, including DJ Khaled, reposted the video. At the end of the game, Chrissy posted comments on the video to further fuel the conversation. While social media went abuzz, MSL's media pitches led to hundreds of stories. The video got more YouTube likes than the Super Bowl ads from Pepsi and Doritos combined, and it ended up ranking top five on Super Bowl ad lists in *Billboard*, *Forbes*, BuzzFeed, and the BBC (The International Business Awards, 2019).

Podcasts

A PR variety show, the "Flack Pack" podcast, resulted from the Washington Media Group's efforts to perfect its podcasting skills (Ragan's PR Daily, 2019d). The public affairs firm developed the podcast with all staff members contributing a variety of segments, such as in-person public interviews and games. All podcast channels carry the weekly 45- to 50-minute podcast, showcasing the firm's talent as they discuss topical issues such as how to manage influencers and the ethics of firms working for authoritarian countries. PR news and PR history are also featured.

As its audience has grown throughout 40 episodes each season, the firm has taken the opportunity to increase its contacts through social media and feels it has served its clients better through its podcasting expertise. A notable success for its ingenuity and broad appeal, Flack Pack earned first place in the podcast category of PR Daily's 2019 Digital Marketing & Social Media Awards.

Augmented Reality

To call attention to the legal voting age in Arizona and activate its audience, the voter initiative "18 in 2018" from Citizens Clean Elections Commission (CCEC, 2019) worked with the Riester agency to create an original augmented reality mural installation to capture the imagination of its target audience. The big idea was that by registering to vote you are "taking flight" into adulthood and initiating your political power.

The *Take Flight* mural, featuring a rainbow-colored 10-foot wingspan, was launched in a prominent location in the Phoenix arts district. To promote sharing of selfies, a similar mural was placed at a popular Tucson concert venue. Just as voting requires our involvement, the mural was meant to be participatory. AR amplified the installation's theme of activating one's political power. To experience it, people would position themselves between the mural's two wings. A partner would download the Shazam app, snap the mural's QR code, and then point at the mural. The AR experience of flapping wings would start when it had the posing person in focus–suggesting they were taking flight. The app, Instagram profile, and paid-digital media all guided users to a landing page for the elections commission, where they could register to vote.

Interactive Microsites

Ferrovial, the Spanish infrastructure company, worked with several NGOs to restore an aqueduct in Colombia to improve access to drinking water. This type of project might typically generate a simple press release. However, the story behind the project was dramatic. To tell it, Colombian comic artists were hired to create an interactive graphic novel—found at www.aguaparalapaz.com (translation: water for peace).

The history of the project's location was a sad one. In the small town of El Salado, 66 people were murdered by paramilitary guerrillas in 2000. Survivors fled to the cities of Bogota and Cartagena. Later, 200 families returned to reclaim their land and their lives. The graphic novel first tells of the Zenú, the region's first inhabitants, and their spiritual connection to water. To tell the returnees' stories, the artists were inspired by the literature of Colombia's own master storyteller, Gabriel García Marquez.

The website combined the comic's mythical narrative with real-life testimonials about El Salado's past violent events, meshing fiction with reality. Interactive elements throughout include ambient noise from an El Salado street to an area map. Also featured are video interviews and photos of those who inspired the story. Shared across social media channels, it earned first place in the *Microsite or Custom Website* category of Ragan's 2019 Digital & Social Media Awards (Ragan's PR Daily, 2019a).

Evaluating Social Media and Looking to the Future

>> LO 8.4   Identify how to measure social media effectiveness, and craft a strategy for staying abreast of trends

Content creation is one of the top services that is driving growth in the PR industry. For that content, basic written and verbal skills are surely important; however, due to the digital nature of much content now, PR leaders must also be stronger in analytics, better at technology, and more creative.

You read about measurement of PR efforts in Chapter 5—essential to establishing the value of your recommended strategies and tactics. To begin to evaluate your social media PR efforts, consider your audience and determine which social channels—and which messages—drive the most traffic to your website or result in your desired outcomes. It's essential to adjust your PR tactics to each platform based on what you learn about their audience demographics and based on the nature of the platform.

Obtaining data analytics is a standard way of measuring social media activity and results: **mentions**, **sentiment**, **reach**, **exposure**, and **engagement**. There are various web metrics tools available to evaluate social media channels. Google Analytics is a free tool developed by Google and probably the one that is most widely used. Two resources from Google, one free and the other for a fee, can get you started with Google Analytics. The free resource offers open courses in the Google Analytics Academy. Its introductory course teaches the basics like implementing tracking code, analyzing reports, and setting up goals and campaign tracking; other lessons cover capabilities that bring app and web analytics together.

Measurement today across multiple communications channels is necessary for reporting. Austin Gaule, media analysis director for the media monitoring company NewsExposure, offers this advice on the value of measurement in public relations (PR):

> PR measurement should start with an evaluation of your current organizational needs and determining how you can tie your measurement to business objectives. Every program should start with defining your KPIs (key performance indicators) that will set the foundation for your analysis.
>
> Choosing a data collection tool that is relevant to your needs is something you will have to keep in mind as well. Traditional media and social media both need separate data collection tools to complete a holistic picture of what is happening in your media space.
>
> Tying your measurement to business objectives and business goals is paramount to proving your success in the public relations space. Looking at

qualitative measures versus quantitative has proven to be the best strategy for public relations professionals in the present day. Measures such as brand loyalty, brand trust, and brand reputation are measures that extend far beyond simple quantitative measures and tell a story.

The PESO Model (developed by Gini Dietrich at Spin Sucks) takes into account paid, earned, shared, and owned media and has been accepted by PR professionals across the world. Measuring across this entire model will give you the full measurement picture of your communications efforts. Finding internal measures from your owned media and combining it with the metrics from your paid media and earned media will prove useful as you evaluate not only your public relations strategy, but it will increase understanding of how these two separate departments need to coexist to reach your organizational goals. Too often, these departments do not work together in unison as they should. Successful measurement programs are rooted in the thinking that public relations and marketing need to work together. (Gaule, personal communication, 2020)

Scenario Outcome

At this chapter's beginning, we provided a real-life scenario requiring VW to respond to a crisis. To review, VW was caught intentionally violating the Clean Air Act. The EPA revealed VW had developed software purposefully designed to deceive the EPA's emissions tests. We asked you these questions:

- How should VW PR have handled this crisis via social media? What repercussions might arise if not handled properly?

- If you were VW's PR counsel, what publics would be critical to communicate with, through which social channels, and with what messaging?

What VW *should* have done and what it *did* offer a critical PR lesson. U.S. VW stopped posting to Facebook and Twitter on Friday, September 18, the day the news broke in the United States. The social media accounts remained dormant for 1 full week, with no responses to comments. Later, VW's CEO posted a statement on the accounts.

Thus, for 8 days after the news, U.S. VW's social media accounts provided no information—only an apology video from the CEO. However, Twitter was exploding with consumer outrage. The U.S. financial news website, The Street, noted in an article headline, "Social Media Shows How Big a Blow Emissions Scandal Is" (Stuart, 2015).

On the ninth day, VW posted an FAQ page directing customers to a customer care phone number and email address. Three months after the news, a *Financial Times* (Milne, 2015) headline revealed, "Volkswagen Blunders Through Communications Over Emissions Scandals: Customers and Investors Have Been Left Exasperated by Carmaker's Public Statements." Five months later, *The New York Times* headlined, "VW's Crisis Strategy: Forward, Reverse, U-Turn," with the opening line, "Someday, Volkswagen's emissions cheating scandal will be studied in crisis communications textbooks. And not in a good way" (Hakim, 2016). Following *The New York Times*, the *Christian Science Monitor's* editorial board stated, "The industry must be as transparent as possible and cooperate with its many stakeholders" (Editorial Board, 2016).

Your advice as PR counsel? If you suggested immediate and comprehensive social media monitoring, followed by escalated and sincere engagement with multiple publics—including employees—you were smarter than the execs at VW.

And beyond the CEO's apology video, you may have suggested other multimedia visual messaging to deliver a more authentic and emotive response.

Lessons learned? In 2019, VW launched the "Drive Bigger" campaign with an ad explaining Dieselgate as impetus for VW's aggressive move into electric vehicles— its effort to recapture environmental high ground lost due to the emissions crisis (Schultz, 2019).

Attempting to put the 2015 emissions scandal behind it, by 2020 VW had embraced a new strategy to "not show a perfect advertising world . . . become more human . . . and tell authentic stories," according to VW CMO Jochen Sengpiehl (Fleming, 2019). It introduced a new logo and brand design and incorporated a female voice to present its vehicles. Interestingly, it also said goodbye to the Beetle, using the Beatles' "Let It Be" (sung by a children's chorus) as soundtrack to a 1-minute-and-30-second animated ad, "The Last Mile," launched on New Year's Eve in 2019. One of the ad's pop culture references included Bravo personality Andy Cohen, host of CNN's New Year's Eve coverage. Cohen teased the ad on Instagram with a paid post, encouraging followers to share pictures of their own Beetles—part of a larger influencer campaign.

WRAP UP

This chapter substantiated the critical relevance of social media in PR today. It traced its historical antecedents and early development through a timeline illustrating social media's exponential growth in the 21st century. This foundational understanding explains why the practice of PR has shifted dramatically in very recent years and must continue to respond and adapt to new platforms and technologies.

To help you recognize and understand how organizations are *best* using social media in PR campaigns, you read about award-winning campaigns in many major platforms and engaged in award-winning case studies. You also got a baseline understanding of the value and need for measuring social media PR efforts and guidance on how to follow social media innovations and success stories in the future.

KEY TERMS

Crowdsourcing 184
Engagement 192
Exposure 192
Hashtags 173
Memes 181

Mentions 192
Reach 192
Return on Investment (ROI) 185
Sentiment 192
Social Network Theory (SNT) 177

THINK ABOUT IT

You will participate in a form of crowdsourcing with your classmates, working together to write a *social media recommendation report* for an organization or situation of your choice (e.g., your university needs to recruit more out-of-state students). Each student is then responsible for one paragraph of the report.

- Use Google Docs or another platform to communicate with one another.
- Begin with a paragraph on the hypothetical or real organization and situation.

- Each student should contribute a paragraph (write your name at the end of it).
- When completed, one student will upload to a class online discussion board.

Each student then posts in the discussion thread: Comment on the experience of writing the report, how it relates to crowdsourcing, and what you learned about social media for PR. Next, each student responds to the comments of at least one other classmate.

WRITE LIKE A PRO

You handle PR for Spaulding Health Research (SHR), headquartered in Detroit, Michigan. SHR has just received $1.4 million funding from the All One World Foundation—for creating a global research initiative on risk reductions for childhood lead poisoning. The funds were awarded to support the human and capital investment needed to launch and sustain this initiative. Sylvia Wallander, president of SHR, attributed its selection to Spaulding's breakthrough research in 2019 on preventing HIV in pregnancies.

Your task is to communicate, via Twitter, with one category of Spaulding's many publics except the media (employees, influencers, researchers in the field, donors, activists, victims of lead poisoning, etc.). Once decided, provide the following:

1. Identify the public.
2. Write the best tweet (280 characters or less) to inspire someone to read, react, and retweet your message. Create and include at least one hashtag.
3. Provide rationale: What was the thought process you used to create "the perfect tweet"?

CASE STUDY

Every Baby Is a Gerber Baby

Situation

Gerber's first contest to find a baby face for its new baby food took place in 1928—and a simple charcoal drawing was the winner. It fast became the "Gerber Baby" symbol, appearing on packaging and advertisements for decades. Then, in 2010 Gerber began holding an annual Gerber Baby contest and awarding winners generously with scholarships plus other prizes and opportunities.

Past winners have reflected diversity and inclusivity, including Kairi of Hmong descent and Latinx Mary Jane. Each Gerber Baby is featured in the brand's social media channels and advertising throughout the year. However, in 2018 Gerber chose Lucas, the first baby with Down syndrome—and partnered with Edible, an Edelman company, to announce him as winner.

Research and Strategy

Edible collaborated with Gerber to create a strategic plan and an earned media strategy, intending to place the story with a top national media outlet. To prepare for the possibility of negative reactions, advocacy groups and NGOs were approached to secure support from credible third parties in advance of the announcement. A crisis and issues management approach was also created to help navigation of this sensitive topic.

Execution

Gerber engaged traditional outlets to announce the news, triggering viral diffusion worldwide. NBC's *Today* show unveiled Lucas as the Gerber winner during its highest rated

8 a.m. hour, reaching more than 4-plus million viewers. According to Edible, "Influencers and advocacy groups publicly shared support, including the National Down Syndrome Society, the Global Down Syndrome Foundation, the Special Olympics and congressmen from Lucas' home state" (Edible, 2018, para. 3). Gerber was a trending topic on Twitter, and stories were featured in prestigious media outlets such as *NBC Nightly News*, CNN, *USA Today*, and *The New York Times*.

Evaluation

Gerber's campaign was named Viral Campaign of the Year 2019 by *PRWeek* and given the platinum award for Best PR Campaign of the Year by the Holmes Report's Global SABRES (Holmes, 2019b). Judges called it one of the most inspiring and moving campaigns for its authenticity. One *PRWeek* judge noted that while it's "hard for brands that are really established to disrupt themselves and do something iconic," the campaign was a "lovely way to contemporize a very old brand" (*PRWeek*, 2019, para. 2). Ultimately, the choice to feature a baby with Down syndrome gave new meaning to the brand's long-standing slogan "Every Baby Is a Gerber Baby."

Engage

- Search to discover how the National Down Syndrome Society, the Global Down Syndrome Foundation, and the Special Olympics perceived and reacted to the choice of Lucas as the 2019 Gerber Baby.

Discuss

- What do you think about Gerber's decision to choose and promote a baby with a disability?
- Is it ethical for a commercial brand to use a child with Down syndrome for PR and marketing purposes?
- Can you think of a client situation involving social media promotion of a child that would trouble you as PR counsel?

Sources: Edible, 2018; Holmes, 2019b; *PRWeek*, 2019.

iStock.com/dolgachov

Corporate Social Responsibility and Community Relations

Learning Objectives

9.1   Understand CSR, its history, and its connection to PR

9.2   Examine how successful CSR activity is part of organizational culture and reputation management

9.3   Evaluate the opportunities and challenges in mounting an effective internal and external CSR campaign

9.4   Understand the PR practice of community relations and its connection to CSR

How Do Smaller U.S. Businesses Practice and Communicate Their Corporate Social Responsibility?

Cheerios partners with the American Heart Association and makes that obvious on its packaging with a heart-shaped cereal bowl, but what do the Blue Goose Market or Graham's Chocolates do to be good citizens and let their communities know?

This is the question posed to eight small Illinois businesses by one of this book's authors (Page & Page, 2013). It's an important question because 89% of U.S. firms had fewer than 20 employees in 2016, according to the Small Business and Entrepreneurship Council (SBE, 2018).

All locally owned, the eight businesses included an insurance company, a coffee shop, a bicycle retailer, an entertainment venue, a sweet shop, a grocery store, a sports club, and a sandwich shop. Half of the businesses were family owned, and employees numbered between 13 and 90.

Small businesses can find that informing the public about their charitable work or efforts at sustainability can be challenging.
iStock.com/4x6

"It's the right thing to do." All owners agreed that "community philanthropy" is their preferred CSR practice, which included donating gift cards, discounted or free products, coupons, rent-free space, and sometimes just cash. A culture of giving flows from employees and family members as well as the consideration of walk-in requests. Their charitable practices are motivated by personal principles and a sense of community obligation. Some of the owners explained, "It's how I was raised." "It comes from my roots in a small town." In all cases, the most common word used when describing their reasons for engaging in CSR was "community." And the biggest beneficiaries of all charitable efforts were children.

"Our acts are seeding more acts." Did they expect anything in return for their good works? A few had no expectations, some placed further philanthropy expectations on the recipients, and others hoped it would build awareness and understanding of who they were. A majority saw their business ethos as playing a key role in building a better community. "We do what we do to bond the community together."

"We do things quietly." When asked if they publicize their charity in any way, however, the response from every participant was not only that they did not, but they felt to do so was somehow distasteful. Indeed, most of the respondents appeared slightly offended by the question and often answered in a reproachful tone. Their answers sometimes derided boasting: "I wouldn't polish my own badge." "We don't go around tooting our own horn." Or their answers indicated some distaste with the question: "That would be bragging." These attitudes carried through any of the various ways questions were asked about how they communicated CSR to the public and the media or what their expectations were of their charitable efforts. Nearly all agreed that their CSR involvement is "strategic," yet most of them had no communication strategy and little structure to measure effectiveness.

(Continued)

(Continued)

Student Challenge

Use the lessons in this chapter to help you answer these questions:

1. Why should the businesses communicate CSR with their publics?
2. What benefits are these local businesses missing from failing to communicate their good works?
3. What methods should the businesses use to communicate their good works?

At the end of the chapter, you'll find some advice. ●

This chapter explains CSR and it origins and reveals how the movement is influencing firms to perform as good corporate citizens with obligations to society and the environment while, at the same time, nurturing the health of their business. You'll find the wisdom for guiding CSR is understanding an organization's multiple stakeholders, ranging from employees to investors. You'll also learn why choosing CSR programs that match up with a firm's brand identity and organizational culture is essential.

Profiles, insights, and cases demonstrate how CEOs lead CSR through example and activism, how employees become more engaged through volunteering, how communities benefit from CSR initiatives, and how PR plays an integral role. How and why certain businesses perform responsibly is explained, covering differences among multinational corporations, benefit corporations, and social entrepreneurships—and the varying roles of PR in each.

Finally, the chapter covers the essential elements of effective CSR communications strategy, including research, traditional and social tactics, evaluation, and an important focus on community relations.

Defining Corporate Social Responsibility and Sustainability Communications: Doing Well by Doing Good, or Is It More Complex?

>> LO 9.1　Understand CSR, its history, and its connection to PR

CSR is the purposeful incorporation of public interest into a business's decision-making. This honoring of a **triple bottom line** (the three Ps)—which refers to *people* (social), *planet* (environmental), and *profit* (economic)—suggests the three performance areas that a company should serve and measure. CSR is widely defined as the sum of "the voluntary actions taken by a company to address the economic, social and environmental impacts of its business operations and the concerns of its principal stakeholders" (Christensen et al., 2007, p. 351).

CSR actions or activities are not required of the company or organization by any government or regulatory body. They are done at a company's discretion. This distinction is one key to considering something to be CSR versus a legal obligation such as paying taxes, maintaining safe working conditions, paying a minimum wage, and so on. While in many European countries there are national policies and legislation surrounding CSR, in the United States, social, environmental, and economic factors drive the implementation of CSR.

Origins and Driving Forces of Corporate Social Responsibility

How CSR became a major PR function can be understood best by looking at public calls for social responsibility and efforts to influence organizational behavior throughout history. In the United States, early movements for the rights of workers, shareholders, and customers versus corporate rights all help explain the history and evolution of CSR (see Table 9.1).

1900s to 1950s

In the early 1900s, a backlash against business began to arise. Large, powerful corporations were accused of lacking concern for employees, community, or society. In 1914, Henry Ford doubled the wages of his Model T assembly line workers; however, he did it specifically to secure his business. In 1929, Eastman Kodak Company offered profit sharing, retirement bonuses, a pension plan, and sickness benefits to its workers.

After the Wall Street crash in 1929 and the subsequent Great Depression in the 1930s and onward, corporations began to be seen as institutions that had social obligations. Philanthropy then became another early form of CSR. In the 1950s, Howard Bowen became one of the first to define social responsibility (SR), citing the obligations of business to pursue policies, make decisions, and follow actions that are desirable for society. He has been called the father of corporate social responsibility.

1960s and 1970s

CSR grew significantly in the 1960s and accelerated in the 1970s. The civil rights movement, along with consumerism and environmentalism, influenced society's expectations of business. Voices demanded the business world be more proactive—stopping to cause social problems and starting to fix them. Legal mandates required equal employment opportunity, product safety, and worker safety. Business philanthropy increased, as did employee improvements, customer relations, and stockholder relations. Businesses also addressed minority hiring and training, environmental concerns, support of education and the arts, urban renewal, and community affairs (Eilbirt & Parket, 1973; Holmes, 1976). Companies began to plan for and organize CSR, assess their performance, and adopt policies and strategies.

TABLE 9.1

Modern Evolution of Corporate Social Responsibility in the United States

TIME PERIOD	EVENT
1900 to 1950s	Corporate power questioned
1960s and 1970s	Business addresses social issues
1980s and 1990s	Call for business ethics and corporate citizenship
21st century	Standards and best practices established

1980s and 1990s

In the 1980s and 1990s, many issues rose to the surface, including businesses' impact on environmental pollution, discrimination in the workplace, consumer abuses, the health and safety of employees, work life quality, deterioration of urban life, and questionable or abusiveness practices of multinational corporations. Concerns for business ethics arose due to notorious instances of corporate wrongdoing—for example, Union Carbide's 1984 disaster in Bhopal and the *Exxon Valdez* oil spill in 1989.

CSR then evolved into subfields of corporate social performance, sustainability, corporate citizenship, and the concept of stakeholder theory. Philanthropy expanded considerably, and CSR became part of business practice. Many early adopters of significant CSR programs include The Body Shop, Ben & Jerry's, Patagonia, Johnson & Johnson, Nike, IBM, and McDonald's.

21st Century

The 21st century established SR standards and best practices. In 2000, 44 businesses signed the United Nation's Global Compact, pledging to align their practices with its principles on "human rights, labour, environment, and anti-corruption" (UN Global Compact, n.d., para. 3). By 2019, more than 9,500 had signed. Well into the first few decades of the 2000s, CSR was becoming fully integrated into business management and governance.

To be clear, this evolution highlights the distinction between CSR and corporate philanthropy. There is a difference between allocating a share of proceeds from product sales to a charity (e.g., Lord & Taylor donating to St. Jude's Hospital during a "special sale") versus integrating sustainable business practices into the company's operations, such as Starbucks, Nike, CVS, and other CSR leaders do. In short, one company is making a charitable donation—no doubt welcomed by the charity—while the other is fundamentally changing the way it does business and how it treats its suppliers and employees. Where would you rather work or do business?

Social Responsibility Is Foundational in Public Relations Today

Behind the more obvious impetus for a company's socially responsible actions—flood victims in need of shelter or beaches needing a cleanup—it is the business's stakeholders who serve as a driving force for organizational change, encouraging more ethical behavior and transparency. Companies and organizations are transforming the way they do business, resulting in a broad spectrum of socially responsible activities and practices aligned with stated organizational values.

A critical role of PR professionals today, whether in agencies or in house, is to serve as counselors to executive management. Guided by the business's values and stakeholders, PR shapes relationship-building programs and communication strategies toward positive outcomes, generating multiple social responsibility (SR) benefits while at the same time building trust, a positive reputation, a competitive market position, and bottom-line rewards.

Ever-Changing Demands of Stakeholders

To develop an SR strategy, it is necessary to recognize and consider an organization's many stakeholders. PR collaborates with leadership to identify and understand

the makeup of an organization's stakeholders and how to prioritize them. This
practice has been studied and analyzed
through research: Over the past decade,
most studies on CSR and PR reveal that
stakeholder concerns are the most dominant perspective (Ho Lee, 2017).

Who Is a Stakeholder?

Collectively, stakeholders are the various groups or individuals who can affect
or are affected by (either voluntarily or
involuntarily) the actions of an organization. An accepted way to categorize stakeholders is into three different groups (see
Figure 9.1), with connecting relationships
among each of them (Chandler, 2017).

**Stakeholders are the various individuals or groups who affect or are
affected by an organization. Understanding the needs and concerns of
stakeholders—for example, by meeting with employees—is one way to
develop a social responsibility strategy.**
PAUL J. RICHARDS / Staff / Getty Images

A pragmatic consideration is to determine which stakeholders have the
capacity to affect a firm's operations and are motivated to act. The answers are often
situational; while the organizational and economic stakeholders may at times be
more *meaningful* stakeholders, the agents and entities not directly connected to
an organization (societal stakeholders) may also become significant. For example,
Exxon's stance on climate change is one that a number of stakeholders may feel is
relevant, yet it is particularly relevant to groups like Greenpeace and 350.org, which
may act to shape the behavior they want from the corporation.

Prioritizing Stakeholders

One way to prioritize stakeholders is by categorizing them as primary and secondary:

- Primary stakeholders have those with some direct involvement in the
  organization—for example, shareholders or owners, employees, customers,
  business partners, and often communities.

- Secondary stakeholders, in contrast, are those without direct involvement
  in the organization but are still affected by it—for example, public or special
  interest groups, competitors, and the media.

FIGURE 9.1

Who Is a Stakeholder?

STAKEHOLDER		
ORGANIZATIONAL	**ECONOMIC**	**SOCIETAL**
• Directors	• Customers	• Communities
• Executives	• Creditors	• Government agencies
• Employees	• Competitors	• Media
• Members	• Suppliers	• Nonprofit
	• Distributers	• NGOs
	• Unions	

TABLE 9.2

Seven Pillars of Strategic CSR

PILLAR	FOCUS
Integrated with firm	Firms incorporate a CSR perspective within their culture and strategic planning process with the leadership, acceptance, and support of top management.
Business relevant	The strategy should have a viable connection to a firm's core operations.
Stakeholder interests	Firms seek to understand and respond to the needs of their stakeholders.
Strategic plan	Objectives should be identified to meet goals through effective tactics.
Optimized value	Firms aim to optimize the value that's created.
Evaluation	A specific plan should be in place to evaluate and analyze the program.
Not short term	Medium- to long-term CSR allows positive relationship management with stakeholders.

Sources: Chandler (2017, p. 248); Parnell, Strategic Public Relations (SPR) Master's Program.

However, the complexities of the issue at hand and instances of stakeholders' competing interests can make prioritizing a challenge. Issues may range widely, from an institutional crisis that places a firm in a defensive mode—such as the crashes of Boeing's 737 Max due to design flaws—to a proactive adoption of environmental practices that can create a leadership platform around an emerging issue—such as many businesses' efforts to reduce their carbon footprint.

What's important to realize is that organizations do not define societal values; they reflect them (Chandler, 2017, p. 93). Ultimately important to CSR as a logical argument, it is in an organization's best interests to recognize and meet needs and desires of the broadest swath of its stakeholders to the best of its ability.

Strategic Benefits of Social Responsibility

A firm and its stakeholders are synonymous in that a firm cannot exist independently of its stakeholders. A firm solves problems that have economic, social, moral, and ethical components and implications. This synergistic relationship between the firm and its stakeholders is why CSR is an important component of business strategy. "CSR is not about saving the whales or ending poverty or other worthwhile goals that are unrelated to a firm's operations and are better left to government or nonprofits," writes David Chandler, author of *Strategic Corporate Social Responsibility: Sustainable Value Creation* (2017, p. 246). "Instead, CSR is about the economic, legal, ethical, and discretionary issues that stakeholders view as directly related to the firm." He proposes seven pillars of strategic CSR (see Table 9.2).

Beyond *strategic CSR*, a company can "do good" by engaging in *responsive CSR* (Porter & Kramer, 2006, p. 89). These social or environmental efforts aren't tied to its business purpose or actions but rather to broader issues peripheral to the firm, such as providing relief to earthquake victims or jobs to refugees. Strategic CSR, however, engages in social or environmental efforts connected to issues that are central to the firm.

Six Practice Areas of Corporate Social Responsibility

Integrating sustainable practices into a business embeds a deeper involvement in social and environmental issues in which companies provide various means of engagement. Breaking these means of engagement down into different categories of activity helps explain how strategic CSR is performed and how it connects to the firm. There are six areas (Kotler & Lee, 2005) where CSR activities typically fall. Although there is no absolute rule to this, by identifying what type of CSR activity the company is practicing (or trying to practice), you can better evaluate its effectiveness in connecting to the business and communicating it to stakeholders. Knowing the six areas also is essential in making recommendations to a client or CEO about CSR engagement (see Table 9.3).

Larger for-profit corporations (e.g., Starbucks) may engage is all six areas of CSR. A good source for exploring firms' activities is the *Reports* page on www.csrwire .com. It features and links to recently published CSR and **sustainability** reports and press releases associated with them. Another avenue is to find links to detailed information and reports on individual corporate websites, usually located under a "social responsibility" or "sustainability" title.

Smaller to medium-sized firms may limit their engagement to philanthropy and volunteering. Other companies that are formed or structured with the priority of benefiting society often focus solely on **socially responsible business practices**. This chapter's special Insights section ("The New Heroes: Social Entrepreneurs") talks about this important sector.

TABLE 9.3

Six Types of Corporate Social Responsibility Engagement

TYPE	DEFINITION	EXAMPLE
Cause promotion	Providing or donating money to support or increase awareness and concern for a cause or charity	Walgreens sells red noses on Red Nose Day to help fund Comic Relief's campaign to end child poverty.
Cause-related marketing	Contributions to a cause or charity-based sales	For each pair of shoes sold, Toms gives customers a choice of causes the company will support.
Corporate social marketing	Support for a behavior-changing campaign to improve safety, health, or the environment	The Allstate Foundation supports the Purple Purse Challenge to fight domestic violence.
Corporate philanthropy	Direct contribution to a charity or cause	JP Morgan Chase funds nonprofits that support small business growth in vulnerable communities.
Community volunteering	Encouraging and facilitating employees to get involved in a cause via time off or sabbaticals	Google offers employees a 6-month paid leave to do charity work.
Socially responsible business practices	Adopting discretionary business practices to support causes or issues	Procter & Gamble reached "zero manufacturing waste to landfill" at 85% of its global sites in 2018—aiming for 100% by 2020.

Successful Corporate Social Responsibility Flows From Business Culture and Builds Reputation

>> **LO 9.2** **Examine how successful CSR activity is part of organizational culture and reputation management**

Successful, ongoing CSR activities have a few key building blocks in common, beginning with a connection to the organization's business and ending with a thorough assessment of their results. Determining how the efforts are impacting the end recipients or cause is only one measurement; learning how various stakeholders interpret your CSR is critical, too. A desired outcome is enhanced reputation, sometimes spurred on by the visibility of an activist CEO.

INSIGHTS

The New Heroes: Social Entrepreneurs

iStock.com/EnchantedFairy

The concept of **social entrepreneurship** started to gain serious attention in the mid-1990s with the Harvard Business School's 1993 launch of the Social Enterprise Initiative. The concept has since gained serious momentum in the 21st century (Harvard Business School, n.d.). Many universities have developed research and training programs and business incubators, offering undergraduate majors and minors, graduate programs, and shorter executive certificate programs to help social entrepreneurs succeed. Social entrepreneurs have been called the "new heroes" (Lauterer, 2005), pioneering breakthrough approaches to some of the world's most pressing problems (Elkington & Hartigan, 2008).

Social entrepreneurship differs from CSR in that the organization's *priority* is to pursue a transformational benefit to society rather than generate substantial financial gain. This does not mean that social entrepreneurs do not make profits (they can be organized as for-profits or nonprofits), but social benefit characterizes their mission.

Social entrepreneurships tend to value relationships, taking a communal versus individualistic orientation; thus, community building is a natural outcome. According to the Skoll Foundation, a promoter of social entrepreneurship worldwide, social entrepreneurs recognize social and environmental needs for change and then develop programs to address and solve the problems (Skoll Foundation, n.d.). For social entrepreneurships, supporting fundraising is often a key objective requiring communication strategies. Some social entrepreneurships obtain the following legal status or certification:

Benefit corporation is a legal status, like a traditional corporation or a nonprofit corporation, that establishes the corporation must have a material positive benefit on society and the environment. In some states, it specifically must consider its effects on all of its stakeholders. Each year it must publish a public report on its performance.

Companies as well-known as Patagonia, Ben & Jerry's, Kickstarter, and Eileen Fisher are benefit corporations, as are lesser known companies, such as Allbirds, Etsy, and Numi Organic Tea.

B Corporation certification differs from a benefit corporation in that it is a certification, not a legal status. B Lab serves as an online hub for B corporation certification, measuring companies' rigorous adherence to SR and sustainability. B Lab partners with B The Change Media, which disseminates stories across print, digital, video, and live event platforms.

B Lab also annually reviews ratings of the more than 1,800 B corporation-certified companies worldwide to determine a list of the top 500 "Best For The World" companies (B The Change Media, n.d.). These companies rank in the top 10% of certified B corporations across all impact areas (governance, workers, community, and environment). In 2019, for example, Colorado's New Belgium Brewing Company was ranked one of the overall best companies. The maker of Fat Tire Amber Ale and a range of Belgian-inspired beers is also recognized by *Outside Magazine* as a best place to work and by *The Wall Street Journal* as a best small business. ●

Key Building Blocks of Corporate Social Responsibility

When it comes to *communicating* CSR, most research indicates that messages about CSR that are perceived as a "corporate fit" enjoy greater credibility and are therefore more effective than messages perceived as not a "fit." Consider Starbucks, whose mission is to "share great coffee with our friends and to help make the world a little better" (Starbucks, n.d.). Its CSR includes ethical and sustainable sourcing of coffee, tea, cocoa, and merchandise; environmental practices in its stores including waste recycling and water and energy conservation; employee benefits like its "bean stock" stock option policy and college tuition support; and its outreach includes youth programs and community service projects. Starbucks's CSR initiatives have a few key things in common (see Table 9.4).

TABLE 9.4

Starbucks Corporate Social Responsibility: Ethical Sourcing

Fit	Tied to the business of the company	Coffee responsibly grown and ethically traded
Buy-In	Acceptance and support of top management	CSR established by former longtime CEO Howard Schultz and now led by CEO Kevin Johnson
Legs	Can and will continue beyond the year of its introduction	From its beginning, has used ethically sourced coffee, reaching 99% in 2017
Objectives	Strategy to meet overall goal through tactics	Developed C.A.F.E. practices in 2004—ethical sourcing guidelines to inform and support coffee producers in the practices and benefits of meeting ethical standards
Measurement	Specific plan to evaluate and analyze program	Trained personnel in third-party inspection and verification process

More Corporate Social Responsibility Building Blocks

Basic components of CSR include stakeholder engagement. Ideal initiatives should be participatory for customers, employees, and any volunteers involved, and the initiatives should adapt well to social media. There is significant PR potential in CSR—for example, announcing the launch, making progress reports, storytelling, and so on. However, the values of the intended audience must also be considered. Personal fit is also critical for positive perception. Thus, adding a personal appeal by demonstrating relevance to the receiver may offset any chance of CSR messaging sending the wrong signal that it's done for promotional purposes.

Prime extensions of CSR are all the crossover applications, including internal communications to employees, advertising and merchandising tie-ins, attracting business partnerships, and providing shareholders with updates.

Positive Impact on Reputation

CSR can positively impact a company's perceived reputation and the health of its business. Cone Communications finds a strong majority of U.S. consumers prioritize companies that are responsible and caring and that advocate for issues, protect the environment, and give back to important causes (Cone, 2018). A 2019 study on Gen Z finds 90% of the Gen Z generation "believe companies must act to help social and environmental issues," and 75% of Gen Z publics "will do research to see if a company is being honest when it takes a stand on issues" (Cone, 2019, para. 4).

Companies are responding to the public's heightened preference for social and environmental responsibility. "What's growing is the boldness of the marketing messages and the commitments that brands are willing to take," according to Crystal Barnes, SVP, Global Responsibility & Sustainability at Viacom. The trend is toward more visible and emotional sustainability messaging, as well as clear positions on social and political issues. Brands are even being personified as "brave brands" or "hero brands" (Nielsen, 2018a, para. 10).

Several sources measure and evaluate businesses' reputation and CSR engagement. The 2019 U.S. RepTrak® 100, produced by the Reputation Institute (2019), measured the reputation of 2,200 companies, ranking the 100 most highly regarded companies. Four of its seven ranked dimensions concern SR: workplace (benefits and culture), governance (ethical behavior, transparency, and fairness), citizenship (taking active stands in bettering the world), and leadership (vision, mission, and accountability). In 2019, these "top 10" companies ranked as most reputable (see Figure 9.2). Significantly, Facebook placed at the bottom of the top 100 list for various weaknesses, including data breaches and weak leadership. And for the first time ever, Google, the company promising to "do no evil," dropped off the top 100 list due to low rankings in governance, citizenship, and leadership.

Netflix jumped an unprecedented 23 spots in 1 year to reach the top spot in the Reputation Institute's 2019 list of America's most reputable companies, due to its innovative content, its corporate responsibility, and its decisive action on important issues. Other awards help explain Netflix's rise in reputation: It took top global ranking as the 2018–2019 "simplest brand experience" (Siegel+Gale, 2020) and the 2019 "most loved brand" in

FIGURE 9.2

Top 10 Most Highly Regarded Companies

1. Netflix
2. Hershey
3. Whirlpool
4. Rolex
5. McCormick
6. Barnes & Noble
7. Hasbro
8. Costco
9. Nintendo
10. Lego

Source: Reputation Institute (2019). https://www.reputationinstitute.com/us-reptrak

America by millennials (Stone & Olito, 2019). From a social perspective, Netflix offers its salaried employees 52 weeks of paid parental leave, to be taken in the child's first year or another time that suits their needs. The Reputation Institute (2019) attributes Netflix's rise to its transition from media repository to content creator and its level of accountability and transparency regarding cultural concerns.

Lesson From the Leader: Take a Stand

Netflix's flagship prestige drama, *House of Cards,* put Netflix on the map as a streaming service, proving the worth of increased investment in original programming. When the #MeToo movement helped to release allegations of sexual harassment against star Kevin Spacey, the network confronted a critical decision: support Spacey while filming the show's final season or banish him, halt production, and risk profitability. They did the latter, and showing the public that doing the right thing was more important than profits (Friedman, 2019).

Netflix continued to take decisive action that reflected its values in 2018. It fired its CCO Jonathan Friedland due to his use of inappropriate language in private meetings. Both the swift Spacey and Friedland decisions set Netflix apart among companies confronting cultural issues. Its accountability and transparency in confronting issues decisively and openly helped to engender a deep level of trust with the public (Friedman, 2019).

Corporate Social Responsibility Communication Is Essential

The 2019 U.S. RepTrak® 100 report notes, "Overall few companies excel in effectively expressing their corporate narrative" (Reputation Institute, 2019, p. 28). The report recommends taking control of the narrative by increasing direct communication (owned and paid). It offers these key takeaways for businesses:

1. Being good is a driver of business.
2. Governance (ethical behavior, transparency, fairness) and citizenship (taking active stands in bettering the world) are the most important drivers of reputation.
3. Companies having positive influence on society and ethical behavior are leading.
4. Executive buy-in is essential.
5. Companies need to better align the reality of good works with perception.

CEOs Take Stances on Social Issues

People want CEOs to speak up on issues linked to business, but this isn't a majority opinion. Corporate CEOs are, in fact, increasingly speaking out about social and environmental issues—many not directly connected to profits (e.g., climate change, income fairness, women's rights, immigration). Eight in 10 American adults agree that CEOs need to speak out when their company's values are violated or threatened, according to a 2018 survey by PR firm Weber Shandwick (Spring et al., 2019). The survey reports nearly 50% of American adults are more likely to buy from a company with a CEO who takes stands on issues these publics agree with. These findings are significantly higher than in the firm's 2017 survey.

Top-level executives at major corporations are increasingly speaking out on social and environmental issues. Former Unilever CEO Paul Polman is well known for his SR leadership.
Victor Boyko / Stringer / Getty Images

However, the same Weber Shandwick survey finds Americans are divided on the CEO's responsibility to speak up or take positions on important social issues in general. A separate survey on CEO activism by the Stanford Rock Center for Corporate Governance (Larcker & Tayan, 2018) finds similar results: For the individuals reacting positively to CEO positions on social, environmental, or political issues, there is a corresponding negative reaction by other respondents. For example, former Starbucks head Howard Schultz is cited in this study both favorably and unfavorably for his stances on racial issues. Both sides tend to come together in approval when the issues are directly linked to the company's business or employees. PR professionals should counsel management that making a closer link to business will help them do more good than harm with speaking out on controversial issues.

For nearly a decade as CEO of Unilever, one of the world's biggest consumer product companies, Paul Polman transformed the company with environmental and socially responsible stewardship through his Sustainable Living Plan (explore it at www.unilever.com/sustainable-living). Early in his 9-year tenure (he stepped down in 2019), Polman acquired brands known for their ecological focus, like Seventh Generation and Tazo Tea. Beyond his SR business sense, he emerged as one of the most prominent corporate voices calling for changes to the status quo, helping the UN create the Sustainable Development Goals and urging world leaders to commit to the Paris climate accord. Polman's SR strategy, first met with skepticism, saw Unilever's stock price more than double during his tenure. According to Polman, "A responsible business model makes your brand stronger and improves corporate reputation, and that is reflected in the share price" (Gelles, 2018).

Communicating Corporate Social Responsibility: Opportunities and Challenges

>> LO 9.3 Evaluate the opportunities and challenges in mounting an effective internal and external CSR campaign

Increasingly, CSR is a clear path for communications professionals to get that proverbial "seat at the table." The ideal executive to manage the CSR process is the communications professional—since this activity is truly a combination of issues management, stakeholder relations (internal and external), media relations, and event planning. Properly planned and executed, CSR touches all aspects of a company's operations and if done well can pay enormous dividends in terms of reputation, shareholder value, and desirability as an employer.

For the large, publicly traded, or multinational corporation, well-communicated CSR helps meet the goals of building corporate reputation, attracting investors, supporting recruitment and retention, and increasing profits. For the smaller socially conscious firm, communicating its mission and practice is essential in helping raise funds as well as build awareness, reputation, and often customers.

The Art of Being More in a World of Change

Mike Fernandez, Senior Vice President and Chief Communications Officer, Enbridge and Professor, Boston University

Photo courtesy of Mike Fernandez

The world we live in is more social and contentious than ever. It is also an era of scientific discovery, technological advancement, and global business and educational opportunity. Because of this, it is an extraordinary time to be a PR professional.

PR professionals are being asked to play bigger roles in their organizations. It is not enough to be a good communicator, writer, event organizer, or adept website and app designer. The complexities of the world require us to think deeply, ask questions, act with urgency, and be problem solvers.

Looking back, I believe I was prepared for this world by my humble beginnings. My mother was raised in an orphanage in South Carolina, and my father was one of nine children in Spanish Harlem (New York City). Growing up, I lived in four states and attended nine different schools, K through 12. Those moves, along with having a foot in both the American and Hispanic cultures, forced me to become adaptable, see change as positive, seize new opportunity, and become a student of people, cultures, and customs.

That orientation would serve me well as a young press secretary in the U.S. Senate, working for Senator Fritz Hollings (D–SC) and also through my long career in PR—including 20 years as a chief communications officer (CCO) at Fortune 100 companies including Cargill and State Farm Insurance—and as a US CEO at Burson-Marsteller and LLYC.

Working in politics early in my career, I learned two very important lessons. One, winning a highly contested campaign (in politics or business) requires talking to more than just your base. And two, it becomes harder to hate someone you have gotten to know and understand, even if you still disagree on the details or approach to an issue.

For example, my first meetings at Cargill with NGOs and community groups were not about establishing CSR initiatives. Instead, they entailed meeting with skeptics and critics who took issue with our complex global supply chain and trying to find common ground.

None of this was easy. What we eventually agreed upon required changing our operations, incentivizing farmers and other suppliers, and working closely with stakeholders so we were clear about timelines and directions. As a result, Cargill not only advanced environmental and societal improvements but did so in a way that provided our customers with the competitively priced, sustainably grown, and responsibly processed food they and their consumers wanted.

Over time, Cargill would receive many honors and recognitions from industry, environmental, and PR groups. For example, in 2014 the Cargill communications team won *PRWeek*'s Global Program of the Year Award. In 2015, Cargill was listed among *Fortune* magazine's top 50 "Change the World" companies making a positive global impact.

And it all started with asking good questions and working with—not always against—others who had different points of view. ●

Source: M. Fernandez, personal communication, 2019.

Communicating CSR

The authors of this book feel that the best way to communicate a company's CSR policy and initiatives is to first focus on the good works themselves. Bring to life the results and benefits, along with a rationale for their fit with the company's values, purpose, and product. Messaging should be shaped to inform both internal and external

A company's CSR efforts must be handled carefully so as not to be seen as self-promoting or engaging in "greenwashing."
iStock.com/bodo23

stakeholders of the company's contribution to society and the environment in a way that engages dialogue. It should be honest and transparent—realizing that the crafting and sending of the message is just one part of the communication process; and reception, interpretation, and engagement among stakeholders a vital part of constituting true communication.

The right way to talk about a firm's CSR has been somewhat problematic up to now. It can be perceived as simply self-promotional, or even **greenwashing**, misleading consumers about the firm's environmental practices or the environmental benefits of a certain product. Fortunately, a lot of recent attention has been focused on the role of PR in effective CSR communications. Ethical awareness and performance characterize today's engaged PR professionals. Both company and professional codes of conduct shape their involvement with CSR planning, performance, and communication.

Today's PR professionals think and perform strategically, advising how CSR initiatives support a company's mission and formulating plans to communicate CSR to key stakeholders, both internal and external. This strategy also involves making logical choices of which communication channels to use. There are many choices, including packaging, events, interviews, websites, ads, newsletters, press releases, social media, and video storytelling. Basically, it's important to talk about CSR—its successes, lessons learned, even trouble spots—and essential to develop strong relationships with media.

Best Practices in Corporate Social Responsibility Communications

Most Americans can't go through a day without interacting with multiple brands. It's a fact of life, and in most cases, preferred brands make life easier, more entertaining, more comfortable, and so on. The close relationship between people and the brands they live with helps explain why corporations that "do good" matter to them. People want to know the impact "their" brands have on social and environmental issues. Many people likely won't read a firm's annual report or CSR report—usually tucked away in a corner of a company website. There are, however, many communication options available.

A Good Starting Point

A successful CSR communications strategy begins with research. What are the values and principles the company has identified and structured past communications on? What do loyal customers know and believe about the firm or product? As CSR engagement should be tied to the firm's purpose and values, talking to customers with familiar language provides an authentic voice to CSR messaging. It rings true.

Also pay attention to the moment, the immediate environment, emerging societal issues, and concerns, and identify how the firm's CSR relates to or addresses them. Your audience is enmeshed in contemporary culture, so signaling the firm is actively addressing a current issue gives it credibility and immediacy.

Finally, remember that two-way dialogue is much better than one-way when it comes to CSR. Turn to social media platforms to know what key stakeholders are talking about, thinking, and feeling to influence how to craft compelling messages.

How to Talk "Corporate Social Responsibility"

In his book *Corporate Responsibility* (Argenti, 2016, pp. 293–296), business professor Paul Argenti shares wisdom gained from his distinguished career in corporate management, responsibility, and communication (see Figure 9.3).

FIGURE 9.3

Seven Tips for Effective CSR Communications

Avoid empty boasting.

- When talking about your CSR activities and outcomes, focus on authenticity by offering substance.

Match rhetoric with action.

- Differentiate your company from those that may be greenwashing by not making empty promises.

Be transparent.

- Tell the truth, good and bad. Being transparent with stakeholders about less-than positive news allows companies to build trust. Avoid ambiguous or confusing language. Simple and direct is more authentic.

Know your audience.

- Identify the issues most relevant to select stakeholders, and know how to reach them with focused messaging.

Create an ongoing dialogue.

- Two-way dialogic communication is the ideal. Both reporting and listening create authentic communication and help you understand the expectations and concerns of your publics and learn to adapt.

Listen . . . and collaborate.

- Beyond knowing who to talk to, know who's talking about you. Engage NGO or nonprofit partners as allies in your communication strategies.

Focus on employee engagement.

- Thoughtful internal communication about CSR can result in a more engaged workforce.

The Beauty of Creative Annual Reports

Most big companies are not only doing CSR but compiling and releasing CSR information in annual CSR reports. The dilemma is that in satisfying the reporting frameworks suggested by the Global Reporting Initiative (GRI), the charts, infographics, and complicated data aren't as accessible for the general public—and even investors can get lost. The adage "Seeing is believing" needs to be acknowledged, so some companies are experimenting with new, highly visual storytelling methods both with their standard reports and in new messaging channels.

For example, Arrow Electronics produced a highly readable 2018 report using dramatic black-and-white photography communicating how its technology touches people, particularly disabled military service members and veterans. The spare use of colorful infographics and maps helped to turn the focus back on the respectful presentation of its black and white images.

As another example, Domtar Corporation is the largest producer of paper in the United States and a leader in sustainable forestry practices. Not only did it produce a traditional print/pdf sustainability report in 2019, but its sustainability webpage offered both an interactive version and a video version of the report (view the interactive version at https://2019sustainability.domtar.com/index.html). On YouTube, you can search for its report, or just search for "CSR Reports" to see the many videos companies have produced to better communicate with their stakeholders.

These cases illustrate the utility in optimizing content, extending to different audiences, and increasing the life span of a story. With media consumption a 24-hour occupation and fast-moving streams of content, creative messaging and channeling is essential today to reach and engage desired audiences.

Community Relations and Corporate Social Responsibility

>> LO 9.4   Understand the PR practice of community relations and its connection to CSR

To illustrate how social responsibility (SR) supports the relationship between a company and one of its stakeholders, let's look at community relations. It's essential for an organization to cultivate good relationships with the communities in which it operates. From local communities come employees and customers—and sometimes donors and investors. PR duties involve fostering and maintaining strategic relationships with community members. They can range from groups who may be impacted by building or relocating a business to diverse publics categorized by age, ethnicity, diversity, or special concerns. Practitioners of community relations must understand the structure, strengths, and weaknesses of a community before setting community outreach goals and objectives for the organization. Socially responsible initiatives are usually a big part of that outreach.

The PR professional who specializes in community relations is typically immersed in the community, humanizing the business by putting a visible and accessible face on it. She or he attends various functions and events and directly meets with community leaders—who may include public officials, educators, religious leaders, and heads of professional organizations and groups defined by special interests or ethnicities.

Cultivating good relationships with the community in which an organization operates is essential for success, and many business leaders make a point of interacting with customers and stakeholders.
Paul Morigi / Stringer / Getty Images

Earning Trust

An Intimate Look at Community Relations

When Comcast expanded its services into a new Illinois county, it hired a local PR practitioner to "open doors" between the utility and area leaders. Several days after hiring the practitioner, Comcast asked his help in boosting attendance at a meet-and-greet designed to introduce the company to the area and to showcase its new products.

Over the years, the PR practitioner had been involved in many community projects and had been a very visible fundraiser for several local charities. He often gave his professional help pro bono for the pet projects of numerous local politicians and community influencers. These were the people he reached out to, and he simply asked them to join him and welcome his new client (Comcast) to the area.

The result was an overflow crowd, far exceeding the expectations of the Comcast executives on hand. The guests included a state senator, a state representative, three mayors, elected officials from several towns, and numerous community influencers. When the guests were asked what brought them to the event, the reason many gave for coming was simple: "Because Bill asked me to."

In other words, the practitioner, through his community involvement, had built up such a large reservoir of goodwill that just his asking was a good enough reason to attend for most.

Businesses Earn Trust as Good Citizens

A business, as a citizen of its community, may benefit from tax breaks, favorable zoning, and a ready employee and consumer base. As a good citizen, at the bare minimum it should be respectful of the environment and society that hosts it, as well as voluntarily support community projects.

The Boston College Center for Corporate Citizenship (BCCCC) studies how companies invest in communities and how these efforts connect to their businesses.

Corporate community involvement programs—such as in-kind and financial donations, employee volunteer days, and enduring nonprofit partnerships—can allow companies to showcase products as well as employee achievements and a firm's values. By using corporate citizenship to bolster community partnerships, firms can shape a workplace culture that strengthens employee commitment and can also build lasting relationships in the communities where they do operate (BCCCC, 2020).

PR supports this engagement via social media, local mass media, event partnerships, outreach to charities, donations, and internal communications with employees, among other efforts.

Public Relations With Diverse Communities

Latinos in the United States: One in Four by 2045

In 2018, the U.S. Hispanic population reached nearly 60 million (Flores et al., 2019). Despite the Trump administration's efforts to curb migration, by 2045 Latinos are expected to comprise about 25% of the U.S. population, according to U.S. Census projections (Frey, 2018b). The World Bank estimates an increase in these numbers as conditions worsen in Latin America due to global warming, which is destroying crops and leading to food insecurity (Amadeo, 2020). With that kind of growth, every single company and governmental entity or political campaign has to think about how they are going to reach this large and fast-growing demographic.

Maria Cardona, principal at Dewey Square Group and founder of its Latino Strategies practice Latinovations, says,

> With this prospect in mind, clients get a real understanding of the potential impact of the Latino community. I counsel them on the kinds of programmatic partnerships that are important to Hispanics for relationships to be authentic: partnering with different community organizations to help reduce the dropout rate, to live healthier, to get better health care, and so on. (M. Cardona, personal communication, 2015)

In light of the rapid growth of the Latino community, outreach tailored to that demographic can be crucial in politics (as seen here at a voter registration event), health, and business.
Thomas Cooper / Contributor / Getty Images

Asian American Community: Breaking the Silence

Asian Americans and Pacific Islanders, while only about 6% of the U.S. population, have outpaced Latino immigration since 2010 to become the fastest-growing minority in the United States, according to New American Economy (NAE), a bipartisan research and advocacy organization (2019). They are also the highest-income and best-educated foreign-born population in the United States (NAE, 2019). According to the Pew Research Center (2012), as a whole group they value marriage, parenthood, hard work, and career success greater than does the general public. However, they uniquely have another not-so-positive characteristic: The Asian American community is disproportionately affected by chronic hepatitis B—one in 10.

The campaign "Breaking the Silence on Hepatitis B in the Asian-American Community" aimed to start a discussion of hepatitis B. Research showed that younger Asian Americans serve as gatekeepers for older Asian Americans who rely on their community for information. So Weber Shandwick PR, APartnership, and Gilead Sciences partnered to develop a 40-minute **unbranded** documentary, *Be About It*. The film followed two families' struggles against this disease that's shrouded by stigma. Its primary subjects were Alan, a news journalist, and AJ, a radiology technician and triathlete. Both had lost loved ones to the complications of hepatitis B. Their stories served as the campaign's centerpieces. You can watch the trailer on YouTube by searching for "Be About It Chronic Hepatitis B Documentary."

The film engaged its target public on an emotional level by presenting the community as people and not just cases. It used storytelling to break the silence and fear. The PR strategy was robust: The film screened at seven film festivals, and more than 100 media placements were secured thanks to local, in-language, and national outreach. Local groups were guided in hosting their own screenings with the help of a community media kit. An unbranded website with educational material engaged influencers to share resources and content. The same materials translated to Chinese, Korean, and Vietnamese were distributed at localized events.

African Americans: Talking About Sickle Cell

The Swiss pharmaceutical company Novartis teamed up with Grammy-nominated singer, film star, and Broadway star Jordin Sparks and the Sickle Cell Disease Association of America, Inc. to launch "Generation S," a national sickle cell disease (SCD) storytelling project. It encouraged people touched by SCD to help inspire the sickle cell community and educate the nation by sharing their personal stories.

Sickle cell disease is a genetic condition affecting African Americans disproportionately. Approximately 1 in 13 African American babies is born with the sickle cell trait, and the disease occurs among 1 out of every 365 births (CDC, n.d.). In fall 2018, the website JoinGenS.com launched to collect stories, photos, audio, and video recordings from people throughout the United States who had been touched by SCD. Beginning in 2019, the website presented an interactive mosaic of the multimedia stories that had been shared while it also continued to collect new stories.

The purpose behind the Generation S campaign is to educate about how the disease affects real people, inspire those touched by the disease to lead strong lives, and to help people understand their family genetic risk factors for passing the disease on to their children. The campaign has a vibrant Facebook presence, and its website offers mobile texting with tips for disease management, reminders of doctor's appointments, and explanations of the science behind the disease.

Fundraising events help bring awareness and education about sickle cell disease. Here, New England Patriot Devin McCourty supports Boston Children's Hospital and its sickle cell research.
Darren McCollester / Stringer / Getty Images

SOCIAL RESPONSIBILITY IN ACTION

Ending the Need for "The Talk"

Procter & Gamble (P&G), the multinational corporation whose brands include Pantene, Ivory, Always, and Gillette, launched the My Black Is Beautiful (MBIB) campaign in 2007, stating its mission was to help improve the way African American women were portrayed in popular culture. It resulted from a poll P&G conducted with Essence Communications. Ten years later, it turned to its agency, BBDO, to create a powerful short video, "The Talk." The video won a Grand Prix in Film at the Cannes Lions creative festival and the Outstanding Commercial Emmy in 2018. The campaign supporting it won the Diversity Communications CSR award from *PR News* in 2019.

Research on Racial Bias

P&G turned to the EGAMI Group, specialists in multicultural communications, to research the impact of racial bias on Black families. The research found that Black mothers have special talks with their children so they are prepared for biases in the near future. For example, Black mothers may caution daughters they may be told they're pretty—for a Black girl—or will tell

their children they must double their work efforts to be successful.

Influencer Focus Groups

To learn how P&G should enter this culturally sensitive space and prepare for potential controversial feedback, EGAMI and P&G/MBIB gathered together five focus groups with multicultural influencers. The results helped to guide the campaign through different phases. EGAMI brought the concept of mothers having to have "The Talk" to the forefront, knowing it would hit home and affect every Black mother and her need to prepare her children.

The Campaign

The campaign content included videos, social media, and influencers. It was designed to inspire the public to #TalkAboutBias in conversations that acknowledged and celebrated Black culture and its broader impact on society. Influencers were also used to advocate for change through their own networks/platforms. ●

Over the past several years, Target's charitable efforts have amounted to 5% of its profit. It funds art museums, disaster relief, and education, and it enlists celebrities like Rocco DiSpirito in assembling meal boxes for foodbanks.
Jamie McCarthy / Staff / Getty Images

Profiles of Community Corporate Social Responsibility Successes and Challenges

Target

The discount store retailer commits its efforts and assets toward supporting the local environment and communities in which it has stores. Since its founding in 1946, it has given 5% of its profit to local communities. In 2019, the store began allowing shoppers to vote on where millions of dollars would be donated—and the list includes 800 nonprofits.

Thanks to Target, art museums for both adults and children across the United States offer free admission to all visitors on select days throughout the year. In support of diversity and inclusion, it supports the National Museum of African American History and Culture, the Smithsonian Latino Center, and GLSEN (Gay, Lesbian, and Straight Education Network), the U.S.-based education organization working on behalf of LGTBQ cultural inclusion and awareness. It has also partnered with the U.S. Soccer Foundation in creating 100 new soccer play spaces across the United States by 2020. The retailer has an independent communications group internally and works with a variety of PR agencies.

H&M

Swedish retailer H&M is the world's second-largest fashion retailer (after Inditex, owner of Zara). H&M has a long history of social consciousness. The Ethisphere Institute named it one of the most ethical companies in the world. It offers a recycling program where anyone can return clothes from any brand in-store, it is a member of the Better Cotton Initiative, and it stocks "conscious" sustainable fashion.

Regarding its supply chain, the retailer was one of the early adopters of the UN Guiding Principles on Human Rights and was among the first global fashion companies to openly release its list of supplier factories. Key suppliers are based in Bangladesh, Cambodia, India, China, and Turkey. H&M receives high ratings for its transparency, its success in tracing most of its suppliers, and its biannual auditing of most facilities in its supply chain.

Yet it isn't always easy to achieve these goals, and H&M struggles to manage its supply chain. In 2013, the Rana Plaza building collapsed in Bangladesh, killing more than 1,100 workers in garment factories providing clothing for H&M, Walmart, and Gap, among others. While H&M had transparency and monitoring systems in place, they could not prevent the conditions that led to this disaster. While it has made progress on its commitments to address labor issues, in 2018 Global Labour Justice reported abuse of female garment workers in factories that supply H&M. And as of 2019, H&M has failed to meet its 2013 promise to pay a living wage to its workers within 5 years (Robertson, 2019).

H&M faced a communications crisis in 2019 when it ran an ad featuring a young Black boy modeling a sweatshirt with the wording "Coolest Monkey in the Jungle."

Social media reacted, debating whether or not it was a racial issue, but a majority of comments were negative against the brand. "We sincerely apologize," responded H&M, stating that the image—and the garment—were removed and acknowledging there was an internal failure that demanded thorough investigation. Racial insensitivity in marketing can have serious repercussions on a brand's reputation (Wood, 2018).

Scenario Outcome

To recap, nearly all the owners of eight small businesses in Illinois reported that their philanthropic giving was "strategic," yet most of them had no communication strategy and little structure to measure the effectiveness of their giving.

Applying lessons from this chapter, you might answer the following questions in this manner:

What benefits are these local businesses missing from failing to communicate their good works?

Seeing this gap as an opportunity rather than a problem, the owners' passion and commitment to CSR engagement offers a pathway *to* strategic management of communication. Thinking only the giving or the event is enough does not consider the loss of impact on the businesses' stakeholders or community members who, by design or accident, were not involved or were less engaged. Without communication, a business loses the potential for expanding awareness of its good works, engaging the larger community in dialogue and action, and nurturing the business while at the same time inspiring more people to do good deeds—a value deeply embedded in these small businesses.

Communicating CSR creates a healthy organization that is fluid and inclusive. It improves employee morale and reinforces positive reputation. A healthy organization communicating its CSR must use a dynamic process responsive to varying needs and conditions and its diverse stakeholders.

Why should the businesses communicate CSR with their publics?

- People want to know about and will support company efforts to be socially responsible.
- The language of SR resonates with people.
- People want to know *why* they should care.
- People value WOM (word-of-mouth) information from trusted sources.
- People care more about *local* CSR.
- People don't actively seek CSR information.
- Telling your own CSR story lets you keep the message authentic.

How should businesses communicate CSR with their publics?

- Determine different stakeholders to reach and address each uniquely.
- Share your compassion and pride by focusing on CSR *results*.
- Place content visibly on the home page of your company website.
- Post photos and media articles in employee lounges.

- Announce CSR on your packaging.
- Use social media to allow quick and easy communication with broad involvement.
- Make your CSR noticeable in store to clients who visit your business.
- Communication that's authentic gives voice to your values and the values of your stakeholders, avoiding the perception that it's "marketing" or even "boasting."

WRAP UP

Five vital takeaways from this chapter are these:

1. CSR should be tied to an organization's core purpose and values.
2. CSR should be connected with and communicated to an organization's multiple stakeholders.
3. The ideal executive to manage the CSR process is the PR/communications professional.
4. CSR communication must be well researched, authentic, and carefully targeted to the personal interests of its receivers.
5. CSR is one of the most appropriate ways to build positive relationships with communities.

KEY TERMS

B Corporation 207
Benefit Corporation 206
Greenwashing 212
Social Entrepreneurship 206
Socially Responsible Business
    Practices 205

Sustainability 205
Triple Bottom Line 200
Unbranded 216

THINK ABOUT IT

You read that a social enterprise's primary objective is social good, not profit. When Aaron Fishman found himself volunteering for an NGO in Bali, he learned the impoverished region shipped its cashew crops to India and Vietnam for processing. He envisioned an opportunity to provide jobs and training and produce uniquely local cashews—processed where they're grown. Read about his story in launching East Bali Cashews (EBC) at www .eastbalicashews.com and explore the website to get a better understanding of a successful social entrepreneurship. Look for evidence on how EBC communicates with its various stakeholders and assess whether or not you think it's doing a sufficient job.

WRITE LIKE A PRO

Imagine the hypothetical bicycle shop, Bikes and Trikes, is an established, locally owned business in your community, founded 30 years ago by its current owners, a husband and wife. While it has a full range of products for the novice and accomplished cyclist, including children's bikes, it also has a secondary stream of business (called Positive Spins) in adaptive bikes and trikes for riders with special needs. It was originally inspired by the needs of a family member. Bikes and Trikes relies on a website to communicate about both business streams and also hosts fundraising events. Its social media presence consists of a Facebook page with frequent posts. It also regularly provides adaptive cycles to participants in the Wounded Warrior Project's Soldier Rides around the country. Drawing from lessons in this chapter, as their newly hired PR consultant, write a 200- to 300-word business memo to the owners of Bikes and Trikes outlining and justifying some recommendations for an improved communications program.

SOCIAL RESPONSIBILITY CASE STUDY

Mastercard's CSR: Global STEM Education Program for Girls

Situation

Cybersecurity and artificial intelligence (AI) are two fast-growing occupations today. Yet globally, women account for less than 20% of high-tech professionals, and only one out of 20 girls chooses a STEM (science, technology, engineering, mathematics) career. Women with STEM degrees are less likely than men with similar degrees to hold a job in a STEM occupation. These women can more likely be found working in education or health care (U.S. Dept. of Commerce, n.d.). The lack of diversity in the STEM fields can be attributed to cultural norms and lingering stereotypical beliefs. Questions of women's ability have been dispelled, as has the mistaken idea that women don't belong in certain careers. There remains, however, an unfortunate gap in confidence between boys and girls when it comes to some STEM areas. For example, one study compared male and female students of a robotics program, finding that males are more confident in all areas except writing (Mantz, 2019). Given the future promise in STEM careers, a strategy to improve girls' confidence is to make them aware of successful women in STEM. One way to do that is through mentors and role models.

Research and Strategy

A poll of Mastercard employees found that 77% derive job satisfaction from volunteering through company programs, consistent with industrywide research that confirms most millennials review a company's CSR record when selecting an employer. Further, Mastercard learned that the 4,000-plus new employees who joined the company through acquisitions needed to be engaged, leading to the decision to position female technologists as role models and mentors in developing a curriculum for girls. To narrow the STEM gender gap, the curriculum would use concrete examples of how science and math standards factor into various professional fields that are vital to Mastercard's operations (such as fraud detection, big data, and cryptology).

Execution

Girls4Tech, the resulting initiative launched in 2014, is an education program developed by Mastercard for young girls worldwide. Tapping into its employees' expertise in payments technology, the goal of Girls4Tech is to inspire girls to build their STEM skills. Its hands-on curriculum is based on global science and math standards that showcase Mastercard's payments technology and the power of its network. The program introduces data analysis, digital convergence, algorithms, encryption, and fraud detection—illustrating the different kinds of interests and skills that girls could pursue in a STEM career. Mastercard's efforts earned first place in the "Community Affairs" category of PR Daily's 2018 Corporate Social Responsibility Awards. It was also named "Campaign of the Year" 2018 by PR News Global. Ultimately, Girls4Tech became the company's first global volunteer program in its 52-year history. It works with a network of global partners to grow the program's reach and impact: Scholastic, American Airlines, Major League Baseball, and the Singapore Committee for UN Women, among others.

Evaluation

By 2019, the program had reached more than 400,000 girls in 25 countries and had been translated into 12 languages. Twenty-six percent of Mastercard's employees have served as role models and mentors worldwide. This success has motivated growth and improvements—for example, expanding the curriculum with deeper exposure into cybersecurity and AI. Mastercard has also launched new programs, including Girls4Tech 2.0 for high school students, emphasizing 21st century work skills like collaboration, creativity, and communication.

Engage

Search online for Mastercard Girls4Tech STEM Program and explore the website's resources and current accolades.

On the website, scroll down to the Girls4Tech and Scholastic section and review some of the exercises, which include "Practicing Cryptology and Fraud Protection" and "Spot the Technology and Encrypt Your Fingerprint."

Do some searches to find any news coverage on this program. Also explore any of its social media participation. From what you find, is their PR team successful in getting the word out about Mastercard's good works?

Discuss

If you were to recommend that Girls4Tech create a program to reach girls younger than 8, what age would you begin with, and what kind of mentoring and activities would you suggest? How would you publicize it? What partners might you enlist?

Sources:

World Economic Forum. (2017). *The global gender gap report, 2017.* http://www3.weforum.org/docs/WEF_GGGR_2017.pdf

U.S. Department of Commerce. (2017). *Women in STEM: 2017 update.* https://www.commerce.gov/news/fact-sheets/2017/11/women-stem-2017-update

Mantz, D. (2019, Sept. 30). How do we get more girls into STEM? Build confidence (and robots). *EdSurge.* https://www.edsurge.com/news/2019-09-30-how-do-we-get-more-girls-into-stem-build-confidence-and-robots

iStock.com/FlamingoImages

10 Employee Relations, Corporate Culture, and Social Responsibility

Learning Objectives

10.1 Describe the importance of employee relations in creating a healthy organization

10.2 Understand how PR supports employee engagement and solves problems during times of change

10.3 Examine the various needs, strategies, and tactics in employee communication

10.4 Identify the strategic connection between CSR and an organization's employees

Scenario

How Can You Inspire 100,000 Employees to Talk About Your Brand?

Intel, one of the early pioneers in the computer industry, conceived a bold vision in 2010: "to create and extend computing technology to connect and enrich the lives of every person on earth" (Hawkins, 2012, para. 1). It was a powerful statement that had a deep impact on its employees.

Changing times. Intel had been admired as a technology star for many years due to its high stock prices, rapid growth, and large bonuses. But beginning in the early 2000s, everything changed when the stock market's value plunged. Hundreds of thousands of technology professionals lost their jobs and any savings invested in stocks. By the mid-2000s, tech companies were restructured and operating with cost cuts and devalued stock options. Employee turnover was high.

In 2010, Intel realized it needed to address the fact that employees lacked an emotional connection to the company.
iStock.com/JasonDoiy

By 2010, however, a defining movement arrived for Intel. While the firm had recovered and transformed into a multifaceted business with diverse products and markets, it realized its customary, top-down communication wasn't working.

Intel wasn't alone. Research revealed that trust in CEOs was low, while trust in employee peers was high—people were listening to each other more than their leaders. Power and titles were becoming a thing of the past, as everyone was always "on." With information always accessible and narratives competing constantly, it was harder to engage people (Spreier, 2013). Yet it required a breakthrough because employee engagement is directly linked to positive business outcomes.

The problem. Employees no longer turned to Intel as their first source of company information. Rather, Twitter and other media channels allowed them to get current news. Company leaders had a challenge: to embrace their employees' media preferences to get them not only to listen to Intel messaging but to motivate them.

Intel decided to connect emotionally with a bold vision. Instead of talking about building the next product, the new vision was rousing and inspirational, showing where the company was headed and how employees could help get there.

How to break through? Intel employees are largely engineers and not always the easiest to reach. The leaders needed to adapt to their media preferences and not force them into unwanted media channels. Leaders also wanted to tap into their thoughts and learn why something may not be working. Employees needed to be part of the solution.

The internal communications team knew its goal was to stimulate employee engagement using digital platforms and interactivity. It knew it needed to abandon the strategic language and bullet points used in the past. The team realized it needed to use many different and creative ways to get through to employees and to inspire the next great innovation.

After reading this chapter, you should be able to answer the following questions:

1. How did Intel connect employees together to encourage conversations with each other and with top management?

(Continued)

(Continued)

2. How did Intel show employees it valued them?

3. Employees can be your best advocates. How did Intel inspire employees to explain to outsiders what they do?

At the end of the chapter, you'll learn the answers. ●

Note: This scenario is excerpted from McVicker (2013).

If all the people who make up an organization or company—from assembly line workers to designers to managers—aren't connecting positively to their work or aren't feeling valued, what's a company to do?

This chapter explains the importance of employee relations, also called internal relations, and how the employee's experience is deeply tied to a healthy corporate culture. PR's support includes counseling company leaders and listening to and communicating with all members of the workforce. The field of internal relations is now a major responsibility of PR (public relations) practitioners. Another growing focus for PR is addressing corporate change. When companies are sold, downsized, or even shut down, PR must work with other departments and executive leadership to successfully facilitate and communicate what it means to employees. The chapter covers how companies have mishandled mergers and acquisitions, juxtaposing the worst practices with the best.

All of this requires communication tactics that are tailored to the corporate culture *and* the media practices of employees. The poster by the coffee machine may need to be replaced by an animated infographic. You'll find strategies for sending messages, inviting interactivity, and hosting employee-created content.

Finally, the high value that a socially responsible company offers an employee—or a prospective one—is explained, proven by research, and illustrated with examples and case studies.

Employee Relations and Healthy Organizations

>> **LO 10.1   Describe the importance of employee relations in creating a healthy organization**

Employee relations, or internal communication, is an important part of creating a corporate culture that will advance an organization's goals.
iStock.com/vm

The one thing that's certain about life is that things change. This couldn't be more true than with businesses and the workplace, whether it's merging personnel from another company, moving to a new location, shifting your brand identity, changing product priorities or strategy, adjusting to ever-changing channels of communication, closing a facility, terminating a product line or service, or encountering a crisis.

At these times, everyone involved needs to transform a little, too. The PR professional, working in an in-house or outside agency capacity, can help drive change for positive outcomes within an organization. People throughout a company often need to understand what's possible during times of challenge or change and what their role is in creating success and meeting business objectives.

For PR/communication practitioners in the United States who handle internal communications, the tasks are broad, including collaborating with and advising top management and facilitating understanding and motivation with varied employees.

Internal Communication

Employee relations. The social, economic, and technological transformations world-wide are challenging companies to strategically handle disruption and innovation. In this rapidly changing environment, attracting, retaining, and engaging workers are vital actions. Sometimes referred to as "internal communication," employee relations focuses on all employees of an organization, from the head executives to the maintenance crew. It's a fast-growing field due to several factors, including a growing distrust of business, shifting workplace dynamics with the entry of millennials and Gen Z, and the blurred lines between internal and external communication.

Depending on the size and structure of an organization, PR will often lead internal communication in partnership with chief executives and human resources. Internal communications' broad goal is to help create and sustain a healthy organizational culture. Its main responsibilities involve social media, employee engagement, counseling leadership, and facilitating change—especially in times of **mergers** and **acquisitions**—along with the accompanying communication challenges and opportunities.

Corporate Culture

The culture of an organization determines how it impacts workers' perceptions and behaviors. It's a filter, sometimes invisible and sometimes very evident, that guides how people interact and work. It affects communication styles and content, employee morale and initiative, and leadership behaviors.

Simply, a culture refers to the personality of an organization and how things are done. A more detailed definition identifies three dimensions to **corporate culture**: what's materially visible (e.g., the physical environment), people's behavior patterns (recurring and influential), and mindsets (widely shared attitudes and beliefs; see Figure 10.1; Katzenback et al., 2016). A healthy corporate culture has been identified

FIGURE 10.1

Three Dimensions to Corporate Culture

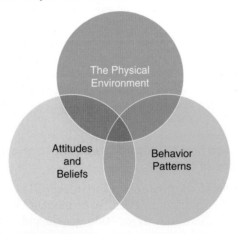

as key to an innovative and successful company. When firms use more relaxed, emotional strategies to impact behaviors, they are considerably more likely to experience lasting change.

Leadership

Supportive leadership is a crucial element of a healthy organization. Employees should have personal and meaningful relationships with management. Trust is key. As supportive leaders, managers should know how to motivate employees to work together, both in times of continuity and of change.

To support a healthy organizational culture, PR works to ensure that both the behavior and communication of management consistently adheres to company values. Company leaders set the tone for organizational culture, and PR advocates that a healthy culture in an organization begins with the example of its leaders.

SOCIAL RESPONSIBILITY

A search of the websites of prominent corporations will likely find the agreed-upon corporate values and vision, often located on the "Our Company" or "About" pages. For example, Coca-Cola states, "We nurture a culture that values how we work as much as what we achieve through inclusivity, empowerment, curiosity, and agility" (The Coca-Cola Company, n.d.). See how the company lives its values (see Table 10.1) by focusing on its core sustainability priorities of women, water, and community well-being.

TABLE 10.1

The Coca-Cola Company Values

VALUES	SOCIAL RESPONSIBILITY ACTIONS
Inclusivity	Coca-Cola's diversity score ranks in the top 20% of large U.S. companies, and its gender score ranks in the top 25% (Comparably, 2020, para. 5).
Empowerment	Coca-Cola's 5by20 program provides women entrepreneurs with business training, access to financial services, and connections with peers and mentors.
Curiosity	The company encourages solutions for providing the highest-quality products and ingredients that are all sourced sustainably and ethically.
Agility	The company returns 100% of water used in its drinks and is committed to collecting and recycling a bottle or can for every one it sells by 2030.

Sources: The Coca-Cola Company, 2020.

Public Relations and Employee Engagement

>> LO 10.2 Understand how PR supports employee engagement and solves problems during times of change

Employee engagement with the goals of the organization is an essential component to the success of the organization's mission. To be blunt, if the employees don't support the mission, how can an organization convince the public to do so?

PR practices and theories, when applied to internal relations and employee communication, are focused on trust, transparency, and commitment, supporting multiple strategies for employee engagement. The foundation for all the strategies—the basis for everything to come—begins with defining the corporate culture for employees of all ranks.

For employees to support the corporation, they must have a clear understanding of the values that are at its core. The company, in turn, must effectively communicate these values through internal PR to its employees before asking for their assistance as advocates.

The stunning downfall of Hollywood movie producer Harvey Weinstein, which was first reported in 2017 by a story in *The New York Times*, began with a toxic workplace culture for women.
JOHANNES EISELE / Contributor / Getty Images

NBA Legends Find Their Voice

Internal communications involves not only employees but members of associations. Chicago-based PR firm and sports marketing agency KemperLesnik teamed with the National Basketball Retired Players Association (NBRPA Legends)—the only alumni association of former NBA and WNBA players. Its purpose is to help players transition into careers after basketball. What weaves the alumni together is their work in the community in collaboration with leading nonprofits and brands, which also helps give them a global reach. However, the association needed to grow membership to 1,500 former players, attract a greater number of younger retirees, and boost sponsorship dollars.

The KemperLesnik team identified the need to develop and implement an integrated marketing and communications program to define and clearly articulate the mission of the NBA Legends and to raise the association's profile to attract members and corporate partnership opportunities. It included these points:

- A messaging strategy and four-pronged communications approach integrated across all traditional, print, and social media channels
- A strategic media relations campaign to significantly increase news coverage of the association as a thought leader
- A structured social media program that reaches and engages fans
- Production and distribution of dozens of videos and graphics over owned online and social channels
- Re-creation of *Legends Magazine*—a glossy read about the pursuits and accomplishments of former players

The Results

Traditional media placements landed in major national publications such as *Bleacher Report*, *The Athletic*, *The Wall Street Journal*, and *Sports Business Daily*. Outstanding Legends served as a unified voice for the Association, being built-in brand ambassadors to the public. All superstars in their own right, they include Tim Hardaway, Sheryl Swoopes, Kareem Abdul-Jabbar, and Caron Butler, among others.

Creation of new dedicated content and graphics was imperative to realigning the brand. Logos and branding assets aided the team in introducing the world to a "refreshed" NBRPA, which helped to support the goal of building younger membership. This also created a consistent and recognizable brand across all social media platforms.

(Continued)

(Continued)

Social media, and the alignment of President & CEO Scott Rochelle as a thought leader in the industry, also breathed new life into the Association. Increased activity via Rochelle's LinkedIn profile, especially through a dedicated video series titled *On Deck With Scott Rochelle*, resulted in added followers, engagement, and—most importantly—sales leads.

A stronger focus on content distribution across Facebook, Twitter, and Instagram also served up major results. During the 2019 All-Star Game Weekend alone, organic Twitter impressions increased year-over-year by 35,600.

Finally, a revamped *Legends Magazine* offered a fresh and engaging read filled with recognizable stars and exclusive stories. The quarterly magazine is delivered to all NBRPA members, as well every NBA team locker room. The content serves as a tool to introduce younger members to the Association, keeping the NBRPA top of mind for those who will be inevitably taking their next step away from the hardwood.

- Case provided by Amy Littleton, Executive Vice President, KemperLesnik, personal communication, 2020. ●

Sources: Johnson, n.d.; Raya and Panneerselvam, 2013.

Public Relations Supports Five Characteristics of a Healthy Organization

Good financial performance is not enough to make a company "healthy." To be successful, organizations need to create and maintain a workplace built on collaboration among its workers at all levels. Certain characteristics should be ingrained in the corporate culture for an organization to be healthy. As you read the following characteristics, you will see many communication and relationship-building tasks that call on the skills of the PR professional—to lead, nurture, or take corrective actions.

Effective Sharing of Goals

Using simple messaging, a healthy organization communicate its business goals with employees throughout the organization. Employees and managers understand the mission and vision of the organization and what is required to reach these shared goals, making every effort to achieve them. Short video messages from the CEO are one effective way to engage employees in these shared goals.

Teamwork

Healthy companies use strategies to develop teams that work together to achieve common goals. Relationship building is an important element. To successfully encourage positive relationships, internal social networks help flatten the corporate hierarchy, letting people collaborate more readily. Both employees and their managers openly assist each other to meet business objectives.

High Employee Morale

Employees know they are valued and in turn value their positions in the organizations and desire longevity and promotion. As a result, productivity is high. Morale can be raised through open lines of communication that allow employees across the organization to contribute ideas and opinions that are freely discussed.

Adapts to Risks, Opportunities, and Changes

Healthy organizations understand the risks to which they are exposed and are proactive enough to take necessary steps to protect themselves. They also know how to recognize and seize good opportunities that allow them to grow. And when there are technological and operational changes, they know how to adapt. The widespread growth of social media presents both threats and opportunities.

Defined Policies and Structure

Organizational policies and structure facilitate the positive function of the business but do not limit innovation and growth. Employees readily understand them and their benefits.

Traits a Corporate Culture Should Exhibit

Constructive Relationships

A successful corporate culture facilitates constructive relationships with fellow employees and management (see Figure 10.2). In its simplest terms, a corporation that has the best relationship with its employees is one that asks, "What do you think?"

Empowerment

Positive corporation administration effectively sends the message that they encourage honest, open, and useful feedback from employees. When management openly respects the input of employees who make suggestions on how to solve workplace challenges and to improve productivity and performance, employees feel empowered to voice their ideas and concerns and feel those opinions will be fairly evaluated and acted upon. Encouraging participation in decision-making and being supportive of creative and innovative approaches no matter where they come from makes employees feel valued. And they will then more easily share their knowledge and experience within the corporate community.

Morality and Honesty

Effective corporate culture provides an organization seen as moral and honest in its business dealings and shows that its integrity is of the same high standards as its employees. People who work for a company want to be proud to say so; they want their friends and neighbors to know they're employed by an honest and ethical company.

FIGURE 10.2

Corporate Culture Traits

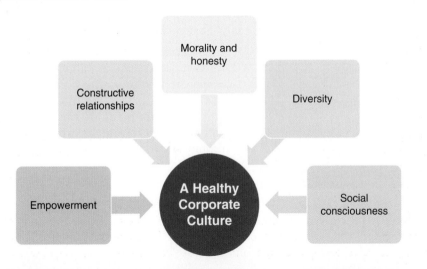

SOCIAL RESPONSIBILITY

Social Consciousness

Today, the trait of social consciousness is highly desirable by employees. It recognizes that social and environmental concerns are corporate responsibilities of interest to employees. The workforce now entering the job market is knowledgeable, and concerned, about their impact on the environment. That concern transfers to their choice of corporations where they would consider working. Is the company committed to sustainable practices? Does it do well by doing good? What does it take from the community versus what it brings to it? And clearly, does it support employees in volunteering during company time, working toward sustainability goals, matching donations to chosen charities, and in other ways that bring together the company and employee as good citizens?

Diversity

A progressive corporation embraces diversity in its workforce and respects the different perspectives a diverse group of employees brings to the organization. By promoting inclusiveness and celebrating the various races, world cultures, genders, religions, sexual orientations, and so on of its workers, the corporation is saying it welcomes all of them on the same level.

Expressing the corporation's core culture and its commitment to the traits and positions listed here is the role of PR both in internal efforts, programs, and communications to employees and in external messaging to outside publics:

- **Company e-newsletters** should reinforce the corporation's belief, for example, that the workplace honors diversity by spotlighting, among other things, the different religious or cultural holidays celebrated by its employees. Likewise, in support of the stated goal of accepting input from all levels, the newsletter should solicit feedback through surveys and polls. Profiling new employees, recognizing achievements, listing internal job openings, and even featuring nearby restaurants are content ideas for successful newsletters.

- **The corporate website** is the place for a bold statement of commitment to positive values. More than a mission statement, this should be a credo, a promise to follow certain guidelines. Putting this where all can see and read gives employees a place they can refer to—and refer their friends and family to also. It is an easy way for workers to say, "This is where I work; these are our values."

- **Internal and external communication** about the company's sustainability and SR (social responsibility) programs addresses numerous audiences. Through internal methods, employees are made aware of the organization's move toward sustainability by the promotion of, for instance, office and plant recycling efforts or the sustainable purchasing of raw goods. Employees are being encouraged to participate in more widespread efforts by joining employee groups to suggest other programs. Externally the

Delta is considered a leader in corporate efforts to create a diverse workplace.
iStock.com/winhorse

greater public should be informed on how the company is "doing good" via traditional methods, such as press releases, signage, and community events as well as through all its digital and social media avenues.

Employee Advocacy

When employees share their support for their company or its products, it can generate both positive awareness and favorable impressions. **Employee advocacy** is an important activity for a company to cultivate to help advance its agenda.

Every employee is a billboard for his or her employer. Unhappy workers, those who feel ignored or unvalued, are not positive spokespeople. The disengaged are likely to spread negativity to others. On the contrary, those who feel included, who are sure their voice is heard, who participate willingly in sustainable and socially responsible efforts, are likely a company's strongest proponents.

The 2020 Edelman Trust Barometer (Edelman, 2020) found that 73% of employees want the opportunity to change society, indicating that companies incorporating an SR/sustainability focus and offering employee volunteer activities are best winning employee trust. If the CEO openly advocates for good, even better: 92% state CEOs should speak out on current issues, such as retraining, the ethical use of technology, and income inequality. In a nutshell, creating a fulfilled and proud employee who authentically shares the company story to others is one goal of PR through internal relations and employee communication.

Mergers and Acquisitions

It is not unusual for one company to acquire another, or for two companies to come together under a single banner, or for a company to sell a business line or division it owns. Every year, hundreds of businesses will be a part of a merger and acquisition (M&A) deal, to be sold by one corporation to another or be merged to create a single company out of two. PR plays a pivotal role in seeking corporate unity, both internally and externally.

A Growing Trend

The year 2019 was the fourth-biggest year for M&As since records began in 1980 and the sixth consecutive year the values of the takeovers surpassed $3 trillion (Croft, 2019). M&A activity is predicted to continue accelerating.

There are numerous reasons why a corporation will divest itself of one of the companies in its portfolio—markets have changed, it's no longer a good fit with the mission of the corporation, and so on. In the same vein, corporations will buy independent companies to strengthen their stake in the marketplace, usually to eliminate some of the competition and other times to acquire the technology the purchased company owns. Mergers are usually created to form a single, stronger company out of two like-minded businesses. A key concern for a successful M&A is corporate integration: the melding of the two company cultures.

Yoga Rooms Versus Boardrooms

Workplace rules vary wildly from corporation to corporation; some offer casual dress, yoga rooms, and free lunches to their employees, while others demand business attire and offer no perks at all. If the traditional company acquires the one with the looser approach and wishes to summarily impose its culture on that company's employees, the result will be unpredictable and likely negative.

While some companies offer free food and on-site yoga classes, others are more straitlaced. Changes to an established corporate culture brought about by a merger or acquisition can be unsettling to employees.
iStock.com/FatCamera

While it may seem easier if the situation is reversed—that is, the corporation with the informal approach acquires the one that is more traditional—the same sort of problems will arise. A worker cannot easily go from a workplace of coats and ties to one of flip-flops and flannel.

When a company is sold outright to a new owner, an important issue that must be considered is the emotional impact this will have on the employees of that organization. They may feel abandoned, betrayed, anxious, and fearful of the future. These emotions must be dealt with in an honest and open manner if the new owners hope to have a successful transition.

M&As Can Often Disappoint

Any of these three events—acquisition, merger, or **divestiture**—will create business opportunities at the same time they create problems. The root of the problems lies in the fact that most corporations have their own way of doing business, a unique approach that it has purposely cultivated, and a corporate culture that has been inculcated in its workforce.

Swift PR response. When one such company acquires another, it gains more than the technology, factories, or storefronts of the other; part of the deal, so to speak, are the employees of the acquired company, along with its corporate culture and workplace habits. Meshing these two groups of strangers into a single workforce with a common corporate culture is an important task that must be accomplished as swiftly as possible. The demands on employee relations can be as challenging as those in crisis situations.

Culture integration is key. According to the *Harvard Business Review* (Martin, 2016), between 70% and 90% of M&A deals fail. The reasons are complex, with a major challenge being the inability to effectively integrate the merging companies. One of the dominant barriers to effective integration is culture: the values, attitudes, and behaviors of the companies' people and how that culture is communicated. A large part of the M&A value relies on soft factors, such as strategic alignment, organizational integration, and low employee resistance.

Sprint and Nextel mismatch. The two communications companies combined in 2005, becoming the nation's third-largest telecommunications provider. The companies hoped to expand by cross-selling their products and services to each other's customers. But problems arose soon after the merger. Many Nextel executives and midlevel managers left the company due to conflicts with company cultures. Sprint had a bureaucratic culture, and Nextel was more entrepreneurial. Nextel focused on customer concerns, and Sprint had a terrible reputation, experiencing the highest customer attrition rate in the industry. It was problematic to integrate their various business functions due to cultural concerns and internal practices. For example, Nextel employees often had to approach Sprint's higher-ups for approval in taking any corrective actions. Consequently, a lack of trust and rapport resulted in inaction or poor execution. The decision early on for each company to maintain separate headquarters made it difficult for executives to coordinate. Ultimately, Nextel was too big and too different for a successful combination with Sprint. The dysfunction, along with stiff competition from AT&T and Apple's iPhone, caused Sprint to cut costs and lay off employees, and in 2008, it wrote off a daunting $30 billion, earning its stock a junk status rating (Dumont, 2019).

Public Relations Strategy

For any of these business transfers or mergers to succeed, PR efforts must follow a communications plan that is open, consistent, and inclusive. The ideal situation is one where a longer planning time is an option, as that will significantly improve the odds of success.

Who's in charge. The first decision that must be made is simple: Who's in charge? In a purchase situation, the obvious PR department to handle communication is from the buyer's side. This will guarantee a single, consistent message—one the new owners want to convey.

When to start. While sensitivity to employees of the purchased company must be observed, the simple truth is their company and its culture no longer exist. It is the role of the PR team to ease those workers, and all of the stakeholders of the former company, into their new reality. As noted, the sooner this process begins, the better—especially if there will be jarring changes to the workplace. Employees need time to adjust and can't be taken by surprise by significant differences that the new regime brings, such as start times, dress expectations, expense policies—every difference, right down to parking space allocation, must be eased in gradually.

What's changed. Equally important to all concerned are the changes to hierarchal structure and departmental language. Who's my new boss? Am I being promoted or demoted? What's the name of my department now? These questions and others must be answered as soon as possible, so employees have time to adapt to the new policies and organizational chart.

How to frame it. At the same time, any message that can be perceived as negative or troubling must be balanced with one that is positive and uplifting. The acquired company's workers must be told of the good this change will bring to their lives, perhaps through new career opportunities or chances for advancement. Highlight the benefits: a better health plan, more liberal vacation or family leave policies, profit sharing—anything significantly better than what they have now.

In a merger of two entities, many compromises will have been made to achieve the merger, especially as it pertains to leadership and mission. These compromises are the ones that affect employees' lives the most and therefore become the core messages the PR team must communicate.

Communication Challenges and Opportunities

>> LO 10.3 Examine the various needs, strategies, and tactics in employee communication

With so many resources focused on the end user of an organization's services or products, it's understandable how the employee may be taken for granted or overlooked. Yet it can't be stressed enough: The workforce is essential to the health and success of a business. Look at it from the employees' perspective: This is a huge part of their lives. Our workplace helps confirm who we are and shapes our identity. Yet at times, the workplace can confuse and alienate. Organizational clarity is needed, and various communication tactics are the means for providing that clarity. The PR professional is tasked with this important responsibility using both two-way and one-way communication strategies.

Need for Organizational Clarity

In today's social reality, where there is more content than attention, employees are often overwhelmed with information. Thus, organizations must communicate a clear vision and direction to employees. This need for **organizational clarity** prompted the Institute for Public Relations to conduct a global study of employees from various business sectors (Kochhar, 2016). Some of its key takeaways include the following:

- The understanding of employee interests and perceptions is the foundation for organizational clarity.
- Strategy and content must connect to employees.

HP "Reinvents Minds" to Nurture Diversity

HP's "Reinvent Minds" campaign promotes employee diversity by highlighting unconscious bias in hiring.
NurPhoto / Contributor / Getty Images

HP, along with Edelman, developed its award-winning campaign "Reinvent Minds" to educate people on the benefits of developing a diverse employee base. The campaign's strategy was to illuminate the widespread unconscious bias and stereotyping experienced in today's hiring process. Despite the reality that the United States will soon become a minority–majority population, this is not well reflected in corporate leadership. Study after study shows "diversity yields better business results," both from building more diverse ideas as well as representing key audiences.

HP Listens to Employees and Community Leaders

First, HP conducted focus groups with its own employee advocacy groups. It then connected with leaders representing diverse communities.

HP needed to hear firsthand of the challenges and experiences various groups face regularly and in hiring practices. The goal was to better understand the issues to address. Information gained from this research led to a creative brief for the overall campaign. The conversations also inspired the creation of a series of short films, some using comments pulled from early meetings.

A Multipronged Campaign

The resulting campaign, Reinvent Minds, consisted of media efforts, job fairs, public speaking, partner events, and several short videos highlighting the challenges diverse groups face in the hiring process. One critical statistic drove the campaign: qualified African Americans are 3 times more likely to get denied a job. HP produced "Let's Get in Touch," focusing on the issue and its own training of all managers to reduce unconscious bias. It led to a partnership with historically Black colleges and universities (HBCUs) of America to launch the HBCU Business Challenge that provides hands-on experience to help prepare students and provide a pipeline to careers. After the success of this initiative, HP devoted subsequent campaigns to women, the LGBTQ community, and Latinos. ●

Sources:

Beaubien, G. (2019a). Best of silver anvil finalist: HP uncovers unconscious biases in hiring. *PRSA.* https://apps.prsa.org/StrategiesTactics/Articles/view/12583/1172/Best_of_Silver_Anvil_Finalist_HP_Uncovers_Unconsci#.XnDvK6hKjIV.

O'Brien, K. (2018). HP continues "reinvent mindsets" campaign with #LatinoJobs recruitment focus. *The Drum.* https://www.thedrum.com/news/2018/04/17/hp-continues-reinvent-mindsets-campaign-with-latinojobs-recruitment-focus

- Listening and encouraging discussion help instill trust and confidence.
- The organizational "voice" should evolve from one of telling to one of facilitating, where employees learn, engage, and question.

Public Relations Communication Tactics

The most common communication tools for employee relations are newsletters, emails, websites, and intranets or internal social media. Other responsibilities are writing executive speeches and developing frequently asked questions for management communication to employees. Relational strategies may involve organizing and managing employee meetings, retreats, workshops, celebrations, competitions, and the like.

According to Cision, the PR management company, employees are increasingly important voices due to their capability to engage with prospects, customers, the media, the general public, and with each other (Mireles, 2015). This ability increases with each technological advance. Thus, listening to employees can provide helpful perspectives. Internal communications employ many of the same strategies and methods used in PR (see the partial list that follows), but in this section, we will take a closeup look at three key tools: intranet, video storytelling, and employee programs.

Intranets

Video storytelling

Employee programs

Real-time information sharing

Mobile technology

Infographics

Messaging customization

Gamification

Internal social networks

Intranet

Intranet is the Internet used specifically inside an organization, closed to the outside Internet community. It allows larger organizations the capacity to coordinate or communicate across departments and locations, centralizing information and interconnectivity. Intranets can carry a wealth of information for organization members, including employee newsletters, tutorials, press clips, project information, employee benefits information, and policies and includes conferencing functions and multimedia. For the PR professional, communication via the intranet is faster, more widely distributed, and more efficient than many alternative printed and electronic media. User interactivity is a growing trend in company intranets. While the intranet has been a steady organizational staple as an employee portal, some intranet innovations include going beyond basic content management and into collaboration, social interaction, mobile apps, and artificial intelligence. Some examples of innovative intranets follow:

- *"Social Chorus" Mobile App.* PVH, corporate head of Calvin Klein, Tommy Hilfiger, and other brands, has a huge base of employees in 40 countries. More than two thirds are retail workers with no access to the types of technology that would connect them to the rest of the company. The mobile app solution allows employees to create personalized news feeds as well as enter photo competitions and access an update call from the CEO. It also promotes advocacy by providing content for employees to share in their personal social media communities (Ragan's PR Daily, 2018a).

- *Tech-Savvy Appeal.* The business software company Workiva is a fast-growing company, with more than 1,400 employees in 18 offices across eight countries (Workiva, n.d.). Unlike other corporate intranets that simply broadcast company information, Workiva's CONNECT creates a community where users collaborate and engage with each other through blogs, customizable profiles, and topic forums. While it integrates aspects of traditional intranets by providing the resources employees need to do their jobs, it has turned the company intranet into a social site that appeals to a younger, tech-savvy demographic—a large part of Workiva's employee base. And reporting company news is reaching new viewers through weekly videos.

- Most people today know Canon from its business in cameras and printers. Founded in Japan in 1937, the Canon name has always been synonymous with photography and visual imagery—from medical to CCTV. The company culture, called *Kyosei,* a Japanese word that means "living and working for the common good," guides how it treats its employees and customers. A unique internal project, Miru (meaning "to see") was designed by the marketing and corporate communications team to bring employees in different countries, and different parts of the company, closer together via a new and engaging company intranet. Its intent was to encourage diverse teams across the company to work collaboratively instead of within their own offices. Canon employs more than 25,000 people throughout 220 countries and regions—with obvious language barriers. The technology of Miru helped empower employees to truly experience *Kyosei,* to live and work together for the common good. It did this by bringing cutting-edge digital and social platforms like Yammer, Skype for Business, and OneDrive into the employees' daily lives—and facilitating the employees' digital dexterity. It's helped shift a culture of "knowledge is power" to one of "knowledge-sharing is power"—no longer rewarding heroes but celebrating collaboration (Canon, n.d.; MSL group, 2016).

Video Storytelling

Video storytelling has the power to engage audiences more quickly and emotionally than text or static visuals; thus, employing narrative storytelling techniques to engage internal audiences is a growing trend. That's because people have a deeper affiliation with messages that tell a story as we tend to interpret them through our own experiences and understanding. Corporate stories that purposefully appeal to employees on a personal level can help bridge barriers, generate understanding, and encourage agreement or loyalty. Consider these examples:

- *Animated Ideas.* ICON Clinical Research, a global provider for the medical industries (ICON Clinical Research, n.d.) created a video to launch SPARK—an internal online idea management and crowdsourcing platform for employees to spark innovation. It told the story of the journey of an idea, illustrated through live action in various global ICON locations and animation of ideas forming, emerging, and developing—essentially the innovation process.

- *Undercover Boss.* Scene: the hospital kitchen. Characters: the hospital executive and the kitchen chef. Plot: The executive discovers the hospital does not get fish already cut and prepared—no, the salmon arrive whole and are cut up right there. Action: Guided by the chef, the executive tries skinning and slicing the fish. It's a short segment, and it's not a new reality show, but rather part of a Johns Hopkins Medicine video series crafted to introduce employees to "Big Jobs Uncovered." This series showing leaders working with frontline staff was prompted by a new president wanting to support employee engagement in a more fun and relatable way (Ragan's PR Daily, 2018c).

Employee Programs

A little more than half of small firms and 82% of larger firms offer employee wellness programs, from simple to extensive; however, research suggests that changing behaviors and getting people motivated to participate at all can be difficult (Appleby, 2019). While ensuring wellness incentives apply across many areas—from foods that workplaces offer to inclusion of spouses or partners in health challenges—the right communication is essential. Companies need to communicate much more persistently, clearly, and creatively—not only to inform but to address employees' doubts, privacy concerns, or lack of self-confidence. Here's an example of a successful communication campaign:

- *Who's Your Reason?* Blue Communications orchestrated an employee wellness campaign for AECOM, an engineering firm with 40,000 employees (Blue Communications, n.d.). The campaign sought to drive engagement in a wellness program through financial incentives—specifically lowering cost increases for employee health care. Those who participated would pay less. The theme "Be well" was illustrated with appealing imagery asking the question "Who's your reason?" to help employees recognize those who rely on them to stay healthy: spouses, children, friends, and even pets. Wellness ambassadors and a variety of media helped communicate the advantages of completing the program. More than 75% of employees did.

Evaluating Employee Communication

Measure and evaluate how communication reaches internal publics, as you would with any PR campaign. Consider your messaging outputs, outtakes, and outcomes.

- Was it well timed?
- Was the content truthful and accurate?
- Did it have relevance for the specific receivers?
- Was it accessed and read or viewed?
- Did it result in its objectives (inform, shape opinion, or encourage behavior)?

Employee Relations and Corporate Social Responsibility

>> LO 10.4 **Identify the strategic connection between CSR and an organization's employees**

A strong commitment to SR is aligned with excellent company reputation. After quality products and services offered at a good value to meet customer needs, the strongest driver of a company's reputation is its positive influence on society (Reputation Institute, 2018a). Reputation is also an emotional bond that inspires employee engagement.

In companies that value sustainability and SR, employees are considered key stakeholders because their feedback can provide insight into issues and how to address them. For example, Starbucks initiated its College Achievement Plan and its FoodShare program out of listening to employee concerns. Employees offer a built-in sounding board for new ideas leading to social and environmental initiatives that everyone can be proud of.

SOCIAL RESPONSIBILITY

Corporate Social Responsibility Engages Employees

While sustainability and green practices are important to many in the workplace, it is in the area of SR where greatest opportunity for employee engagement lies. Many companies have programs that give back to the communities in which they are based; others support national or international issues and charities. The more successful of these corporate efforts are those in which the employees play a direct role in all aspects of the program, from selecting the charity or cause to raising money or to donating time and physical effort. PR takes a vital role internally by promoting the cause and often recruiting employee volunteers. Externally, the story of the good the company has done reflects on the employees and enhances their positive views of their employer.

The biggest, most enduring benefit to employees of companywide CSR programs is the spirit of camaraderie they engender. Side by side as a group, managers and workers work toward a common goal that will benefit others and create a bond that benefits future workplace relationships. It also makes it easier to create support from within the company to advocate for the corporation's business goals.

PR PROFILE

Why Simplicity Is Beautiful in Employee Communication Strategy

Meg Wheaton, Gagen MacDonald

Photo courtesy of Meg Wheaton

What Is a Strategy?

Strategy is the overarching path of how you're going to achieve your goals, and creating the strategy is only the first step. Activating a strategy and making it come to life inside an organization—that's what I'm really passionate about.

Anyone who has kids can attest to the fact that just because you tell them to pick up their socks doesn't mean they're going to. Whether you're at home or at work, simply telling people what to do isn't necessarily going to achieve the outcome that you are seeking. People need a compelling reason to do something or change their behavior, even if it's something as simple as picking up their socks.

How Do We Activate a Strategy?

Create a visual model of your strategy that's simple, impactful, and memorable. The model should include your strategy's pillars or key priorities that will get you the results you are seeking. Try to keep to four pillars, as studies prove that people have a tough time remembering more than that. Use color coding, imagery, and iconography to make the visual model sing.

Understand your target audiences—all of them. Gagen specializes in internal communications, so our campaigns are addressed to employees. For the most part, we are asking them to do something differently or change their behavior. To do this, they need to know what we want them to do (tell them specifically what we need them to do differently) and why we want them to do it (tell them what benefits will come from changing). Holding focus groups, fielding surveys, and talking to people within an organization can help us get at the employee mindset.

Create a compelling story that articulates the change and activates leaders as passionate storytellers. Storytelling is a fantastic way to help

people connect the dots and see themselves inside a strategy shift or culture change. Leaders must connect to both the emotional and rational sides of the brain. Stories are memorable, tactile, and lasting. It's critical that leaders tell stories in their own words and that they "walk the talk." A story isn't a story until everyone can tell it.

Create communications that inspire others. People want to be part of something that is larger than themselves. Create communications that help employees understand the journey as well as the destination and the good that will come from it all. Because everyone consumes information in different ways, you need many different tactics—videos, animations, environmental signage, in-person meetings, digital communications, and so on—to reach all your audiences.

Create impactful experiences that allow employees to see themselves in the strategy. Bring workers together for collaborative, creative sessions where employees can roll up their sleeves and work together to map their own personal paths forward and how they'll contribute to the team effort. Make it fun and make it exciting! ●

Meg Wheaton is managing director at Gagen MacDonald, the leading strategy execution firm based in Chicago.

Source: M. Wheaton, personal communication, 2020.

Corporate Social Responsibility Aids Employee Recruitment and Retention

CSR can be a mechanism for recruiting because it complements purpose-driven work, providing professional fulfillment for workers. More and more employees desire jobs that have purpose and meaning, with expectations that their company is committed to making the world a better place. Research indicates that millennials are the most socially conscious generation since the 1960s. By 2025, those born between 1980 and 1996 will make up three quarters of the global workforce (Catalyst, 2019).

Recent research studies agree that companies' commitments toward social issues have become key drivers for recruiting and retaining employees (Cone Communications, 2016; Peters, 2019). Some of the significant findings include the following:

- 75% of millennials are ready to take a smaller salary to work for a company that's environmentally responsible.

- 40% of millennials said they've picked a past job because the company performed better on sustainability than an alternative job.

- Nearly 70% of employees in all age groups said a company's sustainability plan would affect their long-term commitment to stay.

Girls who attend the Geek Squad Academy, a 2-day technology camp, are taught by Best Buy employees.
Associated Press

Examples of Excellence

Patagonia. Patagonia's mission statement is "Build the best product, cause no unnecessary harm, use business to inspire and implement solutions to the environmental crisis" (Heath, 2019, para. 4). Rick Ridgeway, the company's vice president of public engagement, says the mission "attracts workers who are already committed to sustainable practices before they join the company" (Delisio, 2017, para. 9).

Timberland. When Timberland is recruiting, potential employees often ask about Timberland's Path of Service program. What's attractive about it is the opportunity to participate in a community project for up to 40 paid hours annually. Employees may engage in issues of their choice that they feel passionate about (Delisio, 2017).

Best Buy. Best Buy's Geek Squad participates in an employee CSR program that increases job satisfaction and retention. The Geek Squad Academy (GSA) is a 2-day technology camp for girls and underserved teen populations. In 2019, more than 10,000 students aged 11 to 18 attended camps (Bloomberg, 2019). Employees from both the Geek Squad and the retail division are recruited as camp staff. Since the program's inception in 2007, along with other Best Buy pathway, volunteering, and mentoring programs, the resulting impact on employees has been positive. A formal survey called eVoice revealed that the company experienced an overall employee engagement score of 86 in 2019, leading to higher levels of retention (Best Buy, 2019).

Scenario Outcome

To recap our chapter-beginning scenario, after the tech crash in the mid-2000s, Intel knew it had to transform, and thus, it had to motivate its employees to be innovative. A key problem was how to best communicate with them. Intel's internal communications team developed communications in three broad categories in answer to these questions:

Patagonia attracts workers who are already committed to sustainable practices and, in some locations, those who like to surf on their lunchbreaks.
The Washington Post / Contributor / Getty Images

How did Intel connect employees to encourage conversations with each other? With top management?

The solution was "Connect Me." Intel took employee engagement seriously. To encourage engagement, employees could comment on all intranet articles. Full-time employees could have a company blog. It tapped the "wisdom of the crowd" through forums such as Intelpedia, Ask a Geek forums, and others offering peer-to-peer advice on benefits. Forty percent of employees took advantage of personalizing their intranet home pages in the first few months.

The Intel intranet also encouraged conversations with executives via various methods: personal profiles, blogs, one-to-a-few sessions, and quarterly webcasts.

How did Intel show employees it values them?

The solution was "Value Me." Intel used online platforms to show employees it cared. Fun recognition rewards gave away movie tickets and debit cards. Later, online tutoring was added. Employees also could find information on tuition assistance, health centers, and scholarships. When Intel discovered that employees likely weren't aware of all their benefits, it used social media to raise awareness. For example, stock options were explained in friendly, easy-to-understand language.

Employees can be your best advocates. How did Intel inspire employees to explain to outsiders what they do?

The solution was "Inspire Me." According to Melissa McVicker of Intel, "Intel is a very technical company where it's hard for employees to explain what they do, especially to outsiders" (2013, para. 4). However, an intranet allowed employees to easily share the Intel story. Intel encouraged some of them to start conversations, and before long, it became unnecessary as employees were engaging naturally. "One example is the team who, on their own, turned a code of conduct training course into a fun, Bollywood-style presentation with much greater impact than the conventional version" (McVicker, 2013, para. 4). Intel has learned that engaging 100,000 people starts with a good story.

WRAP UP

In this chapter, you've learned employee relations is a growing and demanding area due to many factors, including a changing workforce, employee diversity, broader communication channels, the complexities of creating a healthy corporate culture, the increased frequency of change due to mergers and acquisitions, and employees' strong desire for a socially conscious workplace.

PR's role in supporting a healthy corporate culture includes counseling management's leadership style, encouraging teamwork, getting and valuing employee input, and supporting volunteer opportunities.

Facilitating employee engagement is a top priority, achieved by creating opportunities for dialogue and collaborative decision-making, encouraging creativity and new ideas, being truthful in your communication, welcoming diversity, and being socially conscious.

Corporate change happens often and can be done poorly or successfully; PR supports success with communication strategies as early as possible in the change cycle. Essential communication and engagement tactics include intranets, e-newsletters, video storytelling, and various employee programs. Throughout the chapter, you've explored the breadth of employee relations and PR's role in it.

KEY TERMS

Acquisitions 227
Corporate Culture 227
Divestiture 234
Employee Advocacy 233

Employee Relations 227
Intranet 237
Merger 227
Organizational Clarity 236

THINK ABOUT IT

Companies benefit from increased employee morale and loyalty. Timberland is a U.S. manufacturer and retailer of footwear, outdoor apparel, and accessories with worldwide operations. The company has a long history of social and environmental responsibility that is ingrained into its corporate culture. Visit Timberland's responsibility website at www.timberland. com/responsibility. Do you get the sense that Timberland is genuine in its commitment to CSR? Now search for "Timberland Path of Service" to learn about its employee engagement. Explore and note the many issues, programs, and opportunities that engage employees.

WRITE LIKE A PRO

In this chapter, you were challenged to solve Intel's internal communication problem. Now apply what you learned to this situation: Over the past 3 years, Hopkins College, a 120-year-old creative and media arts school in a midwestern urban setting, has maintained excellent educational standards and placed graduates in top media positions. However, it has also lost some state funding, eliminated staff and faculty raises, and has experienced increased employee turnover. The leadership wants to reinvigorate a sense of community and motivate dedication in its employees (staff and faculty).

As Intel conceived of a new, bold vision statement—*This decade, we will create and extend computing technology to connect and enrich the life of every person on earth*—now it's your turn. Brainstorm and draft a short vision statement that makes an emotional connection to Hopkins's employees and propose how it would be communicated to engage employees.

SOCIAL RESPONSIBILITY CASE STUDY

IBM's Corporate Service Corps Develops the Leaders of the Future

Situation

IBM has a long history of volunteerism involving employees, developing innovative education solutions through technology, economic development, environmental sustainability, health care, and more. IBM launched its Corporate Service Corps (CSC) in 2008 mainly to develop leadership and engage in CSR. Teams of eight to 15 IBM members work pro bono with volunteers, government, business, and civic leaders in developing nations to assist with critical issues of societal significance. The program is directly aligned with IBM's core value of innovation that matters by harnessing advanced technologies and problem-solving expertise in tackling some of the world's most pressing challenges.

Research and Strategy

Key to success is their partnerships with NGOs like USAID, the Peace Corps, and the Nature Conservancy that assist in providing strategic implementation on the ground for the programs and collaborations with companies such as GlaxoSmithKline and Dow Chemical. Among their goals was to build more awareness of the value of weaving corporate citizenship into overall business strategy. In that process, the company is changing the way people see IBM—as a company that provides services and solves critical problems.

Execution

Inspired by the U.S. Peace Corps, the CSC program has sent more than 4,000 IBMers from nearly 62 countries to serve on more than 1,400 projects in 44 countries. First, teams of IBMers around the world work online for 3 months preparing for each project. Then, the

TABLE 10.2

IBM Corporate Service Corps

COLLABORATIONS	SOCIAL RESPONSIBILITY ACTIONS
Ghanaian Health Service and the Yale School of Medicine	Together with CSC, they work to eradicate HIV transmission from mother to child—initially in Ghana and then throughout sub-Saharan Africa.
NGO CerviCusco	Together, they work to increase cervical cancer screening and treatment in Peru.
The Nature Conservancy	In a joint project, they strategize for conservation and commerce to coexist in Brazil's Amazon rain forest.
Global FoodBanking Network	Together, they work to make nutrition more available in Colombia, Ecuador, and Mexico.
SYSTEMS, PROGRAMS, APPS	SOCIAL RESPONSIBILITY ACTIONS
Knowledge management	CSC developed web-based information management systems in India to enhance eye care.
Disaster preparedness	CSC implemented a system for disaster preparedness in the Philippines, key to relief and recovery there.
Health care programs	CSC developed policies and programs for health care for women and children in Nigeria.
Refugee mobile app	CSC developed a free mobile app to better assist refugees and immigrants in need of medical care in Italy.

Source: Data from IBM.

team takes up residency in the country for 1 month to work with a beneficiary organization to develop recommendations for both immediate and long-term impact. The feedback from the beneficiaries and partners served by CSC teams has been overwhelmingly positive and appreciative. Many of the returning IBMers call their deployments life changing.

Evaluation

The CSC's corporate and nonprofit partnership has produced many positive results (Table 10.2). The corporation also realizes that dedicated employees are inspired to provide exceptional services to clients. Ninety percent of participants say their global IBM experience helped them to develop strong leadership skills. At the same time, it helped them to understand IBM's role in the developing world, strengthened their cultural awareness, and made them better at their jobs. Most employees felt that the program increased their desire to remain at IBM for their career. And in the years since the CSC launch, IBM has helped nurture similar programs at many other companies, including FedEx, John Deere, and JPMorgan Chase.

Engage

- Go to www.IBM.com and explore the breadth of the company's products, services, and industries served.
- Next, go to www.IBM.org to review its social impact and initiatives.

Discuss

- Choose and discuss an IBM initiative that you think is particularly innovative.
- Assume you have the knowledge to participate in any of the initiatives. Which one would you choose, and why? What part of the experience might help strengthen your affinity with IBM?

Sources: IBM, n.d.a, n.d.b, and n.d.c.

11

Corporate Communication and Reputation Management

Learning Objectives

11.1   Understand the environment surrounding the modern corporation

11.2   Describe the core competencies of corporate communications

11.3   Illustrate how SR enhances corporate communications

11.4   Explain the importance of financial communications and investor relations

Scenario
The Starbucks "Race Together" Campaign

Following the controversial police shootings of civilians in Ferguson, Missouri, and New York City, Howard Schultz, CEO of Starbucks, was deeply saddened by the rising racial tensions in the United States. He felt his company needed to address the issue and refused to be a silent bystander. Schultz invited Starbucks employees to participate in internal discussion forums across the nation, where they could come together and discuss race issues in the United States.

As an outgrowth of these forums, Starbucks released a memo to all retail employees, encouraging them to engage customers in conversation about race in the company's stores by writing the words "Race Together" on their paper coffee cups.

The attempts by Starbucks to encourage their employees to engage customers in conversations about race resulted in immediate mockery.
Associated Press

Well intentioned, poorly received. The initiative was well intentioned, but when introduced to customers, it was poorly received. Most people did not want to discuss a topic as complex as race relations while they rushed to get their coffee. The public thought race was an inappropriate topic for a company to address with customers in a retail setting, and the idea was harshly mocked. Late-night talk show hosts ridiculed the initiative, including John Oliver (2015), host of *Last Week Tonight*, who suggested "a conversation about race relations in America is clearly important, but there is a time and a place." At the end of the piece, he advised Starbucks to "just stay in your lane."

A fierce Twitter storm. The campaign was heavily criticized on social media, to the extent that the vice president of corporate communications took down his Twitter account, as he felt he was "being harshly attacked."

A sampling of negative tweets about "Race Together" follows:

Not sure what @Starbucks was thinking. I don't have time to explain 400 years of oppression to you & still make my train. #Race Together

—@ReignOfApril

Yesterday: talk about Love at McDonalds

Today: talk about race at Starbucks

Tmrw: psychoanalysis from guy who makes blizzards at dairy queen

—@MikeIsaac

Would #Starbucks lower their prices in order to offset the emotional cost of discussing #Race Together with a clueless Barista?

—@leviljkm

The only folks about Starbucks baristas discussing race with customers are the suits who run it. Feel-good liberalism at its worst.

—@JamilSmith

The Twitter storm was fierce, but it blew over quickly. The media response was equally critical, and the mainstream press labeled the initiative as poorly executed and gratuitous.

(Continued)

(Continued)

When the practice of writing on the cups ended a week later, most people thought the initiative had been quietly shut down, cut short because of the negative reaction from the public and media.

Did Starbucks suffer lingering damage? Starbucks maintained that writing "Race Together" on cups lasted for its intended run date, March 16 to March 22, 2015, and only played a small role in the overall "Race Together" initiative (Ziv, 2015). The act of writing on cups was meant to serve as a jumping-off point in the conversation, and Starbucks claimed it already had a larger plan in place to address the racial divide. At the end of the chapter, you will learn how this initiative played out.

As you read through the chapter, consider the following:

1. Should companies like Starbucks (or any other retail business) seek to engage customers in a discussion about race relations in the United States?

2. After the rocky start to the campaign, what would you advise them to do next?

3. What program options might have worked better and still be true to Starbucks's corporate culture?

4. Are there some topics or issues that corporations should avoid altogether? Why?

5. Was this an effective social responsibility initiative? ●

Source: Michael, Cauley, and Orengo, 2016.

This chapter offers an overview on corporate communication and reputation management on a global basis in a digital society. It includes important lessons on building relationships between the corporation and its key stakeholders—including the internal audience. Through examples and case studies, you will learn about the skills you need to succeed in a high-stakes environment. It will also focus on the role of corporate leaders and their expectations of the communication team and their outside advisors to protect and enhance corporate reputation.

Finally, it includes short case studies throughout to illustrate the chapter's learning objectives and an opening scenario that puts you in the picture, facing challenges that are part of the daily routine for corporate communication professionals.

The Modern Corporation: Meeting the Challenge

>> LO 11.1 Understand the environment surrounding the modern corporation

To understand the challenges faced by corporate communication professionals, whether they are on staff or serve as outside advisors, you must understand the context and environment of today's corporations. Unless you have worked in a corporate setting, your perceptions are likely driven by the popular media or case studies you've read in class.

The images of corporate life and "big business"—as depicted in TV shows like *Mad Men* or *The Office* and movies like *Horrible Bosses* and *The Devil Wears Prada*—are dramatized for entertainment and effect. In the real world, life as a corporate communicator is no more like these stereotypes than working in crisis communication or politics is comparable to *Scandal* (ABC) or *House of Cards* (Netflix).

Companies Are Multifaceted Organizations

Companies are complex organizations with a variety of stakeholders who interact daily, both internally and externally. These companies are focused on operating profitably, providing quality goods and services to the marketplace, obeying the law, being a good place to work, and being regarded as a good corporate citizen.

In addition, companies—particularly the ones whose common stock is publicly traded on a **stock exchange**—like NASDAQ or the New York Stock Exchange (NYSE)—must comply with required quarterly and yearly reporting of financial results to the public, media, and shareholders. The schedule of publishing financial communication must be adhered to by law and has its own set of rules and requirements. These will be addressed later in the section of this chapter on financial communications.

Communication in a corporate setting can be a high-stakes and challenging activity. You are tasked with representing the company, its products, and its employees to the external market. You may also be involved in communicating with employees—perhaps even globally—depending on the size and scope of the company. Often, you are also responsible for developing or promoting the company's social responsibility (SR) initiatives as well. In some cases, you may be involved—directly or indirectly—in the company's communications with the financial community or government officials.

Finally, you must learn to interpret and convey trends in the marketplace *inward* to management and convey the character and reputation of the company *outward* to the public. This role—as an intermediary between the company and its external stakeholders—can be one of the most challenging and vital.

The Issue of Trust

The Edelman Trust Barometer examines this challenge annually and provides us with some guidance. Since it was first published in 2001, this study has become one of the definitive annual studies on how business, government, NGOs, and the media are perceived by the public and opinion leaders worldwide. Each year, the research results are debuted at Davos, Switzerland, at a high-profile annual gathering of world leaders from politics, business, entertainment, and the nonprofit community.

SOCIAL RESPONSIBILITY

The 2020 study noted a lack of trust globally in the four major social institutions, the study tracks. These include government, nongovernmental organizations (NGOs), the media, and business (see Figure 11.1).

FIGURE 11.1

Edelman Trust Barometer, 2020: Trust in Major Social Institutions

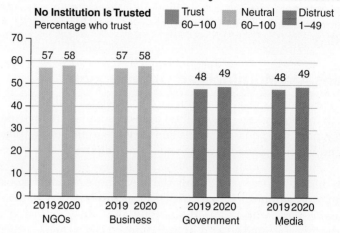

Source: Edelman, "Edelman Trust Barometer," 2020. https://www.edelman.com/sites/g/files/aatuss191/files/2020-01/202 0 %20Edelman%20Trust%20Barometer%20Executive%20Summary_Single%20Spread%20without%20Crops.pdf

FIGURE 11.2

How Much Do You Trust These People to Do What Is Right?

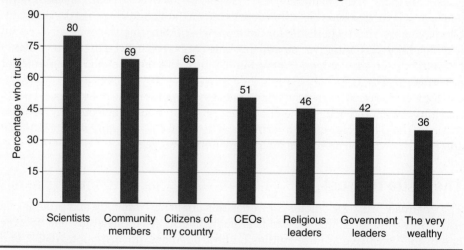

Source: Edelman (2017).

The global study examines the declining level of trust in these institutions among the "informed public" (educated, active consumers of news and information) and the "mass population." The 2020 study also showed a widening gap between the general population and the informed public in the levels of trust in these institutions. The study showed that the more-informed segment had higher levels of trust overall.

Further, the 2020 study shows that 83% of employees globally are worried about job loss due to external forces impacting the workplace, such as the lack of training, cheaper competition, immigration, and automation (Edelman, 2020).

These and other significant results from the research starkly illustrate the polarization and disenfranchisement impacting society, markets, and elections worldwide, as well as the challenges to the modern corporation to respond.

Interestingly, the study shows that among the general population, business is most trusted to keep pace with the changing times as compared to government and the media (see Figure 11.2).

Critical Role for Corporate Public Relations

This is the essence of the challenge for corporate communicators in today's global economy. Communicators must build public trust in their companies or clients while advocating effectively for them at the same time. To do this, a corporate communication team must accomplish the following:

- Identify and engage key stakeholders.
- Secure powerful and impactful media coverage.
- Develop thought leadership opportunities (research, speeches, and events) to promote and enhance executive visibility.
- Promote the corporate brand by creating and leveraging SR initiatives.
- Manage issues and crisis situations as needed to protect the corporate brand.

The basic equation is this: The more balanced, positive news and fewer negative stories (e.g., issues and crisis situations) that appear, the greater the chances the company can increase sales and profits, engage key stakeholders, and build trust. This may sound easy, but as any experienced corporate communicator can attest, it is far from simple. To "solve" this equation, the corporate communicator must be skilled, ethical, honest, as transparent as possible, and accountable to both internal and external stakeholders. "What do stakeholders expect of business today? Certainly, a solid and steady focus on financial returns, but even more [people] say [they expect] action around education, health care, income inequality, and other [social] issues," notes Kathryn Beiser, vice president of global communications for Eli Lilly and Company (personal communication, 2019).

Clearly, this is a 360-degree role and will require your best efforts daily (see Figure 11.3). You will need to understand the company's business strategy, the financial markets, traditional and social media, government and political trends, and the needs and expectations of your fellow employees and external stakeholders.

Commenting on the importance of communicators helping companies drive change and build trust, Gary Sheffer, retired vice president of corporate communication at General Electric and Professor of Public Relations, Boston University, suggests,

> Today, trust is crucial. Customers are more inclined to buy from a trusted company and advocate to others that they do the same. Costs decrease when a company has trusting relationships in its supply chain. Trusted companies retain employees and outperform their competitors. The role (of corporate communications) revolves around earning and preserving this valuable currency of trust. (Haran & Sheffer, 2015, para. 2)

Communication's Place in the Company

All companies—regardless of their structure, size, and ownership (e.g., public or private)—have similar communication goals. They want to communicate results, promote their products or services, be known as a good place to work and a reliable business partner, and earn a reputation as a good corporate citizen. Achieving these goals, as internal and external events unfold, and managing the challenges as they arise are the responsibility of the corporate communicator.

The organizational structure and reporting relationship of the corporate communication function differs from company to company. In some companies, the communication staff is part of the marketing function and reports to the senior executive responsible for marketing, PR, and advertising. These individuals, whose

FIGURE 11.3

Anatomy of the Corporate Communicator

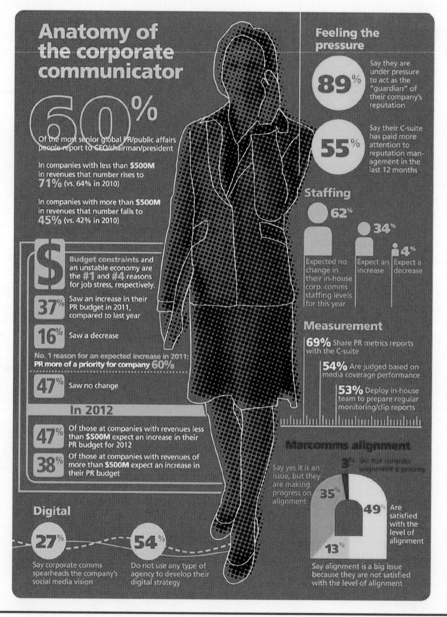

Source: Anatomy of the corporate communicator, *PRWeek*, October 3, 2011. Reprinted with permission from Haymarket Media Group.

title is usually **chief marketing officer (CMO)**, are responsible for overall marketing and the corporate brand.

In other companies the communication function is a separate discipline and reports directly to the chief executive officer (CEO) or president of the organization. Communicators in this role are often referred to as the **chief communications officer (CCO)**. Still other companies have variations on these models, with the communication team reporting to another senior executive, such as human resources (personnel), general counsel (legal officer), or the chief financial officer (CFO)—although these are often the exceptions.

The reporting relationship of the communication function (Figure 11.3) has been debated over the years, and different models continue to be employed. Changes in reporting relationships are driven mostly by external market events (e.g., the trend toward integrated marketing communications in large consumer product companies) or management's changing view on how to structure the communications function.

Page Society President Roger Bolton suggests "there is a lot of ongoing discussion . . . about the CCO's role in relation to marketing and communications convergence, and there is a lot of substance behind that because those two areas are becoming so closely intertwined" (Daniels, 2015, para. 6).

"I don't think we'll see a (consistent) trend toward one model or the other. CEOs want someone who 'gets it' and can run the two functions for them," Bolton adds. "It is OK for each company to have its own approach as long as they understand that marketing and communication have two fundamentally different purposes" (Daniels, 2015, para. 10).

Regardless of whether the communication team reports to the CEO or elsewhere, his or her direct involvement in helping to manage the company and receiving executive support are critical to the success of the effort. A recent study states that "the performance of corporate communication depends heavily on the perceptions, beliefs, and expectations that chief executive officers (CEOs), and other top executives, hold toward communication and its contribution to organizational goals" (Zerfass & Sherzada, 2014).

Core Competencies of Corporate Communications

>> LO 11.2 **Describe the core competencies of corporate communications**

The specific duties of the corporate communication professional include overseeing media relations (see also Chapter 7); branding, special events, and sponsorships (see also Chapter 13); internal or employee communications (see also Chapter 10); and community relations and sustainability communications (see also Chapter 9). These duties, along with **financial communications** for public companies, make up the overall function of corporate communication and are designed to help achieve the strategic goals of the company or organization.

To meet their communications challenges, companies often engage outside PR (public relations) and public affairs firms to assist them in work. According to the research firm IDC, companies spent 3.8% of their marketing budget on PR in 2014—5.7% on branding and content, 1.9% on social marketing, and 1.1% on industry analyst relations (see Table 11.1), all functions that are often handled by an outside PR agency (Comcowich, 2015).

TABLE 11.1

Percentage of Marketing Budget Spent on Corporate Communication Activities

ACTIVITIES	PERCENT OF BUDGET SPENT
Public relations	3.8%
Branding	5.7%
Social marketing	1.9%
Analyst relations	1.1%

Source: IDC.

As such, you do not need to be directly employed by a corporation to be engaged in corporate communication. You can work for a PR agency (like Edelman, Hill & Knowlton, Burson Marsteller, or many others), a management consulting firm (like Booz Allen Hamilton or McKinsey), or be a sole practitioner and still engage in corporate communication.

Corporate Media Relations

Media relations, a topic covered in detail in Chapter 7, is a critical component of communication for today's corporation. Not only is the corporate world a focus of news coverage by the traditional media, both local and national, it is also a hot topic on social media as well. On any given day, you will find stories or conversations on major social media platforms about corporate performance, issues, plans, and strategy. Corporate media relations is challenging, dynamic, and ever changing. This is especially true for "big business" and for publicly traded companies. The explanation for this phenomenon is simple—the number of people and dollar amounts involved are bigger, company news is local *and* global, and the personalities and activities of the CEOs and senior management involved are often compelling.

In looking at the target media for any company or client, you will find a vast array of options and outlets to consider. There are key national publications that track business performance, such as *The New York Times*, the *Financial Times,* and *The Wall Street Journal*; leading business magazines like *Fortune* and *Forbes*; as well as countless broadcast and cable outlets (e.g., CNN, Fox, and MSNBC) and news services (e.g., Reuters and Bloomberg) to contend with and interact daily.

You also need to manage your company's relationship with the local media—both print and broadcast—where your company or client is based and/or has major operations, such as factories or regional offices, including around the world. These publications and local broadcasters have a vested interest in covering your company because you operate in their country or region.

As well, there are numerous online outlets, including Yahoo Finance, Google Finance, Business Insider, Market Watch, and The Huffington Post. Further, the major business media (e.g., *Fortune, Forbes, The Wall Street Journal,* etc.) maintain and update their own websites on a constant basis. Other outlets, including the professional or trade media that cover your industry, are constantly looking for business news from companies—such as updates on corporate performance, management changes, product introductions, and other corporate news. That is the good news—especially if you have a good story to tell.

The bad news is that this constant attention cuts both ways. Should a crisis or issue arise, the same content-hungry local and national media are there to pick up the story and run with it. Managing this two-edged sword and building—or defending—your company's reputation is a critical job for today's corporate communicators. While the stakes can be high at this level, the media relations approach is the same as a smaller organization or nonprofit. The process

United faced a media firestorm in 2017 after the flight staff summoned airport police to remove a passenger from an overbooked flight to make room for a United crew member. The passenger suffered multiple injuries, and video of the incident circulated widely online.
JOSHUA LOTT / Stringer / Getty Images

is about building and maintaining relationships among your company, the media, and all the external stakeholders.

Supa and Zoch (2009, p. 1) suggest that "media relations is the systematic, planned, purposeful and mutually beneficial relationship between a public relations practitioner and a mass media journalist." You can certainly extend that to the digital media as well.

In a corporate setting, the process of media relations requires the PR professional to be available and responsive to media outlets and, selectively, to make senior management available to discuss a major story or industry topic in detail. In turn, reporters can be expected to provide a fair and accurate story as well as to bring in other points of view to balance the story as they see fit. However, while this may sound simple, it is not. Some company executives may "expect" their news coverage to be only positive or flattering. Further, some reporters are out to promote themselves by putting corporate executives in difficult situations or by getting a "scoop" that creates follow-up stories, social media traffic, and a higher overall profile. Fortunately, most reporters are professionals looking to prepare a balanced and interesting story for their readers or viewers.

Your goal as a communicator is to produce an accurate, balanced story that represents the company's point of view, conveys your key messages to target audiences, and meets the reporters' needs. The independence of the media outlet and reporters must be respected, just as the company's point of view should be. That is the basis of the mutually beneficial working relationship of corporate media relations. In short, that is why it called "media relations"—it is a two-way *relationship* and should be respected and cultivated over time.

Digital Media Relations

The most influential recent change affecting the practice of corporate media relations is the proliferation of social media. Social media allows PR practitioners to speak directly to target audiences without interference or alteration by a media gatekeeper, as in traditional media relations. Internet-based platforms have become important direct distribution channels for company information. New media, however, also offers a special set of challenges, as there is often no gatekeeper or control over what gets posted as "news" by companies or so-called "citizen journalists."

The rise of social media platforms such as YouTube, Facebook, Instagram, and Twitter, among others, provide new PR opportunities as well as new risks. You must think carefully about which option is the best for communicating to your target publics. These external stakeholders, in turn, have high expectations for how organizations interact with them online.

Typically, media stakeholders expect corporate communication that meets these criteria:

- Authentic
- Honest
- Candid
- Two-way

Social media often blurs the line between the personal and the professional, so a key proficiency for PR practitioners today is to master managing your organization's online identity and reputation in a balanced and transparent manner.

A 24-Hour-a-Day Job

The ability to communicate directly and interactively via social media has made corporate media relations a 24-hour-a-day job. Reporters expect corporate websites will have up-to-the-second information available without them having to wait for a PR staffer. As a result, your online content must be carefully screened, current, and well organized so that journalists will find the information they need quickly. Absent that, they may go to external activists or even your competitors for comment and information.

Fundamental Practices Remain

Despite these new developments in digital media, the fundamental relationship between the PR practitioner and the journalist remains unchanged. Journalists still want access to accurate information so they can craft a fair and balanced story; PR practitioners still want coverage of client news to be as positive and balanced as possible. Bloggers, Twitter users, and other commentators want interesting, factual, and truthful information as well. And your stakeholders expect to be kept informed on a timely basis.

SOCIAL RESPONSIBILITY

In the end, the mutual dependence between the two camps creates a relationship that serves both parties well. Journalists and digital media outlets need PR practitioners to provide them information for stories, and the PR practitioners need journalists to provide voice and distribution for their messages. Jon Iwata, retired senior vice president of marketing, communications, and citizenship at IBM, summed up the challenge and opportunity of corporate communications in a Distinguished Lecture at the Institute of Public Relations:

> As never before, people care about the corporation behind the soft drink, the bank account or the computer. They do not separate their opinions about the company from their opinions of that company's products and services . . . or its stock, for that matter. People care about the behavior and compensation of the company's executives . . . how the product was produced, and by whom . . . how the company treats its employees and suppliers . . . how it impacts the environment. Now, maybe people always cared about these things—but, really, how much could they know about what was happening inside our companies? Today they have an unprecedented view into the corporation's actual behavior and actual performance. (Iwata & Golin, 2009, p. 2)

On the Job in Media Relations

Applying the core principles of corporate media relations—access to management, transparency, accuracy, and fairness—is a challenging undertaking. As well, it is neither static nor totally predictable because circumstances change and your objectives and the media outlets will not always align. As a corporate communicator, you should assess each opportunity and determine the best course of action. The outcome will depend on the nature of the opportunity or problem.

Is it a positive story (new product, market trend, or management appointment) or a potentially negative one (issue, crisis, or a decline in sales and profits)?

How will management react and comment if they are engaged? Will they listen to your advice?

Other factors to weigh include the following:

Does your company have a point of view on the issue?

Is your management team fully briefed and ready to respond to media questions on the topic?

What are the risks of participating in the discussion?

By answering these questions, and preparing accordingly, your corporate media relations efforts will likely be successful, and your company or client will benefit in an enhanced corporate reputation. Some recent campaigns help to illustrate how different companies responded to the challenge of implementing a corporate campaign with a strong media relations component.

A good example is an effort to publicize the role of the health insurance company Aflac during the implementation of the Affordable Care Act (ACA). Many small businesses needed help in understanding and implementing the required changes in their health insurance required by the ACA. Aflac is a leading insurance company that provides insurance and benefits-related services to the small-business market and is well-known due to its commercials with the Aflac duck.

During the ACA beginning in March, 2010, the company received feedback from its field agents about the confusion and designed a communications program with its agency (Hill & Knowlton) to create more awareness of the changes. Based on field research that showed only 17% of small-business owners understood the ACA and how to comply, Aflac launched an integrated communication campaign with corporate media relations as a key element. The goal was to position Aflac as a source for information and guidance about the ACA for small businesspeople.

Media coverage created by the campaign was extensive, both in the national business press and in the specialized media serving the small-business market. The campaign resulted in more than 700 placements in traditional media and 275 unique stories on social media, as well as extensive coverage in the small-business and insurance trade media (PRSA, 2014a).

Crisis Media Relations

On the other side of the equation, managing bad news or a corporate crisis both have significant media relations challenges. During the global banking and financial crisis, major banks and brokerage firms faced questions about their stability and, in some cases, their survival. The work of the major accounting firms advising these companies was also questioned, creating significant crisis and issues management challenges.

The corporate communicators inside those organizations, and their outside advisors, were front and center on those issues, managing an aggressive media, internal and external pressures, and management teams that were under fire for business practices that threatened the stability of the companies. Government regulators and national politicians were in the mix as well. The stakes were high for

Responding to confusion regarding the requirements for small businesses created by ACA, Aflac launched a media campaign positioning itself as a source of expertise and assistance.
Bloomberg / Contributor / Getty Images

Apple has a strong corporate brand, reinforced by their innovative retail stores and breakthrough technology.
Bloomberg / Contributor / Getty Images

communicators as they sought to balance the legitimate interests of the media, the information needs of the public and government officials, and the expectations of senior management.

Corporate Branding and Reputation

The practice of **corporate branding** is a recent phenomenon and an outgrowth of the trend of reputation management as a key function of corporate communicators. More major companies and their leaders are seeing the value and benefits of building and maintaining a corporate brand as part of their reputation. Simply put, a corporate brand is the attributes of a company that come to mind when you hear the name.

For example, for a company like Apple you might think of innovation. The mention of Starbucks brings to mind high-profile corporate philanthropy or SR. For a company like Tesla, you might think of technology, design, or energy efficiency. Companies like these, and others such as General Motors, Google, and Under Armour, realize that successful corporate branding provides major benefits for their organizations and products. In addition, a strong corporate brand can be a major asset in solidifying reputation when a major issue or a crisis impacts the company. Tom Martin, who was responsible for corporate communications at two Fortune 500 companies (FedEx and ITT), notes,

> Having a strong corporate brand is particularly critical when a company faces a crisis. For example, General Motors faced numerous challenges in the last decade, including the ignition switch failures in 2014 that were blamed in several fatal crashes. The company accepted responsibility, focused on fixing the vehicles, doing right by its customers, and holding itself accountable. By doing the right thing, and by leveraging its strong global brand, sales rebounded within a year to precrisis levels, and public opinion surveys overwhelmingly supported the company and its handling of the crisis. (T. Martin, personal communications, 2017)

Beyond crisis and issues management, creating a powerful brand enhances your business and reputation and paves the way for product launches, new corporate initiatives, and even mergers and acquisitions. Kevin Plank, founder and CEO of Under Armour—the sports apparel and equipment company he launched in 1996—believes in the power of building and living the corporate brand. "Brand is not a product—that's for sure; it's not one item. It's an idea, it's a theory, it's a meaning, it's how you carry yourself and represent the company," Plank told CNBC (2015a).

For companies like Under Armour, the brand is paramount, and the corporate and marketing communications team focuses on it throughout all its communications activities. "We understand that our brand is our signature. It is how our customers, employees and investors see us and how we go to market," explained Diane Pelkey, former senior vice president of global communications and entertainment at Under Armour (personal communication, 2017).

Under Armour has enjoyed a good reputation since its founding, but it has faced major threats to its brand in recent years. For example, when the U.S. speed skating team failed to meet expectations at the 2014 Winter Olympics in Sochi, Russia, the company was blamed because of the new skating suits it had designed, and it fell to the corporate communicators there to manage these challenges (Gloster, 2014). Eventually, the athletes and trainers acknowledged the low medal count was actually due to poor training and on-ice performance, not the new uniforms.

More recently, soon after President Trump was elected in 2016, a casual comment by Plank on an earnings call in early 2017, in which he described President Trump's business experience as an "asset" to business, created a mini crisis for the company. UA employees—and many of the celebrity sports figures (e.g., Cam Newton, Seth Curry, Misty Copeland) who serve as "brand ambassadors" for UA—spoke out amid calls of a boycott. This well-intentioned remark backfired due to Trump's unpopularity with some of UA's key stakeholders. It created a crisis for the corporate communication team that lasted well into 2017.

A strong global corporate brand, such as Coca-Cola's, can have measurable financial value. The value of Coca-Cola's brand rose to $80.83 billion as of year-end 2019 (Guttmann, 2019). This brand value is evident in the universal market acceptance and global consumer awareness of Coke products around the world. Coke products are sold and enjoyed in every country in the world except two—North Korea and Cuba.

Clearly, many factors go into having a successful corporate brand. For Coca-Cola, the quality of its products, creative marketing, and a strong corporate reputation combine to boost overall sales numbers. Without question, the Coke brand creates a unique identity to distinguish the company's products from its multiple global and local competitors. Coke's reputation is due in no small measure to the company's global SR leadership and its commitment to diversity and innovation.

In general, corporate branding employs the same methodology and toolbox used in corporate PR and marketing communication. A strong, well-managed corporate branding strategy adds significant value to the company by helping the corporation implement a long-term vision, create a unique market position in the marketplace, and unlock the potential within the organization (Roll, 2009).

Most often, the task of building and maintaining the corporate brand is the responsibility of the corporate communications team. This is the logical place because the PR function manages the relationships with most of a company's key stakeholders (e.g., employees, customers, investors, the local community, NGOs, issue activists, and the media) and communicates to the external market on behalf of the company.

Special Events and Sponsorships

Companies and organizations often take advantage of major corporate milestones, such as a historical anniversary, a name change, or other major events, to promote the organization and celebrate its contributions to the community or country where it is based. Leading companies will commit to major sponsorships (see Table 11.2),

TABLE 11.2

Examples of Major Global Sponsorships

SPORTING EVENT	SPONSOR
2021 Olympics Tokyo	AirBnB, Alibaba, Atos, GE
2018 FIFA World Cup of Soccer	Coca-Cola, Adidas, Budweiser
2018 Winter Olympics	McDonald's, P&G, Visa

such as the 2018 FIFA World Cup of Soccer (e.g., Coca-Cola, Adidas, Budweiser), the 2018 Winter Olympics (e.g., McDonald's, Proctor & Gamble, Visa), or the 2016 Summer Olympics (e.g., Nissan, GE, Nike). Looking ahead to the Tokyo Olympics in Japan, now scheduled to begin in July 2021, companies are already lining up to serve as high-profile sponsors. Early entrants include returning sponsors like Coca-Cola, GE Panasonic, and Toyota and newer players such as Airbnb, Alibaba Group, and technology-consulting company Atos.

Smaller, less expensive events such as arts and culture sponsorships, employee volunteer days, or local running events also create publicity opportunities for sponsoring companies. These local events connect a company with the community, create goodwill, and enhance company reputation. In both cases, large and small events, it falls to the corporate communication team to leverage these investments. This involves designing strategic plans and PR tactics to create meaningful publicity and product promotions to create brand awareness.

INSIGHTS

Corporate Branding

What is the value of an organization's brand? Companies large and small invest in market research to determine the value of products' brands. Magazines publish lists of the world's most valuable brands, and the highest-ranked ones are likely worth more than the gross domestic product (GDP) totals of some smaller countries. However, the organizational brand (e.g., the value of the company *behind* the products) is often underappreciated. In this digital world, however, organizations are now finding it necessary to focus both on the way they brand the products and services they sell, as well as the "brand" of the organization itself.

A few examples illustrate this:

- In the mid-1990s, Federal Express Corporation made the decision to rebrand itself as FedEx, the name its customers had begun to call the company years earlier. In part, FedEx did this because the name was shorter, easier to say, and already a part of the lexicon of business. But FedEx also recognized that its hundreds of planes and thousands of vehicles were huge, moving billboards. By designing a bold, distinctive corporate brand and prominently displaying it on all its aircraft and trucks—including the famous arrow between the letters—FedEx became a global icon and set itself apart from its primary competitor, UPS.

- An increasingly large number of global companies are embracing the notion that it is difficult to support dozens, or hundreds, of product brands when they stand alone without a strong corporate brand. When these products are linked under a strong organizational brand, it builds employee pride, enhances customer loyalty, and heightens the overall prominence of both the company and its products.

- A few years ago, ITT Industries found itself in competition with strong global brands like GE and Siemens, yet it was still going to market in a fragmented way, with hundreds of individual product brands. By establishing a strong organizational brand and corporate identity, along with a new tagline—*Engineered for Life*—that resonated with its employees and customers, the company was in a better position to compete in the global marketplace.

With the increase in global competition and the pervasiveness of online commerce, organizational branding is more critical than ever before. Customers, employees, and investors are seeking authentic, trustworthy organizations to buy from, work for, and invest in. The corporate brand—properly positioned—provides the beacon by which all stakeholders can navigate. ●

Source: Provided by Thomas R. Martin, executive in residence, Department of Communication, The College of Charleston, and a former communications executive at FedEx and ITT.

Authenticity Is Key to Engaging LGBTQ Audiences

Bob Witeck, President and Founder of Witeck Communications

Early generations of gay and lesbian Americans understandably avoided and feared visibility. They knew that their lives and relationships, at best, were stigmatized and rejected by hostile and often ignorant majorities. Companies likewise feared risk and backlash when seeking gay customers or simply incorporating same-sex themes in their marketing mix.

Where the marketplace once saw little but risk, we can now see ample rewards for companies, causes, and campaigns that are genuinely inclusive. Today we see a dramatic sea change in the acceptance, visibility, and marketing presence of lesbian, gay, bisexual, transgender and queer (LGBTQ) people. What lessons can smart corporate communicators and marketers follow today to effectively communicate with LGBTQ audiences and households?

Never Overlook the Rich Diversity Within the LGBTQ Community

The earliest PR and gay marketing strategies by companies seemed monochromatic and even one-note. They tended to highlight affluent, younger, gay white men, leaving large segments of the community aside or simply in the shadows.

Corporate communicators today are mindful that there is a rich diversity of race, ethnicity, gender, age, physical ability and sexual orientation across the LGBTQ population. In fact, as U.S. Census data reveals, same-sex couples and households tend to be more racially diverse than traditional, opposite-sex couples. If a company wishes to reach the entire LGBTQ audience, they cannot afford to overlook transgender, non-gender conforming and bisexual people too.

Millennials Make a Difference

Early on corporate communicators and marketers feared that reaching out to gay audiences would sacrifice significant numbers of their so-called *mainstream* customers. Millennials, however,

and other youthful consumers today are among the gay-friendliest generation ever—not merely accepting their LGBTQ friends, classmates, siblings and family members but truly advocating for and embracing them. Marketers are smart to tap this "halo" effect in crafting inclusive, mainstream messaging that doesn't shy away or take risks for fear of alienating others.

Most of All, Authenticity Rules

LGBTQ consumers trust companies and brands most that acknowledge and embrace them fully. Before going to market, a company should demonstrate its values through a diverse workforce and fair-minded, nondiscriminatory workplace policies and benefits. When an employer hails its family-friendly policies, do those companies include same-sex couples and diverse families in their policies? Does the brand include LGBTQ spokespersons and senior executives, and will the company sponsor meaningful LGBTQ causes and Gay Pride celebrations along with other causes meaningful to their entire workforce? Will the LGBTQ community feel engaged and honestly rewarded?

According to the National LGBTQ Chamber of Commerce, LGBTQ-owned businesses are also powerful job creators. Nine hundred such companies studied by the Chamber created an estimated 33,000 jobs. Some of the exceptional examples of successful engagement by companies within the LGBTQ market can be found in the hospitality, travel, and tech industries. Companies like Marriott International, Carnival Corporation, American Airlines, along with Apple, IBM, Google, and Intel are considered trailblazers.

The opportunity for corporate leadership in the area is not without risk, but companies and brands that are willing and able to *authentically* embrace the LGBTQ community will, no doubt, be rewarded with brand loyalty and purchase preferences. Considering the LGBTQ market segment was estimated at $917 billion in 2016 by Bloomberg, this seems like smart business (Green, 2016). ●

Bob Witeck has consulted with Fortune 100 corporations since 1993 on their LGBTQ business and market strategies. He is coauthor of Business Inside Out *(2006).*

Source: R. Witeck, personal communication, 2020.

These special events also can serve as unique opportunities to remind employees and other key stakeholders about the mission, character, and contributions of the company and to maintain or expand its service to the communities where it operates. This was the case in the Hertz Corporation relocation, in which the company wanted to maintain ties to its hometown in New Jersey while building new ones as it moved to a new headquarters in Florida (see the Social Responsibility Case Study at the end of this chapter).

For Booz Allen Hamilton, the management consulting firm, the company sought to mark its 100th anniversary by recommitting to its home market of Washington, DC, and providing a way for employees to give back through a companywide volunteer community service effort, reflecting its historic SR focus (see the Social Responsibility in Action box). The corporate communication team was charged with leveraging the event to not only celebrate the company's long history but to look forward to a brighter future as well.

Internal Communications

One key aspect of corporate communication often overlooked is internal or employee communication. In some organizations, corporate communication reports to human resources. The tendency to underestimate the importance of communicating with employees is widespread, but it is often a missed opportunity to create a unified corporate image and a solid reputation inside and out of the company.

Red e App, a mobile platform focused on internal communication and employee engagement suggests,

> If you asked most public relations professionals to point out the hip and sexy practices in the field, internal communications would probably not come to mind. Nevertheless, the field is essential to keeping organizations gelled, providing valuable information inside the company and effectively communicating company goals and visions [externally]. (Kent, 2014, para. 1)

For many companies, especially retailers where the employees interact directly with the public (known as business to consumer, B2C), internal communication is essential to preparing employees to represent the corporate brand in their daily work. As they interact with customers, they represent the company more directly and with more impact than many other forms of communication.

For example, a well-placed news story in a high-profile publication or news broadcast will impress current and prospective customers. However, it can be quickly overshadowed or offset if the message is not reinforced by a knowledgeable and informed employee a customer encounters in a retail or online setting.

Because winning in the marketplace is the primary goal of most companies, it must be for the corporate communication function as well. "To win in the marketplace, you must first win in the workplace," Doug Conant, former CEO of Campbell's Soup, said (Yorizon, 2016). It is imperative to devise a system of internal communication that allows the free flow of necessary and important information employees need to do their jobs. This communication goes way beyond rolling out a new employee benefits program or publishing a newsletter, especially when changes are underway at the company, such as in the Hertz headquarters relocation and Booz Allen Hamilton cases.

Gagen MacDonald, a consulting firm that specializes in internal communications and change management, found in a recent study that the failure rate of many corporate mergers to deliver on the results promised (e.g., cost savings, new markets, or other synergies and improvements) is greater than 50% (Scott, 2017).

Booz Allen Hamilton's 100th Anniversary Campaign: Celebrating a Tradition of Community Service and Market Leadership

To celebrate its 100th anniversary, Booz Allen pledged 100,000 hours of community service.
Jeff Greenberg / Contributor / Getty Images

Booz Allen Hamilton, the Fortune 500 consulting firm, recently turned 100. During its first century, Booz Allen's consultants had played key roles in advising clients on national defense, space exploration, new product development, corporate turnarounds, and even the NFL. Booz Allen's goal for its 100th anniversary celebration was to engage its stakeholders in the firm's vision for the future.

Focus on Service

Against this backdrop, Booz Allen chose a strategy of *partnership and service.* Externally, the firm partnered with respected organizations such as the NYSE, National Gallery of Art, Aspen Institute, and *USS Midway* Museum.

Internally, Booz Allen built on its history of CSR, challenging employees to volunteer 100,000 hours of community service during the anniversary year. Coworkers challenged each other to do more, and top volunteers in the Centennial Community Challenge earned grants worth $25,000 for

charities. At the end of 2014, Booz Allen employees had performed and documented 152,713 volunteer hours of service.

Key Media Took Notice

The 100th anniversary celebration resulted in two prominent positive stories in *The Washington Post*—a business feature in March 2014 ("Company Constant" by Marjorie Censer) and a CSR-focused article in December 2014 ("Booz Allen Marks 100 Years With Emphasis on Giving" by Amrita Jayakumar).

To celebrate the company's historic support of arts and culture, Booz Allen sponsored a major exhibit at the National Gallery of Art in Washington, DC, that drew more than 350,000 visitors.

Target Market Efforts

In San Diego, a key market for the company, Booz Allen sponsored patriotic events at the *USS Midway* Museum on Memorial Day, the Fourth of July, and Veterans Day 2014 and provided a grant to enable San Diego-area school children to attend onboard science lessons.

Social Responsibility Focus

Each element of the anniversary program emphasized the company's community service and SR tradition and recommitted it to more in the future. These efforts were gathered and catalogued in the company's annual report and in all its sustainability reporting as well. ●

Marie Lerch is the former executive vice president of marketing and communications at Booz Allen.

Source: M. Lerch, personal communication, 2017.

Their research notes the most common reason was the failure to successfully combine the corporate cultures and create a sense of common purpose for the employees of the "new" company going forward. In short, the job of communicating to internal stakeholders about the benefits and challenges of the transaction is often not done very well, and the long-term results of the merger reflect this flaw.

Beyond managing high-profile mergers or supporting companywide culture changes, the day-to-day task of communicating to employees is essential to building morale and implementing corporate strategy. The better informed your employees are and the more they understand their jobs, the more successful the company will be in the long run.

Jack Welch, former CEO of GE and a leading commentator on business and management, notes,

> There are three measurements that tell you nearly everything you need to know about your organization's overall performance: employee engagement, customer satisfaction, and cash flow.... It goes without saying that no company, small or large, can win over the long run without energized employees who believe in the mission and understand how to achieve it. (AZQuotes, n.d.).

Corporate Communications and Corporate Social Responsibility

>> LO 11.3   Illustrate how SR enhances corporate communications

SR has become increasingly important in recent years to build and maintain a solid corporate reputation. Research has shown that a profile as an environmentally and socially responsible company pays dividends in terms of product sales, employee recruitment and retention, as well as supports business growth and creates opportunities.

SOCIAL RESPONSIBILITY

Communicating Corporate Social Responsibility

In a corporate communications position, you may be given the task of publicizing the company's good works to your target audiences. The key to success, as noted in Chapter 10, is to make sure that there is a clear business and strategic connection to the CSR activity and that your employees, business partners, and suppliers all understand and support the effort.

A disconnected CSR activity is no different than a business strategy that doesn't fit the company, connect with stakeholders, or make sense to your fellow employees. History has shown that over time, these CSR programs will dissipate and/or fail because the idea does not "stick" to your brand or have relevance for your stakeholders and employees.

Internal and external messages should communicate the company's commitment to SR, its engagement with SR, and the results, benefits, and impacts of SR. Communicating SR enables new market penetration, profiles a product or organization, and converts stakeholders. SR is a powerful driver for consumer demand.

Employee Volunteering and Social Responsibility

Employees also represent a major asset in SR programs. Many leading companies support employee volunteering as a key aspect of their CSR activity. Hertz, as we will learn in Chapter 12, and Booz Allen Hamilton, as noted earlier in this chapter, are good examples but there are many others.

The Points of Light Foundation produces a list of the companies who excel at employee volunteer programs (EVP). They define EVPs as "a planned, managed effort that seeks to motivate and enable employees to effectively volunteer under the leadership of the employer" (Points of Light, 2013). Companies recognized recently by the foundation include the following:

Amway Corporation

Bank of America

BNY Mellon

Cisco

Constellation Energy

Cummins, Inc.

IBM

JPMorgan Chase

Kraft Foods

McKesson

PwC U.S.

The Goldman Sachs Group

The foundation noted best practices in EVP by these companies in the report. They include making employee volunteering part of the corporate culture; time off to engage in EVP through service days companywide; providing grants to support EVP efforts; in-kind contributions of materials and staff to the effort; and celebrating the EVP efforts of its employees with awards and celebrations (Points of Light, 2012).

It should be clear that this is an area of corporate communication that cannot be overlooked. Beyond that, by leveraging the internal audience you can improve your company's chances for success in the marketplace, add depth and dimension to the overall purpose of the company, and reinforce your SR profile.

Today, employee volunteerism is well on its way to becoming a "norm" in terms of one's professional identity. Employees, driven in part by the growing numbers of working millennials, expect their employer to provide ways for them to find purpose at work. (Dorsey & Garlinghouse, 2015, p. 197)

Financial Communications, Media Relations, and Investor Relationships

>> LO 11.4 **Explain the importance of financial communications and investor relations in corporate communications**

Financial Communications

One of the principal differences between corporate communication and working in other settings is the added responsibility of telling the company's story to the financial community. As a public company, you are required to provide accurate and timely information on a quarterly and yearly basis to your stockholders. These complex documents must adhere to a format and provide in-depth information about the company and its financial health.

Quarterly and annual reports permit orderly trading of a company's stock on exchanges like NASDAQ or the NYSE.
Bloomberg / Contributor / Getty Images

This enables the orderly trading of the company's stock on the major stock exchanges, such as the NYSE or the NASDAQ, and supports the free flow of information to the investing public.

Often, the corporate communication team is closely involved in this process, preparing the letter from senior management (usually called the Shareholder Letter) that puts the results into perspective and includes key corporate messages and management's views on the results. The detailed financial information in these documents is prepared by the company's finance and legal staff, usually with the help of outside advisors, including the company's external accounting firm and legal counsel.

It is important to note that companies *must* provide this information simultaneously to the public, media, and investment community. There can be no staging or phasing of information to improve the media response or soften the blow of an issue or crisis. This concept—known as disclosure of information—is a Securities and Exchange Commission (SEC) requirement that requires that everyone, regardless of stature or relationship to the company, gets the same information at the same time. Any deviation from this is considered a legal violation with serious consequences.

Going Public

So you might wonder why companies bother to issue shares and sell them to the public if there are so many restrictions and legal requirements. The short answer to this question is that by issuing shares and selling part of the company to investors, the company has access to a funding source to finance its future growth and expansion. In a sense, the company trades some of its independence for access to outside financial resources necessary to implement its strategy and grow the business.

There are many advantages for a company to "go public" through what is called an **initial public offering** (or IPO). The financial benefit of raising working capital is the most distinct advantage. This capital can be used to fund research and development, support new initiatives, or pay off existing loans from the banks and private investors that helped finance the start of the company.

Also, this is a major transaction and usually generates publicity in major media, making the company and its products known to a new group of customers and investors in the global markets. Subsequently, this heightened awareness often leads to an increase in market share and revenue growth for the company (Balasubramaniam, 2020).

Business, Financial, and Consumer Media

Beyond helping craft the message to the financial community, the corporate communicator is also active in working with the business and financial media who cover public companies. This can include working with leading business magazines (e.g., *Fortune, Forbes, Business Week*), top cable TV business shows (e.g., Bloomberg, CNBC, etc.), and finance-related daily papers such as the *The Wall Street Journal, The New York Times,* and *Financial Times.*

Depending on the location of the company's headquarters and/or its major facilities, daily newspapers and broadcast media nearby will also be interested in covering the company's financial performance—because many employees may live in the area as well.

Here, the usual principles of media relations apply, as discussed previously in Chapter 7. However, it is important to remember the concept of full and fair disclosure applies here as well, and you are *not* allowed to sequence the release of the news—everyone must get the same information simultaneously.

What most communication teams do in this case is distribute the information as required to all parties and then select which media outlets you provide further access to, including interviews with senior management, in-depth briefings, or new product demonstrations. Again, no *new* information can be disclosed, but your target media can get additional perspective from senior management that adds to their coverage. These media strategy decisions should involve thoughtful internal discussion and consideration with your colleagues and advisors before being put into action. Remember, no new or significant information can be provided selectively to any media outlets—only management's perspective or response to the quarterly or yearly results.

Investor Relations

In most companies, the people responsible for the ongoing interaction with the financial community are known as **investor relations (IR)** professionals. These people are highly trained and often have finance backgrounds as well as an understanding of the rules that govern contact with current and prospective investors. Their daily activities include meeting and talking with investors, setting up meetings with stock market analysts, monitoring the daily stock price and trading activity, and advising management on competitive and financial market developments.

As you can imagine, IR is a very specialized function with a demanding and expert audience. It includes major investors on Wall Street and around the world, as well as individual shareholders who buy and trade shares on their own. It requires an understanding of corporate strategy, business conditions, the economy, securities law, and the investment community. The Rivel Research Group, in a recent white paper on the value of investor relations, makes the point that IR professionals are "charged with marketing something equally as important as any of the company's individual products or services—the company's common stock" (Rivel Research Group, 2013, p. 2).

IR best practices call for a close integration with corporate communications to put out unified and consistent messages and leverage each other's effort (National Investor Relations Institute, n.d.). For example, if the PR team places a major story in a key business publication (like *Fortune*) or a leading Wall Street firm (such as Merrill Lynch or Goldman Sachs) issues a positive report about the company's financial performance or corporate strategy, the PR and IR teams can build on that to reach new stakeholders (e.g., media or investors) in their respective areas of focus. This synergy can pay off with a better stock price and an improved corporate reputation.

"Research shows that IR and PR have an undeniable impact on a company's valuation or stock price—because these are the roads by which investors learn about a company's management, strategy and overall investment appeal" (Rivel Research Group, 2013, p. 2). Conversely, research has shown that companies that perform poorly at communicating with the financial community suffer as a result.

Rivel has quantified this differential through their ongoing research. They recently surveyed the U.S. investment community about the value of effective financial communications and found the difference between effective ("good") and ineffective ("bad") IR and financial communications was 30% in a typical company stock price (Rivel Research Group, 2013). This could be the difference between a company's common stock trading at $7 per share or $10 per share. When you are talking about many millions of shares of stock, that is a significant difference in funds to support growth.

In financial communications, the rules may be different, but the desired outcome is the same as for corporate communication. Companies want to maximize their value and reputation. They want to be well regarded in their key markets, in their communities, and by the government and elected officials who regulate and impact their businesses. They want to be viewed as good places to work and have motivated and empowered employees. And finally, they want to be good corporate citizens.

SOCIAL RESPONSIBILITY

Socially Responsible Investing

Companies that are seen as socially responsible create new opportunities for themselves by attracting the interest of investors who value social good.
iStock.com/maxsattana

Companies that are viewed as good corporate citizens have the opportunity to be recognized and rewarded financially for their efforts by individuals known as **socially responsible investors (SRI)**. This investment style invests almost exclusively in companies with a track record of meeting or exceeding environmental, social, and corporate governance (ESG) goals, as well as generating competitive financial returns and a positive societal impact (US SIF, n.d.).

According to the latest *Report on Sustainable and Responsible Investing Trends in the United States*, $12 trillion was invested according to SRI strategies (US SIF, n.d.) at year-end 2018. Clearly, this is a significant source of capital to support growth, and senior management of many leading companies have noticed and are actively positioning their companies as socially responsible to attract this class of investors (US SIF, n.d.).

Attracting investment support from the SRI community is like developing a connection to target media or other external stakeholders. To begin with, you must qualify as a socially responsible company, according to the fund's definition of that term, which can vary. For some, it can be product related—for example, no tobacco, guns or weapons, or oil and gas. In others, it is having corporate policies in place regarding employee benefits, areas of the world where you operate, or having signed corporate pledges on greenhouse gas emissions, energy efficiency, or human rights. With that status in hand, you need to make sure to frequently communicate your progress and activity in the CSR space throughout your communications outreach, including media relations, financial communications, internal communications, CSR, and social media. With a demonstrable track record in hand, the investor relations staff can begin the process of reaching out to SRI funds and telling the SR story to attract new investors.

Some of the leading global companies have had success in reaching out to and attracting SRI to invest in their common stock. While there are hundreds that qualify, a recent list compiled by Kiplinger's Personal Finance (Petruno, 2014) provides some high-profile examples (the company's stock trading symbol is indicated after each company name):

Apple (AAPL)

Gilead Sciences (GILD)

Google (GOOGL)

Johnson Controls (JCI)

Nestle (NSRGY)

Praxair (PX)

Qualcomm (QCOM)

T Rowe Price (TROW)

Xylem (XYL)

Scenario Outcome

At the beginning of the chapter, you were introduced to the Starbucks "Race Together" community relations initiative that began in 2014. However well-intentioned, the concept was not well received at the retail level. Both the traditional and social media criticized the company for overstepping and for not being authentic or realistic.

Commenting on the reaction to the "Race Together" program, then-CEO Howard Schultz responded during a television interview:

> Writing on the cup is a diminutive piece of this issue, and it's not going to last long. It was a catalyst to start this. What's going to last is our company saying that we believe that there is a serious problem in America. We are in almost every community in America, and why not use our stores and our national footprint for good? (CNBC, 2015b)

How did Starbucks respond? Faced with a poor reception of the idea, the company went into crisis mode to clarify its intentions and rebuild trust with its key stakeholders, including the employees who bore the brunt of the negative customer feedback. This included a media outreach program, employee communication activities, and monitoring and responding on social media once the initial storm ended.

The Starbucks corporate media relations team had limited success in turning the story around. The articles that resulted helped explain what the public did not realize—that writing on cups was the tip of the iceberg of a much larger initiative. *The Wall Street Journal* published an article titled "Why Starbucks Takes on Social Issues" that examined why Schultz would continue pushing the race discussion despite the backlash (Kesmodel & Brat, 2015).

Schultz also maintained that performing for his shareholders was top priority: "You have to understand, I spend 90% of my day on Starbucks business—I'm not spending my entire life on the issues of racial inequality, I have a company to run here" (Carr, 2015).

Lesson learned? Most observers feel that the lesson from this case is that the safest stance for a company when it comes to hot-button social issues outside of your business or market focus, such as race, is to be more thoughtful on how and when you engage. Failing that, you must be prepared for the backlash that comes from taking a stand and (in this case) engaging retail customers in a controversial cause or issue. However, consistent with the corporate culture of Starbucks, Schultz seemed determined to continue to use Starbucks' global scale and market position for good.

When new CEO Kevin Johnson took over in 2017, he said that Starbucks will continue to take on social causes and redefine the way for-profit public companies impact social issues (Taylor, 2017). He wasn't wrong.

Starbucks again found itself in the public eye in a racial context. An incident occurred in April 2018 that involved a questionable decision by a store manager in Philadelphia to ask two African American men to leave because she felt they were just waiting in the store, using the restroom and not buying anything. The two men refused to leave, and the manager called the police, requesting to have them removed and/or arrested. As it turns out, the men were contractors waiting to meet a client and had every right to be there.

The incident, which was taped and posted on YouTube by other customers, created another race-related national scandal and a global media sensation for the company. The company responded with a detailed apology and a review of its policies on customer access to their stores and restrooms. Senior management, including founder Howard Schultz, announced the decision to close all of its U.S. locations for a day of sensitivity training to raise awareness of "unconscious bias" and its impact on their retail business. The initial response by the company—including an apology and the closure of the stores—was well received by many. However, others felt there was an underlying and continuing problem at the company that negatively impacted its reputation. Fair or unfair, this was a problem for the corporate communication team to respond to and manage.

Take a minute to discuss in your groups/class how you feel about this incident.

1. Did Starbucks handle this crisis any better than it did the "Race Together" crisis?

2. What else would you have suggested they do to respond to the Philadelphia incident?

3. What should they do to address this problem that many retail and restaurant chains also face?

4. Was their issues and crisis management effort successful?

5. Does it affect your willingness to patronize Starbucks?

WRAP UP

This chapter examined the realm of corporate communication, financial communication, and investor relations. The chapter also detailed and discussed the makeup of today's large corporations and examined how corporate communication fits into the organization—which can differ, depending on the industry and culture of the company.

You read about the multiple responsibilities of corporate communication professionals and discussed each one, including how they support or enhance corporate reputation and promote social responsibility. Finally, the chapter reviewed the complex and important field of financial communications and provided an overview of IR and how it impacts the company's perception and valuation.

As you move ahead in your studies toward a career in PR or public affairs, understanding the complex areas of corporate communication and how they impact the perception of the company will be an important skill to develop. Due to the changing nature of the global marketplace and the media, your commitment to continuous learning and PR skills development can set you apart from your peers as a leading corporate communications professional.

The rewards for succeeding in corporate and financial communication can be substantial over time, but the expectations of the role are challenging and significant.

KEY TERMS

Chief Communications Officer
  (CCO) 252
Chief Marketing Officer
  (CMO) 252
Corporate Branding 258
Financial Communications 253

Initial Public Offering (IPO) 266
Investor Relations (IR) 267
Socially Responsible Investors
  (SRI) 268
Stock Exchange 249
Thought Leadership 251

THINK ABOUT IT

In this chapter, you have learned about the challenge and opportunity of corporate communications in today's companies. Your ability to understand this dynamic environment, should your career take you in this direction, will be a major factor in your success.

Ultimately, most corporate communications professionals seek a "seat at the table" and to be considered as communications strategists, not just tacticians.

Your task is to gather into groups and agree on a company you all admire and are interested in learning more about. Visit the company website and review their SR activities. Based on what you have read so far in the text, suggest a strategy to raise the company's profile with its key stakeholders. This can be a news conference, an article in a key publication, or a community-based event for employees, for example. How would you implement the idea, and what results would you expect?

WRITE LIKE A PRO

Visit the website of a company based in your area that you are familiar with and read about their SR program. If they are active, prepare a short plan to expand awareness of the company's activity on a cause that you are interested in and that relates to their business. If they are not very active or if you feel there are missed opportunities, suggest a strategy and a few tactics to increase their involvement.

Be sure that the issue or cause you suggest is relevant to the company's business and would appeal to their employees. For example, if they are a home improvement company, engaging them in a building or renovation project or teaching home improvement skills to young people makes sense. Raising money for animal welfare programs, for example, is not clearly connected to the company's core business of home improvement and likely won't resonate with the management and employees.

SOCIAL RESPONSIBILITY CASE STUDY

Hertz Hits the Road: Being a Good Neighbor in Florida

Chapter 12's Social Responsibility Case Study discusses the issue management work done by the Hertz Corporation to minimize disruption due to its headquarters relocation from New Jersey to Florida. Through careful planning, the company left New Jersey with its reputation as a good corporate citizen and employer still intact.

After the move, as a new corporate member of the Tampa-area community, Hertz was anxious to get off to a good start. The company continued to work with Ketchum and relied on a CSR-based strategy to build its reputation in its new headquarters market.

Research and Strategy

In January 2016, Hertz officially opened its new headquarters in a suburb of Tampa. At the grand-opening ceremony, which included more than 625 company staff members, the governor, and local and state dignitaries, the company announced significant contributions to the local community and plans for hundreds of hours of employee volunteer work. Hertz also declared its support for local nonprofits, including the Immokalee Foundation, Junior Achievement, the Conservancy of Southwest Florida, Audubon's Corkscrew Swamp Sanctuary, and others.

Execution

The employee volunteer efforts were substantial. The company partnered with Habitat for Humanity of three nearby counties in Florida to sponsor and build three homes. This required more than 400 hours of volunteer time and, in addition to physical labor, included hosting employee team-building days to raise the walls of the homes, finish cosmetic work, and then hand the keys over to the new homeowners at a ceremony.

Other local volunteering efforts included a back-to-school backpack drive, including supplies for the Heights Foundation and the Immokalee Foundation, and a new shoe collection to benefit Laces of Love, which provides new shoes to children in need. Two holiday initiatives were also driven by employee participation: a Thanksgiving food drive to benefit the Heights Foundation and a holiday gift project that benefited both the Shelter for Abused Women and Children and the Children's Advocacy Center of Tampa.

SR efforts continued after the headquarters launch as well. On Hertz's Make a Difference Day 2016, the company hosted several volunteer events, including Interfaith Charities of Southwest Florida and a beach cleanup in partnership with Keep Lee County Beautiful.

Evaluation

Due to these and other community-based activities, Hertz is now an integral part of the Tampa-area community, and its employees feel engaged and welcome in their new home (PRSA, 2014c).

Engage

- After forming into small work groups, visit the Hertz website (www.hertz.com) to acquaint yourselves with the company and review their ongoing sustainability activities.

- Follow that up with some basic research of the area (Tampa metropolitan area and Lee County) in Florida to identify the major issues facing the people and businesses in the area. What are the pressing social issues in the area? How is the government dealing with them?

Discuss

- Look for synergies and identify additional opportunities for local SR activity for Hertz—either in partnership with the city and county government, a nonprofit, or community-based organization.

- For example, should Hertz provide vehicles for driver training, safe driving clinics, or demonstrations of the dangers of impaired or distracted driving? Think of some other ideas that are related to their core business (transportation) that also provide an opportunity for employees and the community to get involved.

  1. How would you organize these?
  2. How might you publicize the events and results?
  3. How would you know you were succeeding?

Source: PRSA, 2014c.

12

Issues Management and Crisis Communication

Learning Objectives

12.1   Demonstrate how issues management is an effective strategy for reputation management

12.2   Differentiate among a crisis, disaster, and problems

12.3   Understand how to prepare for, manage, and communicate during a crisis

Hurricane Maria Devastates Puerto Rico (2017): Changing Perceptions to Encourage Tourism and Boost the Economy

Hurricane Maria Disrupts Puerto Rico's Vital Tourism Industry

In the fall of 2017, Puerto Rico was subjected to a lethal one–two punch from Hurricanes Irma and Maria. According to CNN, Hurricane Maria, which came right after Irma, was the first Category 4 hurricane to make landfall in Puerto Rico since 1932. According to the National Hurricane Center (2012), in a Category 4 hurricane "catastrophic damage will occur. . . . Power outages will last weeks to possibly months. Most of the area will be uninhabitable for weeks or months" (para. 4).

The hurricanes, and the resulting damage, created high-stakes political drama between local officials, the governor of Puerto Rico, and the Trump White House. The political controversy served to shift public attention from the pressing needs of Puerto Rico's citizens in the aftermath of the storm.

Members of the Miñi Miñi community in Loiza, Puerto Rico, help their neighbors leave areas overwhelmed by flood waters after Hurricane Maria hit the island in September 2017.

RP Library / Alamy Stock Photo

None of this was good for the image of the island as a tourist destination. Beyond the immediate devastation, which included casualties approaching 3,000 and property damage exceeding $139 billion, the island commonwealth (which is part of the United States) also saw a dramatic decline in tourism after the hurricanes hit the island.

According to Discover Puerto Rico (a nonprofit destination marketing organization), tourism accounts for 6.5% of Puerto Rico's gross domestic product (GDP) as well as 75,000 jobs in the hospitality and food industries and thousands of others indirectly in the sectors dependent on tourism. Clearly, this natural disaster posed many issues for the island and tourism industry leaders to manage and protect its economy.

To help Discover Puerto Rico, the global PR firm Ketchum was hired as the 1-year anniversary approached to build awareness of the progress the island had made since the storm.

The team of Ketchum and Discover Puerto Rico knew that in disaster situations the media often revisits the original story—and thereby reinforces the negative images, political drama, and devastation. Recent research showed that over 50% of travelers reported that prior media coverage of the storms had negatively impacted their view of Puerto Rico and influenced their future travel plans. Further, an analysis of media coverage of other major natural disasters, including Hurricanes Katrina and Sandy, revealed the tone was typically 90% negative and only 10% neutral or positive. Discover Puerto Rico realized that if it did not balance the media coverage and impact social media conversations, there was a substantial risk that the actual progress the island had made in the past year would be lost in the shuffle.

As you read through this chapter, which covers disaster response, crisis communication, and issues management, consider how you would have advised Discover Puerto Rico to manage this crisis and the related issues for the island's vital tourism industry.

(Continued)

(Continued)

Topics or challenges to consider include these:

- How would you offset the negative elements of the anniversary news stories to focus on the progress made?

- What kind of stories, images, and social media elements could illustrate the progress the island's tourism industry had made?

- Is there a way to minimize the impact of the political drama lingering from the first days of the disaster?

- Which media outlets and influencers would be most important to reach with the story of the progress made in the first year after the hurricane?

At the end of this chapter, you will read about the strategy the agency and Discover Puerto Rico developed and the specific outcomes of the plan they implemented. ●

Source: Adapted from PRSA Silver Anvil Case Study. Beaubien, 2019b.

What is a crisis? Is it a natural disaster like an earthquake, volcano, or typhoon? Or product defects like Samsung's Galaxy 7 smartphone or Takata's automobile airbag? Is it the cyberattacks at Target, Sony Entertainment, Facebook, or the Medicare/Medicaid records at Healthcare.gov? Or is it bad management or questionable business practices (Wells Fargo), sexual harassment (Fox News), gender discrimination (Walmart), or insider trading (Sea World)?

The answer to all of these questions is *yes*. They were all legitimate crises for these companies and countless others. But were they *issues* that became a *crisis*? In most cases, the answer to this question is also yes. Except for a natural disaster, most crises are not a complete surprise. In hindsight, we often find that a crisis could have been prevented, or minimized, if the companies were better prepared. This is where *issues management* comes in to play.

This chapter focuses on issues management and crisis communications. It explores the key differences and details how one—issues management—can prevent or minimize the need for the second—crisis communications. It also addresses how organizations respond to natural disasters and litigation, providing examples of both.

Issues Management

>> **LO 12.1**   **Demonstrate how issues management is an effective strategy for reputation management**

"An ounce of prevention is worth a pound of cure," observed Benjamin Franklin. Although he made this statement in 1736 when speaking about fire prevention, the advice is spot-on when it comes to crisis communications and issues management. When applying this axiom to crisis and issues management today, one might say, "While putting out fires is a critical skill, preventing one may be even more valuable." Crisis is an all-too-common situation facing today's PR practitioners. A crisis can be demanding and multifaceted, requiring preparation of different scenarios, careful managing of the problem, and implementing reputation recovery efforts as required. As such, preventing a crisis—or at least minimizing it—is an important skill set for PR pros to develop. Thus, we first turn to the practice that helps to avoid crises: **issues management**.

The Benefits of Issues Management

Issues management should be viewed as a strategic process that helps organizations detect and respond appropriately to emerging trends or changes in the sociopolitical environment (Dougall, 2008). Think of it as an early warning system designed to see bad things coming. It's like forecasting the weather and preparing for it instead of trying to cope when the storm comes.

Tracking emerging trends over time allows you to understand that organizational problems can crystallize into an issue and erupt into a crisis for an organization and its key stakeholders. Consider the case of Wells Fargo and the crisis beginning in 2016 (and still plaguing the bank today). The practice of aggressively paying cash incentives to branch employees to cross-sell bank services—regardless of customer need—had been in place for years before it exploded into a crisis for the bank. Consider what might have happened if the bank had better controls in place to minimize abuse of this system or if they just eliminated the practice when customer complaints first began to reach branch managers.

A good illustration of risk management or issue monitoring would be an automotive company tracking requests for warranty repairs and noticing a big increase in reported brake problems; or a consumer products company monitoring customer feedback to identify safety issues with a key product. In such cases, an internal group could study these matters, determine if there is an operational or performance problem, and recommend corrective action before experiencing a product recall, litigation, or a decline in sales. Lastly, PR pros should anticipate that any major corporate event—for example, a merger, acquisition, or closing of a facility—can create concerns that need to be addressed in advance before they upset major stakeholders.

The key to understanding issues management is that it is anticipatory and **proactive** as opposed to **crisis communications**, which is **reactive**. Issues management is a form of risk management with a specific focus on the company's reputation, products, and financial performance.

Issue Life Cycle

Figure 12.1 depicts the flow of an issue from origination to a crisis—if corrective action is not taken. If you were to track the Hertz corporate relocation story on this chart (see the case study in this chapter), you would see that the company's attention to the issues management process early on—in the potential and emerging stages— prevented it from becoming a crisis and damaging the company's reputation. "Issues management encompasses the potential, emerging, and current stages of an issue's evolution before it reaches the crisis stage" (Meng, 2009).

Wells Fargo management did not intervene successfully when customer complaints about excessive cross-selling to customers first surfaced in 2016, and the bank experienced a full-blown consumer crisis as a result. Branch employees were later found to have been opening new checking accounts without customer approval and creating phantom accounts for homeless people in order to meet their quota for new accounts.

The high-profile crisis at the bank was well covered by the media, caught the attention of elected officials and government regulators, and impacted the bank's financial performance as well. As the crisis wound down and management and business practices were gradually changed, the bank entered the dormant stage, where it began to repair its image and move forward.

In January 2020, when Wells Fargo released its fourth-quarter and full-year 2019 financial results, new CEO Charles Scharf reported a $1.5 billion charge for costs

FIGURE 12.1

Issue Life Cycle

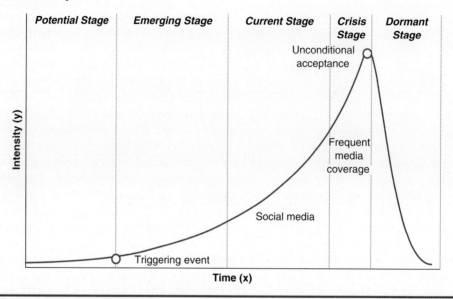

Source: Reprinted with permission from Max B. Meng, MSEd, MA.

stemming from the "fake account scandal," which dates back to 2016. In making the announcement, he commented, "We made some terrible mistakes and haven't effectively addressed our shortcomings" (Eisen, 2020, para. 4). In an early 2020 call with financial analysts discussing the bank's 2019 results, he pledged "fundamental changes" to regain trust. Clearly, more work needs to be done to help Wells Fargo to restore its credibility and reputation.

In summary, issues management is a risk management process used to anticipate and address emerging issues. It allows organizations to clarify or correct a developing problem or situation, hopefully to avoid a major crisis.

Crisis Communications

>> LO 12.2   Differentiate among a crisis, disaster, and problems

The difference between a natural disaster or problem and a crisis is important to clarify. "Disasters are events that are sudden, seriously disrupt routines or systems, require new courses of action to cope with the disruption, and pose a danger to values and social goals," suggests Coombs (2015). He adds that disasters often "are large in scale and require response from multiple government units."

The Organizational Crisis

An organizational crisis, on the other hand, is defined by the Institute for Public Relations (IPR) as "a significant threat to operations that can have long-term, negative consequences to the company or organization involved" (Coombs, 2014b, p. 3). Some crises, the IPR suggests, such as major industrial accidents (like the Exxon Valdez in 1989) and product recalls (e.g., the Tylenol recall by Johnson & Johnson in the fall of 1982) result in injuries and even loss of life. A crisis can also cause major financial losses by disrupting operations, creating a loss of market share, or spawning lawsuits related to the crisis, such as the Boeing 737 Max crisis (2019), which included two crashes that killed 346 people and a worldwide grounding of the planes by the U.S. government.

In cases involving a natural disaster, the company, organization, or government entity may not be at fault, *unless* their response plan is not well managed and/or the situation is made worse by their actions. The chapter-opening scenario, dealing with the impact of Hurricanes Irma and Maria in Puerto Rico, is an example of this. This is true in cases of workplace violence as well, which is usually random, but

FEMA's inadequate response to Hurricane Katrina in 2005 turned the natural disaster into a crisis and led to a congressional investigation. AP Photo / Dave Martin

all companies and organizations should know by now to prepare ahead to prevent it or at least diminish its impact. In such cases, a poor or ineffective response quickly becomes a crisis.

Recent history has provided us with several instances of disasters becoming crises. A well-known example of a poorly managed disaster was Hurricane Katrina, which struck New Orleans and the U.S. Gulf Coast in 2005. The U.S. government estimates that more than $80 billion in property damage was caused by the hurricane and flooding, and the total economic impact to the area included losses in excess of $150 billion (National Center for Environmental Information, 2016).

While the devastating storm was well anticipated due to sophisticated storm tracking by the authorities, it was far worse than expected. Very quickly, it overwhelmed the local government's ability to respond and assist Gulf Coast area residents in recovering.

When New Orleans and the surrounding area were declared a federal disaster area, the Federal Emergency Management Authority (FEMA) was called in to assist. Here is where the situation became a crisis, most experts agree. According to a report prepared on Hurricane Katrina by the U.S. Congress titled "A Failure of Initiative," the Katrina relief effort was poorly handled, supplies were delayed or lost, the process of processing claims and coordinating federal assistance was botched, and the overall situation got worse instead of better once FEMA got involved (United States, 2006). Eventually, the mishandling of the Katrina disaster cost the Bush administration national credibility and political support. As well, FEMA Director Michael Brown, appointed by President George W. Bush in January 2003, resigned in September 2005, 1 month after the crisis.

So if a natural disaster is not necessarily a crisis unless it is mishandled, what constitutes a real crisis, and how do we manage communications before, during, and after?

Jim Lukaszewski, a leading crisis counselor and author of more than 12 books on crisis communications, defines a crisis colorfully, suggesting, "A crisis is a show-stopping, people-stopping, product-stopping, reputation-defining, trust-busting event that creates victims and/or explosive visibility" (Lukaszewski, 2012, p. 210).

Notice that in his definition, Lukaszewski emphasizes the *victim* aspect (e.g., employees, customers, or the public) because he feels that is what creates the emotion and drama and is what the public and the media usually focus on in a crisis. "The principal ingredient of any crisis is the creation of victims," he maintains.

"Avoiding responsibility and shifting blame can become significant barriers for the organization and its leadership to overcome," Lukaszewski (2013) notes.

Eric Dezenhall (1999), a leading crisis counselor and author based in Washington, DC, agrees. He suggests that there are three key elements in any crisis: victim, villain, and vindicator. These categories answer the key questions for the media and the public in a crisis: What happened? Whose fault is it? Who is going to make sure this does not happen again?

Problem Versus a Crisis

"All crises are problems, but not all problems are crises," Lukaszewski (2013) notes. One of the fundamental challenges of issues management and crisis communications is distinguishing a problem from an actual crisis. PR (public relations) practitioners must guard against overreacting and going into crisis mode when confronted with a problem that may be solved without drama.

An example of a "problem" might be limited product availability caused by extreme weather, IT system issues impacting customer service, or a shortage of food/ingredients at a restaurant chain. Solving these "problems" may involve backup systems or alternate shipping options to prevent the problem from becoming a crisis. It is important to note that the PR practitioner or manager who solves a problem or issue *before* it escalates is often more valued than the one who knows what to do when a crisis occurs.

You'll note our focus in this chapter has been on **organizational crises**. These are situations that threaten an organization's stakeholders—shareholders, customers, employees, and so on—and seriously impact performance and generate negative outcomes (Coombs, 2015). For publicly traded companies, the common stock price—and therefore the company's access to the capital markets—can also be impacted. Most often, these crises are attributable to management or operational failures, criminal behavior, or a lack of proper oversight of people and process. The Wells Fargo cross-selling controversy and the Boeing 737 Max crashes are examples of these. The high-profile Samsung's Note 7 phone lithium ion battery crisis was another.

Product Crisis

Beginning in the fall of 2016, the lithium batteries in Samsung's successful smartphone started to spontaneously combust. This situation created major problems for the company with customers and politicians and in the mobile tech marketplace. Soon, government regulators became involved on the safety issue, and the company was forced to issue a total recall of the product. Cost estimates of the impact for Samsung exceed $5 billion (Pandey, 2016), not to mention a major blow to the company's reputation as a technology leader.

Unfortunately, the problems continued after the recall when the replacement batteries and phones experienced the same problems. This created more negative media coverage, which eventually led to a ban on the Samsung 7 phones on all commercial transportation in the United States.

The company responded with an aggressive recall, in-depth testing of the batteries, and an improved manufacturing process. *Forbes* magazine, in a summary article about the crisis, concluded this:

Samsung isn't the first company to have a major consumer recall, nor will it be the last. It's how a company handles a product recall that determines its future success or failure. While it's been a difficult time for Samsung, the company took ownership of the issues, acted quickly, and worked diligently to fix its problems. With its new and improved quality assurance processes and design prowess, Samsung should make a strong comeback. (Lopez, 2017, para. 26)

Following a product-based crisis, a company or organization, like Samsung, will look for opportunities to rebuild or repair their image in the marketplace. Often, these companies will look to their ongoing social responsibility (SR) efforts to rebuild their image and improve employee morale.

Emotional Intelligence and Ethics: Keys to Crisis Management

Mike Paul, The Reputation Doctor®

Mark Mahaney
Times Square NYC

My name is Mike Paul, and I am president of Reputation Doctor® LLC. I have specialized in global crisis communications and reputation management consulting for over 25 years.

I started my career working as a political aide in the New York state legislature. I then went to Washington, DC, and served as an aide to a U.S. senator. In fact, many leaders in PR started their careers in politics, which is a great training ground for crisis, reputation, and issues management. Crisis communications consultants are expected to garner solutions for their clients under great pressure and, usually, in a very short period of time.

After graduate school, I was recruited into Burson-Marsteller's (B-M) management training program and spent time in several practice areas, including crisis communications. It was there at B-M that I realized

crisis communications and reputation management were the professional specialties in PR I loved.

Some highlights of my career to date include helping a U.S. senator get reelected in a very close race; successfully communicating a major cleanup of an oil spill; counseling a global pharmaceutical company to implement a successful rebranding and reputation-building program; counseling a tech company in the midst of major lawsuits; repositioning a major celebrity with substance abuse issues as one of the top actors in the world; counseling two leading professional athletes facing a steroid scandal; counseling leading female actors to speak up with confidence regarding their #MeToo stories; and providing successful litigation-support PR for one of the biggest bank fraud cases on Wall Street.

Based on my experience, my advice for those seeking to work in crisis communications is this: *You must have a strong moral and ethical compass to succeed.*

The most important tool in your crisis tool belt is your emotional intelligence (EQ). Lean on it and trust it—always. Also, always tell your clients and bosses the truth, with love, just like you would a family member you care about. You may be the only one with the courage and expertise to do so, but they will need your honest perspective if they are to survive and move forward. Practice (even in the mirror) makes perfect. ●

Source: M. Paul, personal communication, 2020.

Samsung Employees Participate in a Nationwide Day of Service

Samsung faced a crisis when the batteries in its Galaxy Note 7 began bursting into flames. The company's response included press conferences to explain the issue and instituting a service day for employees to volunteer in their communities.
SeongJoon Cho/Bloomberg/Getty Images

Rebuilding Trust After Samsung 7

As part of its ongoing CSR efforts, Samsung has staged a service day each year for its employees to volunteer in their local communities and show their pride in and commitment to the company. This allows company employees an opportunity to show a different side of the company and begin to rebuild trust and belief in the brand.

"Samsung Gives" Employees' Initiative

In May 2017, Samsung Electronics America held its biannual, companywide Day of Service for employees in New Jersey, New York, Texas, California, Washington, DC, and regional offices. The event, part of the company's overarching "Samsung Gives" initiative, is designed to identify community service opportunities for employees within their own communities.

"Samsung believes in being an active corporate citizen and is committed to giving back to the communities where our employees live and work," said Gregory Lee, president and CEO, Samsung North America. "The Samsung Day of Service allows all employees to serve their communities, work in teams and offer help to causes in need—whether it be feeding the homeless, rebuilding communities or providing workplace training" (Samsung Newsroom, 2017, para. 2).

One Day Benefits More Than 50 Nonprofits

Since its inception, the Samsung Day of Service has provided more than 144,000 hours of service to more than 70 local charities nationwide through year-end 2019. In 2019 alone, thousands of Samsung employees donated hours of service to more than 50 nonprofit organizations within their communities, including the following:

- Local Boys & Girls Club of America
- Grow NYC in New York
- After-School All-Stars in New Jersey
- Special Olympics Texas

Samsung focuses its SR efforts in the United States in the following areas: environment, supply chain, contributions, compliance, and people (communities and employees). It states, "The Corporate Social Responsibility (CSR) vision is to build a society where people, the society and the environment coexist in harmony. As a part of our CSR efforts, we are committed to transparency and delivering important information to our share-holders to continuously build confidence and trust in us" (Samsung, 2016). ●

Could this recall by Samsung have been prevented by earlier intervention or action by the company? While we will never know for sure, it certainly seems that more transparency, better communications, and more attention during the manufacturing process would have helped. The Samsung crisis was a **product crisis** initially, but it became a corporate crisis, and the damage to the overall company brand was a serious side effect that had to be addressed.

Litigation Crisis

Some issues will become a crisis notwithstanding a company's best efforts. But even if the crisis was anticipated, advance preparation should serve a company well. This is usually the case in a litigation crisis driven by a lawsuit and a "trial" in the court of public opinion—as well as the legal system. An example of a prompt and effective response to litigation was the "seasoned beef" ingredients lawsuit filed against Taco Bell. The company was well prepared due to its policy of monitoring consumer feedback and having a litigation response protocol already in place.

After it was accused of using filler rather than meat in its ground beef products, Taco Bell responded aggressively, refuting the claims across multiple platforms and in the media.
Patrick T. Fallon/Bloomberg/Getty Images

- *Taco Bell crisis.* Yum! Brands (Taco Bell's parent company) was sued by consumers contesting the contents of the meat and sauce it uses in its signature tacos. The lawsuit, which was filed by a customer in California, contended the company's "seasoned beef" actually contained only 35% beef and that Taco Bell was lying in advertising that claimed its ingredients were all beef (NPR, 2011). The filing of the lawsuit generated considerable news coverage—mostly negative—and led to late-night talk show hosts and others commentators ridiculing the company.

- *How Taco Bell responded.* Taco Bell declared the claims against it were false and then shared its actual percentages (88% beef and 12% secret sauce), along with the ingredients in the secret recipe itself, which were all-natural products and spices. The company launched a comprehensive campaign to refute the allegations and share the ingredients of its not-so-secret recipe. The effort included local market newspapers and an aggressive social media outreach effort, including a YouTube channel, a dedicated Facebook page, and new in-store signage. Fortunately for Taco Bell, the response plan had a positive impact on the follow-up news coverage, and the story was no longer material for late-night comedians and social media commentators.

- *The result.* Taco Bell's consumers responded very well to the quick and effective campaign. The social media effort was well received, and most comments online supported the company's stance. Soon (less than 4 months later), the lawsuit was dropped, and Taco Bell averted a protracted legal dispute and a PR disaster (Business Insider, 2011).

Preparing for and Managing a Crisis

>> LO 12.3 **Understand how to prepare for, manage, and communicate during a crisis**

Having defined a crisis and provided examples of organizations that have struggled with preparing for a crisis, we can now turn to managing and communicating during and after the crisis. We will also examine how to develop a comprehensive plan to communicate during and after a crisis.

The three stages of crisis communications include pre-crisis, crisis impact, and crisis recovery (Coombs, 2015). Other scholars who have studied and written on

FIGURE 12.2

The Three Stages of Crisis Communications

Precrisis
- Warning signs appear, and the company moves to try to eliminate or reduce the risk.

Crisis Impact
- The actual crisis is underway, and your focus is on managing the situation and providing support to those impacted by the crisis.

Crisis Recovery
- The goal is to return to business as usual as fast as possible while making good on your promises and critically examining the company's response to see how it might be improved. Repairing damage to corporate reputation is also an important effort at this stage.

crisis management include Fink (1986) and Mitroff (1994). Fink is widely quoted and recognized on the topic of crisis, and he proposes a four-stage model—prodromal, acute, chronic, and resolution—using medical terminology. Mitroff suggests a five-stage model—signal detection, probing and prevention, damage containment, recovery, and finally, learning. As these theories have much in common, for our purposes we will focus on the basic three-stage model (see Figure 12.2) in this text.

INSIGHTS

Communications Theory and Crisis Management

Any discussion of issues management and crisis communication would be incomplete without a look at the major communication theory that helps us assess the response by a company or organization facing a crisis. That theory is William Benoit's (1995) image restoration theory (see Table 12.1). Benoit's approach is most often cited in studies of crisis and issues management because it focuses on the process most companies go through when faced with a major crisis.

Benoit's five categories of image restoration include denial, evasion of responsibility, reducing the offensive act, taking corrective action, and mortification.

His communications theory provides a "useful framework to understand and analyze how a company responds to stakeholders about issues that are indicators of a pre-crisis situation that could lead to fraudulent activity of severe business risks" (Cowden & Sellnow, 2002, p. 193). Research shows that "ineffective management of these warning signs can result in a movement from the pre-crisis stage to the crisis stage" (Erickson et al., 2011, p. 207).

In their research "Using Communication Theory to Analyze Corporate Reporting Strategies," Erickson, Weber, and Segovia (2011) apply Benoit's theory to corporate reporting of financial control issues or shortfalls and conclude that "image management is essential to corporations and other organizations." They suggest that if a company is perceived to be responsible for an event or problem (e.g., a crisis) and sought to deny it, dismiss its severity, shift blame, or otherwise evade responsibility versus apologize and take responsibility for corrective action, then "the firm's image will be tarnished and needs to be restored."

Often, students and practitioners confuse Benoit's image restoration theory as a prescribed list that all companies *must* go through in a crisis. This is not the intent of the list. It is best viewed as describing since it closely tracks how companies or individuals in trouble often need to work through several steps before admitting guilt and starting remediation.

To illustrate this, picture a consumer product recall or a government official or celebrity who did something unethical or illegal, and then trace the steps of Benoit's typology.

First, there is a denial and maybe an evasion of responsibility. Then, they might try to claim it was an "accident" or "one-time thing." Next, some try to blame somebody else or minimize the damage, and so on, right on through until, ultimately, they take responsibility and fix the problem—as described in Benoit's table. Some companies or individuals respond appropriately and move right to apologizing and fixing the problem, but many unfortunately do not ever seem to get there.

Benoit's theory is most helpful in assessing where a company is on the image restoration spectrum so you can prepare your communications advice and plans accordingly in order to move to the corrective action stage. By recognizing this process, you can help your clients or the companies you work for move forward to resolving the crisis. ●

TABLE 12.1

Benoit's Typology

Denial	1. Simple denial 2. Shifting the blame	1. Dismissing the idea that the organization had any role or responsibility 2. Suggesting someone else might be responsible
Evasion of responsibility	3. Scapegoating 4. Defeasibility 5. Accident 6. Good intentions	3. Blaming the event on another 4. Not knowing what to do or how to act 5. Suggesting the event was an "accident" 6. Maintaining you meant well
Reducing the offensive act	7. Image bolstering 8. Minimization 9. Differentiation 10. Transcendence 11. Reducing the credibility 12. Compensation	7. Promoting or building your image to offset blame 8. Stating the situation or problem is "not so bad" 9. Maintaining this crisis is much different from other, more serious crises 10. Suggesting your good acts outweigh the damage from this specific issue/crisis 11. Attacking the credibility of the accuser 12. Paying, or making restitution, to victim(s) to set things right
Taking corrective action Mortification	13. Corrective action 14. Mortification	13. Taking steps to stop event from occurring again 14. Admitting guilt, accepting full responsibility, and apologizing to victims

Source: Based on Benoit, W. L. (1995). *Accounts, excuses, and apologies: A theory of image restoration strategies.* Marcombo.

Crisis Plan Development

As noted earlier, a key step in the crisis management process is to identify potential crisis situations, review their potential impact, and plan accordingly. This activity usually occurs in the pre-crisis phase, where planning and preparation take place. To be effective, a crisis communications plan must be current and accurate, with all the necessary information readily available—in advance. There is precious little time to refine and update the plan while a crisis is underway, to be sure. Some crisis experts have equated this with "flying a plane while building it at the same time" (Phelps & Williams, n.d.).

The first step in creating the crisis communications plan is to gather a representative team of employees from throughout your organization—for example, senior managers from operations, human resources, sales and marketing, research and development, security, and so on—to brainstorm the potential things that could go wrong for your organization and then develop a response plan to address them. For example, you can manage a product recall by streamlining your customer communications system to track trends in complaints and establishing a process to implement repairs in the field.

In the event of a lawsuit against the company, you can pre-develop standard responses to lawsuits by topic, which note the following:

a. You do not comment on the specifics of litigation in process.

b. Assure the public and your employees that the company is investigating the matter.

c. State (if applicable) that the company is confident in its case/position.

In a disaster or workplace accident, having the proper protocols in place to manage employee and external communications and monitor social media is critical. As well, an efficient system to get care to those injured and monitor their recovery to keep loved ones and the public informed can be very beneficial.

Larry Smith, president of the Institute for Crisis Management (ICM), suggests that as many as two thirds of crises that occur should never have been a crisis (Bonk et al., 2008, p. 116), thus underscoring the need for issues management. However, he also counsels that companies should be vigilant for problems or issues that could escalate into a crisis and have three essential plans on hand that are current and ready for implementation. These include a crisis operation plan, a communications plan, and a business recovery plan (Bonk et al., 2008, p. 116). These suggestions are consistent with the three stages of crisis as outlined by Coombs.

Prepare a Crisis Checklist

Most experts advocate that companies, nonprofits, celebrities, and elected officials should always have a current and up-to-date crisis plan on hand. One, it provides you with a current overview of potential problems, and two, once the trouble is identified, you can eliminate or minimize it—before it explodes. With a list of vulnerabilities in hand, you can develop your crisis plan. The key steps are as follows:

- *Identify your crisis response team (CRT).* And designate a leader. This may—or may not—be your CEO. Either way, your team should include the necessary subject matter experts and advisors that participated in the brainstorming session.

- *Identify your spokespersons.* You will need articulate and expert managers and a system to respond to media inquiries. Depending on the nature of the crisis, the experts might include medical professionals, engineers, legal counsel, and/or bilingual staff if the situation requires it.

- *Train your spokespersons.* In addition to the subject matter expertise required by the crisis, managers must be able to answer media questions without overreacting and with a sense of the impact of what they say—or don't say.

- *Social media monitoring.* Personnel who know how to monitor social media and respond when necessary are essential as well.

- *Prepare customer-facing employees.* If your company has retail stores or locations, expect that customers will have questions. Preparing staff with materials to respond to customers and the public is critical.

- *Set up monitoring and notification systems.* This is a critical step before, during, and after the crisis. This should include online and traditional media and the customer feedback mechanisms as noted earlier.

- *Create a list of key audiences/stakeholders.* These are the people, both internal and external, that are impacted or who play roles in responding to the situation and the company's performance in addressing it. Understanding who they are and what concerns or motivates them is an important part of crisis preparation and management.

- *Develop holding or stand-by statements.* While you can't predict the specifics of a given crisis, you can predict the situations that *might* arise. Armed with this information, you can prepare templates of news releases, stand-by statements, background research on key areas of your business where a problem could occur, and questions and answers to be adapted and updated when needed.

Crisis Stage

The crisis phase usually begins with a trigger event that challenges the status quo and disrupts normal, daily operations of the company or organization. The crisis management phase ends when the crisis is resolved or under control. In the interval crisis stage, the company or organization is consumed with responding to all its stakeholders (government, media, customers, employees, and the public), as well as solving the underlying problem.

The foundational elements for coping with the active crisis stage should be in the crisis plan. The plan should include all the elements needed—contact information for key executives, key media for outreach, social media monitoring protocols and outreach plan, available trained spokespeople and experts, and so on. However, do not assume that the existence of a plan by itself guarantees a smooth and effective response to the crisis. Crisis counselors like Lukaszewski, Smith, and Dezenhall agree the plan must be current and followed—not left behind on a shelf—and adapted and updated according to the situation and stakes.

Once a crisis is underway, the plan needs to be flexible. Inevitably, the crisis will move and shift in ways not imagined or covered in the basic plan. Here is where the organization and the crisis team need to adapt to the matter at hand while staying true to its overall goals of transparency, accuracy, honesty, and timeliness in its response.

Crisis Recovery

Finally, we have the recovery stage. In this stage, practitioners and scholars suggest the focus should be on two main points:

1. Following through on the promises made during the crisis to your stakeholders
2. Conducting a postcrisis review to assess the effectiveness of the plan and areas for improvement

For many PR practitioners and companies, there is a natural tendency to want to move away from the crisis as soon as possible. However, this can be a major mistake—or a missed opportunity. Instead, convening the CRT; conducting a thorough analysis of what happened, what worked and what did not from your plan; and cataloging mistakes or surprises are significant learning opportunities and will improve ongoing crisis planning. In a way, this is a form of advanced issues management. You can assess your plan's effectiveness, evaluate the response, and close out any outstanding issues that arose during the crisis to prevent or offset a future one.

SOCIAL RESPONSIBILITY

Another important activity during the postcrisis stage is expanding your communications outreach and SR activity to promote positive messages and visibility in the community to offset the lingering reputation effects of the crisis. However, these activities need to be consistent with the company's ongoing sustainability activities, or they risk being seen as not credible or as a cover-up.

Crisis and Social Media

Without question, the dramatic increase in the public's reliance on social media for information and entertainment has had a major impact on the practice of issues management and crisis communications (Jin et al., 2014). To get a sense of how widespread and integral social media has become, let's look at some recent statistics. According to a recent study by Pew Research (Smith & Anderson, 2018), more than two thirds of American adults (68%) use social networking sites such as Facebook and Instagram daily (see Figure 12.3), up from 7% in 2005.

From an issues management and crisis communication perspective, social media can be both a positive and a negative force, as well as an early warning system if it is monitored on a real-time basis. The positive side of social media is that it enables companies and organizations in pre-crisis, crisis, or recovery mode to have direct access to target audience(s) and deliver real-time updates without a time lag, bias, or filter by the media. Companies can post official statements, YouTube videos, situation updates, and instructions for recalls or a fix to the problem on a constant basis, 24/7 and 365 days a year. Social media provides direct access to push out news and updates on a given crisis as well as allows companies to post detailed statements or content to all interested parties on dedicated crisis websites (linked to the main site).

Conversely, the vast array of social media platforms and the public's reliance on them for news and information has a downside. A company in a crisis does not have control of the information being circulated online. As well, there is usually no

FIGURE 12.3

Majority of Americans Use Facebook, YouTube

Percentage of U.S. adults who say they use the following social media sites online or on their cell phone

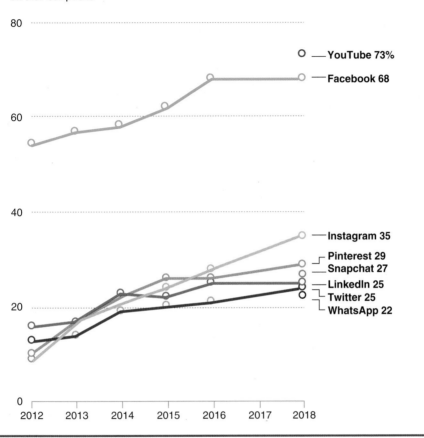

Source: Smith, Aaron and Monica Anderson. "Social Media Use in 2018." Pew Research Center, Washington, DC (March 1, 2018).

gatekeeper who verifies the information that is being posted about the crisis or any comments on the way it is being handled. This will require a constant monitoring of key sites, which include the major ones—for example, Facebook, Twitter, Snapchat, and Instagram. There is also the possibility that activist groups, or "trolls" (people anxious to stir up a controversy generally or bring attention to their cause), might become active since open social platforms are ideal for that purpose.

Examples

In the now-infamous Deepwater Horizon crisis in 2010, early on, a site popped up labeled #BPGlobalPR, which began to post "updates and comments" about the spill and its aftermath, allegedly from the company's PR team. After it became established, it began to post more and more outrageous comments on the disaster, causing the company to step in to correct it and thereby extend the fake site's impact and status in searches. The satirical account quickly surpassed BP America's official Twitter account in terms of followers, and it was able to succeed in part because of BP's limited social media presence when the crisis erupted (Schock, 2010).

BPGlobalPr
@britishpollute

Follow

Instant Updates on the BP Oilspill
http://www.britishpolluting.com/updates/blo
g.html #oilspill #bp #bpoilspill 17:30:01

3:30 PM - 24 Jul 2010

**A Twitter account posing as an official BP source gained attention
during the Deepwater Horizon spill in 2010. It posted increasingly
outrageous comments as its follower count grew.**
Twitter.com/britishpollute

In all phases of crisis management, companies must be vigilant for negative or satirical content that starts on social media. By monitoring this activity, the company can spot trends or issues that could erupt into a full-blown crisis and, hopefully, address them head-on before they gain traction and followers. You must also assess if your company should respond directly on the same site or indirectly on your own site—or other platforms.

This was the case in the example at Taco Bell detailed earlier in this chapter. The company was well prepared to respond to misinformation being circulated by its opponents in the "ingredients" lawsuit. The company used both traditional and social media platforms to respond aggressively without impacting the legal case that was in process. The result was that the crisis was short lived, and the case was ultimately abandoned, as it did not gain traction with the media or the public.

It is worth noting that the traditional media—that is, print and broadcast journalists—often scan social platforms for tips on stories or to identify a crisis in the making and thereby get a jump on a new story. Some news organizations will also cite a Tweet or Facebook post and treat it as news or opinion that serves as the basis for a news story. "When consumers you've never met are rating your company's products in public forums on-line with which you have no experience or influence, your company is vulnerable to a crisis or, at best, a threat to your reputation" (Li & Bernoff, 2011).

Volume, Velocity, and Variety

The need to be vigilant online to identify issues and respond aggressively to a crisis is underscored by recent research by Zignal Labs (2016). Zignal is a San Francisco-based media intelligence firm that defines the crisis environment in relation to a company's digital footprint. It suggests that every crisis needs to be managed with three key (digital) factors in mind—*volume, velocity,* and *variety*—as well as the conventional approaches to crisis communications (see Table 12.2).

The Volkswagen (VW) crisis, following the disclosure that the company had installed a system to deceive U.S.-mandated emission tests, is a case in point. VW, which has long been regarded as a socially responsible company, markets itself as a preferred alternative for green-focused customers around the world.

TABLE 12.2

Key Digital Factors in Crisis Management

DIGITAL FACTOR	MEASUREMENT	EXAMPLES
Volume	The actual amount of data	Tweets, media mentions, shares, and posts on social media
Velocity	The speed at which data, news coverage, and social media chatter is generated	Tweets per second or online news stories per hour
Variety	The types of data generated and the platforms they are shared on	Images and hashtags on Twitter and Instagram, news stories posted and shared, Tweets, and videos on YouTube

Zignal reports that the fallout across the digital and social channels for VW as a result of the emissions scandal was "swift and decisive"—the company went from being highly admired for its engineering expertise, sustainability focus, and fuel efficiency performance to "dead last" in the Harris Poll (2016), which asked Americans to rank "The 100 Most Visible Companies" by quality and reputation.

Gallup reported that due to the high awareness (71% among U.S. consumers surveyed) of the VW scandal, four in 10 people surveyed (41%) were less likely to purchase a car from VW. Gallup also found that 69% of the people said the scandal would negatively impact the VW brand globally (O'Boyle & Adkins, 2015).

Despite Volkswagen's reputation as a socially responsible and eco-conscious company, it installed software designed to cheat emissions tests in its clean diesel line of cars. When the software was discovered, VW faced immediate backlash.
Armando Arorizo/Bloomberg/Getty Images

Beyond the reputation damage to VW, there was a substantial financial penalty and high-level management changes as well. Record-setting fines of $14.7 billion were levied against the company by the U.S. government (Isidore & Goldman, 2016); the U.S. CEO was replaced (Beene, 2016); and the brand's reputation worldwide took a major hit (Harris Poll, 2016). Hans-Gerd Bode, VW's communications chief executive at the time, described the company's experience on social media as a "tsunami" in an interview with *The New York Times* (Hakim, 2016).

Zignal suggests that four trends ring true for every modern crisis:

1. *A modern crisis is fueled by data.* In today's modern marketplace, companies are overwhelmed with massive amounts of data. This data grows and is shared exponentially as a result of the worldwide proliferation of mobile devices and digitally active consumers.

2. *While the nature of a crisis hasn't changed* (e.g., an embarrassing CEO flub or a global product recall), *the digital channels through which a crisis will spread are increasingly fast and ferocious.* For any crisis, brands must prepare for massive volume, increasing velocity, and an expanding variety of digital information.

3. *Conventional approaches (alone) no longer work.* In a modern crisis, the volume, velocity, and variety of data immediately overwhelm traditional crisis management tools and processes. Even the best of existing plans can't adequately address the challenges associated with a crisis that is unfolding and mutating across digital and mobile channels in real time.

4. *Data provides the blueprint for a solution.* While the data deluge poses a clear and immediate challenge for any communications team, data can also provide a path to a solution. Specifically, an analysis of the data can reveal trends, patterns, and insights to empower crisis communications and corporate marketing teams.

With an understanding that data can be both a brand's biggest threat during a crisis and a path to a solution, cross-functional teams must adjust their crisis communications plans. (Zignal Labs, 2016).

Scenario Outcome

At the beginning of this chapter, you read a summary of the challenges facing Discover Puerto Rico and its agency (Ketchum) as they prepared for the 1-year anniversary of Hurricane Maria's devastation of the tropical island. The impact of the storm, right after Hurricane Irma, was tremendous and included thousands of casualties, billions of dollars in damage, and a sharp drop in tourism.

The agency and the tourist authority knew that considerable progress had been made in rebuilding the island and ensuring that the island was "Open for Tourism," as its marketing slogan indicated. However, they also knew from prior research that over 50% of potential visitors surveyed had acknowledged that the media coverage of the storm's aftermath had negatively impacted their travel plans for Puerto Rico.

Clearly, an aggressive and detailed media outreach plan—including key influentials in the travel industry and all forms of social media—was needed. It would require strong visuals, a compelling social media campaign, and outreach to the island's tourism partners (airlines, cruises, hotels, and restaurants) to be successful.

The agency and tourist authority began with a challenge to the media, using the hashtag #CoverTheProgress, and they provided powerful before-and-after visuals, individual stories of local residents and businesses bringing the island back to life, and constant updates of data on improving tourism trends.

An exclusive story on CNN, which had covered the storm and devastation extensively, was organized, and tool kits with images, stats, and customizable social media posts were provided to travel industry partners. Celebrities with personal ties to the island were engaged to post and comment on the revitalization. Finally, a New York media tour with island tourism and government officials participating was implemented right before the 1-year anniversary.

Results

The campaign was a great success. Some highlights include the following:

- *Media coverage of the 1-year anniversary was 70% positive*, with only a 15% negative tone in the anniversary coverage. There was little to no mention of the political drama from the prior year.

- Follow-up research showed a *23% improvement in public perception of Puerto Rico as a desirable destination.*

- *Inbound flight capacity had improved* to pre-storm levels, hotel and resort properties were at or near full capacity, and four new cruise ship visits to the island were added, with more to come in 2020.

- *Media coverage of the campaign #CoverTheProgress was a global success.* The agency recorded more than 1 billion earned media and social media impressions in 4 months, and coverage of the island's revitalization ran on CNN, in *USA Today* and *Forbes,* and in other leading travel trade and hospitality industry media.

- The ultimate media success included Puerto Rico being named as the *"#1 place to go in 2019"* by *The New York Times.*

This case is an excellent example of all three topics covered in this chapter: disaster response, issues, and crisis management. No surprise then that the work of Ketchum and its client was recognized by the PRSA with a Silver Anvil for Issues Management at the awards ceremony in 2019.

Students and practitioners can find many examples of research-based, strategic planning in this case. As well, there are several best practices displayed in how to deal with the aftermath of a major natural disaster and managing the issues and crisis situations they can pose for a company, government, or organization.

WRAP UP

In this chapter, our focus has been on disaster response, issues management, and crisis communications and how they are all interrelated. Definitions of each term were provided and examples cited to show how effective disaster recovery and proper implementation of issues management tactics can offset the need for follow-up crisis communications.

Also, we examined the predominant theory (Benoit's Image Restoration Theory) used by scholars to track how organizations deal with a crisis. Finally, the chapter reviewed the impact of social media and provided guidance on how organizations can monitor and respond online to crisis situations.

Mastering disaster response, issues management, and crisis communications are essential for your growth and development as a PR professional. McKinsey, a leading management consulting firm, said it well:

> Now more than ever, it will be action—not spin—that builds strong reputations. Organizations need to enhance their listening skills so that they are sufficiently aware of emerging issues; to reinvigorate their understanding of, and relationships with, critical stakeholders; and to go beyond traditional PR by activating a network of supporters who can influence key constituencies. (Bonini et al., 2009, para. 4)

KEY TERMS

Crisis 278
Crisis Communications 277
Disasters 278
Issues Management 276
Litigation Crisis 283

Organizational Crisis 280
Proactive 277
Product Crisis 282
Reactive 277

THINK ABOUT IT

Gather in small groups and identify a recent crisis in the news, preferably one involving a social issue or cause, such as the impact of soft drinks on health and wellness of children or an increase in car accidents with teenage victims due to driver distraction from mobile devices.

As you review the coverage, ask yourselves a series of questions:

- What would you have done in that situation?
- What strategies or tactics would you employ?
- How would you measure your progress?
- Most importantly, assess the company's performance *after* the crisis ends. How did they rebuild trust or repair their reputation? What steps did they take to reassure customers, the public, and the government that the situation will not be repeated?

Assessing another company's crisis is a way to test and improve your own plan and response strategies; you will be better off when the time comes. Your ability to see bad things coming, minimize the damage, and protect the company's reputation can enhance your career and make you a more complete PR professional.

WRITE LIKE A PRO

In thinking about the Hurricane Maria scenario that opened this chapter, consider how the island responded to the disaster and the political and social crises that resulted.

Prepare a short paragraph analyzing the case and make suggestions on how things might have been handled better initially to minimize the long-term damage to the island's reputation as a desirable tourist destination. Sample questions include these:

What could the island government and tourism authorities have done in advance to prepare for a more effective initial response?

How might the island's civic and political leaders have better handled the political controversy that developed?

What other stakeholders could the island and its tourism authority have called on to assist?

What role could citizens (not directly impacted by the storm) have played in an outreach program?

Is there a social responsibility angle that might be useful to encourage corporate and public engagement in the recovery efforts?

SOCIAL RESPONSIBILITY CASE STUDY

Hertz Moves Its Corporate Headquarters

In 2013, Hertz, a Fortune 500 company and a leader in the rental car industry, made the decision to relocate its corporate headquarters from Park Ridge, New Jersey, to Fort Myers, Florida (Hertz, 2013). Hertz had been in New Jersey since 1988 and had more than 1,000 working at its headquarters. The company had built up a strong reputation in its home market as a desirable employer and good corporate citizen.

Research and Strategy

The business case for the move to Florida was solid, including tax incentives, a workforce with experience in hospitality and tourism, and other economic considerations. Florida was also the state with the highest concentration of Hertz employees—more than New Jersey or metropolitan New York.

The company knew that this decision would have a major impact on its hometown, specifically its headquarters employees and the local and state economy. It also wanted to minimize the risk of being perceived as having deserted the communities near its corporate headquarters. In anticipation of this, and consistent with sound issues management practice, the company engaged a PR firm (Ketchum) to manage the announcement process and help focus the media coverage on the business case for the decision.

This plan for public and media outreach required research on its impact on local economy and development of an economic case for the move. Ketchum would also need to prepare briefing materials for all the key stakeholders and have them ready before the announcement.

Its reputation for community involvement in New Jersey also had to be supported. Hertz's New Jersey headquarters building was LEED certified, so the company began the process to make sure its new Florida corporate headquarters building would be certified as well. (LEED certification, which stands for Leadership in Energy and Environmental Design, is a status awarded by the U.S. Green Buildings Council and certifies that the building is energy efficient and environmentally friendly. It signifies a commitment to sustainability and energy conservation and can provide tax incentives to the builder and owner for meeting the strict standards.)

Execution

The campaign strategy was to promote the business case for relocating its headquarters and provide details on how headquarters employees were being taken care of to balance the story. Seven hundred employees were to be relocated, and 2,000 head office employees would remain employed at the previous headquarters, thus maintaining a strong presence in its historic headquarters. To minimize the disruption, Hertz also pledged to maintain its community ties in northern New Jersey. These facts needed to be emphasized in the communications materials responding to stakeholder concerns.

The goal of the strategy was to manage the potential negative issue of relocating and balance news coverage of the move to include its key messages and business rationale. The tactics included briefings with headquarters employees, in addition to local officials in New Jersey and Florida, and working closely with key media outlets in both markets to get the story out in a measured and balanced way.

Evaluation

The news did not leak before it was to be announced, which had been a major concern of the executives. News coverage of the move was 93% positive to neutral, and more than 55% of the stories included quotes and key messages from Hertz spokespersons.

Anticipating issues and addressing them in advance led to a smoother announcement and move for Hertz. If the company had decided to simply issue a news release or just hold a press conference, the outcry from the media, politicians, and employees in New Jersey might have prevented or delayed the move.

That outcome would have cost the company money in lost tax incentives, negatively impacted employee morale, and diminished the company's reputation and relationships in both markets. In short, the issue could have become a crisis for Hertz. Instead, both the new location city in Florida and the host community in New Jersey felt their interests had been considered in a responsible way.

Engage

- Break into small groups to do some initial research on Hertz and its SR activity.
- Visit the Hertz CSR site and review its annual report and current activity.
- Visit the sites of some of its main competitors to get a sense of what others in the industry are doing.

Discuss

- What are some of the CSR activities that Hertz should continue in the New Jersey location, and which ones ought to be adapted to Florida?
- Regarding Hertz's competitors (Avis, Enterprise, etc.), what are they doing in their CSR programs that might be of interest for Hertz?
- How can Hertz keep the New Jersey employees engaged in the company's CSR efforts?

Source: PRSA, 2014b.

13

Sports, Tourism, and Entertainment

Learning Objectives

13.1 Identify the opportunities and challenges of sports PR and how CSR initiatives are a fit for both teams and fans

13.2 Explore the scope of the tourism industry and the essential role of PR, gaining insight on socially responsible and sustainability aspects that support organizational goals

13.3 Examine the breadth of PR and CSR engagement within the entertainment industry through the perspectives of talent, agencies, and entertainment companies

Scenario
A Tweet Creates a Crisis for the NBA

For years, the most popular NBA team in China has been the Houston Rockets. This popularity dates to 2002 with the Rocket's drafting Yao Ming as their No. 1 overall pick. Hall-of-Famer Ming spent his entire NBA career as a Rocket and acted as an unofficial ambassador for the league. Because of his popularity in China, the Rockets became the country's adopted hometown team and helped the NBA to grow globally.

However, just prior to the start of the 2019–20 NBA regular season, the NBA became involved in a controversy with China because of a tweet from Daryl Morey, the Rockets' general manager. Morey's tweet caused considerable backlash from the authorities in China, and many parties weighed in on the issue, including Adam Silver, NBA Commissioner.

When Houston Rockets' GM Daryl Morey tweeted in support of Hong Kong protesters, the NBA team suffered immediate backlash from mainland China.

Anthony Wallace / Contributor / Getty Images

On October. 4, 2019, Morey tweeted a message in support of the ongoing protests in Hong Kong. The protests were in opposition to legislation allowing the extradition of criminal suspects to mainland China. The tweet read, "Fight for Freedom. Stand with Hong Kong." Though later deleted, Morey's tweet was not well received by Chinese authorities, who saw the tweet's direct support for Hong Kong as both criticism of and opposition to China's political strategy.

Immediate Backlash

Morey's tweet caused an immediate backlash against the Rockets and the NBA. A statement expressing its "strong dissatisfaction" was issued by the Chinese sponsors, who began to cut ties with the team and the NBA. This meant Morey's tweet could potentially cost the Rockets $25 million in sponsorships.

CCTV (China's state television) said it would cease airing the Rockets' preseason games, and the NBA's exclusive digital partner in China, Tencent, said it was suspending business relations with the Rockets. Fans who had purchased a team pass to view the Rockets 2019 season were offered the option to choose a different team (Stein, 2019).

Two days after Morey's tweet, the NBA, through Silver, released an official statement on the matter.

> We recognize that the views expressed by Houston Rockets general manager Daryl Morey have deeply offended many of our friends and fans in China, which is regrettable. While Daryl has made it clear that his tweet does not represent the Rockets or the NBA, the values of the league support individuals educating themselves and sharing their views on matters important to them. We have great respect for the history and culture of China and hope that sports and the NBA can be used as a unifying force to bridge cultural divides and bring people together. (MacMahon, 2019, para. 2).

Rather than resolving the issue, Silver's comments created more controversy—this time from the NBA's American fan base and U.S. officials. Because it wasn't clear that the league would not impede Morey's freedom of speech, Silver's statement appeared to be a denunciation of Morey's stance.

(Continued)

(Continued)

Student Challenge

As you read through this chapter, consider the following questions. At the end of the chapter, you'll learn how this controversy played out:

How should Adam Silver have responded? Was his initial response adequate?

As this is a free speech issue between a U.S. team and a foreign government, should U.S. government officials have gotten involved? If so, in what way?

Should NBA players have responded? If so, what should they have said? ●

This chapter covers three areas in PR (public relations) that are linked by their popularity as lifestyle interests: the wide world of sports, the allure of travel, and the craving for entertainment. All of them have the pulse of SR (social responsibility) and sustainability running through them.

You'll first read about the PR opportunities and challenges in sports. Athletes and teams are both doing good (foundations and fundraisers) and being bad (crises and damaged reputations). You'll also consider what a stadium's corporate name means to the team—and to fans—and learn when it becomes a PR problem.

Tourism is one of the world's fastest-growing economic sectors. You'll read about PR's role in stimulating interest in a journey, destination, or event; the tasks of handling unexpected threats and crises; and the ever-expanding area of ecotourism.

Finally, entertainment PR touches Hollywood films and actors; spreads across to New York stage plays, publishers, and authors; and reaches out anywhere that on-air and online visuals, voices, and tunes find audiences. You'll also discover all the social and environmental good that entertainers and their industry support.

Opportunities and Challenges of Sports Public Relations

>> **LO 13.1** **Identify the opportunities and challenges of sports PR and how CSR initiatives are a fit for both teams and fans**

Sports are a big part of everyday life. A team's fans follow its ups and downs, cheer its wins, and suffer its losses. Whether high school, minor league, or professional, it becomes intertwined with the lives of its supporters, and the question, *Did you see*

FIGURE 13.1

Sports in the Media

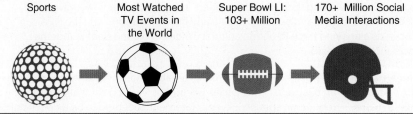

| Sports | Most Watched TV Events in the World | Super Bowl LI: 103+ Million | 170+ Million Social Media Interactions |

Source: Data from Nielsen. (February 5, 2018). Super Bowl LII 50 draws 103.4 million TV viewers, 170.7 million social media interactions.

the game last night, launches thousands of conversations many mornings. A city's pride can swell with a team's good fortune, as happened in Washington, DC, when the Nationals won a World Series after nearly a century of frustration, but a bad run can plunge them into the depression that Atlanta felt when its Falcons lost a Super Bowl in overtime.

Public Relations Plays a Strategic Part in Sports

Sporting events and sports teams benefit from intense PR efforts. These efforts, on all levels, are designed to heighten public knowledge of teams and players—turn them into fans, in other words. It's fans, after all, who buy tickets and team apparel, purchase the products of corporate sponsors and advertisers, and follow the team's exploits in the media. Note the derivation of the word "fans" is from "fanatics," and certainly, many fans are passionate devotees of "their" team.

Sports are also the most watched events on television around the world. In the United States, 19 of the top 20 most-watched television shows in Nielsen ratings history have been Super Bowl broadcasts (Nielsen, 2018b). This includes 2018's Super Bowl LII with 103 million viewers (see Figure 13.1).

Publicists (sometimes called sports information directors) for teams employ numerous PR tactics, including developing and maintaining good relationships with sportswriters and on-air personalities. They compile media kits and the accompanying mounds of statistics, write feature articles on players, handle interview requests from the media, provide website content, and occasionally handle player bookings and appearances.

Social Media's Winning Game

The use of social media, in all its forms and platforms, is a major function for any sports organization's PR department. The Chicago Cubs, for example, use Twitter, Snapchat, Instagram, and Facebook to interact with fans. The club's website carries Wrigley Field information, such as ticket prices and seating charts, upcoming game promotions, and includes help finding a parking space, too. The website also profiles players and team charities and even links to a fantasy league—an online game in which people manage rosters of league baseball players whose real-life statistics score points. All these channels and content are largely the responsibility of the Cubs' PR department.

The Cubs are not alone; the same social media tactics are used by most teams in Major League Baseball (MLB), the National Football League (NFL), the National Basketball Association (NBA), the Women's National Basketball Association (WNBA), Major League Soccer (MLS), the National Women's Soccer League (NWSL), and most college programs. That's a lot of opportunity *online* for PR professionals.

Amy Littleton, executive VP of Kemper-Lesnik, the Chicago-based PR firm and sports marketing agency, offers this advice to aspiring sports PR practitioners:

> Sports PR is not one thing; it is many things. It is broadcasting. It is crisis management. It is player relations and messaging. It is statistics. It is operations. It is fan engagement. And, much more. The key to being successful at sports PR is to be successful at PR. Great PR people can do PR in any industry—so long as they are confident, courageous and curious.

> My advice for getting into the sports PR industry: Get experience. No matter what that looks like—get after it, get experience. Learn and grow.

Chicago Cubs ✔
@Cubs

Follow ⌄

BREAKING in a new glove is one of life's underrated pleasures.

The Chicago Cubs have an active social media presence, sharing information, interacting with fans, and cracking jokes.
Twitter.com/cubs

I recently met with the CEO of Harris Blitzer Sport & Entertainment, which owns, among other things, the Philadelphia 76ers (NBA) and the New Jersey Devils (NHL). Scott started his career getting coffee and making copies for a mid-level manager at the NBA. No job is too small. Be hungry. Be humble. Be smart. And you'll get there. (A. Littleton, personal communication, 2020)

However, not every career in sports PR is with a professional team. In fact, most are not. For the person who loves being associated with sports, the career choices are seemingly endless.

Public Relations Careers for Sports Lovers

The following list identifies some sports and sports-related jobs that may not be obvious and mentions a few of the duties.

- **Minor league teams:** MLB teams all have minor league affiliates on four levels: AAA, AA, A, and Rookie. Hockey follows a similar structure, and the NBA has a roster of minor league teams. All need PR professionals to do the same jobs that are done for the majors.

- **College athletic departments:** Ever wonder why an athlete is considered a Heisman candidate or why a gymnast is profiled as an Olympic hopeful? Thank their school's PR departments for creating the campaigns to raise their profiles. The same department is responsible for all the fan outreach done by the pro teams.

- **Sporting goods:** Wilson, Louisville Slugger, Coleman, Callaway, Bauer, Trek, and Dunlop didn't get to be sports household names without vigorous PR efforts with teams, pro and amateur athletes, and fans.

- **Sportswear:** The same is true of Under Armour, Nike, Adidas, Columbia, and Patagonia. Sportswear companies that enjoy instant name recognition and generally positive brand images have PR campaigns connected to celebrity athletes and professional and college athletic teams.

- **Sports food and drink:** This is an enormous field with many opportunities connecting PR pros to the sports world. It encompasses everything from working with the food manufacturer to retail placements and national awareness campaigns. The energy bar in some cyclist's seat pack didn't get there on its own.

- **Corporate sponsorships:** Sponsored sporting events, especially tournaments and championships, provide great opportunities for a company to put its name in front of the public—and even greater opportunities for PR practitioners. A complete list of sponsored sports events would run to hundreds of names and include college football bowl games, professional and amateur golf tournaments, NASCAR races, bicycle tours, tennis tourneys, and boxing matches, to name just a few.

Suffice to say that opportunities abound for the PR practitioner who wants to live and breathe sports.

Publicizing the Good, Dealing With the Bad

PR professionals working for sports organizations of all sizes—professional and academic—deal with both news that benefits the team and news that casts a shadow on it. Rare is the year that no crisis rocks a sport or team, and dealing with those crises swiftly and honestly is key to keeping the public's support. On the opposite side of the same coin, teams and individual athletes, from pee wee to pro, are involved in good works year-round that benefit their communities. It is an equally important function of PR to highlight these positive activities.

The Right Way to Handle Wrongs

No matter the sport, there is an unfortunate certainty that some athletes will behave badly, and their misdeeds—minor or major—will reflect poorly on their teams, their schools, their own marketability, or even their communities. While it is the function of PR to cast a client in a positive light, it is not acceptable to issue false statements or to knowingly aid in the cover-up of an incident or issue that reflects poorly on them.

Unfortunately, many PR wounds are self-inflicted, usually because of poor decisions made at the onset of the crisis and made worse by poor messaging later. Correcting an earlier PR misstep is much harder that being transparent and forthright from the start.

The NFL spent years denying even the existence of long-term brain injury in its former players, rejecting out-of-hand research that showed a direct link between concussions and chronic traumatic encephalopathy (CTE). Although the league now has an aggressive program to protect players from concussions and their aftereffects, the damage to the league's credibility on any medical issue was substantial and still is not completely repaired.

The same can be said about how the various pro and college leagues have dealt with issues such as domestic abuse, sexual assault, and drug abuse. Even today, those incidents continue to be mishandled by the PR staff of both the teams and the leagues. This can cause damage that will scar an organization for many years.

However unsettling it may be for PR professionals to deal with such a situation, the accusations, and even the arrests, those must be acknowledged and dealt with openly and honestly. Covering up is no solution; it just makes the pain that much worse later on.

The NFL's refusal to acknowledge the long-term impacts of repeated head injuries, known as CTE, harmed both its players and its reputation.
Jamie Squire/Getty Images

Being Good Sports: How Athletes and Teams Give Back to Their Community

The LeBron James Family Foundation has agreed to pay tuition at the University of Akron for thousands of qualifying students.
AP Photo/Karen Schiely

On all levels of athletics—and across all types of sports—good works are performed by individual athletes, teams, and entire leagues to benefit the community.

Big Names Have Big Impacts

Individual pro athletes, especially those with the highest profiles, often have foundations that support causes that have a direct connection to them or their families.

The Mia Hamm Foundation (www.miafoundation. org) founded in 1999 by the soccer star is one example. For the past 20 years, it has raised funds

and awareness of bone marrow and cord blood transplants. Another of its missions is increasing opportunities for young women in sports (Mia Hamm Foundation, n.d.).

Others raise money to aid the towns or states they came from. Eli Manning, retired quarterback for the New York Giants, raised nearly $3 million over a 5-year period to build the Eli Manning Children's Clinic in Mississippi. The clinic reportedly provides outpatient care to more than 75,000 children each year (Powell, 2015).

Basketball superstar LeBron James's Wheels for Education program shepherds select Akron, Ohio, students from third grade through high school. Qualifying students will then enter the I Promise program with a guaranteed 4-year college scholarship to the University of Akron. This act of generosity is expected to cost the James's foundation more than $41 million for 2021 graduates (LeBron James Family Foundation, 2019).

Teams Dive Deep Into Charity, Too

Nearly every professional team's website, regardless of sport, lists the community outreach and charitable giving they support. From sponsoring youth leagues to working with local after-school programs to team members serving holiday meals to the needy, teams are visible in their support of their communities. It is important that the public is made aware of these stories of generosity and engagement. While the bad news will always get coverage, getting out the good news takes effort. The teams' PR departments must make sure that these good works are brought to the public's attention.

From Big Leagues to College Sports, All Do Their Part

MLB has as one of its official charities the Boys & Girls Clubs of America. The NFL foundation funds numerous youth-related programs, and MLS supports the Special Olympics. Colleges and university athletes are also active in lending a generous helping hand. ●

What's in a Name?

Corporations Name Stadiums

Over 700 athletic stadiums in the United States carry the name of a corporation (ESPN, 2017). This figure includes major and minor league baseball parks, soccer stadiums, basketball arenas, and professional and college football stadiums. In fact, on a professional level it is more common for a team to play in a venue bearing a corporate name than not: 26 of 32 NFL teams (Spedden, 2018) and 20 of 30 MLB teams have a company name on the door (Spedden, 2019).

Huge Investments of Millions Each Year

Naming rights for NFL venues aren't cheap, but the fees vary widely. FedEx Field, home to Washington's NFL team, costs the corporation some $7.6 million a year. The San Francisco 49ers play in Levi's Stadium, for which the jeans company pays $11 million a year (Bien, 2013). And following the adage of "everything being bigger in Texas," AT&T is reportedly paying around $19 million annually to have its name on the Dallas Cowboys' home turf (SportsDay, 2013).

Sponsors occasionally change, and with that switch can come some fan adjustments, as when the Chicago White Sox renamed their stadium. Called U.S. Cellular Park since its opening in 2003 (and quickly nicknamed "The Cell" by fans), the Sox now play in Guaranteed Rate Field. Time will tell how fans shorten that name into something less of a mouthful. American sports website Sporting News (Thomas, 2016) offers its opinion on the worst arena and stadium names in sports (see Table 13.1)—names that identify fast-food franchises, mortgage companies, and grocery stores.

Public Relations Values and Risks

From a PR perspective, there can be real value in having your company's name associated with a city or college's team. On-site, your name and logo are on everything from the front door and the roof to the ticket stubs and the concession cups. Off-site, your name gets repeated mentions every time a story about the team refers to the stadium. While such exposure isn't necessarily free because of the naming fees, it most certainly is an efficient way of putting your company's name into the consumer's mind.

TABLE 13.1

Sporting News Tags Worst Arena and Stadium Names in Sports

NAME	LOCATION	SPORT TEAM	TYPE OF BUSINESS
Whataburger Field	Corpus Christi, TX	Hooks, MiLB	Fast food
Little Caesars Arena	Detroit	Red Wings, NHL	Fast food
Guaranteed Rate Field	Chicago	White Sox, MLB	Mortgages
Smoothie King Center	New Orleans	Pelicans, NBA	Beverages
Talking Stick Resort Arena	Phoenix	Suns, NBA	Hotel & casino
Taco Bell Arena	Boise State Univ.	Basketball	Fast food
InfoCision Stadium	Univ. of Akron	Football	Call centers
KFC Yum! Center	Univ. of Louisville	Basketball	Fast food

Source: Thomas. "The worst arena and stadium names in sports." Sporting News, 2016.

There are risks involved for teams and for corporations in the naming rights game; the Houston Astros played in Enron Stadium, named for a corporation that collapsed in scandal. The Astros quickly shed the name and now play in Minute Maid Park. FedEx finds itself in the uncomfortable position of being the stadium sponsor of Washington's NFL team, whose nickname, the Redskins, is offensive to many. The University of Louisville's football stadium had been known as Papa John's Cardinal Stadium, but in 2018 when the pizza chain founder, John Schnatter, admitted to using racial slurs in a phone call, the name was removed. In November of 2019, the university agreed to pay Schnatter almost $10 million over 5 years to terminate the naming agreement that was set to run until 2040 (Keck, 2019).

Tourism: More Than Sightseeing

>> **LO 13.2**   **Explore the scope of the tourism industry and the essential role of PR, gaining insight on socially responsible and sustainability aspects that support organizational goals**

When you think of tourism, what picture comes to mind? Perhaps it's a cruise to the islands of the Caribbean, a bus tour of Italian cities, or maybe a hike among the ruins of Machu Picchu. You may also think of destinations within the United States where you might spend a few days, such as one of the theme parks in Florida, a campsite in Yosemite, or a ski resort in Colorado. Then again, you may associate tourism with sights and places you visit for a day—or even for just a few hours—such as a state fair, a local festival, or a roadside attraction that catches your eye.

You'd be right in any of those definitions of tourism, but you're probably not aware how much impact tourism has on our economy and on the economies of the world's nations. Whether riding a gondola in Venice or eating cotton candy at a county fair, tourists and tourism have an enormous economic impact.

According to the United Nations World Tourism Organization, tourism is one of the largest industries in the world, ranking third behind chemicals and fuels, but ahead of agricultural goods and automotive products (UNWTO, 2018). As one of the major segments in international commerce, tourism represents one of the most important sources of revenue for many developing nations.

The World Economic Forum (2019) reports that in 2018 travel and tourism accounted for 10.4% of the world's gross domestic product (GDP) and currently employs over 10% of the world's workforce, about 319 million people. The percentage of the U.S. GDP attributable to travel and tourism is around 11%, or an astounding $1.6 trillion, and accounts for 7.8 million jobs (World Economic Forum, 2019).

For many years, tourism has had steady growth and is now one of the fastest-growing sectors in the world economy. Tourism today has close links to economic development and includes a growing number of new destinations. Emerging nations are eager to attract travelers and tourists, as the dynamics of tourism have turned it into a prime mover of economic progress.

The Role of Public Relations

The tourism industry, whether it's a nation promoting its heritage or a small town promoting its annual festival, has a single goal: attract travelers and tourists. People want to go places, see things they've never seen, and do things they've never done, and the industry must turn that basic but undirected desire into action. PR is vital in this process. Beyond attracting visitors, communications help them get there and help shape their experience once they arrive.

Promoting the place or attraction is the first step and can include traditional tactics such as story placements in magazines and newspapers, advertising, brochures, and preproduced video news releases for television and online. Now, a strong online presence with social media content is an essential way to attract the interest of tourists.

Public Relations Plan for a Music Festival

Imagine you're promoting a music festival to be hosted in your city. Let's run through your process, from beginning to end.

Music festivals like Coachella in California can attract tens of thousands of people, but first, people need to find out the event is taking place.
Christopher Polk/Getty Images

1. *First use the power of digital and social media.* You want to use these and other online techniques to draw a crowd (see Table 13.2).

2. *Next, you'll want to encourage* partnering airlines, tour operators, and car rental companies to offer special rates and cross-promote on their websites, as you do for them on yours.

3. *Once visitors arrive,* they need to feel welcome, comfortable, and appreciated. Work with local motels and restaurants to not only offer festival packages and discounts, but make them an integral part of the effort to welcome event guests with maps, schedules, and transportation.

4. *Finally, you'll want to have information kiosks* in key locations around the city to help visitors find their way around, get schedules, and obtain discounts—information duplicated on your online platforms.

5. *Once the festival begins,* turn your attention to promoting the events through television placements, news stories, live feeds online, and a festival blog that is written in real time. Also encourage attendees to post their own reviews and comments on social media. The reason you keep promoting is, first, to attract a crowd for the last day or two of the event—encouraging attendance by those people who did not anticipate coming but now want to be in on the fun. Second, showing this year's festival to those who didn't come at all helps build interest for next year's show.

As you can see, there is no one job description that would suit all the tasks that need to be performed by PR professionals for a single event. What's also obvious are the

TABLE 13.2

How to Use the Power of Digital and Social Media

Colorful website	List performers, plus provide links to hotels, restaurants, and transportation options.
YouTube channel	Feature videos of past festivals.
Instagram account	Invite people to virtually explore all attractions.
Twitter feed	Update potential visitors on schedule additions and changes.
Facebook page	Duplicate information and also use it as an interactive question-and-answer tool.

numerous opportunities for employment in the field of PR represented in a single event. No matter your interest—travel, hospitality, social media, or event planning—there's a job for you in PR.

SOCIAL RESPONSIBILITY

Sustainability and Social Responsibility Practices

Hotels

Sustainability goals have become increasingly important in guest attraction and loyalty. Booking.com's 2019 sustainability report (2019) shows a majority of global travelers (about 70%) want to travel sustainably and favor booking accommodations that are eco-friendly.

The hospitality industry has responded, placing itself in the forefront of sustainable practices, which extend from simple in-room cards that encourage guests to reuse their towels and linen to corporatewide practices. Marriott's "Serve Our World" initiative supports local communities and works to protect the environment. Its Ritz-Carlton properties encourage sustainable driving with electric charging stations at hotels around the world. Starwood Hotels and Resorts has a worldwide focus on energy and water. In partnership with Conservation International, the chain committed to a 30% reduction in energy consumption and 20% less water consumption by 2020, from a 2008 baseline (Starwood, n.d.). One way Starwood engages its publics is through video storytelling. Find "Starwood's Water Story: Thinking Beyond Conservation" on YouTube.

State governments are also helping hotels with their sustainable practices. In an effort to reduce the number of plastic containers being discarded by hotels and their guests, California Governor Gavin Newsom signed a bill in October 2019 to ban hotels from supplying travel-sized bottles of shampoo and lotion. The law takes effect in 2023. As of November 2019, the state of New York is considering imposing the same ban (Ebrahimji, 2019).

Indeed, green practices and eco-friendly programs have become so widespread that many travelers not only willingly participate in them but are beginning to expect them. And the booming eco-friendly practices in the hospitality industry provide a plethora of material for PR practitioners, using multiple communication platforms.

Ecotourism

A significant segment of today's tourists wants more from their travel than the familiar sites featured in glossy brochures and on panoramic websites. Not for them is a trip to the top of Paris's Eiffel Tower, a stein of beer at Munich's Octoberfest, or a shopping spree on Tokyo's glittering Ginza. Instead, they're opting for ecotourism by taking a rugged trek to view gorillas in Rwanda, bundling up to see the penguin colonies in Antarctica, or boarding a boat to observe the wonders of the Galapagos Islands.

Many hotels now encourage guests to reuse towels to conserve water, often appealing to their sense of environmental responsibility.
Jonathan Wiggs/The Boston Globe/Getty Images

With the popularity of ecotourism on the rise, so too are concerns about the impact visitors have on areas that, for centuries, were beyond the reach of all but the hardiest adventurers. Now, these areas are playing host to thousands of tourists every year. Their trekking through often-fragile ecosystems can result in permanent and irreversible damage.

Ecotourism presents its own challenges for PR professionals. Promoting a destination such as Las Vegas would mainly focus on getting visitors to the city and describing the fun and excitement they will experience once there. It's hard to imagine a need to include talk of environmental impact.

Promoting ecotourism, however, includes the responsibility to not only attract visitors but the right kind of visitors. In other words, there's a need to let the ecotourists know what is expected of them before they even book their trips. Imagine someone arriving at a camp in Rwanda with false expectations—discovering petting the gorillas is not on the agenda.

Good PR practices will present a thorough and accurate picture of the destination as well as an honest description of the responsibilities of the visitor. Because ecotourists come in contact with the local populace, their visits also affect the lives and well-being of their hosts. It is wise to share information from respected agencies in advance.

Rising ecotourism in places like the Galapagos has led to concern about the impact of thousands of travelers on the ecosystems they are visiting.
In Pictures Ltd./Corbis/Getty Images

Exotic Tourism

Thousands of wealthy travelers take safaris, an exotic vacation that many of us can only imagine or see through amazing video productions. The story of one company in Kenya, Micato Safaris, reveals how animals, their habitat, and Africa's cultural heritage are protected through the company's partnerships with multiple wildlife and wilderness conservation foundations.

One long-term SR effort earned Micato Safaris the "Legacy in Travel Philanthropy Award" by Tourism Cares (n.d.), the charitable community of the travel and tourism industry that has the sponsorship support of American Express. Micato identified a need to educate children, so it formed a U.S. nonprofit, AmericaShare, to focus solely on that effort. Micato and AmericaShare have enabled thousands of Nairobi youth to attend school and to graduate from high school at a rate approaching 100%—from a population where fewer than 50% of boys and 42% of girls graduate. The Nairobi youths that benefit are living in extreme poverty in the city's Mukuru slum, home to 325,000 with low education, public health, and employment rates. It is also where AIDS has been epidemic, with a generation of AIDS orphans.

Micato's education programs fund room and board for youths attending private boarding schools and also help primary students stay in school through supplementing family finances. Local community, church, and tribal leaders guide selections of the recipients. Within the Mukuru community, it also created a community center equipped with a lending library, a learning center for students with disabilities, a nursery school, and in partnership with Johnson & Johnson, provided girls with feminine products and HIV/AIDS prevention information.

To achieve and sustain these long-term community initiatives successfully, Micato recognized the benefit of establishing a U.S.-based nonprofit, AmericaShare, to lead and manage fundraising. It also plays a big role in communicating to donors and travelers. A culture of transparency and accountability was established by using third-party advisors from the community to oversee student selection. In fact, community dynamics, needs, and impacts all influence the charitable operation.

Threats and Crises

Even in times when all seems well, tourism is constantly affected by outside forces and events. PR professionals have to be ready at a moment's notice to cope with all manner of unexpected issues and crises that will seriously affect businesses that depend on tourists and travelers. These include, but aren't limited to, hotels, rental car companies, airlines, tour operators, cruise lines, and airlines—even so far as damaging the entire tourism business of cities, states, and countries.

Most Unforeseen, Few Preventable

From 2008 into 2019, tourism has been affected by every possible crisis—most unforeseen and few preventable. The recession that began in earnest in 2008 reduced disposable income for many families and kept them from taking vacations. The BP Deepwater Horizon oil spill of 2010 blighted the pristine beaches of the southern states that border the Gulf of Mexico, an area just recovering from Hurricane Katrina 5 years earlier.

Travelers who planned to visit Mexico changed their minds in 2011, when drug war violence began reaching the resort towns of Acapulco and Puerto Vallarta. Greece was in the midst of a financial crisis that reached a boiling point in 2012 and saw tourism sharply decline as videos of riots and protests in Athens made potential visitors wary.

INSIGHTS

ECOTOURS and Outdoor Leadership

Ged Kaddick, founder of Terra Incognita ECOTOURS, leads trips to remote and exotic natural destinations around the world. With a website, a blog, and several social media platforms, the business communicates specific values and principles, helping potential clients understand what to expect on an ecotour. By doing so, guests self-select to adhere to those expectations, so no one joins a tour only to be surprised at the destination.

"Our company is committed to the idea that it's our responsibility to leave earth better than we found it, and we impart that belief to our guests," according to Kaddick (personal communication, 2017).

Kaddick's company takes additional steps to "instill in our tourists the concept of making a positive difference rather than a negative impact" (G. Kaddick, personal communication, 2017). For every person who joins one of their ecotours, the company makes a donation to one of the leading conservation organizations working in that area. Their tours are also joined by representative organizations (such as Gorilla Doctors) to explain their mission and provide insight to the tourists.

If the traveler is interested in a more rugged adventure, such as a trek into wilderness areas,

it's very important the promotional efforts also educate potential participants about the hardships they will be facing and the impact their trips will have on the environment. Many tour companies and their leaders ascribe to guidelines created by environmental organizations.

Eric Boggs, expedition faculty for the National Outdoor Leadership School (NOLS), leads backpacking adventures around the world. "It is essential that anyone contemplating joining us understand what they'll be facing. There's no running water, toilets, or beds out here" (E. Boggs, personal communication, 2017). He endorses the principles compiled by the organization Leave No Trace, which stress minimizing impact and respecting the environment, and he uses those guidelines in his treks.

"I've been training my student leaders in *coincidental* socially responsible leadership," says Boggs. "The backpacking trips we've done have essential social and eco-responsible aspects to them; a quick synopsis is what Boy Scouts have always called the 'campsite rule': leaving the place better than you find it—for ecological and social reasons" (E. Boggs, personal communication, 2017). ●

Fear for personal safety after terror attacks had a negative impact on tourism to major destination cities such as Paris, Brussels, Istanbul, and even London. Egypt, after years of political turmoil, has seen a drastic drop in tourists, especially to the well-known sites of Giza.

Each of these examples created enormous challenges for PR professionals, but most have been able to craft messages aimed to reassure and recapture tourists, although not all have been successful.

Spotlight on Mexico

An example of good efforts derailed by unexpected events is what has happened in Mexico. The Tourism Ministry's website, www.visitmexico.com, is aimed at English-speaking tourists. Canadian and U.S. visitors make up 72% of its tourists, approximately 41.5 million visitors annually (L. Gregory, 2019). The website highlights most of the favored destinations and, as to be expected, avoids any negative references to safety. Instead, in 2015 the ministry released numerous reports showing a dramatic lessening of violence, and tourists began to return. Tourism figures released for 2018 showed the industry contributed 8.8% of the country's GDP, with U.S. dollars accounting for nearly $20 billion. With that much at stake, it's easy to see why reassuring visitors their trips will be safe and uneventful is crucial to their decision to come.

Indeed, the Mexican Secretary of Tourism, Miguel Torruco Marques, said in a 2019 interview,

> A quiet, hardworking, safe country is the best promotion for any of its tourist attractions. Warnings are eliminated, perception is eliminated, and above all, it initiates the word-of-mouth promotion by visitors for its proximity, the investments that have already been made, and for its many attractions. Very few places offer turquoise-colored beaches where nature has already provided a water heater. That's an added value in addition to our great historical cultural heritage and gastronomy. (L. Gregory, 2019)

Unfortunately, from 2016 into 2018, flare-ups of violence led the U.S. State Department to issue warnings to U.S. citizens contemplating travel to many of Mexico's states. The effect of these warnings wasn't immediately known, but in 2019, horrific crimes, including a daylight running gun battle by drug cartels in the streets of one city and the kidnapping and murder of American citizens by another suspected drug cartel, played out on U.S. television.

The State Department reissued the travel warning in the starkest terms, advising U.S. citizens visiting Mexico to "exercise extreme caution" because "violent crime such as homicide, kidnapping, carjacking, and robbery is widespread."

How, when, and if Mexico recovers from this ongoing crisis will take years to determine.

Small-Town Festivals Draw Big Crowds

When discussing travel and tourism, it would be a huge mistake to omit those events that many of us will attend this year: small-town festivals. Although not as dazzling as ones hosted by large cities, these fests and fairs draw thousands into small towns and villages and provide a real boost to the local economy.

Small-town festivals, like the Duct Tape Festival in Ohio, can draw large crowds and provide fertile training grounds for aspiring PR professionals.
AP Photo/Rachel Kasunicv

Midwestern Traditions

The city of St. Charles, Illinois, for instance, scheduled its 35th annual Scarecrow Festival for October 2020. As many as 175,000 visitors typically come for the 3 days of the fest, according to the St. Charles Business Alliance (S. Martin, personal communication, 2019). And with them comes a huge economic boost for this town of 33,000.

Further north, the town of Sauk Prairie, Wisconsin, population 3,900, typically hosts up to 50,000 visitors for its decades-old Wisconsin State Cow Chip Throw—which is exactly what you think it is. Director Marietta Reuter says the annual event, held on Labor Day weekend, is a "happy time for all" and a boon to the local economy (M. Reuter, personal communication, 2019). Reuter adds that if you're planning on tossing a chip to bear in mind, "No gloves, but licking your hand for a better grip is allowed." Other fun festivals include these:

- The Duct Tape Festival, Avon, Ohio
- Garlic Fest, Highwood, Illinois
- The West Virginia Roadkill Cook-Off, Marlinton, West Virginia
- National Hollerin' Contest, Spivey's Corner, North Carolina
- National Lentil Festival, Pullman, Washington
- Tarantula Awareness Festival, Coarsegold, California

Good Training Grounds for Public Relations

What all these festivals, and the hundreds like them across the country, have in common is that they attract visitors from well outside their city limits, and those visitors spend money. Although the crowds and dollars won't match those generated by an NFL championship game, they provide a nice boost to their hosts' economy. Also, even on their smaller scale, PR techniques are used to promote them. If you are new to the PR field, look no further than your community's festival to get started. These fairs and fests are great training grounds for aspiring PR professionals.

Entertainment Public Relations: Publicity and Much More

>> LO 13.3   Examine the breadth of PR and CSR engagement within the entertainment industry through the perspectives of talent, agencies, and entertainment companies

From the East to West Coast and in all corners of the world, the entertainment PR specialty flourishes along with the prominence of popular culture personalities, media, products, experiences, and trends. Entertainment PR encompasses a wide range of clients. And while you may think "publicist" when you think of entertainment—getting movie stars and other talent, plus their films, books, concerts, and so on into the "news"—actually, entertainment PR practitioners provide a broad range of services.

Publicists and Celebrities

Let's first consider publicists. They promote the careers of celebrities by generating publicity through diverse methods, including issuing press releases; booking print, radio, and TV interviews; and arranging personal appearances. They look for opportunities to keep their clients in the public's eye and also are proactive in managing risk. Depending on the situation, a strategic communication campaign may be developed to raise, reposition, or rehabilitate a public profile.

Robin Baum (*right*) is considered one of the most powerful publicists in Hollywood, with clients such as Jared Leto.
Kevin Mazur/WireImage/Getty Images

Depending on your own tastes in music, media, and popular culture, you likely are more familiar with some types of celebrities than others. Yet "celebrity" touches a diverse population. Each year *Forbes* magazine releases a list of the top-100 highest-paid celebrities. In 2019, some of those ranking in the top 10 of the list illustrate the wide range of "celebrity" personalities: Taylor Swift, Kylie Jenner, Kanye West, Argentine soccer player Lionel Messi, TV host Dr. Phil McGraw, and the band The Eagles. Death doesn't end a celebrity's earning power, either; some of these top-10 earners passed on decades ago: Michael Jackson, Elvis Presley, golfer Arnold Palmer, cartoonist Charles Schultz, Dr. Seuss, and Marilyn Monroe (Greenburg, 2019).

The Broader Field

In the expansive field of entertainment PR, media relations in general is a high-activity task, due to the need for constant communication with trade, mainstream, and business media outlets (see Table 13.3). PR tactics in entertainment differ for the type of client. Let's look at some examples of *who* needs PR, separated into three categories: talent, general entertainment, and content producers. These lists are certainly not all-inclusive:

- **Talent:** actors, recording artists, musicians, DJs, designers, authors, and models

- **General entertainment:** films, DVD/CD releases, TV and radio programs, video games, novels, magazines, online series, and concerts

- **Content producers:** filmmakers, creative artists, film producers, broadcast and publishing companies; studios, film financiers, and distributors

The following news release headlines and leads, creative and often promotional, illustrate the diverse stories that PR practitioners tell to publicize their clients:

- **Celebrity fashion:** "Jessica Rey Swimwear Takes 'Going Green' to a New Level"—"Timeless style isn't the only forward-looking thing about

TABLE 13.3

Public Relations Services in the Entertainment Industry

PR SERVICES RANGE FROM THE GENERAL . . .	. . . TO THE MORE SPECIFIC
• Strategic communication counsel	• Event & tour support
• Corporate positioning	• Product launches
• Brand enhancement	• Premieres
• Image creation	• Press junkets
• Media relations	• Film festival strategies
• Reputation/issues management	• Awards campaigns
• Litigation support	• Trade shows
• Crisis management/communication	• Red carpets
	• Cause partnerships
	• Sponsorships
	• Product placement

Jessica Rey Swimwear. Designer Rey's latest silhouettes are helping preserve our planet's oceans, too. Rey has partnered with Italian fabric company Aquafil to create designs that incorporate Econyl yarn, composed of 100% regenerated nylon waste, such as abandoned fishing nets, production scraps, and carpet fluff. Prior to launching her career as a designer, Rey was a Hollywood actress starring as Alyssa, the White Ranger on Disney's *Power Rangers Wild Force*. As a Power Ranger, saving the world was part of the routine, but for Rey, now it's for real" (Business Wire, 2017c).

- **Movie theaters:** "Dolby Cinema Showcases Strong Spring Lineup"—"Dolby Laboratories, Inc., today announced 13 new titles, adding to the growing slate of movies to be shown at more than 75 Dolby Cinema locations around the globe. Dolby Cinema enables richer and more action-packed storytelling through Dolby Vision and Dolby Atmos. The result is a dramatically different viewing experience that presents strikingly vivid and realistic images, making viewers feel like they are inside the movie's world" (Business Wire, 2017b).

- **Broadcast and online retailers:** "HSN Ignites Designers' Creativity With the Launch of Its Enchanting Disney *Beauty and the Beast* Collection, Spanning Across Home, Apparel and Accessories"—"Leading entertainment and lifestyle retailer HSN is launching a marketing collaboration with Disney for the release of *Beauty and the Beast* in its all-new live-action adaptation of the animated classic" (HSN Inc., 2017).

- **Television series:** "Cesar Millan Takes on Role as Rescuer and Rehabilitator in New Series"—"*Cesar Millan's Dog Nation* is a new series that follows dog behaviorist Cesar Millan (@cesarmillan) and his son Andre's road trip across America helping groups and individuals that are rescuing and rehabilitating dogs (Business Wire, 2017a).

SOCIAL RESPONSIBILITY

Entertainment Public Relations and Social Causes

Just as with the sports and tourism industries, the entertainment industry is very visibly engaged in CSR. A brief review of initiatives undertaken by entertainment PR agencies, personalities themselves, and media companies and foundations offers a window into their world of giving.

Agencies: A Short List

Entertainment PR firms are guiding clients into CSR initiatives as well as investing in their own.

- The Creative Artists Agency (CAA) Foundation carries the tagline "Using pop culture to create social good." It counsels artists, athletes, and companies on philanthropic strategies, cause marketing, and social change campaigns, with a focus on supporting youth education.

- ICM Partners, a global talent and literary agency, enables employee volunteerism with more than 20 organizations, including the American Red Cross and the Assistance League.

- Havas, the multinational communications firm, offers a sports and entertainment network that specializes in sustainability PR.

- New York's 42West contributes a percentage of its annual profits to various philanthropic and advocacy groups.

Personalities: A Short List

- Actor Leonardo DiCaprio's long commitment to eco-activism began in 1998 when at age 25 he launched a foundation to protect biodiversity and combat climate change.

PR PROFILE

Pro Basketball's Dedication to Community

Arvind Gopalratnam, Executive Director, Milwaukee Bucks Foundation

Following Your Passion

Like any kid, I dreamt about being a professional athlete. I wanted to be Milwaukee Buck, a Milwaukee Brewer, and a Green Bay Packer—a common aspiration for any uber sports fan born and raised in Wisconsin. While my ability to compete at the highest levels did not last much past high school (also common), the love for sports has lived on and been the foundation for my professional development as a corporate PR leader and CSR executive.

As a journalism major at the University of Wisconsin, I took my knowledge and passion for sports and spent 4 years covering Badgers athletics. This path not only also presented me my first leadership experience, serving as sports editor for the *Daily Cardinal* student-run newspaper, but it also developed my passion for communications. On top of learning how to be a written storyteller, being a department leader fostered interpersonal communications skills,

(Continued)

(Continued)

which are core to leading and being a part of any team environment.

Upon graduation, I took a huge life risk, stopped being a journalist, and began my corporate journey at General Electric, initially as a member of the NBC Universal Page Program in New York City (think Kenneth from the NBC sitcom *30 Rock*). After also working with the executive office of NBC Sports and Olympics and learning the inner workings of sports television production, executive, and talent management, I shifted to the next phase of my professional development and into my career as a PR professional for GE Healthcare.

In addition to spearheading global internal and external communications strategy development, executive management, and crisis communications for GE's medical technologies, I was a core leader in the company's Olympics sponsorship. These responsibilities not only took me to over 15 countries and five Olympic Games, but more importantly, they exposed me to the world of corporate philanthropy. As part of GE's contribution to the Olympic Games, it was the company's commitment to leave a legacy gift behind for the host city, and my work afforded me the first chance to develop relationships with local communities and showcase the power of a corporate social responsibility strategy.

My passion for the world of sports has quite literally taken me around the world and back.

Which brings me to today. I'm proud to say, I am a Milwaukee Buck. While not a pro athlete, I'm still part of a pro sports team. As the vice president of corporate social responsibility for the Milwaukee Bucks and executive director of the Milwaukee Bucks Foundation, I am honored and incredibly proud to be a local kid leading an incredible team and a community-conscious organization keen on maximizing its impact on the communities we serve.

Corporate social responsibility cannot just be communication tactic, but instead needs to be a core part of an organizational culture and a business strategy. As with the Bucks and across the NBA, that means investing in professionals willing to connect and build trust with local communities, investing in measurable programs and initiatives, addressing the issues identified by our communities, and using its platform to convene the broader community for better societal outcomes.

The Milwaukee Bucks is way more than just a basketball team. We are also an entertainment company, a real estate developer, a gaming company, *and* a philanthropic organization. We are positively impacting lives across the globe on a daily basis.

Follow your passion, develop relationships with your audience, be a diverse communicator, and be willing to continuously learn, and you too could be in your dream job. ●

Source: A. Gopalratnam, personal communication, 2020.

- Actor Emma Watson, Harry Potter's Hermione, supports gender equality as a goodwill ambassador for UN Women.

- Recording artist and actor Alicia Keys cofounded both the Keep a Child Alive nonprofit to combat HIV and the We Are Here Movement for equality and social justice.

- Actor Mariska Hargitay's nonprofit, the Joyful Heart Foundation, works to address survivors of sexual assault, domestic violence, and child abuse.

- Actor and producer Adrian Grenier cofounded SHFT.com to promote sustainability through multimedia; clients have included Ford, Virgin America, and Estee Lauder.

Foundations and Corporations

The Entertainment Industry Foundation (EIF, n.d.) is the industry's leading charitable organization. Since launching in 2008, its Stand Up To Cancer (SU2C) initiative has funded research through a biennial televised event that features hundreds of celebrities. In collaboration with young filmmakers, it also creates celebrity PSAs to educate youths on the risks of smoking. Other programs include partnering with grocer Albertsons to provide breakfasts to hungry children and partnering with the Bill & Melinda Gates Foundation and ExxonMobil, among others, to coordinate funding for innovative classroom projects.

Major entertainment media companies have dedicated CSR programs (*Variety* Staff, 2016). For example, 21st Century Fox is a founding partner of Ghetto Film School LA, serving disadvantaged communities. Sony Picture Entertainment supports more than 45 organizations, including community arts centers in Los Angeles. Sony also uses its resources to fund and organize a global environmental campaign, Picture This, and Disney's VoluntEARS supports hundreds of nonprofits.

Scenario Outcome

In the NBA case at the beginning of this chapter, you read about negative reactions from the Chinese government to a tweet sent by the Houston Rockets' general manager. You also read about NBA Commissioner Silver's response and subsequent negative reactions to that.

- **You were asked how Silver should have responded and if you believe his initial response was adequate.**

  Due to what Silver said was "confusing" media coverage of the NBA's first statement, a follow-up statement 2 days later clarified, "The NBA will not put itself in a position of regulating what players, employees and team owners say or will not say," Silver stated. "I do know there are consequences from freedom of speech; we will have to live with those consequences" (Riley, 2019, para. 5).

  The following week, Silver emphasized that the NBA supported Morey. "We made clear that we were being asked to fire him, by the Chinese government … we said there's no chance that's happening … no chance we'll even discipline him." Silver noted the NBA did not accede to China's demands. "These American values—we are an American business—travel with us wherever we go," Silver said. "And one of those values is free expression. We wanted to make sure that everyone understood we were supporting free expression" (S. Gregory, 2019, para. 6). Silver said the league is "not only willing" to deal with the loss of millions in revenue, "but we are" (para. 2).

- **You were asked, because this was an issue of free speech, if U.S. government officials should have gotten involved, and if so, in what way?**

  Vice President Mike Pence said, "In siding with the Chinese Communist Party and silencing free speech, the NBA is acting like a wholly owned subsidiary of that authoritarian regime" (Rascoe, 2019, para. 5). And a bipartisan group of U.S. senators and representatives sent Silver an open letter, demanding the league suspend its relationships with China until "government-backed Chinese firms end their 'selective treatment' of the Houston Rockets" (Hoonhout, 2019, para. 6). It also criticized Silver and the NBA for not anticipating "the challenges of doing business in a country run by a repressive single party government" and for not standing up for Morey (Hoonhout, 2019, para. 3).

- **You were asked, should the NBA players have responded to the controversy, and if so, what should they have said or done?**

Players have weighed in, such as Rockets star James Harden, who apologized for Morey's remarks. Expressing his deep appreciation for the Chinese fans, Harden said, "We apologize, we love China, we love playing here," he said. "We appreciate them as a fan base, and we love everything they're about" (Wimbish, 2019, para. 3). Basketball legend Shaquille O'Neal defended Morey for his tweet in support of protestors in Hong Kong when he said, "One of our best values here in America is free speech" (Gajanan, 2019, para. 3). And LeBron James criticized Morey for not considering the potential ramifications of his tweet. "Even though yes, we do have freedom of speech, but there can be a lot of negative that comes with that, too . . . so many people could have been harmed, not only financially, but physically, emotionally, spiritually" (Wimbish & Ward-Henninger, 2019, para. 38).

Questions for further discussion:

- With the financial stakes so high, what moves should the NBA take to ensure a similar controversy doesn't happen again?

- How would you, as a player's publicist, counsel him on responding?

- What is the state of this issue today?

WRAP UP

After exploring the world of sports, tourism, and entertainment PR, it's likely you could see yourself in some role in these exciting fields, especially now that you know how "doing good" is both valued and acted on by athletes and leagues, destinations and agencies, and celebrities and entertainment institutions.

As you've learned, CSR is not viewed as an add-on by many of these athletes, actors, and high-profile personalities; CSR is seen as part of who they are and their public image. The same is true of adventure tours and ecotourism companies, whose core philosophies are rooted in sustainable tourism with a nature-first approach. For sports teams on every level, performing good works that benefit the communities they represent are embedded activities, not afterthoughts. All of these initiatives must be supported by professional communicators to ensure that both the recipients and the organizations benefit.

KEY TERMS

Content Producers 311
Ecotourism 298

General Entertainment 311
Talent 311

THINK ABOUT IT

The lack of diversity in MLB leadership can be seen at the annual managers' lunch reception that brings together managers from both the American League and National League.

A visual snapshot of this group makes it clear baseball's power structure remains overwhelmingly white and male, despite the fact most teams' roster positions are evenly filled with Hispanic, Black, Asian, and white players. There are few non-white managers and fewer still in any part of team ownership.

This lack of diversity extends to the umpiring crews, too—an almost all-white men's group.

With knowledge gained from this chapter, as well as previous chapters, what socially responsible steps do you think the MLB should take to address this problem?

WRITE LIKE A PRO

You are the PR specialist for your city or town's tourism bureau, and you need to create an infographic for its Instagram page. It should feature an upcoming holiday or summer event to attract and engage out-of-area visitors. Once you select the holiday or event, gather facts to build your case—in a clean and visually exciting manner. A good infographic meets the following criteria:

- Address your target audience.

- Be simple.

- Stay focused.

- Show things visually.

- Be a manageable length and size.

- Incorporate "white" space (meaning any space void of content).

Use any of the free infographic generators—for example, Canva, Easel.ly, Piktochart, Infogram, or Venngage.

SPORTS INNOVATION CASE STUDY

The Mouthguard That Became the "Talk of the Show" at CES

Situation

Concussions have dominated sports conversations over the last several years, and contact sports, especially football, have been at the center of that conversation. It's estimated that nearly half of the 3.8 million concussions that occur every year in the United States go undetected. A 2017 study reported the brains of 110 of 111 deceased ex-NFL players exhibited signs of CTE, caused by repeated blows to the head. There is much to be learned about what causes a concussion: Is it the impact location? Is it the impact velocity? Do repeated impacts to the head add up cumulatively to cause a concussion? Attempts to measure head impacts have proven inaccurate. Helmets with impact monitors record impacts *on the helmet*, not *to the brain*. But mouthguards hold more promise, as upper teeth are attached to the skull and therefore more accurately represent impacts to the brain.

Enter Prevent Biometrics, a Cleveland Clinic spinoff that spent 8 years developing technology with the potential to revolutionize the concussion discussion and consequently make it safer for athletes to continue to participate in the sports they love. Its flexible mouthguard—with a circuit

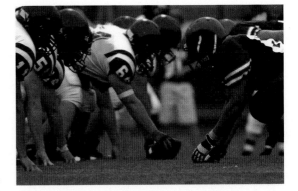

A PR stunt at the Consumer Electronics Show earned widespread media coverage for a new mouthguard.
iStock.com / fredrocko

board, sensors, and Bluetooth—notifies coaches and trainers instantly via an app when a player should be assessed for a possible concussion.

Research and Strategy

To launch its revolutionary mouthguard, Prevent Biometrics hired PR marketing firm Carmichael Lynch Relate. It needed to reach several audiences (coaches, trainers, parents, and researchers) at one time and saw an opportunity to make the company's industry-first technology the talk of the 2018 Consumer Electronics Show (CES). With a shoestring budget, it was up against electronic giants that spend nearly a year preparing for CES (and oftentimes spending millions of dollars for a show-stopping presence). The PR firm focused on using the CES presence to build demand for the product launch through media relations, a provocative in-booth demonstration, and a paid social media strategy to extend the booth experience beyond CES.

Execution

A preshow media event encouraged media to visit the booth. Videos were created with actual in-game footage of mouthguard-equipped athletes receiving impacts, overlaid with the alert sent to the coach on the sideline to demonstrate how the technology works in real time. During CES, the booth featured an engaging interactive demonstration to create buzz: Media members were encouraged to take a rubber mallet and hit a crash test dummy's head as hard as they could—to then instantly see the system at work in real-time action. This also provided a perfect visual for use on social media throughout the show.

Evaluation

The event secured coverage on *CNN Headline News* and Fox News on the morning CES opened. CNN kept a mouthguard for hours and included it in multiple live segments across time zones. This coverage created a groundswell of media interest from influential outlets, including Engadget and Wired, who both deemed the mouthguard a "Best of CES" winner. ABC's *Live With Kelly & Ryan* featured Kelly Ripa swinging the mallet at the crash dummy, helping to send the mouthguard message home to viewing parents. The PR efforts earned 1 billion media impressions, exceeding the client's goal by 600%. Eight months later, 40 teams and 2,500 high school and college football athletes were using the mouthguard system. The work of the PR firm earned it the PRSA Silver Anvil Award of Excellence in 2019.

Engage

- Using the search terms "Prevent Biometrics CES 2018," see the results of their media relations efforts and watch some of the videos demonstrating the device.

- This PR effort involved a stunt that generated significant and widespread engagement and extensive attention. Search online for "PR Sports Stunts" to see how events attract media and fan attention.

Discuss

- Much has been written about the risk of brain injuries in certain sports. Do you think professional sports and school organizations are adequately responding to this risk? How are they communicating this response?

Donna Ward / Stringer / Getty Images

14

Nonprofit, Health, Education, and Grassroots Organizations

Learning Objectives

14.1 Examine the nonprofit industry and illustrate how to plan and manage nonprofit campaigns

14.2 Review the scope of health communication and its need for specialized content

14.3 Identify how PR supports the multiple needs of educational institutions

14.4 Discover and assess how community and special-interest organizations use PR strategies for advocacy

Scenario
How Can We Keep Kids Safe in a World Filled With Risks?

A "Golden Halo" was awarded to Safe Kids Worldwide by Engage for Good, a clearinghouse that supports alliances between businesses and nonprofits. Safe Kids Worldwide was recognized for these accomplishments from three corporate sponsors, among others:

Safe Kids Worldwide partners with companies around the world, including FedEx, to promote ways that kids can work, play, and live safely.
Tommaso Boddi/Safe Kids Worldwide/Getty Images

Johnson & Johnson. J&J is a founding sponsor of Safe Kids. "Since 1988, J&J and Safe Kids have collaborated to teach families about child injury prevention, including water safety, fire safety, bike safety, medicine safety, home safety, and . . . youth sports safety" (Engage for Good, n.d., para. 4).

For example, to help reset the culture of youth sports and encourage its athletes to play *safely,* J&J and Safe Kids created a series of videos titled *Sports Safety 101.* This effort responded to findings that too many injured athletes are hiding that fact to keep playing, are getting hurt due to abusive actions during the game, or are returning to play even if they've suffered a concussion. The video series teaches better habits and better training for all involved: players, their coaches, and their parents.

General Motors (GM). The Buckle Up program resulted from a partnership between GM, the General Motors Foundation, and Safe Kids. Since its launch in 1997, it has expanded from a single focus on child safety seat checks at GM dealerships into a much larger program broadly addressing child safety—everything from heatstroke to teen-aged drivers.

An important arm of the partnership advocates for stronger state laws on child passenger safety. Buckle Up's success is measured by both lives saved and injuries prevented.

When Buckle Up started, almost 6,600 children and youth under age 19 died each year in car crashes. After two decades, that number of deaths has been cut by more than half. More than 2.3 million car seats have been inspected for proper installation, and nearly 800,000 car seats have been provided to at-risk families in the United States.

FedEx. Safe Kids Walk This Way is a program created by FedEx and Safe Kids in 1999 to bring local, national, and global attention to the issue of pedestrian safety. The pilot project that began in three U.S. cities has expanded to more than 225 towns and cities in the United States, as well as in nine more countries around the world.

Since the inception of the program, Safe Kids Walk This Way has reached families in thousands of U.S. communities. With one activity, International Walk to School Day, more than 18,100 FedEx volunteers provided families with life-saving information about pedestrian safety. The partners leveraged online channels, too, creating the interactive infographic about pedestrian safety titled "How to Not Get Hit by a Car."

(Continued)

(Continued)

Student Challenge

Use the lessons in this chapter to brainstorm:

What else should Fed Ex, GM, and Johnson & Johnson do, not only in the United States but in their global markets, to further the cause of children's safety?

Are there contemporary issues?

How should the companies communicate these initiatives?

At the end of the chapter, you'll explore and discover the wider extent of these partnerships—and measure your own solutions against the pros. ●

Source: Engage for Good, n.d.

This chapter first covers PR (public relations) for nonprofits, an extremely broad and expansive category of organizations in the United States—more than 1 million strong and growing. With this robust outlook, PR practitioners can expect ample career opportunities. Especially at the beginning of a PR career, the nonprofit is an excellent training ground (whether through volunteer work or paid employment), particularly for those with social media skills—a cost-efficient tactic for nonprofits.

Another growth area for PR practitioners is health communication. Americans are a more health-conscious population now than ever before and are seeking information and talking about it—online and in person. If your interest is in the field of science and health, opportunities abound with health care organizations and PR firms with health specialties.

The chapter next covers higher education and K–12 schools, which both offer challenging and rewarding careers for strategic communicators—especially in a competitive environment for funding and enrollment. The functions for a PR professional are wide-ranging, including management counsel, internal PR, media relations, capital campaigns, issues management, crisis communication, research, branding, and community relations.

Finally, you'll discover how grassroots community and special-interest organizations use PR strategies and tactics to pursue goals—for example, city residents organizing to promote road safety or to welcome refugees, and larger social movements like the Rainbow PUSH Coalition for social change and United Students Against Sweatshops.

Nonprofits: Size, Impact, and Opportunity for Public Relations Practitioners

>> **LO 14.1** **Examine the nonprofit industry and illustrate how to plan and manage nonprofit campaigns**

Ranging from neighborhood associations without assets that meet a few times a year to major foundations with billions of dollars—like the Bill and Melinda Gates Foundation—a wide variety of nonprofits operate in the United States.

The World of Nonprofits

Figures from the National Center for Charitable Statistics (NCCS) from 2016 show nonprofit organizations registered in the United States topped 1.5 million. This

FIGURE 14.1

Four Common Characteristics of Nonprofits

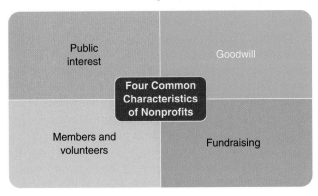

number included over a million public charities and around 100,000 private foundations and other kinds of nonprofit organizations, such as community leagues, fraternal groups, and chambers of commerce. As noted, public charities make up the largest portion by far. The U.S. health care field represents the largest segment of public charities, accounting for more than 55% of nonprofit jobs. These jobs are well paying: Nonprofit social assistance organizations' wages are over 50% higher than those at for-profits in the same field.

Nonprofit organizations are tax exempt and usually have the common characteristics of serving the public interest, fostering goodwill, serving members, recruiting volunteers, and fundraising to support their mission (see Figure 14.1). Nonprofits include what are considered traditional charities that serve the needy to houses of worship, food pantries, environmental organizations, labor unions, and museums. The website www.NCCS.urban.org provides up-to-date information on the nonprofit sector in the United States.

A Healthy Field With Its PR Challenges

Nonprofit employment grew by almost 17% from 2007 to 2016. In the same period, for-profit employment growth was less than 5%—that's job growth of over 3 to 1 (Salamon & Newhouse, 2019). Upon the election of Donald Trump to the U.S. presidency, donations to some nonprofits surged to bolster and protect their operations. However, upon passage of the Federal Tax Cut and Jobs Act in December 2017, a year into the Trump presidency, researchers projected the elimination of tax incentives would have a negative effect on their ability to generate donations from private sources. The Act also doubled exemptions for taxes on estates, thus reducing incentives for wealthy people to form charitable foundations (Salamon & Newhouse, 2019).

Fundraising, Development, and Recruiting

Among the most pressing issues for nonprofits are donor relations and communications (Duffin, 2019). Due to increased funding needs, employment of fundraising managers is expected to grow from 2018 to 2028, according to the U.S. Bureau of Labor Statistics (BLS, n.d.). It will be up to PR practitioners to make sure that charities' missions continue to be communicated broadly, recruiting volunteers and cultivating relationships with donors for them to remain aware and loyal.

Fundraising duties for PR practitioners in nonprofits include supporting or directly soliciting corporate and foundation monetary donations, as well as managing structured capital campaigns. Development goes after big gifts made to universities or hospitals. Often in the seven-figure category, they come from relationships cultivated over time, often decades—thus the term "development." This is how hospitals build buildings and universities endow faculty positions and establish new research institutes.

Other PR duties may include planning and running special events—fostering relationships with the many organizations that help support a cause—plus branding, networking with partners and sponsors, and membership and volunteer support. One study reports that among the top hiring priorities are strengthening the nonprofit's brand, improving organizational culture, and developing employee engagement (Nonprofithr, 2019). Media relations is another need, as PR practitioners maintain media contact with the mainstream press, along with trade and special interest media. Additionally, a key responsibility may be communicating with the nonprofit's multiple publics through direct mail, online media, and social media.

Nongovernmental Organizations

Nongovernmental organizations—often referred to as NGOs—are a category of nonprofit organizations. They are not a part of the government, nor are they operated though a government; however, they often collaborate with governments as well as other groups to partner in addressing common concerns. While not completely voluntary, they are primarily run by volunteers and are funded by donations.

NGOs are organized to perform a variety of service, humanitarian, and investigative functions around environmental and social issues, economic development, health care, and human rights. Typically, NGOs have a global presence; in fact, almost all NGOs based in the United States have some operations outside the United States—such as Human Rights Watch and the Committee to Protect Journalists.

Beyond the multiple outreach and engagement strategies PR practitioners employ in all types of organizations—social media, events, media relations—NGO tactics also include lobbying to influence policy debates and government legislation, as well as fundraising efforts. NGOs may also appoint well-known celebrities as spokespeople, helping attract attention and raise funds, and conduct full-blown communications campaigns that include multimedia PSAs and media kits.

Nonprofits' Use of Social Media

Social media offer a powerful way to allow nonprofits to engage their publics, collect funds, and inspire acts of advocacy. Research into how they do this on Twitter and Facebook offers guidance for messaging strategy to encourage user engagement. One study (Smith, 2018) examined the user engagement of 109 advocacy groups on social media, finding two social media platforms require a different type of communication and a different type of post.

In addition to typical media relations efforts, PR professionals at NGOs must consider fundraising strategies and lobbying efforts to advance the organization's goals.
iStock.com/Steve Debenport

What You Say Versus How You Say It

The study found that for Facebook, communication type—*what* you say—is more important when considering user engagement. For Twitter, post type—*how* you say it—is more important. What does this mean for nonprofits' use of Facebook and Twitter? The researchers conclude that when using Facebook, pay close attention to the content of the communication and make it focused to generate user dialogue. This should result in allowing nonprofits to learn what supporters and stakeholders have to say. A separate study (ICA, 2018) also identified the effectiveness of strong emotive messaging on Facebook. Whether positive or negative, emotion-carrying posts increase user likes, shares, and comments.

When using Twitter, the impact of a single post is enhanced with visual media. While posts may link to visual media, it's better to make pictures or video visible on the platform to increase user engagement plus increase willingness to act. These visual stimuli are more impactful on Twitter than on Facebook; however, visual stimuli are recommended on Facebook as well because they are more likely to be shared than are text or link posts.

SOCIAL RESPONSIBILITY IN ACTION

50th Anniversary of the Stonewall Uprising

When NYC Pride hosted the 2019 WorldPride celebration, it used visual branding to communicate more than 20 events.
Sean Drakes / Contributor / Getty Images

Each year, the nonprofit Heritage of Pride plans and produces the official LGBTQIA+ Pride events for New York City that commemorate the Stonewall Uprising of 1969, which is considered to be the event that ignited the modern gay rights movement. Known also as the Stonewall Riots, they were a series of spontaneous and sometimes violent rallies by members of the gay community in reaction to a police raid on the Stonewall Inn, a gay club in Greenwich Village. In an era of ingrained homosexual discrimination, the response to the raid was liberating for the gay community. Five decades later in June 2019, the city hosted the largest Pride celebration in the world, which stretched through the entire month. In conjunction with the 50th anniversary of the Stonewall Uprising, NYC Pride was awarded the opportunity to host WorldPride—marking the first time a U.S. city hosted the event.

AT&T served as the presenting sponsor of WorldPride NYC, along with numerous other corporations at varying sponsorship levels. The communications campaign involved over 20 events, including the WorldPride Opening Ceremony at Barclays Center, the WorldPride Closing Ceremony in Times Square, the iconic NYC Pride March, and the Human Rights Conference.

With respect to branding for the event, a visual campaign was developed to reflect the entire LGBTQIA+ community with special attention to diversity in race, age, sexual orientation, physical abilities, religious beliefs, and the like. Eboni Munn, NYC Pride's communications manager, cast more than 30 luminaries from the LGBTQIA+ community to speak to the breadth and depth of the community's history, its struggles and triumphs,

(Continued)

(Continued)

and posted their photographs to show their place within the history of the movement.

In all, over 20 events were branded in the original photography campaign for WorldPride NYC | Stonewall 50, and each event image told a different tale—of the event itself and the individuals selected to represent the moment. NYC Pride's official website promoted each event using the campaign images along with event pages

created on Facebook. When all was said and done, more than 5 million people attended the more than 20 events, leading to the largest LGBTQIA+ event in history.

The campaign was winner of PR News's Branding, Content Marketing, Social Networking Campaign, and Viral Campaign awards. ●

Source: PR News, 2019, and NYC Pride, n.d.

Health Communication

>> **LO 14.2** **Review the scope of health communication and its need for specialized content**

Thanks to a broad-based, increased focus on health, people have become more motivated to seek information and interact about their health with each other and with health care providers. Conversely, health care organizations are reaching out more to their members and communities and are actively engaging in public health issues, policies, and crises. Technology has facilitated the growth of digital health care networks and services (e.g., PatientsLikeMe, ZocDoc).

Health Communications in Organizations

A person who works to help others understand more about medical treatments, healthy lifestyle choices, disease prevention, and more is a health communications specialist, according to the Centers for Disease Control and Prevention (CDC, n.d.). Their focus is primarily on disseminating information to the public, which can have a positive impact on the population's health and well-being.

The growth of health awareness and engagement and the evolving health care landscape comes with new communication challenges and opportunities and is a key reason the field of health communications has become a strong growth area in PR. Career opportunities can include focusing on community relations, internal communications, publicity, and fundraising.

PR practitioners working for health care facilities generally handle both internal and external communication needs, programs, and campaigns. Internally, communications are with doctors, nurses, aides, managers, administrators, and patients. Externally, PR specialists disperse news as well as promote services and organize public events.

PR is growing in the health care field, with new opportunities to work on community relations, fundraising, and internal communications and to provide the public with key health and wellness information.
iStock.com/sturti

Health Communication Public Relations Agencies

Many PR agencies specialize in health communications. Clients include pharmaceutical and medical technology companies, health care start-ups, large hospitals, retail pharmacy chains, and nonprofit health organizations.

One respected ranking of North American PR agencies identifies the best "Health Care Agencies of the Year." In 2019, GCI Health ranked first, followed by four finalists. What qualified them for this recognition offers a lesson in best practices.

1. GCI Health is a specialty health care PR and communications agency based in New York City with offices in major U.S. cities, Canada, the United Kingdom, and Singapore. It has long put patients at the center of its purpose, but in 2018, it made the decision to talk about "people" at the center—taking a more holistic view by reaching out to physicians, pharmacists, and other influencers. Additionally, it launched the HealthiHer movement in partnership with Healthy Women and *Redbook* magazine. The platform was developed to address the fact that, when thinking about health, half of all women put others—spouses, children, and parents—ahead of themselves, and HealthiHer is challenging the rest of the industry to join the movement (PRovoke, 2019a). Search for HealthiHer to discover how it communicates with and engages stakeholders.

A WINNING CAMPAIGN FOR GCI

HealthiHer Minds, Bodies, Careers

Wendy Lund, CEO of GCI Health, spearheaded her firm's HealthiHer study, partnering with Healthy Women, a nonprofit health information source, and *Redbook* magazine. The study sought to discover how women manage their health. Their first survey revealed that nearly half of women ages 30 to 60 don't make time to focus on their health but rather take sole responsibility for their family's health care—and consequently experience a lot of stress and anxiety. Then, GCI surveyed women who work in PR and marketing, discovering they're not only stressed but ignore workplace benefits like wellness programs and behavioral health incentives.

How GCI arrived at the resulting HealthiHer initiative can be attributed in part to Lund's track record in health care leadership (Renfree, 2016). She started her 30-year career in the nonprofit world, as marketing vice president for the National League of Nursing and then for Planned Parenthood. After joining GCI in 2010, Lund oversaw the women's health franchise for Bayer, which created the Skyla Make Your Mark contest with partners *Glamour* magazine and its then-columnist, actress Zosia Mamet of HBO's TV series *Girls* (PMLive, n.d.). Creating the HealthiHer movement was a natural progression. When

the HealthiHer survey results first appeared in *Redbook*, an accompanying article coauthored by Joan Lunden, the women's health advocate and broadcast journalist, supported it.

The HealthiHER movement provides holistic support for women's health. On its website, women can find these tools:

- A regular newsletter
- Tools to build health literacy
- Links to measure and monitor one's health
- Links to improve overall health through physical activity
- Tips to avoid smoking, limit alcohol intake, and use sunscreen
- Feminine hygiene tips
- Over-the-counter medicine safety guidelines

It encourages women to join the conversation by posting a photo of their moment of self-care on Instagram, Facebook, or Twitter using #BeHealthiHER. The movement's Facebook page features community posts, photos and instructional and inspirational videos (Healthy Women, 2018). ●

2. DNA Communications (owned by Interpublic Group) is based in London and New York. DNA has spearheaded campaigns focused on leading health issues like addiction, cardiovascular disease, HIV treatment, and diabetes in the Hispanic community. In early 2018, the agency cosponsored the "Super Sick Monday" Super Bowl campaign. That same year it hosted a "Going Beyond Undetectable" conference to transform physician thinking regarding HIV. For its client Exelixis, a drug company needing to engage kidney cancer patients, DNA created a documentary-like video series telling real patients' stories. Thousands of patients responded via postings to the company's Facebook and Twitter pages (PRovoke, 2019a).

3. ReviveHealth (owned by Weber Shandwick/IPG) is based in Nashville. The agency made a big investment in data analytics in 2018, making data and research a core component of its approach to client service and ensuring its work is guided by facts. The agency's most creative and successful initiatives include crafting the "See Goodness" branding for EVP Eyecare, providing Penn State Health with a heroic health system brand in a crowded market, and launching a community movement to bring holistic care to the elderly and underprivileged in inner cities (PRovoke, 2019a).

4. RXMosaic (a Marina Maher/Omnicom agency) is based in New York. RXMosaic calls itself a "healthcare geek," emphasizing science and exploration in its "communications lab." Part of that positioning can be attributed to its emphasis on data-driven work. An example: The agency's Advocacy in Motion system puts real-time analytics and social listening together to advise companies on engagement with organizations and communities. Other products identify health care opinion leaders and microtarget patients with common interests and behaviors (PRovoke, 2019a).

5. Spectrum Science Communications, an independent firm based in Chicago, owes its success to a deep focus on health and science communications— especially biotech and health technology. It developed a compelling patient activation initiative, in partnership with the pharmaceutical company AbbVie, to help skin disease sufferers. It also partnered with the Sepsis Alliance to launch "It's About Time," an awareness and action initiative (PRovoke, 2019a).

PR PROFILE

Health Care Public Relations: A Higher Calling

John Seng, Founder and Former Chair, Spectrum Science Communications/GLOBALHealthPR.

What person hasn't had a family member, or him- or herself, affected by heart disease? Or diabetes? Cancer? Alzheimer's? Or some rare disease? Obviously, health care matters to a lot of people, and it involves everyone.

I believe that health care PR is a "higher calling" specialty for practitioners who make it their choice. Health is central to our lives. And communicating effectively to promote better health through health care PR is more than just storytelling. This specialty works at the intersection of health, science, and communication and offers the perfect career choice for a person who is interested in making a difference in the world.

Health care PR pros must understand how science works in medicine and must be able to communicate creatively and effectively to build awareness and change behavior.

And we must get it right, because lives of people we know and don't know depend on it. Health care PR practitioners wield tremendous power, and we must use it responsibly.

Our reach of influence far exceeds that of the average doctor with her or his patients. A family doctor in the United States sees about 19 patients a day. Don't get me wrong—that's a lot of people for one doctor to care for in the course of a day.

However, when a PR executive writes a blog post, schedules an interview, or conducts an event about a health care topic, the key messages can be seen by tens of thousands, even millions, of people in a day, if not an hour.

Assuming you own strong communications skills, excelling in health care PR comes down to four points:

1. Do you appreciate the life sciences? Can you emulate the curiosity of a scientist and the scientific process?

2. Can you learn to recognize and interpret quality science for storytelling purposes?

3. Will you respect the magnitude of what you do in terms of affecting people's lives and health policy? Do you have a knack?

4. Can you accept the responsibility that health PR experts must maintain to act ethically and responsibly?

Everyone depends on good health to live another day, so health care information must be accurate. If reporters or bloggers get it wrong, people can be harmed. If there's a new, lifesaving drug available but the right people don't hear about it, patients may not survive their disease. If people don't ask better questions of their doctors, they may receive inferior care.

Health care PR work is rewarding and always interesting. If you like science and technology and develop a passion to make a difference in health care, you will love this field. ●

Source: J. Seng, personal communication, 2020.

Health Communication Strategies

Enlisting employees to talk about the organization, keeping customer messaging focused, and sharing customer stories in social media are some of the best communication practices.

- Employee advocacy. Giving employees the freedom—with guidance—to talk about their organization on social media can be more effective than publishing a press release. Journalists increasingly seek real stories on social media, and employees are a valued source as authentic and trustworthy. According to the 2019 Edelman Trust Barometer, "my employer" is the most trusted source among the four societal institutions it evaluates: media, NGOs, the government, or business in general. Trust cements the employee–employer partnership, inspiring employees to engage in advocacy on behalf of their employer (Edelman, 2019).

- Consistent communication strategy. Put health customers at the center at multiple touchpoints; for example, ensure staff members understand the company's brand values and deliver them to customers; provide customers

About a quarter of teens are online nearly all day, making the Internet the best way to reach them.
iStock.com/JackF

with fast, easy access to information; and employ follow-up emails with personalized content.

- Storytelling. Share unique customer experiences and employee profiles in videos, newsletters, and on social media. Some of the most popular platforms like Facebook, Instagram, and Twitter offer easy avenues for storytelling. For example, create and share stories using the Twitter Moments feature, consisting of tweets and multimedia.

Health care publics are often defined by gender, race, age, location, and so on and combinations of those categories. This careful segmentation also affects choices of message delivery via mass media and interpersonal channels. Ninety-five percent of U.S. teens have access to a smartphone, and nearly half say they are "almost constantly" online (Anderson & Jiang, 2018), thus the Internet is likely an ideal source for adolescents seeking sensitive information—especially as it provides a one-way, confidential experience.

An earlier study (Deardorff, 2015) reported that 84% of U.S. teens ages 13 to 18 say they get health information online. The national survey of more than 1,000 teens also reported that nearly one third say they changed their health behaviors based on Internet searches, with medical websites most visited, followed by YouTube. Research draws this conclusion: Online media should be harnessed by communicators as important health information sources for adolescents, and multimedia content is essential.

For sexual health information, teens rely on the Internet as their primary source. One recent study (Starling et al., 2018) found that typically teens search for topics rather than a specific website. The study also found that personal stories were preferred when learning about sexual identity. However, teen-friendly-styled sites were avoided. Teens validated the online information with sex education and life experiences. PR practitioners can find guidance in research like this to influence recommendations for messaging campaigns.

Public Relations Support of Educational Institutions

>> LO 14.3   Identify how PR supports the multiple needs of educational institutions

Educational institutions serve the public as their primary function; thus, an important focus of PR is on two-way communications. PR identifies people's interests and attitudes to enlighten and influence the institution, as well as imparts information and engages publics to cultivate awareness, involvement, and support.

Contemporary conditions of dwindling financial resources, rapidly changing technologies, and an ever-competitive environment are all impacting educational institutions, increasing their communication needs with a wide range of audiences and stakeholders.

The Role of Public Relations in Higher Education

A problem between the general public and higher education is not that people are questioning what universities are actually doing or offering. Rather, the disconnect lies more with how universities are *communicating* what they are doing (i.e., preparing graduates for real careers or advancing research that improves society). This insight came out of the Edelman 2016 survey "University Reputations and the Public" (Edelman Insights, n.d.). Most important to the public is hearing education provides access to top job opportunities.

Therefore, to improve reputation, communications should assure the public that universities are impacting personal lives and society for the better, demonstrating this via media strategies like social networks, content sharing sites, and blogs. The place where the public discusses higher education is online, and while changing rapidly, that's where higher-education communicators should be.

Education journalists say communications staff at educational institutions play a large role in their reporting, according to a 2016 report by the Education Writers Association (CASE, n.d.). Even though one third of respondents admit they often find it difficult to get in-person access to schools and college campuses for reporting purposes, they emphasize that schools' PR efforts are an important part of education coverage. News releases, news conferences, or PR professionals themselves are the top sources of story ideas for 88% of the education journalists surveyed.

Social Media Strategies

As noted earlier, social and digital online content is a preferred avenue for connecting with education publics. *Inside Higher Ed* offers the following advice (Read, 2017).

Align Social Media Goals With Institutional Goals

Social media gives institutions the ability to target information sharing and enables interactive communication among the current student body, prospective students, alumni, and other important audiences. Social media goals need to be weighed in the context of the institution's overall goals. What are the most important issues—retention? New enrollment? Alumni engagement? Next, define what is social media success in support of those goals. This provides clear direction and a measurement for success.

Match Platform(s) With Audience(s)

Decide what platforms connect with the appropriate audiences. Not every platform is appropriate for your needs—some will be better than others at reaching specific audiences. You'll want to research which platform will do the best job of reaching your institution's targets based on their characteristics (demographics, goals, preferences, motivators, etc.). Those are the platforms to focus on.

Define Your Institution's Authentic Social Media Voice

Prior to thinking about the content you'll share on social media, it's important to consider your institution's current social media voice. Is there

Colleges and universities must make clear the ways they improve society and individuals' lives.
Imeh Akpanudosen/Getty Images

a tone? What's its personality and point of view? Consistence is key in all communication, so your social media voice should closely align with your institution's tone and voice. One excellent method of determining voice is to identify the most important three or four adjectives you want your target audiences to think of in describing your institution.

Audit the Institution's Social Media Profiles

The audit must include your institution's primary profile along with any others being managed on the school or department level, including athletics (see Figure 14.2). If you uncover unauthorized accounts, duplicate accounts, and so on, action must be taken to disable, remove, or address those accounts. Then, work closely with those people in charge of the remaining profiles across campus to ensure there's a shared understanding about the purpose and goals for each. Also be sure to optimize all institution-affiliated social media profiles. Here's how:

- Be sure the look and feel of every profile remains consistent with your institution's brand identity, including logos, color schemes, images, and messaging.

- Establish an engagement policy. The policy must clearly articulate expectations for every post and comment as well as the consequences if the policy is violated.

- Draw up a detailed social media editorial calendar, mapping out planned posts for the month that reflect your target audiences and goals. Everything you are aware of in advance should be included, such as posts related to future events, announcements, and content packages such as video or other campaigns. The calendar should also outline the time of day content should be posted and shared to increase engagement (drawn from analytics tools).

- Exploit the full potential of the analytics tools available to you. Regularly review the data to see which posts are getting the most "hits" (greatest engagement), what hours your audiences are most engaged, and so on. Pay close attention to the best-performing content topics and types in order to use that information to shape your planning.

FIGURE 14.2

Consistency Is Key

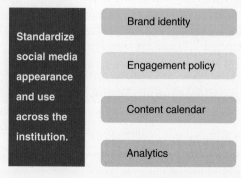

K–12 Education

K–12 education has a long history of active debate and involvement by multiple publics. The National School Public Relations Association (NSPRA, n.d.a) has 1,800-plus members, many of whom serve at one of the 13,500 public school districts in the United States (Educationdata.org, 2018). To better understand the need for and function of PR in education, the NSPRA (n.d.b) identifies and defines 11 major functions provided by PR staff. As you can see by this list (see Table 14.1), working in PR for a school district is an all-encompassing role that demands versatility and offers challenges to communicate with diverse publics. It builds a wide range of PR proficiencies in a specialty that many choose to embrace for the benefits it provides the community.

Multicultural Public Relations and Education

Twenty-first century America will be the most multicultural and pluralistic country on earth, with ethnic connections to every area of the world. By 2045, more than half of the U.S. population will be made up of ethnic consumers (Frey, 2018b). This emerging segment of multicultural consumers is going to demand a different set of engagement touch points as it applies to building relationships with organizations and companies and connecting with their brand stories.

Another priority will be engaging the heavily multicultural talent pool of the next generation. Already, 44% of the current U.S. millennial population is multicultural (Frey, 2018a). This is a generation whose opinions are influenced by social media, cultural preferences, a world view, and a brand's corporate citizenship. Companies

TABLE 14.1

Ten Major Functions of Public Relations in K–12 School Districts

	FUNCTION	GOAL
1.	PR counsel	Takes a proactive stance, anticipating problems and providing solutions
2.	Communication with internal and external publics	Produces all district publications, such as external newspaper and internal newsletter; publicizes student and staff achievement; develops staff and retirement recognition programs
3.	Media relations	Secures local media coverage of district news and serves as media liaison with district
4.	Budget and bond issue campaigns	Promotes community input to budget process and develops budget and bond issue campaigns and publications
5.	Communications planning	Develops communications plan for internal and external publics; develops crisis communications plan
6.	Research	Conducts surveys, polls, and informal research to determine public opinion as a basis for planning and action
7.	Imaging and marketing	Promotes district's brand, strengths, achievements, and its solutions to problems; plans for school district anniversary celebrations
8.	Community relations liaison	Liaises with grassroots organizations, civic associations, and service clubs and helps plan and publicize district's service programs
9.	Information station for the district	Answers public and new resident requests and keeps district's historical records
10.	PR trainer	Provides advocacy, media, and crisis communications training to staff and parent–teacher associations

Source: NSPRA (n.d.). Getting Started. Retrieved from https://www.nspra.org/getting_started.

must create and market a new employee experience in order to resonate with them. Multicultural PR practitioners from all walks of life and diverse backgrounds should have a seat at the table.

HP's Reinvent Mindsets

HP, along with Edelman, developed its award-winning campaign series "Reinvent Mindsets" (PRSA, 2019b) to educate society on the advantages of nurturing a diverse employee base by bringing to light the rampant stereotyping and unconscious bias common in today's hiring environment. Despite the reality that the United States will soon become a minority-majority population, this is not reflected in a variety of community leadership positions, particularly in corporate leadership. However, study after study shows diversity yields better business results, both from building more diverse ideas and representing key audiences.

First, HP conducted focus groups with its own employee advocacy groups. It then connected with leaders representing diverse communities. HP needed to hear firsthand of the challenges and experiences various groups face regularly and in hiring practices. The goal was to better understand the issues to address. Information gained from this research led to a creative brief for the overall campaign. The conversations also inspired the creation of a series of short films, some using comments pulled from early meetings (Beaubien, 2019a).

Partnership With HBCUs

Based on the statistic that, even when qualified for a position, African Americans are three times as likely to be denied (Beaubien, 2019a), HP produced the "Let's Get in Touch" campaign to focus on the issue, drawing from its own training of managers to reduce unconscious bias. The campaign consisted of media efforts, attendance at job fairs, public speaking, partner events, and several short videos highlighting the challenges diverse groups face in the hiring process. It also led to a partnership with historically Black colleges and universities (HBCUs) of America and the launch of the HBCU Business Challenge that provides hands-on experience to help prepare students and provide a pipeline to careers.

Public Relations in Grassroots Organizations

>> **LO 14.4**   **Discover and assess how community and special-interest organizations use PR strategies for advocacy**

Community and special-interest organizations are groups of people who assemble with a like-minded purpose concerning community-level or special-interest issues. They are ordinary citizens from neighborhoods, school districts, cities, or broader boundaries, driven by a common interest or concern. They are not a part of government, nor are they a for-profit business, but they are a grassroots effort that voluntarily forms a collaborative community, self-organized and without governmental support. While some may be incorporated as a nonprofit, others may be informally organized as an unincorporated nonprofit association.

Public Relations Tactics

Depending on the issues and the size of the groups, many traditional PR tactics can help advance the group's mission and produce desired results, including email, letter-writing, and phone call campaigns; websites and social media; and events and public meetings to build community, share information, and get media attention. In situations needing immediate attention and action, they may adopt activist tactics, including unannounced visits to political offices, rallies, vigils, demonstrations, boycotts, and acts of civil disobedience. At the receiving end of activist engagement, best practices for targeted organizations are to personally meet with representatives to share information and perspectives leading to understanding, consensus, compromise, or some mutually agreed-upon resolution.

Women attending the grassroots Women's March on Washington and other cities around the world wore "pussy hats" to signal their unity and their protest of Donald J. Trump's treatment of women.
Credit: Johanna Page

Communication strategies and tactics reflect the context of the issue. It may be a small group, perhaps townspeople advocating for slower speed limits on streets due to a pedestrian tragedy, or a much larger group like Mothers Against Drunk Driving, and still different yet, possibly a large, loosely organized movement like Occupy Wall Street, which formed in response to the late-2000s financial crisis in the United States. The Women's March on Washington on January 21, 2017, offers a good example of a fast-moving response to the surprise Trump victory in the 2016 presidential election.

Sometimes, It Just Takes Two

Two Women's Facebook Posts Inspire Half a Million

With limited resources, grassroots community and special-interest groups can take giant steps toward meeting their goals with strategic online communication. Teresa Shook is credited for the idea of a women's march in response to the 2016 election. The night after the election, Shook, a retired attorney and grandmother of four, suggested a protest on a Facebook page she created. By the end of the evening, there were 40 RSVPs, and when she woke up, there were more than 10,000. On the same evening, Bob Bland, a fashion designer from Brooklyn, also used Facebook to propose a women's protest. (During the campaign season, Bland had already compiled a list of several thousand politically minded followers. After the election, she created T-shirts that read "Nasty Woman," which she sold to raise funds for Planned Parenthood.) Shook and Bland merged their events, other women volunteered to be organizers, and the word spread (Tolentino, 2017).

The organizers wrote a diversity statement to ensure inclusivity and included veteran non-white activists in the leadership. They also clarified that men should participate, writing that the Women's March invites "all defenders of human rights" to attend. The march experienced critical debate and infighting exhaustively on Facebook, acknowledged Jia Tolentino in *The New Yorker:* "Activism is internally contentious by nature. Organization is always tedious" (Tolentino, 2017, para. 10). Yet it grew to one of the largest-ever political demonstrations in Washington, DC, reported at 500,000 (see Table 14.2), with fundraising for the event largely coming in portions of $20 and $30 online donations. "It really remind(ed) me of the Sanders campaign," Linda Sarsour, a Palestinian-American Muslim activist from Brooklyn, told CNN. "A very grassroots, very grass-powered movement" (Krieg, 2017, para. 43).

TABLE 14.2

Headlines Tell Their Story

Beginning on November 12, 2016, with an early report by CNN—"Tens of Thousands Plan Women's March on Washington"—headlines began to tell its evolving story of diversity and magnitude.

"200,000 Expected to Protest Trump the Day After Inauguration"	Townhall	December 17
"Canadian Women to Join Washington March on Day After Trump's Inauguration"	Toronto Star	December 31
"How the Women's March on Washington Has Gone Global"	Huffington Post	January 5
"These Girls From Chicago's Toughest Area Raised $2,000 to Join the Women's March on Washington"	The Tab	January 17
"Latinas Are Playing a Major Role in the Women's March on Washington"	Latina	January 18
"Half a Million People Show Up for D.C. Women's March"	NY Daily News	January 21
"Women's March on Washington Yields Zero Arrests"	The Hill	January 22

INSIGHTS

Activism Is Now the New Normal

Activism is becoming a regular activity for an increasing number of Americans, according to research conducted by the PR firm Ruder Finn (Marshall, 2019). Nearly 9,000 people participated in an online survey, with 500 receiving a follow-up survey. Its key findings reveal that activism is growing and that people have a complex understanding and relationship with companies:

- **Activism is mainstream.** It crosses all age groups. More than half (53%) took recent actions to support a social issue, and most of them had recently done so multiple times. Surprisingly, the most active were Gen Xers, followed by baby boomers; the 25 to 34 demographic was less active, and the 18 to 24 generation was least active. About two thirds of the actions were cause-related (protest marches, petitions, donations, social media activity, volunteering), and one third were related to a company, both pro and con.

- **Media and employers are drivers of action.** News stories and social media are the strongest drivers of actions. Yet people were more likely to be inspired to act in support of a social cause based on the involvement of their employer more so than through influence from family and friends.

- **Companies are under suspicion.** Slightly more than half don't believe companies will act in the best interests of all Americans—

that is, they won't promote a fair economy. Companies that are making positive social impacts, like Apple's commitment to addressing homelessness in California, are helping to change negative perceptions.

- **Activist companies win approval.** But only if true to their brand. Even if their actions on a social cause or issue go against one's personal beliefs, most Americans are forgiving if the firm communicates the importance of the issue. But again, it must be true to the brand. The top five companies most admired for taking social stands: Nike, Chick-fil-A, Apple, Amazon, and Patagonia. While Nike's ad with Colin Kaepernick was controversial, it aligned with the brand and was authentic.

- **Top five issues people care about are diverse.**

  1. Animal health and welfare
  2. The environment and climate issues
  3. Gun control
  4. Children's issues
  5. Women's issues ●

Sources:

Steve Barnes. (2019, Dec. 12). Activism is new normal, says RF study. O'Dwyer's: The inside news of PR and marketing communications. https://www.odwyerpr.com/story/public/13520/2019-12-12/activism-is-new-normal-says-rf-study.html

Monica Marshall. (2019). Activism goes mainstream: A look at who's taking action and why. https://www.ruderfinn.com/wp-content/uploads/Activism-goes-mainstream_report.pdf

After 2017, the Women's March became an annual event in large and small U.S. cities, drawing hundreds of thousands of participants each year—galvanized by the Trump administration policies as well as the #MeToo movement.

Two Bostonians Stop the Olympics

Activism can start small but mushroom when social media and a motivating cause meet. In 2013, a plan was made to bring the 2024 Summer Olympics to Boston. The Olympic boosters promised enormous benefits—with little financial support from the taxpaying public. However, the truth was their plan required billions of dollars in construction of venues using taxpayer dollars, including covering cost overruns.

With little more than a Twitter account, a website, and a PowerPoint presentation, an organization was launched in 2013 whose name spoke for itself: No Boston Olympics—a grassroots effort to battle the private group organizing the city's Olympics bid. Founders Chris Dempsey (2017) and Liam Kerr doubted the benefits the boosters claimed and believed the years of planning would pull attention away from other critical social needs.

No Boston Olympics had a virtually nonexistent budget, but facts led their charge. Research revealed the beneficiaries of past Olympic cities were mainly big businesses, and the losers were the hospitality industry, public housing, and residents. The campaign also garnered community engagement over the secretive pro-Olympics process. A local newspaper labeled the effort to take over a treasured park a secret conspiracy of tycoons and special interests and called on residents to organize to oppose it. No Boston Olympics used focused messaging to identify the damaging side effects of the games—including the excess costs the city and state would be obliged to pay through a taxpayer guarantee.

The United States Olympic Committee (USOC) decided on Boston's bid. It appeared the stage was set for the International Olympic Committee (IOC) to award the Olympic Games to Boston, but 6 months later, Boston residents shocked city leaders by rejecting the proposal to host the Olympics.

The success of No Boston Olympics showed that an underfunded group of diverse and engaged citizens could join together to challenge a powerful group of boosters and ultimately derail the Olympic bid by demanding transparency and accountability and coordinating dissenting voices.

Two Partners Spark a Movement

The connection between school bullying and suicides among gay teens prompted syndicated columnist Dan Savage and his partner Terry Miller to create the "It Gets Better Project" channel on YouTube. In 2010, they posted their first video sharing their own stories of surviving adolescence and the happiness they'd found as adults. In the first week, more than 200 videos arrived, and soon, they were deluged with emails from lesbian, gay, bisexual, transgender, and queer (LGBTQ) adults, teens, and their parents.

Realizing he'd touched on something bigger, Savage sought to turn the viral concept into a lasting movement and asked Blue State Digital (BSD), a digital strategy and technology firm specializing in online advocacy, for help. According to its website, BSD is committed to bridge differences, defend civil and human rights, and help its clients put people first (Blue State, n.d.). Clients have ranged from Obama's presidential campaigns, the NAACP, Google, and the Green Bay Packers.

Partnering with It Gets Better, BSD created the online infrastructure—a digital platform and clearinghouse to drive messaging, fundraising, and advocacy outcomes. The site was designed to get people involved, first by pledging to speak out against anti-LGBTQ bullying, and second, for them to upload their own inspiring stories. As of 2020, more than 625,000 people have taken that pledge of support, some 70,000 people have signed on to say that "it gets better," and the thousands of videos uploaded to the YouTube It Gets Better channel and to www.ItGetsBetter.org have been viewed by millions (It Gets Better, 2020).

Its Twitter (@itgetsbetter) provides constant updates on stories of interest to the LGBTQ community and their supporters, friends, and families, and in 2012, the project earned the Emmy's Governors Award. By 2019, It Gets Better had expanded to 16 countries and had become a fixture at World Pride events. At the 2020 Sundance Film Festival, the It Gets Better House was created for "queer talent to tell their stories."

Scenario Outcome

At the beginning of this chapter, you read about a winner of the Golden Halo Award for nonprofits, Safe Kids Worldwide, and its corporate sponsors GM, FedEx, and Johnson & Johnson. You were asked to stretch your vision beyond the SR (social responsibility) programs listed in this introduction and to recommend new outreach and initiatives.

First, visit www.safekids.org to understand the breadth of this program. Then, to see if you're thinking like the CSR professionals at the three firms, explore their safety SR pages and some specific initiatives through visiting the sites that follow.

FedEx

First, visit www.fedexcares.com and select the "Road Safety" link. There, you will find its report *2019 Road Safety Matters*. Browse this 20-page booklet to discover the other partnerships and initiatives FedEx has engaged in to advance road safety. Who and what did you find? Did you imagine this breadth of partnerships? When you think about road safety, it invites a wide variety of public entities to invest time, money, and talent behind this critical cause. Did you brainstorm an opportunity that FedEx missed?

GM

Visit www.gmsustainability.com/ and under the "Manage" link, select "Community" and scroll down to "Vehicle and Road Safety." Here, you will find GM's story about community safety. Also go to gm.com/our-stories.htlm and search in the Community category. Using your initial knowledge of GM's participation and drawing from lessons in this chapter, how did you imagine GM could extend its good work regarding road safety? How would you communicate it? Did you brainstorm an opportunity that GM missed?

Johnson & Johnson

Visit www.safekids.org/sports-safety-101, and browse the videos, all sponsored by J&J. What do you feel are the most effective parts of these videos? How could you promote more viewing of these videos? How would you extend some of the content of these videos into a WOM (word-of-mouth), interactive, or special-event strategy?

In this chapter, you explored the communication needs of nonprofit, health, education, and special-interest community organizations and the role of PR. You discovered that these specialty areas offer strong career opportunities for the PR practitioner. No doubt you've observed personally the increased communication about health issues and the competitive environment educational institutions are in. And you probably participated in a special-interest community organization—or know someone who did—and realized the importance of strategic communication to advance issues and concerns. By engaging with this chapter's lessons and case studies, you had a trial run at handling the challenges and opportunities confronting a PR professional, from major campaigns like #GivingTuesday to the ad hoc effort of No Boston Olympics.

KEY TERMS

Nongovernmental Organizations (NGOs) 324

THINK ABOUT IT

Nonprofit organizations should use both one-way and two-way communication strategies and content characterized by openness, disclosure, access, positivity, and evidence of collaborations. Analyze a Facebook page of a nonprofit, based on the following criteria:

- Openness and disclosure: Is information available in the About, Founded, and Mission sections?

- Access: Is a website link, along with phone numbers and email information, listed?

- Positivity: Look at the organization's past 10 posts. How many photos and videos are included in them? Engaging visual communication helps build relationships of trust and satisfaction.

- Assurance: Are they actively responding to users' questions in a timely manner?

- Collaborations: Is there evidence of networking and sharing of tasks? Look for organization posts mentioning other groups and partnerships. This content demonstrates the organization's mission and has been shown to support fundraising.

WRITE LIKE A PRO

Word clouds are an eye-catching visualization tool to communicate important information at a glance—whether on an organization's blog, social media platforms, or website. They're also a solution for adding visual interest when you have a lot of text without a ready image. Some free word cloud generators are found at www.wordclouds.com or www.worditout.com.

You will now create a word cloud for a nonprofit organization's blog. First, identify a nonprofit in your local area and find its mission or vision statement on its website. Then, go to the word cloud generator of your choice and create a word cloud by pasting the mission or vision statement into its "Word List" area. Try different colors and fonts to experiment with results. After you're satisfied with the word cloud, save it as a JPEG or pdf or just take a screenshot.

Hit Me With Your Flu Shot

Situation

Flu vaccinations can reduce flu illnesses, ER and doctors' visits, missed work and school, and hospital stays. The 2017–2018 flu season was the worst in the United States since 1976, with the U.S. Centers for Disease Control and Prevention reporting 80,000 deaths from flu. By vaccinating as many employees as possible in a 1-day event, Christiana Care Health System—a chain of private hospitals in eastern states—sought to protect its workers from falling sick and better protect patients and visitors at its facilities. The goals of the campaign were to motivate as many employees as possible to get their flu shot on the day of the event and gain positive media coverage.

Research and Strategy

Research shows influenza outbreaks in health systems are tied to low rates of employee vaccinations. Since the flu season can stretch from December to May, Christiana Care offers voluntary vaccination for its employees October through March and generally achieves over a 90% rate. However, vaccinating employees over several months strains the system. Additionally, past surveys showed nonclinical employees and those not at the system's two major hospitals had low vaccination rates.

As the largest private employer in Delaware, Christiana Care has over 11,000 employees in 70-plus locations in four states. Challenges included employee awareness at all locations, including night workers. To create a catchy campaign name, the event's systemwide planning committee and its entire external affairs department submitted entries. The clear winner was #HitMeWithYourFluShot, with a theme and style built on the Pat Benatar song "Hit Me With Your Best Shot." To address the low vaccination rates among nonclinical employees, a 1-day photo shoot was arranged, with employees serving as models. They posed with flexed arms (to symbolize the strength a flu shot gives the immune system) and neon green bandages.

Execution

These images were featured systemwide on colorful standups, flyers, intranet sites, digital boards, and screensavers. The theme created a buzz among staff and spurred conversation around the campaign. Media was invited to cover the event, and an advance story ran on *PhillyVoice.com* the morning it launched. Employees took "flu shot selfies" and tagged them #HitMeWithYourFluShot, and Gannett's *The News Journal* covered it as a Facebook Live event at the system's city-based hospital. Employees sang "Hit me with your flu shot . . . needle away" while they got vaccinated and told colleagues how fun the event was, which then motivated others to get vaccinated. WJBR-FM, a local top-40 station, broadcast live from Christiana Hospital, and the event featured a photo booth and raffle prizes.

Vaccination kits were dropped off at Christiana Care locations throughout the four-state region, where staff members photographed themselves with

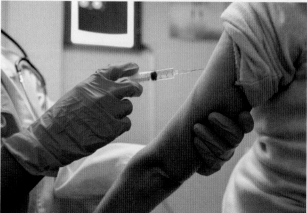

iStock.com / Wavebreakmedia

flexed arms to emphasize their flu bandage, which they then shared on social media. *NBC National News* online did stories on the campaign and, piggybacking off a recent study on the importance of pregnant women getting vaccinated, identified a pregnant employee to speak to *NBC National News*. Three of the top four Philadelphia area television stations broadcast positive stories on the event.

Evaluation

The #HitMeWithYourFluShot campaign resulted in nearly 7,900 employees, volunteers, and allied staff professionals getting their flu shot over a 17-hour time span, propelling the health system close to its overall goal of 10,000. After the event, employees continued to get flu shots, and by January 2019—before the midpoint of the flu season—Christiana Care had vaccinated more than 10,300 members of its workforce. A survey of 700 employees conducted afterward found all respondents were aware of the event.

Engage

In 2019, for the second year in a row, Christiana Care's #HitMeWithYourFuShot campaign succeeded in vaccinating employees—this time more than 8,000 in a single day.

- Search for the company and hashtag to see how the campaign has succeeded in recent years and if new tactics have been used.

Discuss

- If you were leading internal communications and media relations for Christiana Care, how might you improve the campaign next year?

- Consider health and retail facilities in your area that offer flu shots. Choose one and brainstorm how would you apply this type of campaign to its publics or just one segment, such as young children or the elderly.
  Note: #HitMeWithYourFluShot received a 2019 PRSA Silver Anvil Award of Excellence and won first place in the "Cause Marketing Campaign" category of PR Daily's 2019 Media Relations Awards.

Source: PRSA, 2019a.

15

Public Affairs, Government Relations, and Political Communications

Learning Objectives

15.1   Understand the similarities and differences between public affairs and PR

15.2   Understand government relations and lobbying

15.3   Develop an understanding of political communications in the modern era

Infectious disease outbreaks are not infrequent, and each poses its own unique communication challenges. In 2014, an outbreak of Ebola was detected in West Africa. As the disease progressed, it spread across borders in the region. Soon, an international panic was imminent, and people grew concerned that an infected individual could transport the virus to other parts of the world, including the United States.

In late 2019, COVID-19 (i.e., the novel coronavirus) appeared in China and soon created a global panic, leading to record stock market declines and impacting the 2020 presidential primary elections in the United States. As of this writing, the crisis was still underway, but there is no doubt many case studies will be prepared based on how the government and private sector responded.

The Ebola outbreak posed both medical and communications challenges for the government agencies and hospitals involved.
iStock.com/zmeel

In the Ebola crisis, the U.S. government acted quickly at the direction of President Obama, developing a rapid response to protect the health of its citizens and help individuals in Africa. The National Institutes of Health (NIH), which is part of the U.S. Department of Health and Human Services, played a vital role in this collaborative effort.

Two U.S. nurses infected. The growing fear surrounding the outbreak and its potential to spread to the United States reached a peak in the fall of 2014. This was when Thomas Eric Duncan, a Liberian visiting his family in Dallas, Texas, was diagnosed with Ebola and died, following his hospital admission. Two nurses who treated him became infected with the virus while caring for Duncan: 26-year-old Nina Pham and 29-year-old Amber Vinson.

Reports began to circulate in the national media, suggesting flawed safety procedures at the hospital that treated Mr. Duncan. This had the effect of casting doubt on the ability of the medical infrastructure in the United States to prevent the Ebola outbreak that many feared was imminent. Once it was determined that the two American nurses required highly specialized treatment, the decision was made to fly them to hospital facilities with specially trained clinicians and special biocontainment capabilities to isolate and treat such highly infectious patients. As a result, Ms. Vinson was sent to Emory University Hospital in Atlanta, Georgia, and Ms. Pham was sent to the Special Clinical Studies Unit at the NIH Clinical Center in Bethesda, Maryland.

Heightened public concern. In Bethesda, the NIH staff, including communications personnel, had to quickly get ready for Ms. Pham's arrival. Working alongside the clinicians and scientists, the agency's communications staff had to prepare to address several important, but conflicting, concerns:

- How would the agency balance transparency with protecting the patient's privacy?
- How would the agency communicate that Ms. Pham was receiving excellent care while also acknowledging the riskiness of this disease?
- How would NIH balance its pride in having a facility capable of accommodating such a high-risk patient with the heightened public and employee fears about the risks involved?

A comprehensive, science-based communications plan was needed, and the stakes were high for the NIH, its employees, and the citizens living near the hospital. In addition, media interest was at a fever pitch and would likely continue throughout the entire episode.

(Continued)

(Continued)

As you read this chapter, consider the following:

   a. How did the government setting (public affairs) guide the practice of communications?

   b. How are issues and crisis management both *similar* and *different* in this setting—as compared to the private sector?

   c. How should the NIH communications team manage this unique, global challenge?

   d. How was the management of the Ebola crisis different from the coronavirus pandemic in 2020? ●

In previous chapters, you have learned that PR can have many names, depending on the setting where the work is done and the audience you are targeting. In this chapter, you will learn about PR in a government setting—such as at the NIH in the opening scenario—which is usually called *public affairs*. If your career path takes you into the U.S. military, public affairs is the common name for PR work there as well.

As well, you will be introduced to **government relations**, a hybrid of PR, sometimes referred to as **lobbying**. You will also learn about **political communications**, which is usually deployed in election campaigns by elected officials and their senior staff. The goal of this chapter is to make you familiar with each segment and help you understand the differences between them and traditional PR.

Public Affairs, Government Relations, and Political Communications

>> **LO 15.1   Understand the similarities and differences between public affairs and PR**

Let's begin with some definitions to help you understand how public affairs, government relations, and political communications are both different and similar from traditional PR (see Figure 15.1). Later in the chapter, you will learn about these concepts

FIGURE 15.1

Categories of Government-Based Communications

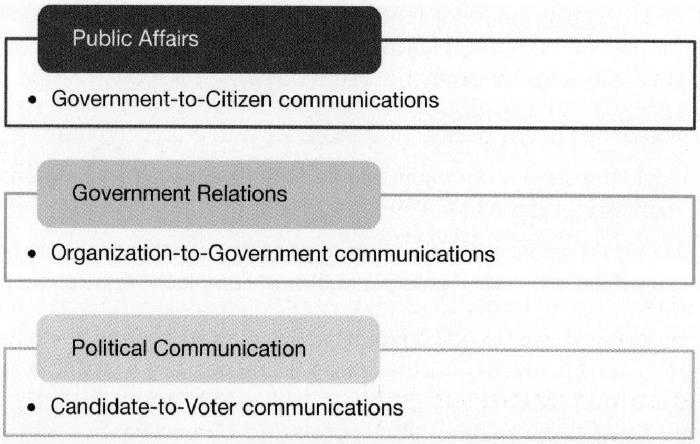

Public Affairs
- Government-to-Citizen communications

Government Relations
- Organization-to-Government communications

Political Communication
- Candidate-to-Voter communications

and review examples of each. Note that a common thread to communications in a government setting is a focus on public service.

- Both public affairs professionals and PIOs (public information officers) focus on *government-to-citizen communications*.

An Overview of Public Affairs, Government Relations, and Political Communication

Public Affairs

Public affairs in a government setting usually combines media relations, crisis communications, issues management, social responsibility (SR), and public information, as well as strategic communications advice. A **public information officer (PIO)** is a related title and function to public affairs and is often used by government agencies. PIOs have a variety of job duties, but written and verbal communication and media relations are the basis for much of what they do. Speechwriting and preparing testimony for public hearings and community meetings are other key duties of a PIO.

It is important to note that government communicators are restricted from promoting a candidate or elected official while working for the government. The Hatch Act, which prohibits this activity for government employees, was passed by Congress and signed by President Franklin Delano Roosevelt in 1939 and updated by President Barack Obama in 2012.

Campaign activities fall into the political communications arena (see the "Applying Public Relations Strategy to Campaigns and Elections" section in this chapter), and there are strict prohibitions against using public money for political purposes. Should a communicator desire to get involved in a campaign, the usual practice is to resign or take a leave of absence and be paid by the campaign instead of the government.

Government Relations

Government relations is the branch of communications that helps organizations communicate with government agencies and elected officials. A comprehensive government relations effort usually includes lobbying of government officials directly. The principal activity of lobbying is direct contact with politicians, regulators, and senior staff to express your organization's point of view.

- Activities in this area focus on *organization-to-government communication*.

Political Communication

Political communication is typically done by a press secretary or campaign communications staff on behalf of an elected official or a candidate for office. This work also entails media relations, social media, speechwriting, and strategic messaging, as well as communications support for get-out-the-vote and campaign fundraising efforts.

- The focus of these efforts is on *elected official (or candidates)-to-public (or voter) communications*.

David Payne, founder and CEO of Codavate, a digital communications and public affairs firm in Washington, DC, distinguishes the terms in this way:

Based on my experience, *public affairs* involves indirect communication aimed at impacting policy and legislative outcomes. *Political communication* consists of regulated speech that influences campaigns for elected office. And *government relations* is a euphemism for direct lobbying of policy makers to influence regulations or laws. (D. Payne, personal communication, 2017)

Public Affairs as Compared to Public Relations

In earlier chapters, you learned that the job titles "public affairs officer" or "public information officer" became more common in government settings, starting early in the 20th century. There's an interesting story behind this shift.

Why Does the Government Call It Public Affairs?

Following the success of publicity agents and publicists in the 1800s and early 1900s, government agencies began to employ PR (public relations) professionals to help shape public opinion. Some business interests were concerned about the potential impact, and they pressured Congress to restrict the allocation of funds to government agencies for publicity purposes. Additional pressure was put on Congress from politicians and activists concerned that "PR" activity could be used to manipulate public opinion against the best interests of the public. As a result, the Gillett Amendment was added to the legislation that created the Interstate Commerce Commission (ICC) in 1913 (Taylor & Kent, 2016).

The White House press secretary is the public face of a presidential administration, often delivering daily briefings to the press.
Cheriss May/NurPhoto/Getty Images; Cheriss May/NurPhoto/Getty Images

Although it came to be viewed as a ban on the government engaging in PR, the amendment didn't specifically prohibit "communications." It simply said that "appropriated funds may not be used to pay a 'publicity expert' unless specifically appropriated for that purpose" (Taylor & Kent, 2016). To address this concern, government officials dropped all references to "public relations" and "publicity" (to avoid the preapproval requirement) and referred to the function as "public affairs" or "public information."

The point is that the government did not stop practicing PR; it just gave the activity a new label and continued to communicate to its citizens (Taylor & Kent, 2016). This practice continues today, and you will rarely find the term "public relations" used to describe communications in a government setting.

Ironically, this process is a classic example of how government relations and lobbying impact public policy. Various stakeholders with competing agendas reach out to elected officials to create new legislation or impact public policy. In this case, the debate was about restricting how—or if—the government practiced PR. Government officials responded by passing legislation to address the issue and established new rules that others must follow in communicating with the public. The effort to curb government spending on communications is an ongoing battle between the party in power and those seeking to limit their communications and promotional activity.

Former White House Press Secretary Josh Earnest defended the practice, noting that it should be a priority for the White House to keep the public informed on essential government services and the president's policies.

"This is important work that requires dedicated professionals who are interested in helping the American people understand exactly what the administration is doing, what we have prioritized and what our success has been in implementing the agenda laid out by the President," Earnest said (Boyer, 2016). More information about the evolution of the role of the press secretary appears later in this chapter.

To be fair, many government communications activities are essential to the well-being of the public. Government public affairs (or public information) teams focus their communications on key areas such as health and wellness, public safety, and information on how citizens can best use government services. For example, information is routinely provided to the public by federal, state, and local government communicators on how to register and vote, how to pay taxes, how to finance a home, or how to pay for college with the support of the government.

According to Aaron Lavallee, deputy assistant administrator of the USDA Food Safety and Inspection Service,

> Public affairs in a government agency setting has three unique aspects as compared to the private sector: First, your communications work is done in a "glass house" since you are working for a government agency. Second, government public affairs teams are typically resource constrained and behind the private sector in terms of technology capability. Third, in government we must answer to many different clients simultaneously—including citizens, political officials, industry and the public. (A. Lavallee, personal communication, 2019)

Summing up, Lavallee adds, "You have the opportunity to work every day to improve the lives of your fellow citizens by facilitating the delivery of essential government services and assistance to them when it is most needed" (personal communication, 2019).

Crisis Management in Governmental Public Affairs

As you read in Chapter 12 on issues management and crisis communications, government communicators are also often called upon to manage crisis situations. These circumstances are usually in response to natural disasters like hurricanes, environmental accidents, and public health challenges, such as the Ebola crisis in 2014 or the COVID-19 in 2020.

Many of the elements of crisis communications are consistent in both settings. Tactical strategies include media relations, social media management, speeches, press conferences, and providing the public with the information necessary to recover, respond, and rebuild. The main difference is that your primary audience is the public versus customers or stockholders. In both cases, the focus needs to be on transparency, credibility and candor—in other words, what is going on, what are you doing about it, and when/how will it get better.

The global coronavirus crisis in late 2019 and early 2020 is a unique case of an external, global crisis that governments across the globe had to manage. National leaders and government communications professionals around the world were faced with protecting public health and safety and communicating to the public to provide information and reassurance about dealing with this new virus. History will show that for some leaders this was not their finest hour. For others, notably state and local officials in the United States and leaders of other countries around the world, the effort to communicate clearly and credibly will be shown to have made a major difference.

South Korea is one country experts feel responded very effectively to the coronavirus crisis by taking decisive action including rapid availability of nationwide testing and constant communication that became a model for other countries to follow. After China and Italy, no other country was harder hit by the virus initially than South Korea.

"The nation's success against the virus is attributable in part to the varied, transparent and innovative ways the government communicated. Importantly, the communication was aimed at both Korean citizens and foreigners living in the country," reported PR News (BGR, 2020).

One PR expert compared the response by the government of South Korea to the iconic crisis management practices found in the 1982 Tylenol crisis (see Chapter 2 case study).

"What are the common threads running through the South Korean and J&J (crisis management) examples? Transparency, honesty, speed and customer service.

PR professionals in the military and law enforcement are known as public affairs officers or public information officers.

Matthew Cavanaugh/Getty Images; Erich Schlegel/Getty Images

The building blocks of effective PR," suggests Frank Ahrens (BGR, 2020), a principal at BGR PR who represents the embassy of South Korea in the United States.

In the United States, however, this was not the case, at least initially. The Trump administration was widely criticized for downplaying the danger posed by the virus and for sharing misleading or incomplete information. When it became apparent that the situation was rapidly worsening, and more candor and concern were required, President Trump changed course and declared a national emergency on March 13, 2020.

The declaration of a national emergency freed up billions of dollars in aid and materials for state and local government to bolster their response to the pandemic. It also signaled to U.S. citizens that the virus outbreak was very serious, and strict precautions had to be taken immediately.

For millions of Americans, the daily routine of work and social activity changed dramatically. Schools were closed, major sporting events were canceled, and citizens were advised to avoid crowds and stay home. With a change in tone from the top and critical disaster assistance, federal, state, and local officials could move forward and respond accordingly.

In the private sector when facing a crisis, communicators focus on multiple stakeholders—customers, employees, and shareholders—and the public. As we have seen in this case, PR pros and leaders in the government sector must focus first on public health and safety. Other factors—including economic impact—must wait to get attention.

Military Public Affairs

In the military, the duties of the **public affairs officer (PAO)** consist primarily of advising senior leaders on media relations and developing issues and assisting their base or unit by developing public and internal communications strategies.

According to the U.S. Army website (www.GoArmy.com), "PAOs plan and execute PR strategies to achieve the desired objectives and evaluate the effectiveness of the programs they undertake" (U.S. Army, 2018). The PAO also manages media relations on behalf of her or his unit or commanding officer. While this is much like the work of a nonmilitary PR professional, the difference is the primary audience and organization doing the communicating is the armed forces and the public and stakes are often much higher.

In addition to meeting the external communications needs of the unit or branch of the military they serve, many PAOs are also responsible for internal communications, including newsletters, publications, digital media, and in-person communications when required. As well, PAOs are responsible for the base or service branch's efforts to address social issues that impact the military, their local community, and society at large.

Government Relations and Lobbying

>> **LO 15.2**   Understand government relations and lobbying

Government relations and lobbying are forms of *organization-to-government com-munications*. The difference is the nature of the communication: indirect (government relations) or direct (lobbying). In most cases, the goal is to advocate your organization's point of view to the government and elected officials. The impetus for this is business related since new laws, or regulatory requirements, add costs or complications to a product or service, and business leaders are necessarily focused on keeping costs down and profits up. Usually, both approaches (government relations and lobbying) are pursued to increase the impact and influence on the process.

"*Lobbying* and *government relations* have come to mean targeted outreach to elected officials by representatives of companies, governments, nonprofits and professional associations as well as regular citizens with the goal of impacting legislation or regulations," according to Popik (2010).

From the government side, however, there are other important considerations—for example, environmental issues, consumer protection, and preserving competition—that must also be weighed by elected officials in their policy making. The decision-making and legislative process is complex, and these communicators are representing their company's interest to the government while decisions are being made on regulations and laws. This involves conversations and meetings with regulators and/or elected officials and their staff.

Government Relations and Public Affairs

In some cases, advocacy can also include indirect communications activity to raise awareness and bring public pressure on government officials through media

Lobbyists from organizations and industries, in this case the National Association of Music Merchants, regularly meet with U.S. senators.
Kris Connor/Getty Images

coverage, petitions, online campaigns, and so on. Government relations departments and agencies use the term "public affairs" to signal this indirect activity.

"Public affairs teams often work in lock step with their government relations colleagues—the distinguishing factor is that public affairs efforts by companies aim to shape policy without stepping foot on Capitol Hill to lobby," explains Lindsay Murphy (2019), executive director of strategic communications at the American Forest & Paper Association, the national trade association of the paper and wood products industry.

Murphy concludes,

Knowing your audience is vital to both approaches, particularly in identifying which elected officials are most likely to be for or against your position. That information drives outreach efforts aimed at influencing key government decision-makers—including which publications and congressional districts are prioritized for media placements and in deploying your social media outreach. Together with the lobbying efforts, this process places your message front and center with decision makers and positions you for success. (L. Murphy, personal communications, 2019)

Why Is It Called Lobbying?

The British Broadcasting Company (BBC) suggests that the term "lobbying" comes from the informal meetings of members of parliament and citizens that took place in the hallways (or "lobbies") of the Houses of Parliament before and after debates. This practice began in the early 18th century.

In the United States, conventional wisdom is that the term originated in the 19th century in Washington, DC, and was used by President Ulysses S. Grant to describe the political operators who frequented lobbies in hotels near the White House. The goal was to gain informal access to the president and the members of his senior staff who often gathered there to enjoy a cigar and some brandy in the evenings. These "lobbyists" would seek out senior administration officials in order to discuss issues and politics in a more relaxed setting.

Applying Public Relations Strategy to Campaigns and Elections

>> LO 15.3 Develop an understanding of political communications in the modern era

Political communication is a dynamic, interactive process for the transmission of information among politicians, the news media, and the public. The process (see Figure 15.2) operates between governing institutions and citizens, links political figures (e.g., candidates, advisors, party officials), and directs public opinion toward authorities (Norris, 2004).

FIGURE 15.2

Transmission of Information in Political Communications Process

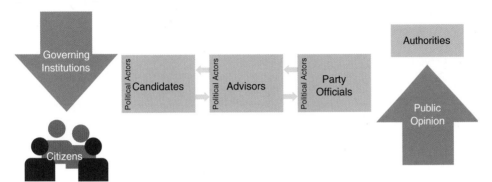

Humana's Campaign for a Healthy Mississippi

In the lead-up to the Obamacare rollout in early 2014, Humana positioned itself as a source of information about the new requirements, as well as a provider of insurance coverage.
iStock.com/SelectStock

Humana (n.d.) is a $27 billion health and well-being company based in Louisville, Kentucky, that offers health insurance and managed care in most of the United States. An excellent example of a combined corporate public affairs and government relations effort was the award-winning work done in Mississippi by Humana and its PR firm Coyne Public Relations.

Focus: Access to Healthcare

In the fall of 2013, the Affordable Care Act (ACA, or "Obamacare" as it became known) was set to launch. Independent research by Gallup showed that one in five people in Mississippi were uninsured and needed to take advantage of the affordable insurance coverage the law provided. However, awareness of the plan and how to enroll was low, and the marketplace for insurance coverage was limited in the state. Clearly, there was a need for an information-based, community outreach effort to increase the number of citizens with health care in the state. Access to health care is a critical issue, and Humana—as a provider of health care insurance—decided to respond with a comprehensive program that leveraged its core competency into an SR outreach program to address the issue.

Challenge: Position Humana Ahead of Competitors

Humana was one of several companies providing health coverage in the state, and it decided to launch a communications campaign to "position itself as a source of knowledge and provide a solution by significantly expanding its coverage" (Humana, n.d.) to serve more Mississippians.

(Continued)

(Continued)

Working with elected officials at the national, state, and local levels, Humana launched a comprehensive campaign. The highly successful campaign featured a dedicated campaign website, RVs equipped with Humana-certified health insurance experts, and a social and traditional media outreach effort to generate awareness of the issue.

When the enrollment period ended in March 2014, nearly 50,000 Mississippians were enrolled from the target areas of the state, and the media coverage of Humana's efforts had exceeded expectations. This campaign illustrates how an **integrated public affairs campaign**—with SR elements—can help position a company as responsive to the community and enhance the company's overall reputation. Further, by working closely with national, state, and local politicians and officials, Humana created strong governmental connections at each level, which may prove useful in the future. ●

Source: PRSA, n.d.a.

Fundamental to Politics

In some way, shape, or form, communication has always been an integral part of politics. Experts have observed that communicating with voters to influence their behavior is an age-old practice. For as long as there have been elections, candidates have worked to persuade the public to favor them (Foster, 2010).

In recent times, political communication represents the best and the worst of communications—especially at the presidential campaign level. In 2008 and 2012, the candidates (Obama and McCain in 2008 and Obama and Romney in 2012) used cutting-edge social media strategies and tactics to convey patriotic messages of hope and change, and the tone was generally civil—with some exceptions. Obama is widely credited with pioneering the use of social media and big data in a major campaign in 2008 (and expanding it in 2012) to increase campaign donations, create supporters, and drive voter turnout.

More recently, President Trump relied heavily on social media, influencers, and state-of-the-art digital strategies to build support ahead of the election in 2016 and again as he seeks a second term in 2020. Since his election, his daily use of Twitter to bypass the media, which he sees as biased against him, has become a staple of his presidential communications arsenal. For example, President Trump posted over 13,000 tweets in 2019 (an average of over 35 per day). His record in office was 142 in one day (Jan. 22, 2020), the second day of his impeachment trial (Pesce, 2020).

On the other side, Democratic challengers to Trump's reelection have also been active users of social media, both in their campaign to get the nomination and in the 2020 campaign against President Trump prior to Election Day in November.

However, neither Vice President Joe Biden nor Senator Bernie Sanders, the last two Democratic candidates for the nomination, were as active as Trump on social media during the 2020 campaign. For example, President Trump's official Twitter (@therealDonaldTrump) has over 74 million followers on Twitter, compared to 9.3 million for Sanders (@SenSanders) and 4.4 million for Biden (@JoeBiden). As well, Sanders and Biden tweeted only a few times a day on average, focusing on campaign events and updates and commentary on the news of the day.

Game of Leapfrog

Michael Cornfield, PhD, has studied and taught online politics since its inception in the mid-1990s. He suggests that the 2020 campaign has featured *one* big change since 2016 and *two* big continuities.

> To begin with the two continuities: "Negative partisanship" continues to dominate appeals to voters: that is, "vote against" instead of "vote for" messages, especially on social media. Second, entertainment value continues to prevail over strategic and civic considerations in the media's coverage of political content. For example, the televised candidate debates appear to have been geared to create confrontational "moments" and follow on news stories that pivot around insult tweets and sharp-edged quips taken from the debates.
>
> The big change stems from the public's reactions to Russian interference in the 2016 elections. In 2020, candidates, voters, and mediators have a heightened sense of suspicion regarding the truth of what they see, hear, read, and share. However, in keeping with the "third-party effect" well documented by social psychology, people worry more about how others may be deceived than about being deceived themselves. The resulting anxiety about "hoaxes" and "echo chambers" permeates and influences political communication today. (M. Cornfield, personal communication, March 2020)

During the 2020 campaign, overall spending on campaign communications—including social media, advertising, and PR and staff—was at record levels due in no small measure to the more than $400 million spent by former New York City mayor Michael Bloomberg as he sought the Democratic nomination. Once he abandoned his quest in early March 2020, spending returned to more "normal" levels, though it still exceeded prior campaign spending, even after discounting the Bloomberg advertising blitz in Super Tuesday states.

Negative Versus Positive

One unintended impact of the "attack"-style strategy used by candidates was a sharp decrease in credibility of social media posts from political figures. In a special study on social media and the 2016 election, a Pew Research Center report found that many users described their online political encounters as "stressful and frustrating," and (as a result) nearly four in 10 took steps to block or minimize the political content (Duggan & Smith, 2016). The 2020 presidential campaign will no doubt prove to exceed these results, given the volume and tone of media activity—both paid and earned.

The Internet and social media are now an essential part of a successful political campaign.
Alice Keeney / Bloomberg / Getty Images

Ringmasters of Political Communications

If politics today seems like a circus, it may be because it shares some of the Big Top's best and worst attributes. Consider two of the leading ringmasters in each domain: one from the past—P. T. Barnum—and one from the present—President Donald J. Trump.

Despite the many similarities in their approach to communications, neither Barnum (see Chapter 2) nor Trump has ever claimed to be a PR pro by trade or training. But in our view, they can both credit their success partially to their genius at generating publicity. In fact, Barnum once told a friend, "All I have, I owe to the press" (Barnum Museum, 2020).

President Trump might well say the same thing: Over the course of his initial presidential campaign in 2016, he earned close to $2 billion worth of free media coverage—twice what Hillary Clinton earned and more than the total of all the other GOP candidates combined. During his presidency, he virtually controlled the news cycle by tweeting furiously. That's not a coincidence—it is deliberate. At the beginning of the 20th century, newspapers played a significant role in telling people what to pay attention to and how to think about it. Without question, in the 21st century, social media has usurped the traditional media as the primary source of campaign news and information.

Like Barnum, Trump knows how to deal with the mainstream media as well. "One thing I've learned about the press is that they're always hungry for a good story, and the more sensational the better," he wrote in *The Art of the Deal*. "If you are a little different, or a little outrageous, the press is going to write about you." Now, you might think that's playing with fire. But just like Barnum, who was known to have posted signs in his museum that said "This way to the egress" to keep people moving toward the exit, Trump is a master of misdirection. "If a reporter asks me what negative effects the world's tallest building might have

on the West Side, I talk about how New Yorkers deserve the world's tallest building," he wrote in *The Art of the Deal*.

In the 2020 presidential primary campaign, he counterprogrammed the Democratic candidates' debates by staging his trademark rallies in the same city—sometimes on the same day. Part stand-up routine, part stream-of-consciousness rant, and 100% a circus-like event, Trump's rallies are similar to the publicity stunts Barnum staged to promote his shows in the late 19th century.

When the COVID-19 global pandemic lead to the cancellation of these rallies in the spring of 2020, Trump was forced to seek other ways to get his message out, including commandeering the podium at the White House daily news briefings on the government's response to the pandemic during March and April. By most accounts, this effort had mixed results (*The New York Times*, 2020).

But Trump knows what the ordinary people want. In his (1987) book, he suggested that "people want to believe that something is the biggest and the greatest and the most spectacular. I call it truthful hyperbole. It's a very effective form of promotion." As for Barnum, he called that "humbug," but he had the same goal. Few of Barnum's attractions ever matched his buildup. But since most were entertained, people accepted the ruse as part of the Barnum experience.

In 2016, voters liked Trump's brashness, and many stuck with him throughout his first term. As the president, he often speaks and tweets in simple, angry terms. He doesn't talk like a politician; he says what some people might be thinking but are afraid to say. They find him entertaining, just like the masses who patronized Barnum's Museum or his circus sideshows over a century ago. Time and history will tell how this all plays out for Trump and his legacy. ●

Source: Dick Martin, author and former chief communications officer of AT&T Corp, personal communication, 2020.

Most experts agree that while traditional media has had to adjust to keep up in political communications, there is no doubt it remains highly relevant. Steven Foster (2010), writing in *Political Communications*, suggests that "it is quite *impossible* to conceive of political communications outside of the nexus linking politician to journalist" (p. 2).

The Changing Role of the Press Secretary

Thomas D. McAvoy / Getty Images

President Franklin D. Roosevelt is credited with appointing the first official White House press secretary (WHPS). Stephen Early was named to the new position in 1932 and charged with interacting with the press on behalf of the president.

Before serving the president, Early was an editor at *Stars & Stripes*, as well as an Associated Press reporter. After accepting the White House position, he obtained presidential approval for some procedures that remain part of the WHPS role. Early received unrestricted access to the president, authority to have his statements attributable to him as press secretary, and permission to offer factual information to the press directly. He also convinced President Roosevelt to conduct twice-weekly presidential press conferences and scheduled them to meet media deadlines (Bailey, n.d.).

The role of the WHPS has evolved and changed since those early days, along with the political process and the media that covers it. In the early days, most press secretaries were former journalists (like Stephen Early), appointed by presidents to look after the White House press corps. More recently, the WHPS has been a political communications professional working as part of the White House staff to shape and manage the president's message and respond to the criticism from political opponents or other leaders.

Mike McCurry, who served as the WHPS to President Bill Clinton from December 1984 until August 1998, suggests that as the link between the president and members of the press, the press secretary has a daunting responsibility. "You're equally distanced between two actors—the President and the media—in this adversarial relationship." And as the voice of the president, McCurry reveals, "By evaluating how the press was likely going to react to a certain statement or a development or a decision, you began to impact the decision itself" (M. McCurry, personal communication, 2017).

During his career, McCurry observed some key differences between a Democratic and a Republican White House. "Democrats tend to believe that the press is going to be on your side because they're all about comforting the afflicted and afflicting the comfortable and speaking truth to power, so they're going to be with the little guy." On the other hand, he says, "Republicans never have that supposition in mind. They're more adept at what we might call corporate communications, and they view the press skeptically, based on their previous experience" (M. McCurry, personal communication, 2017).

McCurry said he was once asked if there is any circumstance under which the press secretary can ever lie to the American public. "And I said, 'By and large, no.' Sometimes, the art of the job is learning how to tell the truth—slowly" (M. McCurry, personal communication, 2017).

Dana Perino, the second woman to serve as the WHPS (for President George W. Bush, September 2007–January 2009), notes that "most people see the press secretary defending the president to the press. But as important as that role is, what people don't see is the press secretary defending the press to the president or members of his senior staff." This, she suggests, illustrates the intermediary role the WHPS has to play on a daily basis (D. Perino, personal communication, 2017).

Under President Trump, a succession of press secretaries—three as of year-end 2019—all but eliminated the traditional daily briefing of the White House press corps, which has been a staple of administrations since the days of Roosevelt and Early. "The number of White House press briefings has slumped under President Trump to the lowest level since they took on their modern format nearly a quarter-century ago," wrote Melissa Quinn in the *Washington Examiner* in January 2019.

In April 2020, Kayleigh McEnany was appointed as President Trump's fourth WHPS. She held her first briefing on May 1, 2020, promising they would be held on a more regular basis (Wise, 2020). McEnany's initial performance drew mixed, partisan views. Sean Spicer, Trump's first WHPS, tweeted "Great debut!" (*Twitter*, May 1, 2020). Joe Lockhart, President Clinton's WHPS, and a CNN commentator, described it as a "shadow briefing" in a Fox news report the same day, (*Fox News*, May 1, 2020).

Without question, the role of the WHPS, and the field of political communications, will continue its evolution due to the dynamic changes in how the public receives news and information about elected officials and candidates for elected office. "We've come a long way in the field of political communications since simple black-and-white TV ads or cozy radio broadcasts," comments Dennis W. Johnson, PhD, an author and expert on political communications.

Today, the world of political communication is robust, multifaceted, and wide open. Politicians must continually figure out the most effective way to connect directly with the voters. For now, it looks like Twitter is dominant—thanks in part to President Trump; a decade from now, who knows? (D. W. Johnson, personal communication, 2017)

Scenario Outcome

At the beginning of this chapter, you read about the challenge the NIH public affairs team faced in 2014 preparing for the arrival of Ebola patient Nina Pham at their Bethesda hospital for care and diagnosis.

The NIH public affairs team was challenged to handle a daily international media presence, respect the patient's privacy, and manage the fears of its local employees and neighbors near its Bethesda, Maryland, hospital and headquarters. While Ms. Pham was being prepared to travel to NIH via a chartered, medically equipped airplane, media inquiries poured in. The NIH communications team anticipated that media would have questions about the care that Ms. Pham was receiving, what this mysterious, ultrasafe clinical unit looked like, and if there was any threat to the community.

How did they respond?

- To provide transparency about the facility's capabilities and what Ms. Pham's care would be like, the team prepared media materials that could be shared proactively with reporters and included the images (e.g., photos and video) that are critical for broadcast media.

- NIH communicators also realized the value of keeping employees and the community informed. The NIH director sent an email to all employees alerting them to the patient's arrival and noted the measures being taken to protect her and the staff as well as the surrounding area. Staff scientists created informational materials for the NIH website explaining the disease and spoke at town hall meetings for all staff to allay concerns.

- Ahead of Ms. Pham's arrival, broadcast outlets and media from national outlets, local Texas stations following Ms. Pham's case, and foreign press from around the globe converged on the NIH campus. Communications staff arrived before dawn to greet satellite trucks at security and direct them to the front of the hospital, where teams of staff from communications offices across the agency worked shifts to assist reporters and supply information, help stage camera shots and stand-ups, and escort them inside the hospital for food and restrooms.

- To ensure that her medical privacy was protected, NIH spokespeople adhered to the American Hospital Association guidelines on describing a patient's condition to the media (i.e., one-word descriptions like "good," "fair," or "serious"). While the NIH most often distributes news in written press releases, in this case in-person press conferences were set up to provide updates for national, local, and cable news channels to ensure that all media present had access to the same information simultaneously. The spokespeople also helped put a face on the scientists and medical staff who were caring for Ms. Pham.

On October 24, 2014, the NIH held a final news conference to announce that Ms. Pham was Ebola free. She appeared at the news conference, smiling and recovered, alongside her family. To help remove the stigma of disease, NIH leaders greeted her with warm hugs at the news conference. Later that day, she received another warm embrace from President Barack Obama in the Oval Office.

Source: Anne Rancourt, section chief, Office of Communications and Government Relations, National Institute of Allergy and Infectious Diseases, National Institutes of Health, personal communication, 2017.

WRAP UP

In this chapter, you read about three exciting and unique areas of strategic communications—public affairs; government relations and lobbying; and political communications. You also explored military public affairs, which has a unique audience and a strategic function within the armed services.

While none of these may be the career path you choose, it is important to know the many options a career in communications has for young professionals so you can make the best choice for yourself.

For example, one option is government-to-citizen communications in public affairs, usually practiced in a government setting. Another is the field of government relations and lobbying that focuses on organization-to-government communications. You may also consider political communications, a PR field that manages elected official (or candidate)-to-voter communication. Finally, if you plan to enter the military (or are already serving) and are interested in communication, the field of public affairs offers a career path to you as a PAO.

KEY TERMS

Government Relations 344
Integrated Public Affairs Campaign 352
Lobbying 344

Political Communications 344
Public Affairs Officer (PAO) 349
Public Information Officer (PIO) 345

THINK ABOUT IT

To help reinforce the key lessons of this chapter, what follows is a series of questions for you to discuss in small groups and then share with the class:

1. What are the principal differences between government-based public affairs work and traditional PR?

2. What is lobbying, and why is it called that?
3. How has the role of traditional media impacted the efforts of government and nonprofit PR to deliver key messages, and how is the media responding?
4. Is SR practiced by government agencies and nonprofits? Research and identify a few examples. (*Note*: www.csrwire.com is a good, searchable source.)

WRITE LIKE A PRO

In this chapter, you read about crisis situations faced by government public affairs professionals. Pick one and answer the questions that follow in a short essay (250 words). You may want to do a media search or visit the website of the agency involved to get information.

What suggestions do you have to improve the crisis management approach used?

What best practices can you identify that other government agencies and companies should consider?

What could have been done differently or better to improve the outcome?

What are the unique challenges a government public affairs office faces in a crisis, and how can these be offset?

SOCIAL RESPONSIBILITY CASE STUDY

The First Ladies Health Initiative: Walgreens Supports HIV/AIDS Screenings in Urban Churches

This CSR initiative funded primarily by Walgreens involves a partnership that includes more than 100 "first ladies"—pastors' wives working with health organizations and volunteers to improve the health of African Americans. The program began in Chicago (Walgreens's headquarters city) with more than 200 pastors' wives and dozens of medical experts convening to learn why HIV/AIDS was disproportionately high among African Americans.

Research and Strategy

The HIV/AIDS epidemic was a serious problem in both Chicago and Los Angeles and, as such, these were the pilot cities. Since AIDS was discovered more than 30 years ago, at least 32,000 Chicagoans have been diagnosed (many of them African Americans), according to the Chicago Department of Public Health. The numbers in Los Angeles are also striking. According to the Los Angeles County Department of Public Health, African Americans accounted for 41% of all new HIV infections in LA.

The Centers for Disease Control and Prevention reported that African Americans represented 44% of new HIV infections in the United States in 2013, even though they make up just 12% of the U.S. population. The AIDS case rate for African Americans was more than 9 times that of whites, and the HIV rate was 7 times greater among Blacks than whites.

Several years prior to the initiative, which began in 2008, the Walgreens Corporation made a commitment to become more involved in the overall health of the African American community, particularly regarding the HIV/AIDS epidemic. The company and its local PR agency (the Danielle Ashley Group) recognized the important role churches play in the African American community, and it was decided to involve the wives of head pastors.

Execution

The goals of the inaugural First Ladies Health Day in 2010 were to furnish about a dozen Chicago churches with Walgreens pharmacists, medical supplies, and volunteer medical

TABLE 15.1

Statistical Information From Chicago and Los Angeles: Health Days Provided by Medical Partners via Patient-by-Patient Surveys (During the Campaign)

	2008	2010	2011	2012	2013
Chicago Luncheon	75 First Ladies	200 First Ladies	225 First Ladies	220+ First Ladies	250+ First Ladies
Chicago Health Day	_____	9,500+ Screenings	15,000+ Screenings	20,000+ Screenings	20,000+ Screenings
No. of participating churches on Health Day	_____	35	40	42	46
Los Angeles Luncheon	_____	_____	100 First Ladies	125 First Ladies	185 First Ladies
Los Angeles Health Day	_____	_____	_____	17,000+ Screenings	15,000+ Screenings
No. of participating churches on Health Day	_____	_____	_____	30	37

Source: PRSA, 2014a.

technicians from associated organizations to provide free health screenings onsite at the churches all in one day. About 20 churches signed on that first year in Chicago. In 2013, the number had grown to more than 45 participating churches. When Walgreens expanded the initiative to Los Angeles, nearly 100,000 free health tests were performed during the six combined Chicago/Los Angeles health days.

Evaluation

In its first 5 years, the Chicago and Los Angeles programs completed 96,500 screenings (see Table 15.1). This successful program was a natural fit, underlining Walgreen's commitment to health care and its hometown (Chicago), as well as an important segment of its national customer base—African Americans in major cities.

Engage

- Visit Walgreens's website and read about its many CSR initiatives around the world.
- Research current statistics about the incidence of HIV/AIDS. Pay particular attention to how it impacts minorities.
- Scan media coverage of CSR initiatives both for Walgreens and its major competitors (e.g., CVS, Rite Aid, etc.).
- Identify what themes or topics tend to get more coverage than others. Determine if having a nonprofit partner impacts success and coverage and gather your data.

Discuss

- This specific case study involves a program launched in 2008, continuing to 2013 (though the program still continues today). What would you recommend that Walgreens do going forward to sustain the momentum?
- Should they broaden the focus beyond HIV/AIDS to the other diseases identified as having a disproportionate impact on the African American community?
- Is there any potential for negative reaction to Walgreens getting involved in a controversial disease like HIV/AIDS? How might they have prepared for this possibility?

- Is there a risk of a program that is focused more on one ethnic group versus all in a city or area? Should they expand this to include free health screenings for everyone?

- How might Walgreens competitors respond with similar SR ideas and programs? Does that matter to Walgreens?

Note: This case is based on a 2014 Silver Anvil winning entry.

Source: PRSA, 2014a.

iStock.com/TommL

16

Global Public Relations and Public Diplomacy

Learning Objectives

16.1   Understand the increasing globalization of PR

16.2   Examine global PR and SR in different organizational settings and countries

16.3   Introduce public diplomacy and its application to economic development and SR

Scenario
"Like a Girl": Positive and Confident

Inside the Cincinnati headquarters of the global consumer products company Procter & Gamble, brand managers for the feminine hygiene category recognized that one of its top products, Always, was being challenged as the market leader. Always was still the global leader in its category, but its biggest competitor was gaining, primarily by connecting with Gen Z girls on social platforms like Facebook and Instagram.

Research reveals issues and directs strategy. Based on research that revealed most young women experience a decline in self-confidence during puberty, the "Like a Girl" campaign was created to empower young girls. By linking the brand with a positive message about self-confidence, the goal was to provide an emotional connection with the target market. This connection would solidify the brand's market position and a "powerful, relevant and purposeful role in this empowerment" (PRSA, n.d.a).

Always's "Like a Girl" campaign was created to empower young girls and, in consumers' minds, link that empowerment to the brand.
iStock.com/diego_cervo

The company engaged its ad agency, Leo Burnett, and its PR firm, MSL, to work together on a new campaign communicating that "Like a Girl" was not an insult but a compliment and a source of pride. The goal was to demonstrate that the Always brand "understands the issues that young girls face." The campaign was launched in 2015, has been continually updated since, and remains a key part of the brand's profile today.

To begin its work, the agency conducted primary and secondary research to track the issues that impact girls' confidence before, during, and after puberty.

From the research, the following became clear:

- More than half of girls surveyed experienced a decline in confidence at puberty.
- Their confidence's lowest point was at the beginning of puberty, but it could last into adulthood.
- The majority (89%) of females ages 16 to 24 agreed that words impact self-confidence—in some cases, for a lifetime.

Linking a product and social message. The agencies reviewed other global campaigns linking a product and a social message to determine the keys to a successful cause-related campaign. Several insights were identified:

- Clear articulation of the idea and proposed response is required.
- Authenticity is critical, especially for this demographic.
- Insights need to be validated with data points.
- Celebrity influencers are important to create visibility.

With the campaign strategy set (i.e., making "Like a Girl" a positive message), the agencies set out to positively connect the Always brand to this critical moment in the lives of young women and build brand loyalty.

(Continued)

(Continued)

Your challenge. As you read through this chapter, imagine you are on the agency account team charged with updating this very successful campaign. Key questions to consider include the following:

1. What media platforms would you leverage?
2. Which organizations or causes might you reach out to and engage?
3. How will you know if the campaign is working?
4. Which celebrities and influencers would you engage to support "Like a Girl"?
5. How can you engage or enlist males in supporting the campaign's message?

At the end of the chapter, you will learn how the original "Like a Girl" campaign was built into a highly successful global marketing communication campaign and why it has received multiple awards for creativity and impact since its launch. As well, updated information about the program's progress and impact since its launch is included. ●

In this chapter, our focus shifts to two areas of dynamics for the PR profession, global PR and public diplomacy. Global PR is one of the fastest-growing segments of the industry as major companies grow and the world shrinks due to the profound impact of digital and social media. Public diplomacy, a newer field, focuses on how communications and PR practices can be applied to support diplomacy, nation branding, and influence building around the world.

We will also examine the relevant career paths and the integration of SR (social responsibility) in global PR (public relations). This is an important discussion because all organizations, national or multinational, must be prepared to interact with global and local stakeholders in a process that researchers suggest "parallels the evolution of public relations as a profession, practice and field of study in every corner of the planet" (Bates, 2006).

Through a discussion of current practices, research, and an exploration of the applicable theories and strategies, this chapter will provide guidance and suggestions to help you understand these trends and the career opportunities they represent.

An Overview of Global Communications

>> LO 16.1   Understand the increasing globalization of PR

The growth of **global communications** is one dynamic challenge for the PR profession. The Business Research Company (BRC, 2020) reports that the global public relations market was valued at about $63.8 billion in 2018, and they predict it will reach $93.07 billion in 2022, following a consolidated annual growth rate (CAGR) of 9.9%.

As you might expect, North America was the largest region in the public relations market in 2018 and is expected to remain so over the next 5 years. The public relations market in North America was forecast to achieve the highest CAGR during 2018 to 2023, followed by Europe (BRC, 2020). However, other areas, notably China and India, are reportedly growing at an accelerated rate as well, the BRC research indicates. The global impact of the COVID-19 virus (which began in late 2019 and is still prevalent at the time of this writing) on the outlook for PR firm revenues has been significant, and growth will likely slow down in 2020 and beyond.

The shift to a global marketplace for communications raises key questions for PR professionals. Some of the more pressing ones include these:

- How do you communicate globally effectively?

- What are the guidelines for success, and which pitfalls should be avoided?

- How do you gain experience in the field?

As **globalization** takes hold, the demand for skilled communicators with a sophisticated worldview increases. Access to the Internet has spread fast across the globe, and thus the stakes and the opportunities for global communications have increased. By all accounts, we are well past the point where any significant news or business or political development is exclusively "local" anymore (Sriramesh & Vercic, 2009).

With the rise of globalization, the potential reach of PR is now worldwide.
ZUMA Press, Inc. / Alamy Stock Photo

What is meant by global PR or communications? The IPR (Institute for Public Relations) defines it as "strategic communications and actions carried out by private, government or nonprofit organizations to build and maintain relationships in socioeconomic and political environments outside their home location" (Molleda, 2009, para. 10). According to Wakefield (2007), global or international PR "boils down to *where the entity is located* and *to which publics it must build relationships with*" (cited in Molleda, 2009, para. 11, italics in original).

In unpacking these definitions and guidelines, you can see the inherent challenges. To be effective, a global communicator must know the company's business and understand the needs and preferences of key stakeholders (e.g., media, government, activists, customers) in each of the markets where an organization operates. Further, you must develop an understanding of *each* market's unique dynamics and characteristics, both economic and social.

To do that, some basic questions must be addressed (Culbertson et al., 2012):

- Is the media free and unrestricted, or is there government control or censorship?

- Is the media active or passive? Does that impact setting agendas and building brands?

- What is the political ideology represented by the government in power?

- What is the development stage and reach of broadband technology, and how do citizens access it (mobile, laptop, or desktop)?

- What are the rates of poverty and literacy, which impact who can purchase and comprehend news coverage and social media material?

- What is the history of activism and major social movements?

- What are the laws and regulations that govern advertising and PR practices?

As with any PR challenge, the key is to know the audience you want to reach. Once you have this information, you can develop new strategies, refine existing communications plans, and create your "story," including the key messages to share locally in each market. This focus on local has always been a hallmark of PR as far back as its origins in the United States and in Western Europe (see Chapter 1). What has changed is the need for companies and enterprises to engage authentically on a global basis. With the advent of social media and the access it provides citizens and consumers to information, corporations, governments, and nonprofits do not have a choice about engaging in global communications, as echoed by Sriramesh and Vercic (2009):

> I wonder whether one should talk any longer about "international public relations" or "global public relations" as a specialty because even "domestic" publics now are multinational and multicultural due to globalization. So understanding the needs, expectations, and values of a diverse set of publics is becoming more important even as it is growing more complex, requiring great skills and thereby becoming more and more strategic and less technical. (p. xxxv)

Storytelling and Global Public Relations

Tom Mattia has overseen global communications for four Fortune 500 companies, most recently Coca-Cola, and was chief communications officer at Yale University. He's also worked in China for 5 years with two global PR firms. Based on his considerable experience, Mattia suggests that developing your corporate "story" is the key. That, along with understanding the local culture and market environment, is essential to success.

"The focus for international communications campaigns is to define and build the organization's narrative or story," Mattia suggests. "Once the narrative has been constructed, one that reflects the DNA of the organization, PR practitioners can mold the narrative to the culture, climate and technical capabilities of the target audience" (personal communication, 2017).

Now retired, Mattia is a senior lecturer at Rutgers University's School of Communications and Information and was recently appointed a Towers Fellow at the University of Texas. Mattia has experienced many different successful communications platforms in his career:

> For example, I might use a different platform to tell the Mars candy story in China than I would to tell the Coca-Cola story in Spain, but in either case, I would begin with the company's basic story. In North America, short, illustrated bursts via Instagram or Twitter can be effective in moving a narrative. In India and Asia, longer-form YouTube videos are very popular. In Europe, there is more opportunity for biting, satirical commentary. The key is never losing sight of the story being told or the market you are trying to impact. (T. Mattia, personal communication, 2017)

Let's look more closely at the cultural adaptation required in China. If your company plans to enter or increase market share there, you need to have your corporate narrative set and adapt it to the way "stories" get told in China. To do that, all parties should be aware that the media is government controlled and social media is monitored and censored.

Based on his experience, Mattia says some global companies in China have managed this "storytelling" process quite well, including Starbucks, Mars, Audi, Samsung, and Apple. Mattia reports that Starbucks and Mars have treated China like a second home and worked hard to develop their own local management talent since entering the market. Now, a few years later, these managers can play major roles in the company's growth in China.

Elsewhere in Asia, the challenge is different, reflecting less government control and a freer media. For example, Oh and Ramaprasad (2003) report that for companies seeking to build awareness and market share in the Republic of South Korea, the halo theory best explains the relationship between foreign multinational companies (MNC), key Korean stakeholders, and the public.

The Halo Effect

The **halo effect** is a term used by communications scholars to describe the positive bias shown toward specific products and services because of a favorable experience global customers have had with other products made by the same manufacturer (Leuthesser et al., 1995). In this situation, the country of origin is the source of the "halo" that extends to products from that country—for example, wines from France, technology from the United States, or fashion from Italy. You will learn more about strategies to build or enhance the perception of the United States, in particular in the discussion of **public diplomacy** later in this chapter.

In Korea, the research of Oh and Ramaprasad (2003) indicates that the perception of an MNC's home country (e.g., the United States) and that country's current relationship with Korea "plays a relevant role in determining the public perception of the MNC" (p. 317). Conversely, a South Korean company seeking to build brand equity in the U.S. market is welcomed in the United States, due to the historically strong relationship between the two countries. Companies like Samsung, Hyundai, and Kia have had much success in building market share in the U.S. market. Korean-based airlines such as Korean Air and Asiana have done well also.

Crisis Considerations

Global companies and their communications styles need to adapt to U.S. market expectations for accountability and transparency, especially in a crisis, as we learned in the discussion of Samsung's Note 7 in Chapter 12. Another recent example occurred on July 6, 2013, when Asiana Airline's Flight 214 crashed while attempting to land at the San Francisco International Airport. Out of 291 passengers, three died and over 180 were injured.

The crisis communication efforts that Asiana undertook following the crash were viewed as insufficient by most U.S. observers. Notable among these was the failure of the senior management of the company to be on-site in San Francisco promptly to personally address the concerns of the passengers and the public.

The company was also criticized for its slow, measured response to the media and to federal and local officials who were investigating the crash. Instead of senior management being on-site immediately after the accident (as the "playbook" for crisis management usually suggests—see Chapter 12), senior

Though a company's story is important across markets, it must be tailored to be delivered in a way that appeals to the audience. Apple is still Apple in China, but the story must be told in a different, culturally appropriate way.
Rik de Groot / Alamy Stock Photo

International crises like the Asiana Airlines Flight 214 crash in San Francisco have driven home the need for cultural intelligence.
Kimberly White / Stringer / Getty Images

management remained in Korea, issuing sympathetic, and sometimes conflicting, statements. The task of managing the crash's aftermath was left to locally based company officials. This created the impression that senior management of Asiana was not engaged or responding directly to the tragedy.

The crash and the crisis management efforts of Asiana demonstrate the need for corporate communication professionals (regardless of their home country) to have cross-cultural competence and training to respond to a crisis or issue the way that is expected in a host country elsewhere in the world.

SOCIAL RESPONSIBILITY IN ACTION

Coca-Cola Creates Brand Loyalty Through Sustainability Efforts in India

Coca-Cola successfully reentered the market in India after buying a local soft drink company and tailoring its message to the diversity of the local market.
DIBYANGSHU SARKAR / Stringer / Getty Images

India is a prized market for many MNCs, especially in the consumer product space. One such global brand, Coca-Cola, had been in India for many years when it was presented with a challenge that eventually led the company to leave the market in 1977. The government passed legislation requiring all foreign companies doing business in India to disclose the ingredients in their products to be allowed to operate there. Since Coca-Cola was unwilling to disclose its secret formula, it decided to leave India to protect its business secrets. When the rule was eased years later, Coca-Cola sought to reenter the market, but its key competitor, Pepsi, had already entered the market in the 1980s through a joint venture with a local company.

Coca-Cola Goes Native

Coca-Cola's response was to acquire the leading soft drink company in India, maintain their native brands, and offer Coke products as well. To regain market share, Coca-Cola customized its marketing communications to address the Indian market with specially tailored messages.

Enter Corporate Social Responsibility

Recognizing the importance of CSR in creating brand loyalty in India, Coca-Cola revised and refocused its sustainability strategy. The company enhanced its existing CSR efforts to emphasize education, water conservation, and health—all areas that their research indicated were the greatest needs in India and where Coca-Cola had global experience and resources.

The Water Battle

The build-out of its CSR platform to support the different communities and regions of India became a valuable resource when the company faced a crisis in 2003. Coca-Cola and Pepsi were both subjected to a ban of sales in India following claims by a local activist group that their products were not safe to drink because of pesticides in the product, allegedly due to poor water purification processes. Coca-Cola overcame the ban and got its products reinstated after a prolonged battle with the activists and the provincial government where the opposition was centered. Coca-Cola proved their product was safe via independent scientific research. They also improved their water management and conservation technology in response to the concerns raised by the activists. These steps were effective in alleviating customer concerns.

Sharing Technology

Later, in another strategic move, Coca-Cola shared the technology it had developed to improve water management with local Indian companies. This enabled them to improve their manufacturing processes and reduce waste. This move further enhanced Coca-Cola's reputation in India as a leading company and social partner committed to sustainability and water management (Kaye, 2005). ●

Cultural Intelligence

The Asiana Airlines crisis illustrates the theory of cultural intelligence, which is defined as the ability to comprehend different beliefs, practices, attitudes, and behaviors in one country or market and apply that knowledge to attain your goals—whether they are political, business, or otherwise.

The case is valuable to global companies seeking to build cross-cultural expertise as they expand globally. Fundamentally, the Asiana Airlines case demonstrates that global companies must learn and adapt to the cultural norms and expectations of the countries where they operate, especially in a crisis situation, if they are to be viewed as authentic (Gomez & Reed, n.d.).

Elsewhere around the world, the challenge is the same. PR professionals need to understand the market and the forces that drive behavior before seeking to enter a new country or manage the company's reputation there. In India, scholars (e.g., Bardhan and Patwardhan, 2004) suggest that MNCs must overcome a history of resistance to entry by foreign businesses into the country. This can be accomplished by understanding the country's expectations for CSR and by developing an affiliation with a locally based company or enterprise to pave the way to market entry. The experience of Coca-Cola in India in the late 1990s and early 2000s illustrates these points (see Social Responsibility in Action: Coca-Cola Creates Brand Loyalty). In South America, research suggests that MNCs will have a smoother road if they "stress the social role of the organization and . . . emphasize an active but intelligent involvement in changing and improving societal conditions" (de Brooks & Waymer, 2009, p. 31).

CEO Activism and Global Public Relations/Corporate Social Responsibility

Activism and taking public positions on political and social issues by CEOs and company leaders is a relatively new phenomenon, yet it is increasing, research indicates. The Edelman Trust Barometer (2020) reports that the world's population increasingly looks to business to lead because the other institutions they track—government, media, and the nonprofit community—have seen steady declines in their trust levels and efficiency compared to prior years. In the area of SR, three out of four respondents agreed a company can take actions to address a key social issue and improve their reputation at the same time.

The 2020 report suggests that trust is built through specific attributes: integrity, engagement, products and services, purpose, and operations. Of these sectors, the agency's research indicates that integrity and engagement are tied as most important. Integrity encompasses ethical business practices, issues management, and transparency. Engagement encompasses employee well-being, customer concern, and frequent communication (Edelman, 2020).

Aaron Chatterji, a professor at the Fuqua School of Business at Duke University, has studied the phenomenon of **CEO activism** and stakeholder expectations and strongly suggests social media has played a major role. "Silence used to be the default posture for CEOs," but social media has changed that significantly, he notes. "It's now a choose-a-side mentality. The middle is harder to occupy. And, with the proliferation of social media, it's kind of like a microphone that is always on. If you're not speaking out, it's more conspicuous" (McGregor, 2017a, para. 11).

SOCIAL RESPONSIBILITY

A recent article in *The Washington Post* cited research by Chatterji and Michael Toffel at Harvard Business School and found that CEO activism—especially as it relates to SR—can "help shape public opinion on controversial social issues and increase interest in buying by consumers who favor the company's point of view" (McGregor, 2017b). Clearly, this is an area where communications professionals will be called upon in the future to advise their clients and senior management teams.

Weber Shandwick, a global PR firm, has been actively researching CEO activism for the past few years. Some of the important conclusions from Weber's most recent research (2018, paras. 1–3) include the following:

- Almost half of Americans (48%) believe CEOs can influence decisions and actions of government.

- Approximately eight in 10 consumers (77%) agree that CEOs should speak out when their company's values are threatened by social issues.

- Half of consumers (46%) would more likely buy products or services from a company whose CEO speaks out on a social issue they care about—only 10% would be less likely to buy.

Working Internationally to Develop Global Public Relations Skills

For many communications professionals, the chance to work internationally can be a significant opportunity for career development and learning. Many senior communications professionals working for (or advising) large, global companies have, at one point in their careers, taken advantage of the chance to learn how business and communications are conducted in different markets. Leading academic institutions are enhancing their communications and business curricula with international residencies to provide this learning opportunity. This is because international experience and training can broaden your horizons and prepare you to be a more effective strategic advisor for your clients and/or senior managers. From a career development perspective, a global posting or training is an attribute that companies and organizations look for in making middle- or senior-level promotions or hires.

Bill Heyman, founder and principal of Heyman & Associates, an executive search firm, suggests the following:

> International PR roles present a high degree of difficulty and show that a candidate can navigate different cultures, manage across distances and time zones—even overcome language barriers. It is a good indication that you are a well-rounded, intelligent person who isn't afraid of a challenge. (B. Heyman, personal communication, 2017)

Richard Marshall, global managing director of corporate affairs for the executive search firm Korn Ferry, agrees adding, "International experience sets candidates apart and puts them in a better position to succeed, in our view" (personal communication, 2017).

Global Public Relations in Different Settings

>> LO 16.2   Examine global PR and SR in different organizational settings and countries

While there are many commonalities in working on a global scale, there are many differences as well. These include managing different languages, media formats, and cultural traditions—all of which will vary depending on the setting. Specifically, a staff or consulting role can be very different in a corporate, nonprofit, or government global setting. Understanding and preparing for these will enhance your chances for success.

Corporate

As you will read in Michael Fanning's profile on the challenges of working internationally (see PR Profile section), companies with operations across multiple countries and continents have numerous (and sometime simultaneous) communications challenges to manage and must use different styles of decision-making.

PR PROFILE

A Manager's Journal: Working Internationally for a Global Corporation

Michael Fanning, Former Global Director of Sustainable Development at Groupe Michelin

I was fortunate to work in communications for several global companies during my career: IBM, The Reader's Digest Association, and finally Michelin. After 10 years as vice president of corporate affairs at Michelin North America, headquartered in Greenville, South Carolina, I had the opportunity to move to the company's global headquarters in France.

Headquartered in Clermont-Ferrand, France, Michelin is a multinational tire manufacturer, distributor, and retailer and is a recognized global leader in sustainable mobility. The global company operates in more than 170 countries around the world, has 112,300 employees, and operates 68 production plants in 17 different countries (Michelin, n.d.).

(Continued)

(Continued)

As Michelin Group's worldwide director of sustainable development, I led the Michelin performance and responsibility process, which charted the company's response to global sustainability challenges. I was also the delegate from my company to the World Business Council for Sustainable Development, headquartered in Geneva.

While serving as the director of sustainable development for Michelin, I led the creation of Michelin's six sustainable development goals for the year 2020 and the company's receipt of the top ranking in its sector on the Dow-Jones Sustainability Index.

In considering a global posting, I loved the thought of cross-cultural assimilation, learning new skills, developing a second-language capability, exploring new countries, and making new international friends. The experience did not disappoint. I came away with a few observations about the value of such a posting:

First, it's easy while living in the United States to get lulled into thinking that our country is at the center of the world. Living abroad opens one up to a diverse way of thinking and different attitudes.

Next, decision-making in a global context can be frustrating for some Americans. At Michelin

headquarters in France, for instance, meetings were not always designed as conduits for action; sometimes, they were opportunities to let everyone make their point, and meetings often ended without clear direction. Decisions would eventually be made by our top executives after taking multiple viewpoints into account.

Finally, the value of developing personal relationships to strengthen business relationships cannot be underestimated. The business lunches and invitations to Sunday meals with families and office celebrations—all these interactions—served to align the personal relationship with the business relationship.

Through this experience, I discovered that the ability to transact business and be an effective strategic advisor was much improved after my time living and working in France. I developed personal relationships with my international colleagues and better understood the global marketplace through first-person work experience outside the United States. Take advantage of the opportunity if you get it; that's my strong advice! ●

Michael Fanning is a former global director of sustainability at Michelin Group.

Source: M. Fanning. personal communication, 2019.

It might be a local event or issue—for example, getting permission to build a new plant or introducing new products and services. Or it may be a companywide challenge that must be managed globally with a sensitivity to local customs and practice. It may also be a company transition, following an acquisition or major strategy shift, to be implemented in multiple countries simultaneously.

Understanding the company's business, strategy, and the markets and countries where the organization operates is critical for success. Further, a working knowledge of which communications tactics work best where—for example, social media in one market, mainstream media in another—is needed. If it is a culture or strategy shift, you must also consider the employee communications aspects of the problem. A case involving IBM undertaking a global identity change serves as a good example.

Nonprofits

Another sector where successful global campaigns are occurring is in the non-profit segment. As with the global efforts discussed elsewhere in this chapter,

Changing Perceptions of a Global Brand

The IBM "Building a Smarter Planet" initiative was designed to solve two key challenges:

- First, IBM had changed its business focus from being a producer of technology equipment (e.g., typewriters) to services (consulting, data management, and analysis).

- Second, the company's brand and identity had changed to match its new strategy. However, the perception of the company remained stuck in the past.

The new strategic direction of the company was "making the world better in our day," with a focus on creating a "smarter planet." This overarching theme, which had marketing, PR, and CSR components, was to be achieved through implementing the new vision and focus on improving both business and society.

The transformation impacted the internal communications team structure at IBM as well: marketing, communications, and citizenship (or CSR) were integrated into one new department. This restructuring ignited "compelling conversations associating the IBM brand with solving clients' toughest problems and positioning IBM as a thought leader in its target industries," said Jon Iwata, senior vice president of marketing, communications, and citizenship.

At the outset, the company set three overarching goals:

- Clarify the identity and brand of IBM to all its key stakeholders.
- Motivate IBM employees to become communications agents to represent the new brand identity.
- Drive a behavior change for the company, merging civic engagement, marketing, and traditional communications into a dominant message to be delivered consistently by employees to customers and stakeholders.

The campaign exceeded the company's expectations by its completion. It spanned more than 170 countries and included input from more than 150,000 IBM employees. It was well received by the market and clients, producing double-digit growth in new and existing client assignments and yielding dramatic revenue growth for the company. Finally, it redefined the company—both to employees internally and externally to clients and prospects—as a firm well positioned for business success and focused on meeting its obligations to its key stakeholders.

"The 'Smarter Planet' initiative proved that a major global corporation could credibly pursue an authentic, positive message of hope and progress even in a cynical world," Iwata noted. ●

Source: Stacks, Wright, and Bowen, 2014.

PR professionals working for nonprofits need to identify the unique aspects of each target market and understand the media mix—social and traditional—that serves it.

Further, nonprofit PR professionals must contend with fewer resources—staff, budget, and technology—than their corporate or agency counterparts have for global campaigns. This is against a backdrop of declining support, both financial and personal, of nonprofits globally by the public, according to recent research on the topic. The 2020 Edelman Trust Barometer research showed that nongovernmental organizations (NGOs) are increasingly viewed as focused on serving the most vulnerable people and are therefore ineffective advocates for the broader global middle class (Edelman, 2020). Thus, the middle class, often a key source of financial support for these charities, is becoming less generous or more selective in which organizations receive their support.

This new reality places a heavier emphasis for the NGO to be creative and resourceful to tie into a trend or a cause that has impact and generates support

The Ice Bucket Challenge, which was started by two Boston College athletes to raise money for a former teammate, raised $115 million in 8 weeks.
John Blanding/The Boston Globe/Getty Images

and enthusiasm among the target audience (e.g., middle-class donors), not an easy task in a crowded digital world.

The "Ice Bucket Challenge," which started locally and grew globally via social media, is a classic case history of how to apply creativity and social media to drive awareness of a cause. The challenge began quietly during the summer of 2014, and its rapid growth was driven by media interest, celebrity participation, social media posts, shares, and retweets. According to the *Boston Globe* (August 14, 2014), Facebook reported 1.2 million videos were posted about the "Ice Bucket Challenge," and more than 15 million people commented or "liked" the videos in less than 2 months. It became a true overnight sensation (Cloutier, 2014).

The campaign started out as a dare between two Boston College athletes to raise money for their former teammate (Pete Frates), and it took off virally almost overnight. The challenge raised $115 million in 8 weeks and generated unprecedented levels of awareness for the disease and the need for a cure. As the campaign grew, the ALS Foundation became the source for information and updates about the disease. The ALS Foundation received support from the government and private sources and a huge increase in donations and awareness. "We have never seen anything like this in the history of the disease," Barbara Newhouse, president and CEO of the ALS Association, said in a statement (ALS Association, 2014).

Not every global campaign for a charity—or any organization—will have the spontaneous, worldwide success of the "Ice Bucket Challenge," although many dream about that outcome when they launch a fundraising effort. Avinash Murthy (personal communication, 2014), suggests four key takeaways from this campaign:

- **Relate the campaign.** Link it to a cause people can commit to—in this case, a debilitating disease, impacting all ages.
- **Keep it simple.** The "Ice Bucket Challenge" only required a mobile device and a social media account to participate (along with a willing participant and a donation).
- **Make it fun.** The "challenge" was entertaining, visual, timely (e.g., summertime), and easy to share, post, or tweet.
- **Celebrity endorsers (influential) are key.** In this case, they were critical to increase views and generate interest in the cause and activity.

Since the original campaign ended, the foundation has worked to extend awareness and fundraising and has developed a new slogan—"Every Drop Counts." They have garnered extensive media coverage, raised more money, and made progress in treating this devastating disease. And they have continued to communicate their progress to sustain the interest and support. The "Ice Bucket Challenge" may have been a spontaneous, organic campaign, but the ALS Foundation leveraged it to build awareness of its work worldwide.

Sadly, Pete Frates succumbed to the disease in late 2019 after raising global awareness and millions of dollars to help find a cure. His family and friends continue to work on the cause, and their efforts, combined with the ALS Foundation, had raised more than $220 million through the end of 2019.

Government

SR initiatives launched by national and local governments is a recent trend that many experts expect will grow in the future. The ability of government officials and agencies to implement specific SR efforts beyond their own agency or government offices is limited because they are public, not private enterprises. However, in the United States and other major countries, elected and appointed government officials are implementing sustainable business practices such as LEED-certified buildings, agencywide recycling, and improved resource and power management. In addition, the public sector is developing outreach programs to assist and support the work of employees and by communities where they have large government complexes or military bases.

The University of Connecticut Office of Sustainability (www.ecohusky.uconn.edu) publishes a newsletter that recently included a list of government-sponsored sustainability initiatives. The projects detailed activities involving small groups of volunteers, city and county agencies, and large partnerships of nonprofits and businesses working with the government on sustainability projects. They range in scale from local neighborhoods and small towns to metropolitan regions and multinational efforts.

Providing communications support for these programs is usually the responsibility of government public affairs and public information offices, which you read about in Chapter 15. By all accounts, this activity is expected to increase for the same reasons it grew in the private sector. Sustainable business initiatives save taxpayer money, support the community, and motivate employees in government roles—just as they do in the private sector. In addition, given the increased expectation on business and nonprofits to initiate new and support existing SR efforts worldwide (Edelman, 2020), governments have a part to play here as well.

Governments worldwide can foster and assist companies to succeed in their SR activity, suggests Jane Nelson (2008), a senior fellow and director of the CSR Initiative at the John F. Kennedy School of Government at Harvard. This is particularly true in areas when the host country or region lacks the infrastructure or political will to solve their most pressing problems alone.

"The ability to identify and prioritize those public goods and issues, and then determine the best strategies for addressing them . . . will be an increasingly important mark of good business (CSR) leadership in the years ahead," Nelson suggests. The role of the government, both in the host country and the home country, is to lend support where possible and recognize and encourage the efforts by companies to help overcome these issues.

Public Diplomacy, Strategic Public Relations, and Social Responsibility

>> **LO 16.3** **Introduce public diplomacy and its application to economic development and SR**

As noted, public diplomacy is a growing field for PR professionals, combining public service, diplomacy, and communications strategy.

An excellent example is the U.S. Secretary of State's Awards for Corporate Excellence (ACE). Established in 1999 by Secretary of State Madeline Albright, the awards recognize U.S.-based companies that are responsible members of their communities where they do business. According to the U.S. Department of State

(DOS; 2019) website, "Together, these companies exemplify some of the most promising and innovative business ideas of the 21st century: that profitability and sustainability are not mutually exclusive, and that sustainability can drive prosperity in the modern economy" (para. 2).

The ACE awards are presented in late October each year to U.S.-based companies in two categories—small to medium enterprises and multinational companies. The 2019 ACE awards focus areas were sustainable operations and women's economic empowerment. Winners included P&G Asia Pacific and PepsiCo India in the MNC category and the Chambers Federation (Democratic Republic of the Congo) and Argilis Partners (Uganda) in the small to medium enterprise category (DOS, 2019).

Previously, companies as large and well-known as Cargill, Intel, and Coca-Cola have been recognized, but smaller companies such as Taylor Guitars, Salman Seafood, and Denimatrix have received awards as well. Earlier in Chapter 5, you learned about the award-winning work of Eco Planet Bamboo in Nicaragua. Research on the characteristics and impact of these companies has suggested a link between the SR activities of these enterprises and the image and reputation of the United States in the host countries. Page and Parnell (2016) have proposed that through this program, U.S. firms function as third-party mediators for U.S. public diplomacy efforts through their global CSR.

Commenting on this connection in 2012, former Secretary of State Hillary Rodham Clinton stated, "The core tenets of corporate social responsibility complement both our diplomatic and development efforts" (DOS, 2012, /para. 1). "[F]or many people around the world, the most direct contact they will ever have with the United States is through American businesses. . . . That's how they learn what we stand for and who we are and what aspirations we share" (para. 7).

These initiatives require the active support and involvement of both the PR and SR teams at these companies to raise awareness and stimulate the participation needed to make the local programs work to maximum effect. The PR practices used vary due to type of CSR initiative, size, and organization of the company, as well as in-country situations. Yet through their corporation-to-government and corporation-to-citizen good deeds, select U.S. firms fulfill the function of public diplomacy, both relational and mediated, in their global CSR.

Public Diplomacy and Public Relations

The practice of public diplomacy is when governments communicate and build relationships with foreign publics to achieve political objectives (Fitzpatrick et al., 2013). Practitioners in public diplomacy may be called public affairs officers (PAOs) or public information officers (PIOs) and are usually government employees. Practicing public diplomacy involves mediated communication, image building, and "soft power," a concept developed by Joseph Nye (1990) that highlights a two-way relational approach versus coercion or payment.

Public diplomacy is fast becoming a new specialization in PR. Due to the tragic events of September 11, government agencies now see the value in creating open dialogue between countries and in relationship-building between government leaders. It is increasingly clear that the United States needs to engage with foreign publics, connect with them, exchange ideas and cultures, and foster two-way, horizontal communication.

Over time, public diplomacy has shifted from a persuasion strategy to an engagement strategy, which involves the following:

- **Focus on mediated communication.** Work with the global news media to emphasize shared core values and frame content to improve public opinion and ideally influence key members of a foreign audience.

- **Focus on branding efforts for country image and reputation.** Once conducted and received successfully, nation-branding campaigns (e.g., tourism promotion, communicating shared values, promotion of technology and innovation, etc.) may provide a strong foundation for better relations (Golan et al., 2015).

- **Focus on a relational soft power approach.** Soft power is built through educational programs, cultural exchanges, language training, and development tools and also through how a country "lives" its political values and its legitimately held and morally driven foreign policies. PR knowledge and skills are regarded as "most important" and "most effective" for public diplomacy, according to a study of former officers in the U.S. Information Agency (Golan, 2013, p. 1251). The similarities between PR and PD are these:

  o Interactive approaches that involve engagement with publics

  o Rejection of propaganda use and disinformation

  o Efforts to influence political opinion formation or policy-making processes

  o The need for understanding and command of global media

As current and future communications professionals, it will be up to you to apply your strategic and tactical communication skills to encourage corporate, government, and nonprofit participation in SR globally and in public diplomacy. This work can make a major difference in the world and improve a company's reputation at the same time—a true win–win situation.

Scenario Outcome

Because *Always* is a global brand, Procter & Gamble set out to develop a global campaign and connect the brand's identity to young women worldwide. The messaging of "Like a Girl" had to resonate across national and cultural boundaries in the United States and adapt to different segments of the global target market. By the end of the initial launch phase, the campaign had been expanded to 20 major markets worldwide.

Independent research has shown that the "Like a Girl" campaign has positively impacted the self-confidence of young women worldwide—76% of girls today have a positive association with the formerly insulting phrase "like a girl," versus only 19% at the start. The campaign has opened the eyes of many others to the damage that bullying can do to a young person's confidence and success later in life.

Paul Holmes, writing about the top 10 campaigns of the decade (which Always topped, according to him), suggests "it was a perfect fit for the Always brand, and it was probably the most successful of all the campaigns . . . in doing what great public relations is supposed to do: building a lasting relationship between the brand and the consumers it is designed to serve" (Holmes, 2019a).

The company's strategy was to take an insult and make it a rallying cry—changing "like a girl" into a phrase that empowered and inspired young women. The centerpiece of the launch campaign was a short video directed by an award-winning documentary filmmaker. It showed how people (especially young women) had interpreted the phrase "like a girl" historically to mean weakness or vanity and revealed the impact this was having on young women worldwide.

The film then revealed how the phrase could be made into a positive statement—that young girls should be proud of doing things "like a girl"—and showcased the achievements of young girls worldwide.

The video was launched through an exclusive with *Advertising Age* (a major trade paper covering marketing and advertising), and soon after, it was previewed on the Always YouTube site. Copies of the video were made available to key influencers and prominent bloggers, asking them to share it on their sites. This had the effect of generating WOM (word-of-mouth) awareness and global visibility for the video and the campaign. Soon after, the hashtag #LikeAGirl and video went viral.

In addition to the social media initiatives, the agency reached out to the online and traditional media to generate coverage about #LikeAGirl and female empowerment. This widespread coverage added to the excitement and buzz about the campaign and stimulated extensive online conversations.

To extend the launch's impact, the Always account team reached out to celebrities to post and tweet about the campaign. The effort started with Vanessa Hudgens and Bella Thorne, but soon, many other well-known female celebrities and opinion leaders joined in. Sarah Silverman, Tyler Oakley, Maria Shriver, Cher, Kristen Bell, Chelsea Clinton, and Melinda Gates all participated with tweets and posts on Facebook and Instagram.

Finally, the agency and its client created a 24-hour, real-time news desk that monitored the conversations online and engaged where appropriate to further amplify the #LikeAGirl campaign.

What began as a social experiment and campaign to bolster the self-image of young girls blossomed into a global movement that changed the conversation online and in the media, as well as impacted young women all over the world.

The program goals were quickly achieved. Postlaunch research from the original campaign showed it had succeeded beyond the team's hopes or expectations:

- 81% of women 16 to 24 surveyed supported Always for creating a movement to reclaim "like a girl" as a positive and inspiring statement.

- The "Like a Girl" launch video was viewed 76 million times on YouTube in more than 150 countries (90% from the United States and the 20 target countries) during the target time period.

- The program earned almost 2,000 media placements around the world on network morning news shows, broadcast networks, print media, and online.

- The program created 290 million social media impressions and 133,000 mentions on Twitter, Facebook, and other major platforms.

By the end of the initial launch period, "Like a Girl" had become a worldwide phenomenon and was a core part of the Always brand message.

At this point, it was decided that the campaign would participate in Super Bowl XLIX (49) in February 2015 with a commercial that asked boys, women, and men to join the #LikeAGirl movement. The new campaign featured a teenage girl who played quarterback on her local tackle football team. It led to 19 onsite interviews at the Super Bowl and four more videos being produced. The Always campaign was a major story in the post–Super Bowl news cycle with more than 1,600 media placements, and it trended nationally on Twitter and Facebook. In turn, these placements, tweets, and posts were echoed online by influential leaders, celebrities, activists, and bloggers—extending the impact of the campaign.

The campaign progress has continued through 2019 and is likely to remain as a staple for the brand going forward:

On its dedicated Always "Like a Girl" page of its website (www.always.com/en-us/about-us/our-epic-battle-like-a-girl), P&G reports some more encouraging statistics and notable accomplishments through year-end 2019:

- Three times more young girls surveyed report they have a positive association of the phrase "Like a Girl."

- 72% of girls responded that they feel society tries to limit their opportunities, but they feel motivated to respond.

- The campaign led to 44 new emojis being added to the Unicode that portray more positive and active images of young women.

- 85% of girls have reported that they feel encouraged to keep trying even after experiencing failure.

"This was a truly global campaign, and perhaps the most powerful example of the decade's dominant trend: purpose-driven brands," Holmes (2019a) concluded.

Note: This case is based on a 2015 PRSA Silver Anvil award-winning entry and includes input from the company (P&G), MS&L, and the company's website. Additional information came from other sources (as noted) to update it through 2019.

Source: PRSA, n.d.a.

WRAP UP

In this chapter, you learned about *global public relations*, which was defined as the strategic communications of organizations in social and political environments outside their home location (Molleda, 2009). You also learned about the concept of *cultural intelligence*—that is, understanding the behavior expected of foreign companies who operate in global markets. (Note: This is often different than the expectations for corporate conduct in their home market.)

Later, you were introduced to a new concept in international communications—*public diplomacy*—which has a lot in common with diplomacy, sustainability, and marketing communications. But it is concerned more with the reputation of countries (e.g., the United States) than with individual companies. The goal is to generate a halo effect for other U.S.-based businesses and improve the perception of the United States as a diplomatic and business partner. These fields represent great opportunities for expanding and building your career in PR.

KEY TERMS

THINK ABOUT IT

As a group activity, look up the ACE award winners on the U.S. Department of State website (www.state.gov) and pick one recent example in each of the two categories (multinational and small to medium enterprises) that is of interest to you and your fellow students.

Summarize the two examples and then propose some next steps for the company to take to expand the program, gain recognition in the United States for its global SR efforts, or launch new, similar activities elsewhere in the company. Present your findings and views to your classmates.

In addition to visiting the ACE awards site, you should review the individual company websites, SR reports, and any news coverage they have received on the SR effort to get a full picture of what they are already doing as part of their outreach efforts.

WRITE LIKE A PRO

On your own, watch the short video *Public Diplomacy and the Role of a Public Affairs Officer* from the USC Center on Public Diplomacy (www.uscpublicdiplomacy.org). It illustrates the critical importance of soft power in public diplomacy. Consider how it might apply as a PR specialty or career internationally.

Prepare a short essay (250 words) on how the U.S. government should or could proceed in promoting the U.S. reputation in developing countries around the world using SR as the focus.

Questions to consider include the following:

- How did the change in the U.S. administration from Obama to Trump impact this activity? What do you think other countries will expect from the US government after the November 2020 election?

- What role does SR and community development by U.S.-based companies play in building America's reputation in the world?

- What PR strategy and tactics lend themselves to supporting this activity?

- Are there countries or topic areas that companies should avoid?

- Is this a career path that might interest you?

SOCIAL RESPONSIBILITY CASE STUDY

Dell Women's Entrepreneurial Network Creates Opportunities for Women

Dell has had a long history of SR since its founding in 1984. As the company grew and developed into an international corporation with operations in more than 50 countries and 110,000 employees worldwide in 2013, it made major commitments to SR throughout its operations. One major goal was to expand opportunities for women entrepreneurs.

Research and Strategy

To define how Dell could make a significant impact with women entrepreneurs, the company conducted qualitative and quantitative research. Dell assembled an advisory board of entrepreneurs, including leading technologists and global ambassadors for entrepreneurship. This group identified several areas for Dell to focus on to accelerate growth for women entrepreneurs: enhanced access to networks, new markets, capital, and technology.

To drive the conversation, the team partnered with the Global Entrepreneurship Development Institute (GEDI) to commission creation of the GEDI Index, a unique tool to measure the rate of female entrepreneurship across 30 developed and developing economies, spanning multiple global regions. The goal of the research was to develop the information to be communicated to academics, business leaders, and government policy makers to create more favorable conditions for women entrepreneurs to thrive. In addition, both the qualitative and quantitative research was used to develop a multifaceted global communications plan.

The program's strategy was to develop personal connections and ongoing dialogues with global women entrepreneurs, influencers, and policy makers, showcasing that Dell is more than an information technology vendor; it is also a trusted business advisor and partner, advocating for the success of women entrepreneurs and the jobs they create globally.

The team positioned Dell as a trusted advisor and advocate for women entrepreneurs and to create a global network of women entrepreneurs to serve as Dell's brand evangelists in media coverage, at events, online, and in sales. In addition, global economic stability was to be promoted by supporting women, innovation, and job creation.

Execution

The Dell Women's Entrepreneurial Network (DWEN) program was launched by the company in 2010. By spotlighting female entrepreneurial success and creating a supportive atmosphere for these new leaders, DWEN helped these new businesswomen share best practices, build opportunities, explore expansion outside the United States, and access capital and technology to support job creation. Networking events were organized or supported to bring entrepreneurs and funding sources together.

An annual global conference of female business founders, CEOs, and other leaders was created to discuss business issues, networking, and technology. At the most recent conference (2017), more than 150 handpicked women leaders representing 19 countries attended. In addition, select reporters representing top-tier publications from over 12 countries covered the conference.

Traditional and social media outreach resulted in 224 articles in key media and 6,522 tweets, reaching 50,000 visitors. This resulted in building an active online community to help company start-ups meet peers and mentors. And an e-book was commissioned and promoted, profiling 10 women entrepreneurs who overcame identified major challenges to be successful.

The company also partnered with the UN Foundation to promote entrepreneurship and job creation globally. This connection led to the appointment of Dell Chairman and CEO (Michael Dell) as the UN Foundation's global advocate for entrepreneurship.

Evaluation

The success of this program led to hundreds of women of all ages and backgrounds launching companies all over the world. Further, it created business opportunities and jobs for related companies and individuals and connected Dell to the growing market of women entrepreneurs. In that sense, it was an ideal recipient of the PRSA Silver Anvil award in 2015 as it connected an SR program to a business opportunity for Dell and enhanced the company's reputation and business at the same time.

Engage

Gather into small groups for an activity to examine this case in the context of Dell's overall CSR efforts and to get a sense of the scope of the problem/opportunity this initiative was designed to address—that is, empowering women globally to start and sustain small businesses.

- Visit the Dell social impact page (https://corporate.delltechnologies.com/en-us/social-impact.htm) and learn more about the company's activities in this area. You will note that they have set areas of interest and priority for their outreach effort.

- Conduct some brief research on the issues facing women in the United States and elsewhere to start and maintain a small business.

Discuss

- Review and discuss your findings within the group. Prepare a series of two or three recommendations to evaluate the program's success (why did it work?) and to make two or three specific recommendations that would improve the program going forward to bring more positive recognition to the company.

Source: PRSA, n.d.a.

GLOSSARY

Absolutism: This is a deontological theory (also called *nonconsequentialism*) that emphasizes duties or rules; what's morally right applies to everyone.

Acquisition: One company takes over another, establishing itself as the new owner.

Active Publics: This is a PR term for people who do something about their beliefs, problems, or opportunities.

Advertising Value Equivalency (AVE): A practice, now largely discredited and abandoned, whereby the impact or value of an article in a publication or a news segment is measured by the relative cost of purchasing that same amount of space or airtime—as you would in a commercial or print ad. Research has clearly indicated that people regard consumer media coverage very differently than they do advertisements or commercials and thus has shown that there is no real "equivalency."

Agenda-Setting Theory: This theory explains that media have a large influence on audiences by choosing which stories to make prominent.

Appropriation: This involves using some aspect of a person's identity that causes mental or physical distress.

Aware Publics: This is a PR term for people who recognize a problem or opportunity.

B Corporation: A certification, not a legal status, of a company's adherence to social responsibility and sustainability standards.

Backgrounder: This is a written document, usually part of a media kit, that provides additional information on an organization and its situation to help a media worker craft a story.

Benefit Corporation: A legal status in which a company must have a positive benefit on society and the environment.

Benoit's Image Restoration Theory: Benoit's theory is most often cited in studies of crisis and issues management by researchers and practitioners. It focuses on how companies monitor issues and manage crises once they occur. Benoit's five categories of image restoration include denial, evasion of responsibility, reducing the offensive act, taking corrective action, and mortification (Benoit, 1995).

Blogger: An individual who writes and posts his or her thoughts about news, issues, or trends on a blog that is then shared, liked, or reposted by others on social media. Some bloggers develop loyal followers and become an important audience for communications outreach to promote a product or service or generate support for a cause or campaign. In this case, they become *influencers* (see definition) and can play an important role in a communications plan or campaign.

Blogging: Chronological posting on an informational website.

Boilerplate: A paragraph appearing at the bottom of a news release, summarizing information about the sending organization.

Business-to-Business (B-to-B), Business-to-Consumer (B-to-C), and **Business-to-Government (B-to-G) Communications:** These are various forms of communications activities defined by the audience. For example, traditional PR focused on promoting a product or service to consumers is referred to as B-to-C; communications efforts that focus on a business audience or customer is referred to as B-to-B; and outreach designed to support the purchase of goods and services by government agencies is referred to as B-to-G.

Cause Promotion: Supporting or increasing awareness and concern for a cause or charity.

Cause-Related Marketing: Contributions to a cause or charity based on percentage of sales revenues.

CEO Activism: This term refers to CEOs and company leaders taking public positions on political and social issues on a local, national, or global basis. It is a new phenomenon, yet one that is increasing, according to research by Edelman (2017). This is in part because activists and *nongovernmental organizations* (*NGOs*; see definition) are increasingly calling for CEOs and company leaders to get more involved in addressing society's problems through social responsibility activities. The rising influence of social media is another contributing factor.

Channel: The medium of communication used to provide information, such as television, radio, email, and so on.

Chief Marketing Officer (CMO) and **Chief Communications Officer (CCO):** These are frequently used titles to denote the marketing or communications function at the senior-most level of the company—in the so-called "C suite" with the chief financial officer (CFO) and chief executive officer (CEO), among others. This is a key career goal for corporate communicators who desire to be close advisors and colleagues of their company leadership.

Cialdini's Influence Principles: Six different cues that trigger mental shortcuts: reciprocation, commitment and consistency, social proof, liking, authority, and scarcity.

Commonsense Theory: A theory that touts using anecdotal information to guide understanding.

Community Volunteering: Employees get involved in a cause via time off or sabbaticals.

Consequentialist Theory: See *Utilitarianism*.

Content Analysis: Research method of examining and categorizing existing communication.

Content Producers: Found in the entertainment field; those involved in content production and/or distribution, such as filmmakers and studios.

Copyright: Legal protection for any creative work that is published, broadcast, presented, or displayed publicly, including online video, audio, imagery, or written work.

Corporate Branding: Just as a product or service—or even a celebrity—can have a brand, so does the company itself. A corporate brand is the product of the combined perception of the company, its products, its people, and its overall reputation. For example, Apple is regarded as an innovative technology company, McDonald's as a leader in the fast-food industry, and Starbucks as a socially responsible coffee company. That is their "brand," and it is the product of considerable effort by communicators and a corporate commitment to be a leader.

Corporate Culture: Shared values, attitudes, standards, and beliefs that characterize members of an organization and guide an organization's goals, strategies, structure, and approaches to labor, customers, investors, and the greater community.

Corporate Philanthropy: Describes charitable activity by an individual or organization wherein materials (in kind) or financial resources (cash or stock) are donated to nonprofit organizations to assist them in achieving their objectives. This is historically one of the most common forms of social responsibility, where companies or organizations would make donations to charities to meet their obligations. Individuals and companies often house these activities in a separate but closely related foundation.

Corporate Reputation: This is a term used by communications professionals to describe how a company (or organization) is perceived by its key *stakeholders* (see definition). Essentially, it is the image or view that comes to mind when you hear a company's name—for example, Apple might be "cool, innovative, or creative," or BP might be more negative with "oil spill, pollution, or controversy" coming to mind.

Corporate Social Marketing: Support for a "behavior-changing" campaign to improve safety, health, or the environment.

Crisis: A crisis is a significant threat to operations that can have long-term, negative consequences to the company or organization involved.

Crisis Communications (or Management): The process by which organizations respond to and manage the situation to minimize damage to products, people, the public, and/or their reputation. Effective crisis management requires the preparation of a crisis plan and the careful application of that plan, adapting as necessary to the evolving situation.

Crowdsourcing: Obtaining information or input from a large number of people, typically via the Internet.

Cultural Intelligence: Refers to the need for company leaders to recognize and comprehend different beliefs, practices, attitudes, and behaviors of a group or market area and then apply that cultural knowledge to attain their goals—whether those goals are political, business, or otherwise. Basically, it means PR pros need to understand the market and the forces that drive behavior before seeking to operate in a new country or to manage their corporate reputation locally.

Cybernetics: A theory of message transmission.

Defamation: The act of making a statement that can be proven to be false, with the intention of causing harm to another's reputation or livelihood (see *Libel* and *Slander*).

Demographics: A term that is used to categorize or analyze the audience for a media outlet or, more broadly, a segment of the population. An example might be middle-class voters, millennials, baby boomers, or senior citizens. PR and research professionals use these categories to break down a large audience or population into smaller groups to identify their media, purchasing, or voting habits.

Deontological Ethics: Ethics that are rules based.

Depth Interview: Research method that searches to answer how and why through a one-on-one conversation.

Diffusion of Innovations Theory: Theory explaining that a new idea or a product must pass through a sequential process with a public to ultimately be adopted.

Digital Analytics: Tools that allow collection, organization, and analysis of online data.

Disasters: These are sudden events that seriously disrupt system routines and require action to cope with them. They may even pose a danger to the system values and goals. Often, disasters are random and cannot be predicted. However, companies or organizations can be held accountable for how well they manage the disaster and its aftermath (e.g., Hurricane Katrina).

Disclosure: This term is used to describe the process by which *publicly traded companies* (e.g., listed on a Stock Exchange; see definition) share significant news and information to all its key publics, stockholders, and the world's financial markets simultaneously. Major corporate news must be disclosed (via a news release and/or a posting on the company's website) to all interested parties in a timely fashion (e.g., as soon as possible). Failure to do so can result in a fine or charges being filed against the company and its management.

Divestiture: Disposition or sale of a business (or a business line, unit, or division) that's owned by a company.

Ecotourism: Environmentally responsible travel to natural areas that promote conservation and provide for beneficially active socioeconomic involvement of local peoples.

Elaboration Likelihood Model (ELM): A major persuasion theory explaining that persuasive messages are received by people through two different routes: central and peripheral.

Employee Advocacy: Word-of-mouth communication by employees on their own online platforms that provides positive public exposure for their company and/or its brands.

Employee Relations: A company's efforts to manage relationships between employers and employees.

Encoded: The way meaning is produced in a message to ensure comprehension by the receiver.

Engagement: A state of attention, comprehension, interest, attitude formation, and/or participation; in social media, interactions people have with content—for example, likes, comments, shares, and retweets.

Evaluation Phase: This is the element in a strategic plan (usually at the end) that allows you to measure progress toward the stated goals and objectives. More complex or longer-term plans can have interim goals (e.g., 5% market share in the first 6 months), which calls for the planner to build in checkpoints where progress can be measured to make sure the plan is on track. This also allows for midplan corrections to messages or tactics if the goals are not being met or if the market or situation has shifted.

Excellence Theory: General theory of PR that explains characteristics of excellent communications.

Exposure: Frequency and time frame of content's appearance on a media platform.

Fair Use: In some situations, under this rule limited use of another's copyrighted work may be allowed without asking permission or infringing on the original copyright.

Fake News: A term that came into popular use during the 2016 presidential campaign. It refers to the proposed practice of publishing news stories online (initially) or in the traditional media that are not based on acts or proven research. The goal of "fake news" is often to discredit an opponent or support a point of view that impacts the candidate or company's reputation and business, usually negatively. This is especially an issue for online news organizations or platforms like Facebook, where posting content without review or validation often occurs. Once posted, it may be liked, reposted, or commented on—giving it perceived validity.

False Light: A term that refers to information either untrue or suggestive of false impressions that is widely publicized.

Financial Communications: This is a category of communications that corporate communicators or investor relations professionals and their advisors engage in routinely for publicly traded companies. The activity consists of preparing the required reports (annual and quarterly reports), communicating with the financial community (current and prospective investors, stock market analysts, etc.), and the financial media (*The Wall Street Journal*, *Financial Times*, and *Bloomberg*) on behalf of the company. Practitioners in this segment must be aware of the *disclosure requirements* (see definition) and make sure all information that is shared is public and available to all.

Focus Group: For communications professionals, this trend means you must consider stakeholders across all the markets where your company or client operates and understand the local factors that impact perception, market acceptation, and reputation.

Framing Theory: A theory that suggests that how something is presented to the audience (called "the frame") influences the choices people make about how to process that information.

Free Speech: The legally protected right to public speech defined by the U.S. Constitution's First Amendment.

Gatekeeper(s): This term is used in theory and practice of media relations to define the person or persons who control access to the media and decide if a story or news item will be published, posted, or put on the air at a TV or radio station. They may be an editor, producer, or the actual reporter themselves. Media relations outreach to these individuals (see *Pitch*) is designed to convince them that the story or news item has merit and would be of interest to their viewers, listeners, or readers.

General Entertainment: Broad category of entertainment products encompassing multiple media, such as TV programs, concerts, and online series.

Global Communications: "Strategic communications and actions carried out by private, government, or nonprofit organizations to build and maintain relationships in social and political environments outside their home location" (Molleda, 2009). Global, or international, PR depends on where the entity is located and which publics it serves.

Globalization: A term often used to describe the worldwide movement toward economic, financial, trade, and communications integration (Business Dictionary, n.d.a).

Government Relations: Defined as "organization-to-government" communications, this is the branch of communications where organizations communicate with government agencies and elected officials. Most often, a comprehensive government relations effort includes *lobbying* (see definition) government officials directly.

Greenwashing: Deceptive messaging that a product or a practice is environmentally friendly.

Halo Effect: A term used to explain the positive bias shown by customers toward certain products because of a favorable experience with other products made by the same manufacturer (Leuthesser et al., 1995). For example, consumers can have a positive predisposition toward a company based on its global reputation and/or the reputation of its home country—for example, a fashion company from Italy or France, a technology company from Japan, or a consumer product company from the United States.

Hashtags: Words or phrases, with a hash or pound sign appearing before them, for use on social media sites.

Immediacy: The quality or experience of something happening now or "being in the moment."

Impressions: This is another tactic designed to measure the impact of news coverage. The concept, which remains in common use though it is controversial and not proven, assumes that PR professionals can report the number of subscribers to a publication or viewers/listeners to a broadcast as the audience reached with a news item or story they placed. For example, an article in a weekday edition of *The New York Times* (with total subscribers of over 5.2 million, including online readers; Tracy, 2020) might be reported as "garnering more than 5 million impressions." The obvious flaw is that no one can say for sure that *all* the paper's subscribers saw and read the paper/article on a given day. Nonetheless, PR firms will use it (maybe with a caveat) as a default way to show the reach and impact of a news story.

Influencer: An individual who develops a following and becomes a "trendsetter" or "opinion leader" (see *Blogger*) and can influence the success or failure of a communications campaign, particularly one that is designed to launch a new product or service. Many PR campaigns make special accommodations to reach out to influencers as opposed to general "word-of-mouth" or "buzz."

Informational Objectives: They are focused on creating awareness of a product, company, or issue by sharing information and attributes.

Initial Public Offering (IPO): An IPO marks the first time a company sells some of its shares (stock certificates representing partial ownership) to the financial

community and the public. This is a major event in the life of a company, as it provides access to capital raised through the sale of its shares. Companies often take this step while relatively new and when they are ready to grow and need the finances to support it.

Inoculation Theory: A theory explaining that inoculation (giving audiences a small dose of an opposing argument and then refuting it) builds their resistance to future opposing messages.

Integrated Marketing Communications (IMC): This is a strategic communications activity combining the activities of advertising, promotion, and public relations to plan, develop, and implement brand-focused communications programs to generate sales or attract customers to a product or service. Increasingly, in the product and brand promotion arenas, the various forms of communications are merging, and a combined, integrated effort is launched to achieve maximum results.

Integrated Public Affairs Campaign: This term describes a comprehensive communications campaign (usually directed at influencing public policy or legislation) that combines the disciplines and activities of government relations, lobbying, *public affairs* (see definition), and traditional public relations. In most cases, these campaigns deal with complex and far-reaching issues or government policy that requires extensive communications activity focused on multiple audiences. A good example would be the ongoing debate and discussion surrounding health care reform, such as the Affordable Care Act (or "Obamacare").

Intranet: A private online network accessible only to an organization's employees.

Intrusion: The intentional disturbance, physically or otherwise, upon the solitude or seclusion of another that causes offense, mental anguish, or suffering.

Inverted Pyramid: The traditional structure of news writing and the writing of news releases.

Investor Relations (IR): This is the practice area where professionals interact with the financial community (investors, analysts, and government regulators) on behalf of a public company. While the process of outreach is very similar to PR (e.g., one-on-one meetings, group presentations, and working with the media), the rules and regulations are very different and the stakes very high. IR professionals typically have financial training and background, along with good communications skills such as writing, speaking, and acting as a spokesperson for management.

Issues Management: Issues management can be defined as an anticipatory, strategic management process that helps organizations detect and respond appropriately to emerging trends or changes in the sociopolitical environment (Dougall, 2008). Think of issues management as an "early warning" system designed to "see" things coming—like forecasting the weather and preparing ahead of time, instead of just coping when the storm happens.

Key Messages: Themes or ideas in a strategic plan that are specially designed to communicate an essential point or view that is critical to accomplishing the overall objectives. For example, it may be a key attribute that differentiates a product from its competition, a benefit that users will derive from trying a new service, or a point of view that differentiates one candidate from another in an election. These messages should be reflected in all communications outreach activity.

Latent Publics: People who are not aware of a problem or opportunity.

Lead: The first paragraph of a news story or news release.

Libel: A written or published statement of defamation.

Litigation Crisis: A crisis driven by a lawsuit (or the threat of one) and that plays out "in the court of public opinion" as well as in the legal system. The case may last for years, but the damage to accused's reputation is immediate. As a result, many organizations decide to settle the case early on rather than litigate for years.

Lobbying: In lobbying, which is also a form of "organization-to-government" communications, the principal activity involves direct contact with politicians and government rule makers to provide a point of view. The goal is to reach them and influence their decision on, or the creation of, new legislation. Lobbying efforts are often supported by traditional public relations efforts designed to generate public support for the issue or policy being discussed (see *Integrated Public Affairs Campaigns*).

Mainstream Media (also **Traditional Media**)**:** Describes the media (e.g., not newer social media platforms) that consist of newspapers, magazines, television (network and local), and radio outlets that have existed in one form or another throughout history. While virtually all media today also offer online news updates, these are viewed as extensions of the pre-Internet versions of the publication or broadcast. A media relations strategy should include strategies and tactics to reach both the "traditional" and "social" media outlets to be complete.

Material Events: News or developments that the Securities and Exchange Commission (SEC), the government agency that regulates the stock exchanges and all investment activity, views as potentially having an impact on the stock price of a *public company* (see definition). This can include a new product or a product recall, a change in senior management, the announcement of a merger or major transaction, a major news or economic event, or annual and quarterly earnings announcements. This process is also referred to as *disclosure* (see definition), and it must be done to all audiences at the same time so that no one has an unfair advantage.

Media Tour: This is a media relations tactic that involves a multicity tour, usually with a celebrity or other spokesperson. The group visits target media outlets and reporters to promote a new product or service. Originated by Dan Edelman, this tactic has become a core tactic for consumer products, fashion, authors, and celebrities to generate news coverage in multiple local markets by bringing the story to them in person.

Memes: Virally transmitted cultural symbols, often a photograph and often captioned.

Mentions: Direct reference or quotes of an entity by a media outlet.

Merger: Two firms combine as a single company.

Microblogging: Short, frequent posts broadcast on social media accounts.

Modern Era of PR: The time period beginning in the early 1900s when public relations moved beyond the era of the publicists and promoters to the current era of applying the strategies and tactics advanced by Edward Bernays and other leaders to corporations and organizations. This era saw the rise of public relations using opinion research to develop strategic plans designed to accomplish defined business objectives, not just create publicity.

Moral Impulse: The human instinct to behave morally.

Motivational Objectives: They are designed to share information and change attitudes and influence behavior.

Noise: Unplanned factors that affect the communication process.

Nonconsequentialist Theory: See *Utilitarianism*.

Nongovernmental Organizations (NGOs): This term describes private sector, voluntary (and usually nonprofit) organizations that contribute to, or participate in, projects, education, and training or other humanitarian, progressive, or watchdog activities. Major worldwide NGOs include the International Chamber of Commerce (ICC), International Committee of the Red Cross, Amnesty International, United Nations Foundation, and the World Wildlife Fund (WWF).

Normative Ethics: Ethical frameworks or theories that present moral standards guiding right or wrong conduct.

Op-Eds: Opinion pieces that usually concern current issues.

Organizational Clarity: Employees have a clear understanding of a company's vision, mission, and strategy.

Organizational Crisis: Situations that threaten an organization and its stakeholders (e.g., shareholders, customers, employees, the public) and can seriously impact performance and generate negative outcomes (Coombs, 2015). These can involve human error, criminal behavior, or deliberate sabotage and usually threaten reputation and/or ongoing operations.

Participant Observation: Research method in which the researcher participates in an activity to observe and better understand the people involved and their perspectives.

Pitch: This is a term used to describe the outreach from a PR professional to reporters (see *Gatekeeper*) to get them to consider a story idea they are proposing to seek news coverage. It likely derives from the concept of a "sales" or "elevator" pitch—and it should be short, to the point, and complete enough to pique their interest to learn more. If a "pitch" is successful, it usually leads to a more involved discussion or exchange wherein the editor or producer decides to follow up and/or develop the story idea.

Political Communications: Defined as "candidate-to-voter" communications, political communication is a dynamic, interactive campaign-based process among politicians, the news media, and the public. The process operates downward from governing institutions toward citizens, horizontally in linkages among candidates, advisors, and party officials, and upward from public opinion toward authorities (Norris, 2004). In recent years, political communication has become increasingly sophisticated with "big data," analytics, and social media playing a more prominent role alongside face-to-face, direct campaigning by the candidates.

Press Event/Publicity Stunt: This is an event or activity specifically designed to draw attention to a product, service, or celebrity and create lots of news coverage or publicity. A "stunt" may involve a trick or a dangerous activity (e.g., a high-wire act between buildings or an attempt at a Guinness record. An "event" is usually more routine and might include a celebrity appearance, a book signing, or a speech. Either way, the media is invited with the hope that news coverage will result and serve to promote a cause or a product.

Primary Research: New research activity undertaken to prepare a communications plan or activity (e.g., a survey, focus group, or other form of research).

Privacy: A right that protects citizens from harm caused by the public dissemination of truthful but private information about them; it is divided into four legal actions: intrusion, disclosure, false light, and appropriation.

Pro Bono Work: This is a term derived from the Latin term *pro bono publica* (which translates to "for the public good" and is usually shortened to "pro bono") and describes professional work undertaken voluntarily and without expectation of payment. In the

PR profession, it describes client work undertaken by an agency or consultancy to support a nonprofit or government agency that lacks the resources to hire a major firm. Pro bono work can be a source of employee engagement and serves as both a recruitment and retention strategy as well as a social responsibility activity for many firms.

Proactive *Versus* Reactive: A company or organization is viewed as proactive if it is monitoring and responding to situations as they are identified, before they erupt (e.g., issues management). Being reactive is when an organization does not act in advance and the situation escalates, requiring an organizational public response (crisis management). If an accident or *disaster* (see definition) occurs for which there is limited ability to prepare, the company is in a reactive mode and must rely on its safety and disaster protocols.

Product Crisis: A case where a manufacturing defect or bad ingredient(s) in a major product (e.g., brakes in a car, faulty batteries in a phone, bacteria in food, or unintended side effects of medicine) create a public hazard and the company is held responsible. A recall is often ordered, and the company must defend its manufacturing process, technology, or reputation as a result.

Public Affairs: There are two uses for this term. It is sometimes used to describe communications outreach and public information activities by government employees to the public in place of the term "public relations" and is a form of "government-to-citizen communications." In a government setting, the practice combines media relations, crisis communications, issues management, corporate social responsibility, public information, and strategic communications advice to elected or appointed officials. Occasionally, the term appears in a business setting, where it usually indicates company-sponsored communications focused on reaching government leaders and elected officials as opposed to the public or other stakeholders.

Public Affairs Officers (PAO): These are communicators working in a military setting. Their primary responsibilities are to advise senior officers/leaders on communications issues, assist them in making well-informed decisions, and translate those decisions into effective military operations. PAOs plan and execute communication strategies to achieve the military unit's desired objectives and evaluate the effectiveness of the programs they undertake. The PAO also facilitates media relations with domestic and international news media on behalf of their unit or commanding officer. Many PAOs pursue active careers in civilian communications after they retire from the military.

Public Company (Publicly Traded Company): This is a company that has decided to sell stock (shares) to the public to raise money (capital) to fund its growth and expansion. This process usually begins with an *initial public offering* (see definition) where the shares are sold to investors for the first time. This is a major corporate event and involves extensive communications and marketing activity as a company travels around the world (referred to as a "road show") to meet with investors who might be interested in purchasing their stock. Once a company has completed the IPO, its stock is listed on a stock exchange (e.g., the New York Stock Exchange or NASDAQ in the United States) and the price is reported on daily by the financial news services. *Material events* (see definition) often impact the stock price, and companies are required to announce (disclose) them promptly.

Public Diplomacy (PD): A process wherein governments communicate and build relationships with foreign publics to achieve their political and diplomatic objectives. Practicing PD involves mediated communication, image building, and "soft power," a concept developed by Joseph Nye (1990) that highlights a two-way relational approach versus coercion or payment. Research has shown that governmental diplomacy is supported by the social responsibility initiatives led by large and small companies in developing countries.

Public Information Officer (PIO): A related title and function to public affairs, often used by government agencies. PIOs have a variety of job duties, but written and verbal communication and media relations are the basis for much of what they do. Speechwriting and preparing testimony for legislative hearings are often duties as well. The focus is on providing information to the public about government services such as registering to vote, obtaining a driver's license, or qualifying for other government benefits. PIOs do not function as advocates for a candidate or elected officials (as a press secretary or campaign staff member would), as they are prohibited by law from doing so.

Publicist (also "Flack"): These are terms, sometimes derogatory (e.g., flack) used to describe PR professionals whose primary (or sole) purpose is to generate publicity for their clients. Most common in the entertainment, fashion, and "celebrity" arenas, this activity is focused on keeping the client visible and in the news to boost their popularity and promote their various projects (e.g., movies, television shows). The term "flack" has its origins in the concept that the publicists take criticisms or questions from the public/media to protect their clients and then assist them in developing a response or creating positive news to offset the potential damage to their reputation or marketability.

Qualitative Methods: Types of research useful to explore attitudes, perceptions, values, and opinions.

Quantitative Methods: Types of research to observe effects, test relationships, and generate numerical data that is considered objective.

Reach: Measurement of audience size; the number of people who are exposed to content.

Reputational Objectives: They are tied to a major event or crisis. The timing can be either short or long term, and they are designed to change perceptions and rebuild reputations or trust after a crisis.

Right of Publicity: Most states allow a citizen to control the commercial use of his or her identity.

ROI: An acronym for return on investment.

Scholarly Theory: Widely tested explanations of human behavior and events generated through systematic research.

Search Engine Optimization (SEO): A process to improve a website's search results.

Secondary Research: Reviewing existing research for new insights or trends. This might include reviewing a recent public opinion survey; scanning news coverage on a topic, issue, or individual; or reading scholarly research for insights on communications theory and its application to a current issue or opportunity.

Sentiment: The analysis of sentiment, also known as opinion mining; identifies the feelings (attitudes, emotions, etc.) expressed through social media communication.

Serifs: On some typefaces, short lines attached to ends of letter strokes.

Slander: Defamation that is spoken.

Social Entrepreneurship: The organization's mission is social benefit over profit.

Social Network Theory (SNT): A theory that examines and explains the web of interrelationships among people and organizations.

Socially Responsible Business Practices: Discretionary business practices to support causes or issues.

Socially Responsible Investors (SRI): This is an investment style that focuses on companies with a demonstrated track record of meeting or exceeding environmental, social, and corporate (ESG) governance criteria and generating long-term competitive financial returns and positive societal impact.

Spiral of Silence Theory: A theory explaining that ideas and opinions expressed in mass media can discourage expressions by people who hold dissenting opinions due to a sensitivity of feeling isolated or rejected.

Spokesperson: This denotes a person or expert associated with a company, organization, or government entity who is authorized to speak to the media on their behalf. You will often see quotes or comments in a news story attributed to a "spokesperson for the company." Often, this can be a PR professional, but it also might be a subject matter expert, a lawyer, or a senior company official if the situation requires it.

Stakeholders: These are people or organizations who have a "stake" in a company/organization. They may include employees, voters, government agencies and elected officials, customers, and prospective employees as well as customers and other similar individuals. Importantly, stakeholders should also be viewed as those people or organizations that are not supportive of your success, such as competitors, activists, and supporters/customers of the competition. Either pro or con, they can be said to have a "stake" in the process. *Note*: There is considerable debate in the PR profession as to whether the media should be considered a stakeholder or a vehicle to reach this audience. Most professionals consider the media to be both—especially in political and governmental communications where the media outlet may have an editorial position on the campaign or issue.

Stewardship: Tactics to maintain relationships with publics after a communication campaign has been executed.

Stock Exchange (NYSE and NASDAQ): These are the major financial markets in the United States and the world. NYSE stands the New York Stock Exchange and NASAQ stands for the National Association of Securities Dealers Automated Quotation System.

Strategic Philanthropy: This occurs when materials donated or the recipient organization has a connection to the core business of the company making the donation (e.g., a computer company donating equipment and supplies to an after-school homework center). This serves a critical need in certain neighborhoods and serves a business purpose for the company as well. These young students become familiar with and used to working with the company's products and equipment and are likely to use them when they move on in their careers.

Survey: Research method that asks both closed questions (multiple choice, yes or no, true or false) and open-ended questions.

Sustainability: Issues or aspects related to conserving the natural environment.

Talent: Entertainment performers, such as actors, DJs, and models.

Teleological Ethics: Ethics that are value based.

Thought Leadership: This is a high-level communications tactic in which a company or organization produces a survey, in-depth research, or a detailed point of view on a major issue or trend in the marketplace or society. Often, the subject matter is related directly or indirectly to the company or organization's business and is designed to show the company is actively studying and following market developments impacting its business.

Triple Bottom Line: Three performance areas a company should serve and measure: people, planet, and profit.

Two-Step Flow Theory: Explains that media can also influence early adopters of new ideas (called "opinion leaders"), who filter the content through their own interpretations and then pass it on to influence certain groups of publics.

Unbranded: The campaign or product is not linked to specific companies.

Upward Flow Theory: Explains how grassroots or general public opinions can influence an organization or political leaders.

Uses and Gratifications Theory: Explains that users of media take an active role by choosing and using certain media to meet various needs.

Utilitarianism: A teleological theory (also called consequentialism) that emphasizes consequences of actions, weighing the greatest good for the greatest number of people.

Virtue Ethics: Ethics that emphasize individual moral character, guided by one's virtue and practical wisdom.

WOM: Word-of-mouth publicity.

Working Theory: Agreed-upon ways of doing things; a hypothesis that has not been tested or proven through structured research.

REFERENCES

Alaimo, K. (2016a). *Pitch, tweet, or engage on the street: How to practice global public relations and strategic communication*. Routledge.

Alaimo, K. (2016b). Updating the generic/specific theory of international public relations: More factors to consider when practicing in new markets. *Institute for Public Relations*. http://www.instituteforpr.org/updating-genericspecific-theory-international-public-relations-factors-consider-practicing-new-markets/

Allstate Foundation Purple Purse. (n.d.). *About us/how we help page*. https://www.purplepurse.com/about-us/how-we-help.aspx

Allstate Foundation Purple Purse. (2014). *Allstate Foundation Purple Purse Silent Weapon: Domestic Violence and Financial Abuse Survey Executive Summary*. http://www.multivu.com/players/English/7253951-allstate-foundation-purple-purse-domestic-violence-awareness/links/7253951-Allstate-Purple-Purse-Survey-Executive-Summary.pdf

ALS Association. (2014). *Ice bucket challenge takes U.S. by storm*. http://web.alsa.org/site/PageNavigator/als_ice_bucket_challenge.html

Amadeo, K. (2020). Donald Trump on immigration: Pros and cons of Donald Trump's immigration policies. *The Balance*. https://www.thebalance.com/donald-trump-immigration-impact-on-economy-4151107

American Academy of Pediatric Dentistry. (2014). America's pediatric dentists bite into problem of rampant tooth decay in little teeth and encourage parents to join the monster-free mouths movement. *Cision PR Newswire*. https://www.prnewswire.com/news-releases/americas-pediatric-dentists-bite-into-problem-of-rampant-tooth-decay-in-little-teeth-and-encourage-parents-to-join-the-monster-free-mouths-movement-242372581.html

Anderson, F. (2014). Measurable objective is critical to successful evaluation. *Measurement Week/IPR*. http://www.instituteforpr.org/measurable-objective-critical-successful-evaluation/

Anderson, M., & Jiang, J. (2018, May 31). Teens, social media & technology 2018. *Pew Research Center: Internet and Technology*. https://www.pewresearch.org/internet/2018/05/31/teens-social-media-technology-2018/

Appleby, J. (2019). How well do workplace wellness programs work? *NPR*. https://www.npr.org/sections/health-shots/2019/04/16/713902890/how-well-do-workplace-wellness-programs-work

Argenti, P. A. (2016). *Corporate responsibility*. SAGE.

Arthur W. Page Center. (1932, March). *Talk on public relations*. http://comm.psu.edu/page-center/speech/talk-on-public-relations

Arthur W. Page Society. (2017). *The CEO view: Communications at the center of the enterprise*. http://awpagesociety.com/thought-leadership/the-ceo-view-communications-at-the-center-of-the-enterprise

AZQuotes. (n.d.). *Jack Welch*. https://www.azquotes.com/quote/540555

B The Change Media. (n.d.). *The 2016 best for the world honorees*. http://bftw.bthechange.com/wp-content/uploads/2016/09/BFoverall-list.pdf

Bailey, K. (n.d.). What is the role of the White House press secretary? *Dummies: A Wiley Brand*. https://www.dummies.com/education/politics-government/what-is-the-role-of-the-white-house-press-secretary/

Balasubramaniam, K. (2020, March 18). What are the advantages and disadvantages for a company going public? *Investopedia*. http://www.investopedia.com/ask/answers/06/ipoadvantagedisadvantage.asp

Ballotpedia. (n.d.). *State sunshine laws*. https://ballotpedia.org/State_sunshine_laws

Banjo, S. (2014). Inside Nike's struggle to balance cost and worker safety in Bangladesh. *The Wall Street Journal*. http://www.wsj.com/articles/SB10001424052702303873604579493502231397942

Bardhan, N., & Patwardhan, P. (2004). Multinational corporations and public relations in a historically resistant host culture. *Journal of Communication Management, 8*(3), 246–263.

Barnhart, B. (2018, April 9). Six brilliant Facebook campaigns (& why they worked). *SproutSocial*. https://sproutsocial.com/insights/facebook-campaign/

Barnum Museum. (2020). *About P.T. Barnum*. https://barnum-museum.org/about/about-p-t-barnum/

Barrett, S. (2020). Steve Barrett on PR: Firms show big US growth before crisis. *PRWeek*. https://www.prweek.com/article/1680841/steve-barrett-pr-firms-show-big-us-growth-crisis

Barthel, M. (2019). 5 key takeaways about the state of the news media in 2018. *Pew Research Center*. https://www.pewresearch.org/fact-tank/2019/07/23/key-takeaways-state-of-the-news-media-2018/

Bates, D. (2006). "Mini-me" history—Public relations from the dawn of civilization. *Institute for Public Relations*. http://www.instituteforpr.org/wp-content/uploads/MiniMe_HistoryOfPR.pdf

Baus, H. M. (1942). *Publicity, how to plan, produce and place it*. Harper.

Beaubien, G. (2019a). Best of silver anvil finalist: HP uncovers unconscious bias in hiring. *PRSA*. https://apps.prsa.org/StrategiesTactics/Articles/view/12583/1172/Best_of_Silver_Anvil_Finalist_HP_Uncovers_Unconsci#.Xmq3pahKiUk

Beaubien, G. (2019b). Best of silver anvil finalist: Signs of progress after Hurricane Maria. *PRSA*. https://www.prsa.org/article/best-of-silver-anvil-finalist-signs-of-progress-after-hurricane-maria

Beene, R. (2016). Michael Horn out as CEO at Volkswagen Group of America. *Automotive News*. http://www.autonews.com/article/20160309/OEM02/160309848/michael-horn-out-as-ceo-at-volkswagen-group-of-america

Benady, A. (2014). The godfather of modern PR Harold Burson on moral responsibilities and controversial clients. *PRWeek*. http://www.prweek.com/article/1281156/godfather-modern-pr-harold-burson-moral-responsibilities-controversial-clients

Benoit, W. L. (1995). *Accounts, excuses, and apologies: A theory of image restoration strategies*. State University of New York Press.

Bernays, E. L. (2015). *Crystallizing public opinion*. Open Road Media. Originally published in 1923. http://www.gutenberg.org/files/61364/61364-h/61364-h.htm

Best Buy. (2019). *Fiscal year 2019 corporate responsibility and sustainability report*. https://corporate.bestbuy.com/wp-content/uploads/2019/06/FY19-full-report-FINAL-1.pdf

BGR Group. (2020). *BGR group team*. https://bgrdc.com/b/bio/1/Frank-Ahrens

Bialik, C. (2011). Publicists pump up value of buzz; don't believe the hype. *The Wall Street Journal*. http://www.wsj.com/articles/SB10001424052702303339904576405683745990342

Bien, L. (2013, May 8). 49ers' Levi's Stadium the 3rd-biggest naming rights deal in American sports. *SB Nation*. http://www.sbnation.com/nfl/2013/5/8/4313344/49ers-levis-stadium-biggest-naming-rights-contracts

Block, E. M. (n.d.). The legacy of public relations excellence behind the name. *Arthur W. Page Society*. http://www.awpagesociety.com/site/historical-perspective

Bloomberg. (2019). *Record-breaking 10,000 teens to receive tech training at geek squad academy camps*. https://www.bloomberg.com/press-releases/2019-05-21/record-breaking-10-000-teens-to-receive-tech-training-at-geek-squad-academy-camps

Blue Communications. (n.d.). Wellness at AECOM. *The American Business Awards*. https://stevieawards.com/aba/blue-communications-wellness-aecom

Blue State. (n.d.). *It gets better: Uplifting LGBTQ+ youth*. https://www.bluestatedigital.com/our-work/it-gets-better/

Blythe, J. (n.d.) *The Schramm model of communication*. http://sk.sagepub.com/books/key-concepts-in-marketing/n46.xml

Bonini, S., Court, D., & Marchi, A. (2009). Rebuilding corporate reputations. *McKinsey & Company*. http://www.mckinsey.com/global-themes/leadership/rebuilding-corporate-reputations

Bonk, K., Tynes, E., Griggs, H., & Sparks, P. (2008). *Strategic communications for nonprofits: A step-by-step guide to working with the media* (2nd ed.). Jossey-Bass.

Booking.com. (2019, April 17). *Booking.com reveals key findings from its 2019 sustainable travel report*. https://globalnews.booking.com/bookingcom-reveals-key-findings-from-its-2019-sustainable-travel-report/

Boorstin, D. J. (1992). *The human image: A guide to pseudo-events in America*. Vintage.

Bortree, D. (2016). *Building legitimacy through video sustainability reports: Trends from 2010 to 2015* [Paper presentation]. Proceedings, 19th *International Public Relations Research Conference*. Coral Gables, FL, United States.http://media.wix.com/ugd/27a53c_f9e0941a0ccb4ad09d89254b8e56bb54.pdf

Boston College Center for Corporate Citizenship. (2020). *Community involvement*. https://ccc.bc.edu/content/ccc/research/corporate-citizenship-news-and-topics/corporate-community-involvement.html

Bowen, S. A. (2009). What communication professionals tell us regarding dominant coalition access and gaining membership. *Journal of Applied Communication Research, 37*(4), 427–452.

Bowen, S. A. (2013). Ethics of public relations. In R. L. Heath (Ed.), *Encyclopedia of public relations* (Vol. 1, 2nd ed.). SAGE. http://go.galegroup.com/ps/i.do? id=GALE%7CCX3719500175&v=2.1&u=trlst298&it=r&p=GVRL&sw=w&asid=12c92cebbd03c1251bb7baf50021307d

Bowen, S. A., Hung-Baesecke, C. J., & Chen, Y. R. (2016). Ethics as a precursor to organization–public relationships: Building trust before and during the OPR model. *Cogent Social Sciences, 29*(1). http://dx.doi.org/10.1080/23311886.2016.1141467

Bowler, T. (2015). Volkswagen: From the Third Reich to emissions scandal. *BBC*. http://www.bbc.com/news/business-34358783

Boyer, D. (2016). White House defends $500 million yearly public-relations budget used to spread Obama's message. *Washington Times*. http://www.washingtontimes.com/news/2016/oct/6/white-house-defends-500-million-yearly-public-rela/

Bates, D. (2019, July 2). PR writer's code of conduct, the time has come. *O'Dwyer's: The inside news of PR and marketing communications*. https://www.odwyerpr.com/story/public/12742/2019-07-02/pr-writers-code-conduct-time-has-come.html

Brandwatch. (2019). *Fake news week 2019: Fake news examples and how they're shared*. https://www.brandwatch.com/blog/fake-news-examples/

Briscoe, T. (2018a). Chicago shelter, Sessions sued after 2 Brazilian boys separated from parents at border transferred here. *Chicago Tribune*. https://www.chicagotribune.com/news/ct-met-heartland-alliance-children-shelter-20180621-story.html

Briscoe, T. (2018b). Chicago group housing 66 separated minors says it's 'a scavenger hunt' to find their families. *Chicago Tribune*. https://www.chicagotribune.com/news/breaking/ct-met-family-separation-chicago-durbin-heartland-alliance-20180622-story.html

Broom, G. M., & Dozier, D. M. (1995). *Using research in public relations: Applications to program management*. Prentice-Hall.

Branson, R. (2013). *Virgin rebel: Richard Branson in his own words*. Agate.

Browne, J., & Nuttall, R. (2013). Beyond corporate social responsibility: Integrated external engagement. *McKinsey & Company*. http://www.mckinsey.com/business-functions/strategy-and-corporate-finance/our-insights/beyond-corporate-social-responsibility-integrated-external-engagement

Buchanan, K. (2018). Virgin Media's sustainability reporting revolution: Q&A with Katie Buchanan. *Briefing Corporate Citizenship.* https://ccbriefing.corporate-citizenship .com/2018/07/30/virgin-medias-sustainability-reporting-revolution-qa-with-katie-buchanan/

Bureau of Labor Statistics, U.S. Department of Labor. (n.d.). *Occupational outlook handbook*, public relations and fundraising managers. https://www.bls.gov/ooh/ management/public-relations-managers.htm

Bureau of Labor Statistics, U.S. Department of Labor. (2020a, January 22). *Labor force statistics from the current population survey.* https://www.bls.gov/cps/cpsaat11.htm

Bureau of Labor Statistics, U.S. Department of Labor. (2020b, April 10). *Occupational outlook handbook*, public relations and fundraising managers. https://www.bls.gov/ooh/ management/public-relations-managers.htm

Burton, C. (2014). Exclusive: Meet Judy Smith, the real-life Olivia Pope. http://abc7chicago.com/entertainment/exclusive-meet-judy-smith-the-real-life-olivia-pope/324838/

Business Dictionary. (n.d.a). Globalization. http://www .businessdictionary.com/definition/globalization.html

Business Dictionary. (n.d.b). Nongovernmental organizations (NGOs). http://www.businessdictionary.com/definitions

Business Insider. (2011). *9 PR fiascos that were handled brilliantly by management.* http://www.businessinsider .com/pr-disasters-crisis-management-2011-5-taco-bells-seasoned-beef-meat-filling-lawsuit-2011-9

Business Research Company. (2020). *Public relations global market report 2020.* https://www.thebusinessresearchcompany. com/report/public-relations-global-market-report

Business Wire. (2017a, February 9). *Cesar Millan takes on role as rescuer and rehabilitator in new series*, Cesar Millan's Dog Nation. http://www.businesswire.com/news/ home/20170209005948/en/

Business Wire. (2017b, February 9). *Dolby Cinema showcases strong spring lineup.* http://www.businesswire.com/news/ home/20170209005564/en/

Business Wire. (2017c, February 0). *Jessica Ray swimwear.* http://www.businesswire.com/news/ home/20170209006179/en/

Canon. (n.d.). http://downloads.canon.com/nw/about/ corporate-pub/canon-story-2016-2017-e.pdf

Carr, A. (2015). The inside story of Starbucks's race together campaign, no foam. *Fast Company.* https://www .fastcompany.com/3046890/the-inside-story-of-starbuckss-race-together-campaign-no-foam

Carroll, A. B., & Buchholtz, A. K. (2014). *Business and society: Ethics, sustainability, and stakeholder management.* Nelson Education.

Carufel, R. (2017, April 7). Deep research and expert media targeting earn Duffy & Shanley huge coverage for client Deepwater Wind's offshore wind farm campaign—and a gold bulldog award. *Bulldog Reporter.* https://www .bulldogreporter.com/deep-research-and-expert-media-targeting-earn-duffy-shanley-huge-coverage-for-client-deepwater-winds-offshore-wind-farm-campaign-and-a-gold-bulldog-award/

CASE. (n.d.). *Research and news of note: Public relations efforts top source for education journalists.* http://www.case.org/ Publications_and_Products/September_2016_BriefCASE/ Research_and_News_of_Note_September_2016/Public_ Relations_Efforts_Top_Source_for_Education_Journalists.html

Catalyst. (2019). *Generations-demographic trends in population and workforce: Quick take.* https://www.catalyst .org/research/generations-demographic-trends-in-population-and-workforce/

Cayce, M. (2015). Public relations confidentiality: An analysis of PR practitioner–client privilege in high profile litigation. *Public Relations Review, 41*(1), 14–21.

CDC. (n.d.). *Sickle cell disease.* https://www.cdc.gov/ncbddd/ sicklecell/data.html

Centers for Disease Control and Prevention. (n.d.). *What is health communications?* https://www.cdc.gov/ healthcommunication/healthbasics/whatishc.html

Chadwick, P. (2017). Defining fake news will help us expose it. *The Guardian* (U.S. edition). https://www.theguardian .com/media/commentisfree/2017/may/12/defining-fake-news-will-help-us-expose-it

Chandler, D. (2017). *Strategic corporate social responsibility* (4th ed.). SAGE.

Christensen, L. J., Peirce, E., Hartman, L. P., Hoffman, W. M., & Carrier, J. (2007). Ethics, CSR, and sustainability education in the *Financial Times* top 50 global business schools: Baseline data and future research directions. *Journal of Business Ethics, 73*(4), 347–368.

Cialdini, R. (2001). *Influence: Science and practice* (4th ed.). Pearson.

Cision. (2012). How social media is changing PR. *Beyond PR.* http://www.prnewswire.com/blog/how-social-media-is-changing-pr-4406.html

Cision. (2016). *State of the media report.* http://www.cision .com/us/resources/white-papers/state-of-the-media-2016-report/? clid=whitepaper-ty

Cision. (2017, April 13). *How your news release can help the media do their job: Cision's 2017 State of the Media Report.* http://www.cision.com/us/2017/04/how-your-news-release-can-help-the-media-do-their-job/ and http://www.cision.com/us/resources/white-papers/the-cision-2017-state-of-the-media-report/? clid=whitepaper-ty

Cision. (2019). *Cision's 2019 global state of the media report.* https://www.cision.com/content/dam/cision/Resources/ white-papers/2019_Q2_SOTM_report.pdf

Citizens Clean Elections Commission. (2019). *Clean elections youth voter campaign "18 in 2018" nominated for a national award.* https://www.azcleanelections.gov/media/pr-week-awards

Citizens United v. FEC, 130 S. Ct. 876 (2010).

Cloutier, C. (2014). Facebook: 1.2 million #IceBucketChallenge videos posted. *Boston Globe.* https://www.bostonglobe .com/business/2014/08/15/facebook-million-icebucket challenge-videos-posted/24D8bnxFlrMce5BRTixAEM/ story.html

CNBC. (2015a). *I am American business*. https://www.cnbc.com/id/100000662

CNBC. (2015b, March 18). Starbucks CEO Howard Schultz: "Race Together" campaign [Television series segment]. In *Mad Money*. CNBC.

Cobb, J. G. (1999). This just in: Model T gets award. *The New York Times*. https://www.nytimes.com/1999/12/24/automobiles/this-just-in-model-t-gets-award.html

The Coca-Cola Company. (n.d.). *Mission, vision, and values*. http://www.coca-colacompany.com/out-company/mission-vision-values

The Coca-Cola Company. (2020). *Better shared future*. https://www.coca-colacompany.com/shared-future

Comcowich, W. (2015). How much should companies spend on marketing & PR? *CyberAlert*. http://www.cyberalert.com/blog/how-much-should-companies-spend-on-marketing-pr/?replytocom=89418

Comparably. (2020). *Diversity at the Coca-Cola Company*. https://www.comparably.com/companies/the-coca-cola-company/diversity

Cone. (2015). Cone communications millennial CSR study, 2015. http://www.conecomm.com/research-blog/2015-cone-communications-millennial-csr-study

Cone. (2018). *2018 Porter Novelli/Cone purpose premium index: How companies can unlock reputational gains by leading with purpose*. https://www.conecomm.com/research-blog/purpose-premium

Cone. (2019). *2019 Porter Novelli/Cone Gen Z purpose study*. https://www.conecomm.com/research-blog/cone-gen-z-purpose-study

Cone Communications. (2014, June 19). *Cone Communications and Johnson & Johnson awarded PRSA's 2014 silver anvil award of excellence*. http://www.conecomm.com/news-blog/cone-communications-and-johnson-johnson-awarded-prsas-2014-silver-anvil-award-of-excellence

Cone Communications. (2015). *CSR & millennials: Overview*. https://conemillennialcsr.com/millennialoverview

Cone Communications. (2016). *Employee engagement study*. http://www.conecomm.com/research-blog/2016-employee-engagement-study

Confessore, N., & Yourish, K. (2016, March 15). $2 billion worth of free media for Trump. *The New York Times*. https://www.nytimes.com/2016/03/16/upshot/measuring-donald-trumps-mammoth-advantage-in-free-media.html

Conway, D. (2012). Copyright and the PR professional in the digital age. *Bulldog Reporter*. https://www.bulldogreporter.com/copyright-and-pr-professional-digital-age/

Coombs, W. T. (2014a). Crisis management and communications. *Institute for Public Relations*. http://www.instituteforpr.org/crisis-management-communications/

Coombs, W. T. (2014b). State of crisis communication: Evidence and the bleeding edge. *Research Journal of the Institute for Public Relations, 1*(1), p. 3. http://www.instituteforpr.org/wp-content/uploads/CoombsFinalWES.pdf

Coombs, W. T. (2015). *Ongoing crisis communication: Planning, managing, and responding* (4th ed.). SAGE.

Cowden, K., & Sellnow, T. L. (2002). Issues advertising as crisis communication: Northwest Airlines' use of image restoration strategies during the 1998 pilot's strike. *Journal of Business Communication, 39*(2), 193–219.

Creel, G. (1920). *How we advertised America: The first telling of the amazing story of the Committee on Public Information that carried the gospel of Americanism to every corner of the globe*. Harper & Brothers.

Crisis Communications Strategies. (n.d.). DoD joint course in communications. *University of Oklahoma*. http://www.ou.edu.deptcomm/dodjss/groups/O2C2

Croft, A. (2019). The year in M&A: "Super mega" deals and a fourth-quarter surge put dealmakers on top in 2019. *Fortune*. https://fortune.com/2019/12/31/super-mega-mergers-deals-2019/.

Culbertson, H. M., Jeffers, D. W., Stone, D. B., & Terrell, M. (2012). *Social, political, and economic contexts in public relations: Theory and cases*. Routledge.

Curtin, P. A., & Boynton, L. A. (2000). Ethics in public relations: Theory and practice. In R. L. Heath (Ed.), *Handbook of public relations* (pp. 411–421). SAGE.

Cutlip, S. M., Center, A. H., & Broom, G. M. (1994). *Effective public relations*. Prentice Hall.

Cutlip, S. M., Center, A. H., & Broom, G. M. (2000). *Effective public relations*. Prentice Hall.

Daniels, C. (2015). How the CCO role is changing—It's complicated. *PRWeek*. http://www.prweek.com/article/1342255/cco-role-changing-its-complicated

Davie, G. (n.d.). *Gatekeeping theory*. https://masscommtheory.com/theory-overviews/gatekeeping-theory/

de Brooks, K. P., & Waymer, D. (2009). Public relations and strategic issues management challenges in Venezuela: A discourse analysis of Crystallex International Corporation in Las Cristinas. *Public Relations Review, 35*(1), 31–39.

Deardorff, J. (2015). Teens turn to Internet to cope with health challenges. *Northwestern Now*. https://news.northwestern.edu/stories/2015/06/teens-turn-to-internet-to-cope-with-health-challenges/

Delisio, E. R. (July, 2017). How companies can engage employees to support the core sustainability missions. *Green Edge*. https://greenedge.co.za/2017/06/29/companies-can-engage-employees-support-core-sustainability-missions/

Dempsey, C. (2017, May 2). No Boston Olympics: How and why smart cities are passing on the torch. *No Boston Olympics*. http://www.nobostonolympics.org/

Dezenhall, E. (1999). *Nail 'em! Confronting high-profile attacks on celebrities & businesses*. Prometheus Books.

Diaz, E. (2019, June 28). Where we stand on immigration. *Heartland Alliance*. https://www.heartlandalliance.org/where-we-stand-on-immigration/

Dorsey, A., & Garlinghouse, M. (2015). The power and unrealized promise of skilled volunteering. In *Volunteer engagement 2.0: Ideas and insights changing the world* (pp. 197–209). John Wiley & Sons.

Dougall, E. (2008). Issues management. *Institute for Public Relations*. http://www.instituteforpr.org/issues-management/

Dozier, D. M. (1985). Planning and evaluation in PR practice. *Public Relations Review, 11*(2), 17–25.

Dozier, D. M., & Broom, G. M. (1995). Evolution of the manager role in public relations practice. *Journal of Public Relations Research, 7*(1), 3–26.

Dozier, D., & Grunig, L. A. (1992). Organization of public relations function. In J. E. Grunig (Ed.), *Excellence in public relations and communication management* (pp. 395–418). Routledge.

The Drum. (2019). *Octopus group: Tudder "Tinder for cows."* https://www.thedrumprawards.com/the-drum-pr-awards-2019/most-effective-use-of-social-media/tudder-tinder-for-cows

Duffin, E. (2019). U.S. nonprofit organizations: Biggest challenges 2019. *Statista.* https://www.statista.com/statistics/502411/us-nonprofit-organizations-biggest-challenges-for-fundraising/

Duggan, M., & Smith, A. (2016). The political environment on social media. *Pew Research Center.* http://www.pewinternet.org/2016/10/25/the-political-environment-on-social-media/

Dumont, M. (2019). 4 biggest merger and acquisitions disasters. *Investopedia.* https://www.investopedia.com/articles/financial-theory/08/merger-acquisition-disasters.asp

eBiz/MBA. (2020). *Top 15 best social networking sites & apps.* http://www.ebizmba.com/articles/social-networking-websites

Ebrahimji, A. (2019). California bans travel-size plastic shampoo bottles from hotels. *CNN Travel.* https://www.cnn.com/travel/article/shampoo-plastic-bottles-ban-trnd/index.html

Economy, P. (2017, May). A 5-step social-responsibility action plan. *Inc.* https://www.inc.com/peter-economy/a-social-responsibility-action-plan-for-2014.html

Edelman. (2010). *Citizens engage! Edelman goodpurpose study 2010—Fourth annual global consumer survey.* http://ppqty.com/GoodPurpose2010globalPPT_WEBversion (1).pdf

Edelman. (2014). *2014 Edelman trust barometer.* https://www.edelman.com/research/2014-edelman-trust-barometer

Edelman. (2015). *Edelman's position on climate change.* http://www.edelman.com/who-we-are/values-and-mission/edelmans-position-climate-change/

Edelman. (2016, January 17). *2016 Edelman trust barometer finds global trust inequality is growing.* http://www.edelman.com/news/2016-edelman-trust-barometer-release/

Edelman. (2017). *2017 Edelman Trust Barometer: Executive summary.* http://www.edelman.com/executive-summary/

Edelman. (2019). *2019 Edelman trust barometer.* https://www.edelman.com/sites/g/files/aatuss191/files/2019-02/2019_Edelman_Trust_Barometer_Global_Report.pdf

Edelman. (2020). *2020 Edelman trust barometer.* https://www.edelman.com/trustbarometer

Edelman Insights. (n.d.). *University reputations and the public.* http://www.slideshare.net/EdelmanInsights/university-reputations-and-the-public

Edelman, R. (2014). *The rise of communications marketing.* http://www.edelman.com/insights/intellectual-property/the-rise-of-communications-marketing/

Edible. (2018). *Gerber® photo search.* https://www.edible-inc.com/project/gerber-photo-search.

Editorial Board. (2016, April 24). Long road to trust for the car industry. *Christian Science Monitor.* http://www.csmonitor.com/Commentary/the-monitors-view/2016/0424/Long-road-to-trust-for-the-car-industry

Educationdata.org. (2018). *How many public schools are there in the U.S.?* https://educationdata.org/number-of-public-schools/

EIF. (n.d.). *About.* http://www.eifoundation.org/

Eilbirt, H., & Parket, I. R. (1973). The practice of business: The current status of corporate social responsibility. *Business Horizons, 16*(4), 5–14.

Eisen, B. (2020, Jan. 14). Wells Fargo CEO: A wonderful bank that made "some terrible mistakes." *The Wall Street Journal.* https://www.wsj.com/articles/wells-fargos-results-sink-on-legal-reserves-11579007417?mod=searchresults&page=1&pos=20

Elliott, S. (2011). Redefining public relations in the age of social media. *The New York Times.* http://www.nytimes.com/2011/11/21/business/media/redefining-public-relations-in-the-age-of-social-media.html?_r=0

Elkington, J., & Hartigan, P. (2008). *The power of unreasonable people: How social entrepreneurs create markets that change the world.* Harvard Business Press.

Ember, S. (2016). New York Times Co. reports loss as digital subscriptions grow. *The New York Times.* http://www.nytimes.com/2016/05/04/business/media/new-york-times-co-q1-earnings.html

Engage for Good. (n.d.). *Safe kids worldwide.* http://engageforgood.com/halo-award/2016-golden-halo-award-nonprofit/

Entman, R. M. (1993). Framing: Toward clarification of a fractured paradigm. *Journal of Communication, 43*(4), 51–58.

Erickson, S. L., Weber, M., & Segovia, J. (2011). Using communication theory to analyze corporate reporting strategies. *Journal of Business Communication, 48*(2), 207–223.

Erz, A., Marder, B., & Osadchaya, E. (2018). Hashtags: Motivational drivers, their use, and differences between influencers and followers. *Computers in Human Behavior, 89.* http://www.espn.com/sportsbusiness/s/stadiumnames.html

ESPN. (2017, January 14). *Sports business: stadium naming rights.*

Facebook. (n.d.). *Stats.* http://newsroom.fb.com/company-info/

Feldman, E. (2015). How to handle copyright's 50 shades of gray. *Cision.* http://www.cision.com/us/2015/12/how-to-handle-copyrights-50-shades-of-gray/

Ferreira, A., & Teles, S. (2019). Persuasion: How phishing emails can influence users and bypass security measures. *International Journal of Human-Computer Studies, 125*(5), 19–31.

Fink, S. (1986). *Crisis management: Planning for the inevitable.* American Management Association.

Fitzpatrick, K., Fullerton, J., & Kendrick, A. (2013). Public relations and public diplomacy: Conceptual and practical connections. *Public Relations Journal, 7*(4), 1–21.

Flecha, J., Ortiz, M., & Dones, V. (2017). Risk communication: The media content effect on brain drain—The case of Puerto Rico. *Communication & Society, 30*(3), 97–107.

Fleming, M. (2019). VW overhauls its brand for a "new era" as it attempts to put emissions scandal behind it. *MarketingWeek*. https://www.marketingweek.com/volkswagen-brand-redesign/

Flores, A., Lopez, M. H., & Krogstad, J. M. (2019). U.S. Hispanic population reached new high in 2018, but growth has slowed. *Pew Research Center*. https://www.pewresearch.org/fact-tank/2019/07/08/u-s-hispanic-population-reached-new-high-in-2018-but-growth-has-slowed/

FOIA. (n.d.). *Freedom of Information Act*. https://www.foia.gov/

Fontein, D. (2016). The best time to post of Facebook, Twitter, and Instagram. *Hootsuite Blog*. https://blog.hootsuite.com/best-time-to-post-on-facebook-twitter-instagram/

Fortune. (2017). *World's most admired companies*. http://fortune.com/worlds-most-admired-companies/

Foster, S. (2010). *Political communication*. Edinburgh University Press.

Freeman, C. P. (2009). A greater means to the greater good: Ethical guidelines to meet social movement organization advocacy challenges. *Journal of Mass Media Ethics, 24,* 269–288.

Frey, W. H. (2018a). The millennial generation: A demographic bridge to America's diverse future. *Brookings*. https://www.brookings.edu/research/millennials/

Frey, W. H. (2018b). The US will become "minority white" in 2045, Census projects. *Brookings*. https://www.brookings.edu/blog/the-avenue/2018/03/14/the-us-will-become-minority-white-in-2045-census-projects/

Friedman, D. (2019, April 3). Netflix: #1 corporate reputation in the United States. *RepTrak*. https://insights.reputationinstitute.com/blog-ri/netflix-1-corporate-reputation-in-the-united-states.

FTC. (2009). *FTC publishes final guides governing endorsements, testimonials*. https://www.ftc.gov/news-events/press-releases/2009/10/ftc-publishes-final-guides-governing-endorsements-testimonials

Gajanan, M. (2019). "Daryl Morey was right": Shaquille O'Neal weighs in on NBA–China controversy. *Time*. https://time.com/5708184/shaquille-oneal-daryl-morey-nba-china/

Galvez-Rodriguez, M., Haro-de-Rosario, A., & Caba-Perez, C. (2018). Improving citizens' online engagement via community managers: An explanatory study. *Information, Communication & Society, 21*(10).

Garfield, B. (1999). Ad age advertising century: The top 100 campaigns. *Ad Age*. http://adage.com/article/special-report-the-advertising-century/ad-age-advertising-century-top-100-campaigns/140918/

GCI Health. (2019). *The HealthiHer movement: Enoucraging women to make their health a priority*. https://www.provokemedia.com/agency-playbook/sponsored/article/the-healthiher-movement-encouraging-women-to-make-their-health-a-priority

Gelles, D. (2018). Paul Polman, a "crucial voice for corporate responsibility," steps down as Unilever CEO. *The New York Times*. https://www.nytimes.com/2018/11/29/business/unilever-ceo-paul-polman.html

George-Parkin, H. (2019). Nike slips behind Adidas in corporate reputation rankings. *Footwear News*. https://footwearnews.com/2019/business/retail/nike-adidas-corporate-reputation-1202758821/

Gibson, W. (2014). How organizations should handle false, defamatory Reddit posts. *PR Daily*. http://www.prdaily.com/Main/Articles/17649.aspx

Girion, L. (2003). Nike settles lawsuit over labor claims. *LA Times*. http://articles.latimes.com/2003/sep/13/business/fi-nike13

Gitlin, T. (2003). *The whole world is watching: Mass media in the making and unmaking of the new left*. University of California Press.

Global WebIndex. (2019). *Gen Z audience report*. https://www.globalwebindex.com/hubfs/Downloads/Generation_Z_report_2019.pdf?utm_campaign=Gen%20Z%20report%202019&utm_source=hs_automation&utm_medium=email&utm_content=71833136&_hsenc=p2ANqtz-9hZacahs1gB4YO2_CATRFYZtY1NSO71XsFJRIIixwKgC6awr9brnHr6C8-n1c06xRLeKQpiA6v07AFOtSWc6lLdNoO4w&_hsmi=71833136

Gloster, R. (2014, February 19). Under Armour goes to damage control instead of cold in Sochi. *Bloomberg Technology*. https://www.bloomberg.com/news/articles/2014-02-17/under-armour-goes-for-damage-control-instead-of-gold-at-olympics

Goffman, E. (1974). *Frame analysis: An essay on the organization of experience*. Harvard University Press.

Golan, G. J. (2013). *An integrated approach to public diplomacy*. SAGE.

Golan, G. J., Yang, S.-U., & Kinsey, D. F. (2015). *International public relations and public diplomacy*. Peter Lang.

Goldenberg, S. (2015). Edelman ends work with coal producers and climate change deniers. *The Guardian*. https://www.theguardian.com/environment/2015/sep/15/edelman-ends-work-with-coal-and-climate-change-deniers

Gomez, D., & Reed, E. (n.d.). The need for cultural intelligence. *Arthur W. Page Society*. http://www.awpagesociety.com/attachments/c41877da2bcd2e784530e629e003dec046743055/store/15fb6cb1e84b2c4e026b43edf0efbf4fb46dde3d0beb4feb7a5b2b8fc006/AsianaAirlinesCaseStudy.pdf

Gordon, R. (2009). Penn defends firm post-Maddow show. *PRWeek*. http://www.prweek.com/article/1272801/penn-defends-firm-post-maddow-show

Gottfried, J., & Shearer, E. (2016). News use across social media platforms 2016. *Pew Research Center*. http://www.journalism.org/files/2016/05/PJ_2016.05.26_social-media-and-news_FINAL-1.pdf

Granger, R. (2018). Aflac's CSR efforts fit the bill: How a duck helped strengthen the company's reputation. *PRSA*. https://apps.prsa.org/StrategiesTactics/Articles/view/12273/1158/Aflac_s_CSR_Efforts_Fit_the_Bill_How_a_Duck_Helped#.XtvMXjpKhPY

Granovetter, M. S. (1973). The strength of weak ties. *American Journal of Sociology, 78*(6), 1360–1380.

Green, J. (2016). LGBT purchasing power near $1 trillion rivals other minorities. *Bloomberg*. https://www.bloomberg.com/news/articles/2016-07-20/lgbt-purchasing-power-near-1-trillion-rivals-other-minorities

Greenburg, Z. O. (2019). The world's highest-paid entertainers 2019. *Forbes*. https://www.forbes.com/celebrities/#116890b5947d

Gregory, D., & Kirschenbaum, J. (2012). *Chester Burger*. https://jmc492pr.wordpress.com/2012/02/page/7/

Gregory, L. (2019). Mexico's secretary of tourism shares new strategies. *Travel Pulse*. https://www.travelpulse.com/news/destinations/mexicos-secretary-of-tourism-shares-new-strategies.html

Gregory, S. (2019). The losses have already been substantial: Adam Silver addresses fallout from the NBA–China controversy. *Time*. https://time.com/5703259/adam-silver-nba-china-time-100-health-summit/

Griffin, E. (2017). *Theories covered in 9th edition*. http://www.afirstlook.com/edition_9/theory_list

Grunig, J. E. (1992). *Excellence in public relations and communication management*. Mahwah, NJ: Lawrence Erlbaum Associates.

Grunig, J. (2013). *Excellence theory*. https://excellencetheory.wordpress.com/2013/09/27/pr-professional-3-qa/

Grunig, J. E., & Hunt, T. (1984). *Managing public relations*. Holt, Rinehart and Winston.

Grunig, L. A., Grunig, J. E., & Verčič, D. (1998). Are the IABC's excellence principles generic? Comparing Slovenia and the United States, the United Kingdom and Canada. *Journal of Communication Management, 2*(4), 335–356.

Guttmann, A. (2019, Aug. 9). Coca-Colas brand value from 2006 to 2019. *Statista*. https://www.statista.com/statistics/326065/coca-cola-brand-value/

Hakim, D. (2016, February 26). VW's crisis strategy: Forward, reverse, u-turn. *The New York Times*. http://www.nytimes.com/2016/02/28/business/international/vws-crisis-strategy-forward-reverse-u-turn.html?_r=0

Hannah-Jones, N. (2017, January 23). When Ida B. Wells married, it was a page one story. *The New York Times*. https://www.nytimes.com/interactive/projects/cp/weddings/165-years-of-wedding-announcements/ida-wells-wedding

Haran, L., & Sheffer, G. (2015). Is the chief communications officer position going the way of the dodo? *PRWeek*. http://www.prweek.com/article/1339638/chief-communications-officer-position-going-dodo

The Harris Poll. (2016). *The Harris poll releases annual reputation rankings for the 100 most visible companies in the U.S.* http://www.theharrispoll.com/business/Reputation-Rankings-Most-Visible-Companies.html

Harvard Business School. (n.d.). *Social enterprise: About history*. http://www.hbs.edu/socialenterprise/about/Pages/history.aspx

Hawkins, W. (2012, June 11). Connecting & enriching the lives of every person on earth. *Intel*. https://blogs.intel.com/csr/2012/06/connecting-enriching-the-lives-of-every-person-on-earth/#gs.6csfhj

Healthy Women. (2018). *HealthiHer*. https://www.healthywomen.org/content/article/behealthiher

Heartland Alliance. (n.d.). *Facts about our shelters*. https://www.heartlandalliance.org/facts-about-our-shelters/

Heath, A. (2019, Feb. 14). Spotlight on Patagonia: Core values key to employee engagement. *wethrive*. https://wethrive.net/blog/spotlight-patagonia-core-values-key-employee-engagement/

Heath, D., & Heath, C. (2007). *Made to stick: Why some ideas survive and others die*. Random House.

Heath, R. L. (Ed.). (2001). *Handbook of public relations*. SAGE.

Hertz. (2013). *Hertz announces corporate headquarters relocation*. http://newsroom.hertz.com/2013-05-07-Hertz-Announces-Corporate-Headquarters-Relocation

Ho, B., Shin, W., & Pang, A. (2017). Corporate crisis advertising: A framework examining the use and effects of corporate advertising before and after crises. *Journal of Marketing Communications, 23*(6).

Ho Lee, T. (2017). The status of corporate social responsibility research in public relations: A content analysis of published articles in eleven scholarly journals from 1980 to 2015. *Public Relations Review, 43*(1), 211–218.

Holmes, P. (2017a, May 1). "Public relations": Now more than ever. *The Holmes Report*. https://www.holmesreport.com/long-reads/article/%27public-relations%27-now-more-than-ever

Holmes, P. (2017b, March 30). 2017 global communications report predicts convergence of marketing and PR. *The Holmes Report*. https://www.holmesreport.com/latest/article/2017-global-communications-report-predicts-convergence-of-marketing-and-pr

Holmes, P. (2019a). *Always #LikeAGirl tops our top 10 campaigns of the decade*. PRovoke. https://www.provokemedia.com/long-reads/article/always-likeagirl-tops-our-top-10-campaigns-of-the-decade

Holmes, P. (2019b, Oct. 24). *Gerber's "every baby" campaign takes home platinum award at global SABREs*. https://www.provokemedia.com/latest/article/gerber's-every-baby-campaign-takes-home-platinum-award-at-global-sabres

Holmes, S. L. (1976). Executive perceptions of corporate social responsibility. *Business Horizons, 19*(3), 34–40.

Holtzhausen, D. R. (2015). The unethical consequences of professional communication codes of ethics: A postmodern analysis of ethical decision-making in communication practice. *Public Relations Review, 41*, 769–776.

Hoonhout, T. (2019). AOC joins Cruz, Sasse, others in letter to NBA's Silver condemning league for "betrayal of American values." *National Review*. https://www.nationalreview.com/news/china-nba-dispute-legislators-condemn-league-for-betrayal-of-american-values/

HSN, Inc. (2017, February 19). HSN ignites designers' creativity with the launch of its enchanting Disney *Beauty and the Beast* collection. https://globenewswire.com/news-release/2017/02/09/915638/0/en/HSN-Ignites-Designers-Creativity-With-the-Launch-of-Its-Enchanting-Disney-Beauty-and-the-Beast-Collection.html

Hu, X., Rodgers, K., & Lovrich, N. P. (2018). "We are more than crime fighters": Social media images of police departments. *Police Quarterly, 21*(40).

Humana. (n.d.). Humana believes everyone should have access to affordable, quality healthcare coverage. https://

closethegap.humana.com/how-we-are-closing-the-gap/mississipi-story-health-insurance-access/

Hyundai Motor America with Ketchum. (2015). Driving on hydrogen—Launching Hyundai's Tucson fuel cell vehicle. http://apps.prsa.org/SearchResults/Download/6BE-1502AG1553/0/Driving_on_Hydrogen_Launching_Hyundai_s_Tucson_Fue

IBM. (n.d.a). *Education & workforce development.* http://www.ibm.com/ibm/responsibility/initiatives.html#cce

IBM. (n.d.b). IBM Corporate Service Corps. http://www.ibm.com/ibm/responsibility/corporateservicecorps/pdf/CSC-Benefits_Infographic.pdf

IBM. (n.d.c). IBM's Corporate Service Corps and the Global FoodBanking Network. http://www.ibm.com/ibm/responsibility/corporateservicecorps/pdf/GFN_case_study.pdf

ICA Conference Paper. (2018). *Emotion contagion and stakeholder engagement on nonprofit organizations' Facebook sites: A big data perspective.* http://web.b.ebscohost.com.proxygw.wrlc.org/ehost/detail/detail? vid=9&sid=b85db963-6bca-4218-9a5a-4c28bdb89242%40pdc-v-sessmgr01&bdata=JnNpdGU9ZWhvc3QtbGl2ZQ%3d%3d#db=ufh&AN=135748405

ICON Clinical Research—Launch Video for Spark. (n.d.). The American Business Awards. https://stevieawards.com/aba/icon-clinical-research-launch-video-spark

Inglespc. (n.d.). *A brief history of social media (1969–2015).* http://inglespc.com/a-brief-history-of-social-media-1969-2012/

Inside Social Media. (2009). *Intel's social media policy.* https://insidesocialmedia.com/social-media-policies/intel-social-media-policy/

Institute for Public Relations. (n.d.). PR measurement standards. http://www.instituteforpr.org/wp-content/uploads/Standards-dos-and-donts-09302014.pdf

Institute for Public Relations. (2015). Barcelona principles 2.0. *AMEC.* https://amecorg.com/barcelona-principles-2-0/

International Business Awards. (2019). *MSL: Consumer PR for Pampers.* https://stevieawards.com/iba/msl-consumer-pr-pampers

Isidore, C., & Goldman, D. (2016). Volkswagen agrees to record $14.7 billion settlement over emissions cheating. *CNN Money.* http://money.cnn.com/2016/06/28/news/companies/volkswagen-fine/

It Gets Better. (2020). *Home.* http://www.itgetsbetter.org/

Iwata, J., & Golin, A. (2009). Toward a new profession: Brand, constituency and eminence on the global commons. *Institute for Public Relations.* http://www.instituteforpr.org/global-brand-constituency-eminence/

Jin, Y., Liu, B. F., & Austin, L. L. (2014). Examining the role of social media in effective crisis management: The effects of crisis origin, information form, and source on publics' crisis responses. *Communication Research, 41*(1), pp. 74–94. Originally published 2011. 10.1177/0093650211423918

Johnson, R. (n.d.). The top 10 characteristics of a healthy organization. *Chron.* http://smallbusiness.chron.com/top-10-characteristics-healthy-organization-20452.html

Jurnecka, R. (2015). Volkswagen Golf is the 2015 *Motor Trend* car of the year. http://www.motortrend.com/news/2015-volkswagen-golf-is-the-motor-trend-car-of-the-year/

Kaplan, T. (2005). *The Tylenol crisis: How effective public relations saved Johnson & Johnson.* http://www.aerobiologicalengineering.com/wxk116/TylenolMurders/crisis.html

Katz, A. J. (2016). Led by A. Holt, NBC *Nightly News* is now no. 1 for 20 consecutive seasons. *Adweek.* http://www.adweek.com/tvnewser/led-by-lester-holt-nbc-nightly-news-is-now-no-1-for-20-consecutive-seasons/305030

Katzenback, J., Oelschlegel, C., & Thomas, J. (2016). Ten principles of organizational culture. *Strategy+Business, 82.* http://www.strategy-business.com/article/10-Principles-of-Organizational-Culture? gko=71d2f

Kaye, J. (2005). Coca-Cola India. *Artur W. Page Society.* http://www.awpagesociety.com/study_competitions/2005-case-study-competition

Kaye, L. (2011, March 28). SAP 2010 CSR report boasts US$470M in energy savings. *Greengopost.com.* http://greengopost.com/sap-2010-csr-report-boasts-us470m-energy-savings/

Keck, M. (2019). *U of L and John Schnatter reach settlement over stadium naming rights.* http://www.louisvilleblogs.com/?cat=10426

Kelly, K. S. (2001). Stewardship. In R. Heath (Ed.), *Handbook of public relations* (pp. 279–289). Thousand Oaks, CA: SAGE.

Kent, A. (2014). 10 internal communications thought leaders you should follow. *Red e APP.* https://redeapp.com/2014/12/22/10-internal-communications-thought-leaders-you-should-follow/

Kesmodel, D., & Brat, I. (2015). Why Starbucks takes on social issues. *The Wall Street Journal.* http://www.wsj.com/articles/why-starbucks-takes-on-social-issues-1427155129

Ketchum. (2016). *Home.* http://www.ketchum.com

Kim, C. M., & Brown, W. J. (2015, Winter). Conceptualizing credibility in social media spaces of public relations. *Public Relations Journal, 9*(4). http://www.prsa.org/Intelligence/PRJournal/Vol9/No4/

Kim, S., & Ferguson, M. A. T. (2014). Public expectations of CSR communication: What and how to communicate CSR. *Public Relations Journal, 8*(3). https://prjournal.instituteforpr.org/wp-content/uploads/2014KIMFERGUSON.pdf

Kochhar, S. (2016, Summer). Organizational clarity: The new engagement for internal communications. *Public Relations Strategist, 22*(2). https://apps.prsa.org/Intelligence/TheStrategist/Articles/view/11587/1129/Organizational_Clarity_The_New_Engagement_for_Inte#.XtRSHzpKhPZ

Kotler, P., & Gertner, D. (2002). Country as brand, product, and beyond: A place marketing and brand management perspective. *Journal of Brand Management, 9*(4), 249–261.

Kotler, P., & Lee, K. (2005). *Corporate social responsibility: Doing the most good for your company and your cause.* Wiley.

Krajewski, J. M. T., Schumacher, A. C., & Dalrymple, K. E. (2019). Just turn on the faucet: A content analysis of PSAs about the global water crisis on YouTube. *Environmental Communication, 13*(2).

Krieg, G. (2017, January 19). Police injured, more than 200 arrested at Trump inauguration protests in DC. *CNN Politics*. https://www.cnn.com/2017/01/19/politics/trump-inauguration-protests-womens-march/index.html

Kuczynski, A. (2000, May 8). In public relations, 25% admit lying. *The New York Times*, sec. C, p. 20, col. 5.

Lahav, T., & Zimand-Sheiner, D. (2016). Public relations and the practice of paid content: Practical, theoretical propositions and ethical implications. *Public Relations Review, 42*(3), 395–401.

Lapeer Downtown. (2018). *Art on Nepessing St.: A celebration of the arts in downtown Lapeer, Michigan*. http://cms5.revize.com/revize/greaterlapeer/AoN%20Fact%20Sheet%202018.pdf

Larcker, D. F., & Tayan, D. (2018). 2018 CEO activism survey. https://www.gsb.stanford.edu/faculty-research/publications/2018-ceo-activism-survey

Lauterer, S. (2005). *Oregon public broadcasting: Calvert underwrites PBS documentary celebrating social entrepreneurship*. http://www.businesswire.com/news/home/20050606005339/en/Oregon-Public-Broadcasting-Calvert-Underwrites-PBS-Documentary

LeBron James Family Foundation. (2019). *About us*. https://www.lebronjamesfamilyfoundation.org/about/

Lester, P. M. (2014). *Visual communication: Images with messages*. Wadsworth.

Leuthesser, L., Kohli, C. S., & Harich, K. R. (1995). Brand equity: The halo effect measure. *European Journal of Marketing, 29*(4), 57–66.

Leveille, D. (2015). VW scandal threatens "made in Germany" image. *PRI*. https://www.pri.org/stories/2015-09-23/vw-scandal-threatens-made-germany-image

Lexico Oxford Dictionary. (n.d.). *Public relations*. https://www.lexico.com/en/definition/public_relations

Li, C., & Bernoff, J. (2011). *Groundswell: Winning in a world transformed by social technologies*. Harvard Business Review Press.

Long, K. (2011, October 7). Anatomy of the corporate communicator. *PRWeek*. https://www.ragan.com/Main/Articles/Infographic_Anatomy_of_the_corporate_communicator_43749.aspx

Lopez, M. (2017). Samsung explains note 7 battery explosions, and turns crisis into opportunity. *Forbes*. https://www.forbes.com/sites/maribellopez/2017/01/22/samsung-reveals-cause-of-note-7-issue-turns-crisis-into-opportunity/#52fd729724f1

Lukaszewski, J. (2013). *Crisis communications: What your CEO needs to know about reputation risk and crisis management*. Rothstein Associates.

Lukaszewski, J. E. (2012). Managing the victim dimension of large-scale disasters. *Leadership and Management in Engineering, 12*(4), 210–221.

Luo, M., Want, N., & Bigman, C. (2019). Effects of opinion climate, efficacy messages, and publicness of social media on intentions to retransmit anti-binge drinking message on Facebook. *CyberPsychology, Behavior & Social Networking, 22*(11).

MacMahon, T. (2019). *Tweet: Statement from NBA re: Daryl Morey's controversial tweet*. https://twitter.com/espn_macmahon/status/1181007488856072192

Marklein, T. (2016). Impressions are a sham: The path to better media metrics. *Institute for Public Relations*. http://www.instituteforpr.org/impressions-are-a-sham-and-the-path-to-better-media-metrics/

Martin, D., & Wright, D. (2015). *Public relations: How to practice PR without losing your soul*. Business Expert Press.

Martin, R. L. (2016). M&A: The one thing you need to get right. *Harvard Business Review*. https://hbr.org/2016/06/ma-the-one-thing-you-need-to-get-right

Marzilli, T. (2014). Carnival cruise lines—In perspective. *YouGovBrandIndex*. http://www.brandindex.com/article/carnival-cruise-lines-perspective

Mastercard. (2015). *MasterCard works with Apple to integrate Apple Pay*. http://newsroom.mastercard.com/digital-press-kits/mastercard-powers-mobile-payments-safe-and-simple/

McCombs, M. E., & Shaw, D. L. (1972). The agenda-setting function of mass media. *Public Opinion Quarterly, 36*(2), 176–187.

McElhaney, K. A. (2008). *Just good business: The strategic guide to aligning corporate responsibility and brand*. Berrett-Koehler.

McGregor, J. (2017a). What millennials want from their CEOs: Activism. *The Washington Post*. https://www.washingtonpost.com/news/on-leadership/wp/2017/07/24/what-millennials-want-from-their-ceos-activism/? utm_term=.084323cd83d8

McGregor, J. (2017b). The cost of silence: Why more CEOs are speaking out in the Trump era. *The Washington Post*. https://www.washingtonpost.com/news/on-leadership/wp/2017/02/17/the-cost-of-silence-why-more-ceos-are-speaking-out-in-the-trump-era/

McKeever, B. (2018, December 13). The nonprofit sector in brief 2018. *Urban institute*. https://nccs.urban.org/publication/nonprofit-sector-brief-2018#finances

McKinsey Global Institute. (2017). *Jobs lost, jobs gained: Workforce transitions in a time of automation*. McKinsey & Company.

McQuail, D., & Windahl, S. (1993). *Communication models for the study of mass communications*. Routledge.

McVicker, M. (2013, May 19). *Engaging the social workforce*. https://issuu.com/mslgroupofficial/docs/engaging-the-social-workforce

Meng, M. (2009, February 5). *Issue life cycle clarifies difference between "issues management" and "crisis management."* http://www.alexanderps.com/Index/BLOG/CC888933-80F7-4617-A3BC-1B63C45C6776.html

The Mia Hamm Foundation. (n.d.). *Mission*. http://www.miafoundation.org/index#/mission

Michael, C., Cauley, M., & Orengo, L. (2016). The third place on a third rail Issue: An analysis of Starbucks' race together initiative. *Arthur W. Page Society*. http://www.awpagesociety.com/attachments/7615245b5d1bb6a740d82c0b099b31d30dc2cf20/store/1b2a6ddf451cf14676f0415b54d8ac628451de30ff38edafbaa06041f0df/Starbucks+Case+Study+3.25_FINAL.pdf

Michaelson, D., & Stacks, D. W. (2011). Standardization in public relations measurement and evaluation. *Public Relations Journal, 5*(2), 1–22.

Michaelson, D., & Wright, D. (n.d.). *A practitioner's guide to public relations research, measurement and evaluation.* http://amecorg.com/wp-content/uploads/2012/10/16JuneDavidMichaelsonandDonaldK-APractitionersGuide.pdf

Michelin. (n.d.). *Michelin.* http://www.michelin.com/eng

Miller, K. S. (1999). Public relations in film and fiction: 1930 to 1995. *Journal of Public Relations Research, 11*(1), 3–28.

Milne, R. (2015, December 2). Volkswagen blunders through communications over emissions scandal. *Financial Times.* https://www.ft.com/content/b9f35440-98ed-11e5-bdda-9f13f99fa654

Mireles, A. (2014). PR is facing challenges, but they're NOT insurmountable!" *Cision.* http://www.cision.com/us/2014/11/pr-is-facing-challenges-but-theyre-not-insurmountable/

Mireles, A. (2015, January 15). PR and internal communications: Changing with the times? *Cision.* http://www.cision.com/us/2015/01/pr-and-internal-communications-changing-with-the-times/

Mitroff, I. I. (1994). Crisis management and environmentalism: A natural fit. *California Management Review, 36*(2), 101–113.

Molleda, J.-C. (2009). Global public relations. *Institute for Public Relations.* http://www.instituteforpr.org/global-public-relations/

Morris, C. (2019). Exploring social video app TikTok—how 3 brands are benefitting. *Agility PR Solutions.* https://www.agilitypr.com/pr-news/public-relations/exploring-social-video-app-tiktok-how-3-brands-are-benefitting/

MSLGroup. (2016, February 19). *Behind the scenes at Canon.* http://blog.mslgroup.com/behind-the-scenes-at-canon/

MSNBC. (2009). *The* Rachel Maddow Show *transcript 03/05/09.* http://www.msnbc.com/transcripts/rachel-maddow-show/2009-03-05

Multivu. (n.d.). *Make your mark.* http://www.multivu.com/players/English/7123753-bayer-skyla-glamour-make-your-mark-contest/

The Museum of Public Relations. (n.d.). *Pioneer—Edward Bernays.* https://www.prmuseum.org/pioneer-edward-bernays?rq=Bernays

The Museum of Public Relations. (2018, March 21). *Belle Moskowitz: The first woman to serve as political consultant.* https://www.prmuseum.org/blog/2018/3/21/belle-moskowitz-the-first-woman-to-serve-as-political-consultant

Myers, C. (2013). Free speech v. social media: Is your policy legal? *Institute for Public Relations.* http://www.instituteforpr.org/free-speech-v-social-media-is-your-policy-legal/

National Center for Environmental Information. (2016). *Billion-dollar weather and climate disasters: Table of events.* https://www.ncdc.noaa.gov/billions/events

National Hurricane Center. (2012). *Saffir-Simpson hurricane wind scale.* https://www.nhc.noaa.gov/aboutsshws.php

National Investor Relations Institute. (n.d.). *Global IR considerations.* https://www.niri.org/resources/resource-libraries/free-resources/wp-global-ir-considerations

National Park Service. (n.d.). *John Muir.* https://www.nps.gov/yose/learn/historyculture/muir.htm

Neff, J. (2014). *Ten years in, Dove's "Real Beauty" seems to be aging well.* https://adage.com/article/creativity-news/ten-years-dove-s-real-beauty-aging/291234/

Nelson, J. (2008). CSR and public policy: *New forms of engagement between business and government.* Corporate Social Responsibility Initiative Working Paper No 45. John F. Kennedy School of Government. Cambridge, MA: Harvard University. https://www.hks.harvard.edu/m-rcbg/CSRI/publications/workingpaper_45_nelson.pdf

New American Economy. (2019, July 9). *Spotlight on Asian Americans and Pacific Islanders in the United States.* https://research.newamericaneconomy.org/report/spotlight-on-asian-americans/

Newberry, C. (2018). Eight social media security tips to mitigate risks. *Hootsuite.* https://blog.hootsuite.com/social-media-security-for-business/

Newell, A. (2015). How Nike embraced CSR and went from villain to hero. TriplePundit. http://www.triplepundit.com/special/roi-of-sustainability/how-nike-embraced-csr-and-went-from-villain-to-hero/

Newton, J. (2005). Visual ethics theory. In K. Smith, S. Moriarty, G. Barbatsis, & K. Kenney (Eds.), *Handbook of visual communication* (pp. 429–444). Routledge.

The New York Times Staff. (2020, April 25). Trump suggests daily briefings no longer worth his time as White House considers replacing health secretary. https://www.nytimes.com/2020/04/25/us/coronavirus-news.html

Nielsen. (2018a). *The evolution of the sustainability mindset.* https://www.nielsen.com/us/en/insights/report/2018/the-education-of-the-sustainable-mindset/

Nielsen. (2018b, Feb. 5). *Super Bowl LII draws 103.4 million TV viewers, 170.7 million social media interactions.* https://www.nielsen.com/us/en/insights/article/2018/super-bowl-lii-draws-103-4-million-tv-viewers-170-7-million-social-media-interactions/

Nielsen. (2019). *It's in the bag: Black consumers' path to purchase—Demographics.* https://www.nielsen.com/us/en/insights/report/2019/its-in-the-bag-black-consumer-path-to-purchase/

Nike. (2006). Nike named top 10 for social responsibility reporting. *Nike News.* http://news.nike.com/news/nike-named-top-10-for-social-responsibility-reporting

NOLO. (n.d.a). Defamation, slander and libel. http://www.nolo.com/legal-encyclopedia/defamation-slander-libel

NOLO. (n.d.b). *The "fair use" rule: When use of copyrighted material is acceptable.* http://www.nolo.com/legal-encyclopedia/fair-use-rule-copyright-material-30100.html

Nonprofithr. (2019). *2019 talent management priorities for nonprofits.* https://www.nonprofithr.com/2019tmpsinfographic/

Norris, P. (2004). Global political communication. In F. Esser & B. Pfetch (Eds.), *Comparing political communication: Theories, cases and challenges* (pp. 115–150). Cambridge University Press

NPR. (2011). *Taco Bell faces lawsuit over "seasoned beef."* http://www.npr.org/2011/01/25/133218485/Taco-Bell-Faces-Lawsuit-Over-Seasoned-Beef

NSPRA. (n.d.a). *Getting started.* https://www.nspra.org/getting_started

NSPRA. (n.d.b). *In their own words: Value of NSPRA.* https://www.nspra.org/info

NYC Pride. (n.d.). *Our mission.* https://www.nycpride.org/about/

Nye, J. S. (1990). Soft power. *Foreign Policy, 80,* 153–171.

O'Brien, K. (2018). HP continues "reinvent mindsets" campaign with #LatinoJobs recruitment focus. *The Drum.* https://www.thedrum.com/news/2018/04/17/hp-continues-reinvent-mindsets-campaign-with-latinojobs-recruitment-focus

O'Boyle, E., & Adkins, A. (2015). Can Volkswagen salvage its damaged brand? *Gallup.* http://www.gallup.com/businessjournal/187472/volkswagen-salvage-damaged-brand.aspx

Oh, M.-Y., & Ramaprasad, J. (2003). Halo effect: Conceptual definition and empirical exploration with regard to South Korean subsidiaries of US and Japanese multinational corporations. *Journal of Communication Management, 7*(4), 317–332.

Oliver, J. (2015, March 23). *Last Week Tonight.* HBO. https://www.youtube.com/watch?v=D0CXoMBJbpI

Page, J. T., & Page, W. S. (2013). *The state of micro CSR: Small businesses in a sample of U.S. firms.* Presented to the 2nd International CSR Communication Conference, Aarhus, Denmark.

Page, J. T., & Page, W. S. (2018). Taylor guitars: Guardians of the forest. In B. Brunner & C. Hickerson (Eds.), *Cases in public relations: Translating ethics into action.* Oxford University Press.

Page, J., & Parnell, L. (2016). U.S. secretary of state's award for corporate excellence. In J. Fullerton & A. Kendrick (Eds.), *Shaping international public opinion: A model for nation branding and public diplomacy* (pp. 221–239). Peter Lang.

Pandey, A. (2016). Samsung Galaxy Note 7 debacle to cost company over $5 billion. *IBT.* http://www.ibtimes.com/samsung-galaxy-note-7-debacle-cost-company-over-5-billion-2431578

Perrin, A. (2015). Social media usage: 2005–2015. *Pew Research Center.* http://www.pewinternet.org/files/2015/10/PI_2015-10-08_Social-Networking-Usage-2005-2015_FINAL.pdf

Perrin, A., & Anderson, M. (2019). Share of U.S. adults using social media, including Facebook, is mostly unchanged since 2018. *Pew Research Center.* https://www.pewresearch.org/fact-tank/2019/04/10/share-of-u-s-adults-using-social-media-including-facebook-is-mostly-unchanged-since-2018/

Perrin, A., & Kumar, M. (2019). About three-in-ten U.S. adults say they are "almost constantly" online. *Pew Research Center.* https://www.pewresearch.org/fact-tank/2019/07/25/americans-going-online-almost-constantly/

Perry, E. I. (2009, March 20). Belle Moskowitz. *Jewish Women: A comprehensive historical encyclopedia.* https://jwa.org/encyclopedia/article/moskowitz-belle

Pesce, N. L. (2020, Jan. 23). Trump hits uncharted Twitter territory while reacting to his impeachment trial.

MarketWatch. https://www.marketwatch.com/story/this-is-trump-unleashed-these-charts-show-that-the-president-is-tweeting-and-speaking-more-than-ever-2019-09-23

Peters, A. (2019). *Most millennials would take a pay cut to work at an environmentally responsible company.* https://www.fastcompany.com/90306556/most-millennials-would-take-a-pay-cut-to-work-at-a-sustainable-company

Petruno, T. (2014, October 11). 10 stocks for socially responsible investors. *Kiplinger.* https://www.kiplinger.com/slideshow/investing/T052-S003-best-stocks-for-socially-responsible-investors/index.html

Pew Research Center. (2012, June 19). *The rise of Asian Americans: Chapter 5—Family and personal values.* https://www.pewsocialtrends.org/2012/06/19/chapter-5-family-and-personal-values/

Peyok, S. (2019). More investors exploring nature-based growth opportunities. *Triple Pundit.* https://www.triplepundit.com/story/2019/more-investors-exploring-nature-based-growth-opportunities/84531

Phelps, R., & Williams, K. D. (n.d.). From routine to crisis: Handling an escalating IT incident. *Everbridge.* http://ems-solutionsinc.com/wp-content/uploads/2015/11/From-Routine-to-Crisis-Handling-an-Escalating-IT-Incident.pdf

Piasecki, A. (2000). Blowing the railroad trumpet: Public relations on the American frontier. *Public Relations Review, 26*(1), 53–65.

Plowman, K. D., & Wilson, C. (2018). Strategy and tactics in strategic communication: Examining their intersection with social media use. *International Journal of Strategic Communication, 12*(2), 125–144.

PMLive. (n.d.). Bayer partners with *Glamour* on female empowerment. http://www.pmlive.com/pharma_news/bayer_partners_with_glamour_on_female_empowerment_598152?SQ_ACTION=clear_design_name&full=true

Points of Light. (2012). *News flash: Just released—Trends in excellence, innovations in employee volunteering.* http://www.pointsoflight.org/blog/2012/03/28/news-flash-just-released-trends-excellence---innovations-employee-volunteering

Points of Light. (2013). *Nominations open for 2013 corporate engagement awards of excellence from points of light.* http://www.pointsoflight.org/press-releases/nominations-open-2013-corporate-engagement-awards-excellence-points-light

Popik, B. (2010, January 30). Lobbyist (lobbying). *The Big Apple.* https://www.barrypopik.com/index.php/new_york_city/entry/lobbyist_lobbying/

Porter, M. E., & Kramer, M. R. (2006, December). Strategy and society: The link between competitive advantage. *Harvard Business Review, 84*(12), 78–92.

Poushter, J. (2016). Smartphone ownership and Internet usage continues to climb in emerging economies. *Pew Research Center.* http://www.pewglobal.org/files/2016/02/pew_research_center_global_technology_report_final_february_22__2016.pdf

Powell, N. (2015, April 11). *Giants' Eli Manning named one of the top philanthropists under 40.* http://www.nj.com/giants/

index.ssf/2015/04/giants_eli_manning_named_one_of_the_top_philanthro.html

PR Daily. (n.d.). *Japanese paint company earns significant coverage for its CSR effort.* https://www.prdaily.com/awards/media-relations-awards/2019/winners/media-relations-campaign-of-the-year-under-50000/

PR News. (2016). *PR News 2016 CSR awards: Annual report.* http://www.prnewsonline.com/awards/csr-2016/annual-report

PR News. (2019). *PR News digital awards.* https://www.prnewsonline.com/go/2019-digital-pr-awards/?id=463774

Praccreditation.org. (n.d.). *Laws for PR professionals.* http://www.praccreditation.org/resources/documents/APRSG-Law-Ethics.pdf

PRovoke. (2019a). *2019 healthcare agencies of the year.* https://www.provokemedia.com/events-awards/agencies-of-the-year/2019-agencies-of-the-year/north-america/healthcare-agencies-of-the-year

PRovoke. (2019b). Global PR agency rankings 2019: Networks rebound after dismal 2017. https://www.provokemedia.com/ranking-and-data/global-pr-agency-rankings/2019-pr-agency-rankings/top-10

PRSA. (n.d.a). *Awards.* http://www.prsa.org/awards

PRSA. (n.d.b). *Code provisions of conduct.* http://apps.prsa.org/AboutPRSA/Ethics/CodeEnglish#Provisions

PRSA. (n.d.c). *Member code of ethics.* http://apps.prsa.org/AboutPRSA/Ethics/CodeEnglish

PRSA. (n.d.d). *The four-step process.* https://apps.prsa.org/Learning/Calendar/display/5520/The_Four_Step_Process#.XTcfsehKiUk

PRSA. (2014a). *Health care reform essentials: Aflac supports small business owners in the new health care reality.* http://www.prsa.org/searchresults/view/6be-1404a04/0/health_care_reform_essentials_aflac_supports_small.WFLL77GZPvE

PRSA. (2014b). *Hertz hits the road.* https://apps.prsa.org/Awards/SilverAnvil/Search?pg=1&saYear=2014&sakeyword=hertz&saCategory=&saIndustry=&saOutcome=

PRSA. (2014c). *The new Hertz.* https://apps.prsa.org/Awards/SilverAnvil/Search?pg=1&saYear=All&sakeyword=Hertz&saCategory=&saIndustry=&saOutcome=#

PRSA. (2015). *Allstate foundation purple purse.* https://apps.prsa.org/Awards/SilverAnvil/Search?pg=1&saYear=All&sakeyword=Purple+Purse&saCategory=&saIndustry=&saOutcome=

PRSA. (2018). *Orlando's big thank you: Highlighting a welcoming and grateful destination.* https://apps.prsa.org/SearchResults/Download/6BE-180621109/0/Orlando_s_BIG_Thank_You_Highlighting_a_Welcoming_a

PRSA. (2019a). *#HitMeWithYourFluShot.* https://apps.prsa.org/Awards/SilverAnvil/Search?pg=1&saYear=All&sakeyword=hitmewithyourflushot&saCategory=&saIndustry=&saOutcome=

PRSA. (2019b). *HP combating unconscious bias (a.k.a. "Caucasians are better than African-Americans at math and science?!").* https://apps.prsa.org/Awards/SilverAnvil/Search?sayear=All&pg=1&saindustry=&sakeyword=hispanic&saoutcome=&sacategory=

PRSA. (2019c). *#RepresentLove.* https://apps.prsa.org/Awards/SilverAnvil/Search?pg=1&saYear=All&sakeyword=tinder&saCategory=&saIndustry=&saOutcome=

PRSA New York. (2016). *John W. Hill award.* http://c.ymcdn.com/sites/www.prsany.org/resource/resmgr/Docs/Press_Releases/2016_Big_Apple_Chapter_Winne.pdf?hhSearchTerms=%22John+and+W+and+Hill+and+Award%22

PRWeek. (2016). *Harold Burson turns 95.* http://www.prweek.com/article/1383080/harold-burson-turns-95

PRWeek. (2018). *Rankings tables: PRWeek agency business report 2018.* https://www.prweek.com/article/1457605/rankings-tables-prweek-agency-business-report-2018

PRWeek. (2019, Mar. 22). *PRWeek U.S. awards: 2019 winners.* https://www.prweek.com/article/1579436/prweek-us-awards-2019-winners

Purdue Online Writing Lab. (2020). *Associated Press style.* https://owl.purdue.edu/owl/subject_specific_writing/journalism_and_journalistic_writing/ap_style.html

Quinn, M. (2019). Under Trump, number of White House press briefings has sunk to historic low. *Washington Examiner.* https://www.washingtonexaminer.com/news/under-trump-number-of-white-house-press-briefings-has-sunk-to-historic-low

Quoteswise. (n.d.). *P. T. Barnum.* http://www.quoteswise.com/p-t-barnum-quotes.html

Ragan's PR Daily. (2018a). *Fashion company reaches deskless employees with mobile app.* https://www.ragan.com/awards/employee-communications-awards/2018/winners/mobile-app/

Ragan's PR Daily. (2018b). *Innovative CSR campaign involving toasters lights up social media.* https://www.prdaily.com/awards/corporate-social-responsibility-awards/2018/winners/social-media-campaign/

Ragan's PR Daily. (2018c). *Video pairs Johns Hopkins Medicine leaders with staff doing unusual jobs.* https://www.ragan.com/awards/employee-communications-awards/2018/winners/informational-video/

Ragan's PR Daily. (2019a). *Digital graphic novel brings an infrastructure story to life.* https://www.prdaily.com/awards/digital-pr-social-media-awards/2019/winners/microsite-or-custom-website/

Ragan's PR Daily. (2019b). *Japanese paint company earns significant coverage for its CSR effort.* https://www.prdaily.com/awards/media-relations-awards/2019/winners/media-relations-campaign-of-the-year-under-50000/

Ragan's PR Daily. (2019c). *University offers themed GIFs to drive student engagement on Instagram.* https://www.prdaily.com/awards/digital-pr-social-media-awards/2019/winners/instagram-stories/

Ragan's PR Daily. (2019d). *What began as an exercise in learning to podcast evolves into a PR variety show.* https://www.prdaily.com/awards/digital-pr-social-media-awards/2019/winners/podcast/

Rascoe, A. (2019). Pence chides NBA, Nike for "losing their voices" on China. *NPR/KCLU.* https://www.npr

.org/2019/10/24/773025664/pence-chides-nba-nike-for-losing-their-voices-on-china

Raya, R. B., & Panneerselvam, S. (2013). The healthy organization construct: A review and research agenda. *Indian Journal of Occupational and Environmental Medicine, 17*(3). 10.4103/0019-5278.130835

Read, L. (2017, January 5). #HigherEd: Making social strategic. *Inside Higher Ed.* https://www.insidehighered.com/blogs/call-action-marketing-and-communications-higher-education/highered-making-social-strategic

Regester, M., & Larkin, J. (2008). *Risk issues and crisis management in public relations: A casebook of best practice.* Kogan Page.

Renfree, M. (2016, January 26). Top women in PR: Wendy Lund. *PRNews.* http://www.prnewsonline.com/awards/topwomen2016_lund

Reputation Institute. (2018a). *2017 global reptrak 100.* https://www.reputationinstitute.com/research/Global-RepTrak-100.aspx

Reputation Institute. (2018b). *Campbell's and Nike rise to the top, Amazon falls in Reputation Institute's 2018 US reptrak® 100.* https://www.reputationinstitute.com/about-ri/press-release/campbells-and-nike-rise-top-amazon-falls-reputation-institutes-2018-us

Reputation Institute. (2019). *The reptrak program.* https://www.reputationinstitute.com/us-reptrak

Riley, C. (2019). NBA chief Adam Silver says profit can't come before the league's principles. *CNN Business.* https://www.cnn.com/2019/10/08/media/nba-adam-silver/index.html

Rivel Research Group. (2013). *Harnessing IR's power to impact a company's valuation.* http://www.rivel.com/PDFs/power.pdf

Robertson, L. (2019). How ethical is H&M? *Good on You.* https://goodonyou.eco/how-ethical-is-hm/

Rockland, D. (2010). *Ketchum.* https://www.ketchum.com/

Roll, M. (2009). Benefits of the corporate brand. *Branding Strategy Insider.* http://www.brandingstrategyinsider.com/2009/07/benefits-of-the-corporate-brand.html.WFCOj3eZOIY

Sacks, M. A., & Graves, N. (2012). How many "friends" do you need? Teaching students how to network using social media. *Business Communication Quarterly (75)*1, 80–88.

Sainz, M. (2019). *Five ingredients for success for partnerships in fragile economies like South Sudan. Ethical Corporation.* http://www.ethicalcorp.com/five-ingredients-success-partnerships-fragile-economies-south-sudan

Salamon, L. M., & Newhouse, C. L. (2019, January). The 2019 nonprofit employment report. *Nonprofit Economic Data Bulletin,* no. 47. Available at cccss.jhu.edu.

Saltzman, J. (2011). The image of the public relations practitioner in movies and television, 1901–2011. IJPC. https://www.ijpc.org/page/ijpc_pr_practitioner

Samsung. (2016). *Corporate social responsibility.* https://secureus.samsung.com/us/aboutsamsung/investor_relations/corporate_governance/corporatesocialresponsibility/

Samsung Newsroom. (2017, May 19). *Samsung employees nationwide swap the office for day of service.* https://news.samsung.com/us/samsung-employees-nationwide-swap-the-office-for-day-of-service-samsunggives/

Sanchez, M., Cohen, J., & Eldeib, D. (2018). *Immigrant children sent to Chicago shelters are traumatized and sick, in some instances with chicken pox or tuberculosis.* https://www.propublica.org/article/heartland-chicago-shelters-immigrant-children-sick-traumatized

Sanchez, M., Eldeib, D., & Cohen, J. S. (2019). *After controversy, Heartland to close four Illinois shelters for immigrant youth.* https://www.propublica.org/article/heartland-illinois-shelters-four-to-close-immigrant-youth

Savage, D. G. (2002). Nike takes ad liability case to high court. *Los Angeles Times.* http://articles.latimes.com/2002/oct/15/local/me-nike15

SBE. (2018). Facts & data on small business and entrepreneurship. http://sbecouncil.org/about-us/facts-and-data/

Schock, N. (2010). Handling a fake Twitter account: @BPGlobalPR leaves lasting impression on crisis communications. *PRSA.* http://www.prsa.org/Intelligence/TheStrategist/Articles/view/8757/1019/Handling_a_Fake_Twitter_Account_BPGlobalPR_Leaves.WDsNB3eZPfA

Schooley, S. (2019). *SWOT analysis: What it is and when to use it.* https://www.businessnewsdaily.com/4245-swot-analysis.html

Schroeder, A. (2015). Pioneer in public relations: Doris Fleischman. *CulpWrit.* https://www.culpwrit.com/2015/08/07/pioneer-in-public-relations-doris-fleischman/

Schultz, E. J. (2019). VW bids farewell to the Beetle with big New Year's Eve campaign. *AdAge.* https://adage.com/article/cmo-strategy/vw-bids-farewell-beetle-big-new-years-eve-campaign/2224206

Scott, S. (2017). *Why most M&As don't reach their full potential.* https://www.gagenmacdonald.com/2015/the-hard-stuff-in-a-successful-ma/

Seitel, F. P. (2013). *The practice of public relations.* Pearson.

Seymour, C. (2016, March 17). *PR News 2016 CSR awards: Annual report.* https://www.prnewsonline.com/awards/csr-2016/annual-report

Shir-Raz, Y., & Avraham, E. (2017). "Under the regulation radar": PR strategies of pharmaceutical companies in countries where direct advertising of prescription drugs is banned—The Israeli case. *Public Relations Review, 43,* 382–391.

Siegel+Gale. (2020). *The world's simplest brands 2018–2019.* https://simplicityindex.com/

Skin Cancer Foundation. (n.d.). *Bob Marley shouldn't have died from melanoma.* http://www.skincancer.org/news/melanoma/marley

Skin Cancer Foundation. (2016). *The dangers of skin cancer in skin of color.* http://www.skincancer.org/prevention/skin-cancer-and-skin-of-color

Skoll Foundation. (n.d.). *About the forum.* http://skoll.org/skoll-world-forum/about/

Sleek, S. (2015). The curse of knowledge: Pinker describes a key cause of bad writing. *Association for Psychological Science.* http://www.psychologicalscience.org/index

.php/convention/the-curse-of-knowledge-pinker-describes-a-key-cause-of-bad-writing.html

Smith, A., & Anderson, M. (2018, March 1). Social media use in 2018. *Pew Research Center.* https://www.pewresearch.org/internet/2018/03/01/social-media-use-in-2018/

Smith, H. (2020, January). Harold Burson, public relations giant often called upon during a crisis, dies at 98. *The Washington Post.* https://www.washingtonpost.com/local/obituaries/harold-burson-public-relations-giant-often-called-upon-during-a-crisis-dies-at-98/2020/01/12/cf4541a6-33c5-11ea-9313-6cba89b1b9fb_story.html

Smith, J. N. (2018). The social network? Nonprofit constituent engagement through social media. *Journal of Nonprofit & Public Sector Marketing, 30*(3).

Smith, R. (2011). *Agenda-setting, priming & framing.* http://faculty.buffalostate.edu/smithrd/PR/Framing.htm

Smith, R. D. (2013). *Strategic planning for public relations* (4th ed.). Routledge.

Sodexo. (2019). U.S. Department of Labor presents Sodexo with platinum HIRE vets medallion. *CSR Wire.* https://www.csrwire.com/press_releases/43187-U-S-Department-of-Labor-Presents-Sodexo-With-Platinum-HIRE-Vets-Medallion

Spangler, T. (2018). Cord-cutting keeps churning: U.S. pay-TV cancelers to hit 33 million in 2018. *Variety.* https://variety.com/2018/digital/news/cord-cutting-2018-estimates-33-million-us-study-1202881488/

Spedden, Z. (2018). NFL stadiums without naming rights deals for 2018. *Football Stadium Digest.* https://footballstadiumdigest.com/2018/03/nfl-stadiums-without-naming-rights-deals-for-2018/

Spedden, Z. (2019). Current MLB ballparks without naming rights deals. *Ballpark Digest.* https://ballparkdigest.com/2019/03/21/current-mlb-ballparks-without-naming-rights-deals/

SportsDay. (2013, July). *Report: AT&T naming rights for Dallas Cowboys' stadium $17–19m a year.* https://www.dallasnews.com/news/2013/07/25/report-att-naming-rights-for-dallas-cowboys-stadium-17-19m-a-year/

Spreier, S. (2013, July 4). *How global trends affect employee communication and engagement.* http://blog.mslgroup.com/how-global-trends-affect-employee-communication-and-engagement/

Spring, M., Gaines-Ross, L., & Massey, P. (2019, March). CEO activism in 2018: The purposeful CEO. *KRC Research.* https://www.webershandwick.com/wp-content/uploads/2019/03/CEO-Activism-2018_Purposeful-CEO_FINAL_3.7.19.pdf

Sriramesh, K., & Vercic, D. (2009). *The global public relations handbook: Theory, research, and practice* (Rev. ed.). Routledge.

St. John, B. (2006). The case for ethical propaganda within a democracy: Ivy Lee's successful 1913–1914 railroad rate campaign. *Public Relations Review, 32*(3), 221–228.

Stacks, D. W. (2010). *Primer of public relations research.* Guilford Press.

Stacks, D., & Michaelson, D. (2010). *A practitioner's guide to public relations research, measurement and evaluation.* Business Expert Press.

Stacks, D. W., Wright, D. K., & Bowen, S. A. (2014). IBM's smarter planet initiative: Building a more intelligent world. In J. V. Turk, J. Paluszek, & J. Valin (Eds.), *Public relations case studies from around the world* (pp. 3–20). Peter Lang.

Starbucks. (n.d.). *Company information.* https://www.starbucks.com/about-us/company-information

Starling, M. S., Deardorff, J., Nuru-Jeter, A., & Cheshire, C. (2018). Late adolescent user experiences with online sexual health resources: A qualitative study. *American Journal of Sexuality Education, 13*(4).

Starwood. (n.d.). Global citizenship environmental initiatives. *Starwood Hotels and Resorts.* http://www.starwoodhotels.com/corporate/about/citizenship/environment.html?language=en_US

Stein, M. (2019). China conflict mutes NBA new season buzz. *The New York Times.* https://www.nytimes.com/2019/10/12/sports/basketball/nba-china-hong-kong.html

Stimson, S. (2013). *Why the PR industry lacks diversity.* https://www.theguardian.com/careers/pr-industry-lack-diversity

Stone, M., & Olito, F. (2019). From Amazon to Colgate, these are the 25 most loved brands in America. *Business Insider.* https://www.businessinsider.com/amazon-netflix-home-depot-among-americas-most-loved-brands-2019-4

Stuart, E. (2015, September 25). Volkswagen's big scandal—Social media shows how big a blow emissions scandal is. *The Street.* https://www.thestreet.com/story/13301990/1/volkswagen-s-big-scandal-social-media-shows-how-big-a-blow-emissions-scandal-is.html

Supa, D. W. (2014). The academic inquiry of media relations as both a tactical and strategic function of public relations. *Research Journal of the Institute for Public Relations, 1*(1), 1–15.

Supa, D. W., & Zoch, L. M. (2009). Maximizing media relations through a better understanding of the public relations–journalist relationship: A quantitative analysis of changes over the past 23 years. *Public Relations Journal, 3*(4), 1–28.

Sutter, K. (2012). The growing importance of more sustainable products in the global health care industry. *Johnson & Johnson.* https://www.jnj.com/_document? id=00000159-6a81-dba3-afdb-7aeba25f0000

Talkwalker. (2020). *The global state of PR.* https://www.talkwalker.com/case-studies/global-state-pr-2020

Taylor Guitars. (n.d.). Chapter 4: Transforming a sawmill. *The Ebony Project.* https://www.taylorguitars.com/ebonyproject/transforming-a-sawmill/

Taylor, K. (2017). Starbucks' new CEO tells us he'll never be Howard Schultz—and that's great news for the brand. *Business Insider.* http://www.businessinsider.com/interview-with-starbucks-new-ceo-kevin-johnson-2017-4

Taylor, M., & Kent, M. L. (2016). Towards legitimacy and professionalism: A call to repeal the Gillett Amendment. *Public Relations Review, 42*(1), 1–8.

Ten Berge, D. (1990). *The first 24 hours: A comprehensive guide to successful crisis communications.* Blackwell.

Terilli, S. A., Splichal, S. L., & Driscol, P. J. (2007). Lowering the bar: Privileged court filings as substitutes for press releases in the court of public opinion. *Communication Law & Policy, 12*(2), 143–175.

Thomas, C. (2016, August 24). The worst arena and stadium names in sports. *SportingNews*. http://www.sportingnews.com/other-sports/list/worst-arena-stadium-names-guaranteed-rate-field-little-caesars-kfc-yum-center-oco-coliseum-taco-bell-arena/1hujyc2ubxqvp1i0b994h9phqv

Tolentino, J. (2017, January 18). The somehow controversial women's march on Washington. *New Yorker*. http://www.newyorker.com/culture/jia-tolentino/the-somehow-controversial-womens-march-on-washington

Tourism Cares. (n.d.). https://static1.squarespace.com/static/54de6549e4b054179782b0eb/t/555f803ce4b097314db898b0/1432322108313/micatocasestudy.pdf

Tracy, M. (2020, February 6). *The New York Times tops 5 million subscriptions as ads decline*. https://www.nytimes.com/2020/02/06/business/new-york-times-earning.html

Trinder, S. (2020). Twitter picks 2019's most creative brand campaigns. *PRWeek*. https://www.prweek.com/article/1671380/twitter-picks-2019s-creative-brand-campaigns

Trump, D. J., with Schwartz, T. (1987). *The art of the deal*. Random House.

Tsetsura, K. (2011). Cultural and historical aspects of media transparency in Russia. In *Ethical Issues in International Communication* (pp. 172–182). Palgrave Macmillan.

Tye, L. (2002). *The father of spin: Edward L. Bernays and the birth of public relations*. Macmillan.

UN Global Impact. (n.d.). *Our mission*. https://www.unglobalcompact.org/what-is-gc/mission

United Nations. (n.d.). *Global compact*. https://www.unglobalcompact.org/what-is-gc

United States. (2006). A failure of initiative: Final report of the select bipartisan committee to investigate the preparation for and response to Hurricane Katrina. *U.S. G.P.O.* https://www.uscg.mil/history/katrina/docs/USHouseOfRepKatrina2006MainR1eport.pdf

UNWTO World Tourism Organization. (2018). *Tourism highlights*. https://www.e-unwto.org/doi/pdf/10.18111/9789284419876

USC Annenberg Center for Public Relations. (2019). *Global communications report, PR: Tech, the future of technology in communication*. http://assets.uscannenberg.org/docs/2019-global-communications-report.pdf

U.S. Army. (2018). *Careers & jobs*. https://www.goarmy.com/careers-and-jobs/browse-career-and-job-categories/arts-and-media/public-affairs-officer.html

U.S. Census Bureau. (2011). *2010 census shows America's diversity*. https://www.census.gov/newsroom/releases/archives/2010_census/cb11-cn125.html

U.S. Department of State (n.d.). *Secretary of state's award for corporate excellence*. https://2001-2009.state.gov/e/eeb/ace/

U.S. Department of State (2012). *Remarks at the 14th annual award for corporate excellence*. https://2009-2017.state.gov/secretary/20092013clinton/rm/2012/11/201147.htm

U.S. Department of State. (2014). *Award for corporate excellence 2014*. https://2009-2017.state.gov/e/eb/ace/2014/index.htm

U.S. Department of State. (2019). *Winners for the 2019 secretary of state's award for corporate excellence*. https://www.state.gov/winners-for-the-2019-secretary-of-states-award-for-corporate-excellence/

US SIF. (n.d.). *SRI basics*. http://www.ussif.org/sribasics

Variety Staff. (2016, August 2). *Corporate citizenship programs seize the chance to give back*. http://variety.com/2016/biz/spotlight/10-entertainment-corporate-philanthropy-wme-caa-1201828893/

Verčič, D., Grunig, L. A., & Grunig, J. E. (1996). Global and specific principles of public relations: Evidence from Slovenia. In H. Culbertson & N. Chen (Eds.), *International public relations: A comparative analysis* (pp. 31–65). Routledge.

Wakefield, R. I. (2007). Theory of international public relations, the Internet, and activism: A personal reflection. *Journal of Public Relations Research, 20*(1), 138–157.

Walden, J., Bortree, D., & DiStaso, M. (2014). This blog brought to you by . . . exploring blogger perceptions of a product endorsement policy and reviews. *Journal of Communication Management, 19* (3), 254–269.

Weber Shandwick. (2017, July 24). *CEO Activism in 2017: High Noon in the C-Suite*. https://www.webershandwick.com/news/ceo-activism-in-2017-high-noon-in-the-c-suite/

Weber Shandwick. (2018, July 25). *CEO activism in 2018: Half of Americans say CEO activism influences government*. https://www.webershandwick.com/news/ceo-activism-in-2018-half-of-americans-say-ceo-activism-influences-government/

Weber Shandwick. (2019, May 29). *Employee activism in the age of purpose: Employee (up)rising*. https://www.webershandwick.com/news/employee-activism-age-of-purpose/

Whirlpool Corporation. (2016, August 2). *Care Counts™ school laundry program exposes link between clean clothes and attendance*. http://www.whirlpoolcorp.com/care-counts-school-laundry-program-exposes-link-between-clean-clothes-and-attendance/

Whirlpool Corporation. (2019). *Education has a laundry problem: Whirlpool helps fight back by expanding landmark program to schools across nation*. https://www.multivu.com/players/English/8589951-whirlpool-care-counts-school-laundry-program/

White, D. M. (1950). The "gate keeper": A case study in the selection of news. *Journalism Quarterly, 27*(4), 383–390.

Whytas, K. J. (2016). *Impact of a brand crisis on nation branding: An analysis of tweets about VW's emissions crisis* (unpublished master's thesis). University of South Florida, Tampa, FL.

Wiener, N. (1988). *The human use of human beings: Cybernetics and society*. Da Capo Press.

Wimbish, J. (2019). Rockets' James Harden apologizes for GM Daryl Morey's controversial tweet about Hong Kong. *CBSSports.com*. https://www.cbssports.com/nba/news/rockets-james-harden-apologizes-for-gm-daryl-moreys-controversial-tweet-about-hong-kong/

Wimbish, J., & Ward-Henninger, C. (2019). NBA–China issue: Latest news resulting from Daryl Morey's Hong Kong tweet, what it means for the league. *CBSSports.com*. https://www.cbssports.com/nba/news/nba-china-issue-latest-news-resulting-from-daryl-moreys-hong-kong-tweet-what-it-means-for-the-league/

Wise, A. (2020, May 1). "I will never lie to you": Trump's new press secretary revives briefing. *NPR*. https://www.npr.org/2020/05/01/849019976/trumps-new-press-secretary-revives-white-house-briefing

Wisner, F. (2012). *Edelman and the rise of public relations*. Eight Communications.

Wood, S. (2018). H&M under fire, loses brand collaborator The Weeknd. *PR News*. https://www.prnewsonline.com/hm-under-fire-loses-brand-collaborator-the-weeknd/

Workiva. (n.d.). *About Workiva*. https://www.workiva.com/about

The World Economic Forum. (2019). *The travel & tourism competitiveness report 2019*. https://www.weforum.org/reports/the-travel-tourism-competitiveness-report-2019

Wynne, R. (2014). The real difference between PR and advertising. *Forbes*. http://www.forbes.com/sites/robertwynne/2014/07/08/the-real-difference-between-pr-and-advertising-credibility/-c5e46a322700

Yorizon. (2016, December 5). *To win in the marketplace you must first win in the workplace*. https://www.yorizongroup.com/news-blog/to-win-the-marketplace-you-must-first-win-the-workplace/

Yu, L., Asur, S., & Huberman, B. A. (2011). What trends in Chinese social media. *arXiv*. https://arxiv.org/pdf/1107.3522.pdf

Zed, O., & Dasher, S. (2019). Dove: A purpose-driven brand in a crisis of sincerity—The struggle to navigate rising expectations of corporate responsibility. *Page case study competition grand prize winner*. https://docs.google.com/gview?url=https://page.org/attachments/186ec25755d3ca0b1baa4821b35cb4749e31b692/store/5b558cb29c2b06bfe3dea04fbcf5db1fc7e19b6a326d4678db2e15d25a83/DOVE_-_A_PURPOSE.case.pdf

Zeng, L., Zhou, L., Pan, P., & Fowler, G. (2018). Coping with the milk scandal. *Journal of Communication Management, 22*(4).

Zerfass, A., & Sherzada, M. (2014). *Corporate communications from the CEO's perspective: How top executives conceptualize and value strategic communication*. Paper presented at the 17th International Public Relations Research Conference, Coral Gables, FL.

Zignal Labs. (2016). *10 ways big data will modernize your crisis communications plan*. http://go.zignallabs.com/crisis-communications-ebook

Ziv, S. (2015). Starbucks ends phase one of race together initiative after grande fail. *Newsweek*. http://www.newsweek.com/starbucks-ends-phase-one-race-together-initiative-after-grande-fail-316043

INDEX